T5-BAM-373

The Religious Dimension in Hispanic Los Angeles

Clifton L. Holland

THE RELIGIOUS DIMENSION

IN HISPANIC LOS ANGELES

a Protestant Case Study

William Carey Library

533 Hermosa Street • South Pasadena, Calif. 91030

Holland, Clifton L 1939-
The religious dimension in Hispanic Los Angeles.

Thesis (M. A.)--Fuller Theological Seminary.
Bibliography: p.
1. Mexican Americans--Religion--Los Angeles.
2. Mexican Americans--Los Angeles. 3. Los Angeles--Religion. I. Title.
BR563.M49H64 280'.4'0979494 74-5123
ISBN 0-87808-309-X

In accord with some of the most recent thinking in the academic press, the William Carey Library is pleased to present this scholarly book which has been prepared from an author-edited and author-prepared camera-ready manuscript.

Published by the William Carey Library
533 Hermosa Street
South Pasadena, Calif. 91030
Telephone 213-799-4559

PRINTED IN THE UNITED STATES OF AMERICA

To my wife

LINDA JOYCE

In sickness and in health,
For richer or for poorer...

Contents

Figures

Abbreviations

AB	American Baptist
AG	Assembly of God
BBF	Baptist Bible Fellowship
CBA	Conservative Baptist Association
FSQ	Church of the Foursquare Gospel
GARB	General Association of Regular Baptists
IND	Independent Protestant (non-Pentecostal)
IND BAPT	Independent Baptist Churches
IP	Independent Pentecostal
LAM	Latin American Methodist (United Methodist)
LACCC	Latin American Council of Christian Churches
P	Pentecostal
PRES	Presbyterian (United Pres., U.S.A.)
SB	Southern Baptist
SDA	Seventh-Day Adventist
UCC	United Church of Christ

Foreword

Increased awareness of minority problems during the last two decades has been closely associated with the demands of these minorities to have fuller participation in all aspects of American life. The larger community has been confronted with social unrest largely created by conditions it does not always understand.

The issues raised by minority Americans, such as Mexican Americans, are important to the community at large. At stake not only is the fairness of the present social and economic facts as they apply to all Americans, but more compelling, the survival of our major institutions and social order.

Awareness and knowledge about the hispanic community is something that needs to be acquired by all responsible groups and individuals. It is for this reason that I am especially happy for the publication of this volume and strongly recommend its study to the entire church community in the American Southwest.

The stated purpose of the author of this well-documented volume is to "make a socio-religious analysis of the heterogeneous Mexican American population of Los Angeles." This book is a unique effort by a religiously oriented writer to investigate with the tools of the social scientists the Mexican American experience in the United States.

A social scientist is not an impartial and "culture free investigative agent," and throughout this book the influence of the Anglo perspective is made evident by the author's choice of descriptive adjectives and other uses of the language which indicate that he is the product of his own nurture and environment. However, what is important is that the author proceeds in a creditable way, as a social scientist, to bring to the attention of the religious community some of the shortcomings of past missionary efforts directed to the Mexican American people.

The Hispanic population growth in the Southwest in the last 20 years has been phenomenal. In 1950 the U.S. Census Bureau reported 758,400 people of Spanish surname in California. The number increased more than fourfold by 1970 to more than 3,100,000. Projecting population factors such as birthrate and immigration from this base, it is anticipated that Mexican Americans will constitute a majority of the people in this state within the next 25 years. This fact alone is reason enough for the church to take a very close look at the history, culture, and present problems of the Hispanic American.

Taking the historical perspective one can say that the Mexican American was here before the Anglo came. California missionary activity began in the middle of the 1700's with Catholic priests sent from the interior of Mexico, who with the help of the native Indians, founded the early missions. These missions later blossomed into cities such as Los Angeles, San Francisco, San Diego, and others. When California passed to American hands in 1850, new social forces came into play changing a once pastoral land into areas with highly concentrated urban centers. Beginning with the goldrush of 1849, California continued its rapid growth with the extension of the railroads, the opening of large fertile valleys to irrigation/agriculture and the development of industry and commerce. By the turn of the 20th century, Mexican Americans who once owned large tracts of land called "ranchos," found themselves dispossessed. They were made into common laborers, and by the thousands were used to develop modern mining, agriculture and industry.

The Protestant efforts to preach the gospel to the Mexican American at the end of the 19th century and early years of the 20th were based on the premise that the Christian gospel would benefit Mexicans both by saving their souls and integrating them into the successful Anglo society that was taking root in California. Church leaders noted that Mexicans suffered great hardships, serving at the lowest levels of the developing labor market. All major denominations working with the Mexican community established "Christian centers" to care for their medical, social, economic and educational needs. The relatively rapid Protestant growth in the early part of the century must be seen in the light of the initial interest of church leaders to meet the Mexicans' needs. Conquered militarily, deceived by unscrupulous Anglo businessmen and neglected by their own church, Mexicans were viewed as a missionary field within the American borders.

The efforts of the early pioneers were not followed in later years. The church was not able to persuade other groups to deal with Mexican Americans in a fair and honest way. Although the land prospered, Mexicans did not share in the benefits. With the start of the revolution in Mexico in 1910, thousands of additional Mexicans came into the United States further depressing the economic status of the Mexicans already here.

When the depression came, tens of thousands were deported or otherwise persuaded by governmental agencies to leave the country. The early interests of the Anglo church in helping improve the social and economic conditions along with the salvation of their souls now gave way to a narrower perspective of concentrating on the "spiritual" needs at the expense of the "whole gospel to the whole man."

Today, the social unrest that exists in the Mexican American community has sometimes erupted into violence. But pressure for change also comes through more peaceful means such as efforts to unionize farmworkers to achieve better pay. Mexican Americans have staged peaceful demonstrations to reform the welfare system, the educational system, and in the case of "Catolicos por la Raza" in Los Angeles, to reform the church itself.

Mexican Americans in the Southwest believe that all existing laws and political arrangements are stacked against them and that the day of their liberation from second-class citizenship is still far off. In this belief, of course, they are amply supported by all socio-economic indicators. Mexican Americans in the Southwest have less income, less schooling, the worst housing conditions, the worst health facilities, and poorer and fewer jobs than the population at large.

This book is a well-documented study that invites the church to take a second look at the important work of expressing God's love to an exploited and abused minority. The church must take a strong stand condemning the exploitive attitudes of American business towards Mexican Americans and the indifference of government and other major institutions in our society. It is the role of the church to effectively speak to the entire community concerning the moral issues inherent in a majority/minority relationship. This work by Clifton Holland persuasively argues for a deep Christian involvement in the social issues of our day. It may be that in seeking to help our brothers, we may save our own soul.

Vahac Mardirosian
May, 1974

Acknowledgments

There are many people who have had a significant part in bringing this study to completion. Some have provided inspiration and encouragement, while others have given technical assistance and critical evaluation. Others have supported the project in a variety of ways.

First of all, this study would never have been attempted without the inspiration and encouragement of Drs. Donald A. McGavran and Ralph D. Winter of the School of World Mission at Fuller Theological Seminary, Pasadena, California. Other faculty members, especially Alan Tippett, Charles Kraft, C. Peter Wagner, and Roy Shearer, made invaluable contributions during regular class sessions and in private conversations.

I owe a special debt to Dr. Ralph Winter, who was my thesis advisor during the early stages of research and writing, and to Dr. C. Peter Wagner, who gave valuable encouragement and guidance as my mentor, beginning with Dr. Winter's sabbatical and continuing to the end of the thesis project.

The extensive and original nature of the research required for this study placed great demands on my time, energy, and finances; and it would have been impossible to complete the study without the help of the following individuals and organizations: The Department of Language Missions of the Southern Baptist Convention, through the kindness and encouragement of the Rev. Oscar Romo and the friendship of Taylor Pendley, provided a research grant during the summer of 1970 which enabled me to spend three months in full-time research and interviews; Mr. Jack Lightbody and Mr. Ken Bowen provided needed typewriters and duplicating services; Mrs. Mary Anne Voelkel and Mrs. Edna Sawnor sacrificially translated valuable source materials from

Spanish; the Lake Avenue Congregational Church staff (Pasadena, California) and the Pathfinder Class provided much needed support and encouragement; and Mr. A. William Cook, General Coordinator of the Institute of In-Depth Evangelism (INDEPTH), granted me the time needed to complete the writing and revision of this study, while serving on the INDEPTH staff in San José, Costa Rica.

Special thanks to Mr. Paul Remington and Mr. David Pretiz who did most of the artwork; to my colleagues at the Institute of In-Depth Evangelism who gave valuable input and evaluation for Part III; and to Mrs. Betty Manchester who helped with the final stages of preparation, duplication, and submission of the thesis to McAlister Library of Fuller Theological Seminary.

My appreciation goes to many other individuals--librarians, pastors, denominational officials, and many others--who contributed in a variety of ways to the documentation of this study.

There is no way to adequately express the value of the assistance given by my wife, Linda, in terms of the preparation of the many drafts of the manuscript; her patience and longsuffering with my mistakes, revisions, and slowness; and her constant encouragement, sometimes "forceful", but mostly gentle. And to my children, Richard and Suzan, I ask for their forgiveness and understanding for my self-imposed isolation during the many months of research and writing.

To each one who contributed to this study, I offer a genuine, heartfelt "thank you". As you read the completed work, I trust that each of you will feel that your part was worth the time, effort, and sacrifice.

San José, Costa Rica
October 1973

Introduction

When Diaz Ordaz was president of the Republic of Mexico, he stated that the large Mexican American population of Los Angeles, California constituted one of the most important concentrations of Mexicans in the whole world, so much so that Ordaz termed Los Angeles "the second city of the Mexican Republic" (Loory 1970:2).

The Spanish-surname (SSN) population of Los Angeles County in 1970 was estimated to be over 1.2 million people. One-fifth of the total SSN population live in the *barrios* of East Los Angeles, where the largest riot involving Mexican Americans in the history of the United States occurred on August 29, 1970. The other four-fifths of the Hispanic population live in scattered communities throughout the greater Los Angeles metropolitan area.

Challenged by the strategic concentration of the large, urban Mexican American population of Los Angeles County, this author began to ask questions concerning the role that the *Hispanic Protestant Church* (used collectively of all Spanish-speaking Protestant congregations) has within the life of the Mexican American "community", which is generally presumed to be dominantly Roman Catholic. This initial curiosity about the role of the Hispanic Protestant Church soon turned into a serious analysis of *the religious dimension in Hispanic Los Angeles*.

The present study began in September 1969 as part of the requirements for the degree Master of Arts at the School of World Mission and Institute of Church Growth, Fuller Theological Seminary, Pasadena, California.

OVERVIEW OF THE RELIGIOUS DIMENSION

Careful research was needed to find answers to many important questions concerning the growth history and the present ministry of the Hispanic Protestant Church and its component denominational bodies in Los Angeles County. In terms of the internal or "church-directed ministry", the following questions were raised:

- What is the present size and influence of the Protestant Spanish-speaking community in Los Angeles County?

- How many Spanish language churches and Anglo American churches with Spanish-speaking departments or missions are located in the county?

- What is the denominational affiliation and growth history of these churches?

- How have Hispanic churches in Los Angeles County grown in the past in relationship to each other and to other Hispanic churches in the Southwest? In relationship to Anglo American churches?

- What factors have stimulated or hindered the growth and maturity of Spanish-speaking churches in Los Angeles County?

- What problems are the churches now facing and how are these problems being resolved?

- Where are the pastors of Spanish-speaking churches being trained and what kind of training are they receiving?

- What about lay training and leadership--what is being done in this vital area in the life and ministry of local congregations?

- And what of the self-image of the Hispanic congregations--how do they conceive of themselves as an organism, their reason for existence in the plan of God, and their purpose or mission in the world?

These and other important questions were asked in an attempt to gain the widest possible perspective of the life and ministry of the Hispanic Protestant churches, their members and adherents.

Since the Church does not exist for itself alone, it is necessary to consider not only the "church-directed ministry", but also the "world-directed ministry" of the Hispanic Church.

During the past twenty-five years, many changes have taken place within the Mexican American *barrios* in Southern California, and especially within Los Angeles County. Young men returning from the Second World War and the Korean Conflict have provided new, educated leadership (thanks to the educational benefits of the G.I. Bill) for their communities and renewed hope among their people for correcting social injustices that have long existed in the *barrios*. Many *barrio* residents have been forced to relocate in other areas because of freeway construction, industrial expansion, and urban renewal projects (termed "Mexican removal projects" by some Mexican American leaders). Hundreds of thousands of new immigrants from Mexico, Central America and the Caribbean, as well as thousands of migrants from other states and other parts of California, have added to the growing problems of unemployment, lack of adequate housing, poor health, deficient and inadequate school systems, unequal opportunities for social and economic mobility, growing civil disobedience among young people, police harassment, and denial of civil rights that are commonplace in the *barrios* of Los Angeles County, and particularly of East Los Angeles.

The nature and intensity of Mexican American socioeconomic problems are a challenge to the Christian Church, whether Protestant or Catholic. The people in the *barrios* are *questioning the relevance of religious institutions that fail to demonstrate the reality of the Gospel of Christ in terms of social justice*. To a growing number of Mexican Americans, the validity of the Church is revealed as "the people of God" take constructive social action toward meeting the multidimensional needs of suffering minority groups and by standing with these suppressed peoples in their struggles against social injustice.

It is important for the Christian Church to ask: What has been the influence of religious beliefs and attitudes among Mexican Americans either for or against personal and collective involvement in improving the socioeconomic condition of *barrio* residents? What attitudes and corrective action have various Anglo and Hispanic denominational bodies taken concerning the broad range of social problems represented within the Hispanic population? Are Hispanic churches growing or declining because of their stand on, or their lack of involvement in, social issues? Is the Hispanic Protestant Church a relevant voice within the Hispanic communities of Los Angeles County, does it have a relevant life-style that demonstrates the radical demands of the Gospel of Christ, and what will be the Church's future role within the growing Hispanic population?

Part I of *The Religious Dimension in Hispanic Los Angeles* examines the origin and development of the Hispanic American population in terms of immigration, urbanization and assimilation.

Then, in Part II, the historical development of Hispanic Protestant denominations is traced in Southern California, particularly within Los Angeles County. The religious dimension in Hispanic Los Angeles is analyzed, in Part III, from the dual perspective of Anglo-Hispanic relationships and of the internal growth and development of the Hispanic Protestant Church. Special emphasis is given to the dilemma of the "introverted" church; the dynamics of church growth; the process of evangelism, conversion, and discipleship; and the development and training of Hispanic leadership.

This study is an evaluation of the direction that Hispanic congregations and denominations are now moving, and raises questions concerning the direction towards which they ought to be moving. It is hoped that denominational leaders, pastors and laymen in the Spanish-speaking churches, as well as key leaders in Anglo American churches and in administrative positions within the denominational structures, will be stimulated to do three things: (1) to reevaluate the role and function of the Hispanic Protestant Church based on a serious study of the social history of Hispanic Americans in the Southwest; (2) to reevaluate the goals and priorities of Hispanic Protestant ministry, while seeking the following results: revitalization and renewal of attitudes, structures, and ministries; balanced four-dimensional church growth (conceptual, incarnational, organic, and quantitative); and the development of a credible witness to the Lordship of Christ. And, (3) to commit themselves to the emergence of a revitalized Hispanic Church, experiencing balanced growth and giving credible witness to the Lordship of Christ, in order that *all* men (brown, white, black, etc.) will experience Christ's reconciliation and liberation in their relations with God and with their neighbors.

Most importantly, *the local congregation* must rediscover its reason for existence in the plan of God, which is to be His agents in the world for the vertical reconciliation of men to God and for the horizontal reconciliation and liberation of men to men, thus demonstrating a credible witness to the person of Jesus Christ in the power of the Holy Spirit, so that men will be brought to decision, discipleship, and obedience to Jesus Christ as Lord and only Savior in the visible fellowship of His Church in the world. The local congregation must become both a "reconciled community" and a "reconciling community" and so demonstrate that Jesus is Savior and Lord, both in the Church and in the world. When the local congregation becomes a vital, relevant, and servant-centered organism as God intended it to be, then the "Body of Christ" will have become an incarnational reality in the life of the local community, as men are reconciled to God and to each other through the liberating, healing-fellowship and service of the Church of Jesus Christ.

The author believes that "church growth" analysis (as articulated by the Institute of Church Growth and School of World Mission at Fuller Theological Seminary, Pasadena, California) is an important tool for evaluating the four-dimensional aspects of the Church's growth. Church leaders need to have a comprehensive understanding of the state of the Church in any specific geographical area and within each homogeneous unit that makes up the socio-cultural mosaic. Pastors and lay leaders should study, gain an understanding of, and communicate to others the principles of "balanced church growth", in order that: (1) cells of disciples can be greatly multipled among responsive homogeneous units in each local area throughout the world for the glory of God; and (2) that the causes of nongrowth and stagnation in the four dimensions of growth can be isolated and eliminated for the benefit and vitality of the Body of Christ, and in fulfillment of the Church's mission in the world as the servant of Christ.

METHODOLOGY

In order to obtain an overall perspective of the Mexican American people and their problems throughout the United States, and especially in Southern California, an analysis was made of the general literature available in books, pamphlets, articles, theses, and dissertations. Careful attention was given to studies dealing with the Mexican American population in Los Angeles County. Especially helpful were the libraries of California State College at Los Angeles, Occidental College, the University of Southern California, the School of Theology at Claremont, and Fuller Theological Seminary.

One of the aims of this study was to determine the actual size of the Mexican American population in Los Angeles County in 1970. Since no data was then available from the 1970 census, data from the 1960 census served as a starting point and projections were made from it based on the rate of population growth between 1950 and 1960. Changes in the Spanish surname population were uncovered by the *Special Census Survey of South and East Los Angeles* conducted by the California Department of Industrial Relations in November 1965. The single most helpful volume in terms of up-to-date projections of SSN population in the Southwest and in analyzing general Mexican American problems was Leo Grebler's *The Mexican American People: The Nation's Second Largest Minority* published in 1970. Finally, projections based on early returns from the 1970 census were released in January 1972 by the Census Bureau in Washington which gave figures on "Spanish American" population (new designation used by the 1970 census) for each state. The Los Angeles County Regional Planning Commission also released similar projections for the county by city and unincorporated areas (August 1972).

A second objective was to determine the geographical location of the predominantly Mexican American neighborhoods in Los Angeles County. These neighborhoods are called *barrios* or *colonias* and are generally lower socioeconomic housing areas. Data was accumulated on the size and density of the SSN population in each congressional district and statistical area of Los Angeles County as well as for each city, when available. This information was obtained from the 1960 Census of Population, the Los Angeles County Welfare Planning Council, the Superintendent of Los Angeles County Schools, and other public and business sources.

Another objective was to compile a directory of the total number of Spanish-speaking non-Catholic churches in Los Angeles and Orange Counties. Information was needed on the name and location of each church, the pastor's name, and the denominational affiliation, if any. This list was difficult to obtain and many sources and methods were used: existing directories of denominational and interdenominational organizations, interviews with pastors and denominational officials, area telephone directories and many hours spent driving through the *barrios* in search of unlisted churches. Two hundred twenty-six Hispanic churches were verified to exist in Los Angeles and Orange Counties, and these churches were plotted on a 72" x 72" wall map of the two-county area, with each church represented by a small, red dot. The resulting visual aid shows the geographical distribution of Spanish-speaking churches in the greater Los Angeles area and provides a basis of comparison with the distribution and density of the SSN population.

After obtaining a listing of all known Spanish-speaking churches in Los Angeles County, it was then possible to proceed with a fourth objective. This consisted of making a survey of each church using a printed questionnaire which was brief and yet comprehensive. The forms were sent out in July 1970 with an enclosed, self-addressed stamped envelope, and were personally addressed to the pastor of each church, when known. The purpose of this questionnaire was to obtain statistics on church membership and average attendance so that the size of the total Protestant "community" (adherents) and the size of the active church membership (communicants) could be determined. Questions were asked about the history of each church: when founded, membership statistics, the name of the present pastor and how long he has served the church, etc. The questionnaire also requested information on the composition and nativity of the membership, ministerial training, leadership education, and church extension. The results of this survey are graphically presented in the thesis along with a careful analysis of the results. Also, as a check on the accuracy of the information received on the questionnaires, over one hundred churches were visited and interviews were conducted with denominational officials, pastors, laymen, and community leaders. A pictorial directory of over seventy churches was compiled based on a cross-section of each denomination.

The final objective of this study was to analyze the historical growth characteristics of the Spanish-speaking churches in the milieu of Southern California and Los Angeles County. Reasons for growth and nongrowth were evaluated from both an internal and external viewpoint: the organizational structure of the church, type of leadership, forms of worship and service, composition of the membership, doctrinal position, denominational and interdenominational relationships, attitude toward the community and the world, as well as the environmental influences such as the location of the church in the community, the attitude of the community toward the church, problems within the community, and the nature of the church's response to those problems, etc. Only when accurate "church growth" factors are identified and evaluated can realistic solutions to complex socioeconomic and ecclesiastical problems be found.

To my knowledge, this is the first thorough growth history of the Hispanic Protestant Church in Los Angeles County. Therefore, it is hoped that whatever limitations or inadequacies are present in this study will be corrected by others who will be able to "zero in" on specific issues and provide additional insight and analysis of both the problems and the solutions.

PURPOSE

The purpose for this study of the religious dimension in Hispanic Los Angeles is four-fold: First, to apply the "church growth" methodology of socio-religious analysis to the heterogeneous Mexican American population of urban Los Angeles County, in order to stimulate the critical study of Hispanic churches in other areas of the United States. Secondly, to aid my own cross-cultural understanding and appreciation of the growth problems of the Christian Church among people who speak a different native language and who have a different cultural orientation than mine. In the third place, and no doubt of greatest importance, to stimulate and encourage the Hispanic Protestant Church toward a continuous state of socio-religious revitalization and four-dimensional church growth, in order that she may exercise her prophetic ministry of reconciliation and liberation within the growing Hispanic American communities of the Southwest and the nation. And, finally, that Anglo Protestant church leaders, and through them Anglo Protestants in general, may repent of their past failures in relationship to the Hispanic American community and to the Hispanic Church, and may develop a new relationship with them that will reflect the radical demands of the Gospel of Christ.

Clifton L. Holland

PART I

The Setting: Immigration, Urbanization, and Assimilation

1.

An Analysis of Mexican Immigration to the U.S.

Immigration from Mexico has accounted for a significant portion of the total influx of peoples to the United States in this century. Between 1925-1929, and again in the period 1955-1964, Mexico contributed more than fifteen percent of all immigrants to the United States (Figure 1). Although immigration records for the early years of this century are notoriously incomplete, at least 1.3 million Mexicans entered the U.S. for permanent residence between 1910 and 1964 (Grebler 1970:64). Added to this figure are the millions of illegal immigrants, commonly referred to as "wetbacks", who have crossed the U.S.-Mexican border and now reside mainly in the Southwest.

Along with the high birth rate of the Mexican American population, immigration from Mexico has been a primary source of the rapid growth of the "Hispanic population of Mexican descent" in the United States. Therefore, an understanding of the growing Mexican American population in our society today will depend a great deal upon a careful analysis and understanding of the factors related to Mexican immigration, which will provide the setting for analyzing the heterogeneous Mexican American population in urban Los Angeles County, California.

DISTINCTIVE FEATURES OF MEXICAN IMMIGRATION

Leo Grebler, in *Mexican Immigration to the United States*, defines five distinctive features of Mexican immigration (1966: 7-11). The first significant wave of Mexican immigration began

Figure 1

MEXICAN IMMIGRANTS COMPARED WITH ALL IMMIGRANTS

1900-1964

Fiscal years	Mexican	Mexican as % of total Immigration	Mexican Immigration as % of total Mexican Population (decade average)
1900 - 1904	2,259	0.07	0.17
1905 - 1909	21,732	0.44	
1910 - 1914	82,588	1.60	1.52
1915 - 1919	91,075	7.77	
1920 - 1924	249,248	8.98	2.83
1925 - 1929	238,527	15.68	
1930 - 1934	19,200	4.50	0.15
1935 - 1939	8,737	3.21	
1940 - 1944	16,548	8.13	0.24
1945 - 1949	37,742	5.78	
1950 - 1954	78,723	7.16	0.97
1955 - 1959	214,746	15.34	
1960 - 1964	217,827	15.35	-

Source: Grebler 1966:8, 22; Young 1930:19

in 1909-1910 which was about the time when European immigration had reached its peak and began to decline. Mexican immigration gathered momentum during the 1920s, declined significantly during the 1930s, and increased again greatly after World War II (Figure 1). The fact that a continuous stream of immigrants from Mexico, both legal and illegal, have reinforced the Mexican American population is important in understanding the present problems of acculturation (cf. Samora 1966:8, 9). In the case of most European groups, when the rate of immigration declined and nearly ceased, the rate of acculturation increased greatly.

Secondly, migration across the Mexican border is distinguished by a variety of movements: permanent legal immigrants; illegal immigrants; Mexican nationals who live in Mexico but commute daily to jobs in United States border cities; agricultural workers who come for seasonal employment on their own volition, on contract, or under the bracero program (now terminated); or the many tourists, businessmen, students, and visitors who enter for limited periods. Figure 2 compares legal, illegal, and contractural labor as sources of Mexican immigration between 1910-1969.

The third distinctive feature of immigration from Mexico is its intensity. Since 1955, Mexico has supplied more permanent-visa immigrants than any other single country. Mexico is also the largest source of non-immigrant visitors, tourists, students, and temporary workers. In addition, there have been large numbers of illegal immigrants--far more than legal immigrants (cf. Figures 1-3).

Fourthly, migration from Mexico occurs along a 1,600 mile border that has few natural obstacles to impede movement:

> The river bed of the Rio Grande in certain seasons is so dry that it is possible to cross on foot at many places. At other times and places, men can swim across (hence the term "wetback"), or they have come on ferries run by human bootleggers. West of the Rio Grande the boundary cuts across hundreds of miles of desert land. Wire fences erected in the vicinity of important points of entry have been extended over time, but many of them present no serious problem to the "border jumper". Consequently, it has always been difficult to control migration across the Mexican border. In fact, this was once a favorite point of illegal entry for non-Mexican aliens who were barred from immigration or believed they would be excluded (Grebler 1966:9).

Figure 2

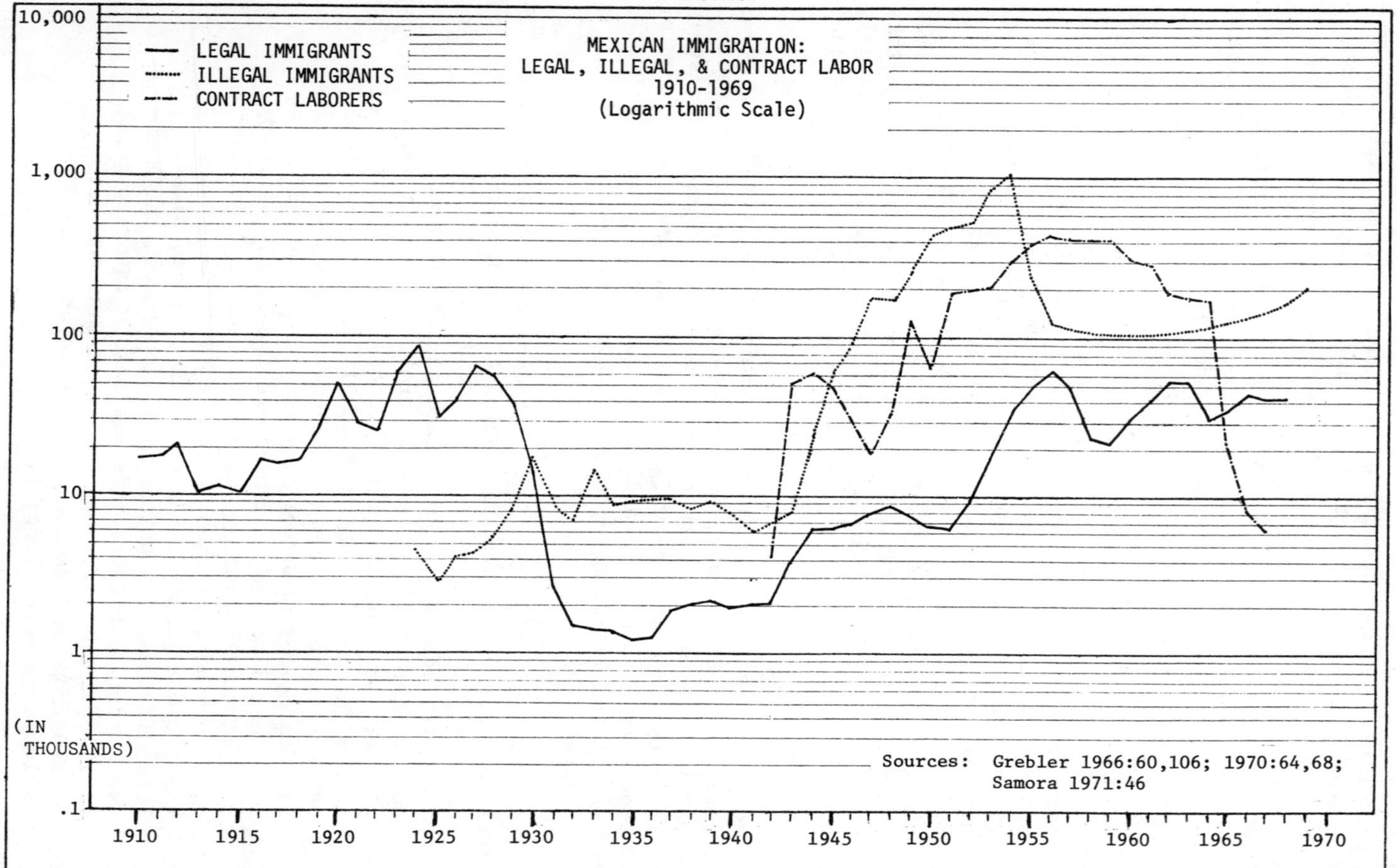

MEXICAN IMMIGRATION:
LEGAL, ILLEGAL, & CONTRACT LABOR
1910-1969
(Logarithmic Scale)

LEGAL IMMIGRANTS
ILLEGAL IMMIGRANTS
CONTRACT LABORERS

10,000
1,000
100
10
1
.1
(IN THOUSANDS)

1910 1915 1920 1925 1930 1935 1940 1945 1950 1955 1960 1965 1970

Sources: Grebler 1966:60,106; 1970:64,68; Samora 1971:46

The Mexican border country has many common geographic, cul-
ural, and economic characteristics. Both sides of the interna-
ional border have similar natural resources and a dry climate
nich requires irrigation for agricultural development. Mexican
ultural patterns persist throughout the Southwest in matters
uch as language, diet, and architecture. The desire for great-
r economic opportunity has provided an incentive for large
umbers of Mexican people to enter the United States by any
vailable means.

In the fifth place, the intentions of Mexicans coming to the
nited States seems to have been less certain, and much more
aried, than those of millions of European immigrants. In con-
rast to the Europeans who had made an enormous and irrecover-
ble committment to entering the United States, many Mexican
mmigrants have come to this country as an experiment, an adven-
ure, or as a temporary economic expedient:

> In the case of many Mexicans, the commitment involved in going North was much less momentous or permanent. If a Mexican entered on a regular immigration visa, he could return without incurring extraordinary emotional or monetary cost. If he came for temporary employment and liked the experience, he found it often not too difficult to stay and, being unfamiliar with the ways of impersonal bureaucracy, may have given little thought to the technicalities of his legal status. Many of those who slipped in illegally to begin with could hope to go back some time and re-enter properly. Moreover, large numbers of Mexican immigrants, especially those of the earlier periods who came from a society with more locally oriented loyalties, may have had a perception of the international boundary which was at variance with its formal significance (Grebler 1966:10).

The record of Mexican immigration has also been marked by
oth voluntary and involuntary return movements. Many immi-
rants freely returned to Mexico during the Great Depression of
he 1930s, but thousands of others were forcibly returned to
exico by local U.S. authorities. This mass repatriation was a
evice to relieve local communities of welfare and unemployment
roblems. In a later period, 1954-1956, the Immigration and
aturalization Service apprehended and either deported or re-
uired over three million illegal Mexican immigrants to return
o Mexico (Figure 3). Nothing comparable to these episodes has
ccurred in the experience of other immigrant groups. These
epatriations undoubtedly had a significant influence upon the
ttitude of many Mexican Americans toward the host society--
specially regarding the nature of governmental authority and
onstitutional rights.

Figure 3

MEXICAN ALIENS EXPELLED FROM THE UNITED STATES

1910-1964[1]

Fiscal years	Deported[2]		Required to Depart[2]	
	Mexican	Mexican as % of total aliens "deported"	Mexican	Mexican as % of all alie[ns] "requested t[o] depart"
1910 - 1914	1,181	7.4	-	-
1915 - 1919	3,534	29.9	-	-
1920 - 1924	5,096	23.5	-	-
1925 - 1929	15,434	27.3	-	-
1930 - 1934	35,535	42.8	39,380	75.4
1935 - 1939	23,030	52.6	24,805	56.5
1940 - 1944	17,078	64.6	40,191	60.7
1945 - 1949	70,505	83.2	785,326	93.4
1950 - 1954	63,515	72.9	3,841,562	98.3
1955 - 1959	25,113	59.0	237,093	56.0
1960 - 1964	20,490	53.7	67,170	44.8

[1]The reported figures refer to cases rather than persons and inclu[de] double-counts of individuals expelled more than once.

[2]Different procedures apply to these two types of compulsory repat[ri]ation. Deportations are based on formal procedures including hear[]ings and appeals. In the case of aliens "required to depart," the Immigration and Naturalization Service presents its evidence of illegal entry to the alien or his representative and gives him the option to depart voluntarily in order to avoid formal deportation proceedings. This is usually applied to first offenders. Aliens who choose this option are not debarred from subsequent legal admission if they qualify. In contrast, aliens who have been deported generally are ineligible for later legal admission.

Source: Grebler 1966:28

THE HISTORICAL RECORD OF MEXICAN IMMIGRATION

The problem of tracing the volume and impact of immigration from Mexico is difficult because the number of immigrants who entered legally by permanent visa accounts for probably less than half of the number who have entered illegally. John Burma stated that from thirty to fifty percent of all Mexican immigrants have entered the United States illegally (1954:42). Some of the reasons for large numbers of illegal migrants in the early 1950s are given by Burma:

> The high rate of illegal entry arose not only from the long, poorly patroled border and the desire of the Mexican to emigrate, but also from the fear and ignorance of immigration laws, inability to meet the legal requirements, especially literacy, loss of time and expense involved in red tape, willingness of employers to hire "wetbacks", and particularly from the fact that the $18.50 fee is far too great for many immigrants to pay (1954:42).

Early statistics on Mexican immigration are incomplete and inaccurate, and statistical classifications have also changed over the years. Grebler makes the following comment on the absurdity of relying upon the official immigration figures as a reliable record of the total immigration from Mexico:

> The arithmetic exercise of deducting from the gross immigration the involuntary departures (not to speak of the voluntary ones) yields the absurd finding that more Mexican aliens left this country in the 1950-1954 period than were ever reported as immigrants in all of the preceeding years (1966:18).

Therefore, since it is impossible to present a consistent record of immigration from Mexico, the following analysis represents only a rough estimate of the total number of Mexican immigrants in each period. The historical divisions used here are based upon Grebler (1966:17-37).

The Period before 1910: Lack of Controls

One of the early mass migrations occurred when large numbers of Mexicans from Sonora along with other Latins trekked to the California gold fields beginning in 1848 (McWilliams 1968b:129). According to Pitt, by 1850 the Mexican *Cholos*, Chileans and Peruvians outnumbered the 15,000 native *Californios* (1970:52-53). Between 1850-1900, farm workers, cowboys, and shepherds crossed the border in both directions as if no boundary existed (Burma 1954:40). It was only in the period 1907-1908 that comprehensive controls, patterned after those at the Canadian border, were instituted. In 1911 the Commissioner General of Immigration reported that at least 50,000 temporary workers and illegal migrants were arriving annually in normal years, while the official statistics recorded only 24,000 immigrants for the period 1900-1909 (Figure 1). Grebler reports that "Mexican laborers were employed in border areas and beyond as agricultural workers, also in mining, railroad construction and maintenance, and other nonagricultural jobs" (1966:19).

1910-1919: The Mexican Revolution and Emergent United States Labor Demands

The Mexican revolutionary period, beginning in 1910, was a major expulsionary force for thousands of upper and middle-class refugees who felt threatened by the revolution, as well as for a great horde of lower-class peons who sought to escape from the harsh years of bloody conflict. According to Landes, over one million people were killed during the revolution: "Leaders killed each other; followers and bystanders were jailed, starved, killed; typhus spread, and the dead were hung from trees; homes, crops, and livestock were set afire" (1965:54). One observer, writing in 1920, reported:

> Lifting our eyes to *suffering and struggling Mexico*, we are reminded that our task reaches vitally into a situation which has already cost the United States half a billion dollars--Mexico at least $400,000,000; led to the violent death of 300,000 Mexicans; caused the death, by pestilence and famine, of 500,000 more Mexicans, *and hurled across the Border not less than one million people seeking safety, work, education and opportunity*. 665 American citizens have lost their lives in Mexico, and some 80,000 United States troops have been required to patrol the Border (*Journal of the Latin American Mission* 1920:26, italics mine).

Nearly nine-tenths of the total Mexican population lived in rural areas where large numbers of agricultural workers were landless, indebted peasants. These masses were immobile geographically as well as socially. The revolution released the peasant population from immobility:

> The new mobility injected into Mexican society under these circumstances expressed itself in internal migrations as well as movements across the border. Many Mexicans went from rural to urban areas in their own homeland because safety and order were relatively

> greater in the cities. Mexico's total population is estimated to have declined between 1910 and 1921 as the revolution (and later the influenza epidemic) took its toll, but the urban population increased by one-tenth. In many cases the decision to seek refuge in a Mexican city or across the border was probably a matter of happenstance, proximity, kinship relations, or previous experience in the United States. One can also assume that the migration intentions even of those who came to this country on permanent visa were generally quite uncertain. There was always the hope for remigration when Mexico would return to normalcy (Grebler 1966:20).

In addition to the push of the Mexican revolution, *the emerging American labor demands* provided an impetus to Mexican migration to the United States. Government irrigation projects, made possible by the Reclamation Act of 1902 which provided federal funds for large-scale land reclamation, made wide areas in the arid West available for agricultural development. California, Arizona, and Texas profited the most from these projects and irrigated farming was soon a reality in the following areas: the San Joaquin, Imperial, Salt River, Mesilla, and Lower Rio Grande valleys. According to McWilliams, "irrigation has had more to do with the economic growth of the Southwest than any other single factor" (1968b:175-177).

The semi-desert character of most of the Southwest meant that before crops could be planted, cultivated and harvested, farm workers had to clear away the brush, level the ground, and construct an irrigation system from a main canal. McWilliams states that

> It was not easy to find in these years a large supply of labor that would brave the desert heat and perform the monotonous stoop-labor, hand-labor tasks which the agriculture of the Southwest demanded. Under these circumstances, the use of Mexican labor was largely noncompetitive and nearly indispensible.... Virtually all of the phenominal [agricultural development] in the Southwest was made possible by the use of Mexican labor (1968b:176-178).

World War I greatly increased the demand for thousands of new workers, not only in agriculture, but also in manufacturing and mining, and in expanding the nation's transportation system. The supply of domestic labor often failed to meet this demand, especially in agriculture:

> Farm laborers flocked from the country to the cities, immigration from Europe had been curtailed, and manpower was later drawn into the armed services. Much

> of the agriculture of the Southwest, especially in California and Texas, depended heavily on seasonal, foreign, low-wage labor which was satisfied with minimal housing and primitive working conditions.
>
> Under these circumstances, growers could make a case for opening the gates at the Mexican border. Mexicans were close at hand and, in view of the economic distress accompanying the revolution, were only too willing to join the succession of foreign groups imported to meet the labor demands of agricultural enterprises (Grebler 1966:21).

1920-1929: Mass Migration

During the decade of the 1920s, immigration from Mexico reached a new peak with about 490,000 entering on permanent-visa along with hundreds of thousands of illegal migrants (Figure 1). In Mexico, the consequences of the revolution had depleted both capital and resources; it caused smaller production in many vital industries; and it frightened away most foreign investors. The masses were freed from peonage, but agrarian reform was proceeding very slowly. Although human losses during the revolution had been great, there were still more hungry people in Mexico in the late 1920s than in 1910 (1966:23).

The new era of prosperity in the United States attracted the landless peons as never before (Figure 2). There was a continuing demand for new workers in agriculture as well as unskilled labor in manufacturing and service industries. Mexican immigrants supplied the needed low-wage labor:

> To trace the story of Mexican immigration to the United States is to trace the rise of the great regional industries--railroads, mining, citrus fruit, sugar beets, winter vegetables, cotton. The flow of Mexican population into each state coincides with its emerging development and prosperity (Burma 1955:40-41).

McWilliams, in *North From Mexico: The Spanish-speaking People of the United States*, discusses the important contribution of Mexican labor in the Southwest in this period:

> Testifying before congressional committees in the "twenties", the principal employers of Mexican labor in the Southwest presented facts and figures showing that Mexicans had been a vital factor in the development of agricultural and industrial enterprises valued at $5,000,000,000. Starting with a scant

> production in 1900, the Southwest was by 1929 producing between 300,000 and 500,000 carloads of vegetables, fruit, and truck crops--forty per cent of the nation's supply of these products. Most of this development took place in less than two decades and was directly based on the use of Mexican labor which constituted from sixty-five to eighty-five per cent of the common labor used in the production of these crops.
>
> From 1900 to 1940, Mexican labor constituted sixty per cent of the common labor in the mines of the Southwest and from sixty to ninety per cent of the section and extra gangs employed on eighteen western railroads. *Obviously the transformation of the Southwest which has occured in the last forty years was largely made possible by the use of Mexican labor.* Conversely, the employment of Mexicans in the Southwest has been of enormous importance to Mexico in this same period. Some guage of this importance may be found in the fact that from 1917 to 1927, Mexican immigrants sent a yearly average of $10,173,719.31 in remittances to families in Mexico (1968b:185-186, italics mine).

1930-1939: Exodus

The Great Depression of the 1930s drastically reduced all foreign immigration and produced an unusual reverse movement of former immigrants back to Mexico. American agriculture was in trouble long before the general slump in business. Mexican immigration declined drastically after 1929 so that by 1930 only 12,000 Mexicans entered this country legally (Grebler 1966:106). As the Depression intensified, large numbers of Midwestern farmers and workers were displaced and became a new source of low-wage labor for Western agriculture. This, along with the improvement of the Mexican economy, greatly reduced immigration to the United States (Figure 1).

An important feature of this era was the repatriation of over one hundred thousand people of Mexican descent--both United States citizens and aliens. Although some Mexicans returned to their homeland voluntarily, the majority of those repatriated were "expelled" (Figure 3) by local authorities and private welfare agencies with the cooperation of the Mexican government (Grebler 1966:25; McWilliams 1968b:193).

In his analysis of the impact of the repatriations of the 1930s, Leo Grebler states:

> In all probability, they had a significant impact on the relations between the Mexican-American minority

> and the host society. Only a few years earlier, many of those now ejected had been actively recruited by American enterprises. When they were shipped off as surplus, or when those who remained saw others returned to Mexico sometimes regardless of their legal status, *the experience probably served to strengthen their mistrust of the host society, add to their feeling of alienation, and confirm their worst views of government as something to fear and avoid* (1966:29, italics mine).

1940-1949: Birth of the Bracero Program

The growing demand for agricultural and unskilled laborers in the U.S. economy during World War II was initially met by large numbers of unemployed domestic workers. Requests for temporary admission of unskilled Mexican workers by employers in sugar beet, cotton, and vegetable growing areas began to increase in late 1941, and by the spring of 1942, requests were granted for railroad workers.

The development of a controlled recruitment program for "temporary workers" was organized under bilateral government agreement in August 1942; it was termed the "bracero program". The United States Government acted as the labor contractor and the Mexican Government as the recruiting agent. This agreement was "officially" designed to eliminate some of the undesirable and inequitable features of the previously unregulated period:

> This innovation included a number of special features to safeguard the national interests of the two governments in conducting their war effort and to protect the Mexican migrants. The latter were to be exempted from military service. No discrimination against them was to be allowed.... Transportation expenses for the round trip and living expenses en route were guaranteed. Wages were to be paid at the prevailing local level, with a minimum of initially 30 cents per hour. Work was guaranteed for three-quarters of the contract periods. The U.S. government was to see to it that adequate housing and sanitary facilities were provided. Braceros could buy merchandise at places of their choice. An amount equal to 10 percent of each worker's earnings was to be placed in a Mexican savings fund on which he could draw after his return. *To protect domestic labor, Mexican workers were to be admitted only to fill demonstrated shortages* (1966:30-31, italics mine).

Although the Bracero Program was terminated in August 1945, it was reinstated in 1951 to meet the so-called manpower shortage resulting from the Korean War. The program reached its peak in 1956 when 445,000 workers were admitted for temporary agricultural employment (Figure 3). However, the program came to an end in December 1964 (Grebler 1966:29,60).

The illegal immigration of wetbacks continued to be a problem in the Southwestern states, according to Grebler, even after the institution of the Bracero Program. Mexican laborers could save time, inconvenience, and expense by illegal migration rather than traveling to the Mexican recruitment centers, paying the official fees and the unofficial commissions extracted by middlemen. American agricultural employers hired both legal and illegal immigrants who worked side by side on the ranches and farms; the wetbacks saved the growers both time and money as well as inconveniences that the Bracero Program demanded. [For a detailed history of this problem see Samora (1971), *Los Mojados: The Wetback Story*]. Wetbacks continued to be a major problem well into the 1950s as Figure 3 indicates: cases of expulsion climbed from 57,000 in the early 1940s to nearly 856,000 in the later years.

However, both the *braceros* and the wetbacks constituted a problem for domestic labor. According to Wollenberg:

> These immigrations from Mexico, both official and illegal, had a profound effect on resident farm workers of Mexican origin. To put it simply, wages were kept down and bargaining positions remained weak as long as a supply of temporary migrant labor from Mexico was available (1970:145).

1950-1959: Renewed Mass Immigration and the Expulsion of the Wetbacks

In the early 1950s the number of legal immigrants began to accelerate rapidly--from 6,841 in 1950 to 65,047 in 1956 (Grebler 1966:106). In the decade of the 1950s, nearly 293,500 immigrants were admitted from Mexico which accounted for more than fifteen percent of the total immigration to the United States in that period (Figure 1). Permanent immigration accelerated along with the increased number of temporary workers under the Bracero Program. Over 400,000 *braceros* were admitted to the United States each year between 1955 and 1959 (1966:60).

In 1952 Public Law 283 made it a felony "to willfully import, transport, or harbor illegal aliens" and was aimed at channeling the flood of temporary farm workers into the orderly and regulated Bracero Program. The Immigration and Naturalization

Service reported in 1953 that, for every agricultural laborer admitted legally, four aliens were apprehended by the Border Patrol. For the entire decade of the 1950s, a total of over four million Mexican aliens were deported or required to depart from the United States (Figure 3).

The effect of this large-scale deportation on the attitude of Mexican Americans is discussed by Grebler:

> The mass repatriations of this period were bound to affect the relationship between the Mexican-American community and the host society, as did those of the 1930s. The community was deeply involved to the extent that some of its members with long residence status in this country were apprehended and sent back to Mexico because their papers were not in order. This meant disruption of family and kinship ties and could not help but strengthen feelings of alienation from American society and mistrust of government. Also, the methods employed in the round-up were often less than gentle or considerate. *On the other hand, growing sections of the community were opposed to the importation of temporary workers who were often in competition with resident Mexican-Americans, and especially to the wetback traffic.* Ever since the first attempts to organize Mexican farm workers in the late 1920's, the regulation and restraint of immigration has been one of the stated objectives of many Mexican-American organizations. Stricter law enforcement conformed to this position. At the same time, many members of the group felt protective toward the individuals who were apprehended, especially when kinship ties were involved, or expellees had been employed by persons of Mexican descent (1966:35, italics mine).

1960s: A New Era of Controls

During the first half of the 1960s, Mexican immigrants on permanent-visas continued to constitute over fifteen percent of the total number of immigrants; about 218,000 were admitted between 1960-1964 (Figure 1). Beginning in 1963, however, the United States Government initiated a new procedure that required persons wishing to immigrate to the U.S. on the assurance of jobs by American employers to have the job offer endorsed by the U.S. Department of Labor. Such an endorsement was dependent upon an investigation by the State Employment Service and a finding that "no sufficient supply of domestic workers was available for the job and that employment of the alien would not adversely affect the wages and working conditions of such workers" (Grebler 1966:36). This requirement made the granting of visas dependent upon an official evaluation of the labor market impact of a job offer; it had the affect of modifying the principle of applying no quantitative restrictions to natives of the Western Hemisphere (1966:37).

The termination of the Bracero Program in 1964 was another significant factor in regulating the flow of Mexican immigration. Agriculture in the Southwest has historically depended upon large numbers of foreign low-wage farm workers to meet its labor demands. The exclusion of *braceros* from California and Texas agriculture has resulted in major changes in respect to agricultural output, food prices, union organization, and technological changes within Southwestern agribusiness as foreseen by Grebler (1966:37).

1970-1972: Continuing Problems with Illegal Aliens

In California during 1971, over 117,000 illegal Mexican aliens were apprehended by the Border Patrol and other local law enforcement agencies and were returned to Mexico. In the Los Angeles area alone, it is estimated that there are between 200,000 and 300,000 illegal aliens; and in the entire United States, estimates go as high as 1.5 million (West 1971:3). Federal officials "plead with employers not to hire the illegals on grounds that it deprives U.S. workers of jobs and depresses the wages of U.S. workers who can't or won't accept the low wages the illegal aliens are willing to take" (Bernstein 1972a:1). Immigration agents warn employers that by hiring illegal Mexican immigrants more illegals will be encouraged to cross the border with forged papers or with help from organized gangs of alien smugglers (1972a:1).

The scope of the illegal alien problem in California has prompted the state legislature to create a law to curb the hiring of illegal aliens. Proposed by assemblyman Dixon Arnett (Republican, Redwood City), the *Arnett Act* was signed into law by Governor Reagan in November 1971. This law became the first one enacted by a state government to deal with the national illegal Mexican alien problem, and it was proposed because the U.S. Congress had failed to enact similar legislation. The California alien work law makes it a misdemeanor for an employer to knowingly hire an illegal alien and prescribes a minimum fine of $200 for a convicted employer. The new law is aimed at "those well-known employers who regularly hire large numbers of illegal aliens and who are constantly raided by immigration authorities" (Bernstein 1972a:1,12; West 1971:3).

The Arnett Act has stirred up a great deal of controversy, both pro and con, in the Mexican American community. In November

1971, the "Los Angeles Committee for the Defense of the Bill of Rights" filed a suit for an injunction to prohibit operation of the Act (*Los Angeles Times* 1971b). The Los Angeles Superior Court, in February 1972, declared the Arnett Act unconstitutional "because federal law dealing with immigration preempts the field, and because the state law is too vague in defining illegal aliens" (Bernstein 1972a:12). This ruling has been appealed by advocates of the measure, however.

Initially, California agribusiness and management organizations were opposed to the Arnett bill because they felt that the burden of proof in determining whether or not employees were illegal aliens was a hardship on the employer. However, after the new law went into effect, opposition grew among Mexican American community leaders against the Act. At least four principal reasons are given for this opposition: (1) "It hurts Mexican Americans who are fired or laid off because they cannot prove citizenship to wary employers"; (2) "the law has imposed an added hardship on illegal aliens, some married and supporting families, who cannot establish the legitimacy of their status because of stringent U.S. immigration laws"; (3) "there is no such thing as an illegal alien," some argue, since the Treaty of Guadalupe Hidalgo gave Mexicans free access to the conquered Mexican territory in the Southwest, since individuals have a right to emigrate to improve their socioeconomic status, and since the U.S.-Mexican border is an arbitrary boundary imposed by a conquering nation; and (4) the Act causes increased human suffering because it deprives "hard-working, honest people of financial support for themselves and their families" (del Olmo 1972:12).

Other Mexican American leaders, however, are much in favor of the Arnett Act, even though they are sympathetic with the plight of the illegals. Supporters of the measure argue that illegal aliens "adversely affect employment opportunities for Mexican Americans, lowering their wages by competing for work if not taking potential jobs outright" (1972:1). The illegals compete in a temporarily depressed labor market with unemployed young Mexican Americans and usually win because they are willing to work for lower wages and under more difficult working conditions. Cesar Chavez of the United Farm Workers Union argues that "too many farm worker's strikes [are] broken by growers who bring in Mexican laborers to gather crops at struck farms" (1972:1). In addition to stopping this practice, the Arnett Act also punishes employers who consistently hire illegals to take advantage of "cheap Mexican labor." This has been a perpetual problem in the field of California agriculture since early in the 1900s.

Both sides in this controversy over the new legislation have many strong supporters within the Mexican American community.

Bernstein says that "the dispute has divided the Mexican American community as no other issue has done in modern times" (Bernstein 1972a:1). However, the majority of people in the *barrios* "are maintaining a cautious middle ground" because of their divided sympathies. Meanwhile, the illegal alien problem continues to mount in Southern California with 25,000 aliens apprehended in Los Angeles in 1971 (1972a:1).

According to Dionicio Morales of the Mexican American Opportunity Foundation, "this situation pits a poor Chicano against a poverty stricken Mexican and between the two of us our struggle makes someone else rich" (del Olma 1972:12). Morales contends that the problem is too big for the State of California to adequately deal with and that the U.S. and Mexican governments will have to cooperate in solving a complicated, international socioeconomic situation (1972:12).

SOCIOECONOMIC FACTORS IN MEXICAN IMMIGRATION

The analysis of socioeconomic factors which have caused the expulsion of mass migrations from Mexico and of the forces within the United States which have attracted migrants must be considered as to both long and short-term effects.

Economic Betterment

The most significant and obvious factor is the *enormous income disparity* between Mexico and the United States:

> When the large and persistent differential in real per-capita income is considered the secular condition conducive to immigration from Mexico, it becomes irrelevant whether underemployment or unemployment or poverty in Mexico acts as a push, or actual and expected incremental income in the United States as a pull (Grebler 1966:79,80)

Within Mexico, the fruits of economic progress are unevenly distributed: "Extremely large and possible growing income disparities can be observed between urban and rural areas, between the Federal District (which included Mexico City) and the rest of the country, and among different regions" (1966:82). Great masses of the Mexican people live in dismal poverty and have furnished a vast migration potential. Oscar Lewis, a controversial anthropologist, graphically depicted what he has called the "culture of poverty" within Mexico in three important studies: *Five Families* (1959), *The Children of Sanchez* (1961), and *Pedro Martinez* (1964).

In view of the enormous income disparity between the two countries, Grebler raises the question of why more Mexicans have not migrated to the United States. Some of the reasons he gives are the following: cultural differences, the language barrier, and failure of the poor and less educated people of Mexico to realize emigration as a realistic possibility or option for economic improvement (Grebler 1966:82).

Social Aspirations

Grebler discusses the important function of social aspirations as a migration variable:

> Of course, migrants are propelled to move by their individual appraisal of relative income opportunities, and by their levels of aspiration for themselves and their children, rather than by abstract disparities of per-capita real income. The latter are merely quantified expressions of the immigrants' notion that they can do better elsewhere, with expectations of incremental welfare reckoned vaguely against the monetary and psychic cost of moving.... The expectations themselves may have varied between permanent relocation and mere desire to make enough money to return to Mexico and live there at a higher standard. *Several Mexican community studies indicate that small towns (where this phenomenon can be observed more easily) contain large numbers of returned immigrants who have used their incremental U.S. earnings to improve their level of living within the context of their homeland's culture* (1966:82,83, italics mine).

One such community study was made by John Armstrong, about 1948, in the rural-agricultural area of Chavinda in western Michoacan. Armstrong summarizes the cultural determinants of migration in terms of the relationship existing between the migrant and his society:

> It is noted that fear of violence, a concomitant of political antagonism, is a persistent cause of migration, and everyone recognizes migration as an essential means of personal economic and social advancement. Apart from the very rich and the very poor (who need not, or cannot migrate) Chavinda is found to be a community of returned migrants, who have used the money earned in the United States to improve their lot within the context of their own culture.
>
> In conclusion, it is found that all aspects of Chavindian culture are involved as determinants of

> migration since individual needs, definable in its terms, can be fulfilled by means of migration (1949:i).

Thus, the huge post-war migration of temporary workers from Mexico into the United States has been an important source of income for many Mexican nationals and has, perhaps, reduced the desire of many for permanent relocation. Knowledge of the mass repatriation of illegal immigrants in the 1930s and 1950s on the one hand, and the difficulties encountered in obtaining visas for permanent legal immigration to the U.S. on the other hand, have no doubt deterred many Mexicans from coming to this country.

Social and Geographic Mobility

A significant factor in the early emigration of Mexicans was the Revolution of 1910, which greatly affected the social and geographic mobility of the lower classes:

> By liberating masses of people from peonage, the revolution made it possible for a dormant migration potential to become effective. *If the income disparity is viewed as a sufficient secular condition to induce migration, the mobility injected into Mexican society by the revolution can be said to be the condition necessary for income differentials to be perceived and acted upon.* This process has probably extended beyond the end of the revolutionary era itself. Improved communication, greater awareness of a new social organization, and progressive urbanization all helped to convert the migration potential into actual movement. Without this transformation of Mexican society, proximity could not have produced permanent relocation on any large scale (Grebler 1966:84, italics mine).

This social upheaval resulted in a large-scale movement from the rural areas to the cities, from both rural and urban areas towards the north of Mexico, and from the border areas into the Southwestern United States. One observer from this period gives an informative description of the new arrivals:

> From 1910 to 1929, revolutions in Mexico drove [various] classes of Mexicans to our borders. Mestizos, or Mexicans of mixed Spanish and Indian blood, came from various parts of Mexico to escape being forced into the army or being killed by the invaders. They immigrated to find new homes where they could enjoy quiet and freedom and better opportunities for their children. Others came, after hearing glowing accounts from friends or relatives who had already entered the United States (Smith 1933:9).

Important contributing factors to this great exodus were: first, the railroad connections which provided the means of mobility for poverty stricken *cholos* from Central Mexico into the Southwestern states (Figure 4); and secondly, the emerging demands of U.S. labor markets which recruited large numbers of Mexican workers. For example, McEuen reported that in 1914 employment agencies, representing the various railroads, sent their agents or "rustlers" into northern Mexico to recruit unskilled laborers by offering wages about twice as high as normally received in Mexico. Contracts were offered to Mexicans arriving by rail in El Paso, Brownsville, and other points at the rate of $1.00-$1.25 per day for six months or a year, with free transportation back to El Paso if workers completed the full term of their contract. "Reinforcements are received," according to McEuen, "about every six months and the supply of this class of labor is kept abnormally high and as a result wages are kept very low " (1914:11-12).

American Business Cycle

The relationship of the role of the American business cycle to the volume of Mexican immigration is another important factor. Grebler states:

> At the risk of oversimplification, one may say that the findings indicate a close association between immigration and economic cycles in the receiving country. The association between emigration and business fluctuations in the country of origin is less clear or strong (1966: 84).

The volume of immigration seems to be more closely related to long economic cycles such as the period of the early 1920s, the depression of the 1930s, or the rising prospects of the post-war years.

Prospects for Continued Immigration

In analyzing the migration potential over the next generation, Grebler argues that Mexico's economic growth cannot accelerate greatly enough to counteract the high rate of population growth--about 3.5 percent annually. Also, the rural section of the Mexican economy is plagued by backward technology, under-employment, unrest among the landless masses, and the inefficiency of the *ejido* system. The rural areas have been the primary source of emigrant peoples and this pressure is most likely to persist for many years (1966:93,94). The continuing poverty of Mexico, however, will cause large masses of the population who are unable to maintain a minimum standard of living to consider migration into the United States as the only possible way of improving their economic situation (1966:95).

Figure 4

RAILROADS IN THE AMERICAN SOUTHWEST AND MEXICO, 1914

Sources: Quick 1960:VIII,IX: Josephy 1965:348-349; Fogelson 1967:47; McWilliams 1968b:175-176

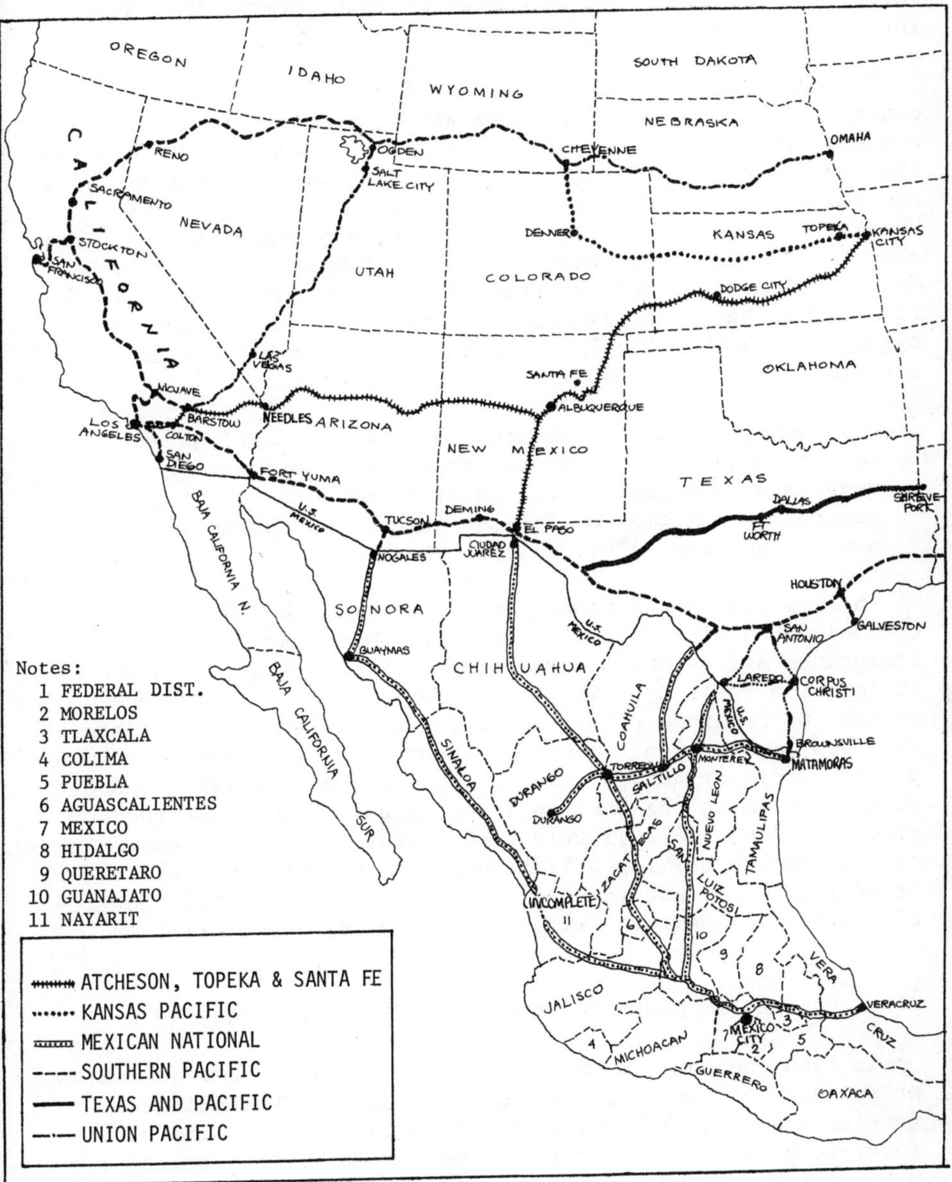

Another major source of migration potential is the rural-urban migrants of Mexico's cities whose hope for a better life has failed to materialize. As technological advances are made in Mexican agriculture, more farm workers will be forced to migrate to the cities. There they will greatly increase the surplus urban labor market. Movement across the northern border will merely be an extension of this internal migration (Grebler 1966:94).

The changing immigration policy of the United States is another factor affecting the immigration potential in the coming decade. The termination of the Bracero Program in 1964 and the 1965 amendments to the Immigration and Nationality Act are indications of a stricter control policy by the U.S. government. Whereas American agricultural and other business interests were able to strongly influence the flow of temporary workers from Mexico to meet their labor demands until recent years, this influence has been greatly reduced because of the pressure from organized labor in the United States and from Mexican American political organizations. According to Grebler:

> Now these [business] interests have been subordinated to consideration of domestic employment, protection of wages and labor standards, and the consequences of unrestrained immigration for the success of the anti-poverty program (1966:96).

In 1965 the United States Senate adopted the 1965 Act (P.L. 89-236) which fixed a ceiling of 120,000 a year for New World immigrants and established a Commission of Western Hemisphere Immigration to study immigration problems and to make recommendations to Congress prior to the January 1968 effective date of this new legislation. There was hope that this Commission would perform an important function by devising an equitable and durable solution to the Mexican immigration problem, but the Commission did not fulfill this task. What the future consequences of the 120,000 ceiling will be depends upon how the ceiling will be administered, but it will no doubt have an overall restrictive effect on Mexican immigration (Grebler 1970:80-81).

CHANGES IN HISPANIC AMERICAN POPULATION: 1960-1970

In 1960 the total number of persons who were born in Mexico or who were of Mexican or mixed parentage in the Southwest totaled more than 1.7 million (Figure 5). This accounted for forty-five percent of the total Mexican American population of 3.8 million in 1960. The remaining fifty-five percent of the Spanish-surname population were "natives of native parents."

Figure 5

ESTIMATED MEXICAN AMERICANS
IN THE UNITED STATES, 1960

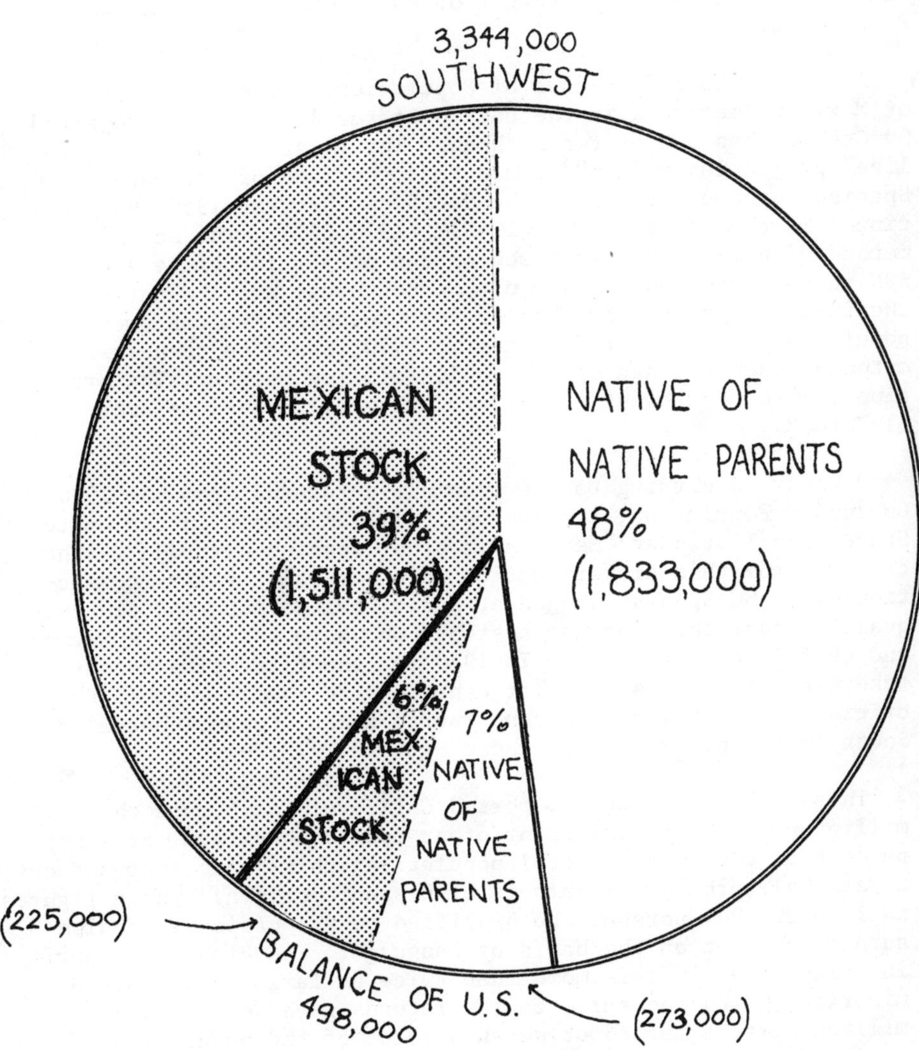

U.S. TOTAL 3,842,000

Source: Grebler 1966:2

This classification represents children of earlier immigrants or descendants of the original Hispano-Mexican settlers who became citizens in 1848 when the Southwest territories were incorporated into the United States through the Treaty of Guadalupe Hidalgo. (Figure 5 is Grebler's breakdown of the Mexican American population in the Southwest based on the 1960 Census of Population).

Prior to the 1970 Census of Population, the estimated number of Mexican Americans in the United States in 1970 was projected by Grebler based upon two methods. The first was a "straight-line" projection which "assumes that the rate of increase of Spanish-surname persons in the Southwest between 1950-1960 continued in the decade of the 1960s" (1970:607). The second method of projection was based on the proportion of persons of SSN in the total population of the Southwest and the nation. The figures computed by Grebler for the total Mexican American population of the United States in 1970, based on these two methods, show a range of 5.3 to 5.8 million people. The projection for the Southwest was 4.7 to 5.2 million Mexican Americans (1970:608).

However, according to the incomplete returns from the 1970 Census of Population, at least 9.3 million people in the United States are listed as "Mexican or other Spanish heritage". The criteria for this classification were several: family connection with the Spanish language, additional persons who did not qualify under the language test but who have a Spanish surname, and self-identification. "In 1970 for the first time census takers asked persons in a large nationwide sample whether their origin or descent was Mexican, Puerto Rican, Cuban, Central or South American, or none of these" (Burke 1972:29).

This preliminary data reported California with more than 3.1 million persons of Mexican or other Spanish heritage, or sixteen percent of the state's total population; this means that one out of six California residents is of Hispanic origin. These figures include 363,000 persons who qualified on the basis of Spanish-surname but not on the basis of language. The Hispanic minority in California (16%) is more than twice as large as the Negro minority, which the early census returns gave as totaling 1.4 million persons, or about seven percent of the population of the state (1972:1,29).

One often hears generalizations or stereotypes about "*the* Mexican American subculture" or "*the* Negro subculture" that tend to reinforce the idea that ethnic or racial minorities are homogeneous populations. One of the purposes of the present study is to demonstrate the heterogeneity of the Mexican American population, especially in urban Los Angeles County in Southern California.

The existence of great diversity within this growing population in the greater Los Angeles area has important implications for Christian leaders who are concerned about the spiritual, social, and physical well-being of a minority group that constitutes over seventeen percent of the county's seven million population.

2.

The Mexican American Mosaic in the Southwest

A continuing problem among Anglo Americans is the tendency either to make or to accept broad generalizations about the "distinctive characteristics" of the large Hispanic (SSN) population of Texas, New Mexico, Colorado, Arizona, and California, an area in which ninety-five percent of the SSN population are Mexican Americans. Rather than being a homogeneous population, the Mexican Americans of the Southwest have distinctive regional variations, and within each region there are subcultural, subgroup, and personal variables that defy attempted generalizations. Each local community is not static but dynamic, as many outdated anthropological case studies bear witness. Twenty-five years of rapid industrial and urban expansion in Southern California in the post-war period, for example, have transformed isolated Mexican *barrios* into urban and suburban ethnic neighborhoods, and have transformed rural-oriented, unskilled laborers into cosmopolitan industrial workers. The urban industrial centers of the Southwest contain Mexican Americans in all phases of transition and acculturation into the complex patterns of modern American urban society.

While recognizing that wide diversity exists within the Mexican American population of the Southwest, Anglo Americans should be aware of the traditional, rural folk-Catholic orientation of the Mexican masses which has been translated by the immigration of millions of Mexicans to the cities and towns of the Southwest, and from which the urban Mexican American is now emerging with a strong commitment to biculturalism.

Admittedly, there is a danger of over-simplification and distortion in trying to analyze Mexican American diversity and the historical process of its development. However, this author has attempted to honestly evaluate both the general and divergent characteristics of Mexican Americans in the Southwest in the hope that concerned Anglo Protestants may achieve a greater degree of *understanding* and *identification* with them as part of the Christian's ministry of reconciliation and liberation in the world. The resultant degree of understanding and identification by Anglo churchmen should lead to a balanced strategy of inclusive ministry to the diversified Hispanic "community". This strategy should be developed with a strong commitment to constructive spiritual and social involvement with the Hispanic population, as well as a commitment to Hispanic self-determination and the principle of biculturalism. Therefore, the following discussion (Chapters 2-4) will attempt to answer two important questions: (1) What *kind* of minority is the Hispanic American minority, or more specifically, the Mexican American minority, and (2) How do both the distinctive and divergent characteristics of the Mexican American population relate to the *religious dimension* in Hispanic Los Angeles?

THE *MEXICAN* AMERICAN

The Hispanic American minority in the Southwest is predominantly a *Mexican* minority. In the same way that the Republic of Mexico demonstrates the variety and diversity of personality types and life-styles based on numerous population variables--*subcultural, regional, racial, socioeconomic, religious,* and *personal*--so also does the *Mexican* American population of the United States.

Subcultural Variables of Mexican Immigrants

Although Latin America in general contains certain common cultural denominators, there is also significant social and cultural variation. Wagley and Harris have identified a variety of Latin American *subcultures*, with each one having a somewhat different *modal personality*. By definition, "subcultures" are "variations of a larger cultural tradition and represent the way of life of significant segments of the Latin American population" (Wagley & Harris 1965:43). The term "modal personality" is used to distinguish "the central or dominant personality characteristics more or less shared by all members of an ethnic group" (Keesing 1958:430).

These subcultural types represent the variables found in Mexico and are here briefly identified in order to trace the origins of the contemporary Mexican American population. Wagley and Harris have described nine basic typologies (these categories are not meant to be absolute, but only representative) in a preliminary attempt at "ordering the universe of Latin American cultural materials" (1965:42-69):

(1) *Tribal Indian*, comprising the cultures of the few remaining aboriginal peoples.

(2) *Modern Indian*, resulting from the fusion of aboriginal and, in the main, sixteenth and seventeenth century Iberian institutions and culture patterns.

(3) *Peasant*, carried by the relatively isolated horticultural peoples of Latin America (and frequently by the lower classes of small isolated towns), who are called variously *Mestizos*, *Cholos*, *Ladinos*, *Caboclos*, or other local terms.

(4) *Engenho Plantations* [*Haciendas or Fincas*], the subculture of the workers on family-owned estates.

(5) *Usina Plantations*, the way of life on the large modern corporation-owned agricultural establishments.

(6) *Town*, the way of life of the middle and upper class inhabitants of the numerous settlements serving as administrative, market, and religious centers throughout Latin America.

(7) *Metropolitan Upper Class*, characteristic of the highest socioeconomic strata in the large cities and of the owners of plantations.

(8) *Metropolitan Middle Class*, characteristic of an emerging group of big-city professional and white-collar workers and owners of medium-size business.

(9) *Urban Proletariat*, characteristic of a mass of unskilled and semiskilled industrial and menial workers in the larger cities.

Wide *regional variations* exist within each of these subcultural types throughout Latin America as seen, for example, in the differences between the Peasant populations of central Mexico and lowland Brazil. "They are called 'types'", according to Wagley and Harris, "because their content differs according to the environment, history, and distinctive local traditions of the nation or subregion in which they are found" (1965:43).

In terms of Mexico, the hacienda land tenure system of the pre-revolutionary era was *an economic and social matrix* that kept at least eighty-four percent of the Mexican population landless, indebted, and poverty-stricken in 1910. According to Herring,

> The hacienda...represented a little world within a larger nation. Its broad acres converged on the great manor house, to which its owner brought his fine city friends on a few festal occasions each year; clustered around were barns, shops, and stables; next to the house stood the church, and sometimes the school-house; trailing off from the center were the peons' adobe quarters, windowless and floorless. It was a self-contained community: the cornfields furnished the food; the maguey (agave), the drink; the forests, the charcoal which was the chief fuel; and the cotton fields, the clothing.... Economically, the hacienda was a laggard in a nation that boasted of progress (1955:346).

These large family-owned estates were controlled by a few thousand land barons that represented the old Mexican aristocracy. Although there were a few "high-minded and generous *hacendados* who made brave attempts to improve the lot of their workers [*peónes*]...these were brave exceptions." More commonly, wrote Herring,

> overbearing masters treated their men as slaves, (which they were in fact, though not in law), working them for unconscionable hours, flogging them for infraction of petty rules, shooting down rebels in cold blood, and appropriating the more comely daughters and wives for their casual pleasure. There were neither police nor courts of appeal for such victims; the benefits of civilization were reserved for the masters (1955:347).

Social Mobility

Deliverance came to the Mexican masses through the Revolution of 1910 which freed millions of *peónes* from bondage to the soil and gave them the needed mobility to migrate to the larger towns and cities, to the northern border areas of Mexico, and into the Southwestern United States. The largest volume of this flood of immigration came from the Peasant, Hacienda, and Town subcultures of the Mexican interior.

The external stimulus to emigration was the growing demand for new workers in agriculture as well as semi-skilled laborers in manufacturing and service industries in the United States. Mexican immigrants provided the needed low-wage labor supply, often at the instigation of labor recruiters who were agents for the railroads and other commercial interests in the Southwest. Between 1910 and 1930, more than 650,000 Mexicans *legally* entered the U.S. but many additional thousands entered *illegally* and moved more or less at will back and forth across the border (Figure 2, Chapter 1).

Geographical Origins

In 1930 Gamio estimated that the majority of the immigrants at that time came from the central plateau, which was predominantly a rural-agricultural area (1930:17). According to Broom and Shevky, a secondary source was the northern states bordering Texas where the primary ports of entry are located (1952: 150-158). More recent studies on the geographical origin of the *braceros* indicates that the central plateau has furnished most of these temporary migrants (Grebler 1966: Appendix C-3). This area includes the states of Chihuahua, Coahuila, Durango, Zacatecas, Guanajuato, Querétaro, Aguascalientes, and parts of San Luis Potosí, Jalisco, and Michoacan (cf. Figure 4).

The bulk of Mexican immigration has originated from two processes: continued migration from rural areas, and the movement of recent rural-urban migrants within Mexico who have not been absorbed into the urban economy. The agricultural section of central Mexico, which comprises nearly half of its population, is characterized by *widespread and severe poverty* and large-scale unemployment. Surplus farm workers tend to migrate to the cities but usually arrive "without the needed skills or adaptive capabilities" to form a permanent part of the urban economy. The Central Mesa continues to be the primary source of emigration along with the border areas which are now furnishing a larger portion than before. The northern areas are usually only a temporary place of residence for migrants from Mexico's interior before immigrating to the United States (1966:76).

Racial Variables

Although the U.S. Bureau of the Census identifies most Americans of Mexican descent as "white persons of Spanish surname," they are in fact a racially mixed population and have been considered as such by Anglos in the Southwest since the early frontier period. California Governor Young's "Mexican Fact-Finding Committee" in 1930 reported that fifty-nine percent of the total population of Mexico was classified as *mestizo*, twenty-nine percent as *Indian*, ten percent as *white*, and two percent *others*, according to the Mexican government. This report states that "the bulk of the immigration from Mexico into the United States is from the pure Indian or the Mestizo stock of the Mexican population" (Young 1930:42-43). The racial composition of Mexico had changed somewhat by 1954, according to Rycroft and Clemmer who reported the following classifications: Indian, twenty percent; mestizo, sixty percent; Negroes and mulattoes, five percent; white and others, fifteen percent (1963:29).

Religious Variables

Gamio evaluated the religious and ethical attitudes of the Mexican people in 1930 and distinguished two "social groups": the first group represents those "who find themselves in accord with fundamental and universal ethical principles, and who do not need, or do not think they need, the moralizing influence of religion"; the second group is "composed of those that possess varied special and characteristic religious concepts that they believe to be, or which in reality are, the motives of their ethical behavior" (1930:108). The former group consisted of an extremely small number of individuals who belonged mostly to the "cultured middle classes." The latter group "embraces almost all the population of Mexico."

Three general systems of religious behavior will briefly be described as a background for our analysis of Mexican immigration. The original religious orientation of Mexico consisted of *the Pre-Colombian animistic religious systems* of the early Indian tribes. Superimposed on this polytheistic base was the *Catholicism* of the Spanish conquerors who came both with the cross and the sword, to baptize those who submitted to their religious and political rule and to slay those who refused.

Eugene Nida has called the resultant admixture of Catholicism and pagan Indian beliefs and practices "Cristo-paganism" (1961:1). There has been an uneven mixture of these two systems, however, due to the natural processes of undirected selection, reinterpretation, and uneven social acceptance by the newly "converted" indigeneous populations (Luzbetak 1966:119-121). Nida distinguishes at least three different syncretistic levels within the Roman Catholic system:

> On the one level there is the almost purely indigeneous religious system preserved by the *brujo* 'sorcerer' and the *curandero* 'medicine man' with only a superficial addition of Spanish holy words, incantations, and Catholic images. At the other extreme there is the typical church-centered worship of the town-dwelling and Spanish-speaking Roman Catholic, whose beliefs and practices are quite orthodox, except for a scattering of Indian magic and beliefs about native herbs and medicines and possibly about some evil spirits in a distant cave. But in between these two extremes there are varying degrees of Cristo-paganism, a kind of two-headed system which has two distinct, but non-contradictory, orientations. On the one hand, the person looks to the "God of heaven", the "priest", and the "church", and in this he is a good Roman Catholic. On the other hand, he also looks to *Dios Mundo* "the God of the world" (owner of the mountains, valleys, rivers, and springs), the sorcerer, and the *Ermita* 'local shrine'" (1961:1-2).

The folk-Catholicism of the Mexican lower classes, with its various degrees of syncretism, was mainly due to the Church's inability as well as its failure to provide adequate catechetical instruction in sound theology (Luzbetak 1966:128). Grebler advances the opinion that the "nominal" Catholicism of the lower classes principally resulted from "a chronic shortage of priests," especially after the Revolution, and for this reason Mexican Catholic immigrants were largely "ignorant about their religion, with tenuous loyalties to the institutional Church and formal Catholicism" (1970:449-450). Gamio, however, has demonstrated that "a greater number of churches, convents, and monasteries sometimes out of proportion to the number of inhabitants" were located in the central plateau where the majority of immigrants originated (1930:115). This region is described as a "fanatical" stronghold of Catholicism and for this reason the spread of Protestantism had made little advance prior to 1930.

During the colonial period in Mexico, the Catholic Church established itself as a landowner of vast tracts of land and became tremendously wealthy and politically powerful. However, during the independence movement in the early 1800s, the Church lost much of its wealth and power due to the reform laws established and enforced by a strong anticlerical movement. At the time of the Revolution in 1910, the Church had regained some of its lost power through the patronage of Porfirio Diaz, but there was still a very strong anticlerical movement that extended down to the Mexican masses (Gamio 1930:112-113). This movement also conditioned the attitudes of Mexican immigrants towards the American Catholic Church in the Southwestern states (Grebler 1970:449-450).

The third religious system to be considered is that of *Protestantism* which had its origins in the period 1857-1914. In spite of heavy persecution and opposition, at least seventy-nine mission stations had been established in twenty-five states and the Federal District of Mexico by 1914. When all of the American missionaries were recalled in 1913-1914 because of the violence and turmoil of the Revolution, they left behind approximately 30,000-35,000 communicant members and a Protestant community of 150,000 (slightly more than one percent of the total population). The states with the strongest Protestant activity were Chihuahua, Coahuila, Jalisco, Nuevo León, San Luis Potosí, Sonora, and the Federal District. The strength of the Protestant work was notably in the northern states along the U.S. border and on the fringes of the Central Mesa (Leslie 1923: 69,92-93,120-121).

According to McGavran, Huegel, and Taylor, the Mexican response to Protestantism by 1963 had mainly come from the lower lasses and from the following regions: the revolutionary ranhos and *ejidos*, the northern border areas, the liberal cities such as Monterey and Torreon), and especially the Federal Disrict (1963:30,36-41). However, Gamio states that prior to 1930 he growth of Protestantism had mainly come from the middle lasses, who were "too intelligent to accept the neo-paganism f the Indians" and had no privileged status to protect as did he upper classes who are traditionally conservative (1930:114).

'sychological Variables

Turning to the psychology of the Mexican in our attempt to nderstand the background of the *Mexican* American minority in he United States, Samuel Ramos, a noted Mexican philosopher, as analyzed the "Mexican national character" in his *Profile of an and Culture in Mexico*. Ramos' major thesis is that a deep ense of inferiority is felt by a great many Mexicans as a reult of the prolonged contact between Mexico and European ulture:

> It seems to me that *the sentiment of inferiority* in our race has a historical origin which must be sought in the areas of the Conquest and Colonization. But it did not really begin to manifest itself until the time of the Independence movement, when the country had to define its own national physiognomy. Being an extremely young nation, it attempted--overnight--to reach the level of traditional European civilization. It was then that the conflict broke out between ambition and the limits of natural capacity. The solution seemed to be imitation of Europe, its ideas and its institutions, creating thereby certain collective fictions which, when we have interpreted them as fact, have artificially solved our psychological conflict (1962:9,10).

Ramos sees some of the expressions of Mexican character as ays of compensating for this *unconscious* sense of inferiority. here is *no* real somatic or psychic inferiority within the Mexian, but only a *feeling* of inferiority. Ramos clarifies his osition in this way: "What I maintain is that the Mexican ndervalues himself, committing in this way an injustice to his erson.... I of course do *not* claim that this psychological exlanation is a valid generalization for *all* Mexicans, for some ossess other modes of character whose mechanism should be exlained by other scientific principles" (1962:9, italics mine). This reference to other "modes of character" allows for the ubcultural variable which we have previously examined in the ypologies of Wagley and Harris. Whether Ramos' psychological onstruct covers all nine subcultural types is open to question.]

Briefly stated, Ramos' construct is the following: Given the innate personality variables that are possible in man, the environmental and cultural determinants in the Mexican context tend to create a strong *sense of inferiority* which is manifested in the Mexican's irrational distrust of himself, others and the world in which he lives. The Mexican is *strongly fatalistic*, which is a reflection of his general distrust of a chaotic world. He engages in *self-deception* in his quest to achieve a comfortable self-image by imagining that he has become what he would like to be. His downtrodden ego finds salvation in the cult of *machismo* (virility or masculine superiority). This conflict between his fictitious and his real personality causes him to be *hypersensitive* in his relationships with others. Thus, his *fatalistic* view of life and his *distrustful* attitude towards others have been culturally and historically determined by the fact that he was born a *Mexican* (cf. Octavio Paz 1961).

It is obvious that a great many Mexicans have developed a healthy self-image as well as mature interpersonal relationships. That they have refused to allow the feeling of inferiority to dominate their lives is evidence of man's ability to achieve a relative self-control and to rise above the environmental and cultural forces that converge upon him. While keeping these *psychological variables* in view, Ramos' interpretation of the modal personality of the Mexican appears to be generally valid.

Age, Sex, and Occupational Variables

When Mexican immigrants are compared with all other immigrants as to age, sex, and occupation, the analysis reveals substantial differences in all three areas and for all periods for which data was available. Immigrants from Mexico include a greater percentage of males and tend to be grouped in the lower-grade occupations and in the productive age groups (14-40 years). Grebler emphasizes, however, that "In many ways the age, sex, and occupational characteristics of Mexican immigrants of *recent years* resemble those of Europeans who came to the United States in an earlier epoch" (1966:43).

Between 1910 and 1964 Mexican immigrants who came legally to the United States were heavily concentrated in the *occupational classification* "laborers *except* farm and mine" and underrepresented in all other classifications, especially "white-collar" categories (Grebler 1966:103). It may seem unusual that immigrants were over-represented in the first category, "laborers other than farm and mine", when, as we have seen, the majority of the immigrants were from the rural farming states of the Central Mesa. Grebler explains this apparent contradiction:

> Rural origin...does not necessarily give a full description of occupations and skill levels or of exposure to urban experience. Rural Mexico includes part-time or even full-time artisans as well as agricultural workers. Traditional handicraft in many cases has qualified rural people for other occupations. Moreover, much of the rural population lives in the small towns which dot the Mexican landscape, and this means a degree of quasi-urban orientation as well as an admixture of urban job experience. This observation may help explain the apparent contradiction between the over-representation of non-agricultural occupations among immigrants (relative to the Mexican labor force) and the persistent significance of the rural segment as a source of newcomers to this country (Grebler 1966:76).

The majority of illegal aliens were temporary farm workers, who considered this type of migration as an alternative to permanent relocation. Many permanent immigrants were employed in agricultural jobs for only part of the year and held other jobs requiring additional skills for the remaining months. In recent years the labor demands of our changing economy have made it far more difficult to absorb unskilled immigrants than in the earlier years when European immigration met the needs of our rapidly growing industrial economy. Today, the highest rates of unemployment and the longest periods of unemployment are found among the unskilled laborers (1966:45-50).

The characteristics of Mexican immigrants have a significant bearing upon the type of impact that is made upon the recipient society. These effects include the labor market, school systems, and various social institutions, including both the Catholic and Protestant Churches. These characteristics also seriously affect the rate of acculturation of the migrants and their socio-economic expectations.

THE MEXICAN *AMERICAN*

Now that brief evaluations of the variables as well as the general tendencies within the Mexican milieu have been given, let us consider the divergent characteristics and historical development of the Mexican *American* minority in the Southwest, by the way of comparison and contrast.

Minority Group Origins

The war between the United States and Mexico ended in 1848 with the signing of the Treaty of Guadalupe Hidalgo by which Mexico ceded an extensive territory, about one-half of its national domain, to their imperialistic conquerors. According to McWilliams,

> All citizens of Mexico residing within the ceded domain were to become citizens of the United States if they failed to leave the territory within one year after ratification of the treaty. Only a few thousand Mexican nationals, perhaps not more than 1,500 or 2,000 took advantage of this provision; the rest became citizens by default (1948:51).

The Treaty of Guadalupe Hidalgo also guaranteed specific property and political rights to the Spanish-speaking population, which was composed of the descendents of the original Spanish colonialists and later settlers from Mexico. This "native" population was allowed to retain its language, culture, and religion, which in effect was a guarantee of cultural autonomy (1948:51-52). As we have previously noted, large numbers of Mexican immigrants came to California during the Gold Rush, still larger numbers arrived in the Southwest between 1910-1930, and mass immigration has continued since World War II.

The U.S. Bureau of the Census has used various classifications over the years to distinguish Americans of Mexican descent as well as immigrants from other Latin American countries. For example, the 1960 census used the classification "Spanish surname population" and distinguished the following categories: native born of foreign parentage, native of native parents, and native of mixed parentage. The 1970 census broadened the SSN classification to that of "Mexican or other Spanish heritage". Mexican Americans constitute over ninety-five percent of the Hispanic heritage population in the Southwest (Grebler 1970:601-608).

Social Class Structure

During the early years of Mexican immigration and continuing into the mid-1940s, the dominant characteristic of Anglo and Mexican community life was a "*caste-like system*" that separated "Mexicans" from "Americans" in almost all social situations. An overwhelming majority of the Mexican population were lower-class laborers who were segregated in employment, housing, schools, and public accomodations; they were also widely deprived of normal community and local government services, political and union representation, equal consumer services, and social interaction with Anglos, except occasionally in employee-employer relationships--and often even this was handled through a Mexican foreman for a crew of laborers.

The only exception to this caste system was in the case of upper-class "Spanish" Americans who were either the descendants of the white Spanish aristocracy of the Southwestern colonial period or upper-class refugees from the Mexican Revolution--including "political exiles, lawyers, men of letters, doctors, engineers, and journalists" (Ortegon 1932:20). Although the few Spanish families were usually accepted in the Anglo American social world, even to the extent of intermarriage, the "old family" aristocracy themselves discriminated against lower-class Mexicans in the Southwest, which was no different from the practice of the upper-class elite in Mexico. Upper status Mexican Americans, therefore, have experienced minimal discrimination by Anglos and have usually been free to reside outside of the Mexican *colonias*, attend Anglo schools, and ignore most of the other caste restrictions, especially if they had light complexions and spoke good English. However, this tended to be true *only* in the larger Southwestern cities with large concentrations of Mexican Americans, but not true of the smaller towns (Grebler 1970:322-324).

The Mexican American caste system was greatly modified in Southern California during and after World War II because of the occupational and geographical mobility that resulted from expanded job opportunities, especially in Los Angeles, primarily due to the extensive manpower demands of wartime industrialization and to post-war commercial and industrial development. According to Grebler, "labor shortages were so great that discrimination in hiring and upgrading was sharply reduced; job qualification standards, especially with regard to formal schooling, were substantially relaxed" (1970:217). The SSN population of Southern California drastically shifted from a rural-agricultural base prior to 1940 to urban-industrial employment by the early 1950s, a trend which has continued in later decades although the occupational progress of Mexican Americans in industrial employment has proceeded at a slower rate than in the peak war years. The process of caste modification, or "caste leakage" as Grebler calls it, resulted from the large-scale migration of Mexican Americans from the strongholds of the caste system--the rural towns of the Southwest--to the larger cities in Texas and California and to Midwestern industrial centers, like St. Louis, Chicago, and Detroit. As a result, some Mexican Americans achieved not only geographical and occupational mobility but upward social mobility as well (1970:324).

Grebler identifies a third type of class structure that appears among larger cities in California, and in some of the northern states, where greater social mobility has allowed a growing Mexican American middle-class to come into existence, especially during the 1950s and 1960s. New upward mobility was achieved as a by-product of World War II and the Korean Conflict in which many Mexican Americans valiently participated.

They reaped the benefits of job training and new skills acquired during their military service, also the benefits of post-war educational, housing, and loan provisions from the G.I. Bill of Rights. In the military, Mexican Americans received an exposure to Anglos which they had never had before, as well as exposure to other people and cultures in many parts of the world. Veterans returned to their home communities with high expectations and with a much higher level of acculturation than before the war. Although some became discouraged by continued discrimination and unequal opportunities that they encountered in their old *barrios*, others, equipped with new job skills and higher education, achieved middle-class status and a new respectability in the Anglo community (1970:325).

In the process of achieving geographical and socioeconomic mobility in the post-war period, a growing number of Mexican Americans have opted to cut their ties with the ethnic community and to merge into Anglo middle-class society; some have done so with marked success. These individuals have achieved the mobility to work with Anglos, to live in Anglo neighborhoods, to send their children to Anglo schools, and to identify themselves with a prestigious social class subculture, thereby receiving needed status and self-esteem from the Anglo middle class value system rather than through identification with the ethnic community. However, the price usually paid for identification with the Anglo middle class, rather than with the ethnic community, was alienation from other Mexican Americans:

> A typical pattern is that of dissociation from Mexican friends and schoolmates in high school in order to move increasingly in Anglo circles in high school, in college, and in work. It may end in anonymity and, perhaps, then a conscious decision for reidentification with Mexican Americans and even a conscious decision to enter or return to the barrio (Moore 1970:113-114).

Socially mobile Mexican Americans in Los Angeles who choose to live in predominantly Mexican housing areas ("Colonies" with greater than 45% SSN) are individuals who are seeking to retain their ties to the ethnic community, whereas those who choose to live in predominantly Anglo areas ("Frontier"--less than 15% SSN) are attempting greater assimilation to Anglo society (cf. Figure 16). Grebler explains the difference in these two prestige systems:

> The middle-class Colonists tend to be people who may obtain status rewards from their fellow ethnics on the basis of money (like the skilled workers) while avoiding the possible status deprivation commensurate with their low job prestige in the large society. For example, a

> highly-paid truck driver of Mexican descent may be able to get more out of life by staying in a predominantly Mexican area, where both his income and his occupation receive deference because they are above the norm. On the other hand, highly-paid white-collar workers tend to leave the Mexican areas. This may be because both their income and their occupation permit them to be comfortable without the extra prestige support of the ethnic group (1970:379).

Many socially mobile Mexican Americans have the option of finding support and identity either in the ethnic community or in the status rewards of Anglo middle-class society. The availability of such an option varies with the aspiration level and felt needs of the individual and with time and place: "It is greater for the Mexican American now than it was in the past, and greater in large California cities than in small Texas towns" (Grebler 1970:319).

Socioeconomic Variables

The social class system of Mexican American communities varies from rural to urban areas, between urban or rural areas, and within urban areas. All *barrios* are not the same and there are many variables that determine neighborhood differences: historical development, opportunity structure, socioeconomic level, degree of ethnicity, etc. Increasing social-class differentiation among Mexican Americans points to a serious modification of the concept that *most barrios* are enclaves of "traditional Mexican folk-society", especially in Southern California:

> Despite great obstacles, this population as a whole is clearly moving further away from lower-class Mexican traditional culture and toward Anglo-American middle-class culture, so that both its cultural status and its social-class status are changing. It is true that immigrants in many ways reinforce the traditional patterns locally, but they are coming from a changing Mexico much more urbanized and industrialized than the Mexico known to the immigrant of two, three, or four decades ago. The latest waves of immigration have come from socioeconomically higher, more urbanized strata of Mexican society. Mexican-American migrants also come in important numbers from other states of the Southwest, particularly from Texas and New Mexico. The communities from which they have come are generally more traditionally oriented than Southern California Mexican-American communities (Penalosa 1967:407,408).

Examples of Social Stratification. The traditionally-oriented *barrios* are usually in agriculturally-oriented areas where the caste system is still strong. The isolation of Mexican American communities from Anglo society seriously retards acculturation and upward social mobility. Clark's study of Mexican American community life in San Jose, California in the mid-1950s identified two perspectives concerning *barrio* social classes. From the perspective of the Anglo, only two classes were evident: a lower class (the poor and less acculturated) and a higher class (equivalent to the Anglo middle class). However, the Spanish-speaking community itself distinguished three classes: *La alta sociedad* (the upper class), *los medianos* (the middle class), and *los de abajo* (the lower class). These classes were distinguished by differences in income, standard of living, occupation, speech, property ownership, and ethnic identity (1970:16-18).

The lower class was composed of migrant farm workers (including *braceros*), the temporarily employed, the unemployed, and those on public assistance (welfare). The middle class consisted of steadily employed blue-collar workers who were buying their own homes, sending their children to school, acquiring a few luxuries, and trying to live as comfortably as possible in their "insulated" *barrios*. Those in *la alta sociedad* were the more successful Mexican Americans who had higher incomes, better homes, more education, fluency in English, greater prestige in the community, and more residential mobility. According to Clark, "many of the more 'successful' Mexican-Americans in San Jose are traitors to their own people, disassociate themselves from other Spanish-speaking groups, and ally themselves with Anglos" (1970:18). The upper class lived in more expensive houses, had white-collar jobs, attended Anglo churches, and were members of Anglo organizations (1970:16-33).

Madsen (1964:29-43), in the context of rural Hidalgo County in South Texas, distinguished five social stratums which more closely resemble the structure of Anglo society. The top stratum was composed of wealthy "old Spanish families" and below them wealthy families without distinguished ancestry who achieved their status through vertical mobility: owners of large businesses, ranches, or farms and professionals--mainly doctors and lawyers. The middle class was divided into two levels (upper-middle and lower-middle) which were distinguished "only in terms of those who are financially better off or worse off" than any specific Mexican American of the middle class. The occupations represented by the middle class included: "migratory labor contractors, store proprietors, small farm owners, mechanics, clerks, stenographers, and other white-collar workers" (1964:36). The lowest class was also divisible into two levels: a lower-lower class composed of unskilled migrant laborers, either immigrants of first generation Mexican Americans, who resided in both rural towns and urban centers; an upper-lower class consisting of steadily employed unskilled and semiskilled workers in agriculture, construction, manufacturing, and other low-skill occupations.

Although these social distinctions help us understand the background of Mexican Americans who have migrated to large urban centers like Los Angeles, the urban social stratification system is better explained by Penalosa's study of Pomona, California in the early 1960s. The lowest level was composed of the very poor, the least acculturated, and the unskilled. The next level contained the majority of Mexican American workers, the steadily employed unskilled and semiskilled. The third level includes skilled craftsmen, small businessmen, sales personnel, technicians, and other lower level white-collar workers--those who have achieved a "modest degree of success". The top level, which Penalosa considered the equivalent of the Anglo middle class, consisted of substantial businessmen, large land owners, professionals and other upper level white-collar workers. This class was composed of "the most successful and most acculturated individuals of the Mexican Amerian community" (1963:28-31,289-293,324,353-354; Heller 1966:17).

Class Stratification in Los Angeles County. Grebler (1970) and Sheldon (1966) help us zero in on Los Angeles County's class stratification system with studies from the period 1961-1966. According to Grebler, "income is...the major indicator of class position. Not only is income the most general means for the acquisition of most types of status, but the other commonly used indicators (education, occupational level, occupational prestige, neighborhood reputation) are equivocal" (1970:225-226).

Mexican American socioeconomic levels in Los Angeles County for the period 1965-1966 are shown in Figure 6, and comparisons made with Mexican social classes and with SSN income in California in 1960. The previous discussion of upper, middle, and lower classes among the Mexican American population, especially Penalosa's analysis, is adequate to describe the social stratums used in Figure 6. The family income levels for Los Angeles County are significant at the upper and lower extremes: only fifteen percent had incomes above $10,000 while thirty-four percent earned less than $5,000. However, Los Angeles County is somewhat better represented than the Southwest as a whole in terms of poverty-level income: only fourteen percent of Mexican American families in the county earned less than $3,000 compared to 34.8 percent of all SSN families in the Southwest (1970:197, 305).

Figure 6

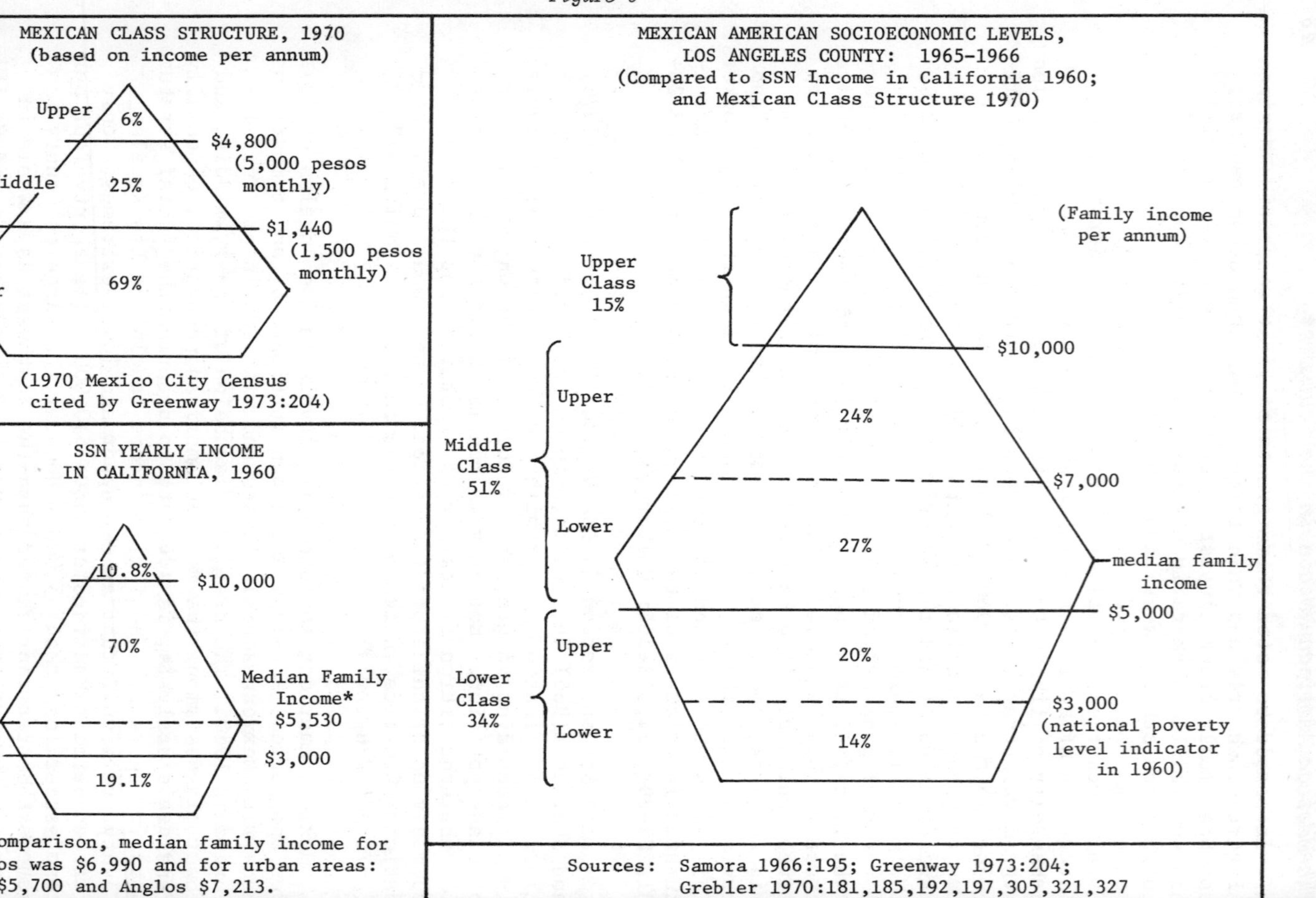

MEXICAN CLASS STRUCTURE, 1970
(based on income per annum)
Upper
6%
$4,800
(5,000 pesos monthly)
Middle
25%
$1,440
(1,500 pesos monthly)
Lower
69%
(1970 Mexico City Census cited by Greenway 1973:204)
SSN YEARLY INCOME IN CALIFORNIA, 1960
10.8%
$10,000
70%
Median Family Income*
$5,530
$3,000
19.1%
*By comparison, median family income for Anglos was $6,990 and for urban areas: SSN $5,700 and Anglos $7,213.
MEXICAN AMERICAN SOCIOECONOMIC LEVELS, LOS ANGELES COUNTY: 1965-1966
(Compared to SSN Income in California 1960; and Mexican Class Structure 1970)
(Family income per annum)
Upper Class 15%
$10,000
Middle Class 51%
Upper
24%
$7,000
Lower
27%
median family income
$5,000
Lower Class 34%
Upper
20%
$3,000
(national poverty level indicator in 1960)
Lower
14%
Sources: Samora 1966:195; Greenway 1973:204; Grebler 1970:181,185,192,197,305,321,327

It should be noted that the social class divisions used in Figure 6 are only approximations of possible class lines based on SSN family income levels in Los Angeles County in the mid-1960s. Also, these class divisions represent the internal stratification of the area's Mexican American subsociety and should not be confused with Anglo class structure. By comparison, however, at least one economist was bold enough to challenge the myth of the American middle class by pointing out the absurdity of trying to stretch the "middle class" label from the lower boundary of $5,000 to the upper boundary of $40,000: "The difference between life-styles of a family earning $9,000 a year and one earning $30,000 a year is too broad to permit a common label" (Parker 1972:22).

Parker proposed, for the sake of exposing this "myth", that the middle class constitutes seventy percent of the American population, the upper class ten percent, and the lower class twenty percent. He then goes on to show that "economic equality is not a prominant characteristic of contemporary American society" (1972:22).

> According to statistics, the upper half of the so-called middle class received 46 per cent of the nation's total money income. At the same time, the lower half of the middle class received 22 per cent or, in other words, less than half the amount received by the upper group....
>
> Inequality of income is only one part of the problem in the myth of the middle class in America. Figures show that for the poor, life is marginal. And for the bottom segment of the lower-middle class, who might be called the "New Poor", economic danger is never far away. Income is spent almost entirely for day-to-day maintenance of life; liquid assets and debt purchasing are the chief means for the accumulation of comforts, such as appliances, a car or a college education. And debt purchasing, whatever its popularity, can impose not only exorbitant costs in the form of inflated interest charges, but a heavier psychological burden in the loss of a sense of freedom (1972:22).

The occupational distribution of Mexican Americans, used as an indicator of general income level and potential, aids our analysis of urban SSN population in the Southwest. Figure 7 shows the occupational distribution and classification of urban SSN males in the Southwest in 1960 compared to urban Anglos. Only 18.8 percent of urban SSN males in California are in white-collar occupations compared to 56.6 in low-skill jobs, whereas urban Anglos are classified as 46.3 percent white-collar and only 26.7 percent low-skill. Grebler does not

FIGURE 7

OCCUPATIONAL DISTRIBUTION OF
URBAN SSN MALES, SOUTHWEST, 1960

Occupational Category	Anglo	SSN
Professional	15.1%	4.6%
Manager and Proprietor	14.7	4.9
Clerical	7.8	5.5
Sales	9.2	4.1
Craftsmen[1]	21.5	18.2
Operatives	15.8	25.4
Private household	0.1	0.1
Service	5.4	8.4
Laborers (non-farm)	4.4	15.8
Farm laborers	0.6	7.3
Farm managers	0.7	0.6
Occupations not reported	4.7	5.1

OCCUPATIONAL CLASSIFICATION
URBAN SSN MALES, 1960

White-Collar Occupations[2]	Anglo	SSN
Southwest	46.9%	19.0%
California	46.3	18.8
Low-Skill Occupations[3]		
Southwest	26.3%	57.0%
California	26.7	56.6

Notes:

[1]Grebler considers "craftsmen" to be neither white-collar nor low-skilled worker because of high average earnings; craftsmen, however, are included in the category "blue-collar workers".

[2]Includes the following occupational categories: professional, managerial, clerical, and sales. Farm managers are excluded.

[3]Includes the following occupational categories: operative, laborer, farm labor and foreman, and service workers

Source: Grebler 1970:209-212,626-627

place "skilled craftsmen" in either category for obvious reasons; craftsmen are normally included, however, in the category "blue-collar" workers where they rank high in average earnings and unionization.

Mexican Americans in Los Angeles County had the highest occupational representation in the following industries in 1965-1966: construction; manufacturing; wholesale and retail trade; and transportation, communication, and public utilities, with the highest number employed in manufacturing (1970:304). Large numbers of women, for example, were employed in the sweatshops of the garment industry, located in the basements and upper floors of dilapidated buildings in Los Angeles' Wholesale District, where thousands of Mexican Americans and Mexican nationals work in small, non-union factories for wages that range from $35 to $75 per week (Bernstein and Del Olmo 1971:1, 15). California's billion dollar clothing industry is the tenth-ranked industry in the state and employs 54,000 garment workers in Los Angeles County, with "the overwhelming majority of them Mexican-Americans, Mexican nationals, blacks and Orientals" (Boyarsky 1972:4,7,10,12).

In the period 1961-1963, Sheldon conducted a study of East Los Angeles as part of the Laboratory in Urban Culture of Occidental College. Sheldon noted that

> social class differences are becoming increasingly significant as more and more Mexican-Americans achieve higher levels of education and move up the socioeconomic ladder without changing their identity; they remain persons of Mexican descent instead of becoming "old Spanish", as was formerly the custom when being "Mexican" carried greater stigma (1966:126).

Nevertheless, Mexico continues to strongly influence Mexican American life in Los Angeles due to continued high in-migration and to "extensive visiting back and forth across the border" (1966:129). The heterogeneity of Los Angeles' Mexican American population is seen in the following comment by a Mexican American leader, quoted by Sheldon: "[a recent study] lists nine different types of people of Mexican descent living in Los Angeles, but I don't see myself or my friends as fitting into *any* of these groups" (1966:129).

Sheldon's study used two sample groups in an attempt to observe contrasting life-styles and levels of community dynamics: first, an area aggregate consisting of "a random sample of residents in a typical census tract in East Los Angeles" was chosen, mainly composed of "working-class" Mexican Americans; the second sample consisted primarily of middle and upper-middle class Mexican Americans, drawn from active members of leading Mexican American organizations in Los Angeles County.

Using ethnic and Anglo organizational affiliations as a measure of acculturation to Anglo middle-class society, the working-class sample "tended to belong to no voluntary organizations or, at most, only one. Only 13.7 percent belonged to any formally organized group other than nominal membership in church groups and labor unions." By contrast, the middle-class sample "tended to belong not to just one but to many different groups." According to Sheldon, "an unknown number have merged so completely with the dominant society that they have, for all intents and purposes, lost their identity as Mexican-Americans" (1966:137). An analysis of Mexican American organizations and leadership will be presented later.

While Sheldon's working-class sample (lower-lower and upper-lower, see Figure 6) revealed that "patterns of self-concept, ways of life, daily living practices, and other variables among the urban working-class" were not significantly different from those described by Saunders, Samora, Simmons, and Madsen from studies in rural areas or small towns in Texas, New Mexico, and Southern Colorado, the middle-class sample showed greater variation. The urbanized Mexican American of the middle-class "has chosen a set of values different from those traditionally associated with working-class Mexican-Americans and also different from those describing urban-Americans who live in the ghetto" (1966:147).

The composite description of the urban, middle-class Mexican American given by Sheldon includes the following factors:

> ...optimism, mobility, high regard for education, active in political organizations, and a high civic spirit. He, his family and his friends are in the process of becoming middle-class Americans, while at the same time retaining much of the heritage of the parent culture. He still identifies himself as Mexican-American, is bilingual, has strong ties to Mexico, and many of his attitudes and values relating to the family, religion, compadrazgo, and politics have a strong ethnic flavor. Yet the neighborhood in which he lives, the house and its material comforts, the family's recreational patterns, the type of employment, the amount of money he earns, and his high educational achievement--all these characteristics--are American and middle class. It is likely that [his] children will complete the task of assimilation that was begun by [his] parents when they first decided to cross the border into the United States (1966:156).

Demographically, the model urban, middle-class Mexican American is age 40-50, is a second generation American and a college graduate, has three children, is married to a Mexican American, owns his own home ($20,000-$25,000 value in 1963), and lives in "a predominantly Anglo neighborhood with less than 25 per cent Mexican-American population." Employed as a medium level white-collar worker, he earns from $8,000 to $14,000 per year (1963), works primarily with Anglos (conversely, with few or no Mexican Americans), and has two medium-priced cars, a radio, television, telephone, etc. Although he is a Roman Catholic, about fifteen percent of his friends are Protestants; but he is not very active in church-related organizations. The model man is politically active, however, and is a registered Democrat, usually voting a straight Democratic ticket. In terms of informal social relationships, he has many friends in many parts of Los Angeles, with ninety percent of them living outside his immediate neighborhood; he visits his friends often and many are Anglos. By contrast, most of the working-class sample "tended to have social contacts only within their extended family or in the neighborhood" (1966:146-156).

Upward Social Mobility

The characteristics of Mexican Americans in the rural Rio Grande Valley of South Texas may or may not typify Mexican Americans in urban Los Angeles. The differences between these areas tend to be far greater than the similarities. Mexican Americans living in urban areas tend to reflect the various socioeconomic levels of their heterogeneous urban environment. According to Penalosa, "Mexican American subculture in its most common variant [in Southern California] is probably best regarded as a variant of American working-lower class culture" (1967:410). The *rural-to-urban migration* that changed the orientation of Mexican Americans in Los Angeles County, mainly stimulated by rural poverty during the Depression and by the growing opportunities for upward mobility in urban areas during the Second World War and in the post-war years, did not seriously alter the rural orientation of Mexican Americans in many areas of the Southwest, at least not to the same degree as in Southern California.

Agricultural labor, rather than being a desirable occupation, is considered by most Mexican Americans to be only a means of survival. Although adjustment to an urban milieu may be difficult, unskilled agricultural laborers are willing to risk being socially dislocated by moving to an urban center and starting anew at the bottom of the class stratification system. Many rural-urban migrants view *geographical relocation* as a means of upward social mobility, but only a few are able to rise significantly above their previous socioeconomic level (Grebler 1970:

341-342). Moreover, there are significant regional differences between urban areas:

> In Los Angeles the native born attain higher-income levels, and comparatively few of the Mexican bred reach the middle classes. In San Antonio, those born in the city are not much more likely to live above the poverty level than those born elsewhere in Texas or even in Mexico (Grebler 1970:344-345).

Second and third generation Mexican American urbanites in Los Angeles are usually able to achieve a high degree of upward social mobility than did their parents because of greater opportunities for better education, occupational diversification, higher income, residential mobility, accelerated acculturation, higher levels of aspiration, and greater opportunities for self-fulfillment. Nevertheless, many emerging middle-class Mexican Americans,

> instead of comparing themselves with their parents and congratulating themselves on how far they have come, compare themselves with others in the Anglo world and depreciate their accomplishments. Instead of looking ahead to a better future, they often look behind in fear of the abyss from which they have climbed (1970:342).

However, those who demonstrate fear or apprehension about their present and future socioeconomic stability are usually those who have painfully climbed up from a background of poverty and discrimination, rather than individuals who were raised in an Anglo neighborhood by middle-class parents who spoke good English and instilled middle-class values. The Anglicized second or third generation middle-class Mexican American has little common experience with those who have climbed up the hard way (1970:342-343,433-439).

Grebler has shown that Mexican American *upward social mobility* in Southern California is accelerated by migration from rural to urban areas, by migration to an urban area as a child rather than as an adult, by native-birth rather than immigration from Mexico, by being a second or third generation urban resident rather than a recent arrival, by residence in "Frontier" areas (predominantly Anglo neighborhoods) rather than in Mexican "Colonies", and by birth to middle-income and highly acculturated parents rather than to parents of the struggling lower-class who have had few opportunities for acculturation (1970:337-343). Figure 8 lists some of the major variables in the urban Mexican American milieu of Los Angeles County which influence social mobility. This listing of variables is meant to be representative rather than exhaustive of possible social mobility influences, although at first glance it may appear to be the latter.

Figure 8

VARIABLES WITHIN THE URBAN MEXICAN AMERICAN MOSAIC IN LOS ANGELES COUNTY

Nativity variables:

- Mexican-born (+ all Mexican variables)
- Native of Mexican-born parents
- Native of mixed parentage (one parent born in Mexico)
- Native of native parents (second, third generation, etc.)
- Native of Texas/New Mexico/Colorado/Arizona/Other
- Native of California
- Citizenship: native/naturalized/alien

Immigration/migration variables:

- Immigrant from Mexico to California (direct or via other Southwestern states)
- Migrant to California from Texas/New Mexico/Colorado/Arizona/other
- California subregional migrant (from rural/suburban/urban area to Los Angeles County)
- Immigration status: legal, illegal, contract, green-card; temporary/permanent

Time/age variables:

- Recent immigrant/migrant (less than one year, five years, etc.)
- Older immigrant/migrant (more than five, ten years, etc.)
- Length of time in present: house/apartment, neighborhood, school, church, job, voluntary organization (political, social, educational, religious, recreational, etc.)
- Age at time of immigration/migration; urbanization; neighborhood change; education, language, acculturation attainment; organizational affiliation, etc.

Regional variables: rural, suburban, urban

- Rural-urban migrant, semi-migrant, permanent resident
- Interurban/suburban/rural migrant
- "Rur-ban" orientation: recent rural-to-urban migrant; semi-migratory--part farm, part industrial; commuter--live in rural/urban area, work in rural/urban district
- Composition of neighborhood
  - Resident of mixed Hispanic or other ethnic/racial neighborhood
  - Resident of *Colonia* (45% or greater SSN)
  - Resident of Mixed Anglo-Mexican American neighborhood (Intermediate: 15-44% SSN)
  - Resident of Anglo neighborhood (Frontier: Less than 15% SSN)

Regional variables (Continued)

Socioeconomic level of neighborhood: Low, middle, high-income, or mixed
Housing: renters or owners--resident/absentee; type, size, age, and condition of housing (safe, substandard, blighted); accessibility by car or public transportation; proximity to place of employment, business and recreational areas, schools, churches, medical centers, etc.
Type area: incorporated/nonincorporated; type and quality of public services; rating--standard/blighted; zoning and density; trends--static, private development, urban renewal
Public safety: crime rate + type offenses; quality of police/fire protection; condition/width of streets, lighting, water drainage, traffic intensity; health hazards, etc.

Personal variables:

Age, sex, intelligence, physical features; personal habits/values/goals, childhood home life (numerous variables), nuclear/extended family ties (strong, informal, weak); personality/self-image/self-identity, personal motivation/aspirations/expectations (low, medium, high), acceptance/participation in Protestant Ethic/Anglo middle-class values; attitudes toward majority society/other minorities, friendship contacts/working associates (M-A, Anglo, others); single/married (to M-A, Anglo, other); personal morality; social/anti-social behavior (variable standards); need levels: psychological, safety, love and belongingness, self-esteem, and self-actualization

Assimilation variables:

Types of assimilation
- Cultural or behavioral (acculturation)
- Structural (integration of Anglo social groups and institutions)
- Marital (intermarriage/amalgamation)
- Identificational (with dominant WASP middle class)
- Attitude receptional (absence of prejudice)
- Behavior receptional (absence of discrimination)
- Civic (absence of value and power conflict)

Assimilational retardation factors: segregation/discrimination in employment, housing, education, civil rights; attitudes toward culture change, host society, native subcultural group; ethnic/socioeconomic group identification; need level fulfillment

Language/acculturation variables (four generalized stages of language transition):

Spanish-speaking, no English (Stage #1)

Language/acculturation variables (Continued)

Spanish-speaking, some English (Stage #2)
Functionally bilingual (Stage #3)
English-speaking little or no Spanish (Stage #4)
(Various degrees of acceptance/reflection of Anglo middle class values)

Occupational/Employment variables:

Unemployed/employed (temporary/permanent)
Part-time/full-time, seasonal/nonseasonal, temporary/permanent, semi-migratory (part farm/part industrial)
Agricultural/industrial/commercial/educational/religious/public service/etc.
Types of vocational training and experience: "Blue-collar" (skilled, semi-skilled, unskilled)/ "White-collar" (clerical, sales, managerial, professional, etc.)
Mobility of occupation, employment, rank, income, job type
Wage earner/salaried/self-employed
Working associates: M-A, Anglo, Negro, Other
Type of on-the-job training and rate of advancement, atmosphere, personal satisfaction, job security, health benefits, union/nonunion, etc.

Socioeconomic variables:

Low income group: lower-low/upper-low
Middle income group: lower-middle/upper middle
Upper income group: lower-upper/upper-upper
Upward social mobility: low, medium, high potential
Factors retarding upward mobility: socioeconomic class, minority group status, education, assimilation variables, personal variables, need level/aspirations

Educational variables:

No formal schooling: literate/illiterate (Spanish/English, both/neither
Elementary education: various grades completed
Secondary Education: Junior High/Senior High--various grades completed
Vocational education or training: various levels of training and proficiency
College or university education: Junior college/upper division/post-graduate level; secular/religious (Bible Institute/Seminary)
Residence school/correspondence school
Day school/night school; part-time/full-time
Quality of education; attitude toward school experience; peer group pressure; quality of counselling received; motivation to stay in school; aspirations/expectations toward future schooling/employment; etc.

Political/ideological variables:

- Attitude toward social change/community involvement: support status quo; constructive criticism of establishment/power structure; anti-establishment
- Politically active/inactive (registered/nonregistered voter)
- Vote issues/personalities; informed/uninformed voter
- Conservative/moderate/liberal/radical
- Republican, Democrat, Third Party/Ethnic party: AM.GI Forum, CMAA, La Raza Unida, MAPA, CSP, CSO, LULAC, etc.
- Degree of involvement: vote, officiate, recruit, organize, campaign, hold office, etc.
- Non-partisan voluntary organizations: educational, fraternal, social, recreational, etc.

Religious variables:

- Identify with or member of Catholic/Protestant Church, sect, cult, none; non-Christian religion
- Member/nonmember: active/nominal/inactive/indifferent
- Polity: congregational, presbyterian, episcopal, other
- Organization church/representative congregation
- Exclusive/inclusive ministry toward various socioeconomic classes, other ethnic/racial minorities, recent immigrants/migrants, language/acculturation group levels, age groups
- Theological conservative/moderate/liberal/radical
- Confessional/pietistic; Pentecostal/Non-Pentecostal
- Prosyletic/nonprosyletic (evangelistic/nonevangelistic)
- Voluntary associations by: age, sex, interest, election, appointment; denominational/interdenominational
- Type and quality of leadership: clergy/laity, male/female, youth/young adult/older adult (+ all other variables)
- Type of religious instruction/leadership training: pre-membership classes, catachism/church school classes, neighborhood or school release-time religious instruction, informal group study and discussion; teacher training courses (in local church or regional center), on-the-job training, leadership seminars; religious colleges, institutes, and seminaries (residence, extension, correspondence)
- Stability/change in communal group: harmony, tension, conflict, disorder, renewal
- Church growth and development: quantitative, organic, conceptual, incarnational
- Attitude/involvement in local neighborhood, identification with local/regional community problems, type/degree of social action

(What important variables have been omitted? What others would you suggest?)

Sources: McWilliams 1948; Winter 1962; Gordon 1964; Arnoff 1967; Read, Monterroso, Johnson 1969; Grebler 1970; McGavran 1970; Carter 1970; Cabrera 1971

Intergenerational mobility is closely associated with education and acculturation levels rather than with parental occupation and skill levels. Penalosa states that "the most important factor [promoting upward social mobility] is the degree of acculturation to the American middle-class way of life" (1963:42). "Having had a father who was a skilled worker or a white-collar worker", observes Grebler, "seems to have made little difference to the present generation's chances for higher income.... Present income is somewhat more closely related to parental education than to occupation" (1970:337). On the other hand, continuing adherence to traditional Mexican cultural values and a failure to become acculturated to Anglo middle-class culture are factors retarding the upward social mobility of the Mexican American.

The social class stratification of the Mexican American, based on a variety of social mobility factors, is strongly reflected in the type of neighborhoods where various social classes reside. Mexican Americans with higher income, occupation, and education levels tend to live in Frontier areas whereas those with lower income, occupation, and education levels tend to live in Colonies. The Intermediate areas are more equally divided on each of these levels. However, differences in ethnic and social class identity--whether one chooses to identify with the ethnic community or with Anglo middle-class subculture--influence the residential patterns of Mexican Americans with higher and medium incomes. Grebler's study shows that

> Although half of the high-income people in Los Angeles live in predominantly Anglo areas, so do more than a quarter of the low-income people. And although more than two-thirds of the poorest people live in Colonies, so do more than one-fifth of the high-income people (1970:327).

Low-income Mexican Americans are probably over-represented in Frontier areas due to census tract distortions--small barrio concentrations of low-income Mexican Americans that are statistically overpowered by heavy concentrations of Anglos in the same census tracts.

At all periods of transition from being a lower-class, unskilled *Mexican* laborer to becoming a well-education, acculturated, and financially secure Mexican *American* of the upper-middle class, the Spanish-speaking population of the Southwest has had to struggle with the problems of limited employment and educational opportunities, segregated and inadequate housing, poor health and welfare services, and limitations on their political and civil rights. For many Mexican migrants, geographical relocation, whether from Mexico to the United States or from rural to urban areas, has not always resulted in an improved socioeconomic status. Recent Mexican American arrivals to East Los Angeles, a "port of entry" for thousands of displaced farm workers from the Central Valley and other Southwestern agricultural areas, often are people who lack the basic language and trade skills needed to compete in an urban economy. In the words of one Mexican American spokesman, these rural-to-urban migrants come "looking for an opportunity, but it is *the poverty of opportunity* that they must overcome" (Rowan 1968:10; italics mine).

Subculture of Poverty

Grebler has shown that poverty is a massive problem in the Southwest: over 1,450,000 families were living in poverty (annual income under $3,000) in 1960; 66.4 percent were white, 16.7 percent were SSN, and 17.0 were non-white--there were many more by 1970 (1970:197-202). Nationally, there are "some 18 million families, numbering more than 50 million individuals [who] live below the $3,000 'poverty line'" (Lewis 1966:19). Poverty is a lack of money and a lack of earning power; it results from, and is complicated by, a host of factors: unemployment and underemployment, low levels of education and high dropout rates from school, poor housing and poor neighborhoods, urban renewal and freeway construction (Mexican and black "removal"), broken families and broken lives, large families and poor health. These factors are part of a complex socioeconomic problem that faces American society. The American "dream" of equal opportunity is considered by the poor--white, brown, and black--to be a gigantic hoax. If this "hoax" is to be dispelled then "America must consciously, deliberately, and rationally create a society that eliminates poverty" (Winter 1971:11-16).

American Attitudes About Poverty. The hoax is subconsciously reinforced by the attitudes of many Americans who believe that the poor themselves are to blame for their own poverty. According to Clark (1970:74): "The notion that the prime cause of poverty is indolence is shared not only by many Anglos but also by some...Mexican-Americans who enjoy adequate incomes." The so-called "lazy Mexican" theory is disproved by the high percentage of Mexican Americans who work as unskilled or semiskilled laborers, which usually requires "strenuous physical exertion." The economic problems of lower-class Mexican Americans "stem not from unwillingness to work but rather from poor job opportunities, low wages, and seasonal periods of unemployment," especially for the least acculturated (1970:74).

A recent survey (1971) by Joseph R. Feagin of the University of Texas, under a grant from the National Institute of Mental Health, discovered that the majority of Americans believe that "the main causes of poverty involve such personal shortcomings as laziness, lack of thrift, loose morals and drunkenness.... The poor are themselves responsible for their plight and society is not to blame." The success of the War on Poverty (Figure 9) and other national anti-poverty programs, according to Feagin, "must await a further shift in basic American attitudes and values...[if] major improvements in the economic structure of the American system" are to be realized.

The people most likely to believe that poverty results from character defects were "white Protestants or Catholics...aged 50 or over with middle-income and middle-educational status." But on the other hand, those most likely to believe that "poverty has roots in society failures" tended to be non-white Protestants or Jews, aged 30 or younger, poor and less well educated. Factors cited by the latter group for producing poverty were: low wages, inadequate schooling, job scarcity, racial and ethnic discrimination, and exploitation by the rich.

There are many forms of exploitation that the wealthy perpetrate on the poor. One form is influencing public opinion against welfare reform and vast injections of money to aid the urban, suburban, and rural poor. While protesting subsidies to the poor, vested industrial and commercial interests encourage and thrive on huge subsidies to farmers, the petroleum ndustry, the communications industry, aerospace manufacturers, and the multifaceted extensions of the military-industrial complex. However, the guaranteed-income provisions of the Family Assistance Plan and Aid to Families with Dependant Children program are denounced by many Americans as "a giant step toward a Welfare state." Mitchel Ginsberg, of Columbia University's chool of social welfare, commented: "The United States is ubstantially a welfare state already--it's just a question of welfare for whom" (1972:23).

Culture-of-Poverty Model. One of the important contribuions of Oscar Lewis has been to distinguish "between poverty, which is financial, and the subculture of poverty, which is a way of life shared by some poverty-stricken people" (Burma 1971: 9). Lewis stated in *Scientific American*:

> Among the 50 million U.S. citizens now more or less officially certified as poor, I would guess that about 20 percent live in a culture of poverty. The largest numbers in this group are made up of [very low income] Negroes, Puerto Ricans, Mexicans, American Indians and Southern poor whites (1966:25; 1968:196-197).

Figure 9

THE POVERTY CYCLE*

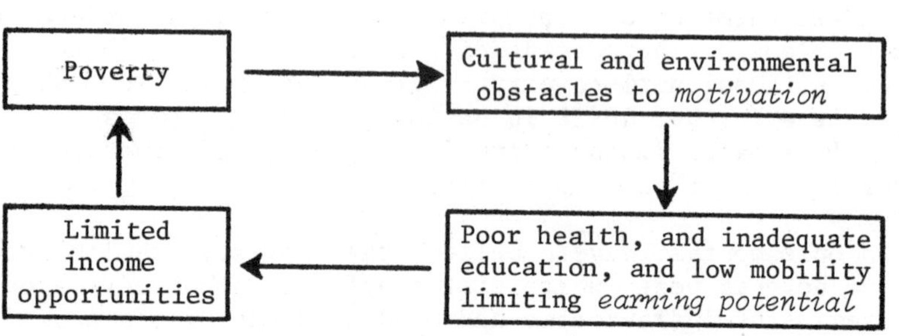

The sources of poverty are not listed in chronological sequence. The vicious cycle, in which poverty breeds poverty, occurs through time, and transmits its effects from one generation to another. There is no beginning to the cycle, no end. There is, therefore, no one "right" place to break into it: increasing opportunities may help little if health, educational attainments and motivation are unsuitable; making more education available may bear little fruit unless additional employment opportunities exist; altering adverse environmental factors may not be feasible or effective unless access to education and ultimately job opportunities is enhanced.

Programs to attack each of the three principal stages in the poverty cycle may be directed at one or more of three levels: (1) *prevent* the problem from developing, (2) *rehabilitate* the person who has been hurt, and (3) *ameliorate* the difficulties of persons for whom prevention or rehabilitation are not feasible. Each type of "treatment" is associated generally with a separate stage in the life cycle. Prevention of poverty calls for attention principally to youngsters (and to their parents, insofar as parents' attitudes and values affect the children). Rehabilitation of those missed by preventive efforts, or for whom these efforts were ineffective, seems best designed for adults in their productive work years. Amelioration of poverty seems called for in the case of the aged, the physically and mentally disabled, and those for whom prevention and rehabilitation are ineffective.

*This document was a staff memorandum of President Kennedy's Council of Economic Advisors, which represents the government's War on Poverty strategy at its early stages in 1963.

Source: Moynihan 1968:9

According to Lewis, the characteristic life-styles of people iving in a "culture of poverty" tend to closely resemble those f people in other areas who are also living in poverty, re-;ardless of racial or ethnic differences:

> This style of life transcends national boundaries and regional and rural-urban differences within nations. Wherever it occurs, its practitioners exhibit remarkable similarity in the structure of their families, in inter-personal relations, in spending habits, in their value systems and in their orientation in time.... The con-cept of the *culture of poverty* may help to correct mis-apprehensions that have ascribed some behavior patterns of ethnic, national or regional groups as distinctive [or inherent] characteristics (1966:19).

'or example, the distinctive characteristics of the "Mexican .ational character" identified by Ramos (Chapter 2) are re-arkably similar to what Lewis describes in his culture-of-overty model.

Seventy traits are listed by Lewis as characterizing the ulture of poverty, which he groups into four major categories: the relationship between the subculture and the larger society; he nature of the slum community; the nature of the family; and he attitudes, values, and character structure of the individual" 1966:21).

Although the culture of poverty may come into being in a 'ariety of historical contexts, it tends to develop in societies 'ith a definite set of conditions:

> (1) a cash economy, wage labor, and production for profit; (2) a persistently high rate of unemployment and underemployment for unskilled labor; (3) low wages; (4) the failure to provide social, political, and eco-nomic organization, either on a voluntary basis or by government imposition, for the low-income population; (5) the existence of a bilateral kinship system rather than a unilateral one; and finally, (6) the existence in the dominant class of a set of values that stress the accumulation of wealth and property, the possibil-ity of upward mobility, and thrift and that explains low income status as the result of personal inadequacy or inferiority (1968:187-188).

The culture-of-poverty model, according to J. Alan Winter, s based upon three related hypotheses:

> (1) that the way of life of the poor in many nations

> comprises a relatively unique configuration of behavioral patterns and values; (2) that the configuration constitutes a true culture or subculture and not a mere set of transient adaptations to objective conditions; and (3) that this configuration is most likely to appear among the poor in a class-stratified, highly individualized capitalistic society (1971:17-18).

The characteristics of the culture of poverty were further detailed by Winter (1971:19):

1. The lack of effective participation and integration of the poor in the major institutions of the larger society...

2. ...a minimum of organization beyond the level of the nuclear and extended family.

3. On the family level the major traits...are the absence of childhood as a specially prolonged and protected stage in the life cycle, early initiation into sex, free unions or consensual marriages, a relatively high incidence of abandonment of wives and children, a trend toward female- or mother-centered families,...a strong disposition toward authoritarianism, lack of privacy,...and the competition for limited goods and maternal affection.

4. On the level of the individual the major characteristics are a strong feeling of marginality, of helplessness, or of dependency and inferiority.

Other factors cited by Winter (1971:19) were:

> A high incidence of...weak ego structure [self-image], confusion of sexual identification, a lack of impulse control [as seen in spending habits],...little ability to defer gratification and to plan for the future, [and] a sense of resignation and fatalism....

Many criticisms have been voiced against Lewis' culture-of-poverty model for a variety of reasons. While it is true that some of the criticisms detailed in Winter's *The Poor: A Culture of Poverty or a Poverty of Culture?* (1971) point out genuine weaknesses in Lewis' theory, other criticisms only seem to point out the weaknesses of the critic--mainly his own bias or commitment to other theoretical systems. For example, both Willie and Liebow criticize the "subcultural" dimension of the theory, that is, the emphasis on "cultural transmission" of a poverty subculture from parent to child. Liebow argues that the persistence of a culture of poverty reflects the persis-ence of the objective conditions to which it is a response," uch as racial and ethnic discrimination and powerful political, conomic, and social forces that create the conditions and cir-umstances for poverty to exist and be perpetuated (1971:22-23, 31-136). However, Lewis seems to make this very point in his ntroduction to *La Vida* (1968:188):

> The culture of poverty is both an adaptation and a re-action of the poor to their marginal position in a class-stratified, highly individualized, capitalistic society. It represents an effort to cope with feelings of hope-lessness and despair that develop from the realization of the improbability of achieving success in terms of the values and goals of the larger society. Indeed, many of the traits of the culture of poverty can be viewed as attempts at local solutions for problems not met by existing institutions and agencies because the people are not eligible for them, cannot afford them, or are ignorant or suspicious of them.

While it is true, as Glazer points out, that various ethnic roups and cultures have varying attitudes toward "dependency", hat changes within a society also affect individual motivation nd family strength, and that "a culture of poverty may be ostered by the very social policies and programs that seek to liminate poverty," still the concept that "something like a ulture of poverty exists" and will require major structural hanges in American society to eliminate the conditions which erpetuate poverty is one that is strongly supported by Grebler 1970) and others (cf. Moynihan's *On Understanding Poverty*, 968, especially the Appendix, pp. 343-397).

Grebler's conclusion in *The Mexican American People* is very ignificant for our present study:

> One basic assumption of American ideology has been that *social mobility* is potentially available to *all* members of society. On this assumption, no sizeable and readily identifiable groups of people were to be permanently sub-ordinated. Such a social system would be without a permanent proletariat. *The ideology has always ignored the condition of most Negroes and American Indians and, as this volume has demonstrated, the condition of most Mexican Americans as well.* All three groups were long considered beyond the pale. But the ideology conformed to the experiences of enough other people to be per-ceived as broadly valid (Grebler 1970:595, italics mine).

Characteristics of the Poor. At least one question seems to be yet unanswered: "Who are the poor"? While "all agree that those living in poverty are persons and households that have considerably less than average financial and other resources," there doesn't seem to be agreement on where to draw the poverty-line, or what constitutes "minimum adequacy" and on how many Americans can be considered "poor". The poor, however, include both those who "happen" to be temporarily suffering from low income levels--the aged, sick, disabled, or victims of economic dislocation (such as in a depression or recession, either local or national)--and the "chronic poor" who are unable "to make ends meet" because of lack of language ability, education, skills, ability, or character inadequacies (regardless of the reason). According to Blum and Rossi, "the 'poor'...are those whose income is low (excluding the disabled, the retired, and the temporarily poor), who are unable to cope successfully even at a minimum level with their poverty and who present a problem to society" (Moynihan 1968:350-351).

This segment of the poor is described as the "lower-lower class" and have the following characteristics (1968:351-352):

1. Labor-Force Participation. Long periods of unemployment and/or very intermittent employment. Public assistance is frequently a major source of income for extended periods.

2. Occupational Participation. When employed, persons hold jobs at the lowest level of skills, for example, domestic service, unskilled labor, menial service jobs, and farm labor.

3. Family and Interpersonal Relations. High rates of mental instability (desertion, divorce, separation), high incidence of households headed by females, high rates of illegitimacy; unstable and superficial interpersonal relationships characterized by considerable suspicion of persons outside the immediate household.

4. Community Characteristics. Residential areas with very poorly developed voluntary associations and low levels of participation in such local voluntary associations as exist.

5. Relations to Larger Society. Little interest in, or knowledge of, the larger society and its events; some degree of alienation from the larger society.

6. Value Orientation. A sense of helplessness and low

sense of personal efficacy; dogmatism and authoritarianism in political ideology, [and religion] with strong beliefs in magical practices. Low "need achievement" and low levels of aspirations for the self.

Cohen and Hodges (1963:303-334) have shown that when lower-ower class behavior patterns of Negroes, Mexican Americans, nd Anglo-Saxons in Central California were compared, "there ere no significant differences in their values systems"--a conirmation of Lewis' thesis. Figure 10 illustrates the minor ifferences between racial and ethnic groups when the socioconomic class variable was held constant, as well as the comon variables shared by all lower-lower socioeconomic classes. y contrast, Anglo middle-class variables are hypothesized to how both the similarities and differences between ethnicity nd socioeconomic class levels. According to Irelan and Besner, ho draw upon the Cohen-Hodges study, "a continuously low inome is directly associated with certain life situations...in ur society" (1968:1-12):

Poorer, more crowded living quarters, reduced access to education and recreation, occupational restriction to simpler, manual types of work--these and similar characteristics of the very poor are sufficiently obvious to need no underlining. The result of these circumstances is a set of life conditions which is not so obvious. They consist of four general limitations: (1) comparative simplification of the experience world [limited alternatives and opportunities], (2) powerlessness [social and political impotency and helplessness], (3) deprivation [lack of resources and opportunities for upward social mobility], and (4) insecurity [concerning health, housing, employment, the future, and himself]....

Constant, fruitless struggle with these conditions is likely to produce estrangement--from society and from other individuals, even from oneself.... The alienation of the poor is graphically seen in their feelings of: (1) powerlessness, (2) meaninglessness, (3) anomia, and (4) isolation.... There are four distinctive themes peculiar to lower class behavior, all apparently the result of a deprived, alienated condition: fatalism, orientation to the present, authoritarianism, and concreteness [stress on material rather than intellectual things, concrete verbal style, pragmatism, and anti-intellectualism].

One need only read the many case studies of "Mexican nerican subculture" by Tuck (1946), Griffith (1948),

Figure 10

LOWER SOCIOECONOMIC CLASS VARIABLES COMPARED WITH MIDDLE CLASS VARIABLES

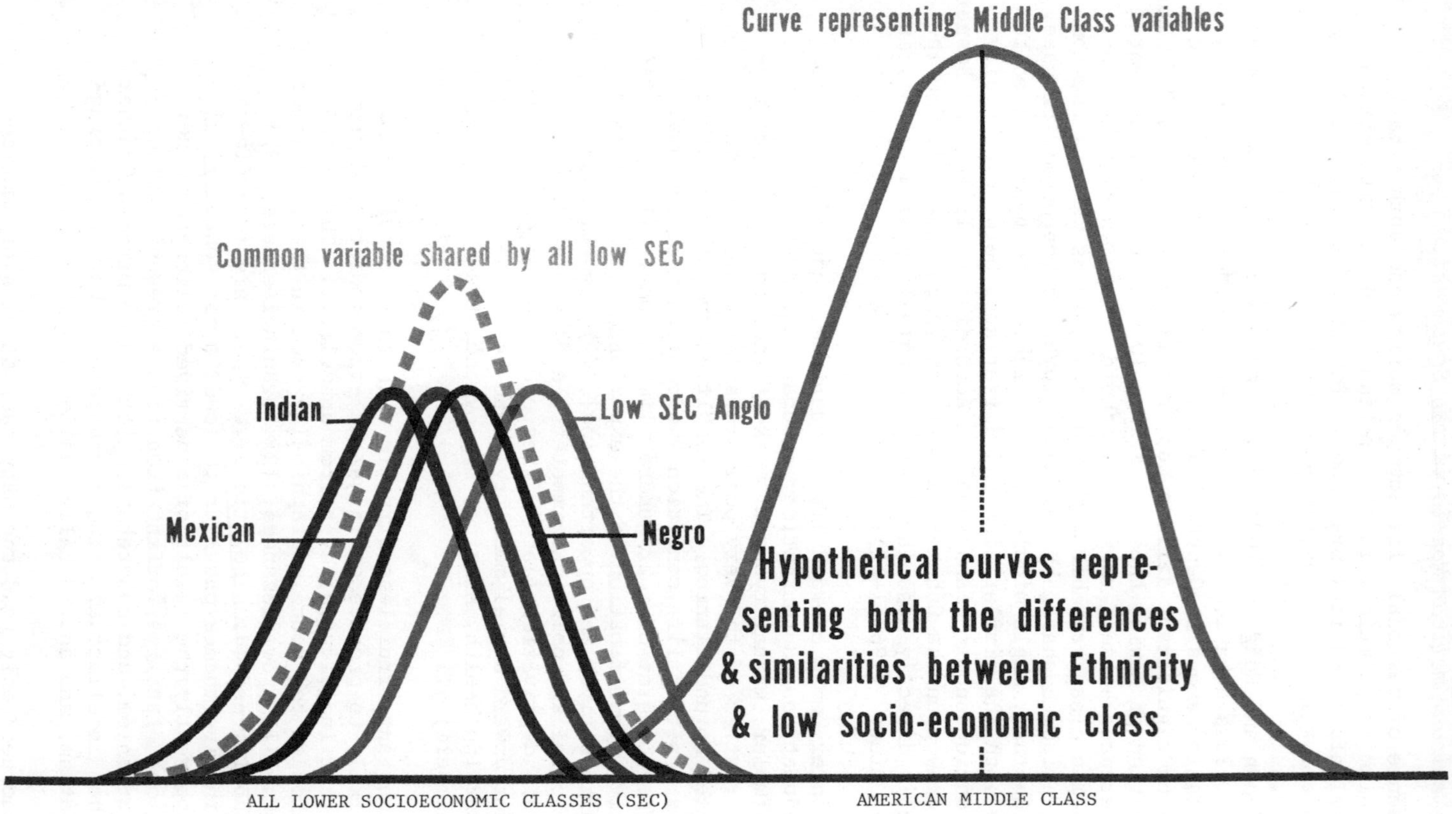

Sources: Cohen and Hodges 1963:303-334; Casavantes 1969:2-3.11

Clark (1959), Madsen (1964), Rubel (1966), and others to observe the obvious parallels with the "subculture of poverty" in American society (see Burma 1970:17-28 for a fuller discussion of these parallels, also Chapter 4 of the present study). What America needs is a sincere desire and commitment to impart to the future a new attitude toward the marginal members of our society, and to actively participate in creating structural changes in our social institutions that will rid the poor of the "poverty of opportunity" in their quest for upward social mobility. Motivation for such change should not be hard to find:

> ...you have trampled and crushed beneath your feet the lowly of the world, and deprived men of their God-given rights, and refused them justice. No wonder the Lord will deal with you in His anger...(Lamentations 3:34-36).

Geographical Distribution

The Mexican American population is heavily concentrated in the Southwestern states of Texas, New Mexico, Colorado, Arizona, and California. Only thirteen percent or 498,000 out of 3.8 million Mexican Americans in 1960 lived outside of these five states (Grebler 1966:51). Most of the legal immigrants from Mexico intended to reside in this area as shown in Figure 11. In the 1910-1929 period, Texas attracted the majority of immigrants, whereas in the period 1955-1964 California had gained a distinctive majority. By 1970 California's Hispanic heritage population had grown to 3.1 million compared to 2.0 million in Texas (Figure 11).

Concentration in the Southwest. Grebler raises two important questions relating to the geographical distribution of Mexican immigrants: "Why have the Mexican immigrants and their children remained so heavily concentrated in the Southwest? And why has there been such a remarkable shift away from Texas and Arizona to California?" (1966:53). Grebler's answer to the first question is as follows:

> Concerning the concentration in the southwest region, immigrants from many countries have tended to remain clustered in certain areas; Mexicans are not unique in this respect. *Immigrants have always been attracted to places where they have relatives or can expect to find large numbers of their own ethnic group, can use their mother tongue without embarrassment, rely on landsmen for employment, housing, and help in orienting themselves to a strange environment, and have access to community organizations composed of like people.* In the case at hand, a natural base was provided by the

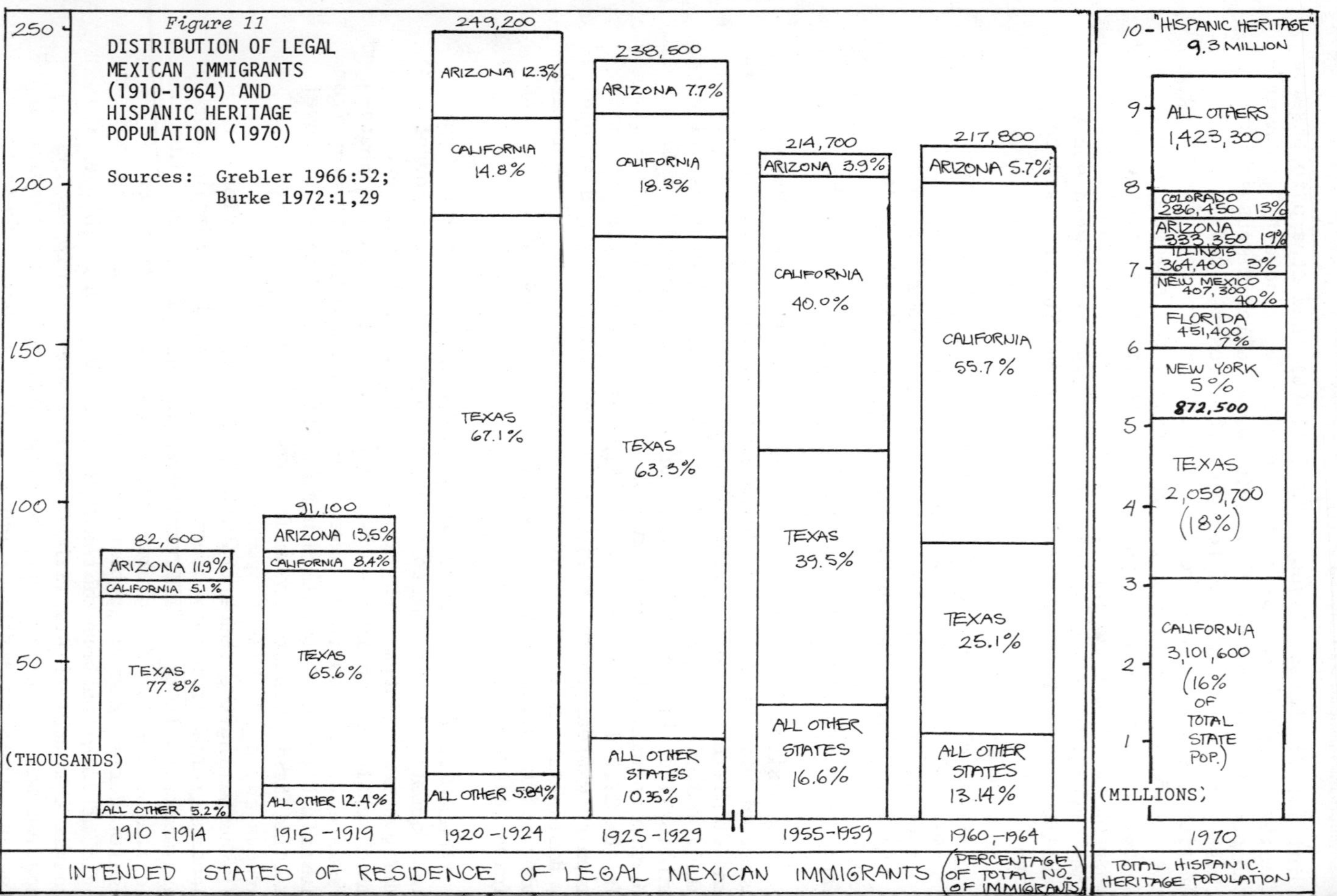

Figure 11
DISTRIBUTION OF LEGAL MEXICAN IMMIGRANTS (1910-1964) AND HISPANIC HERITAGE POPULATION (1970)
Sources: Grebler 1966:52; Burke 1972:1,29
250
200
150
100
50
(THOUSANDS)
82,600
ARIZONA 11.9%
CALIFORNIA 5.1%
TEXAS 77.8%
ALL OTHER 5.2%
91,100
ARIZONA 13.5%
CALIFORNIA 8.4%
TEXAS 65.6%
ALL OTHER 12.4%
249,200
ARIZONA 12.3%
CALIFORNIA 14.8%
TEXAS 67.1%
ALL OTHER 5.84%
238,500
ARIZONA 7.7%
CALIFORNIA 18.3%
TEXAS 63.3%
ALL OTHER STATES 10.35%
214,700
ARIZONA 3.9%
CALIFORNIA 40.0%
TEXAS 39.5%
ALL OTHER STATES 16.6%
217,800
ARIZONA 5.7%
CALIFORNIA 55.7%
TEXAS 25.1%
ALL OTHER STATES 13.14%
1910-1914
1915-1919
1920-1924
1925-1929
1955-1959
1960-1964
INTENDED STATES OF RESIDENCE OF LEGAL MEXICAN IMMIGRANTS (PERCENTAGE OF TOTAL NO. OF IMMIGRANTS)
10 - "HISPANIC HERITAGE" 9.3 MILLION
9
8
7
6
5
4
3
2
1
(MILLIONS)
ALL OTHERS 1,423,300
COLORADO 286,450 13%
ARIZONA 333,350 19%
ILLINOIS 364,400 3%
NEW MEXICO 407,300 40%
FLORIDA 451,400 7%
NEW YORK 5% 872,500
TEXAS 2,059,700 (18%)
CALIFORNIA 3,101,600 (16% OF TOTAL STATE POP.)
1970
TOTAL HISPANIC HERITAGE POPULATION

initial presence of colonial settlers from Mexico in the Southwest, acquaintance with the area through early informal border crossings, and the first wave of immigration during the Mexican revolution. Under these conditions, *the continued concentration in this region can be viewed as a cumulative, self-reinforcing process.* Also, the Southwest offers a climate and landscape compatible with the experience and preferences of many Mexican immigrants. Both psychic and physical proximity or resemblance may have tended to keep them in the area. And, in many cases, *poverty* coupled with uncertainty or ignorance of opportunities elsewhere may have been a roadblock to further costly moves (1966:93,95; italics mine).

Migration Toward California. In the period 1910-1929, ɜxas and Arizona were far more accessible to immigrants from ɜxico than was California because the largest portion of the ɜxican border is contiguous with those two states. In terms E distance and cost, Texas and Arizona made immigration ısier in that the principal rail connections with Mexico ɜre on their borders, whereas a trip to California required long journey by railroad from Mexico through Texas, New ɜxico and/or Arizona, or a difficult overland journey through ıe thinly populated desert region of Baja California which ɔrders California (Figure 4, Chapter 1). The initial stimuıs for immigration to Texas was the need for large numbers of ;ricultural workers whereas California's growing farming areas ıd a sufficient supply of Chinese, Japanese, and other Asian ırm workers until World War I (1966:55).

After 1915, California's rapidly expanding corporation farmıg, termed the "agribusiness", began to experience serious ınpower shortages which opened the door for "cheap Mexican ıbor". The principal reasons for this shortage of farm workɾs were: (1) extensive government irrigation projects that ıabled millions of additional acres throughout the state to ɜ cultivated; (2) growth of domestic and international ırkets for agricultural produce during and after World War I; 3) corresponding increases in agricultural production; (4) ıcreasing dependence on large numbers of low-wage, seasonal ırm workers during a variety of harvest seasons throughout ıe state; and (5) the diminishing supply of Asian laborers ɜsulting from a growing racial hostility toward Asiatics by ıglo Californians and the resulting alien restriction laws--;ainst the Chinese in the 1870s and 1880s and against the ıpanese between 1913-1924. By the early 1920s, many California ɾowers as well as whole agricultural districts had become deɜndent upon Mexican labor, especially the Imperial Valley. ɜnters of population on both sides of the Mexican border grew rapidly, enlarged by the daily arrival by rail of migrants from the Central Mesa; these centers became great farm labor reservoirs for Southwestern agriculture (Galarza 1964:23-25,29; Wollenberg 1970:105-112,138-140).

California growers, with holdings both large and small, established associations such as the California Fruit Growers Exchange for the marketing of products and the large-scale recruitment and distribution of seasonal, non-union farm workers. According to Galarza, "The dependence on seasonal farm labor in numbers out of all proportion to the year-round work force became a characteristic of commercial agriculture" (1964:25). In some agricultural districts, the seasonal work force ranged from a few hundred workers in the off-season to 10,000-20,000 at peak harvest time during the late 1920s and early 1930s. Although Mexican migrant workers normally spent half the year planting and harvesting crops throughout the state, the winter months were usually spent in the rural and suburban *colonias* of Southern California, where a growing number of nonmigrating workers had permanently settled (1964:25-26).

However, as Figure 11 indicates, California did not overtake Texas as the intended state of residence for Mexican immigrants until the period 1955-1959. The decade of the 1950s witnessed the significant growth of California's Spanish-surname population--in fact California accounted for about three-fifths of the entire SSN population growth in the Southwest during that period (Grebler 1970:109). The state's SSN growth continued to increase at the fantastic rate of over 117 percent between 1960 and 1970, from 1.4 million to 3.1 million. This latter figure is over a million more than the SSN population in Texas in 1970 (Figures 11,12).

Although California's Hispanic growth was more spectacular during the 1960s than in the 1950s, an analysis of the more recent decade must wait until more information becomes available from the 1970 census and other reliable sources. However, Grebler has provided an important analysis of SSN population growth in the late 1950s:

> Nearly 60 percent of the Mexican-American interstate movers between 1955 and 1960 went to California, although the state accounted for only one-third of the Spanish-surname population in the Southwest in 1950 and two-fifths in 1960. Of those coming from abroad in the 1955-1960 period, 63 percent were located in California in 1960, though some of them may have first resided in other states. In contrast, only 17 percent of the Spanish-surname interstate movers between 1955 and 1960 went to Texas, and few went to the smaller

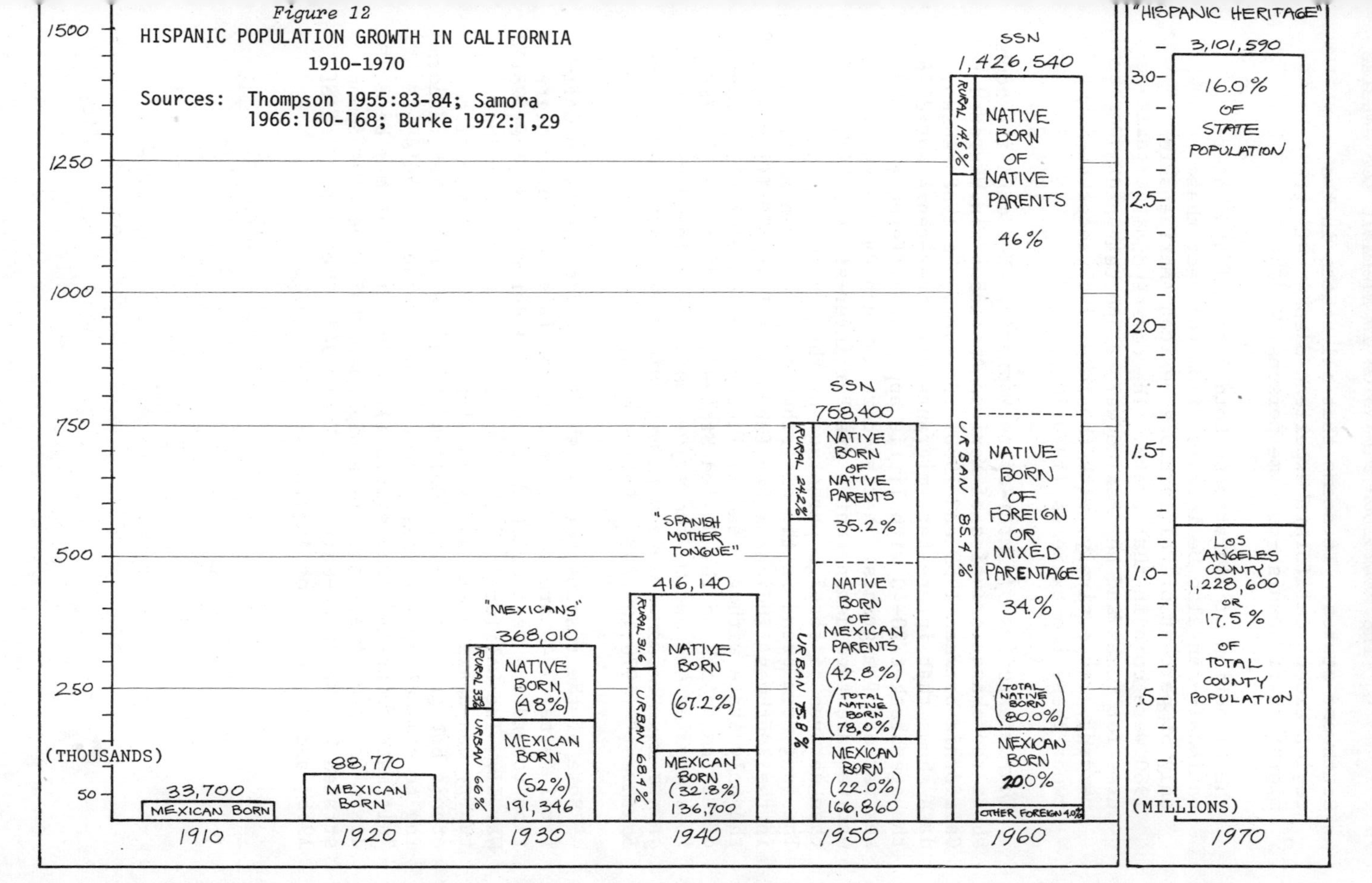

Figure 12

HISPANIC POPULATION GROWTH IN CALIFORNIA 1910–1970

Sources: Thompson 1955:83-84; Samora 1966:160-168; Burke 1972:1,29

> Southwest states. It seems that all states in the region except California experienced some net out-migration of Spanish-surname persons.
>
> The direction of migrations--both internal and international--can also be inferred from the fact that only 55 percent of California's Mexican Americans in 1960 were born in that state. The corresponding figures for Texas and New Mexico were 81 percent and 87 percent, respectively, with the remaining states between these two extremes (1970:109).

Characteristics of Inter-state Migrants. Not much is known about the characteristics of Mexican Americans who migrated to California between 1955 and 1960. However, the 1960 census data shows that inter-state migrants were over-represented in the age bracket 20-40 with little apparent difference in the sex ratio of migrants. Native-born Mexican Americans of native parentage demonstrated greater inter-state mobility than natives of foreign parentage or those born in Mexico. The long-term trend in the distribution of Mexican Americans in the Southwest indicates two factors: first, "California is the only state with a steadily increasing share of all persons of Mexican stock in the United States"; and secondly, *by 1960 "Los Angeles had become the major destination for Mexican immigrants and Mexican-American in-migrants from other areas of the Southwest"* (1970:109,298; italics mine).

Some of the reasons for the shift away from Texas to California after 1940 are seen in the great internal Anglo migration toward the west coast that occurred during and after World War II. The California "dream" of unlimited economic opportunity has drawn millions of Americans of various racial and ethnic backgrounds to the "Golden State", a dream that, according to some observers, has made California the nation's "ultimate frontier" (Davie 1972:1). However, what may be a dream for some Americans is a nightmare for others as demonstrated by the "Zoot-Suiter Riot" of 1943, the Watts Riot of 1966, and the East Los Angeles Riots of 1970.

3.

The Mexican American in Urban Los Angeles

Urban Los Angeles County constitutes one of America's largest population centers, not only of Anglo Americans but also of various racial and ethnic minorities. Out of the county's seven million population in 1970, over 1.2 million were Mexican Americans, 760,000 were blacks, 150,000 were Orientals, and almost 25,000 were American Indians. While close to 100,000 whites moved out of the county between 1960 and 1970, over 900,000 new minority group residents were added (Hebert 1972: 1,26).

Rapid urbanization in Los Angeles County has increased pollution, blight, congestion and poverty. In the past thirty years, more than four million people, two million jobs, and 700 square miles of land area development have been added by urban growth (Hebert 1970:1,5). However, such unrestricted urbanization has aggravated such problems as isolation, hostility, poverty, and personal disorientation. Not enough concern and effort have gone into improving the quality of urban and suburban life in terms of human opportunities and environmental control. Transportation and housing are critical problems for the growing urban poor who inhabit dilapidated, blighted areas throughout Los Angeles County. And the growing alienation of large minority populations in the black ghettos and the brown *barrios* threatens the traditional isolation-insulation system of the declining Anglo population. The great "fragmented metropolis" is becoming more fragmented.

But there are healthy signs of change--talk of modern rapid transit, restricting population growth, developing a strategy for "city survival", greater participation of minorities in local government, a new black mayor. The quest for "community" is still going on and the need for reinterpretation and integration of community life is a growing reality. This chapter is a brief history of the quest of the Mexican American minority for equal opportunity and participation in the American Dream.

THE GROWTH OF HISPANIC LOS ANGELES

The town of Los Angeles, founded in 1781 as *El Pueblo de Nuestra Señora La Reina de Los Angeles*, was one of three major Spanish settlements in what later became Los Angeles County, the other two were located around the missions at San Gabriel and San Fernando. After the American occupation in 1846, Los Angeles remained "semi-gringo" until the land booms of the 1870s and 1880s brought in enough Anglo Americans to constitute a majority of the population. By 1880 Mexican Americans constituted only twenty-one percent of the total population of Los Angeles (Pitt 1970:121-123,262-263).

The 1880s

Most of the Spanish-speaking residents of Los Angeles in 1880 lived in "Sonoratown", an area extending east from the old Plaza to the river and south to the Southern Pacific Railroad yards. The area north of the Plaza, called "Nigger Alley", which had been inhabited predominantly by Mexicans prior to 1870, was filled with Chinese laborers in the period 1876-1880 (1970:264-265). By 1885, a small manufacturing complex had been established along the Los Angeles River near the Plaza area where Chinese and Mexicans "still rented rooms in dilapidated and overcrowded adobes and shacks amid rundown hotels, gambling dens, and houses of prostitution" (Fogelson 1965:138-139). The Spanish-speaking population of Los Angeles totaled 12,000 in 1887, but in proportion to the Anglo inhabitants, Mexican Americans composed less than ten percent of the total population (Pitt 1970:273).

From 1900 to 1920

Thousands of Mexican laborers were brought to Los Angeles by Henry Huntington, beginning around 1902, to build the Pacific Electric Railway system throughout Los Angeles and Orange Counties. "Others", according to Nadeau, "were brought in for harvest work in the burgeoning citrus industry and for maintenance work on the rail lines of the Southern Pacific and the Santa Fe" (1960:239). In the early 1900s the Southern Pacific Railway was employing at least 4,500 Mexican workers on its rail lines in Southern California (McWilliams 1948:169). While the wages paid to Mexican workers were higher than they received in Mex-ico, they were "insufficient to provide anything but the barest living conditions in Los Angeles" (Nadeau 1960:239).

Mexican immigrants, by the tens of thousands, poured into Southern California after 1910 and established small colonies in many parts of Los Angeles and in the rural countryside. The major concentration of Mexicans in 1914, according to McEuen, was "north of the Plaza or within a mile of the Los Angeles River" (1914:38). Most of the housing in the growing industrial area on the west side of the river, what is now the Wholesale District, was occupied by Mexicans. McEuen stated that "the Mexican will usually pay high rent for poor accomoda-tions near the center of the city rather than move to the out-lying districts where rents are lower and accomodations better" (1914:39).

The number of house-courts and shacks multiplied in Los Angeles "as the demand for Mexican housing became acute with high land costs and rising rents" (McWilliams 1948:223). In 1912, about 20,000-30,000 Mexicans were living in the house-courts of Sonoratown, in the small shacks and houses that dot-ted many nearby hillsides, and in various railroad and agricul-tural labor camps of Los Angeles. By 1916, many working class immigrants of various nationalities were living in house-courts and shacks throughout the city. Out of 1,200 courts surveyed in 1916, only about 300 were occupied exclusively by Mexicans, although many other courts no doubt had large numbers of Mexi-can inhabitants (1948:223). An investigation of the "shack problem" in Los Angeles in 1913-1914 revealed that Mexicans in-habited only thirty-eight out of 305 shacks surveyed in several areas of the city (McEuen 1914:41). Poverty, it seems, was not exclusively a Mexican problem in early twentieth century Los Angeles.

McEuen distinguished three types of Mexican housing in Los Angeles in 1914: (1) house-courts consisting of barracks-like rows of small, two-room habitations (renting for $6 per month) built around a courtyard, with common toilets and wash-ing facilities; (2) bungalows or cottages consisting of three rooms on the average, with from one to four houses on a lot and a common outhouse; and (3) shacks constructed of everything imaginable--scrap lumber, old berry boxes, discarded stoves, gunny sacks and tarred paper--with as many as six shacks on a single lot (1914:39-47).

Many newly arrived Mexicans were forced, due to lack of housing in the Central District, to obtain quarters east of the Los Angeles River in the Boyle Heights area, or to con-struct their own small houses and shacks in numerous "gulches and arroyos where land was cheap and undesirable" to Anglos. Mexican colonies were established on the east side of the river at East First Street and Wellington, on Fickett Street between Seventh and Hollenbeck, at Ninth and Hollenbeck, at North Main and Mission Road, and several smaller housing clusters on both city and county land (1914:38-39).

The 1920s

The trend of movement to areas east of the Los Angeles River that began prior to 1920 continued among Mexican Americans during the boom years of the 1920s. Thousands of Mexican immigrants and interstate migrants who arrived in Los Angeles in the 1920s searched for housing in the Central District only to be disappointed by overcrowded housing conditions and by high rents and property values. Consequently, many Mexicans were forced to find housing in outlying districts to the east (Young 1930:177). In addition, rising land values in the downtown area resulted in the large-scale construction of new office and commercial buildings, a corresponding reduction in the number of available housing units, and the relocation of many industries to less expensive nearby districts, particularly in Southeastern Los Angeles near the rail lines (Fogelson 1967: 147-151). According to McLean, "it was found necessary that ground in the center of the city should be improved with buildings which would give an adequate return upon the value of the property. The whole development, coming rapidly, placed a bomb under the Mexican colony" (1928:146).

Real estate companies bought up large tracts of hilly pasture land between Boyle Heights and Montebello which were then subdivided and sold in small lots to recent immigrants. The older sections of Boyle Heights and new subdivisions in the Wabash and City Terrace districts were heavily populated with Jewish immigrants from Eastern Europe, whereas the districts farther east, particularly in Belvedere and the new subdivision of Maravilla Park, were largely filled with Mexican immigrants (Vorspan 1970:118-119). The Belvedere district, located in county territory east of Indiana Street,

> was divided into fifty-foot lots, and sold out to Mexicans on small payments. There were no sewers, no sidewalks, no playgrounds; and the only restriction as to the number of houses which could be built upon a single lot was the size of the lot.... Mexicans bought property, lost it through the failure to make payments, and then bought again.... Everywhere there were the usual evidences of over-crowding and inadequate housing, for the families were not only large, but were augmented by the aunts and uncles and cousins coming from Mexico who,

> with ready hospitality, were entertained until they could build for themselves.... It seemed as if all Mexico were moving to Belvedere" (McLean 1928:146-147).

By 1930 the Mexican population in Central Los Angeles was mainly concentrated in seven communities (Figure 13): Belvedere Park (the largest and most densely populated), Maravilla Park, Boyle Heights, Palo Verde (also known as "Chavez Ravine"), Lincoln Park, the Central District, and Rose Hill (later known as "Happy Valley") (Ortegon 1932:14-18,65).

Belvedere Park was characterized as the "largest and most progressive" Mexican colony. The majority of the residents owned their own homes and a large number were "American-born Mexicans" who spoke English with no noticeable foreign accent. By contrast, Maravilla Park, located to the east of Belvedere, was characterized by the "extreme poverty" of its inhabitants--"large families, with as many as twelve, living in shacks and eating practically nothing" (1932:15). Over 45,000 Mexican Americans lived in the Belvedere-Maravilla Park District in 1930 and at least six "large modern public schools" in the area were "practically 100 per cent Mexican" (Young 1930:177).

The Los Angeles County Health Department surveyed housing conditions in Maravilla Park in 1928 and reported that, although two-thirds of the Mexican families were living in their own homes, out of 317 houses surveyed "211 were rated as mere shacks and the remaining 106 as bungalows and semibungalows." Sanitary conditions were very poor; only ten dwellings had flush toilets and the rest had outhouses. The overall rating of housing and living conditions in the district, based on a "home index score card", was "poor". The majority of the workers were classified as unskilled laborers whose "average annual family income was only $795" (1930:178).

Although the Boyle Heights District was predominantly composed of European immigrants, with a large population of Russian Jews, there also were a considerable number of Mexicans. According to Ortegon, "the educational and living conditions of the Boyle Heights District is far superior to any other of the Mexican colonies of Los Angeles...the predominant type of this colony is that of the middle class" (1932:17).

Palo Verde, or Chavez Ravine, was "particularly isolated within a circle of hills and [was] like a picturesque fragment of old Mexico...one feels as if one passed to an entirely foreign city." Living conditions in Palo Verde, located in the hills between Elysian Park and North Broadway, resembled the poverty found in Maravilla Park. McWilliams contributed the following graphic description of this barrio in the mid-1940s:

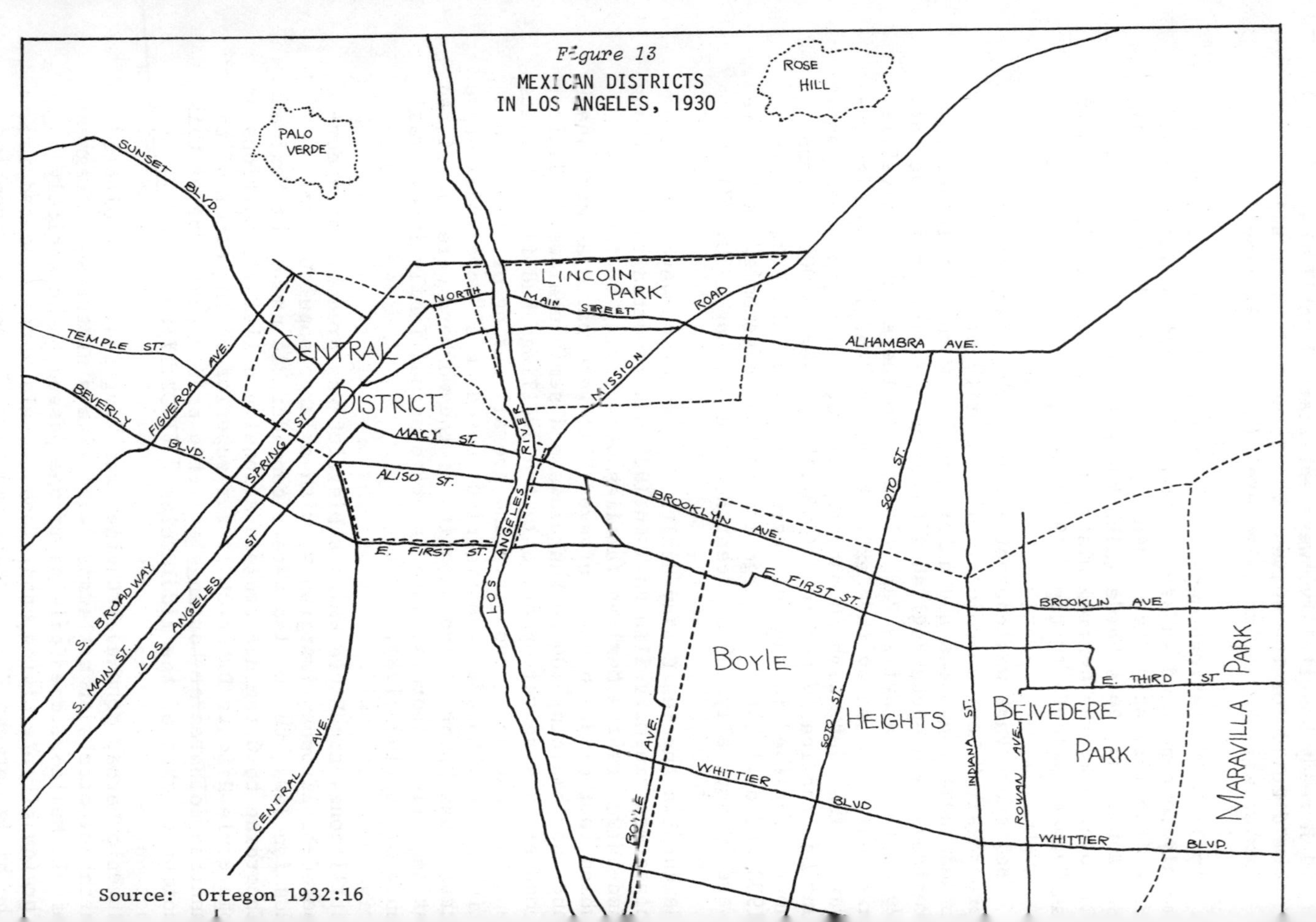

Figure 13

MEXICAN DISTRICTS IN LOS ANGELES, 1930

Source: Ortegon 1932:16

> Shacks cling precariously to the hillsides and are bunched in clusters in the bottom of the ravine.... Goats, staked out on picket lines, can be seen on the hillsides; and most of the homes have chicken pens and fences. The streets are unpaved; really trails packed hard by years of travel.... The houses are old shacks, unpainted and weatherbeaten. Ancient automobile bodies clutter up the landscape and various "dumps" are scattered about. The atmosphere of the ravine, as of *El Hoyo* and other pocket settlements, is ancient, antiquated, a survival--something pushed backward in time and subordinated (1948:224).

Although Rose Hill ("Happy Valley") was a new Mexican colony in 1930, it soon came to have the same characteristics as Palo Verde. This isolated community is located among the steep hills north of Lincoln Park where Huntington Drive winds its way northward to the elegant Anglo suburbs of South Pasadena and San Marino, which are only a few minutes drive from the poverty of the Mexican colonies in East Los Angeles (Ortegon 1932:16,18).

The Lincoln Park District had many similarities with Boyle Heights in the early 1930s. There large numbers of middle class Mexicans lived among other nationalities. Between 1910 and 1930, growing numbers of Mexicans settled in this district, which is located on North Broadway, North Main, Alhambra Avenue, and Mission Road to the east of the Los Angeles River (McEuen 1914:38-39; Ortegon 1932:16-17).

Very few Mexican families owned their own homes in the Central District of Los Angeles in 1930, even though large numbers still lived in the old Mexican settlement ("Sonoratown") north and east of the Plaza. This area, between the Plaza and the river and from North Broadway south to East First Street, was still considered the center of the Mexican community: the oldest Catholic church in Los Angeles, *Nuestra Señora La Reina de Los Angeles*, was located on the Plaza--"until 1876 the Plaza Church enjoyed the distinction of being the first and only place of Catholic public worship in the city of Los Angeles"--and Spanish-speaking shops, businesses, and amusements predominated in the area (1932:6,17-18; Young 1930:177). It was not until the late 1930s that this sizeable community was reduced by urban renewal projects which replaced old Mexican neighborhoods with new factories, a modern union railroad terminal, multi-storied office buildings, and the enlargement of the Civic Center (Schermerhorn 1953:2-3).

During the 1920s and early 1930s, the area between Boyle Heights and the city limits of Alhambra, Monterey Park, and

Montebello became heavily populated with semi-migratory agricultural workers. Some migrated locally, as the season demanded, in the planting, cultivating, and harvesting of citrus and other fruit and nut crops, as well as vegetables and sugar beets. Many others followed the seasonal harvests throughout the state with the result that many neighborhoods in East Los Angeles were largely depopulated in the Spring and repopulated in the late Fall. According to Sheldon, "these people were looked down upon by the more stable residents of the local *barrios* [*Los Locales*] and were classified as *Los de Abajos*, "the lowly ones" (1966:133; Galarza 1964:32).

In the good years, Mexican migrant families earned enough money to return to East Los Angeles and other *barrios* in Los Angeles County and to provide for their minimum needs throughout the winter months. However, in the bad years, when poor health or transportation placed limitations on family earnings, many Mexican families returned to Los Angeles worse off than when they left (Young 1930:178). McWilliams states that when migrant families became stranded in the San Joaquin Valley at the end of the harvest season, some "townspeople would provide ...from public funds...just enough gasoline to make the trip back over the Ridge Route to Los Angeles, where welfare and charitable agencies took care of them during the winter months" (1948:174).

For at least part of the year, mainly the winter months, thousands of needy Mexican families received financial and medical assistance from public and private welfare agencies in Los Angeles County. During the decade of the 1920s, the number of Mexicans on county relief accounted for one-fourth to one-third of the total case load and received over one million dollars per year in welfare and medical assistance (Servín 1970:84-87).

Fluctuations in Community Life: 1930-1970

Mexican American community life in Los Angeles and neighboring *barrios* experienced many fluctuations prior to 1940. In the period 1910-1930, most fluctuations were mainly caused by seasonal employment in agriculture. However, during the midst of the Depression, in the early 1930s, Mexicans by the tens of thousands returned to Mexico as *repatriados*, either voluntarily or involuntarily. In 1934, Emory Bogardus, commenting on this mass movement, wrote:

> The Mexicans who have "gone back" include: (1) those who have voluntarily packed up their belongings and returned by car or train; (2) those who have returned under polite coercion; and (3) those who have been deported. The

second group is composed of many Mexicans who have been told by county or other public welfare agencies that if they would depart their transportation expenses to the border would be paid, but if they did not accept this proposition they would be denied further welfare aid (Servín 1970:89).

Between January 1930 and December 1933, over 311,700 Mexicans returned to their home land and approximately ninety percent of these were repatriates from the United States. Most returned to their native villages and towns (about 80 percent), some to the large cities (15 percent), and about five percent to government repatriation colonies (1970:89-90).

Grebler cites instances of forced repatriation of Mexicans from Detroit, Saint Paul, and Los Angeles, but the exact number of cities that instituted this procedure and the total number of repatriates are unknown. Records of the Los Angeles County Board of Supervisors indicate that at least 15,000 Mexicans were repatriated via fifteen "special trains", with about 1,000 Mexicans in each shipment, by the Department of Charities between 1931 and 1934 (Grebler 1970:524). However, McWilliams, writing in 1933, states that "more than twenty-five special trains" carrying Mexican repatriates left the Southern Pacific Station between February 1931 and April 1932; over 11,000 were repatriated from Los Angeles in 1932 alone. One shipment, consisting of three special trains, left Los Angeles in December 1932 with over 6,000 Mexicans (McWilliams 1948:193).

Therefore, it seems likely that between 30,000-40,000 Mexicans were repatriated from Los Angeles County in the early 1930s. This is confirmed by another observer, Samuel Ortegon, who made the following statement in May 1932, based on statistics he received from the Mexican Consulate: "approximately 10,900 have left for Mexico within the last twelve months... due to recent action by the Los Angeles County authorities..." (1932:65). The implications of this mass repatriation policy will be discussed in a later section.

Fluctuations in Mexican American community life after 1940 were many and varied in Los Angeles. Thousands of Mexican Americans were drafted into the armed services during the Second World War, and later during the Korean conflict, and established a distinguished record of military service. Their accomplishments were well-recorded by Raúl Morín in *Among the Valient: Mexican Americans in World War II and Korea* (1966).

In the agricultural districts, Mexican American youths were drafted so fast in comparison with others that land owners of large farms and ranches, faced with manpower shortage, voiced stern protests with local draft boards" (Servín 1970:101). Many Mexican aliens living in the United States were also drafted but, faced with the opportunity of becoming naturalized citizens during their military service, most returned to their communities after the war as citizens. Rapid acculturation took place among Mexican Americans in the armed services as a result of greater exposure to Anglos, new opportunities for educational and vocational training, and new multicultural experiences and awareness. Returning G.I.s had a growing self-awareness of what it meant to be a Mexican *American*, a more positive self-image, and a greater optimism regarding their future role in American society, no longer as a subordinated minority but as "full citizens" (1970:100-105).

However, those who stayed at home were less optimistic about the future and more dissatisfied with the past and present. While new job opportunities had opened up during the war for Mexican Americans in manufacturing, wholesale and retail trade, the service industries, and notably in the construction trades, there was continuing frustration and anger over their subordinate status--the denial of civil rights in employment, housing, education, union and political representation, police protection and government services. The memories of forced repatriation to Mexico during the Depression, the war-time "Zoot-Suit Riots" in Los Angeles, and the continuing problems of unequal educational opportunities, unemployment, job discrimination, and poor housing not only brought discouragement to many *barrio* residents who were non-veterans, but also contributed to the disillusionment and pessimism of many G.I.s who had once hoped for a better life.

LOS ANGELES COUNTY IN 1970-1972

The rapid and continuous growth of Los Angeles has produced a great fragmented metropolis of over seven million people, the nation's third largest city and a "trading, manufacturing, financial, transportation, and recreational center for a vast area, increasingly oriented to international transactions" (Grebler 1970:289). Although Mexican Americans are the nation's second largest minority, in Los Angeles they are number one. Since 1930, Los Angeles County (Figure 14) has had the largest concentration of Mexican Americans in the United States. According to the 1970 census, the county's 4,000 square mile area had a SSN population of over 1.2 million people, or about 17.5 percent of the total population (Figure 12). Whereas the Hispanic community increased by 113 percent between 1960 and 1970, the county's black population growth was only 64.3 percent. In 1970 the Negro population numbered 762,844, which is 10.9 percent of the county total. By contrast, Los Angeles County had

Figure 14

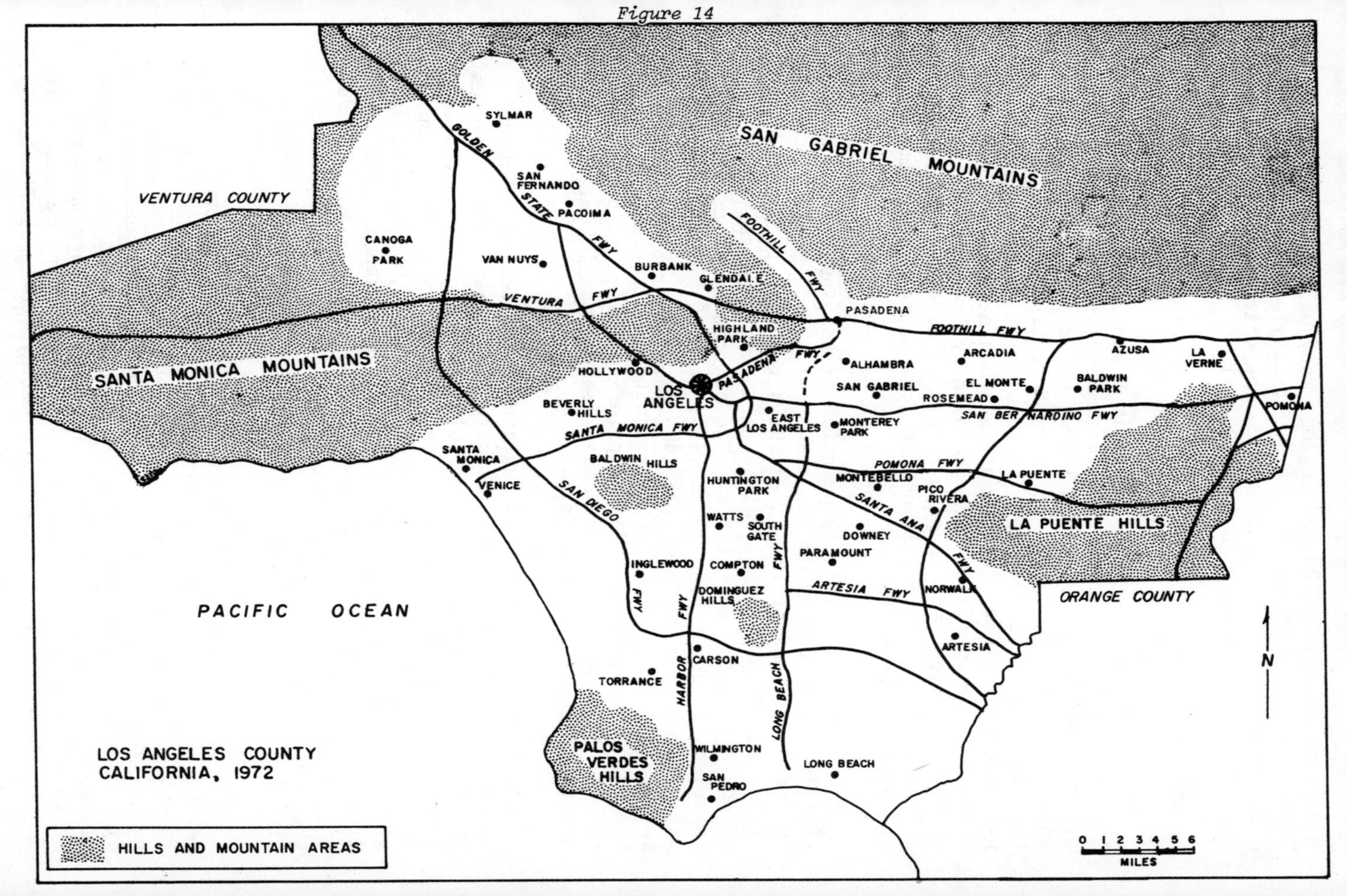

LOS ANGELES COUNTY
CALIFORNIA, 1972
HILLS AND MOUNTAIN AREAS
0 1 2 3 4 5 6
MILES
N
VENTURA COUNTY
ORANGE COUNTY
PACIFIC OCEAN
SAN GABRIEL MOUNTAINS
SANTA MONICA MOUNTAINS
LA PUENTE HILLS
PALOS VERDES HILLS
BALDWIN HILLS
DOMINGUEZ HILLS
SYLMAR
SAN FERNANDO
PACOIMA
CANOGA PARK
VAN NUYS
BURBANK
GLENDALE
PASADENA
HIGHLAND PARK
HOLLYWOOD
LOS ANGELES
BEVERLY HILLS
SANTA MONICA
VENICE
EAST LOS ANGELES
ALHAMBRA
SAN GABRIEL
MONTEREY PARK
ARCADIA
EL MONTE
ROSEMEAD
AZUSA
BALDWIN PARK
LA VERNE
POMONA
MONTEBELLO
PICO RIVERA
LA PUENTE
HUNTINGTON PARK
WATTS
SOUTH GATE
DOWNEY
PARAMOUNT
INGLEWOOD
COMPTON
NORWALK
ARTESIA
CARSON
TORRANCE
WILMINGTON
SAN PEDRO
LONG BEACH
GOLDEN STATE FWY
FOOTHILL FWY
VENTURA FWY
PASADENA FWY
SANTA MONICA FWY
SAN BERNARDINO FWY
POMONA FWY
SANTA ANA FWY
SAN DIEGO FWY
HARBOR FWY
LONG BEACH FWY
ARTESIA FWY

a decline of nearly 100,000 Anglos, many of whom had fled from growing social problems in the inner-city and in some of the older suburbs and had retreated to the white middle-class sanctuary of Orange County (Hebert 1972:1).

Overview of Hispanic Growth

Many *barrios* were established in Los Angeles County between 1910 and 1970. Prior to 1920, most were located in agricultural areas. During the 1920s and 1930s, other *barrios* came into existence in areas adjacent to urban centers like Los Angeles. From the 1920s to the 1970s, as a succession of upwardly mobile Anglos pulled out of older, deteriorating urban neighborhoods, which eventually became areas characterized by low-rent houses and apartments often kept in poor repair by absentee landlords, these "blighted" areas were filled with low-income Mexican Americans and other minorities.

The Hispanic heritage population of Los Angeles County grew rapidly during the 1920s and numbered 250,000 by 1930. However, the repatriations of the early 1930s resulted in a marked decrease in SSN population, although an increase was again recorded during the late 1930s. The Mexican American community increased to about 385,000 in 1950, totaled 576,700 in 1960, and doubled to more than 1,228,600 by 1970. Mexican American in-migrants came mainly from agricultural districts in other Southwestern states and Mexico prior to 1940, or from newly mechanized farming areas or other urban areas in California and the Southwest in the post-war years.

In addition to the rapid immigration of Mexicans, other Spanish-speaking nationalities were also drawn to Los Angeles. In 1960, the non-Mexican SSN population of Los Angeles County numbered about 30,000 compared to 546,800 Mexican Americans. The Latin community included approximately 4,000 Cubans, 3,000 Nicaraguans, 2,600 Argentines, 2,000 Panamanians, 2,000 Costa Ricans, and smaller numbers from Colombia, Guatemala, Ecuador, and Brazil. However, no figures were given for the size of the Puerto Rican population, mainly because they are all U.S. citizens (U.S. Census Bureau 1963b:489,492).

The non-Mexican Latin population greatly increased in the period 1965-1971, when an estimated 20,000 Cuban refugees were resettled in the Los Angeles area. All social classes are represented among the Cuban population but there seems to be a disproportionate number of well-educated members of the upper classes. Although no one area of the county is considered a Cuban stronghold, large numbers can be found in the inner-city and in the *barrios* of San Gabriel Valley (Castro 1971b:1,4-5).

Distribution of SSN Population

In 1970 the Economic and Youth Opportunities Agency (EYOA), a federally-funded poverty planning agency, made an estimate of the SSN population distribution in Los Angeles County by Poverty Planning Areas and Community Action Agencies. Although the total SSN population estimate for the county was 200,000 short of the official census count of 1.2 million, the geographical distribution, as represented in Figure 15, is considered an accurate proportional representation of Hispanic population based on SSN pupil enrollment in each of these areas. Those familiar with Los Angeles will be quick to notice an obvious distortion in the SSN distribution shown in Figure 15, which is the result of an arbitrary EYOA boundary division between the East Los Angeles and Central-Northeast Areas. This distortion gives the latter area prominance over East Los Angeles as the major urban concentration of SSN population. The extreme southern part of the Central-Northeast Area includes districts which range from forty-five to seventy-five percent SSN and are districts that are contiguous with and usually considered part of the "East Los Angeles" area. Also, several cities have been included by the EYOA in the latter area which are not typically considered part of East Los Angeles: Vernon, Huntington Park, Maywood, Bell, Cudahy, Bell Gardens, Montebello, and Monterey Park. Nevertheless, most of these cities have large concentrations of Mexican Americans who have moved out of East Los Angeles.

By comparing the estimated distribution of SSN population in 1970 (Figure 15) with the density of SSN people in Los Angeles County by census tracts in 1960 (Figure 16), a better understanding of the general location of Mexican American housing areas in 1970 is obtained. [For a specific breakdown by census tracts of communities within the county that had greater than five percent SSN population in 1960, see Appendix I, Figure A. It should be noted that area designations in Figure A are not the same as these used by the Economic and Youth Opportunities Agency as shown in Figure 15. For community and area locations correlated with Figure A consult the Welfare Planning Council 1965:8,22,23.]

Although Figure 16 shows SSN population density in 1960, the changes in SSN pupil enrollment in Los Angeles County public schools between 1966 and 1971 confirm that the Hispanic population remains concentrated in "Colony" (greater than 45% SSN) and "Intermediate" (15-44% SSN) areas (cf. Appendix I, Figures B, C, D). The greatest increases in SSN population between 1960 and 1970 were in the following districts: East Los Angeles-Montebello; Alhambra, South San Gabriel, Rosemead, El Monte, Baldwin Park, West Covina, Bassett and Duarte (San

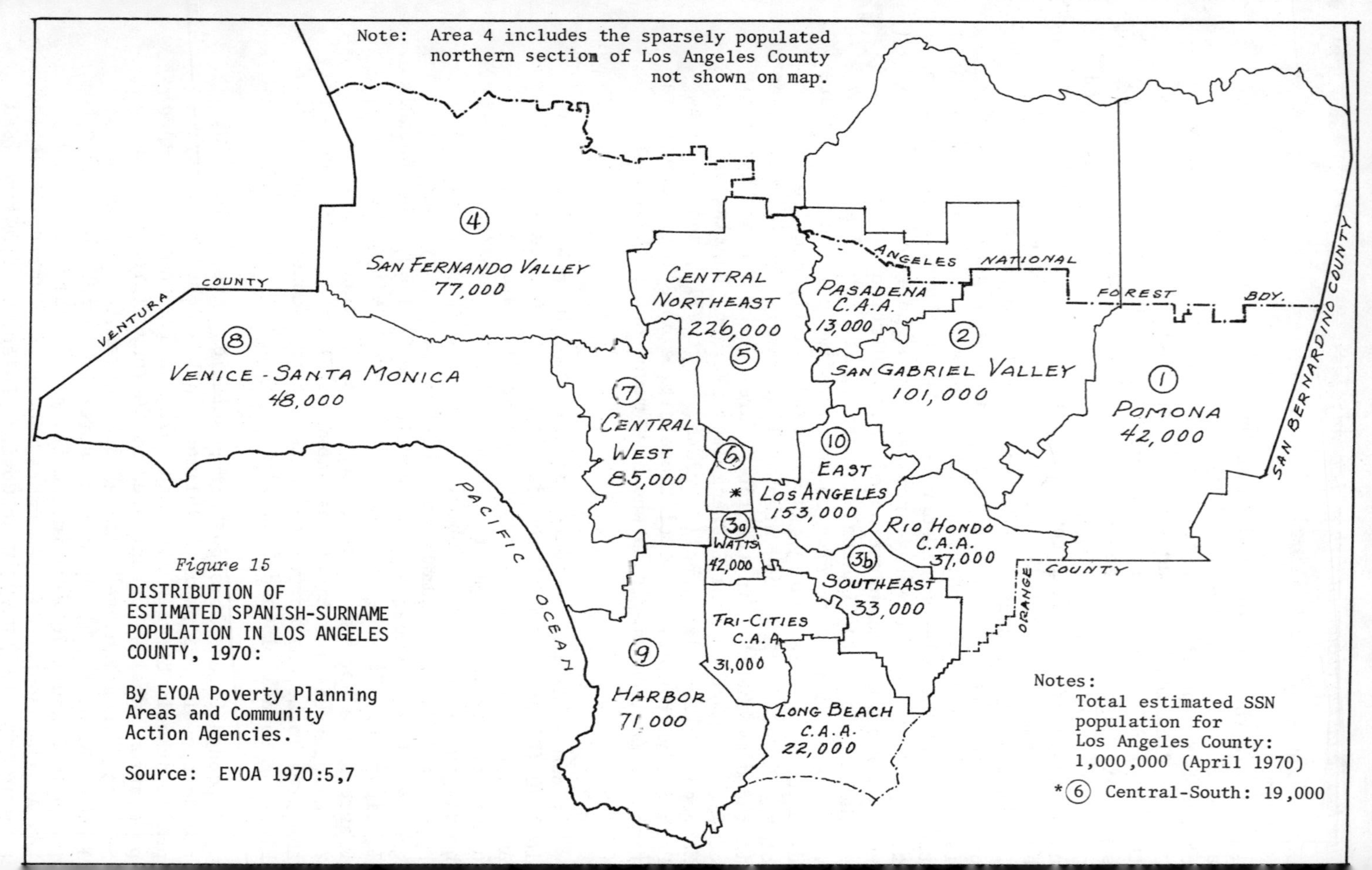

Figure 15

DISTRIBUTION OF ESTIMATED SPANISH-SURNAME POPULATION IN LOS ANGELES COUNTY, 1970:

By EYOA Poverty Planning Areas and Community Action Agencies.

Source: EYOA 1970:5,7

Figure 10

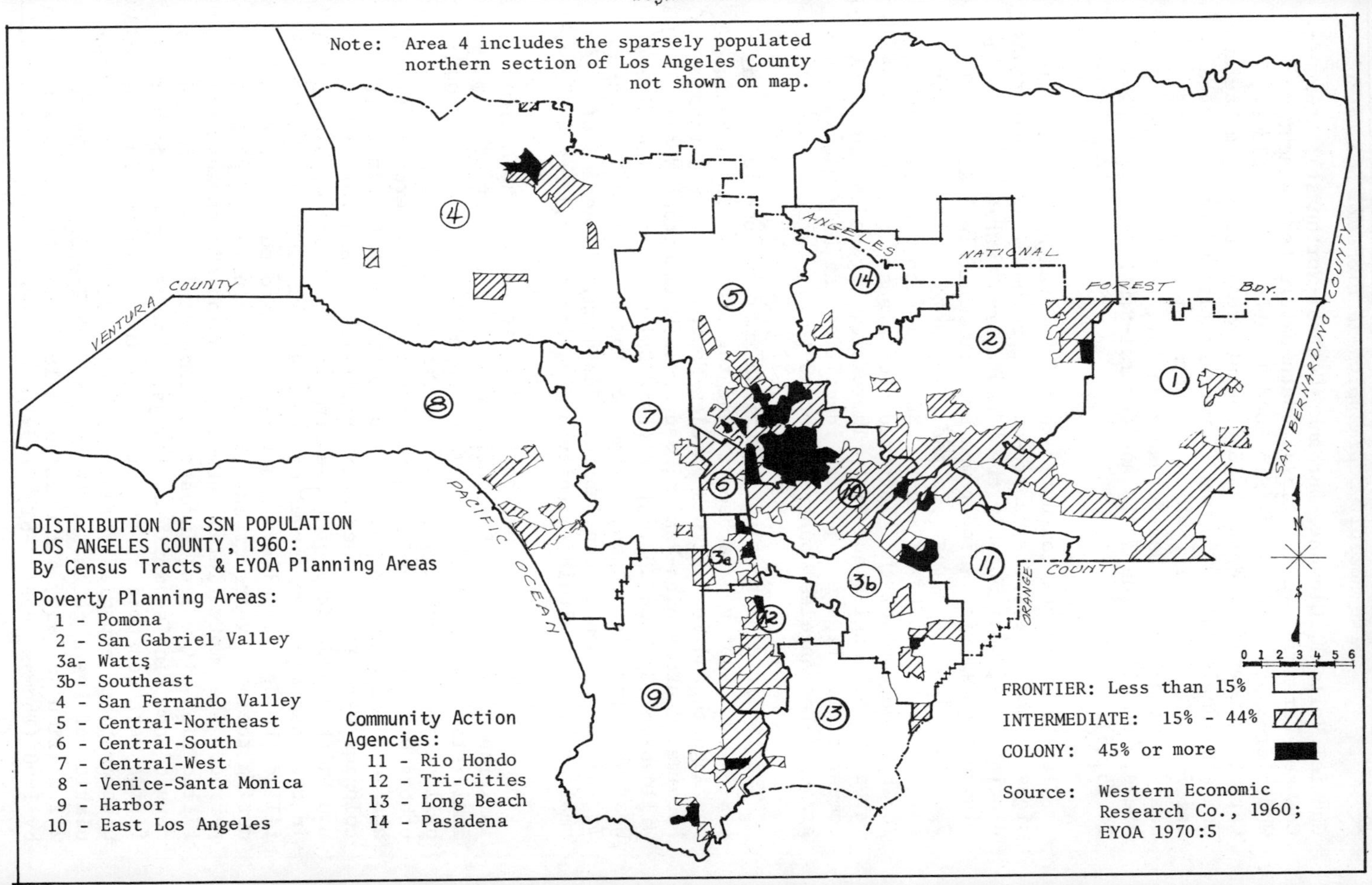

Note: Area 4 includes the sparsely populated northern section of Los Angeles County not shown on map.
VENTURA COUNTY
ANGELES NATIONAL FOREST BDY.
SAN BERNARDINO COUNTY
ORANGE COUNTY
PACIFIC OCEAN
N
S
0 1 2 3 4 5 6
DISTRIBUTION OF SSN POPULATION
LOS ANGELES COUNTY, 1960:
By Census Tracts & EYOA Planning Areas
Poverty Planning Areas:
1 - Pomona
2 - San Gabriel Valley
3a- Watts
3b- Southeast
4 - San Fernando Valley
5 - Central-Northeast
6 - Central-South
7 - Central-West
8 - Venice-Santa Monica
9 - Harbor
10 - East Los Angeles
Community Action Agencies:
11 - Rio Hondo
12 - Tri-Cities
13 - Long Beach
14 - Pasadena
FRONTIER: Less than 15%
INTERMEDIATE: 15% - 44%
COLONY: 45% or more
Source: Western Economic Research Co., 1960; EYOA 1970:5

Gabriel Valley); Glendale-Burbank (Central-Northeast); Lynwood-Compton-Paramount (Tri-Cities); Southwestern Long Beach; Whittier-Santa Fe Springs (Rio Hondo); Artesia, Bellflower, Cerritos, Lawndale, Norwalk (Southeast Area); La Puente-Hacienda Heights, Rowland, and Pomona (Pomona Area); and the Los Angeles Unified School District which includes parts of the Harbor, Santa Monica-Venice, San Fernando Valley, and Central-Northeast Areas, and all of the Watts and Central-South Area (cf. Figures 14,15,16).

[It should be further noted that EYOA area names and divisions do not necessarily correspond to normally accepted area distinctions, most notably the "Pomona Area" category which includes several cities and towns more commonly included in the San Gabriel Valley area. In addition, some distortion is present in the census tract map of SSN population density (Figure 16) because some of the "Intermediate" areas are thinly populated by both Anglos and SSN. Therefore, Figure 16 should be compared with Figure 14, which identifies the hill and mountain areas of Los Angeles County that tend to be sparsely populated.]

The traditional centers of Mexican American population in Los Angeles County have been around the old Mexican Plaza in Los Angeles and in East Los Angeles-Montebello, San Fernando-Pacoima, Santa Monica-Venice, San Pedro-Wilmington, Watts-Willowbrook-Compton, Norwalk-Artesia-Dairy Valley, Pico Rivera-West Whittier-Los Nietos, La Puente, Pomona-La Verne, Azusa-Irwindale, El Monte, San Gabriel, Pasadena, and dozens of smaller *barrios* within the city of Los Angeles and its suburbs.

Many of these older neighborhoods were settled by Mexican immigrants fleeing the Revolution or during the period of mass immigration in the 1920s. Some settlements sprang up in foothill citrus communities in the San Gabriel and Pomona Valleys; others were settled by field workers in the San Fernando Valley and in a large portion of the southeastern county; still other colonies were established near industrial areas, rail lines, and brickyards. Many of these semi-rural *barrios* were engulfed in the vast suburban sprawl of new Anglo subdivisions that filled the nearby valleys and farm lands around Los Angeles during the boom years of the 1920s and again in the post-war period. The empty fields between towns and cities were soon filled with oil wells, industrial-commercial areas, and endless rows of new single-family dwellings. Orange groves and bean fields were consumed in the spread of industrialization and urbanization, especially in the post-war years. The total population of Los Angeles County surged from 936,000 in 1920 to 2.2 million in 1930, 4.1 million in 1950, and to over six million by 1960 (Thomas 1959:80-81, 87-99).

For many Anglos, the Mexican American, isolated in his urban or suburban *barrio*, is an invisible part of the landscape as he cruises along the freeway at seventy miles per hour on his way home to his "safe" middle-class suburban neighborhood. For still other Anglos, particularly in the San Gabriel Valley and in cities like Glendale, Lynwood, and Long Beach, the rapid increase of Mexican American families in deteriorating neighborhoods has forced him to realize that one out of every six residents of Los Angeles County have Spanish surnames. However, many urban Anglos have had long exposure to the problems of changing neighborhoods--both brown and black--in the areas like Pasadena, Central-West Los Angeles, and Compton. Five examples of contemporary Mexican American community life are here presented to illustrate the present situation in Los Angeles County, with problems both old and new.

East Los Angeles

Although this designation is often ambiguous, "East Los Angeles" (cf. Figure 14) is here defined as "a series of neighborhoods, including both city and unincorporated county districts, extending from the Los Angeles River east to the ring of incorporated suburbs" (Sheldon 1966:135-136). Two of the major subregional divisions are located within the City of Los Angeles, Boyle Heights and Lincoln Heights, while East Los Angeles (as defined by the 1960 census) is an unincorporated county area that includes the subcommunities of City Terrace, Belvedere, and Maravilla Park. For purposes of the present study, "East Los Angeles" is an area bordered on the west by the Los Angeles River, on the north by Mt. Washington, Highland Park, and El Sereno districts, on the east by the cities of Alhambra, Monterey Park, and Montebello, and on the south by Commerce and Vernon.

Population Characteristics. The distinguishing feature of East Los Angeles is the high concentration of Mexican Americans and other Hispanic descent people within this large area--about six miles from east to west and 4.5 miles from north to south. In 1960 East Los Angeles contained thirty-five census tracts with greater than forty-five percent SSN population; thirteen of these had greater than seventy-five percent SSN and eighteen were 60-74 percent SSN (Figure 16). The total Hispanic population of the area was approximately 138,700 with the subregional breakdown as follows: Boyle Heights 50,140 (66.8% of the total population), Lincoln Heights 17,865 (56.9%), and East Los Angeles 70,765 (67.1%) (Figure A, Appendix I).

According to a special census of "East Los Angeles" in 1965, the subcommunities of Boyle Heights, City Terrace, and East Los Angeles had a SSN population of 134,870 which was more than seventy-five percent of the total population of the area [Note: this special census did not include Lincoln Heights, and City Terrace was listed separately from East Los Angeles which makes this information difficult to correlate with 1960 census data.] Between 1960 and 1965, six percent of the residents of East Los Angeles moved into the area from other parts of California or from other Southwestern states; seven percent were new arrivals from Mexico or other Latin American countries. Although the total population decreased by eight percent, the SSN population increased by 7,400 in the period 1960-1965. In terms of age distribution, fifty-three percent of the population was under twenty-five years; thirty-seven percent were under the age of fourteen. The condition of area housing was listed as: seven percent "dilapidated", twenty-eight percent "deteriorating", and sixty-five percent "sound". The average rent for a house or apartment was seventy-five dollars per month. Only about thirty-six percent of the housing units were owner occupied, whereas the majority were controlled by absentee landlords. The unemployment rate for East Los Angeles was 7.7 percent for men and 6.8 percent for women in the labor force. The median family income in 1965 was only $5,106 which had to meet the needs of a family of four to five persons (U.S. Bureau of the Census 1966a,b). The corresponding median family incomes for urban areas in California in 1960 were as follows: Anglo $7,213; SSN $5,700; and non-white $5,061 (Grebler 1970:181).

Area Variables. East Los Angeles is an area of few contrasts and many similarities. Many middle and upper class Mexican American businessmen and professionals have their offices in one of several important business districts in East Los Angeles. Sheldon, writing in 1966, stated: "East Los Angeles today is dominated by active, educated Americans of Mexican extraction" (1966:135). However, in 1965-1966, only about twenty percent of the residents in Los Angeles County's largest *colonia* had yearly incomes above $6,000, while forty-two percent ranged from $3,600-$5,999 and forty-five percent earned less than $3,600. By comparison, only about fourteen percent of the total SSN population in Los Angeles County in 1960 earned less than $3,000 per annum, which was the national poverty-level indicator (Grebler 1970:305,327). East Los Angeles is composed predominantly of low-skilled and low-income blue-collar workers. The high-income and high-prestige workers tend to move out of colony areas to intermediate or frontier areas. According to Grebler, "those above the poverty line who choose to live in the Colonies tend to be persons whose general status attributes --especially job prestige and education--are relatively low" (1970:332).

While East Los Angeles continues to attract migrants from the rural Southwest and immigrants from Mexico, an increasing ımber of upwardly mobile Mexican Americans are leaving the ›lonies for better housing and opportunities in the suburbs-- ıe San Fernando and San Gabriel Valleys, and western Los ıgeles and the southeastern communities. Many families, both ›wer and middle class, were forced to find housing outside of ıst Los Angeles due to extensive freeway construction in the '50s and 1960s; the poor drifted to other urban low-cost housıg areas throughout the city while the growing lower-middle .ass had a much wider choice of residential areas and housing.

Overcrowding and poor housing characterize most Mexican ıericans both in East Los Angeles and throughout Los Angeles ›unty, which are conditions that are mainly due to their low ıcome and large family size. Compared to non-whites, Mexican ıericans have a higher median family income. But in terms of ːr-capita income, Mexican Americans lag behind non-whites beıuse of the larger size of Mexican American families, which 'eraged 4.3 persons in Los Angeles County in 1960 compared to 0 for the total population. [The median per-capita income ›r Californians in 1960 was: Anglo $2,255; SSN $1,380; and ›n-whites $1,482 (1970:126)]. Consequently, Mexican American ımilies must make greater sacrifices in housing quality and ›ace, which results in severe overcrowding. In addition, ːxican American tenants receive poorer housing than do others .ying comparable rents, regardless of income bracket (1970: ᵌ3-185,262-265,305).

In East Los Angeles, although some communities like Hollen-.ck Heights and Boyle Heights contain many large, older homes .ich have been converted to apartments or rooming houses, most ' the housing consists of "small, four-or-five room frame or .ucco single dwellings, often two or three on tiny (30 X 50) ›ts." Many of these homes were built in the 1920s and usually ›nsisted of little more than shacks, but most have been slowly ıproved upon and enlarged over the years. According to Sheldon, 'his is not a slum area in the eastern-city sense, but it is .fined as one of the two most extreme poverty areas and is con- dered among the least desirable sections of Los Angeles in .ich to live" (1966:136). In the mid-1960s, East Los Angeles .d five city and county projects that provided low-cost housing ›r low-income families.

Although some expensive and well-built homes can also be ›und in East Los Angeles, the area is generally characterized "blighted" or "deteriorating". According to the Los Angeles ›mmunity Analysis Bureau in 1971, Boyle Heights and Lincoln ›ights are among the top ten "seriously blighted" communities thin the City of Los Angeles, along with other Mexican Ameri-.n housing areas like El Sereno, Mt. Washington, Wholesale, ysian Park, Downtown, University, Santa Barbara, Wilmington, and Pacoima which were rated among the top twenty most seriously blighted areas. City Terrace, Belvedere, and Maravilla Park were not listed in the bureau's report because they are located outside the city limits in an unincorporated county area. [Note: the "blighted" rating is determined by a series of factors: "education, housing, income production, public safety, calculated general blight, an ambiance rating and, finally, an overall integrated blight rating" (Hebert 1970:10).]

Community Problems. East Los Angeles has been at a critical stage of internal tension and frustration for many years. Local and state government officials have often tried to deal with community problems by a policy of "Mexican removal"--routing as many freeways as possible through the area. So far, at least 16,000 Mexican Americans have been displaced by freeway construction: "The San Bernardino is one of six freeways that slice up an area three miles square in East Los Angeles. No other place in the state can match this concentration" (Pastier 1971:7).

The nation's largest Mexican American *barrio* has been traditionally gerrymandered into political impotency, but many community leaders are now active in a legislative reapportionment movement to obtain greater political representation for Mexican Americans at both the local and state level (Gillam 1971:3,30). Other Mexican American leaders are pushing for the incorporation of "East Los Angeles" so that it can establish its own municipal government and police department. However, a similar effort in 1961 failed by a narrow margin, a factor attributed to strong opposition from powerful groups outside the community, and to internal dissention among Mexican American leaders (Sheldon 1966:145).

The high rate of juvenile delinquency in East Los Angeles, along with high drop-out rates among junior high and high school-aged Mexican Americans, are but symptoms of larger and more basic community problems. In 1968, thousands of Mexican American students boycotted several East Los Angeles high schools to protest against the inability of the Anglo-controlled educational system to deal with language and cultural differences and the resulting high drop-out rate of students from predominantly Mexican American schools, and to publicize their demands for educational reform, particularly the establishment of bilingual and bicultural programs for *Chicano* students (Burma 1970:279-294)

An estimated fifty percent of Mexican American youths in some East Los Angeles high schools drop out of school. Many of them turn to organized gangs and juvenile delinquency because of their inability to enter the job market (Rawitch 1971:1,20). According to a recent study by the Manpower Research Center at UCLA, "marijuana selling and other illegal activities are the biggest source of income for young workers in the Watts and East Los Angeles areas where unemployment has reached disastrous proportions." In 1971 the unemployment rate in East Los Angeles for all men aged 16 to 24 was thirty percent, but for teenagers alone, thirty-four percent were without jobs. The UCLA study reported that more than a third of the *Chicano* teenagers surveyed in East Los Angeles had dropped out of high school (Bernstein 1972b:1,12).

Growing bitterness and frustration among younger Mexican Americans in East Los Angeles, stimulated by a lack of improvement in long-term community problems--unemployment, poor housing, lack of adequate educational opportunities, lack of political representation, and strained police-community relations--are cited as principal reasons behind the destructive riots that took place in East Los Angeles in August and September 1970 (Del Olmo 1971:3,22). Although there are growing tensions between the majority of Mexican Americans in East Los Angeles and young *Chicano* militants, Mexican Americans both young and old are restless for significant social changes that will improve the quality of community life in East Los Angeles.

Echo Park District

Many urban neighborhoods that surround Downtown Los Angeles have been labeled "blighted" for more than twenty years. However, the circle of blight is not yet complete around the Central City. The exception is Echo Park, a multiracial, multiethnic hilly neighborhood located between the Hollywood Freeway, Elysian Park, and the Golden State Freeway and bordered on the west by the Silver Lake District (cf. Figure 14). Although this changing community was approximately thirty percent SSN in 1960, by 1970 the SSN population had increased to seventy percent. Dial Torgerson stated that "Echo Park is becoming a near slum and a much-in-demand middle-class community at the same time. It is going up and down simultaneously" (1971:1).

Community Tensions. City planners are trying to save "outer fringe" communities like Echo Park from further deterioration by replacing substandard housing units and limiting population density. Community leaders have opposed plans for new federally-funded low-cost housing in order to stop the influx of the urban poor. The neighborhood is geographically divided between deteriorating flatland housing and middle class hillside plots; home values range from $5,000 to $40,000. Echo Park boosters claim that their community is "one of the few really successfully blended communities in the city of Los Angeles...with islands of different kinds of people living together in harmony" (1971:1). However, community harmony is being shaken by disruptive forces from within.

Echo Park was for many years a fairly stable and serene near downtown neighborhood, surrounding picturesque Echo Park Lake. Other notable landmarks include Angeles Temple, built in the late 1920s by Foursquare evangelist Aimee Semple McPherson, and home of the L.I.F.E. Bible College. The area includes a "thriving, 24-hour-a-day business district at Sunset Blvd. and Echo Park Ave.," where the community's heterogeneous population does much of its shopping. In addition to the large Latin population (Mexican Americans, Mexican nationals, Cubans, Central and South Americans), various neighborhood blocks are inhabited by groups of Orientals, Filipinos, Ukrainians, and Yugoslavians, in addition to many "hippies" and interracial couples. The racial and ethnic mixture of the community is seen in the diversity of pupil enrollment at Elysian Heights Elementary School: "58 Oriental children, 11 black children, 118 Anglos, and the rest of the 460 students were Spanish surname" (1971:1).

Neighborhood Change. The Echo Park area has changed in stages. Many oldtimers owned homes there from the time the suburb was developed in the 1920s. But as the older population began to die out, their heirs, who had moved to newer suburbs, sold the newly acquired properties to absentee landlords. When the Chinese community expanded into and developed the Alpine area, an old Mexican neighborhood that was adjacent to the colony in Chavez Ravine--bulldozed to make room for Dodger Stadium in the late 1950s--the poorer residents were forced to move due to the construction of the new higher-rent housing. Many of these dislocated Mexican Americans moved into low-rent houses and apartments in the Echo Park District, along with others who were forced to move from the Temple District when city inspectors condemned large numbers of rat and roach-infested slum buildings. The absentee landlords of Echo Park rented their unpainted and deteriorating properties for $85-$100 per month to many welfare families from the Alpine and Temple areas.

Although some Echo Park residents accuse the Latin community of causing the rapid deterioration of flatland housing areas and turning them into slums, community deterioration is mainly due to the characteristic problems of the urban poor (1971:1):

> ...the spread of blight is not just a movement of any racial or ethnic group, nor is it simply a deterioration of housing. Blight is something the helpless, hopeless poor bring with them, whatever their background or color.
>
> It is a willingness to be victimized and to victimize. Victimized, they think by unscrupulous landlords, the merchants and the schools, the angriest poor bring vandalism and violence to wherever they move.

...youths from impoverished, disadvantaged families, coming to "La Echo Park" from areas with histories of gang warfare, found themselves unable to achieve, advance or even cope. They turned to gangs again.

According to a recent community study of the Silver Lake-cho Park area by UCLA sociologists, Echo Park will soon be-ome "entirely Latin American." Much of the area's unused creage is zoned for apartments which, if developed for that urpose, will greatly increase the population density and urther the ghettoization process. In December 1970 plans ere announced for the construction of ninety-four low-rent ousing units to be developed under a federally-subsidized rogram. A group of property owners banded together to stop he project and to push for a zoning rollback to keep down ousing and population density. The present density is only bout one-third of the maximum allowed by present zoning. The roblem many property owners face is: "How much density will e enough to stimulate new building?" Torgerson quoted one ommunity spokesman as saying: "People must be allowed to uild units from which they can make a decent return, or here'll be no new building" (1971:2).

Answers to Urban Problems. The problems facing the residents f Echo Park are characteristic of many other urban communities n Los Angeles. High density housing encourages overcrowding nd blight. Deteriorating neighborhoods must be rebuilt in rder for property owners to profit from their investments. Low-ent housing stimulates the influx of the urban poor and leads o community deterioration. In 1971, Echo Park was ranked eight-enth in a list of twenty communities threatened with blight; it eceived the following rating compared to citywide medians 1971:2-3):

Sound housing: 86% (compared to 92% citywide); renters--as opposed to home owners--64% (citywide 55.6%); median rent $80 (citywide $98).

Education: high school dropout rate 39% (citywide 27%); scores on 10th grade reading tests 26.3 (citywide 30.5).

Income: median earnings $5,965 per year (citywide $7,132); number of white collar workers 30% (citywide 39%).

Public safety: reported felonies per 100 persons .93 per year (citywide .98).

Other factors used as indicators are recreational facilities, health and accessibility via car or transit system.

City planners evaluate community blight status by watching educational, home ownership, and construction trends (1971:103). Persons with less education are less capable of producing income and, consequently, live in low-rent housing areas. Absentee property ownership often results in the further deterioration of older housing areas because such owners want to make as much profit as possible, while holding down the cost of property maintenance. Resident owners usually take pride in the upkeep of their property and are more careful in the selection of renters. Many Echo Park properties have two houses on a lot, with resident owners living in one house and renting out the other one. The properties of absentee landlords tend to deteriorate at twice the rate of those of resident owners. The construction of new low-cost housing provides better homes for some urban workers but invites the in-migration of low-income families from neighboring areas to fill the vacated and deteriorating housing.

The answers to these problems seem strangely evasive, but answers must be found in order to improve the quality of community life for all residents--including Echo Park's seventy percent Spanish surname population, many of whom are poor. The replacement of substandard housing units has often resulted in prohibitive rents for many low-income families and the out-migration of the very poor to other low-rent housing areas. Extensive urban renewal projects have often been used to rid an area of the urban poor without providing for new housing that low-income families can afford. Consequently, the poor are often opposed to both urban renewal and freeway construction projects.

Rosemead

There are many divided communities in suburban Los Angeles County, one of which is Rosemead. This residential community of 41,000 inhabitants is located on the San Bernardino Freeway between San Gabriel and El Monte, in the South San Gabriel Valley (cf. Figure 14). It is a community not only divided by the eight lanes of the San Bernardino Freeway, but also by class and ethnic lines. The north side of the freeway is predominantly white and middle class, while the south side is mainly composed of low-income Mexican American families who have moved out of East Los Angeles in search of something better. South Rosemead is almost identical in composition to the adjoining Mexican American communities of South San Gabriel and South El Monte, whose residents have also largely come from East Los Angeles. The families in these areas have exchanged urban poverty for suburban poverty (Turner 1972:1).

SSN Population Growth. In 1960 Rosemead was only 7.6 percent Spanish surname. But by 1972, forty percent of the city's esidents were Mexican American, most of whom lived south of the reeway (1972:1). The Garvey Elementary School District, which ncludes South San Gabriel and south Rosemead, had over fifty ercent SSN pupil enrollment during the school year 1970-1971 nd added almost 1,000 SSN pupils between 1966 and 1970. By contrast, the Rosemead Elementary District, located north of the reeway was only twenty-four percent SSN in 1970 and increased y only 180 SSN pupils in the period 1966-1970 (Figure B, ppendix I).

Community Problems. The differences between north and south osemead are a major source of tension between area residents. ırner cites a 1969 survey of the south Rosemead-South San abriel area which reveals that twenty-three percent of the amily heads had annual incomes of $4,000 or less. Many of the rea's streets were in poor condition and were without sidewalks; any were unlighted. Some community leaders believe that conditions are just as bad on the south side of Rosemead and San Gabiel as conditions in East Los Angeles--unemployment, inadequate ousing, unequal educational opportunities, juvenile delinquency, rug abuse, police brutality, and many families on welfare .972:1).

Mexican American Community Organization. Mexican American mmunity leaders, like Ed Hernandez and David Froba, insist at Rosemead City councilmen, none of whom are Mexican American, e insensitive to and ignore the problems of the Mexican American community. But, for the first time, the community is organ-ing itself for constructive action: "the Bienvenidos Community nter, [organized in January 1970] has been used as a rallying int for community activity" (1972:1). This center has become place for discussing Mexican American community problems and om which grievances have been presented to the city council, e schools, and the Los Angeles County Sheriff's Department, ich is responsible for public safety in Rosemead since the ty lacks its own police department.

Bienvenidos Community Center has not only been an agency for ganizing community action, but also provides the following rvices (1972:5):

1. Family services such as a food co-op and welfare advice.
2. Delinquency prevention through a youth center and camping activities.
3. A job clearing house for adults and juveniles.
4. An education center where school dropouts can earn credits toward a high school diploma.

The Center grew out of a previous organization called "Rosemead Community at Work" and is funded by the Economic and Youth Opportunities Agency of Greater Los Angeles. To many city fathers, having a poverty agency in Rosemead was an insult--"for years, they'd been saying they had no problems; then the federal government funds a poverty agency in town" (1972:5).

Demands for Change. Mexican American leaders are organizing the community for constructive changes. The greatest sources of tension concern the County Sheriff's Department, local government and community schools. Froba and Joe Sanchez organized "Citizens Concerned About Police Brutality" to protest the shooting death of a seventeen-year-old Mexican American youth by a deputy sheriff in October 1971. Mutual distrust characterizes the relationship between the Sheriff's Department and the Mexican American community. Chicano spokesman are calling for Rosemead to establish its own police force subject to local control and with community representation in law enforcement. Some police officials agree with the policy of community representation: "We need to recruit people from the community and then put them back out on the street as deputies...we need people-oriented recruits" (1972:5).

The Mexican American community is restless for adequate representation on the city council and has accused the all-Anglo council of reluctance to seek federal funds for community development projects. Plans are being made by *Chicano* leaders to elect Mexican Americans to the city council during forthcoming elections. The lack of political representation for Rosemead's SSN community will no doubt soon change since the SSN population is now almost fifty percent of the total community (1972:1,5).

Chicano activists have also organized opposition to a proposed realignment of school districts in the Alhambra-San Gabriel-Rosemead-El Monte area. This territory is presently divided into two high school districts--Alhambra City and El Monte Union. The Los Angeles County Board of Education has proposed a four-district split which would create a unified school district in each of the following cities: El Monte, Rosemead, San Gabriel, and Alhambra-Monterey Park. Proponents of the four-district realignment stress the need for "community identity in a school district," for reestablishing local control and thus insuring quality education. On the other hand, stated Turner (1971:6,7):

> Rosemead residents--Anglos and Mexican-Americans--assailed the four-way alignment, contending it leaves their proposed district ethnically unbalanced and with an insufficient property tax base.... The proposed Rosemead Unified District...would have the highest percentage of Spanish surnames [42%] and the lowest amount of assessed valuation per student [$7,900].

Mexican American leaders in Rosemead and South San Gabriel 'iewed the county proposal as a plot "to get rid of Chicanos .t San Gabriel High School." It was estimated that the re- .lignment would decrease San Gabriel High's SSN enrollment by .bout 500 students, to approximately twenty-eight percent SSN. 'his decrease would result from shifting students to Rosemead :igh School who live in south Rosemead and now attend San ;abriel High School (1971:5).

Thus, the gerrymandering of school districts to deprive the oor of equal educational opportunities is as real a problem .s the gerrymandering of political districts to eliminate Mexi- .an American representation. The unequal opportunities of the oor, whether urban or suburban, continue to be a major problem .n Los Angeles County in the 1970s.

'asadena

One of the concrete escape routes from the congested Los .ngeles downtown area is the Pasadena Freeway, built in the .ate 1940s as the prototype of modern highway construction but .ow seriously overcrowded and confined to the narrow Arroyo eco. Not only is the Pasadena Freeway an escape route for uburban Anglos who work in the Central City and live in the nce-elegant city that lies in the lower foothills of the San ·abriel mountains, but the much-used freeway is also a migra- ion route for the growing Spanish surname population of Cen- ral and East Los Angeles (cf. Figure 14).

Community Change. Although Central Pasadena had under 3,000 panish surname residents in 1960, amounting to 8.3 percent of he area's total population, Pasadena's SSN community in 1970 'as estimated to number 9,000. According to Martin Ortiz, di- 'ector of the Mexican American Studies Center at Whittier Col- ege, "about 7,000 are of Mexican descent...others are largely :ubans and Puerto Ricans" (Berkenshaw 1969:1). The increase in SN population is reflected in pupil enrollment figures between .966 and 1970, an increase of 618 SSN pupils. The Pasadena 'nified District had 2,666 SSN students in October 1970, which 'as 9.2 percent of the total enrollment (Figure B, Appendix I).

Pasadena has witnessed tremendous community changes since the id-1940s when the city was a dominantly white, middle and upper :lass sanctuary of the affluent. The enrollment of white stu- ents in Pasadena public schools decreased from 90.5 percent in 946 to 58.3 percent in 1970, with a decline of 4,600 white stu- ents in the period 1963-1970. Between 1946 and 1970, the :ity's racial and ethnic minority population increased in size 'rom 9.5 to 41.7 percent, based on school district statistics of tudent enrollment (Austin 1970:1). The racial and ethnic com- osition of Pasadena, as reflected in pupil enrollment for the school year 1970-1971, was 53.9 percent white, 33 percent black, 9.3 percent Spanish surname, 2.8 percent Oriental, and 1.0 percent other minorities (Austin 1971b:6).

Since Pasadena is Los Angeles County's fifth largest city, with a total population of 123,800 in 1970, the extent of minority population increase in such a large, formerly white suburb points to a significant trend in the county's minority distribution. The overcrowded urban poor are seeking better living conditions and greater opportunities in the suburbs, and by so doing are forcing the Anglo majority society to *face* its responsibility for improving the quality of community life for all residents. However, the "white flight" from integrated neighborhoods and schools is evidence of the dominant society's reluctance to *accept* responsibility for improving the socioeconomic condition of the urban and suburban poor.

Minority Education. The white exodus from Pasadena has increased since the 1970 federal court decision to enforce the integration of Pasadena schools in order to achieve equal educational opportunities and to eliminate *de facto* segregation. The Pasadena Unified School District's thirty-four schools and 30,600 students were integrated during the school year 1970-1971. The Fall enrollment statistics showed a decline of 2,212 white students and an increase of 703 minority students over enrollment figures for the previous year. School officials predicted the continued decline of white students for the 1971-1972 school year--by approximately 1,700--and the increase of minority pupils--about 330 blacks and 100 Spanish surname. If these projections were accurate, minority students would have totaled fifty percent of Pasadena's pupil enrollment in the Fall of 1971 (Austin 1971b:6).

In the Spring of 1970, a group of Mexican American students and parents presented a list of eight demands to Pasadena's Superintendent of Schools, Ralph Hornbeck:

> The demands were for Mexican-American studies in high school curriculum; more Mexican-American teachers; Mexican-American counsellors sensitive to Mexican-American student problems; cessation of alledged discrimination in the Pasadena Unified School District; more Mexican-American literature in school libraries; permission for the MECHA organization (a Mexican American student organization with chapters mainly on college campuses) to establish branches on Pasadena high school campuses; establishment of a committee of Mexican-American students to meet with the school board on a regular basis to discuss problems that might arise; permission for Mexican-American youth organizations to

wear jackets to school and to hold meetings on campus (Leiren 1970:4).

Hornbeck, conceding that most of these "demands" were legitimate grievances, announced plans for recruiting additional Mexican teachers and counsellors, curriculum changes that would add courses on Mexican American history and literature, and a curriculum committee composed of student, teacher, and community representatives. The proposed committee would meet with the Department of Instructional Services "to promote student and community involvement in developing curriculum as it relates to the contributions of the Mexican American" (1970:4).

In March 1971, the "Mexican American Educational Committee" presented five specific requests to the Pasadena Board of Education that summarized continuing Mexican American educational concerns (Austin 1971a):

1. Establishment of a preschool program at Garfield Primary School, which has 30.5% Spanish surname pupils.
2. Employment of more bilingual teachers and aids in the schools.
3. Review of the district's "target area" schools for special federally-funded educational programs in terms of the Mexican-American enrollments.
4. Extra pay to bilingual aids and teachers for their additional duties of translating and interpreting.
5. Appointment of a Mexican-American, recommended by the Mexican-American Educational Committee, to fill the district's Intergroup Educational Department consultant position....

Maxine Casso, an advisory member of this committee, explained that these five "requests" were made directly to the Board of Education because school administrators had failed to act on previous proposals submitted by her committee: "the frustrations of the community have mounted to such proportions that we have no alternative but to come before this board" (1971a). Casso pointed out that, of $800,000 in federal funds received by the district under the Elementary and Secondary Education Act Title I, "only $13,000 was alloted to assist the Spanish speaking student" (1971a):

> The primary role of the Compensatory Education Act was to provide special educational services to children from low income families and for students who because of language, cultural, economic and environmental handicaps are unlikely to achieve at grade level.

> As I go around the community I find many of our families are living on poverty level income but because they are not on welfare they are being excluded from our program.... Many parents are deeply concerned about this.... [They] want equal education for their children.

Other concerns of the Mexican American community are for helping high school dropouts complete their education, aiding Mexican American students in achieving college and university education, providing summer tutorial programs for elementary and secondary pupils who are behind in grade level achievement, expanding "English as a second language" (ESL) programs for Mexican Americans who have low proficiency in English, and changing an Anglo-controlled educational system that deprives Mexican American children of equal educational opportunities and that restricts their social mobility. Berkenshaw describes the historical process that has kept many Mexican Americans from receiving equal educational, occupational, and life-time mobility opportunities (1969:1):

> The cycle...has gone like this: A Mexican child, speaking only Spanish, enters school but soon discovers that he does not understand the teacher, who speaks only English, nor she him.
>
> She may sympathize with him but he finds himself shunted to the side as the class moves on. It has been estimated that it takes two to three years before the child can effectively speak English and by then he is far behind. Faced with the keen competition from his Anglo classmates and withdrawn from school activities, he waits for the day he can quit school.
>
> Without the education he can fill only the menial jobs. His withdrawal in school overlaps in his adulthood, preventing him from seeking help that might be available in the community.

The principle of establishing and maintaining racially and ethnically integrated and balanced schools is an attempt to provide a heterogeneous school and classroom environment in which pupils of all races, ethnic groups, socioeconomic backgrounds, and achievement levels have equal educational opportunities. However, the segregation of minority pupils has often been practiced not only within school districts, but also in individual schools by grouping students according to achievement levels. Austin quotes from a report by the "Emergency School Assistance Program Committee" of the Pasadena Board of Education in order to explain this problem (1971c:1,3):

Social mobility is a long-stated goal of American education. Ability grouping or tracking blocks this upward social mobility for it is the children of the less affluent--the poor, the children of the black ghettos and the brown barrios--who make up most of the low ability classes in our schools.

...Studies in the past 10 years show ability grouping is detrimental to the low achiever because it stigmatizes children, lowers the child's self-image, results in low motivation and produces and perpetuates low results.

Barrio Problems. Segregated schools and classrooms are not ıe only problems that Mexican Americans have faced and are now ıcing. Phil Gutierrez, who was raised and educated in Pasadena ıd is now Director of Spanish-speaking Affairs for the Pasadena ommission on Human Need and Opportunity (PCHNO), remembers ougher times for the area's Mexican Americans--"subtle preıdice from the Anglos, harrassment from the police, indifferıce from the city itself...But there is a change...It's not .g and it's not dramatic, but I've lived here all my life and can see it" (Birkenshaw 1970:3).

Gutierrez was raised in *Chihuahuita*, one of Pasadena's Mexiın American *barrios* located on the east side of the city, where migrants from the Mexican state of *Chihuahua* settled in the ırly 1900s:

Settled after the turn of the century when the area was largely in agriculture, [*Chihuahuita*] is now hemmed in tightly by middle class homes and a utility right-of-way and [Eaton Wash]. Their homes, while generally small and close together, are nonetheless neat, many with lush gardens of flowers and shrubs (1970:1).

Although many Spanish-speaking families now live in older, eteriorating housing between Colorado Boulevard and Villa treet in Pasadena's Central District, the traditional Mexican ıerican areas have been *Chihuahuita* and the South-West Barrio, ocated south of Colorado Boulevard and between Arroyo Parkway ıd the Union Pacific Railroad tracks. Many of the *barrio* homes .ong Pasadena Avenue and adjoining streets have been condemned ıd destroyed by the City of Pasadena, while other low-income exican American housing has been consumed by freeway construcion and urban development projects.

Mexican immigrants acquired homes in the South-West Barrio, ıe of the city's early industrial areas, about the same time *ihuahuita* was settled. The few Mexican businesses established ı the pre-World War II era were located among the manufacturing and packing plants along Arroyo, Raymond, and Fair Oaks Avenues. Mexican families, forced to leave this area, have been dispersed throughout the Central District, especially in low-rent properties between North Lincoln and North Fair Oaks and in the east-west strip through the middle of the city mentioned earlier. Most of the housing in these areas is old and seriously deteriorated; the neighborhoods are blighted and only inhabited by Pasadena's black and brown minorities who can't afford housing elsewhere.

Another *barrio* deserves special mention although it is no longer in existence. The South Arroyo Parkway Barrio, once labeled Pasadena's second largest concentration of Mexican Americans, consisted of a white stucco house-court of about thirty units where "up to fifty families [lived] in sleazy, cockroach infested bungalows in an area of one acre" (Chamberlin 1970). The Pasadena Health Department condemned this court in the Spring of 1970, all families were out by the summer, and it was destroyed soon thereafter. Many families had a hard time finding housing that they could afford in other neighborhoods. An angry young *Chicano* spokeswoman, Vibrana Chamberlin, wrote the following statement in the Pasadena *Eagle* in March 1970:

> It is not an exageration to describe the South Arroyo barrio as a captive colony of desperately poor Chicanos unable to adapt financially to the high housing costs in Pasadena. And Pasadena is not moving to provide housing for low income families. This city is pushing its low income families out.
>
> The barrio atmosphere, with its Chicano folk culture, Spanish language and close knit family life style offers the Chicano a home atmosphere in the alien, bureaucratic Anglo world. But the Latino barely steps into the barrio to discover that his home is to be destroyed due to an urban plot to change the Chicano neighborhood into an urban atrocity of concrete and asphalt. These environments are not designed for human living. For they are designed by self-seeking bureaucrats who view community planning simply as ventures in business and profit.

Fortunately, not all of the *barrios* in Los Angeles County have suffered the same fate as Pasadena's southwestern *barrios*.

Hick's Camp Barrio

About 1918 when a river-bottom Mexican labor camp near El Monte was washed out by the flood-swollen Rio Hondo, the destitute families were aided by Los Angeles County health authorities and the Red Cross to establish a new camp site on the high ıst bank of the normally dry river bed (McWilliams 1948:217-.8). There on a twenty-one acre plot where land was cheap, .cks Camp became a permanent landmark in an unincorporated ›unty area across the Rio Hondo from El Monte (cf. Figure 14), ıd just north of the Southern Pacific Railroad line (Castro ›72:7).

Barrio Characteristics. Many residents of the *barrio* have .ved in Hicks Camp since the early 1920s. Little has changed ıring the past fifty years in the small community of about ›rty families--the streets are still unpaved, there are no ›wers, and the residents live in dilapidated, unpainted sub-:andard housing. According to Stingley,

> It had been a simple community, with churches, taverns, a baseball field and even a meeting hall--places long since rotted down. Hicks families are poor. Their earnings don't match the cost of living. They live in their shacks because they can't afford to move elsewhere (1970:2).

Community Organization. After decades of neglect by both ıe City of El Monte and the County of Los Angeles, *barrio* ›sidents formed the Hicks Urban Development Action Committee. ›quests for assistance were taken to city and county officials, ıt no action was forthcoming. However, people somehow hoped ›r something better:

> What the families visualized were good homes that did not rattle with each breath of wind, or become aquariums with each rain. They dreamed of things not unusual in these times--sidewalks, sewers, paved streets, and maybe a nice park where the old people could sit and the children could play (1970:2).

Neighborhood Redevelopment. But miracles do happen. In :tober 1969, County Supervisor Frank G. Bonelli went to Hicks ımp to discuss with its residents plans for a federally-›onsored redevelopment project that would include new low-›st housing for Hicks' families without relocating them else-ıere. However, Bonelli also proposed a 236-unit low-rent ›artment complex that created serious barriers to the success : the project.

The Anglo residents of Arden Village, another unincorporated :ea to the north of Hicks Camp, organized opposition to ›nelli's redevelopment plan by initiating annexation proceed-ıgs with El Monte for their area. Since the annexation of :den Village would have to include the adjacent Hicks Camp :ea to receive approval from the County Local Agency Formation

Commission, the annexation petition blocked Bonelli's request for federal funds to underwrite the county redevelopment project. Opposition from Arden Villagers arose from their concern that "the additional low-rent apartment complex would add to present police problems in the economically disadvantaged Mexican-American area...and would overload the area's schools as well" (1970:2).

For awhile, the redevelopment of Hicks Camp seemed like a remote possibility. But the neighborhood committee and Bonelli continued to pursue their goal and by January 1972 a compromise solution had been agreed to by city, county, and federal officials. The federal Department of Housing and Urban Development (HUD) approved the new redevelopment plan and granted $1.9 million for the combined federal-county project--two-thirds of the required funds will be provided by the U.S. government and one-third by Los Angeles County.

The approved plan eliminated the proposed 236-unit apartment complex and absolved El Monte from any financial responsibility in the project. County funds will be used to initiate the redevelopment of Hicks Camp and the federal government will reimburse the county. The HUD grant means a new lease on life for thirty-six families in one of the county's poorest *barrios* (Castro 1972:7):

> Federal approval means Hicks Camp will be the first community redevelopment for the county in which poverty-level residents of the area themselves participated in the planning.
>
> Approval means the area will receive new housing, paved streets instead of the present dirt ones; sanitary sewers, parks and recreational areas and a light industrial development that will act as a buffer zone between the housing and industrially used land nearby.
>
> ...there [will] be no relocation of barrio families to other areas...Single family dwellings for the existing families in the area [will] be built in addition to a similar number of dwelling units for senior citizens from other low income areas.

Value of Social Action. These recent developments in the Hicks Camp Barrio should provide hope and incentive for residents of other *barrios* in Los Angeles County to organize for social action. Community organization is needed to secure outside funds for redevelopment projects in the county's *barrios*; to enlist *barrio* residents in self-help projects through organizations like Rosemead's Bienvenidos Community Center; to form pressure group committees that can articulate Mexican American ievances before city councils, police commissions, school ards, management and labor organizations, and the general blic; and to secure Mexican American participation and representation in local government, law enforcement, education, and e labor market. Effective community organization should proce constructive changes in the local system for the benefit the Mexican American community, especially the urban and burban poor.

4.

The Assimilation of the Mexican American

Throughout Los Angeles County and Southern California exist hundreds of Mexican colonies where hundreds of thousands of Mexican Americans have lived in forced isolation from the mainstream of American society. The *colonias* have changed little over the years--dilapidated, substandard housing in an area or district where Anglos refused to live, always on the other side of something: a river bed, railroad track, industrial or agricultural area, or more recently, a major highway or freeway. The historical patterns of discrimination in employment, housing, education, and civil rights have seriously limited the opportunities for assimilation and have reinforced minority group attitudes for self-determination as a defense against majority group exclusion.

Disfranchized Mexican Americans, including many who have been citizens for several generations, are now entering a new era of community organization and political representation. In communities where Mexican Americans are the majority population, significant change is but a vote away. Anglos are becoming aware of this and are "running scared" in fear of losing their place of privilege in the community, or simply running--to new cities and neighborhoods. New Mexican American political organizations are signing up new voters, entering Mexican American candidates for office, influencing the appropriation of federal poverty funds, and shaking up the Anglo Establishment at many levels. New faces and voices are being seen and heard within the social institutions of the dominant society. We can hope that a truly integrated, pluralistic society will emerge in America with "liberty and justice for *all*".

The relationship between the host society and the Mexican American minority will now be explored in terms of the interaction between the national society and its component subsocieties, the assimilation models that characterize Anglo society, the types and levels of assimilation that characterize the Mexican American population, the factors that have hindered Mexican American assimilation, and the emergence of leadership and political representation among the Mexican American minority. Finally, the role of religion in the assimilation process and in the development of Mexican American leadership and politicalization is evaluated as an introduction to Part II, which traces the historical development of Hispanic Protestant churches in Southern California, and specifically within Los Angeles County.

NATIONAL SOCIETY AND SUBSOCIETIES

The large-scale immigration of millions of Mexicans to the United States in this century (cf. Figures 1 and 2, Chapter 1), along with massive immigration from Europe and to a smaller extent from Asia during past centuries, has resulted in a significant interaction of diverse cultures. This interaction has created an American cultural mosaic of various ethnic minority groups in various stages of assimilation to the dominant society.

Culture and Subculture

Culture is a given society's way of life and consists of "prescribed ways of behavior or norms of conduct, beliefs, values, and skills, along with behavioral patterns and uniformities based on these categories" (Gordon 1964:32-33). In *Assimilation in American Life*, Gordon wrote:

> ...just as we speak of the national culture as representing the cultural way of life or cultural patterns of the national society, one may think of the ethnic subsociety as having its own cultural patterns, these patterns consisting of the national cultural patterns blended with or refracted through the particular cultural heritage of the ethnic group; this blend or amalgam we may call... the *subculture* of the ethnic subsociety (1964:38).
>
> ...the term "subculture" [represents] the cultural patterns of a subsociety which contains both sexes, all ages, and family groups, and which parallels the larger society in that it provides for a network of groups and institutions extending through the individual's entire life cycle (1964:39).

American national society, then, is a composite of various subsocieties with their respective subcultures, and it is through these subcultures that various immigrant populations have preserved their self-identity and common sense of peoplehood. An ethnic subsociety, states Gordon, is "any group which is defined or set off by race, religion, or national origin, or some combination of these factors" (1964:27).

Social Relationships

Ethnic groups have a variety of relationships with each other and it is these relationships which constitute the "social structures" of the national society. Gordon defines "social structure" as:

> ...the set of crystallized social relationships which its members have with each other which places them in groups, large or small, permanent or temporary, formally organized or unorganized, and which relates them to the major institutional activities of a society, such as economic and occupational life, religion, marriage and the family, education, government, and recreation (1964: 30-31).

Furthermore, there are two basic group classifications which represent these crystallized social relationships, the primary group and the secondary group (1964:33-32):

> The primary group is a group in which contact is personal, informal, intimate, and usually face-to-face, and which involves the whole personality, not just a segmentalized part of it. The family, the child's play group, and the social clique are all examples of a primary group. They are primary in that they are first both from the point of view of time in the "socialization" process--that is, the process by which the growing child is indoctrinated into the values of his culture--and from the standpoint of their importance in molding human personality.
>
> In direct contrast, the secondary group is a group in which contacts tend to be impersonal, formal or casual, non-intimate, and segmented, in some cases face-to-face, in others not. We belong to many an "interest" organization, for instance, in American society, most of whose other members we never see....

The influence of the ethnic group on primary and secondary group relationships within the social structures of the national society is explained by Gordon:

> The network of organizations, informal social relationships, and institutional activities which makes up the ethnic subsociety tends to pre-empt most or all primary group relationships, while secondary relationships across ethnic group lines are carried out in the "larger society", principally in the spheres of economic and occupational life, civic and political activity, public and private nonparochial education, and mass entertainment. All of these relationships, primary and secondary, are contained within the boundaries of common political allegiance and responsibility to the politico-legal demands and expectations of American nationality (1964:37).

Assimilation Trends

The dynamics within the American cultural mosaic have created the phenomena of diverse ethnic groups, not just as forms of survival from the periods of mass immigration, but as distinct self-perpetuating forms of social organization based on the composite characteristics of race, religion, and national origin. According to Glazer and Moynihan, "the assimilating power of American society and culture operated on immigrant groups in different ways, to make them...something they had not been, but still something distinct and identifiable" (1963:13-14).

Whereas later immigrants from northern Europe were able to successfully blend with the "old stock" of original American immigrants who were predominantly "white Anglo-Saxon Protestants", other immigrant groups, such as southern and eastern Europeans, Africans, Asians, and Latin Americans, have not been readily assimilated. The cultural and structural separation of ethnic groups in America has been due in part to the desire of many immigrants to retain their own communal identity and subculture on the one hand, and to the prejudices and discrimination of the dominant society on the other hand (Gordon 1964:236).

The myth of the American "melting-pot" is exposed by the continued existence of diverse ethnic groups within American society, long after the termination of mass immigration from the countries of origin. Modern American society is fragmented by racial, religious, and cultural minorities who are demanding equal opportunities for participation in the structures of national society. Even after the declining influence of national origin among some immigrant groups, the distinctives of race and religion continue to be the major focus of self-identity, as seen in Will Herberg's *Protestant--Catholic--Jew* (1960) and Glazer and Moynihan's *Beyond the Melting Pot* (1963). However, ethnicity continues to be the major source of identity for millions of Spanish-speaking people in the United States, along with religion (Catholic or Protestant) and national origin (Mexican, Puerto Rican, and Cuban).

Subcultural Diversity

There is a strong tendency to think of the subsociety and its subculture as homogeneous; but, as we have already demonstrated in the case of the Mexican American minority, great diversity exists within the social structure of a given minority group (Chapter 2). Gordon advances the theory that ethnic groups are themselves fragmented by social class differences, rural or urban residence, and the region of the country lived in, and that these factors combine to form "the basic large social units which make up American society and which bear and transmit the subcultures of America" (1964:47). Thus, an individual is not simply a white Catholic of Mexican descent but a lower-middle class white Catholic living in urban Southern California, or a lower-lower class white Catholic living in rural South Texas.

However, Gordon argues that rural-urban and regional residence are less important factors than social class differences in determining the composition of American subsocieties. The ethnic group and social class are becoming "increasingly important as the principal background factors making up the subsociety with its subculture in American life" (1964:51). The concept of "ethclass" is therefore proposed by Gordon to explain the relationship between the ethnic group and the social class stratification systems (1964:39-54).

Not only do individuals find self-identity in their ethnic group--based on common bonds of race, religion, and national origin--but also in their social class through commonalities of income, occupation, education, interest, tastes, and status. Social class stratification is based on differences in economic power (wealth and income), political power in the community and nation, and social status. These three factors have a reciprocal relationship--"that is, those who are high in economic power tend to be high in political power and in social status, and so on" (1964:41).

The influence of social class on cultural behavior, social participation, and group identity, are discussed by Gordon (1964:52):

(1) With regard to cultural behavior, differences of social class are more important and decisive than differences of ethnic group. This means that people of the same class tend to act alike and to have the same values even if they have different ethnic backgrounds. People of different social classes tend to act differently and have different values even if they have the same ethnic background.

(2) With regard to social participation in primary groups and primary relationships, people tend to confine these to their own social class segment within their own ethnic group--that is, to the ethclass.

(3) The question of group identification must be dealt with by distinguishing two types of such identification from one another--one the sense of peoplehood [the ethnic group is likely to be the group of historical identification]..., the other a sense of being truly congenial with only a social class segment of that "people" [participational identification in the ethclass].

Grebler, however, has suggested that, at least for some highly acculturated Mexican Americans of the middle and upper classes, the locus of group identity may be in a social class segment of *another* ethnic group, such as the Anglo middle or upper class (1970:319-320):

> ...we suggest that social-class subculture (rather than ethnicity) does the most adequate job of providing its members with a focus of positive identity and belonging at its upper level. At the lower-class levels, ethnic and religious groups can provide an alternative focus of identity....

Although "something like an ethclass system" may exist within American society, the status rewards that an upwardly mobile ethnic individual may receive through identification with the Anglo middle or upper class, rather than through continued identification with the ethnic group, may provide strong motivation for him to attempt assimilation to the dominant society. Changes in education, occupation, and income along with accompanying changes in interests, tastes and values tend to increase upward social mobility and the formation of primary group relationships with persons of higher social rank, either in the ethclass or in the Anglo middle or upper classes (1970: 319-320; Gordon 1964:55-56).

Mexican American Subculture

It is in this context, then, that a generalized "Mexican American subculture" may be said to exist. Burma comments on the "unique way of life" that the Mexican American ethnic minority is said to share:

> The parent Mexican culture, which is itself something of an amalgam, has been introduced into the United States by immigrants each year for many decades. Those persons

> entering our borders from Mexico tend to find themselves in a different situation requiring new adaptations for success. In actual practice the immigrant and his children retain, or retain in modified character, some of the old Mexican culture traits. Also they accept and use, either directly or in modified character, some of the new Anglo culture traits. The result is a mixture, a reasonably fluid one, of the parent cultures, a mixture which quite properly may be considered a Mexican American subculture, with traits and characteristics which stem from both cultures, but whose configuration is unique, and whose amalgamation certainly is different from either of the parent cultures. Because of its dynamic nature, this hybrid culture is shifting, changing in time and place, and Mexican Americans do not all partake of it to the same degree (1970:20).

The subcultural heritage of the Mexican American minority consists of cultural norms brought to the United States by Mexican immigrants and which were entrenched in the *barrios* of the Southwest, as well as of cultural adaptations based on the "cumulative domestic experiences of enforced segregation...over a number of generations" (Gordon 1964:38). However, the rapid urbanization of Mexican Americans in the Southwest since World War II, especially in Southern California, has produced a wide variation in behavior, attitudes, and beliefs so that the stereotyped "Mexican American subculture" is rapidly becoming fiction (Grebler 1970:422-423).

MODELS OF ASSIMILATION

Three major goal-systems of assimilation have characterized American ideology during the periods of mass immigration and continue to represent Anglo attitudes toward racial and cultural minorities within American society. Gordon summarizes these goal-systems for us:

> [The] three central ideological tendencies may be referred to as "Anglo-conformity"..., "the melting pot", and "cultural pluralism". In preliminary fashion, we may say that the "Anglo conformity" theory demanded the complete renunciation of the immigrant's ancestral culture in favor of the behavior and values of the Anglo Saxon core group; the "melting pot" idea envisaged a biological merger of the Anglo-Saxon peoples with other immigrant groups and a blending of their respective cultures into a new indigenous American type; and "cultural pluralism" postulated the preservation of the communal life and significant portions of the culture of the later immigrant groups

within the context of American citizenship and political and economic integration into American society (1964:85).

Anglo-Conformity Model

According to Gordon, the Anglo-conformity model of assimilation has been "the most prevalent ideology of assimilation in America throughout the nation's history" (1964:89). This "umbrella" term covers a variety of attitudes about immigration and assimilation but "all have as a central assumption the desirability of maintaining English institutions (as modified by the American Revolution), the English language, and English-oriented cultural patterns as dominant and standard in American life" (1964:88). However, related attitudes to this assumption were the now "discredited notions about race and 'Nordic' and 'Aryan' racial superiority together with the Nativistic political programs and exclusionist immigration policies which such notions entail" (1964:88).

The Anglo-conformity model received its most popular expression in the "Americanization Movement" in the early 1900s. The program of Americanization was carried out through thousands of settlement houses in the urban centers of America, and it was, according to Gordon,

> ...a consciously articulated movement to strip the immigrant of his native culture and attachments and make him over into an American along Anglo-Saxon lines--all this to be accomplished with great rapidity. To use an image of a later day, it was an attempt at "pressure-cooking assimilation" (1964:98-99).

The social problems created by unrestricted mass immigration shocked most Anglo Americans into taking emergency measures to alleviate the resultant threat to Anglo social institutions. It was hoped that the Americanization program would remake the diverse populations of foreign immigrants and improve the problems of housing, sanitation, morals, education, and government that their presence created. Gordon quotes a spokesman of the Americanization movement who wrote in 1909:

> Our task is to break up [immigrant] groups or settlements, to assimilate and amalgamate these people as a part of our American race, and to implant in their children, so far as can be done, the Anglo-Saxon concept of righteousness, law and order, and popular government, and to awaken in them a reverance for our democratic institutions and for those things in our national life which we as a people hold to be of abiding worth (1964:98).

The Americanization crusade bogged down during the late 1920s, although settlement house programs continued on into the 1930s, but amidst strong demands for restrictions on new immigration. Meanwhile, American nativism emerged in discriminatory anti-Asian, anti-Negro, anti-Semitic, anti-Mexican, and anti-Japanese movements that sought to eliminate and subordinate those ethnic groups that were considered "unassimilable" (1964:101-103).

However, the Anglo-conformity doctrine cannot be automatically equated with racism, although "it would appear that all racists...have been Anglo-conformists"; but all Anglo-conformists have not been racist (1964:103). Gordon states that

> The non-racist Anglo-conformists presumably are either convinced of the *cultural* superiority of Anglo-Saxon institutions as developed in the United States, or believe simply that, regardless of superiority or inferiority, since English culture has constituted the dominant frame-work for the development of American institutions, newcomers should expect to adjust accordingly (1964: 103-104).

Nevertheless, both these examples of non-racist Anglo-conformity attitudes are but conscious or subconscious expressions of Anglo American *ethnocentrism*, an attitude derived from a strong belief in the *cultural superiority* of Anglo American social institutions which represent the middle and upper class values of the core society, a society that is predominantly "white Anglo-Saxon Protestant". Anglo ethnocentricity shows itself in overt acts of racial and ethnic discrimination, as well as in covert prejudicial attitudes such as: "If you are going to live in America than you should speak English and act like *most* Americans!"--like most white Anglo-Saxon Protestant Americans, that is (Gordon 1964:72-73,103-104).

However, as Gordon points out, an ethnocentric attitude not only characterizes Protestants of the core society but also Catholics and other religious groups who have aspired to middle class "Wasp" affluence and now share to a large extent the values of the core culture. According to Gordon, "the great mass of white Catholic parishioners do not appear to act differently from their Protestant...counterparts" in terms of "social separation in primary group relationships and communal life," either in respect to the Hispanic descent population or to Negroes within American society (1964:200-201).

After discussing the Anglo-conformity model of assimilation, Gordon comes to an important conclusion. The dominant focus of the Anglo-conformity model has been on the acculturation or behavioral assimilation of the immigrant to the behavior and attitudes of the dominant society. It was assumed by advocates of this doctrine that *if* an immigrant--except for non-whites--did become successfully acculturated, then he would be able to enter the social institutions of the larger society at the primary group level, become fully assimilated within the dominant group, and all prejudice and discrimination against him would disappear. However, Gordon argues that this has *not* occurred:

> From the long-range point of view, the goal of Anglo-conformity has been substantially, although not completely, achieved with regard to *acculturation*. It has, in the main, not been achieved or only partially been achieved with regard to the other assimilation variables (1964:105).

The presence of prejudice, discrimination, and exploitation by the dominant society on the one hand, and the natural tendency of ethnic and racial minorities to preserve their valued heritage on the other hand, has severely retarded the assimilation process, especially among the Negro, the Indian, and the Latin American minorities (1964:108-109; Grebler 1970:595).

Although the behavioral assimilation of minority groups has been strongly encouraged by Anglo Americans, they have *not permitted* racial and ethnic minorities to be *structurally integrated and assimilated* within American society, except for a few highly acculturated members of the middle and upper classes. Structural assimilation has been hindered by the tendency of minority groups to *confine* primary group contacts to members of their own groups, and the tendency of Anglo-Americans to *restrict* primary group relationships to those of their own group, especially to those of the same social class level. Gordon summarized the problem in this way:

> If structural assimilation in substantial fashion has not taken place in America, we must ask why. The answer lies in the attitudes of both the majority and the minority groups and in the way in which these attitudes have interacted. A folk saying of the current day is that "It takes two to tango." To utilize the analogy, there is no good reason to believe that white Protestant America ever extended a firm and cordial invitation to its minorities to dance. Furthermore, the attitudes of the minority group members themselves on the matter have been divided and ambiguous (1964:111).

The Melting Pot Model

In 1782 when this model of assimilation was first introduced, the primary source of immigration to America was from Germany,

Sweden, and France and the problem that faced the "white Anglo-Saxon Protestant" English colonists was whether or not to blend culturally and biologically their racial stock with "the stocks and folkways of Europe." Although this concession was granted in that early period, the "melting pot" has become a myth in respect to most racial and cultural minorities who did not come from Northern Europe (1964:115-122).

In the early 1940s, Ruby Jo Reeves Kennedy investigated the intermarriage of ethnic groups in New Haven, Connecticut and, because of her findings, suggested a revision of the "melting pot" model. The revision was termed a "triple melting pot" which was based on religious divisions rather than on national origins. The New Haven study showed that the rate of in-marriage (or endogamy) among "various national origins groups," although high prior to 1870, began decreasing steadily from that year and continued to 1940 (from 91.2 percent in 1870 to 63.6 percent in 1940). "But while there was a decreasing emphasis on national origins lines in choosing a mate, there was still a considerable tendency to marry within one's own religious group" (1964:123). Hence, the origin of the "triple melting pot" theory which postulates that marriages within American society are mainly confined within one or another of the three major religious groups--Protestants, Catholics, and Jews (1964: 122,123).

Will Herberg expanded and defended the "triple melting pot" model in *Protestant-Catholic-Jew* (1960) in which he argues that the religious community provides the primary context for group and self-identity within American society as the ties of national origin decrease. "Not to be a Catholic, a Protestant, or a Jew today," states Herberg, "is, for increasing numbers of American people, not to be anything, not to have a *name*..." (1960:40).

Cultural Pluralism

American society is now composed of several "pots" or subsocieties, three of which are containers marked "Protestant, Catholic, and Jew," but other subsociety containers are also in existence resulting from their failure to be melted down; these are the nation's racial and cultural minorities. Hence, the classification of American society as a "multiple melting pot", a culturally pluralistic society (Gordon 1964:130-131).

Many factors have contributed to make ethnic groups a seemingly permanent part of the national society: isolated or segregated ethnic settlements in both rural and urban areas; the perpetuation of ethnic social institutions, including native language schools, churches, clubs, and other formal and informal organizations; the establishment of native language newspapers and other literature, and including in more recent times, motion pictures, and radio and television programs and stations (especially Spanish-speaking); the desire of many members of an ethnic community to retain their traditional way of life and to resist major innovation and change; and the patterns of employment, housing, education, social life, and civil participation that the dominant society allows or enforces.

The key variable is, again, structural assimilation and the interchange of minority group goals and attitudes with those of the majority society. Gordon redefines the American situation as "structural pluralism" rather than cultural pluralism: "Structural pluralism...is the key to the understanding of the ethnic makeup of American society, while cultural pluralism is the minor one" (1964:159).

The major problems facing our pluralistic society are how to reduce or eliminate racial and ethnic prejudice and discrimination and how to control value conflicts between separate subsocieties. Within this context, Gordon projects an idealized model of the pluralistic society:

> ...the sense of ethnic peoplehood will remain as one important layer of group identity while, hopefully, prejudice and discrimination will disappear or become so slight in scope as to be barely noticeable. Value conflict, where it exists, is to be fought out in the arena of the ballot box and public opinion, but the goal is to keep such conflict at a minimum by emphasizing the areas of flexibility, permitted alternatives, and free choice in American life and by refraining from imposing one's own collective will as standards of enforced behavior for other groups (1964:158).

In regard to the long-range goals concerning ethnic communality within American society, Gordon proposes that fluidity and moderation be maintained "within the context of equal civil rights for all, regardless of race, religion, or national background, and the option of democratic free choice for both groups and individuals." "Ethnic Communality", according to Gordon, "will not disappear in the foreseeable future and its legitimacy and rationale should be recognized and respected" (1964: 264-265).

The roadblock in arriving at the "idealized model of cultural pluralism" is, according to Grebler, *the continued subordination of racial and ethnic minorities by the dominant society* (1970: 319). The structural integration and assimilation of ethnic minorities will not take place simply by *allowing* ethnic groups the right of self-determination, but rather by *removing* the obstacles that the larger society has placed in the path of socioeconomic mobility for the nation's minorities. "American pluralism", states Grebler, "can assume true validity as a national ideal only if our major institutions can transform themselves speedily and ensure the participation of minority members in the process" (1970:594). Institutional resistance to change must be overcome so that an "open system" is established and maintained for all minority members of our society which will guarantee equal opportunities for socioeconomic mobility, for structural integration, and for active civic participation within our national society.

ASSIMILATION VARIABLES

The dual tendency has existed within American society for ethnic groups to conserve their cherished traditions and values on the one hand, and to desire conformity with national ideals and values on the other hand. When different cultures come into continuous first-hand contact with one another, changes occur in both cultural patterns in varying degrees; this process is defined as "acculturation" or behavioral assimilation (Gordon 1964:61,71).

Whereas "acculturation" is the term commonly used by anthropologists to describe what happens "when peoples meet", sociologists are more apt to use the term "assimilation". Gordon discusses at length the uses of these terms and then breaks down the concept of assimilation into relevant variables which lend themselves to systematic analysis (Figure 17). Although we have referred to some of these assimilation variables throughout our study, specifically in the discussion of assimilation models, we will now take a closer look at behavioral assimilation or acculturation.

Acculturation Levels

By acculturation, we mean basically the change of Mexican subcultural patterns analyzed in Chapter 2 to those of American society, the behavior patterns and values of the "white Anglo-Saxon Protestant" core culture (Figure 18). Madsen (1964) distinguished three levels of acculturation among Mexican Americans in South Texas, and these levels represent the general acculturation stages of the total Mexican American population.

The *first level* of acculturation is that of the "traditional" folk culture of northern Mexico modified in the context of rural South Texas. This group often consists of low-skilled, lower-class manual laborers, many of whom are recent immigrants; however, all social classes and skill levels may be represented

FIGURE 17

ASSIMILATION VARIABLES

SUBPROCESS OR CONDITION	TYPE OR STAGE OF ASSIMILATION
Change of cultural patterns to those of host society	Cultural or behavioral assimilation (or acculturation)
Large-scale entrance into cliques, clubs, and institutions of the host society, on primary group level	Structural assimilation
Large-scale intermarriage	Marital assimilation (or amalgamation)
Development of sense of peoplehood based exclusively on host society	Identificational assimilation
Absence of prejudice	Attitude receptional assimilation
Absence of discrimination	Behavior receptional assimilation
Absence of value and power conflict	Civic assimilation

Source: Gordon 1964:71

---

among new arrivals. Representing the first step in the "Americanization" process, it is at this level that traditional Mexican concepts are exposed to the advanced technology of American industry, and where recent immigrants are challenged by the possibility of upward social mobility (1964:2).

The *second level* of acculturation represents the rising upper-lower or lower-middle class who are caught in the conflict between two competing value systems (Figure 18). According to Madsen, those at this stage

> ...were born into folk society but have had enough education and experience outside of their own group to recognize the conflict between the Mexican values they learned

Figure 18

CONFLICTING CULTURAL SYSTEMS

Anglo Middle-class Cultural Characteristics	"Traditional" Mexican American Subculture	Culture of Poverty Characteristics
Oriented to the future (including emphasis on punctuality)	Oriented to the present (little importance given to punctuality)	Oriented to the present (unable to postpone gratification or to plan for the future)
Success-oriented	People-oriented	People-oriented
Stress on "Doing" (change, flux)	Stress on "Being"	
Materialistic orientation: "acquiring things"	Relational orientation: friendships and family (personalism)	Mixed materialistic/relational orientation
Nuclear family	Extended family (familism)	Extended family
Individualism ("ego assertion", independence)	Paternalism, authoritarianism, "Dignity of the Individual"	Authoritarianism, Matriarchal, "Weak ego structure"
Equalitarianism (male-female roles, female assertion)	Male-domination (*machismo*)	*Machismo*/confusion of sex roles
Rationalism (orderliness, progress)	Traditionalism (conformity of the individual, stability of roles and functions)	Traditionalism, Provincialism, anti-intellectualism
Acculturation/assimilation	Enculturation	Enculturation
Utilitarianism	Dramatism	Concreteness (simplistic verbal style, pragmatism)
Manipulation of the universe ("Master-over-Nature")	Fatalism, resignation ("Subjugation-to-Nature")	Fatalism (helplessness, dependence, inferiority)
Protestant Work Ethic (thrift and hard work for future success, "work" as a virtue)	Work to satisfy present needs (low level of aspiration)	Work to satisfy present needs (high level of unemployment, low level of aspiration)
Political compromise and issue orientation	Non-compromise and personality-orientation (*caudillismo*)	Non-joiners of voluntary organizations

Sources:		
Nida 1960:53-55 Saunders 1960:193-204 Heller 1966:19-21	Sheldon 1966:140,145 Burger 1969:241-251 Carter 1970:42-47	Lewis 1966:19-25, Winter 1971:17-28 Ireland 1968:1-9, Burma 1970:17-28 Casavantes 1969:2-4,11

> from their parents and the values of United States [core] society.... On the same level of acculturation are individuals who are *consciously attempting culture transfer* from Mexican American culture to that of the dominant society (1964:3, italics mine).

Within this group, usually composed of second and third generation Americans of Mexican descent, an *identity crisis* is taking place that is characterized by severe anxiety as individuals struggle with the problems of their ethnic past, present, and future--with both their self-identity and their group-identity. This second level of acculturation includes many who are functionally bilingual (Madsen 1964:2-3).

At the *third level* are Mexican Americans who have successfully acquired the behavior patterns and values of the Anglo English-speaking majority society. In the rural setting of South Texas, only Mexican Americans of the middle and upper classes, usually third generation Americans who have rejected their Mexican cultural heritage, have completed this transition (1964:3).

Madsen identifies these acculturation levels as "conceptual constructs" since acculturation is taking place on all three levels. Also, conflicts between Anglo and Mexican value systems, although most common on the intermediate level, exist on the other two levels as well. It is important to also recognize that "retreat from the intermediate level of value conflicts, back into folk society, occurs frequently" (1964:3). This stage of retreat from or rejection of Anglo culture may be thought of as a fourth type of acculturation, although Madsen identifies only three levels. Madsen, summarizing the acculturation process, states:

> The three levels of Mexican American acculturation frequently represents a three-generation process...[and] are further correlated with the class structure. In general, Mexican American folk society consists of lower-class, manual laborers. Acculturation is actively pursued by the middle class. Here, value conflicts are keenly felt and solutions are sought through Americanization. By whatever criteria one judges successful acculturation among Mexican Americans it is generally a middle-or upper-class phenomenon (1964:3).

Language Variables

Another method of analyzing acculturation is on the basis of language usage. Grebler cites Fishman's study of language shifts that "a typical immigrant to a new country" experiences:

> In the first stage of acculturation in the United States, English is used only in a few spheres, such as work, where the mother tongue cannot be used; in the second stage, immigrants not only use English in an increasing number of spheres, but it creeps into their casual conversation; in the third stage there is a maximum overlap between languages and spheres of life; and in the final stage, English has almost entirely displaced the mother tongue (1970:426).

Applying these shifts in language to Mexican immigrants and the Mexican American population, *the initial stage* requires little use of English, especially if the individual lives in a Colony and works primarily with other Mexican Americans; this is notably true of migrant farm workers. If the Spanish-speaking population is relatively isolated in a rural area or in a large concentration of other Spanish speakers, then the persistence of the native language may continue for several generations. Many Spanish-speaking "islands" exist in both rural and urban areas and there are notable regional differences as seen, for example, between San Antonio and Los Angeles and between urban neighborhoods in the same city (1970:424,426-427).

The *second stage* is characterized by increasing use of English as contacts with the dominant English-speaking society increase. However, the use of the mother tongue predominates in the home and in friendship contacts. The learning of English in an urban area like Los Angeles is encouraged in the public schools, in employment, in dealing with government agencies, by mass media, and perhaps through church attendance. Grebler comments that

> ...the shift from Spanish to English is most fruitfully considered not only in terms of generational and chronological changes in language usage of the individual, but also in terms of a community milieu which may inhibit or enhance the possibilities of retaining Spanish or adding English (1970:427).

In the *third stage*, the number of bilingual individuals has reached its maximum peak and biculturalism is a growing reality. The greatest incentive for becoming fluent in English is often attributed to the desire to improve one's economic and occupational position. Residence in Intermediate or Frontier areas provides greater opportunities to converse with Anglos in English, both within the local neighborhood and in the larger community in various activities: casual conversation, business transactions, education, church activities, and employment. However, "the generational shift is notable...in cases where omestic life is still primarily a domain of Spanish for adults, ut has become a domain of English for children" (1970:428). ntergenerational tensions are created when children of immi- rants begin to experience high degrees of pressure for accultur- tion from teachers and classmates in the public schools, and hen the children's values and behavior begin to conflict with hose of their parents because of differences in acculturation. owever, the language of the home and with friends may be Spanish r English, or bilingual, depending on the linguistic ability and thnicity of relatives and friends, who may be either Mexican mericans, other Latins, or Anglos (1970:427-428).

The *fourth stage* represents "the non-Spanish-speaking *agrin- ado*, the Mexican American who has reached the point where he is n contact only or primarily with English speakers. Such a per- on would also live in a predominantly Anglo neighborhood" (1970: 28). Just as the first stage represents those who are so iso- ated from the English-speaking society that they speak only a ew words of English, so the fourth stage represents those who re generally so isolated from the Spanish community that they know nly a few words of Spanish. The Mexican American who is mono- ingual in English is probably an urban resident of an Anglo eighborhood whose parents were middle-class and spoke only nglish in the home (1970:428).

rban Variables

Grebler's Los Angeles sample in 1965-1966 showed that fifty- ix percent of the Mexican American population were functionally ilingual; that is, they were conversationally fluent in both anguages. Only one percent were *unable* to "converse comfortably" n either language. Eighty-four percent of the respondents were ore comfortable speaking Spanish than English and only seventy- ne percent could function well in English. In terms of those onversationally handicapped in English, a higher percentage ere reported in Colony areas and among low income families. he converse was also true; the number of respondents who were onversationally handicapped in Spanish was higher in Frontier reas and among those with higher incomes (1970:424-425).

Generally speaking, higher levels of acculturation and English anguage ability, at least for Los Angeles County, are found mong Mexican Americans in Frontier and Intermediate areas than n Colony areas, especially among upper income families. Greater nteraction with Anglos in the neighborhood, at work, and in the ommunity facilitate greater English language ability and behavior- l assimilation. For children and young people, the public chools, the peer group, and the family have the greatest influ- nce on language ability, either in developing fluency in Spanish r English. On the other hand, the greater the isolation of

Spanish-speaking people in their local environment--in housing, education, employment, churches, and the larger community--the fewer opportunities and incentive they will have for acculturation and English language learning.

In the Los Angeles area, the use of Spanish in mass media is an important factor in the persistence of Spanish in the community. Los Angeles has a Spanish language television station and several all-Spanish radio stations, in addition to motion pictures, newspapers, magazines and other literature. Grebler discovered that "in the predominantly Mexican neighborhoods of Los Angeles...more people prefer the Spanish-language radio stations ...than the English-language stations, and this preference also holds for poorer respondents in intermediate neighborhoods" (1970:429). However, the preference for Spanish language television programs and newspapers was much lower, with the highest number in each category being medium and low income respondents in Colony and Intermediate areas (1970:430-431).

The distinctive cultural traits of Mexican Americans in Los Angeles vary with social class, neighborhood ethnicity, and nativity. The more highly acculturated Mexican Americans tend to be those with higher income, living in predominantly Anglo areas, and native-born urbanites (1970:439). Grebler states that

> Mexican Americans do not appear to possess distinctively traditional values of the kind frequently attributed to them. Much like other Americans, and probably much like other urbanites in industrial countries, most want to get ahead in their work; they want work that gives them intrinsic satisfactions; many hope for job security and higher income (1970:438).

We have not said a great deal about the Mexican American family, nor have we contributed much on the traits of the traditional Mexican American folk subculture. Much has been written on these subjects and we have tried to show, more than anything else, that these "traditional" stereotypes are deceptive and characterize few urban Mexican Americans. Grebler's Los Angeles survey data "indicate a substantial departure in the contemporary family from the traditional patriarchy. The departure is greatest among the young, the more well-to-do, and those living outside the Mexican colony" (1970:361).

In the process of mobility away from the lower class and the expedients of poverty, the role models of the Anglo middle class and the greater opportunity structure of an urban environment (cf. Figure 19) have greatly modified the internal structure of the "traditional Mexican family". The indications are that the extended family, *compadrazgo* (godparents), male and female roles,

Figure 19

ACCULTURATION/LANGUAGE VARIABLES

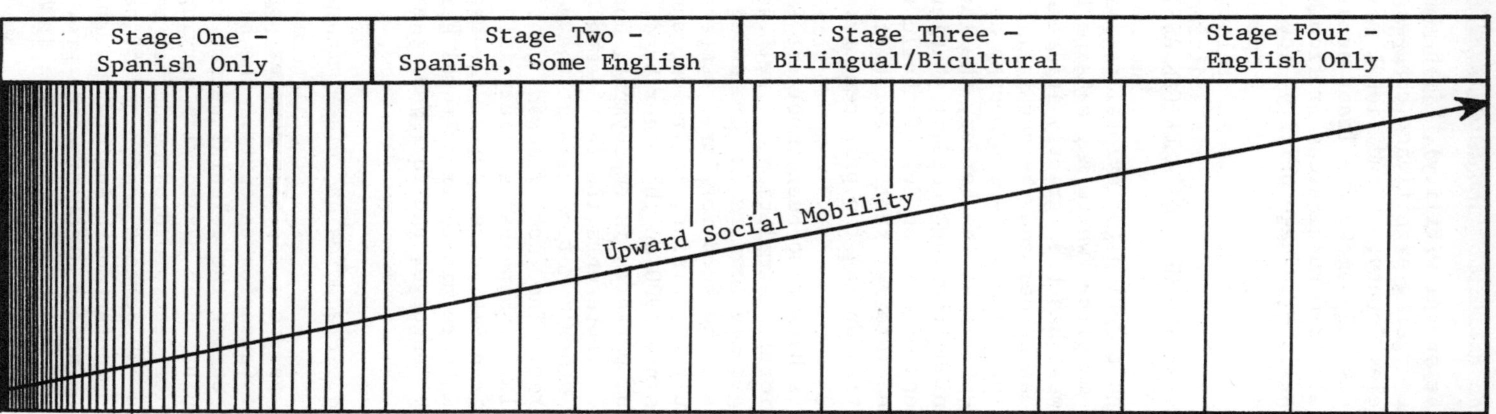

Source: Grebler 1970:296-297,426-427

machismo (masculine sexual virility), birth control, and child raising are all undergoing significant changes in the urban milieu of Los Angeles County. "Traditional Mexican American Subculture" survives only among the least acculturated and the most recent arrivals from rural areas or from Mexico, those with the lowest English-language ability, education and income (1970:350-372).

FACTORS RETARDING MEXICAN AMERICAN ASSIMILATION

The rate of acculturation (behavioral assimilation) of Mexican immigrants to mainline "white Anglo-Saxon Protestant" culture in the Southwest has been greatly influenced by the proximity of the Mexican border and the constant influx of new arrivals from Mexico. The *self-reinforcing process* of a high mobility of movement across the border, the large and continuously growing Spanish-speaking resident population, and the resulting entrenchment of Mexican folk-Catholic culture in the Southwest have been internal factors acting to retard the process of acculturation during the past century.

External factors have also been important in slowing down the rate of behavioral assimilation, as well as other types of assimilation. *Anglo-American racial prejudice and hostility* on the one hand, and the need for large numbers of low-wage laborers in agriculture, mining, railroads, and manufacturing in the Southwest since 1900 on the other hand, have together created the present patterns in employment, housing, education, and political under-representation that demonstrate *Anglo racial and ethnic discrimination* against the Mexican and his native-born children. The *lack of social justice* in majority-minority group relationships has severely influenced the attitudes of many Mexican Americans *against* the assimilation process, causing them to retain their cultural heritage and the use of the Spanish language, and to *reject* the Anglo value system.

The Pattern of Anglo Prejudice and Discrimination

Mexican Americans are a racially complex population with varying degrees of Caucasian ancestry. The blending of Indian and Spanish blood during the colonial period resulted in a large mestizo population in Mexico with varying shades of skin color, but with a tendency to produce darker complexions. As Mexican immigrants--29 percent Indian and 59 percent mestizo in 1930--came into contact with Anglo Americans in the Southwest, Anglo racial prejudice and discrimination grew to become a dominant factor in inter-group relationships. In *North from Mexico*, McWilliams wrote:

> Mexicans are related to Indians by race and culture with the Indian part of their cultural and racial inheritance being more important than the Spanish. Mexicans were consistently equated with Indians by the race-conscious Anglo-Americans. Quite apart from the question of how much Indian blood flows in the veins of the Mexican minority, *Mexicans are regarded as a racial minority in the Southwest* (1948:208,209).

Not only was this true during the early frontier period, but Anglo prejudice and intolerance continued to manifest itself in later periods as well. Consequently, argues McWilliams, "persistent discrimination has repelled the immigrant from the value-side of Anglo-American culture" (1948:214). This fact is seen in the following statement from 1914:

> All other races [in Los Angeles] meet the Mexicans with an attitude of contempt and scorn and they are generally regarded as the most degraded race in the city. The Mexicans respond to this attitude with one of defiance, pride, hate, and extreme dislike. They are clannish and exclusive and marriage with other races is rare. Consequently *the spread of American customs among them is very slow and their amalgamation and assimilation does not progress rapidly* (McEuen 1914:36, italics mine).

Nor was the situation much improved by 1930 when the State of California reported:

> Americanization teachers in California frequently comment upon the fact that few Mexicans ever become American citizens, even after securing their first papers. The Mexicans are described as proud of their country of birth and slow to assimilate.... *Undoubtedly, the willingness, or urge, to become citizens is a matter which can be developed in aliens largely by the attitude of the natives surrounding them.* The fact that in many localities in California the Mexicans are *prevented* from living in the same districts with [Anglo] natives, or with already assimilated groups of foreign born, is militating against Americanization efforts. The same is true of the *social isolation* to which Mexicans are subjected in many communities.... We should not expect the Mexicans to be eager to become citizens when they are made to feel that they are persons with whom we [Anglo Americans] do not desire to associate (Young 1930:72; italics mine).

Remi Nadeau, in *Los Angeles: From Mission to Modern City* (1960), states that Los Angeles has had a long history of racial hatred and bigotry as seen in the "Chinese Massacre" in

1871, the "Sleepy Lagoon Case" of 1942-1944, the "Zoot-suiter Riots" of 1943, and the "Bloody Christmas" of 1951, to name but a few examples (1960:239-245). His following comment is noteworthy:

> Like the Mexicans, [the Negroes] were chiefly relegated to the most menial and unskilled employment; their low income brought low living conditions, poor sanitation, high hospitalization rates, and above-average juvenile delinquency. Unfortunately, the established Los Angeles community often tended to interpret these statistics on the basis of *inherent racial characteristics* rather than on the environmental conditions to which the Mexicans and Negroes were traditionally assigned (1960:239; italics mine).

The Problem of Stereotypes

There has been a strong tendency among many Anglo Americans, often supported by older sociological and anthropological studies, to characterize some ethnic or racial minorities with the general personal traits and life-styles of people living in a subculture of poverty and identifying these characteristics as "inherent" rather than learned qualities. This has often been done regardless of the diversity and dynamics of change within these groups, or of the environmental factors that have caused the so-called "culture of poverty". Such deceptions tend to fortify existing ethnic and racial *prejudices* and *stereotypes* among members of the dominant society, while also strengthening their attitudes of racial and ethnic superiority. The resulting intolerance finds expression in continuing discriminatory policies and behavior and in other forms of social injustice (Moore 1970:1-6).

"The Mexican Problem". An example of the type of sociological studies that reinforced Anglo prejudice and misconception is one by William McEuen, who evaluated the situation among rapidly growing numbers of Mexican immigrants in Los Angeles in 1913. McEuen's statement concerning the nature of "the Mexican problem" is one that characterizes many similar studies in the 1920s and 1930s:

> The problems presented by this *race of ignorant, illiterate, and non-moral people*, complicated by their low plane of living, their tendency to crime, and their bad housing conditions, are serious to the extreme and urgently demand the attention of all Christian reformers and social workers.... Education is the key to the solution of these problems; for *the Mexicans are essentially a race of children* (McEuen 1913, Vol. 2, No. 1:5; italics mine).

"The Mexican Problem", according to McWilliams, was defined in terms of the social consequences of Mexican immigration: unskilled labor, low wages, poor housing, welfare, adult illiteracy, language barrier, poor education, high juvenile delinquency, high rates of disease, and "inadequacies and weaknesses of the Mexican character." Rather than focusing attention on the basic issue in Mexican immigration (i.e., the exploitation of "cheap" Mexican labor), "the Mexican Problem" analysts focused primarily upon the consequences of the mass immigration of poverty-stricken Mexican workers (1948:178,206-207,215-217).

Unfortunately, this type of deception not only characterized many sociological studies but also many official government reports. For example, the "Mexican Fact-Finding Committee" of 1930 sponsored by Governor C. C. Young of California reported that the tuberculosis rate among Mexican immigrants, while "due in part to poverty," was mainly the consequence of "a fundamentally susceptible [racial] stock." In addition, the high rate of crime and delinquency among Mexicans in California was reported to be "an index of racial and national characteristics and also an index of the...lack of adjustment of Mexicans to American customs and standards" (1930:82-83,87). The Young report, according to one observer, discounted "the effects of squalid living conditions and [absolved] the dominant society of blame for those conditions and of responsibility for rectifying them" (Servín 1970:82).

Mexican Criminality. Another example of "official" fact-finding which perpetrated racial and ethnic stereotypes was a report given to the Los Angeles County Grand Jury in 1942 by Lieutenant Edward D. Ayres of the "Foreign Relations Bureau" of the Los Angeles County Sheriff's Department. This report was compiled in the aftermath of the "Sleepy Lagoon Case" in which nine members of a Mexican American street gang were convicted of second degree murder in the mysterious death of a rival gang member. Their conviction was based on circumstantial evidence and all nine youths were later acquitted, but not until the defendants had served nearly two years in San Quentin Prison. Ayres' report was an attempt to prove to the Grand Jury during the course of the trial that "the Mexican-American is criminally inclined because his ancestors [the Aztecs] practiced human sacrifice." Whereas Anglo-Saxon youths were said to fight mainly with their fists, the Mexican resorted "to knives and other lethal weapons" because his desire was to kill or at least to draw blood. Therefore, concluded Ayres, "the [Mexican] race must be punished, at least the biologically depraved part of it" (1970:110-111).

Although this "official police report" was widely criticized and denounced by leading social scientists and community leaders,

Ayres was strongly supported by the Sheriff of Los Angeles County, Eugene W. Biscailuz, and by the Chief of Police of the City of Los Angeles, C. B. Horrall. The rationale behind Ayres' report led to continued public support for mass arrests of Mexican American *pachucos* (see McWilliams 1948:239-243), blatant racial and ethnic discrimination against Mexican Americans in local newspapers, and eventually was responsible for the permissive attitude taken by the average Anglo citizen, the police, and the local newspapers in Los Angeles during the so-called "Zoot-Suiter Riots" in 1943. During the week of June 3-10, thousands of servicemen and civilians were allowed to roam the streets and indiscriminantly assault Mexican Americans and other minorities (mainly blacks) in a repulsive wave of racial hatred and violence. McWilliams has accurately described this brutal event:

> Marching through the streets of downtown Los Angeles, a mob of several thousand soldiers, sailors, and civilians proceeded to beat up every zoot-suiter they could find. Pushing its way into the important motion picture theaters, the mob ordered the management to turn on the house lights and then ranged up and down the aisles dragging Mexicans out of their seats. Street cars were halted while Mexicans, and some Philippinos and Negroes, were jerked out of their seats, pushed into the streets, and beaten with sadistic frenzy. If the victims wore zoot-suits, they were stripped of their clothing and left naked or half-naked on the streets, bleeding and bruised (1948:248).

Although the 1943 Grand Jury of Los Angeles County investigated the riots, as well as the general problem of juvenile crime and delinquency in Los Angeles, their investigation refused to acknowledge the obvious truth about the depth of racial hatred and discrimination against the Mexican American community. However, according to many observers, the indifference of the general public and municipal officials, the inflamatory reporting of the *Los Angeles Times*, and the irresponsible action of the Los Angeles Police Department were jointly to blame for failing to halt the initial rioting and disorder which was initiated by a group of servicemen.

The angry servicemen were out to avenge a series of attacks on sailors who had been beaten and robbed on the Mexican eastside by zoot-suited *pachucos*. However, Robin Scott has documented the fact that tension had been brewing for many months between the *pachucos* and the servicemen because the Anglos often came to the eastside in search of "pick-ups"--Mexican *pachuquitas* whom they considered something less than virgins--in hope of having a "night-on-the-town" just before going overseas. "When the soldiers and sailors dated the Mexican-American girls they invited conflict with the zoot-suited boys [and] the servicemen were usually badly beaten" (1970:117-118, 120-123).

Public opinion, inflamed and controlled by local newspapers, had come to regard *all* zoot-suiters as "Mexican juvenile delinquents" and, therefore, deserving of all the harrassment they received. According to Scott,

> the stereotype of the zoot-suiter as an undesireable Mexican allowed the people of Los Angeles to feel relieved of any moral obligations to Mexican-American youth and sanctioned widespread hostile crowd behavior against the zoot-suiters (1970:116,122-124).

Mexican American Solidarity. Prior to the 1940s, many Mexican Americans avoided the use of the word "Mexican" because of its derrogatory use by Anglos, while preferring to identify themselves as "Spanish Americans" or "Latin Americans". The self-identity of the Mexican American since the mid-1940s, however, has been strongly linked to his growing concept of *La Raza*, a sense of "peoplehood"--of racial and cultural solidarity. In its broadest use this term refers to all Latin Americans, but in the Southwest it commonly refers specifically to the Mexican and those of Mexican descent:

> *La Raza* has remained a deeply evocative term--stronger than "Mexican American", appealing simultaneously to a sense of solidarity with the most vulnerable of the group--the *exploited* and *unacculturated*--and with the most successful members of the group, all of whom reflect glory on *La Raza*. Its vagueness is particularly functional as a term of solidarity with a group whose cultural and genetic diversity in Mexico and historical and inter-regional diversity in the United States make more specific symbols of cohesiveness difficult (Grebler 1970:380-381; italics mine).

Armed with a new sense of self-identity and self-respect, angry Mexican American leaders in Los Angeles County were still opposing the continued widespread use of dishonest stereotypes of "all Mexican Americans" in the early 1970s. *Chicano* leaders recently challenged the Pomona School District for its alleged misuse of a chapter from William Madsen's *The Mexican-Americans of South Texas* in a tenth grade Anthropology class (Diebold 1970:1,3). In this specific incident, an anthropology teacher erroneously applied Madsen's profile of a comparatively small, homogeneous, agriculturally-oriented Mexican immigrant community to "Mexican American culture" in general. Leaders in the

Chicano movement have also objected to the "Frito Bandido" commercial and other commercials on radio and television that depict Mexican Americans as "lazy, shiftless, criminal types," with resulting damage both to the self-image of Americans of Mexican descent and to the improvement of good relationships between Anglos and the Spanish-speaking community (Salazar 1970b).

The Pattern of Employment

McWilliams argues that "the basic factor *retarding* the assimilation of the Mexican immigrant, at all levels, has been *the pattern of his employment*"(1948:215; italics mine). The universal pattern prior to World War II was that large employers in certain industries employed large groups of unskilled Mexican laborers and payed them the lowest possible wages:

> With few exceptions, *only a particular class of employers* has employed Mexican labor in the Southwest: large-scale industrial enterprises; railroads; smelters; copper mines; sugar-beet refineries; farm-factories; large fruit and vegetable exchanges. These concerns have employed many Mexicans, in gangs, crews, and by families as in the sugar-beet industry. *It was not the individual who was employed but the group* (1948:215; italics mine).

This practice of isolating groups of Mexicans in undesireable types of employment, states McWilliams, has "arbitrarily limited the immigrant's chance for the type of acculturation that comes from association with [Anglo] workers on the job" (1948:216).

By far, the largest number of immigrants prior to World War II were employed in particular industries for specialized tasks which were undesireable to Anglos because of the location or the type of employment. In 1914 McEuen reported that

> ...Mexicans form a large element in the labor supply of Los Angeles and meet the need for low-class unskilled labor satisfactorily without encroaching to any great extent upon the fields of employment occupied by Americans and other high-class labor. They compete entirely with the low-class foreign labor such as the Chinese, the Japanese and the Hindu, to which they are generally preferred (1914:31).
>
> [The Mexicans] are employed largely by the railroads and street car companies in the maintenance-of-way Department, by the brickyards, gas company, construction companies and other employers of common labor (1914:23).

However, by 1930, nonagricultural labor in Southern California only accounted for about twenty-five percent of the male labor force, whereas agriculture totaled seventy-five percent (Young 1930:209-210). Often the seasonal and migrating character of Mexican agricultural workers provided few opportunities for the immigrant to learn Anglo American ways by example and imitation.

Although the Mexican American population achieved far greater occupational and geographical mobility during World War II as the result of serious domestic labor shortages, there was still considerable employment discrimination in the post-war era. For example, Grebler's study in the late 1960s demonstrated that

> Mexican Americans are concentrated in the lower-wage jobs of most of the occupational categories...and tend to earn less than Anglos even when they hold comparable jobs in the same occupational class; Spanish-surname workers are likely to be clustered in industries which provide unsteady employment and in the low-wage firms even in the same industry.... The unfavorable occupational patterns of [Mexican Americans] result in considerable measure from factors not associated with education (1970:214-215).

Grebler's findings support the allegation that Mexican Americans in California have unequal employment opportunities, especially in craft unions, large industrial firms, and local, state, and federal government jobs, including high underrepresentation in the category "fire and police protection" (1970:219-227,229-246).

The Pattern of Residence

Another major factor retarding the acculturation of the Mexican has been his *pattern of residence* in the Southwest. Throughout this five-state area are scattered thousands of Mexican colonies where literally millions of immigrants and native-born Mexican Americans have lived in isolation from the mainstream of Anglo society.

Segregated Housing. Prior to 1940, the *colonias* mainly consisted of unpainted, weather-beaten, and dilapidated bungalows or shacks which were invariably located on the other side of something--a railroad track, a river bed, an industrial area, or a major highway--away from the Anglo side of town (McWilliams 1948:215-217).

Governor Young's 1930 report on the status of the Mexican housing problem in California stated that the Mexican, "like various other foreign-speaking immigrants in the United States, tends to live in colonies, retaining his traditions and a mode of life not always satisfactory to his American neighbors" (1930:176). However, the reasons for Mexican segregation in colonies was far more complex than a simple self-reinforcement process as the Young Report goes on to describe:

> The tendency of the Mexican to live in a racial group is strengthened by several conditions. On arrival he seldom speaks English and consequently is dependent upon the Spanish-speaking group for adjustment to his new environment. The Mexican commonly performs unskilled and consequently low-paid work, so that his choice as to quarters is restricted. In Mexico the laboring classes [about ninety percent of the population in 1930] have been used to very simple living with only the most primitive sanitation, and owners are naturally reluctant to rent their buildings to Mexican tenants if others can be found. In addition, there exists a [racial] prejudice against the Mexican which manifests itself in the common classification of the Mexican as "not white" (1930:71-72).

Many of the larger employers in the pre-World War II period provided their workers with segregated housing in labor camps or company towns in order to keep them exclusively in their employment, which by so doing seriously limited their opportunities for acculturation. Grebler mentions one example:

> The brickyard, typically located at the edge of a town, is a case in point. Isolation was carried to an extreme in a settlement in Los Angeles County just outside of Montebello, where the Simons Brick Company erected a walled, wholly Mexican company town--complete with church, school, store, and other community facilities. The company was managed in a spirit of paternalistic benevolence, but *its workers were effectively isolated from the larger community* (1970:89; italics mine).

Other examples of similar isolation are not hard to find: small railroad "section houses" or old railroad cars on little-used sidings, the shack towns of remote mining camps, the rural labor camps of migrant farm workers, and the segregated permanent *colonias* in towns and cities throughout the Southwest.

Although the majority of the Mexican work force in California prior to 1940 participated in the great migration of seasonal labor from the mid-winter harvest of truck crops in the Imperial Valley in the south to the harvest of fruits, vegetables, and cotton in the San Joaquin and Salinas Valleys in the north, usually moving and working together as family units, many migratory workers spent part of the year in urban centers like Los

Angeles and worked in nonagricultural jobs. According to Grebler, "for these workers and their families, then, there was less differentiation between urban and rural residence or farm and nonfarm work than there was for most immigrant groups" (1970:88). This same pattern of mixed rural-urban work and migration can be demonstrated from other Southwestern states as well (1970:87-88; McWilliams 1948:169-183).

Types of Colonias. Throughout Southern California, in both urban and rural areas, Mexican Americans were segregated from growing Anglo communities decade after decade. Housing sites were determined by several factors: "low wages, cheap rents, low land values, prejudice, closeness to employment, undesireability of the site [to Anglos], etc." (McWilliams 1948:217). The size of the Mexican *barrios* varied from a small cluster of bungalows or shacks to colonies containing several thousand residents who were spread over a wide area, usually near an agricultural or industrial district.

The permanently segregated *colonias* of this region often grew up at the site of older agricultural labor camps where rows of weather-torn tents and hastily constructed shacks once stood, often alongside an irrigation ditch or river bed such as "Hicks Camp" near El Monte. At camps on the outskirts of Whittier, Montebello, and El Monte, for example, a common practice among landowners was to rent small plots and permit the renter to construct his own shack; these camps usually lacked adequate sanitation and were menaced by widespread disease (Young 1930:178-179).

Other colonies emerged around the older Mexican *barrios*, some of which could be traced to the pre-1900 era of the early California missions and Spanish settlements. New Mexican colonies were often constructed along the expanding railroad right-of-ways, like the large colony at San Fernando which was mainly the outgrowth of an early railroad labor camp, or at Watts where, in 1906, Mexican railroad families bought small plots for "a dollar down and a dollar a week".

> The Cholos came to work on the railroads being built [by Henry E. Huntington] to Long Beach and Los Angeles Harbor at San Pedro, another to Santa Ana and a fourth to Redondo Beach. They first lived in box cars with their families, later in tents, and finally in rows of four-room houses, each house occupied by two families with a common shelter outside for wash days for the women (Smith 1933:6-7).

The Mexican Americans in Los Angeles were confined to undesirable districts such as Watts and East Los Angeles, subdivided exclusively for them, and to deteriorating urban neighborhoods, like the near downtown areas and Boyle Heights where the Anglos were unwilling to remain. Middle class Anglos had a high level of residential mobility whereas Mexican Americans, regardless of socioeconomic class, were generally restricted to the blighted and deteriorating areas of the city. Unrestricted residential mobility characterized a growing number of Anglos in Los Angeles:

> As older houses deteriorated, commercial facilities expanded, and ethnic ghettos spread, homeowners in the central district, who gained from rising property values and felt little attachment to any particular tract, moved--often more than once--to outlying subdivisions. There they erected newer and more comfortable homes (Fogelson 1967:195).

Neighborhood mobility was significantly different for ethnic and racial minorities--mainly Mexicans, Negroes, and Asians--in their quest for better housing, schools, and community environment:

> A few secure and successful Mexicans, Negroes, and Japanese, who shared with native [Anglo] Americans the rustic ideal, attempted to acquire private homes in residential suburbs after the First World War. But as the prevailing concept of good community excluded races other than white and classes other than middle, they found themselves barred from subdivisions in greater Los Angeles by restrictive covenants.... Even where [restrictive covenants] had never been imposed or had already expired, [racial and ethnic minorities] often encountered the resistance of nearby property owners (1967:200).

However, residential segregation was not as strictly enforced against Mexican Americans as against Negroes, especially after World War II. Except in the case of Watts where Mexicans and Negroes lived together in the same neighborhood, these two minorities had a strong tendency to live apart from each other, each trying to preserve their own ethnic cohesiveness in response to majority society exclusion (Grebler 1970:277-288).

Racial and ethnic minorities in Los Angeles "were discriminated against as individuals, frustrated as spouses and parents, offered only the most menial employment, and confined to the least desireable neighborhoods," observed Fogelson. "In a metropolis that promised a fuller life and opportunity, their subordination and segregation was particularly appalling" (1967: 203). So much, then, for "the California dream".

Everywhere, whether in urban or rural areas, the Mexican population was segregated from Anglos. In the suburban "citrus-belt" communities of Los Angeles and Orange Counties which were dominated by the California Fruit Growers Exchange, homogeneous Anglo citrus-grower colonies were effectively "insulated" from the Mexican *barrios* just as Mexican citrus laborers were invariably segregated from the Anglo communities. Writing in the mid-1940s, McWilliams described these commonplace communities:

> Throughout the citrus belt [along the foothills of Los Angeles, San Bernardino, Riverside, Orange, and Ventura Counties, and in certain lowland areas], the workers are Spanish-speaking, Catholic and dark-skinned, the owners are white, Protestant, and English-speaking. That both groups are highly homogeneous is a circumstance that serves to widen the gulf of social distance that separates the one from the other. While the towns deny that they practice segregation, nevertheless, segregation exists.... Mexicans attend separate schools and churches [predominantly Spanish-speaking congregations], occupy the balcony seats in the motion-picture theaters, and frequently [have] separate places of amusement [or special-day usage of public swimming pools].... The whole system of employment, in fact, is perfectly designed to insulate workers from employers in every walk of life, from the cradle to the grave, from the church to the saloon (1946:219).

The sharply defined social organization of these communities was symbolized, according to McWilliams, by the Protestant Church, the "Sunkist" orange, and the "no trespassing" signs that were found throughout the citrus belt. Rigid class and status lines existed between the orthodox Protestant grower-dominated communities of the citrus belt and the poverty-ridden and politically powerless Mexican "serfs", a system that was strongly maintained until the late 1940s (1948:215-221).

Numerous Mexican labor camps and colonies could be found throughout California's inland agricultural valleys by the mid-1920s, from the Imperial Valley on the Mexican border to the rich acreage of the northern San Joaquin Valley and the truck farms of the coastal Salinas and Santa Clara Valleys. The same social caste system that characterized the suburban citrus areas of Los Angeles and Orange Counties was also the dominant pattern in the rural agricultural areas. For example, in the Imperial Valley where Paul S. Taylor studied Mexican labor problems in the 1920s, the following pattern was evident:

> One of the most striking aspects of the Mexican labor situation in the Imperial Valley is the concentration of Mexican town population in colonies *geographically apart* from the American community.... Most of the Mexicans outside of Calexico are poor, and *poverty* leaves them little choice of residence outside of the cheapest quarters. Furthermore, there is the natural tendency to gravitate toward the places where, in a strange land, others of one's language, class, and culture may be found. Finally, there is the *social pressure* from the American community, which generally does not desire Mexicans as neighbors. A symptom of this pressure is the *race restriction* sometimes included in the deeds to property.... The Mexicans in the valley are sensitive to the *social ostracism* which they face, and do not force themselves in where they feel the pressure against them.... The separation of rural Mexicans from American neighborhoods is as clear as the separation prevailing in the towns (Young 1930:176; italics mine).

The extent of the social caste system that dominated Southern California over a period of many years, especially in the suburban agricultural communities of the greater Los Angeles area, is seen in the fact that Los Angeles County, from 1918 to 1949, was the first-ranked agricultural county in the nation with a vast assortment of citrus and field crops and a marked dependence upon irrigated farming and "cheap Mexican labor" (Thomas 1959:75,87).

However, the rapid population growth of the Los Angeles area in the post-war years, the transformation of vast tracts of agricultural land to industrial and residential use, and many other visible signs of rapid urbanization and social change erroded the caste system of the suburban communities and replaced it with a semi-caste, and in some cases a "dual mobility system", in an expanding network of heterogeneous population centers (cf. Chapter 2).

The Pattern of Education

The dominant pattern of Mexican American residential segregation throughout Southern California and the Southwest, mainly due to Anglo discrimination in employment and in nearly every aspect of community life, also resulted quite naturally in the establishment of segregated Mexican schools. The Young Report noted that at least fifty-eight public elementary schools in Southern California during the school year 1927-1928 were composed of from 90 to 100 percent Mexican American pupils, with the majority of these located in Los Angeles, Orange, and San

Bernardino Counties. These schools, it was reported, were predominantly Mexican because each "district is inhabited by virtually none but Mexicans" (Young 1930:177).

De Facto Segregation. The determining factor in the existence of predominantly Mexican schools was the Anglo community's policy of *de facto* segregation which was accomplished, in some cases, by the gerrymandering of school districts (McWilliams 1948:280-284; Carter 1970:67-81). Even in mixed Anglo and Mexican districts and schools an effective ethnic and social class cleavage was maintained throughout the Southwest (1970:81-95).

Although *de jure* segregation was enforced against native American Indians and against Chinese, Japanese, and other Asians, a system of *de facto* segregation (widely enforced as though it had legal sanctions) effectively isolated both Negroes and Mexican Americans throughout Southern California. According to McWilliams, the segregation of Mexican children in public schools came about "largely through default of any determined resistance on the part of Mexican-Americans"; but once the policy was established, "segregated schools were defended and rationalized" by Anglo educators and enforced by strong public opinion (1948:280-281).

It was not until 1945 that the common practice of Mexican American segregation in public schools was challenged in the federal courts. In that year, Gonzalo Méndez, a naturalized Mexican immigrant who had lived in Southern California for twenty-five years, filed a civil suit (*Mendez vs Westminster School District*) against school officials in Orange County in behalf of thousands of Mexican Americans with children in segregated schools. Orange County school officials defended segregation on the basis of Mexican racial and ethnic "inferiority", which necessitated separate schools and pedagogical procedures, and on the basis of the health hazard of exposing Anglo pupils to "dirty" Mexicans.

However, a federal district court, and later the Ninth Circuit Court of Appeals, ruled that segregation of Mexican pupils was illegal by California laws and that it violated the "equal protection" clause of the Fourteenth Amendment. The court found that it was not a matter of "some" Mexican children who "might" have a language problem or who "might" be coming to school dirty, but that it was *all* Mexican children who had been segregated (1948:281-282). Grebler, refering to the problem of school segregation in this period, states:

> The *intent* to segregate was clear in some school districts, where non-Mexican children were transported to their schools by routes which bypassed or even crossed

> through the zones having schools attended only by Mexican American children. The *custom* of segregation was clearly revealed in court findings that in some instances, in place of tests to determine whether a language handicap necessitated provisional segregation, the decision to segregate or not was based mainly on the Latinized or Mexican name of the child (1970:173).

The *Mendez vs Westminster* decision stimulated similar civil rights suits on behalf of Mexican Americans in other Southern California towns and in other Southwestern states, most of which were also successful. These important court rulings of the late 1940s "laid the legal groundwork for the subsequent desegregation decisions of the 1950s, which also argued on the First, Fifth, and Fourteenth Amendments to the Constitution" (Grebler 1970:172).

Although Spanish-surname pupils in California's public schools in the early 1970s are not as severely isolated as black students, there is still a serious imbalance that must be corrected if racial and ethnic minorities are to receive "equal educational opportunities" as ruled by the State Supreme Court in 1963:

> The right to an equal opportunity for education and the harmful consequences of segregation require that school boards take steps, insofar as reasonably feasable, to alleviate racial imbalance in schools regardless of its cause (California State Board of Education 1971:10).

The need for racial and ethnic balance in California schools is seen by the fact that "nearly 59 percent of all Negro pupils attended predominantly Negro schools, and nearly 29 percent of Spanish surname pupils attended predominantly Spanish surname schools" (1971:5). In addition, seventy-four percent of all Negro pupils in the state and forty percent of all the SSN pupils were in "minority schools", i.e. schools with fifty percent or more minority enrollment (1971:Appendix, Figure 4).

Los Angeles County had a large share of the state's racially and ethnically imbalanced and minority schools in 1970-1971. Thirty-two school districts had schools with a racial or ethnic "imbalance" (i.e. schools that deviate more than 15 percent from district mean in any racial or ethnic group) and twenty-five districts had schools with fifty percent or more enrollment of minority pupils (1971:Appendix, Figures 3,5).

The Mexican American Population Commission reported that Los Angeles County's SSN pupil enrollment in 1970-1971 was 279,500 or 19.1 percent of the total number enrolled (1971:16). The

Los Angeles Unified School District had the greatest share of SSN pupils in the county: 141,450 or twenty-two percent of the total enrollment. Other districts with large SSN enrollments were Montebello (13,600), El Rancho (9,600), Hacienda-La Puente (8,580), and Norwalk-La Mirada (7,180). On the other hand, districts with over fifty percent SSN enrollment in Los Angeles County were: Los Nietos (South Whittier), El Rancho (Pico Rivera), Valle Lindo (South El Monte), Garvey (South San Gabriel, Rosemead), Montebello, and Mountain View (Five Points, El Monte). [For a more complete breakdown of Los Angeles County school districts consult Appendix I, Figures B, C, D; however, no breakdown was available for individual schools within the Los Angeles Unified School District.]

In regard to religious education, the Archdiocese of Los Angeles reported 39,812 SSN pupils enrolled in 351 parochial schools or 24.1 percent of the total student enrollment in 1970. Although the Archdiocese includes Orange, Ventura, and Santa Barbara Counties in addition to Los Angeles County, an estimated ninety percent of the total SSN enrollment of the Archdiocese was located in Los Angeles County. This means that about ten percent of all SSN pupils enrolled in Los Angeles County schools were attending parochial schools in 1970 (Mexican American Population Commission 1971:19).

Although no data were available on the ethnic and racial breakdown for individual Catholic schools within the Archdiocese, the general policy of parish-related parochial schools dictates a policy of *de facto* segregation of Mexican American pupils, since Mexican Americans are typically assigned to their own parishes. The low economic level of most of the all-Mexican parishes in Los Angeles meant that few could afford to build and maintain a parish school without outside help. Grebler reports that "only 30 percent of the Los Angeles parishes in heavily Mexican-American areas had parochial schools in 1948 as against 58 percent for all other parishes" (1970:459). However, by 1960, because of an intensive school building program launched by Archbishop McIntyre in 1948, "practically every parish in East Los Angeles had a parochial school" (1970:459).

This massive program of parochial school building was designed to aid the integration of Mexican Americans into the dominant society, but instead of Americanization to "white Anglo Protestant society" the program was geared to speed acculturation to "white Anglo Catholic society." Secular public schools were viewed as agents of acculturation to Protestant ideals and a threat to the Catholic Faith. Thus, socialization to American Catholicism, plus a secondary emphasis on combating juvenile delinquency, was a dominant theme in the program of building parochial schools in Mexican American areas during the 1950s and 1960s (1970:459-460).

Role of Public Education. The role of public schools within American society has been traditionally one of socialization: the *enculturation* of children from the dominant society and the *acculturation*, or Americanization, of children from diverse ethnic groups through the educational process. According to Carter:

> *Socialization* involves bringing the child into membership in society by teaching him certain behavior, expectations, roles, and personality characteristics. *Enculturation* is the corollary and interrelated activity of teaching the values, knowledge, and skills of the parent culture (1970:14, italics mine).

The common segregation and isolation of Mexican American pupils based on local social and cultural practices on the one hand, and the attempt by public schools to acculturate Mexican Americans to the norms of "white Anglo-Saxon Protestant" society on the other hand, have often created diverse conflicts which have seriously affected the lives of pupils, their families, teachers, and school administrators. These conflicts tend to have crippling effects on the self-image and expectations of individual Mexican American students, while also pointing out the hypocritical incongruities between national ideals and prevalent local community practices (1970:13-16,53-57; Dworkin 1970:397-409).

The problems of low academic achievement and high underrepresentation of Mexican American pupils in Southwestern schools have come into being through a complex, interrelated social process. Many educators and sociologists attribute these problems mainly to the "culturally deprived or disadvantaged" background of Mexican American pupils (Carter 1970: 35-63). An example of this viewpoint is given by Celia Heller:

> ...ambitious and mobility-oriented young Mexican Americans are indeed handicapped as compared with their Anglo American peers. In most cases, they are born into larger families, their family training includes little emphasis on mobility values and behavior conducive to advancement, they acquire few such skills in school, their youthful world lacks visible models of achievement, they are not well aware of existing opportunities. Moreover, their ethnic identification and sense of group loyalty, however praiseworthy on other grounds, encourage behavior in keeping with traditional values and norms--and these may hamper mobility. The values of masculinity, honor, politeness, and leisure and the modes of conduct consistent with these values are a rationally unnecessary and

> heavy baggage on the road to conventional advancement, although they are cultural and psychological assets for those securely established at or near the top of the social pyramid (1966:104).

Others argue that the major failures have been within the educational process itself: the attitudes and policies of educational administrators; the influence of school facilities, curriculum, and staff; the composition and intergroup attitudes of the student body; the attitudes, characteristics, and pedagogical techniques of teachers; and the characteristic and resultant practice of ethnic separation and isolation, together with the exclusion of Spanish language and culture (cf. Carter 1970:65-130). However, Carter argues that

> in reality...the home culture, the personality of the child it produces, the practices and policies of educational institutions, and the nature of the community are a complex intertwining of causes and effects (1970:36).

Some progress has recently been made in unraveling some of these cause and effect relationships. For example, a direct association has been established between the individual student's school achievement and home-related factors, according to the Los Angeles School Study of 1968 (Grebler 1970:165-166; Carter 1970:18-19):

1. The most consistent and important influence is family educational level as expressed primarily in *parental aspirations* for pupils' educational attainment.

2. *Pupil attitudes and values* are an important source of influence (perhaps a measure of home acculturation to middle-class orientations).

3. *School type* (a measure of socioeconomic and ethnic composition) substantially affects the performance of Mexican Americans at elementary and junior high but less at senior high level.

4. *Language spoken at home*. The exclusive use of English as the home language contributes consistently and positively for Mexican-American pupils at all grade levels.

5. *Family economic level* contributes less to the performance of either ethnic group than does family educational level.

Commenting on the results of this study, Carter states that *"the academic success of a Mexican-American child depends on the degree to which his home has been oriented to Anglo middle-class culture,"* at least in the present system of general education (1970:19; italics mine). But, as we have seen, the process of Mexican American acculturation and assimilation has been retarded at every level by persistent Anglo discrimination which has resulted in continued long-term effects on the upward social mobility of the nation's second largest minority.

Carter's study of *Mexican Americans in School: A History of Educational Neglect* is a recent confirmation of McWilliam's earlier evaluation of the relationship between the Anglo-controlled educational process and the ethnocentrism and self-interest of the dominant Anglo society. The result has been the perpetuation of Mexican American minority status and impotency:

> [Anglo] society and its schools produced an adult Mexican American population prepared for participation in the agricultural economy of the traditional Southwest. The school was, and in many geographic areas still is, "successful" in equipping most Mexican Americans with the knowledge and skills appropriate to low status: minimum English language ability, rudimentary reading and figuring skills, and the values necessary to a law-abiding, although nonparticipating and essentially disenfranchised, citizen. *The fact that the school failed to Americanize or to raise the group status of so many Mexican Americans was evidence of its success. Local society functioned well with an easily controlled, politically impotent, and subordinate ethnic caste.* School practices evolved that functioned to perpetuate the social and economic system by unconsciously encouraging the minority group to fail academically, drop out early, and enter society at the low status traditional for Mexican Americans, thus producing the human types necessary to perpetuate the local society. Mexican American failure to achieve well in school contributed to the Anglos' belief that they had innately inferior intelligence, that they were lazy, passive, fatalistic, and lacked initiative. *This self-reinforcing circle of circumstances became well established in the Southwest and persists to the present* (1970:204-205; italics mine).

Problems and Solutions. According to the 1960 census, the median years of school completed by SSN persons age twenty-five or over in the Los Angeles-Long Beach (SMSA) area was 8.9

years, an increase from 8.1 in 1950. There was a marked differentiation in educational attainment between native-born Mexican Americans and the Mexican born, with the native-born completing at least twice as many school years as the foreign-born (Grebler 1970:149,154).

This record of low academic achievement suggests a high drop-out rate for Mexican American students in Los Angeles County: "More than one-third of Mexican American children enrolled in Los Angeles secondary schools drop out before completion. In some schools, slightly more than half are able to finish." In addition, "Mexican American pupils usually score lower than others in four dimensions of achievement: academic grades, deportment, achievement test scores standardized against a national norm, and I.Q. test scores" (Moore 1970:83-84).

Whereas teachers, school administrators, and the Anglo community in general tend to place the blame for low educational attainment of Mexican American students on their "culturally deprived" home environment, Mexican American community leaders and many concerned educators are *demanding drastic improvements in the whole system of minority group education*, usually in the form of implementing a genuine program of bilingual education rather than continuing patch-work "compensatory and remedial programs" (Grebler 1970:158-195; cf. Valentine 1971:137-157 for a "Bicultural Model of Afro-American Behavior").

Although *bilingual educational programs* are considered by a growing number of educators as the key to surmounting the tremendous language barrier that prevents thousands of students from receiving an adequate education in the United States, there is obvious confusion and oversimplification in what is meant by "bilingual education". By simple definition, bilingual education is "instruction in two languages and the use of those two languages as mediums of instruction for any part of or all of the school curriculum" (Lara-Braud 1971b:3). In practice, however, the rationale for and program of bilingual education finds many expressions.

There are two distinct types of bilingual programs, each with its own rationale. "One-way" programs are geared to help Spanish-speaking students make the transition into English instruction as soon as possible. Spanish is only used as a medium of instruction until students are proficient enough in English to use it without difficulty in the classroom. No attempt is made to improve either the quality of children's Spanish or to make Spanish a medium for teaching curriculum content to native English-speaking students (Carter 1970:187-188).

The "two-way" bilingual program has a distinctively different approach and purpose: "a two-way school instructs children from two linguistic communities (for example, Spanish speakers and English speakers) in both languages, so that children from each community learn both their own and the other group's language" (Clark 1970:188). For the native Spanish-speaking student, two-way programs allow him to learn curriculum content in his mother tongue as well as developing reading skills and verbal proficiency in Spanish. English is taught as a second language (hence the term ESL programs).

However, developing proficiency in both Spanish and English is only part of the problem for many Mexican Americans who are presently "unfit" or functionally illiterate in either language. For the most part, they are victims of an educational process under which minorities--brown, black, or just plain poor--develop a negative self-image with resulting personal disorientation, insecurity, and low life-time mobility.

The purpose of bilingual education, then, should be to aid in the development of a healthy self-image among Mexican Americans, especially lower income young people, through a program of cultural appreciation and self-awareness--to develop young people who function well in both cultures, with a dual pride in being both Mexican and American. Thus, "bicultural" instruction is an important part of a bilingual program that has as its purpose the structural integration of Mexican Americans in a truly pluralistic society (Cabrera 1970:19-20,68).

Although some may consider the terms "bilingual" and "bicultural" to be practically synonomous, Carter makes an important distinction between them:

> In a bilingual school two languages are used for instruction, and in a bicultural school two languages and two cultures are used. The curriculum in many bilingual schools is drawn exclusively from the dominant Anglo culture and merely translated into another language. In a bicultural school, the content, method, and sequence of instruction are drawn from two cultures (1970:189).

If the trend toward the growing frustration and alienation of Mexican Americans from Anglo society is to be remedied, then serious consideration must be given to bilingual-bicultural programs rather than trying to force Spanish-speaking children to suppress their native culture in the process of learning an exclusive Anglo cultural system. Public schools must restructure their educational programs so that Spanish language and culture become assets rather than liabilities for Mexican Americans and other Hispanic minority children (Cabrera 1970:14-16).

The search for identity and self-esteem, for self-fulfillment and social mobility, may not end in frustration for many Mexican American young people if the educational "Establishment" and Anglo middle class society in general can be reprogrammed to accept cultural diversity, especially biculturalism, as a distinct advantage rather than as a handicap. It may not yet be too late. A good beginning has been made in many colleges and universities with the establishment of ethnic studies programs. Although some of these efforts may be only token attempts at biculturalism, hopefully true biculturalism will soon emerge (Cabrera 1970: 17-20).

The advantages of bicultural programs for Mexican Americans has been considered, but there are definite advantages for Anglo Americans as well:

(1) the development of a broader cultural perspective within American society with an appreciation of the diversity of peoples and cultures in a shrinking world;

(2) the lessening of Anglo ethnocentrism while gaining a greater degree of self-understanding, a greater tolerance and acceptance of cultural differences, a greater respect for all socioeconomic classes and the value of each individual, and a greater flexibility in making structural changes in society that will benefit the marginal man;

(3) the recognition of bilingualism and biculturalism as goals worth seeking with diligence so that a genuinely cosmopolitan, world-oriented and pluralistic American society may emerge from the darkness of Anglo ethnocentricity, bigotry, and destructive self-interest, not only at the national level but also within the structures and institutions of local social systems in local communities.

Sources of Prejudice and Discrimination

From the foregoing study we have seen that Anglo Americans have had strong attitudes of prejudice and have consistently practiced discrimination against Mexican Americans and other minority groups in American society. It is imperative that we seek for a better understanding of the causes of prejudice and discrimination and that we focus our energies on preventing and eliminating their continuation.

In the first place, what is meant by prejudice and discrimination? The term "prejudice" describes an attitude or a feeling, and is therefore *covert*, whereas "discrimination" describes an *overt* act. By definition, "prejudice" is a preconceived judgment or opinion, usually negative, based on insufficient knowledge or understanding of a person or group of persons; it is an unreasonable attitude or bias toward selected categories of people based on stereotyped concepts rather than direct experience, or a preconceived opinion that distorts one's perception or understanding of certain categories of people during periods of direct observation or experience. "Discrimination", on the other hand, refers to concrete actions, to unequal treatment of individuals or groups for a variety of reasons.

Burma discusses some of the sources of discrimination and prejudice, which he classifies as psychological, cultural, or egoistical. The "frustration-aggression theory" explains prejudice and discrimination as the result of the emotional and psychological needs of an individual:

> Possibly the person is frustrated in his attempt to achieve goals--a common condition--and feels a desire to aggress against what he considers the blocking agency. In some cases this agency is not subject to aggression; e.g., it may be world conditions; it may be an act which has already occurred and cannot be recalled; it may be a force against which he cannot aggress because it would seriously and successfully retaliate against him; or it may be the person does not even know the source of his frustration. In such circumstances this frustration may lead to feelings of anger which are relatively undirected, and are called "free-floating hostility." This hostility, this frustration, may seek a subject [a "scapegoat"], even though this subject is not the cause, against whom to aggress with reasonable safety: a wife, an institution, or a minority group (1970:58).

Another source of group prejudice and discrimination may be attitudes and behavior patterns passed down from parent to child through the process of enculturation and uncritically absorbed by them. A related source is varying degrees of ethnocentrism that characterize individuals within an ethnic group. Members of a cultural group tend to regard their way of life as inherently superior to other cultural groups and use their own culture as a standard for the appraisal of other cultural systems (1970:59-60).

A final source to be considered is that of "naked self-interest". Often the things most desired in a society are inadequate to meet the demand, such as economic and political power, social status, prestige, material goods, friendship, organizational membership, good housing, higher income, etc.

"In some cases," explains Burma, "discriminatory behavior does 'pay off' in terms of securing cheap labor, segregated housing areas, political power through disfranchisement of a part of the potential electorate, or additional income achieved through unethical business practices," such as charging higher prices, paying lower wages, or selling inferior merchandise (1970:58).

There need not be any deep-rooted prejudice resulting from frustration or aggression involved in the economic exploitation of individuals or groups. Naked self-interest furnishes sufficient motivation for discriminatory practices against selected ethnic groups and social classes, such as segregating school districts or classrooms (for quality education); gerrymandering political districts (for greater political power); and maintaining unequal employment opportunities, low educational attainment, low wages, and poor housing (for greater socioeconomic power).

Burma argues that "when a society prevents an individual from achieving his fullest growth and making his greatest contribution, not only is that person harmed, but so is his family, his community and his nation" (1970:59). In addition, those who discriminate against minority groups are sowing the seeds of their own destruction by adding to the frustration and aggressive tendencies of those who are being exploited. On the individual level, observes Burma,

> The person subjected to prejudice and discrimination suffers in a variety of ways. He receives psychic wounds which, to use a crude analogy, may be constantly open sores, very frequently re-irritated and re-inflamed, never able to heal, and resulting in constant pain; or they may be wounds which partially heal, whose pain diminishes or temporarily disappears only periodically to be ripped open again for the whole process to be repeated; even if the wounds do heal, they may leave psychic scars which are permanently disfiguring or distorting (1970:59).

The Mexican American Response

Mexican Americans have demonstrated a variety of individual and group responses to Anglo prejudice and discrimination and their accumulative effects (1970:60-61):

1. Disassociation from the Mexican American community and consciously seeking identification and acceptance within Anglo society.
2. Retreating within Mexican American subculture and avoiding contact with the Anglo world.
3. "Using discrimination as an excuse for not trying to

achieve, for dropping out, for being a failure by the standards of both communities, but protecting one's ego by saying it is all 'their' fault."

4. Active participation in *Chicano* organizations which seek to advance and strengthen the concept of *La Raza*, of racial and cultural pride and a sense of "peoplehood".
5. Non-violent social action through various pressure groups--community, service, and religious organizations, labor unions, political parties, etc.
6. Violent social action by personal physical violence, rioting, looting, selective vandalism, and other forms of civil disobedience and criminal activity.
7. "Accepting a certain amount of prejudice and discrimination as inevitable, but ignoring it, and participating in both communities with as much ease and freedom as possible; being cautious about one's behavior, selecting it in terms of the group with which one is at the time [in order] to be as acceptable and successful as possible in both groups."
8. "Ignoring possible prejudice and discrimination and actively seeking for oneself the best elements of both cultures; practicing the cultural pluralism approach... and trying rationally to choose the best adaptations."
9. "In connection with any of the above reactions, holding prejudice against the Mexican American group (self-hatred), against Anglos, against Jews or Blacks, or any other minority and by so doing transferring one's frustration and aggression to a scapegoat."

In conclusion, it is obvious that greater assimilation of Mexican Americans to the dominant society has not taken place because the necessary degree of tolerance between Anglo and Mexican American has often failed to develop. Anglo prejudice and self-interest have consistently frustrated the hopes and aspirations of many Mexican Americans who have desired to become "first-class citizens". Mexican Americans have often been repulsed by the "superior values" of the white Anglo-Saxon Protestant majority society, while developing a growing conviction that rejection of their Hispanic cultural heritage was too great a price to pay for Anglo acceptance. Recent trends within the Mexican American community--the quest for self-identity, the growth of *La Raza Nueva*, the development of a new type of leadership, the emergence of new political parties and action groups--signal that a new day has dawned for the nation's second largest minority.

THE POLITICALIZATION OF THE MEXICAN AMERICAN

The history of social injustice experienced by Mexican Americans in Southern California, and throughout the Southwest and the nation, is still being written. The civil rights "guaranteed" by the Treaty of Guadalupe Hidalgo to all Mexicans who chose to remain within the annexed territories in 1848 proved to be a cruel deception. Today, Mexican Americans are still struggling for the civil liberties that most Anglo Americans take for granted. Large numbers of Mexican Americans remain outside of our so-called system of "representative democracy" which supposedly guarantees the right of equal opportunity to all citizens, regardless of race, religion, or national origin. The unavoidable question is "Why?" Partial answers have emerged in our study thus far (Chapters 1-4), but other possible answers will now be considered as we trace the rise of Mexican American minority group consciousness and politicalization.

Conflict and Political Submergence (1848-1920)

Following the American conquest of the Southwest in 1846-1848, widespread violence and disorder existed as the new state (Texas 1845 and California 1850) and territorial governments (New Mexico, Arizona, Colorado and Nevada) sought to consolidate their gains among the scattered frontier settlements. United States control on the recently acquired territories was shaky at best, with recurring clashes between Anglos and Mexican "Americans" in Texas, New Mexico and California, and continued Indian resistance throughout the Southwest. Abortive rebellions, guerilla warfare, and bandit activity by embittered Mexicans continued throughout the decade of the 1850s, especially in Texas and California, with some "pseudo-military" raids from Mexico into the U.S. occuring in the 1870s (Juan Cortina) and as late as 1916-1917 (Pancho Villa). However, the period of overt violence between gringos and Mexicans in the Southwest came to an end about 1865 (Moore 1970:139-141).

Conflict in California Gold Fields. Mutual distrust and hatred between Anglos and Mexicans in California was particularly severe. The lawlessness and violence of the Gold Rush period was felt throughout California--from the northern gold fields to the dusty streets of Los Angeles. Thousands of Mexican *cholos*, Chileans and other Latin Americans arrived in the gold fields during 1848-1850 and were concentrated mainly in the "southern mines". But gold-hungry Yankees--goaded by mixed feelings of nationalism, racism, jealousy and fear--refused to recognize any distinctions between Latin Americans, lumping them all together as "greasers" (McWilliams 1948:57); and through a combination of fraud, violence and legislation (Foreign Miner's Tax) drove them from the mining districts.

Thousands of Mexicans and Chileans were expelled from the mines in 1849 and 1850, with most Chileans returning to their native land while large numbers of Mexicans merely retreated to the towns and villages of Southern California, where they were fused with the native Spanish-speaking Californians (Pitt 1970: 48-68).

Civil Disorder in Los Angeles. In "semi-gringo" Los Angeles, where the Spanish-speaking population out-numbered the Yankees until the 1870s, growing resentment about the lack of civil order and civil rights--in terms of injustice to Mexicans and native Californians--climaxed in an open "race war" in the mid-1850s. Los Angeles developed one of the worst reputations of any town during the Gold Rush period, with the number of criminals that terrorized the town rivaling the several thousand wild dogs that nightly prowled the streets. A high rate of crime and the low number of criminals brought to trial in Los Angeles led to the emergence of vigilante justice with its lynch-law tribunals, most of the lynchings involving Spanish-speaking victims. Mexican law breakers were severely punished, while most "Yankee evildoers" were not prosecuted (1970:148-166).

Troublemakers of all kinds drifted to Los Angeles, but especially in evidence were resentful Mexicans who had been brutalized by peonage in Mexico, by the Mexican War, and by cruelty and injustice in the mining camps and towns of California. Although a small number of Mexicans came to California as criminals, others turned to robbery, murder, and banditry in response to the violence and injustice that they encountered. Mexican bandit groups roamed the hills of California from north to south, some with bands of 500 men, during the decade of the 1850s (1970:75-82, 167-180; McWilliams 1946:58-61).

Social Injustice in California. Although many minority groups suffered severe injustice in California during the period 1849-1860, none suffered more than Latin Americans, particularly the Mexicans. All "greasers" were considered to be "innately" criminal and immoral. No justice existed for Latin Americans either in or out of court because of the double standard that prevailed--all "greasers" are guilty and all Yankees are free from prosecution in cases involving "greasers". Both the regular courts and the improvised lynch courts were equally severe: "they...inclined toward quick and final punishments such as whipping, branding, ear cropping, banishment and hanging" (1970: 70). The high number of Mexicans whipped, banished or hanged, either legally or illegally, between 1849 and 1860 is witness to the cruelty, violence and injustice of the Gold Rush era (1970:69-71).

The history of social injustice toward California's Spanish-speaking population prior to 1900, not only included the landless lower classes, but also the owners of the large ranchos who controlled millions of acres throughout California prior to 1850. The northern ranchos were "stolen" from the Spanish land grant families by thousands of ex-miners who "squatted" on the land and eventually acquired title to vast holdings through the legal treachery of the Land Law of 1851 (1970:83-103).

The large ranchos of Southern California, although subject to some squatter invasions, were mainly lost through mortgages, taxes, and bankruptcy. Although rich in land, the land grant families had little cash reserves and were forced to mortgage or sell most of their holdings by the late 1860s, mainly as a consequence of three disastrous events: the decline of the cattle trade in the late 1850s, the floods of 1860-1861, and the severe drought of 1862-1864 (1970:108-109,245-248; McWilliams 1946:61-63).

Political Participation. Native Californians took part in the constitutional convention of 1849 and contributed to key provisions dealing with voting qualifications, taxation, state boundaries, and the publication of state laws (Pitt 1970:43-47). Particularly during the decade of the 1850s, the Spanish-speaking "sought and obtained practically every imaginable public office," although there was a notable decline in their leadership and influence after 1856 (1970:147).

Although Spanish-speaking Californians were numerically overwhelmed in the northern counties during the Gold Rush, they retained their superiority in the southern counties until the early 1870s. However, by 1880, the estrangement of the Hispanic population from California politics was complete, although a quarter of the population of Los Angeles County was still Spanish-speaking (1970:262-263).

Between 1880 and 1920, the Spanish-speaking Californians were politically powerless, functionally disenfranchized, and victimized by various types of civil injustice which we have previously considered. Moreover, the beginning of large-scale Mexican immigration to California after 1910 intensified the problems of Anglo discrimination and prejudice, of mutual distrust and suspicion, of the exploitation of "cheap foreign labor" by the emerging California "agribusiness" and its related financial and political power structures.

Hispanic Organizations. The only type of Hispanic organizations traceable to this period were the mutual benefit societies, which probably existed even prior to the Treaty of Guadalupe Hidalgo. However, after the American conquest, mutual benefit societies (such as *La Alianza Hispano Americana*, founded in 1894) attempted to protect Mexican Americans "from the necessity of dealing with the larger community by providing death benefits and sometimes insurance against accident or sickness" (Briegel 1970:161-163; cf. Grebler 1970:542-543).

The Politics of Accommodation and the Turmoil of Labor (1920-1942)

The rapid immigration of Mexicans to the Southwest between 1910 and 1930 created new problems and intensified old ones, both in terms of the internal social structure of the Hispanic American population and in relationship to the dominant Anglo society. In this period, the first Mexican American political organizations emerged with an attitude of accomodation to the *status quo* in an effort to conserve what few gains the newly emerging Mexican American middle class and the older aristocratic upper class had attained. However, the working classes rebelled against Anglo domination in the form of "militant trade unionism".

Political Accommodation. Although the Anglo power structure maintained an effective caste system throughout the Southwest in regard to the general Hispanic population of lower class workers, Hispanic Americans of the upper classes made few political demands and exerted little pressure for recovering the lost civil rights of the Spanish-speaking masses. The 1920s and 1930s were characterized by "the politics of accommodation" among the middle and upper class Hispanic Americans, which was an adaptation to the injustices prevalent within the established social order, controlled by Anglos for the benefit of Anglos (Moore 1970:143-144).

The *Orden Hijos de America* (Order of the Sons of America) was founded in San Antonio in 1921, not to inaugurate a social movement for Mexican American equality and civil rights, but as a movement of native and naturalized American citizens to publically differentiate themselves from the hordes of low status Mexican immigrants who were pouring into the Southwest. According to Cuéllar, "the implication was that Mexican Americans were more trustworthy to Anglos than Mexican nationals, and also more deserving of the benefits of American life" (Moore 1970:142). This organization took no partisan stand but rather concerned itself with "training members for citizenship," which meant affirmations of loyalty to the United States of America and the disarming of Anglo suspicions concerning Mexican disloyalty and subversive activity in the post-World War I period when the "Red scare" was dominant (1970:143).

The *League of United Latin-American Citizens* (LULAC), organized in 1929 at Corpus Christi, Texas, emerged as a "protective device" by middle class Mexican Americans who were sensitive to

Anglo anti-Mexican attitudes, especially at a time when a national debate was raging over the problems of Mexican immigration. The social and economic vulnerability of the Mexican American middle class in the late 1920s led LULAC members to adopt a twofold policy in an effort to appease Anglo fears: (1) "To develop within members of our race the best, purest and most perfect type of a true and loyal citizen of the United States of America" and (2) "we shall oppose any radical and violent demonstration which may tend to create conflicts and disturb the peace and tranquility of our country" (Moore 1970:143).

The few Spanish-speaking Americans who were able to vote in this period were usually under the control of Mexican American or Anglo political bosses who actively supported the *status quo* of Anglo domination and Mexican American subjugation (cf. Grebler 1970:556-557). Hispanic Americans were generally denied "the normal channels of political expression" in all of the border states except New Mexico. As Moore described the situation,

> The alien, of course, had no voice, but the settled and native-born were also efficiently disenfranchised, either by means of the poll tax and the open primary (as in Texas) or by simply being overwhelmed in numbers and by political manipulation (as in California).... The massive and irresponsible manipulation of this politically voiceless minority depended on the domination of state legislatures by the big agricultural, railroad, and mining interests (1970:24).

Militant Trade Unionism. Anglo belief in "the docility of Mexican labor" was challenged by periodic labor conflict, predominantly among agricultural workers. Mexican immigrants, once they became conscious of their subordination in the Anglo social structure, attempted to rebel in the form of "militant trade-unionism" which, according to McWilliams, made them "the pioneers of the trade-union movement in the Southwest" (1948:189).

Denied participation in the Anglo political system, Mexican workers began to organize for self-protection against the oppressive system in which they found themselves. As early as 1903, Mexican sugar-beet workers went on strike at Ventura, California, and this was followed by other strikes by Mexican railroad workers in Los Angeles (1910 and 1920); by field workers in Wheatland (1913) and grape-pickers at Fresno, California (1922); and by Mexican miners in Arizona (1915 and 1917). However, most of these early labor organizing efforts were temporary and largely unproductive (1948:190-191).

The Industrial Workers of the World (IWW),"an anarcho-syndicalist" organization formed in Chicago in 1905, launched a drive to organize migratory farm workers in California about 1910. The famous "Wheatland Riot" of August 1913 resulted from a clash between the IWW and growers who maintained "barbaric" working conditions and housing for farm workers. Throughout the state, local police and vigilante committees (composed of self-styled "good citizens") initiated violence against IWW organizers and striking workers, which caused Governor Hiram Johnson to raise the question concerning who were the "real anarchists"--the IWW or the "good citizens" (Bean 1968:294-296).

Urbanization, Poverty and Repatriation. By 1920, many Mexican Americans were demonstrating attitudes and tendencies similar to other immigrant groups: (1) desire for greater economic security, better housing and health care, and education for their children; (2) turning from agricultural to industrial employment; and (3) migration to urban areas for greater employment opportunities. Although some workers were absorbed by the growing industrial development of the cities, thousands more were forced to depend solely on agricultural employment. Many migrant farm workers spent the winter months in the larger cities of the Southwest and often were forced by their poverty to seek city or county welfare services--to go on "relief".

The growing agricultural depression of the 1920s, culminating in the Great Depression of the early 1930s, affected the Mexican American population in a variety of ways. Declining prices, decreasing wages, and rising unemployment produced more and more poverty. The decline in wages was accelerated by the large-scale migration of dispossessed small farmers and sharecroppers from the "dust-bowl" states to California, where they hoped to obtain employment, land and food for their hungry families--Mexicans and "Okies" and "Arkies" all competing for the same jobs, and not enough jobs and not enough income to provide food, clothing and shelter for poverty-stricken families (Moore 1970:25-26; Steinbeck 1939:212-220).

By 1934, half of the farm laborers in California were poor Anglos (dust-bowl refugees) and no more than a third were of Mexican descent (Moore 1970:26). The unemployed Anglos had nowhere to go, but welfare authorities had found a solution to the "Mexican problem"--repatriation.

The repatriation by railroad of tens of thousands of Mexicans from Los Angeles and other large cities throughout the United States during the Depression was organized and executed with official sanction from local authorities, as well as with the consent and encouragement of the Mexican government. The "polite coercion" used by local welfare bureaus to accomplish the mass repatriation of Mexicans was done "irrespective of the wishes or legal standing of the individuals involved." Many repatriated "Mexicans", it seems, were actually U.S. citizens whose rights "to citizenship in their native land were explicitly denied or not taken into account." Many other repatriates were naturalized citizens who were unfortunate enough to be poor and on relief and who, without benefit of legal sanctions, were "forced" to leave their adopted homeland with what few possessions they could carry by hand (Grebler 1970:524-526).

There is no record of organized protest by Mexican American organizations, no Anglo institution aided those who wanted to remain in the United States, and "almost no voice of contemporary dissent by Anglos was heard" protesting the mass repatriations. The ethnic community had been intimidated into subjection by a long history of contact with government agencies, and the Anglo community was accustomed to pursuing a policy of self-interest at the expense of minority group rights. According to Grebler, "the procedure of those days, with all of its bureaucratic overlay, is painfully reminiscent of the later removal of Japanese from the West coast during World War II." Tragically, the rights of American citizenship have often been withheld from certain minority groups by the dominant society whenever it seemed expedient for the "common good" of the Anglo majority, regardless of the constitutional legalities involved (1970:525-526).

Farm Facism of the 1930s. Many Mexican agricultural workers refused to accept the subordinate status imposed upon them by big business agriculture in the Southwest. The exploitation of Mexican field workers forced them to organize for self-protection in the late 1920s and throughout the 1930s. The first stable union organization, *La Confederación de Uniones Obreras Mexicanas*, was established in Southern California in 1927 with 3,000 workers in twenty locals throughout the region. The first strike called by the new union was in the Imperial Valley during the cantaloupe harvest of May 1928 (see Wollenberg 1970:141-143); the second was called two years later, in 1930, when 5,000 Mexican field workers struck Imperial Valley growers. In 1933, 7,000 Mexican workers in Los Angeles County participated in the largest agricultural strike in California history up to that time. Other important strikes occured in the Imperial and San Joaquin Valleys during 1932-1933 (cf. Grebler 1970:531-532), and again in Los Angeles and Orange Counties in 1936. The strikes in California "were duplicated wherever Mexicans were employed in agriculture"--Arizona, Idaho, Washington, Colorado, Michigan and Texas. For example, over 6,000 Mexican pecan-shellers were involved in a prolonged strike in San Antonio during 1934 (McWilliams 1948:191-194).

Commenting on the agricultural labor turmoil during the 1930s, McWilliams wrote (1948:194-195):

> With scarcely an exception, every strike in which Mexicans participated in the borderlands in the 'thirties was broken by the use of violence and was followed by deportations. In most of these strikes, Mexican workers stood alone, that is, they were not supported by organized labor, for their organizations, for the most part, were affiliated neither with the CIO nor the AFL....
>
> In two decades, [Mexican immigrants] had learned to protest, in a typically American fashion, against an annual family wage of $600; against poor housing; and, above all, against discrimination.... Once their commendable efforts toward self-organization were crushed--with violence and gross brutality, with mass arrests, deportations, and "repatriations"--the immigrants became demoralized and momentarily abandoned any attempt to establish a *rapprochement* with the Anglo-Americans.

Almost without exception, California growers, as well as growers in other states, claimed that these strikes were "the work of outside agitators or radicals who had stirred up contented workers" (Wollenberg 1970:143). Growers, police officials, and local newspapers and politicans placed the blame on Communists, radicals, and the IWW. However, the California Bureau of Industrial Relations, in an official report on labor turmoil in the Imperial Valley during the major strike of 1928, "concluded that there was no evidence pointing to professional agitators or members of radical groups as organizers of the work stoppages" (1970:143-144).

However, the wretched conditions of agricultural workers and the complete absence of restraints on the abuses of growers throughout California during the 1930s "opened the door to the most extreme radicals." The left-wing Cannery and Agricultural Workers' Industrial Union (CAWIU), an avowed arm of the Communist Party, led strikes among grape pickers in Lodi and cotton pickers in the southern San Joaquin Valley during 1933, and later among field workers in the Imperial Valley in 1934. According to Bean, "Employer-vigilante groups, sometimes deputized by county sheriffs, did not hesitate to use violence in crushing these strikes, and the 'union' was dissolved when its Communist leaders were arrested and convicted under the state criminal syndicalism law" (1968:414).

All farm labor organizing efforts were opposed by the forces of California agribusiness, mainly through the Associated Farmers of California, who maintained anti-organizational units throughout the state and worked closely with "law enforcement" officers. Anti-strike vigilante forces, armed with shotguns, pick handles, and gasoline, burned down migrant labor camps and assaulted striking workers, while receiving the enthusiastic support of local and state police officials. Known labor organizers and union members were denied employment, ordered out of the county, or arrested. Consequently, unionization efforts were notably unsuccessful during the "farm facism" period of the 1930s (1968:496-498).

The exploitation of Mexican American agricultural workers--economically, socially, and politically--was sufficient cause and incentive for the prolonged period of social turmoil that bitterly emerged during the 1930s. Although this social struggle was partially submerged during World War II and in the post-war era, its history is still being written, both in the fields and in the industrial centers of California and the Southwest.

The Political Awakening of Mexican Americans (1942-1965)

Several profound social changes occurred among the Mexican American population during the 1940s, which brought them into new contact with Anglo American society and new exposure to the larger world around them.

Urbanization, Military Service and Discrimination. The growing labor demands of wartime industry drew hundreds of thousands of Mexican nationals and their native-born children from rural to urban areas, with many coming to Los Angeles. At the same time, hundreds of thousands of Mexican Americans were drafted into or volunteered for the armed services and traveled to many foreign countries, thereby gaining a greater awareness of and appreciation for cultural diversity.

The process of Mexican American urbanization in Southern California brought with it a realization that the rural areas of the Southwest did not have a monopoly on discrimination and prejudice. The "Sleepy Lagoon Case" and the "Zoot-Suiter Riots" of 1942-1943 brought to shocking reality the subordinate position of Mexican Americans, in spite of their improved economic condition as a result of wartime prosperity. In Los Angeles, and in the surrounding cities and towns that rapidly grew to form a great metropolis during the early 1940s, recent urban Mexican American migrants "could find only poor housing, the lowest unskilled employment, and restricted access to schools and other public facilities" (Moore 1970:145).

In the new urban environment, however, many Mexican Americans became increasingly dissatisfied with their traditional pattern of political accomodation and their subservient social status. In the immediate post-war years, a new type of leadership emerged in the *barrios* that was not only dissatisfied with the past but began to press for significant changes, both in their local communities and in the larger social matrix of American society.

The World War II era has often been described as the beginning of the Mexican American political awakening and the development of minority group consciousness. According to John Martinez,

> The opportunities for employment, the new horizons acquired from military service, and the educational opportunities through the G.I. Bill of Rights meant that for the first time large numbers of Spanish-speaking moved into the skilled, business, and professional classes. It follows that new voices were soon heard; the educated began articulating and analyzing the plight of their ethnic group. The response was a political awakening of great numbers of people (1966:49).

Growing Political Participation. For the Spanish-speaking, politics, rather than continuing to be a means of pacifying the fears of Anglos regarding Mexican American citizenship, became a social instrument for achieving certain goals and rewards for the benefit of all Hispanic Americans, and a means of protecting themselves from the abuses and exploitation of the dominant society (Martinez 1966:48). Southern California became the focal point for the new social and political awakening.

The initial expression of greater Mexican American political participation appeared in the form of "Unity Leagues" in many towns in Southern California. Ignacio López, publisher of a bilingual Pomona newspaper, provided the inspiration and leadership for numerous Unity League chapters, which focused their efforts on voter registration drives and supported Mexican American candidates for public office--mainly for board of education and city council seats (Briegel 1970:167; McWilliams 1948:280).

Another "grass-roots" organization that has made a significant contribution to Mexican American politicalization is the Community Service Organization (CSO), established in Los Angeles in 1947. The significance of the CSO is described by Moore:

> The guiding idea of CSO was to cope with concrete and immediate social, economic, and political problems.... In general, CSO pressed for full and equal rights for Mexican Americans. The new emphasis was the extra

> appeal for active and increased participation by as many elements of the community as possible. Therefore, in contrast to previous organizations, CSO tended to be more egalitarian. Under the influence of an outside catalyst (Saul Alensky's Industrial Areas Foundation) it became a group that no longer served as the vehicle of a relatively few and successful Mexican Americans. Although the leadership tended to be middle class, on the whole it made an effort to recruit members of the working class and other lower-class elements, including new arrivals from Mexico (1970:146).

The method of CSO was to develop indigeneous community leadership for organized action "directed against restricted housing, police brutality, segregated schools, inequitable justice, and discriminatory employment," which were all problems that faced Mexican Americans throughout Southern California (1970:146). CSO members organized nonpartisan voter registration drives; put pressure on public housing authorities, the Fair Employment Practices Commission (FEPC), and law enforcement authorities; sponsored legislation to provide old age pension benefits for resident non-citizens; and supported the unionization of agricultural workers (1970:146-147; Sheldon 1966:140-141).

The CSO functioned as a politically powerful organization throughout California in the late 1940s and through the 1950s, but declined somewhat in influence during the 1960s due to a lack of leadership and finances. More recently, the CSO has reasserted positive leadership, with assistance from antipoverty funds, for a program of consumer education among low-income families in East Los Angeles (Moore 1970:147; Briegel 1970:168-169).

Beginning in the 1950s, new college-educated Mexican American leaders emerged who rejected the "grass-roots" approach in favor of "pressure group" organizations. The Council of Mexican-American Affairs (CMAA), organized in Los Angeles in 1953, sought to change the image of Mexican Americans from blue-collar to white-collar workers; to persuade the Anglo community that "bilingual and bicultural citizens do not suffer a disadvantage" (Briegel 1970:171); to develop Mexican American leadership; and to promote unity and coordination of efforts among Mexican American organizations (Sheldon 1966:139). Although CMAA has experienced many internal tensions and organizational problems, this organization has represented the Mexican American community at many conferences, hearings, and social functions to make the larger community aware of Mexican American problems and grievances. The Educational Committee has pressed for improved opportunities for Mexican American students and educators, has sponsored educational scholarships, and has more recently administered several Operation Headstart centers in Los Angeles County *barrios* (Briegel 1970:171-173).

The first Mexican American organization to openly proclaim itself as being actively political was the Mexican American Political Association (MAPA), founded in 1958 under the sponsorship of the California Democratic Party. The new organization pursued the following aims:

> to seek the social, economic, cultural and civil betterment of Mexican Americans and other persons sympathetic to our aims; to take stands on political issues and present and endorse candidates for public office; to launch voter registration drives throughout California; and to encourage increased activity within the political parties (Sheldon 1966:142).

MAPA immediately began to establish local chapters throughout California in assembly districts with large concentrations of Mexican Americans.

MAPA's organizational efforts, however, were unfruitful in the California elections of 1960 because strong public interest in the national presidential race, mainly centered in the Democratic Party's "Viva Kennedy! Clubs", distracted attention from local MAPA campaigns. But MAPA successfully endorsed three candidates in the congressional elections of 1962: Edward Roybal was elected to the U.S. House of Representatives, and Philip Soto and John Moreno were voted into the California State Assembly. Since 1962, MAPA has had only limited success in the election of Mexican American candidates to public office (Briegel 1970:174-175).

The potential of statewide Mexican American organizations like MAPA is seen in the successful (but temporary) overthrow of the Anglo dominated government of Crystal City, Texas in 1963 by PASSO (Political Association of Spanish-Speaking Organizations), which staged the upset with support from the Teamsters Union and the Catholic Bishops' Committee for the Spanish-Speaking. This victory was a forewarning to other Anglo-controlled Southwestern cities where Mexican Americans constitute the majority population, an omen of the potential collective voting power of the heretofore politically dominated Spanish-speaking minority. The balance of power may soon shift in hundreds of communities throughout the Southwest as Mexican Americans become organized and unified around common political objectives (Moore 1970:147-148).

The development of Mexican American politics, although hindered by inadequate funding and staff, has shown a marked transition from paternalistic and accomodating organizations such as LULAC, to social action groups like CSO that have attacked the structures of injustice and brought pressure for meaningful change, and to active political organizations like MAPA which take a stand on political issues and support the election and appointment of Mexican Americans to public office. The American G.I. Forum and PASSO in Texas have also had important roles in the politicalization process of the Mexican American minority.

Braceros vs. Unionization. Important changes also occured in the area of farm labor during the period 1942-1965, which set the stage for successful union organizational efforts during the late 1960s.

The Bracero Program (see Chapter 1), introduced in the summer of 1942, was an "emergency" measure to meet the agricultural manpower crises that resulted from the draft and from wartime industrial development. California's surplus farm labor pool of the 1930s was quickly drained of manual laborers by growth in the manufacturing, transportation and service industries in Los Angeles, San Francisco and San Diego during the early 1940s (Galarza 1964:41-45).

The agribusiness has exerted strong control on Southwestern politics, not only in the pre-World War II period as we have seen, but also in the post-war period. This is demonstrated by the fact that the so-called "emergency" that brought the Bracero Program into existence continued for over twenty years. The Bracero Program was finally terminated by Congress in 1964, much to the displeasure of big business agriculture in the Soutwest. Theoretically, *braceros* could only be used to fill proven labor shortages and not to displace domestic workers (1964:47). However, in practice, domestic workers were forced to compete with "substandard *bracero* norms" which kept wages and working conditions at a deplorable level. *Braceros* formed a "captive labor force" that could be shuttled from harvest to harvest and was a highly efficient means of increasing the profits of agribusiness, while at the same time preventing domestic workers from becoming unionized and receiving the benefits of workers in other industries--the right of collective bargaining, health insurance, unemployment compensation insurance, and other fringe benefits (Servín 1970:179-184).

When the Bracero Program came to a close, growers were forced to offer better wages and working conditions and thereby attracted sufficient domestic labor to insure a bountiful harvest, thus refuting their previous claims that a shortage of workers threatened the harvest and that the Bracero Program should be continued (1970:197-199; Bean 1968:501).

During the post-war years, Mexican American community and labor leaders actively protested against the Bracero Program and the unregulated flow of "wetbacks", both of which constituted unfair labor competion for domestic workers. This two-fold evil depressed wages, destroyed the power of collective bargaining, froze out local labor, and made unionization of farm workers impossible. Referring to the *bracero* era, McWilliams stated that "the annual influx of imported farm workers and 'wetbacks' had so thoroughly demoralized the labor market that any thought of organization was unrealistic" (1948: 14-15).

However, termination of the Bracero Program opened the door for farm labor reform and effective unionization of field workers. In 1964, Congress passed the Economic Opportunity Act which provided grants to agencies assisting migrant farm workers, and amended the National Housing Act to provide for direct loans for farm-labor housing construction. Then, in 1966, the new Federal minimum-wage law was extended to farm workers. But these measures were only token attempts at improving the deplorable conditions in which migrant farm workers were forced to live (Bean 1968:505-506).

Although previous organizational efforts among farm workers in California had been notably unsuccessful due to the extreme poverty, disorganization, and demoralization of the workers on the one hand, and to the powerful domination of California agriculture by the "agribusiness" (the combined power of growers, canners and packers, shippers, land companies, financial institutions, agricultural investors, politicians, government and law enforcement agencies) on the other hand, a new labor movement emerged in the early 1960s that awakened the public conscience to the plight of migrant farm workers.

Beginning in 1959, the AFL-CIO launched a new drive for farm labor organization through the Agricultural Workers Organizing Committee (AWOC), led by veteran union officials. Then, in 1962, a new independent union led by César Châvez began to successfully organize farm workers with a strong "grass-roots" appeal. Châvez had helped to build the CSO into a strong organization during the 1950s, first by organizing chapters throughout the state, and later as general director of the organization. Because of his commitment to helping farm workers organize against the agribusiness power structure and the illegal use of *braceros*, Châvez resigned from the CSO in 1961 to lay the foundation for establishing the National Farm Workers Association (NFWA), which was organized statewide in California in 1962. When the NFWA joined AWOC members in a strike against grape growers in the Delano area of Kern County in September 1965, a new era began in behalf of the civil rights of the Mexican American minority (Bean 1968:503-504; Nelson 1970:227-235

The Radicalization of Mexican American Politics (1965-)

Although the Negro Civil Rights Movement was launched in the early 1950s, it was not until the mid-1960s that social reform for Mexican Americans really got underway. Militancy among Mexican Americans in the 1960s was demonstrated in: (1) the national NFWA-AWOC boycott against non-union grape growers that began in 1965, and in the NFWA-sponsored march on Sacramento from Delano which covered 300 miles in 25 days (March-April 1966); (2) the "Albuquerque Walkout" of March 1966 when national Mexican American leaders boycotted the Equal Employment Opportunities Commission hearings because of the commissioners' alledged indifference to Mexican American problems; (3) the 1966-1967 "guerilla warfare" of Reies López Tijerina and his followers who formed the *Alianza Federal de Mercedes* to recapture the lost Spanish land grants of New Mexico (a march from Albuquerque to Santa Fe to dramatize the *Alianza* cause was made in July 1966, as well as an armed assault on the courthouse at Tierra Amarilla, New Mexico in June 1967); (4) the birth of the *Chicano* movement among Mexican American youth (1966); and (5) the nationally publicized high school walkouts in East Los Angeles by Mexican American students in March 1968. However, only the organization of farm labor and the growing *Chicano* movement will be considered here since these two movements have had the most significance for Mexican Americans in California during the past decade.

The Unionization of Farm Labor. The California Grape Boycott, led by Chávez and characterized by nonviolent methods, began in 1967 through the combined efforts of the NFWA and AWOC in an attempt to bring decent working conditions, a living wage, and collective bargaining to Mexican American farm workers. By April 1966, the NFWA was recognized by two large wine grape growers in the Delano area as the sole bargaining agent for their field workers, which was the first such recognition of a farm worker's union by major California growers. The two victorious unions merged in 1966 to form the United Farm Workers Organizing Committee (UFWOC), with Chávez as director. Soon contracts had been signed with ten major wine grape growers, and in 1967-1968 the boycott was extended to table grape growers throughout California because of their continued unified resistance to all organizational efforts for their field workers. It was not until the summer of 1970 that California table grape growers admitted defeat and signed two-year or three-year contracts with UFWOC. The new pact with twenty-six major growers brought approximately eighty percent of California's table grape crop under UFWOC contracts and covered 7,000-8,000 workers during peak harvest season (Harley 1970).

By August 1971, the UFWOC held over 200 labor contracts with California growers which covered an estimated 55,000 workers. The workers covered by these contracts had authorized the UFWOC to be their sole bargaining representative. Summarizing union accomplishments, Ron Taylor wrote: "UFWOC officials administer a 1.8 million health and welfare benefit fund for union members, operate two medical clinics, 22 field office-service centers and 44 boycott offices scattered across the nation" (1971:1).

The UFWOC extended the boycott to wine grapes in 1971 and iceberg lettuce in 1972 in order to extend union benefits to more field workers. The boycott of lettuce, one of California's largest and most valuable crops, has made measurable economic impact on some vegetable growers in the Imperial and Salinas Valleys. Four large companies had signed UFWOC contracts by August 1972 and about 200 others were resisting the boycott, with many growers protesting that their workers were already represented by the Teamsters Union or didn't want union representation (Aarons 1972:3H).

Teamster contracts were signed with vegetable growers dating from the summer of 1970, only after growers became fearful that the UFWOC would soon strike their farms to follow up the grape boycott victory. Moreover, the Teamster-grower pact impossed the union on ninety percent of the field workers, none of whom had the opportunity of chosing their own bargaining agent. Most of the growers chose to deepen their ties with the Teamsters Union, which had represented packers and shippers for a number of years, rather than submitting to pressure from Chávez and the nationwide boycott. "Chávez's threat," commented Leroy Aarons, "is that his contracts, in contrast to the softer Teamster pacts, shift much of the grower's traditional power to the union. The UFW threat is political as much as it is economic" (1972:3H).

Chávez and the UFWOC have received strong support from several AFL-CIO member unions (Wollenberg 1970:148-149), the National Council of Churches (Grebler 1970:500-502), various Catholic organizations (1970:461-467), and substancial support from segments of the general public who are developing an awakening social consciousness (Wollenberg 1970:149). The lettuce boycott, however, has probably not been as successful as the previous grape strike. Nevertheless, Chávez has made tremendous gains against the power structure of the agribusiness in spite of competition from the Teamsters.

Several recent developments have further strengthened Chávez' bargaining position with growers who use migrant farm labor, not only in California but throughout the United States. In February 1972, the UFWOC was officially accepted into the AFL-CIO as a full-fledged member union and was renamed the United Farm Workers of America (UFWA). Then, in September 1973, a crucial agreement was reached between the UFWA and the Teamsters (mainly worked out between AFL-CIO president George Meany and Teamsters chief Frank Fitzsimmons, although Châvez took part in the final phase of the negotiations) whereby the UFWA will represent *all* field workers and the Teamsters will have jurisdiction over cannery and other non-harvest workers (*The Miami Herald* 1973:2A).

The Chicano Movement. The second major socio-political development among Mexican Americans in California during the post-war period has been the emergence of the *Chicano* movement. Its origins have been traced by Cuéllar to a series of conferences held at Loyola University in Los Angeles during the summer of 1966:

> As originally conceived by its Catholic sponsors, the conferences were to create a fairly innocuous youth organization for middle-class Mexican students attending various colleges throughout California. Very quickly the movement grew beyond the intent or control of its sponsors (Loyola has never been very noted for its interest in Mexican American education) and it drew in yet others, not students and not middle class, who were attracted by the ideology of *chicanismo* (Moore 1970:149).

The *Chicano* movement is extremely heterogeneous in that it cuts across social classes, regions, and generations to form a radical new form of social protest and a quest for self-determination. Its broad base includes the followers of Tijerina in New Mexico, Rodolfo (Corky) Gonzâlez in Colorado, and Châvez in California. Gonzâlez' efforts through The Crusade for Justice have mainly been in terms of urban social action; he has also had strong influence outside of Colorado, mainly through the organization of regional youth conferences.

Chicanos are attempting to re-educate and awaken a new social consciousness among Anglos by various forms of protest against specific and long-standing grievances, such as police brutality (cf. Grebler 1970:532-534). Confrontation with the Anglo power structures is the prefered method of achieving desired social change, even though militant protest occasionally leads to violence. For example, the East Los Angeles Riots of August 1970 were occasioned by a rally sponsored by the Chicano Moratorium Committee and resulted in a violent confrontation with sheriff's deputies.

The "*Chicano* revolution", however, had its beginning during the high school "blowouts" in East Los Angeles in 1968. Young

Chicano activists staged a militant protest against Anglo educators who refused to listen and respond to student grievances. The "blowouts" were an explosive type of anger in response to long-term Mexican American frustrations. That the 1968 student walkouts were an *organized* protest is a significant factor, which reflects the development of new student organizations in California during the late 1960s (Burma 1970:279-294; Cuéllar 1970:150).

The ideology of *chicanismo*, which has been largely shaped by Mexican American student activists, focuses on both the socioeconomic and cultural predicament of the Mexican American people. Americans of Mexican descent are viewed as the children of a conquered people--dominated by Anglo imperialism and economically and culturally exploited. Deprived of his land and his civil rights, the Mexican American became only "a cheap source of wage labor" for the economic exploitation of Anglo capitalists. The economic expansion of the Southwest is viewed essentially as a "dehumanizing process" in that the Mexican was transformed into a "rootless economic commodity" and was forced to live in poverty, regardless of whether he lived in rural or urban areas (1970:151).

In terms of the cultural exploitation and suppression of Mexican Americans by Anglo society, *Chicanos* are particularly angered. The "Americanization" process of the Anglo-dominated educational system has deprived Mexican Americans of an autonomous cultural life. Consequently, *Chicano* young people tend to feel personally and culturally disoriented. In the process of self-discovery, the *Chicano*, instead of being ashamed of his "Mexican-ness", has developed a new sense of racial and cultural pride, particularly symbolized in his concept of *"La Raza"*--a sense of collective identity based on common history, culture, and ethnic background. Cuéllar calls this a movement of "cultural nationalism" (1970:153).

Chicanismo is a socio-cultural revitalization movement that has found expression, not only in a new sense of "peoplehood", but also in "cultural" activities--development of greater fluency in Spanish; emergence of *Chicano* theater groups; development of literary arts (newspapers, magazines, articles and books) and establishment of ethnic studies programs for high school and college students (1970:153).

In terms of political awareness and participation, many young *Chicanos* view conventional political activity as producing few changes in socioeconomic conditions, even though there has been no open repudiation of traditional political methods. Conservative Mexican American leaders and organizations are commited to working *within* the system to achieve political leverage for social change, whereas many *Chicanos* speak of "revolutionary activity" to achieve radical social change for the benefit of the oppressed Mexican American minority. The life-style and writings of Ché Guevara and Camilo Torres provide them with inspiration, as well as the Mexican revolutionary tradition. The ideology of the Cuban Revolution has had a strong appeal for the "Brown Berets" and the "Chicano Liberation Front", two of the more radical *Chicano* youth organizations (1970:150-151).

The *Chicano* movement, however, represents much *more* than young Mexican American "radicals" who are rebelling against the Anglo Establishment. Within the movement are groups of well-educated Mexican American professionals who are turning away from public demonstrations to pursue meaningful political activity. *Chicano* activists have been signing up Mexican American voters (in Texas since 1969 and in California since 1970) for a new third party, *El Partido de la Raza Unida* ("The Party of the United People"), which they hope will increase political leverage for electing Mexican American candidates to public office (*Los Angeles Times* 1971d:3,23).

The emergence of *La Raza Unida Party* (PRU) points to the growing political sophistication of *Chicano* activists who during the past few years have learned that, although militant demonstrations get a lot of attention, they usually don't change the traditional balance of power. *Chicanos* are now trying to develop enough political muscle to bring about positive social changes that will benefit the traditionally voiceless Mexican American minority.

La Raza Unida represents a "slap in the face" of the Democratic Party, which tends to take "the Mexican American vote" for granted (on the other hand, the Republican Party has never fared well among Mexican Americans). In a special 48th Assembly District election in Los Angeles in November 1971, PRU took credit for the defeat of the Democratic candidate by pulling away part of the Mexican American vote. *La Raza Unida* is conveying a new message to Mexican Americans; it is calling *barrio* residents to abandon their traditional Democratic allegiance and to form a strong third party that would be a base for political control of Mexican American communities (Del Olmo 1971b:3,22; 1971c:1,10).

The potential effect of *La Raza Unida* on local elections is seen in the success of the new party in South Texas where, in 1970, PRU won over twenty school board and municipal government positions in three predominantly Mexican American counties (*Los Angeles Times* 1971d:23). In Texas and Colorado, *La Raza Unida* is an officially recognized third party, whereas in California (as of January 1972) PRU had not yet achieved official status and its candidates must run as independents.

At the state and national levels, the impact of the Mexican American vote could determine the balance of power in close elections, not only in Southwestern states, but also in other states with large Hispanic populations, such as New York, Illinois, and Florida. The potential of Mexican American voters has grown more powerful since the passage of the 1970 Voting Rights Act, which eliminated literacy requirements for voting, and by the increased interest in voting by newly franchized younger *Chicanos* (Foley 1971:18,19).

Patterns of Mexican American Leadership

It may seem strange to many Anglo Americans that "the Mexican American" has not yet developed the ability to speak with a mass voice to promote the common good of his minority group. The truth is, as we have attempted to point out throughout the preceeding chapters of this study, that Mexican Americans are *not* a homogeneous group; they do not have a common voice nor have they achieved mutual agreement on many issues; and they are fragmented by heterogeneity at every level (Martinez 1966:47-62).

Minority Group Consciousness. Only in the post-World War II era have Mexican Americans begun to develop the ability to work together on a large scale to achieve a common goal or to rally around a common cause. Only with the development of a minority group consciousness have Mexican Americans realized their structural separation from the Anglo American power structures and only with the development of Anglo political sophistication (excluding the possibility of violent revolution and the collapse of the system) will the Mexican American people be truly integrated into the structures of power in America (Cabrera 1971:32-37,68).

Emergence of Leadership. Mexican American leadership for social reform has been notably lacking for many years of their history. The political voice of Mexican Americans was subjugated and accommodating to Anglo domination until the social awakening that accompanied the post-war period of economic development, which freed many Mexican Americans from poverty and gave them some upward socioeconomic mobility. Political awareness and participation has been the corollary of upward social mobility.

Although a large number of middle-income Mexican Americans have become apathetic to the problems of their working class "brothers", a growing number of acculturated Mexican Americans who have achieved status and recognition in Anglo society--as businessmen, educators, lawyers, and other types of white-collar workers and professionals--have retained their ethnic ties and are providing new leadership for Mexican American communities. Some affluent Mexican Americans, as the result of a growing social consciousness or perhaps guilt concerning the continuing discrimination and unequal opportunities of their disadvantaged "brothers", have been stimulated to greater political and social action in order to improve the opportunity structure of *all* Americans of Mexican descent within the framework of a culturally pluralistic society.

In addition, there are a growing number of college-educated Mexican Americans who have become well informed concerning the historical development of Mexican American social injustice, and who have commited themselves to remedial social action. According to Sheldon,

> The existence of Anglo-type Mexican-American young men and women dedicated to the advancement of Mexican-Americans is a phenomenon of recent years. It represents a breaking of the traditional working-class pattern of limited and informal relationships outside of the extended family. Perhaps the phenomenon of an emerging middle class may be related also to acculturation, to a growing awareness of the methods needed to be effectual in urban Anglo society (1966:144-145).

Types and Problems of Leadership. Mexican American leadership continues to be fragmented and competitive, lacking both funds and political power and struggling with the problems of compromise and coalition, of diplomacy and radicalism. José Villarreal has identified several types of political leaders within the Mexican American community (1966:28,30):

> There is the angry, militant young intellectual, usually a lawyer or educator, driven not only by a zeal to deliver his people, but also by personal ambition...
>
> There is also the older, embittered veteran who has fought the hard fight (many times alone), whose ambition has been thwarted by the passage of time and who sees the newcomers receiving state appointments and otherwise reaping the fruits of his labor...
>
> There is also the other ancient, who has given his time and himself to the cause, but has no ambition for either wealth or position. He just wants his world made better...
>
> There are also crooks, those who are out only for what they can get, quickly but not necessarily honestly. They are not a force within the Mexican-American community, any more than they are a force in the Anglo community. They are an irritant to both, but that is all...
>
> Finally, there is the tool, the *Tio Tomas* (Uncle Tom), who, for an appointment to a minor office or responsibility, will betray his people, while professing that he is doing good for them. There is for the politician,

after all, a value to having a Spanish surname listed on his staff. And for the Mexican staff member, it is justified as proof that Mexicans can improve themselves.

There are other kinds of leaders within the Mexican American community as well--both internal and external leaders (Figure 20). Each one has an important role and function in serving the Hispanic population, with some individuals being more capable and more effective than others. Grebler has outlined some of the major problems in the development and maintenance of leadership:

> One is the problem of validation: the built-in conflict between acceptance in the dominant society and approval by the Mexican American community. Another issue is the high degree of fragmentation and parochialism that results from the many varieties of organizations and leaders. In addition, Mexican-American leadership is not exempt from the familiar generational conflict (1970:551).

The Role of Religion. The important roles of the Catholic priest and the Protestant minister deserve special consideration, along with the roles of their respective congregations, lay leaders, and ecclesiastical machinery. This, of course, raises the important question of the role of religion, in general, in respect to Mexican American assimilation and the development of community leadership. What function have religious attitudes, beliefs and behavior had, for example, in the liberation of the Mexican American from socioeconomic and political exploitation by Anglo Americans? In developing an enlightened Christian social conscience and active community participation? In the reorientation of both individuals and groups concerning Christian values and priorities?

Although the Catholic Church admittedly has more direct influence over Mexican Americans than do Protestant churches and denominations, the remaining chapters of this study concern themselves mainly with the Protestant side of the religious dimension. However, it should be noted that major changes are occurring within Mexican American Catholicism, especially in terms of goals and types of ministry among the Spanish-speaking population (cf. Grebler 1970:449-485).

Recent trends within the Archdiocese of Los Angeles show encouraging signs that the Catholic Church is awakening socially. On Christmas eve 1969, a newly formed *Chicano* group called *Catōlicos por la Raza* ("Catholics for the People") staged a militant protest at St. Basil's Roman Catholic Church in Los Angeles. This new group challenged Cardinal McIntyre's

Figure 20

A TYPOLOGY OF MEXICAN-AMERICAN LEADERSHIP

INTERNAL LEADERS

<u>Social</u>

Heads of ethnic clubs and societies
The economically secure

<u>Political</u>

Party committeemen
Professional politicians
Field representatives of professional politicians

<u>Economic</u>

Merchants whose economic base rests in the *barrio*
Professionals (lawyers, doctors, etc.) who depend upon the *barrio* for income
Labor intermediaries

<u>Professional</u>

Teachers and school administrators
Social workers
Community organizers
Police officers
Other civil servants

<u>Religious</u>

Priests or ministers
Laymen

<u>Informal social workers</u>

A man or woman who has a reputation for solving social problems (housewives, small businessmen, notary publics, etc.)

EXTERNAL LEADERS

<u>Anglos</u>

Social organizers from labor, community, and church groups
Experts from government, universities, and political groups

<u>Mexican Americans</u>

"Subsidized leaders" employed by local, state, or national organizations or government agencies
Independent individuals (college professors, school teachers, etc.)

Source: Grebler 1970:549

conservative approach to solving Mexican American problems. The December melee was an attempt to awaken Anglo Catholics to the plight of the Mexican American minority in Los Angeles; it was a demand that the Archdiocese become more relevant to Mexican American needs. Richard Cruz, a spokesman for *Católicos por la Raza*, said: "The true nature of our protest is that we want the Catholic Church to identify with the struggle of our people to obtain self-determination and to give us spiritual leadership" (Dart 1969:10).

Apparently, the December protest was well-timed with the dynamics of internal change within the Archdiocese of Los Angeles stimulated by the spirit of Vatican II (Davis 1972:8,10). In January 1970, Cardinal McIntyre "retired" as head of the Archdiocese and Archbishop Timothy Manning was appointed as his successor. Manning promised that the Church would "take a fresh look at social problems and other issues which have wracked it in recent years" (Thrapp 1970a:1).

Then, in February 1970, Manning established the Interparochial Council of East Los Angeles, composed of Catholic laymen, priests and nuns from twenty-one parishes in the East Los Angeles area. Evidently, the new Council grew out of recommendations from the East Los Angeles Association of Catholic Priests (organized in 1967), but no doubt pressure from *Católicos por la Raza* helped to bring the Council into existence. It would appear that Manning has opened the way for greater participation by Mexican Americans in the policy-making decisions of the Church at the local level, particularly in reference to the needs of the Spanish-speaking minority (Thrapp 1970b:1; Dart 1971b:26).

Another evidence of this trend was the February 1971 appointment of Father Juan Arzube as new auxiliary bishop, which made him only the second bishop of Hispanic heritage among the present 250 bishops within the U.S. Catholic Church. The other Hispanic American bishop is Patrick F. Flores, who was named auxiliary bishop of San Antonio in March 1970 (Dart 1971a:1).

These and other changes introduced by Archbishop Manning have revitalized many facets of the Catholic Church in Southern California and have given Manning the reputation for being "one of the most socially progressive Catholic officials in America" (Davis 1972:7). Nevertheless, Manning has been criticized by some *Chicanos* for appointing an Ecuadorian (Father Juan Arzube) as auxiliary bishop instead of a Mexican American, and for only "throwing crumbs" to appease Mexican Americans when the Church should be doing much more to aid their social progress. The Archdiocese of Los Angeles is the fourth largest in the nation and probably the second richest (after New York), with assets in 1972 of $352.42 million (1972:7,10).

The depth of the social separation between Anglo and Spanish-speaking Catholics has led to the creation of a national association of Mexican American priests that is seeking greater representation for Hispanic Catholics among the Irish-Catholic power structure (cf. *Newsweek* 1971:82) of the American Catholic Church. The PADRES (*Padres Asociados para Derechos Religiosos, Educativos y Sociales*) was founded in October 1969 in San Antonio, Texas and is "dedicated to helping the Church identify more closely with the social, economic and educational needs of the Spanish-speaking in the U.S." (*Catholic Almanac* 1970:99). The potential strength of this organization is seen in the following factors: one-fourth of all Catholics in the U.S. are of Hispanic descent, the new organization already has over 80 full members (Mexican Americans) and 67 associate members (non-Mexican Americans), and the national chairman for 1972 was Bishop Patrick Flores of San Antonio (Dart 1971c:8). At their second national convention in Los Angeles in October 1971, the PADRES discussed the possibility of creating a "National Chicano Church", a separate Spanish-speaking vicariate in the United States accountable only to Rome, if adequate representation for Hispanic Catholics was not forthcoming in the present ecclesiastical structure (Thrapp 1971b).

The Mexican has experienced a long series of conflicts with Anglo society: military conquest; exploitation of his private property; exploitation of his wage-labor; denial of his right to labor organization for collective bargaining; denial of his rights as a U.S. citizen (the repatriation of the 1930s); denial of his rights to "equal opportunity" in housing, employment, education, and health care; and deprival of his civil rights by police brutality, illegal arrest, exclusion from juries, gerrymandering of political districts, and disfranchizement of his vote (due to literacy, language, property, residence, or citizenship requirements) (cf. Rowan 1968:1-69). The reality of these grievances cannot easily be denied by Anglos who have taken the time to study Mexican American history or to examine the contemporary injustices that are prevalent throughout the Southwest in respect to Hispanic Americans.

It is imperative, therefore, that the Christian Church--both Catholics and Protestants--raise the question of its role in eliminating social injustice, in helping to improve the socio-economic status of Hispanic Americans, and in aiding their structural integration into Anglo American society. The challenge, according to Grebler,

> is to impart a new thrust to the future--to create the conditions in which the Mexican American people can become more active participants in our society, can develop their individual abilities without hindrance,

> and are free to make personal choices with regard to their cultural identity (1970:595).

The tension, of course, is how to balance the Church's *internal* ministry (its pastoral function) with its *external* ministry (its servant function). For many Protestants, the issue narrows down to whether the mission of the Church is "evangelism" and/or "social action", or the problem of balance between these two areas of ministry. Anglo Protestants have had mixed motives and have demonstrated numerous inconsistencies in their ministries among Hispanic Americans, both in terms of pastoral and service goals and functions, both in evangelism and social action.

It is sometimes "overlooked" by many Christians that churches are social institutions which reflect the beliefs, attitudes and behavior of society at large, society itself being the incarnation of *both* good and evil in a matrix of individual and collective confusion and conflict. The ideal of what the Church *ought to be* is often confused with *what it is* in reality. All that has been said about Anglo and Hispanic society so far in this study is also reflected in the various religious subsocieties that comprise parts of the whole. Churches are composed of people from all classes, races and cultures, with each local congregation reflecting these differences in varying degrees. Both individual churches and denominational bodies, however, tend to be stratified along class, race and subcultural lines. The Church is in the process of transition from its present imperfect state toward the biblical ideal of being the incarnate Body of Christ, filled with the Holy Spirit, united in its faith and purity, motivated by love, and sent forth into the world to reconcile alienated men to God and to one another.

The chapters which follow trace the history of Protestant Hispanic denominations and congregations in Southern California, with all of their problems and imperfections which are a reflection of the incongruities of American society in general. Finally, the role of the Church in society is evaluated from the biblical perspective of what the Church *ought to be* in fulfillment of her pastoral, priestly, and prophetic ministry in the world as "the people of God."

PART II

The History of Hispanic Church Development

5.

An Overview of Hispanic Church Development

Two methods of historical analysis have been used in Part II to trace the origin and development of Hispanic churches and missions in Southern California and Los Angeles County. Chapter Five represents a *synchronic* (a horizontal cross-section in time) analysis of the growth history of Hispanic Protestant Church development at specific periods when enough data was available to obtain an overview of total Hispanic Protestant activity in Los Angeles County, or in the city of Los Angeles. Because of the meager historical sources on which to base the horizontal analysis of Hispanic development, it was necessary to usually depend upon one major source of information for each period of time analyzed. However, other sources have been used to clarify, amplify, confirm or contradict the major source of information, in addition to the author's critical evaluation of the total available data. Chapters Six through Ten represent a *diachronic* (a vertical or "through time") analysis of various denominations that have established Spanish-speaking churches and missions from the pioneer period to the present.

ANGLO AMERICANS IN SOUTHERN CALIFORNIA

When California was admitted to the Union in September 1850, Southern California had experienced few changes through American control and settlement. Only three small towns existed in all of Southern California: San Diego, Los Angeles and Santa Barbara. However, smaller settlements were to be found around the old Spanish missions and on some of the large *ranchos* that dominated the economy of Southern California, a region that had a total population of only 6,367 in 1851 (McWilliams 1946:64).

The Cow Counties

For many years the unpopulated Southland was termed the "cow counties" by northern Californians. Between 1849 and 1862, the demand for beef in the northern mining districts and in the rapidly growing towns of San Francisco and Sacramento sent great herds of cattle northward, often more than 25,000 head every year. The Southern California *rancheros* grew rich on the cattle trade and Los Angeles quickly became a frontier boom town with a "hellhole" reputation during the 1850s and 1860s (Nadeau 1960: 41-42).

The cattle market was declining by the summer of 1854 due to the saturation of the northern market by large numbers of cattle and sheep brought into the state from Missouri, Texas, and Mexico. The serious droughts of the early 1860s finally destroyed the cattle trade in Southern California--everywhere dead cattle and horses littered the ground. Many rancheros were forced to sell their holdings at great losses, and others were lost to foreclosure proceedings and for nonpayment of taxes. Much of the remaining land was mortgaged at very high interest rates and was soon lost to all but a few *Californios*. Carey McWilliams, in *Southern California Country* (1948:49-69) and *North From Mexico* (1948:88-94), and Leonard Pitt (1970: esp. 275,282-283,296) have well portrayed "the decline of the Californios" and the conquest of their land by gringo settlers prior to 1890.

Gringos Devour the Land

The population of the small towns in Southern California began to increase as mining declined in the north and the temporary miners returned to their previous agricultural occupations. Some of the newly arrived Anglo Americans who had been farmers in the Midwest and East realized that the large *ranchos* of the *Californios* had great potential for agricultural development, as well as for cattle raising. Greedy Anglos surveyed the land with hungry eyes and began to seek ways to convert the land to agriculture. Thus, according to Nadeau:

> ...the old feudal regime, reaching its Golden Age in the cattle boom of the fifties, found itself under the pressure of the American frontier. The Mexican treaty of 1848 had guaranteed to existing landowners in the conquered territories the continued possession of their holdings. But to the gringo the first question was, Exactly who were the owners and what did they really own? ...To the law-loving American mind the unscrambling of land titles was a first order of business in the new state. Accordingly, Congress provided for a Land Commission to review and determine all claims...

> the commissioners opened hearings at San Francisco and Los Angeles in 1852.
>
> The Land Commission has since been attacked as the origin of injustice against the native Californians.... What hurt the Californians far more was the provision in the Land Acts for government appeal to the courts. With this license lawyers kept the land cases in litigation for years, draining owners of their slim cash reserves, forcing them to borrow money at usurious rates of interest or to convey part of their domain in legal fees in order to defend their rights. Forty percent of the rancho lands in Los Angeles County was pared from its owners to satisfy the expense of litigation. Some, unable to pursue their cases, forfeited their whole domain (1960:46-48).

While the land titles were being contested, American squatters settled on some of the choicest farm land and defended the land with force of arms. Land speculators acquired large tracts of land and subdivided them into smaller plots, which stimulated the rapid development of small towns and farms. Nadeau wrote:

> The American conquest of the land had now begun in earnest. For their part the Californians joined the ancient ranks of the world's dispossessed.... Nor was it litigation alone that attacked the old regime. In 1849 the Americans introduced into California one of their stateside institutions--the property tax. By the early 1850's the tax was being applied heavily upon undeveloped land-holdings for the avowed purpose of forcing sale and subdivision (1960:48).
>
> With this last, miserable struggle the gringo possessed the physical corpus of California. It was accomplished through a combination of Spanish self-delusion and American avarice. It was not a planned campaign; no body of men sat down and agreed, "Now we will take the land from the Californians." The contest was one of individual skirmishes, permitted under American law and excused by the callous American business customs of the day. The gringo had completed his conquest, not by the barbarity of the sword but with the civility of the sheriff's hammer (1960:58).

Agricultural and Commercial Development

The first American town to be founded in Southern California was at El Monte, located near the San Gabriel River, where Phineas Banning established a relay station for his new stage line.

Beginning in 1850, El Monte had been a stopping-off place for wagon trains traveling to Los Angeles on the Santa Fe Trail from Independence, Missouri, or over the northern Mormon Trail through Utah to San Bernardino and Los Angeles. A Mormon colony was established in 1851 at San Bernardino, near El Cajon Pass, when Jefferson Hunt led a party of about 500 Mormon settlers into the valley, where they bought land from the Lugo family. Although most of the Mormons returned to Utah in 1857, San Bernardino became an important transportation center. And it was in 1857 that the Anaheim grape colony was established near the Santa Ana River, in present Orange County, by a group of German farmers from northern California (Hine 1960:19,22-23).

Between 1851 and 1855, Banning established a transportation empire throughout Southern California. In addition to his stage line, Banning's wagon trains, drawn by teams of mules, carried supplies south to Fort Yuma on the Colorado River and north to the mining settlements along the Kern River. The transcontinental Butterfield Stage Line also established a regular line between San Francisco, Los Angeles, San Bernardino, and San Diego. Remi Nadeau developed a lucrative freight hauling business headquartered in Los Angeles and extending to the mining districts along the Kern River and in the Owens Valley, and to the Colorado River in the east. The Cerro Gordo silver mine near Owens Lake provided more than a fourth of the export trade from San Pedro harbor between 1869 and 1874, and Nadeau's mules consummed a large share of the local barley and hay crop (Nadeau 1960:61). In 1869 Banning completed the Los Angeles and San Pedro Railway, the first rail line in Southern California, which provided an important commercial link between those two points. This twenty-one mile connection further stimulated the growth of small farms throughout the region.

By 1870 a land boom came to Southern California as real estate promoters began to sell new land to the flood of Anglo immigrants that came from northern California during 1868 and 1869. Real estate prices in one year jumped 200 percent as investors discovered that the land would yield rich quantities of every known crop, given an adequate supply of water. Barley and corn were the preferred crops in Southern California during these early years because they required little or no irrigation. After 1868, however, the underground water supply of the Los Angeles basin was taped to provide irrigation water for the blossoming farming industry (1960:60-61).

William Wolfskill pioneered the cultivation of orange trees in the Southland in the 1840s, but it was not until the introduction of the Washington naval orange in the early 1870s that the citrus industry was developed. Agricultural development proceeded at a fast pace:

> By the 1870s the landscape was dotted with windmills, their whirling blades creaking a constant song of gringo enterprise. A whole new range of irrigated fruit and vegetable crops was opened, and Los Angeles County land took another jump in value...a new economy had descended upon southern California. A patchwork of fields and orchards had spread across hills that had known only the hoofs of longhorn cattle. Whole communities--Compton, Santa Ana, Riverside--sprang to life as local marketing centers. Several were founded by colonies of farmers who combined to dig an irrigation canal from a nearby river (1960:61-62).

In 1873 the Southern Pacific Railway began laying rail lines throughout Los Angeles County in anticipation of completing the main line between San Francisco to Los Angeles. Nadeau commented:

> Wherever their iron advanced whole new towns--from San Fernando in the north to Pomona in the east--burst into life. With their farm boom recharged with railroad fever, the new Los Angeles boosters were riding high. Throughout the county the birth of towns and the planting of new crops had brought an unprecedented flow of coin. Cultivated acreage quadrupled within six years (1960: 67-69).

There were some setbacks, however. In 1875, financial panic swept Southern California as several banks failed and businesses went bankrupt. The population of Los Angeles declined from 16,000 in 1876 to 11,000 by 1880. The Board of Trade, established in 1873 under the leadership of Robert Widney and John Downey, ceased to exist.

But the tide of prosperity turned after 1876 when the Southern Pacific Railroad completed its line between San Francisco and Los Angeles and linked the Southland with the transcontinental railway. In 1881, a second rail line to the Pacific was completed when the Southern Pacific and the Santa Fe met at Deming, New Mexico. These rail links opened midwestern and eastern states as a market for Southern California agricultural products and provided the needed transportation to attract people from the East. While Los Angeles boosters launched an extensive advertising campaign to attract eastern farmers and investors, the Southern Pacific Railroad provided "emigrant trains" to stimulate western migration.

In 1885 the Santa Fe completed its own transcontinental line to the Pacific Coast through El Cajon Pass and into Los Angeles over the Los Angeles and San Gabriel Railway. A competitive rate war began between the Southern Pacific and the Santa Fe in

1886 and fares dropped from $100 to $5 for a first-class ticket between Los Angeles and Kansas City, Missouri. Although the fares increased again, for nearly a year the rate was under $25. The hordes of new arrivals to Southern California were predominantly middle-aged couples from the Midwest with money to invest. Real estate promotion began in earnest as huge tracts of land were subdivided and sold as individual lots (Figure 21).

By the middle of 1887 prices had increased 400 to 500 percent in a single year and "the Great Boom" reached from Santa Barbara to San Diego. Whole towns emerged from the planner's drawing board--Burbank, Fullerton, Whittier, Monrovia, Hollywood, Azusa--more than a hundred towns and thousands of orchards and farms emerged between 1880-1888. However, the great land boom of 1886-1887 collapsed toward the end of 1887 when local banks began tightening their loan policies and refused to accept land as security unless it was located in a well established community.

> With speculative capital cut off, the promoters found themselves overextended. Prices sagged, then tumbled. By April 1888, everybody was scrambling to get out of the way. Fortunes and would-be fortunes were swept away. With payments defaulted, whole townsites reverted to the original owners (Nadeau 1960:80).

By tightening credit policies and then easing controls a few months later, the banks averted a serious financial disaster. However, newcomers to Los Angeles returned home at the rate of over a thousand per month. From a population of 80,000 in 1887, Los Angeles declined to 50,400 by 1890, but this was still five times the pre-boom population.

At the turn of the century, the population of Los Angeles totaled more than 102,000 and the county area 170,300. The discovery of vast oil deposits within the city limits of Los Angeles in 1892 stimulated migration and new investments. By 1897, the city oil fields were producing 1.3 million barrels per year. Major oil fields were discovered at Santa Fe Springs in 1919 and at Signal Hill in 1921.

Between 1900 and 1910, Los Angeles constructed the Owens Valle Aqueduct to provide the growing Southland with adequate water for continued agricultural and commercial development. Tourism broug thousands of new residents to Southern California from the East, and the construction industry stretched to keep pace with the ar rapid expansion. The Los Angeles Chamber of Commerce, the Calif Fruit Growers Exchange, the railroads, and other large investors the California "dream" all contributed significantly to the trem dous population growth of Southern California.

Figure 21

RAILROAD FEVER AND LAND SPECULATION
SOUTHERN CALIFORNIA, 1887

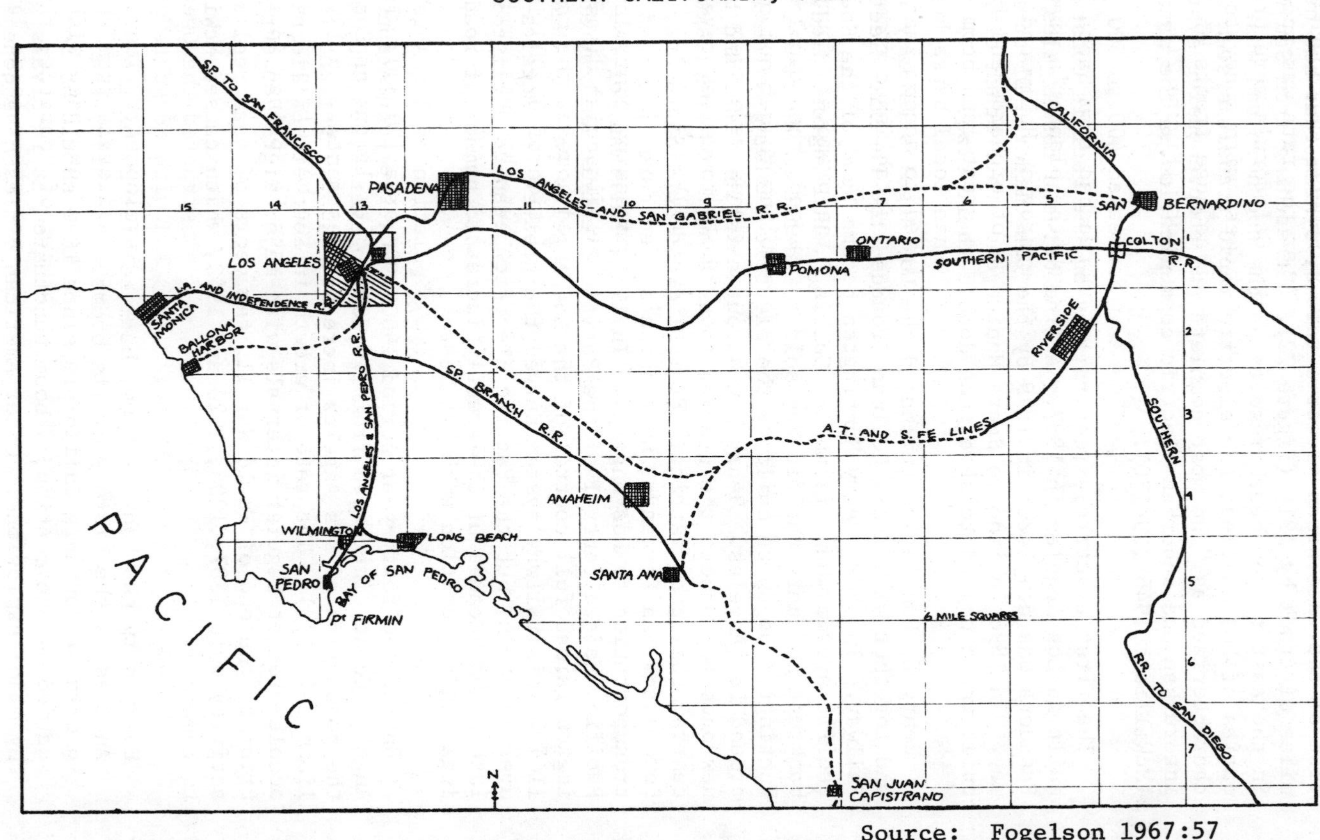

Source: Fogelson 1967:57

An important feature of Southland development was the construction of the interurban electric railway system that had over 1,000 miles of track by 1915 (Figure 22). Stretching from San Bernardin in the east to the beach resorts on the southern and western boundaries of Los Angeles, the electric rapid transit system was characterized as "the most complete and comprehensive system of interurban and suburban electric communication in the nation" (McWilliams 1946:129-130).

The first electric street railway on the Pacific Coast was built in Los Angeles in 1887. A line between Los Angeles and Pasadena was completed in 1895 by the Consolidated Electric Railway. In 1896, a line to Santa Monica and other beach cities was built which helped to more than double their size.

Henry E. Huntington purchased the Los Angeles Railway in 1898, and together with Isais Hellman, founded the Pacific Electric Railway. In 1900, Henry Huntington became head of the Southern Pacific system when his uncle, Collis P. Huntington, died. But the bankrupt Southern Pacific was sold to Edward H. Harriman, and Henry Huntington began to build up the electric railway system in and around Los Angeles. Henry bought out existing lines and built new ones to connect the growing towns around Los Angeles with the central business district. From Riverside and Santa Ana, from Pomona and San Fernando, Huntington's "red cars" provided rapid transportation to Los Angeles. In 1911, Harriman, of the Southern Pacific, gained control of the Pacific Electric Railway and Huntington gained full control of the Los Angeles Railway (Nadeau 1960 116). This railway system served the greater Los Angeles area for over 50 years, but the Pacific Electric began to decline in the late 1940s because of the greatly increased number of road crossings and competition with bus lines.

During the forty-year period 1900-1940, the population of Los Angeles County increased from 170,300 to over 2,285,000, while the population of Los Angeles increased 1,535.7 percent (McWilliams 1946:113). The rate of growth in Southern California has accelerated at regular intervals with major migration surges. Prior to the end of World War II, the years of peak real estate activity were 1887, 1906, 1923 and 1943, which caused McWilliams to comment:

> Every city has had its boom, but the history of Los Angeles is the history of its booms. Actually, the growth of Southern California since 1870 should be regarded as one continuous boom punctuated at intervals by major explosions. Other American cities have gone through a boom phase and then entered upon a period of normal growth. But Los Angeles has always been a boom town, chronically unable to consolidate its gains or to integrate its new population (1946:114).

Figure 22

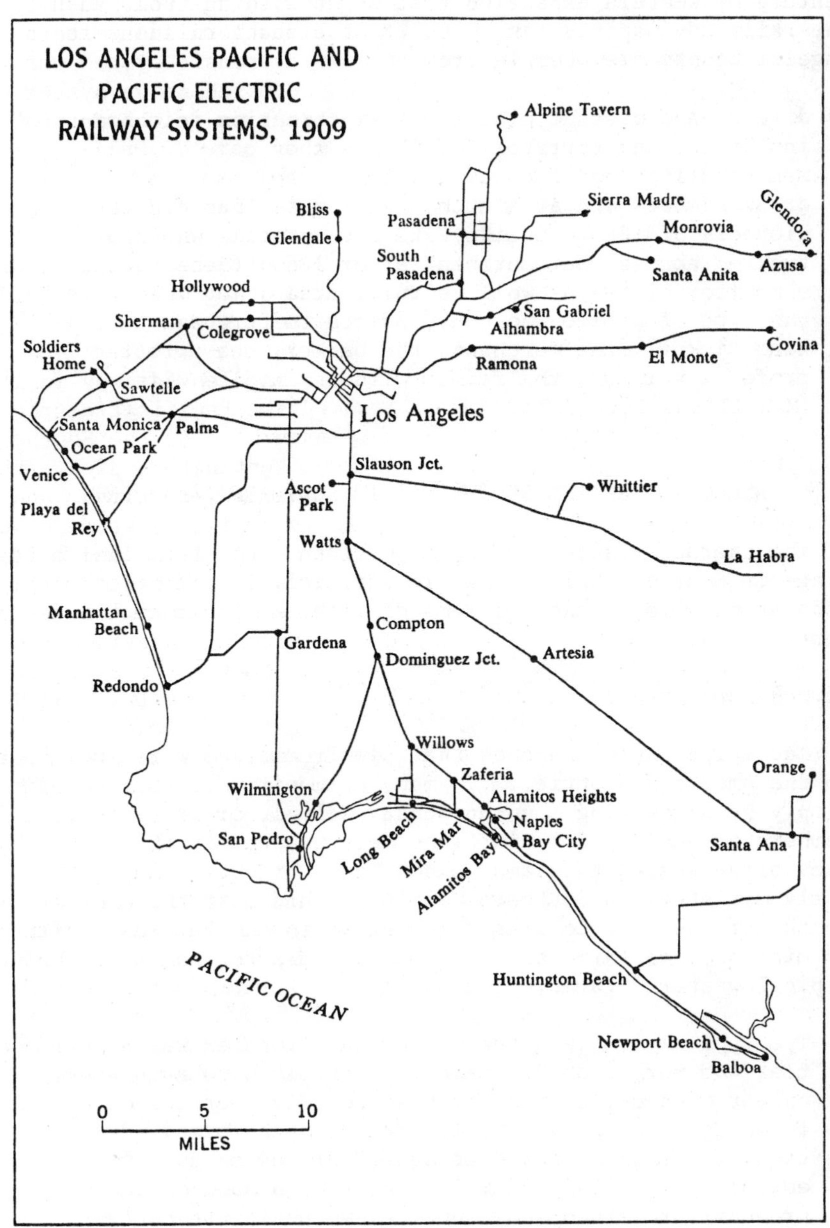

Source: Fogelson 1967:93

The land booms of Southern California have attracted a different type of settler than did most settlements during the century of western expansion that began with the Gold Rush. The railroad-inspired land booms that brought millions to Los Angeles County drew people from

> diverse and distant places rather than from neighboring states and territories. Since they came in Pullman cars instead of covered wagons, they came in great numbers and at a much faster rate than did the pioneers of 1849. Unlike Pike County folks who had trekked across the continent after 1850, these people came from cities as well as rural areas, and they were the type of people who could afford to purchase a railroad ticket: the merchant, the banker, the uprooted professional man, the farmer with an invalid wife (McWilliams 1946:127).

ANGLO PROTESTANT BEGINNINGS IN SOUTHERN CALIFORNIA

The characteristics of Anglo American Protestant church beginnings in Southern California are extremely important in order to understand some of the problems of later Hispanic church development.

Church Development

The early Anglo churches that slowly emerged were indigenous to the American frontier. In many communities a church began simply by organizing a union Sunday school, or if sufficient members of several denominations were present in the community, they often shared the same school house or social hall. Most early ministers in Southern California had left the Midwest, the South, or the East to make a new start in the Far West, either as miners or as farmers. William Warren Sweet has described the typical western "farmer-preacher":

> Tye typical Baptist preacher on the frontier was a settler who worked on his land five or six days each week, except when called upon to hold weekday meetings or funerals. He was generally without much formal education, for there was a deep-seated prejudice against educated and salaried ministers, though some of the preachers received some support, which in the early days was paid in kind (1950;217).

Baptist churches in Southern California were usually formed through the initiative of a licensed or ordained farmer-preacher after settling in a new community. In this period of western expansion, the Baptists and Methodists both had about the same number of church members and the Presbyterians had half again as many. Whereas the Baptist preacher simply came with the people as part of the western migration, the Methodist preachers were usually sent west to form churches, and the Presbyterian ministers were called to serve a church by a previously formed congregation. A considerable number of early Presbyterian ministers were also school teachers in the small western towns and a large proportion of their time was taken up with teaching responsibilities (Sweet 1950:214-215).

As the Anglo population of Southern California began to grow after 1850, small denominational churches grew out of union services in the small towns. During the late 1860s and the decade of the 1870s, as more churches were planted in new settlements and the size of denominational groups increased along with the rapidly growing population, regional and state associations of churches were formed (see chapters 6-10).

Unstable Beginnings

Although a great many small churches came into existence in Southern California between 1850 and 1900, many did not continue for more than a few years. Ivan Ellis has suggested some reasons for the disbanding of many Baptist churches in this pioneer period. Some local congregations ceased because the pastor migrated along with many of the townspeople to other areas. The migratory nature of the early population was a strong factor in the disappearance of many churches, along with a lack of adequate pastoral leadership, or for that matter, a lack of any real leadership. Occasionally several small churches united to form a more stable congregation. This pioneer period was also characterized by denominational competition as the size of the communities increased. Whereas a few people with previous membership in a specific denominational body might meet together temporarily with another group, a new congregation would be formed when sufficient numbers of their own denomination migrated to the area. Occasionally the entire population of a small community relocated in another area (1938:163-165).

However, the disbanding of a majority of Baptist churches was the result of community stagnation, according to Ellis. Over half the churches that disbanded between 1850 and 1938, were located in villages that never grew into towns or had such slow growth that the church folded. Some towns had too many churches for the size of the population, so there was a strong tendency either to unite with another local church of the same denomination or to dissolve the congregation and join another church. Sometimes an entire community slowly ceased to exist as the population moved to an area with a greater potential for agricultural development (1938:165).

Growth in Stability

Problems experienced by Baptist churches during the pioneer period were avoided during later years, according to Ellis. Competition with other denominations in Los Angeles County was eliminated when a comity council was organized about 1913. Transient communities were cared for by temporary missions rather than by permanent churches. The quality of the pastoral leadership was improved. New churches were seldom established without first raising the question of the potential for growth in the new area. Denominational expansion in a new area was discussed with state and city mission boards and the comity council. By 1938, new churches began with greater numerical strength and more adequate facilities. With more attention given to developing a well-rounded church life, churches failed less frequently than before (1938:165-166).

Anglo Church Growth

Anglo Protestant church growth in Southern California, in all periods of its development, has mainly resulted from the relocation of church members from other parts of the United States to the local area. Since the land boom of the 1880s, Southern California has experienced one of the highest rates of population increase in the nation. The rapid growth of Anglo Protestant churches and denominations in the Los Angeles area is well known, but the fact that rapid increases in membership were due to *relocation growth* is seldom mentioned. Increases in Anglo Protestant membership because of *conversion growth* has often been a minimal factor, although a high percentage of the children of church members have also joined their parents' church (*i.e., biological growth*).

Anglo Attitudes

The attitudes of Anglo American settlers who migrated to Southern California in the pioneer period need to be seriously evaluated because this will help us understand later problems in the period of Hispanic church growth. When Protestant churches were established in Los Angeles and in the surrounding countryside, the type of religious expression usually found was that of the Midwestern farmer. And his church was a transplanted institution in the same way that whole communities were transplanted from Iowa, Illinois, or Indiana.

The majority of Anglo American settlers in Southern California were strongly *biased* and *discriminatory* against Indians, Mexicans Asians and Catholics (Bean 1968:162-171). The pioneer settlers cared little for the problems of the indigenous Indian population that struggled to survive in Southern California. The many years of previous conflict between Indians and frontiersmen had hardened Anglos to the plight of the Indian. The Indian population of California declined from 100,000 in 1846 to a mere 16,000 by 1900 (Bean 1968:169). The main causes for rapid decrease in the Indian population were disease, violence and general oppression of the Indian by Anglos (Wollenburg 1970:1-42).

Americans were also *strongly anti-Mexican* because of bitterness and hatred that developed during the period of the Mexican War, and because of competition from Sonoran miners who dominated the southern Sierra Nevada gold fields (McWilliams 1968:127-137). According to McWilliams, racial and ethnic stereotypes were dominant in this period: "To the early American settlers, the Mexicans were lazy, shiftless, jealous, cowardly, bigoted, superstitious, backward, and immoral"(1968:99). The strong Protestant orientation of the majority of Anglo settlers also made them characteristically *anti-Catholic* (Moore 1970:36; McWilliams 1968: 100-103). Strong hostilities existed between Northerners and Southerners during the decade of the 1860s as well. Anglos in California also discriminated against the large Chinese population who worked the mines, built the railroads, or labored in the fields (Wollenburg 1970:61-100).

Anglo settlers were highly motivated by the concept of "manifest destiny" in the period of westward expansion. Their strong *individualism* and *ethnocentricity* hindered their relationships with minority groups on the American frontier. Their attitude of Anglo-Saxon *racial superiority* caused them to be intolerant of racial and ethnic minority groups (Pomeroy 1965:277-280). Individualism, economic self-interest, and intolerance, then, characterized Anglo Americans during the period of western migration. The attitude of most Anglo American settlers could perhaps best be characterized by the phrase "God helps those who help themselves".

HISPANIC PROTESTANT ORIGINS IN SOUTHERN CALIFORNIA: 1890s

One of the earliest known Protestant efforts to establish an organized ministry among the Spanish-speaking people in Southern California was the creation of the *California Spanish Missionary Society*. This interdenominational society was organized in 1897 through the vision and determination of Alden B. Case of Pomona. Case became the society's first "general missionary" and wrote a pamphlet in June 1897, entitled *Foreign Work at Home for Our Spanish Neighbor*, in which he and his supporters stated their case for developing evangelistic work among the Hispanic population.

The Condition of the Hispanic Population

Recalling the past history of Spanish California, Case wrote about the inundation of the original *Californios* by the heavy migration of American settlers:

> These ancient possessors of the soil have seen the Protestant English-speaking race come in upon them in wave after wave of immigration until they themselves have been well nigh submerged by the flood. Today we call them foreigners and in speaking of efforts for their welfare put it under the head "foreign work at home" (1897:5).

With few exceptions, according to Case, most Spanish-speaking Californians were reduced to circumstances of poverty or extreme distress. The Hispanic population resented the treatment they received from Anglos and drew closer together as a people. Case visited many Mexican homes and found them to be "very humble", and he observed many cases of protracted illness accompanied by extreme poverty. The Mexicans assisted one another with their scant provisions while the well-to-do American neighbors did little to help. Although Case felt that the problem of poverty among the Spanish-speaking population was a major concern, he considered other afflictions of equal importance: ignorance, immorality, jealousy, drunkeness, and numerous fatalities that resulted from frequent fighting (1897:5-6).

The superintendent of Congregational Sunday school work in Southern California, H. P. Case, probably a relative of Alden Case, estimated that the Spanish-speaking population of California was about 50,000 persons and that they were largely "un-Americanized" and unassimilated to "American life". Three reasons are given for this "undesirable" condition. First, the Mexicans are a "conquered race" as a result of the U.S. military invasion of Mexico and the annexation of the Southwestern territories to the United States, which was never fully accepted by the Mexican people.

Secondly, the *Californios* are an "outwitted people" because deceitful Anglo businessmen and land promoters were able to take advantage of the Spanish-speaking land owners due to the languag[e] barrier and the *Californios'* lack of knowledge of American laws. In twenty-five years, the *Californios* passed from being the richest land owners in California to being "tenants at will", a condition that is mainly attributed to the legal trickery and manipulation of greedy Anglo Americans who coveted the vast tracts of land that formed the family-owned *ranchos* of Southern California (See Leonard Pitt, *The Decline of the Californios*, 1970:104-119,282-283).

The third reason given by H. P. Case is that the Spanish-speaking population constitutes a religiously separate people because they are Roman Catholics who are now residing in a dominantly Anglo American Protestant society. The *Californios* considered the action of the California State Legislature on the issue of the separation of church and state to be "an effort of their conquerors to suppress their religion," especially the decision to tax church property. Consequently, many Spanish-speaking people were "hostile toward even well-meant efforts to acquaint them with the simple Gospel" (Case 1897:6).

Whereas the Mexicans had received fairly adequate religious care during the period of Spanish Missions, according to Alden Case, the Roman Catholic Church severely neglected the Spanish-speaking population in the 1890s in preference to the English-speaking population, as did the Protestants. The Spanish language was only rarely employed in the Catholic services and many Mexicans felt that the Church cared little for their spiritual needs. Consequently, attendance at Mass was very low (1897:6-7).

Case was equally appalled by the lack of missionary concern on the part of the pioneer Protestant settlers of Southern California toward the Hispanic population:

> Protestants of all denominations have been so busy providing for their own churches, homes and work that year after year and decade after decade have gone by without our having yet even seriously planned to give the Gospel to those among whom we have come (1897:7).

However, some American pastors and laymen felt strong compassion for the plight of the Mexicans and sought to do something to alleviate their physical and spiritual distress. Apparently it was Case's concern for the Mexicans, along with the interest of these ministers and laymen, that led to the formation of the California Spanish Missionary Society. No other missionary society was active in Southern California, with the exception of a small Presbyterian work, and Case considered the area to be extremely neglected and offering many opportunities for Christian ministry. "It seems incredible," said Case, "that the Protestant Christians of California have attempted so little for the evangelism of this people right at our doors" (1897:6-7).

Early Evangelistic Efforts by Alden Case

Case had been a missionary for eleven years in Mexico under the American Board of Commissioners for Foreign Missions prior to his coming to Southern California in 1896, primarily due to the illness of his wife. Because of his knowledge of the language and his concern for the spiritual welfare of the large

Spanish-speaking population, Case immediately began to "evangelize" among the scattered Mexican colonies. In one year of ministry, regular services were established at five locations: Redlands, Chino, Santa Ana, San Bernardino and Piru, with occasional services at other points. At some locations, such as Redlands, Case was aided by the Epworth League of the Methodist Church (1897:9).

Prior to the formation of the California Spanish Missionary Society, Case had no regular financial support, although he tried to support himself by teaching the Spanish language. However, this severely restricted his ministry among the Spanish-speaking people. When time permitted, Case traveled all over Southern California at the invitation of many churches of various denominations and conducted evangelistic services in Spanish. A "stereopticon" was often used to attract people to the services that were usually held on Saturday evenings and Sunday mornings (1897:9).

The pastor of the Methodist Episcopal Church at Piru invited Case to conduct a series of eight evening meetings for the Spanish-speaking people, which resulted in the permanent establishment of a Mexican mission. At least twenty-one conversions were recorded during the week of meetings and all of the new converts requested church membership. This experience apparently revolutionized the Piru Methodist Church by bringing them to realize "what an unusual field of opportunity [lay] at their door to minister to their Mexican neighbors." Several church members, including the pastor, began studying Spanish so that they could more effectively minister to their Spanish-speaking community (1879:11).

Case encouraged many pastors and laymen in churches throughout Southern California to study Spanish and to initiate ministries among the Mexican population. At least fifteen people were engaged in language study in 1897, according to Case, among whom were pastors and their wives, Sunday school teachers, and "singers". Case strongly encouraged laymen to actively participate in Hispanic ministries (1897:12).

The California Spanish Missionary Society

The California Spanish Missionary Society began as an informal organization in January 1897 but steps were underway in June of that year to establish it on a more permanent basis. A Board of Directors was formed representing the various Protestant denominations that were interested in ministry to Spanish-speaking people. The officers of the society served without salary, except for Case who received about thirty dollars per month as general missionary (1897:14). According to LeShana, several

Quakers from Whittier helped to support the society and served on the board in 1898 (1969:131). It is not known how long this society was in existence or what its success was in terms of establishing permanent Spanish language churches. [However, Case published his memoirs in 1917 entitled *Thirty Years Among the Mexicans: In Peace and Revolution*, which undoubtedly contains much valuable information up to 1917, but a copy of this book could not be located by this author.]

The primary aim of the California Spanish Missionary Society was "to push forward along the lines undertaken by Reverend Case as soon as additional workers and means of support could be secured." There were many opportunities for ministry among the Spanish-speaking population but not enough workers to initiate ministries among them. Rather than encouraging individual churches to begin Spanish worship services and Sunday schools, the Society encouraged all of the Anglo churches in a town to establish a united effort (Case 1897:12).

The preferred strategy of ministry was for one church to be given the specific responsibility of initiating Hispanic work with the aid and encouragement of other churches. This work was to be coordinated by a local evangelistic committee under the supervision of the general missionary of the Society. The specific responsibility for developing a local Spanish-speaking congregation was given to a Mexican preacher, who was expected to associate himself with the church sponsoring the Mexican mission in that town.

Another aim of the Society was to distribute evangelical literature freely among the Spanish-speaking population and to place a Bible in every Mexican home. While the spiritual welfare of the Mexican people was the primary concern, additional measures were also sought to promote ministry to the physical, social, and educational needs of the Hispanic community (1897:12).

Other Early Hispanic Ministries

Robert Grant of Los Angeles was also engaged in evangelistic work among the Mexican population in various neighborhoods in the city. Grant probably was a printer by trade since Case states that he was active in publishing evangelical literature for Spanish work, not only in California, but also sending literature to Mexico and Central and South America as well (1897:10).

Miss E. L. Schultz, who had recently returned from Peru where she was a missionary with the Methodist Episcopal Church, opened a day school for Spanish-speaking children at San Bernardino in 1896-1897. She had an active visitation ministry among the Spanish-speaking families of that city, but she had no assured financial support from any group. In regard to children's work, Case felt that a great need existed for a Protestant orphanage for Mexican children and that the best location for this work was in Santa Ana (Case 1897:12).

Although various attempts had been made at different times by English-speaking churches to minister to the Mexican people in the local communities, these attempts were often frustrated due to the lack of capable leaders who could minister effectively in Spanish. Consequently, wrote Case, "these efforts, while praiseworthy, have been fluctuating and with little permanent results." Case notes one exception, however:

> Some seven years ago,...Rev. A. M. Merwin, a returned missionary from South America, commenced work among the Spanish speaking people of Los Angeles and vicinity. He has now charge of three churches, one in the city, one in San Gabriel and another at Azusa. About 200 Mexicans have been received into these churches. In several other places occasional or regular meetings are conducted by Mr. Merwin and his assistants (1897:10).

This earlier ministry by Merwin represents the first recorded Spanish-speaking ministry by Protestants in the Los Angeles area, and the Presbyterians have the distinction of being the first denomination to begin such a ministry.

THE RELIGIOUS DIMENSION IN 1914

The next historical insight into the development of Hispanic ministry among the Spanish-speaking population in Los Angeles is given by William W. McEuen in a Master's Thesis entitled "A Survey of the Mexicans in Los Angeles" (1914). However, McEuen's main interest was the socioeconomic status of the Mexican population.

The Mexican population in the city of Los Angeles increased from 8,917 as recorded by the 1910 census to between 20,000-40,000 people in 1914 (McEuen 1914:4). The majority of the Mexican male population was classified as "lower-class peon laborers McEuen estimated that in addition to the number of Mexicans living within the city of Los Angeles, there were perhaps as many more who passed through the city on their way to one job or another throughout Southern California, especially during harves season (1914:5). It is noted, however, that the 1920 census gives the total "Foreign-Born White Mexican Population" of Los Angeles County as 33,644 (Young 1930:46). However, this figure does not include native-born Americans of Mexican descent or "non-white" Mexican immigrants. Another source estimated the

Mexican population of Los Angeles to be 20,000-30,000 in 1913 (*El Mexicano* Vol. 1, No. 7:4).

Socioeconomic Overview

Because of the revolutionary conditions in Mexico, many thousands of immigrants had arrived in Los Angeles and were living in overcrowded "shack" towns, which were classified by authorities as "dilapidated, tumbled-down, and unsanitary" (McEuen 1914:33). About fifty percent of the Mexican population were men, which included between 12,000-18,000 in the labor market. Most were common laborers who were "employed largely by the railroads and street car companies in the Maintenance-of-way Department, by the brickyards, gas company, construction companies and other employers of common labor" (1914:23). However, "in the summer-time whole families are to be found working in the walnut orchards and in the fruit drying and canning industries in and around Los Angeles"(1914:26).

McEuen confirms McWilliams' observation concerning the pattern of Mexican housing and employment and the realism of Anglo prejudice and discrimination:

> The Mexicans form a large element in the labor supply of Los Angeles and meet the need for low-class unskilled labor satisfactorily without encroaching to any great extent upon the fields of employment occupied by Americans and other high-class labor. They compete almost entirely with the low-class foreign labor such as the Chinese, the Japanese and the Hindu, to which they are generally preferred (1914:31).
>
> All other races [predominantly the Anglos] meet the Mexicans with an attitude of contempt and scorn and they are generally regarded as the most degraded race in the city. The Mexicans respond to this attitude with one of defiance, pride, hate and extreme dislike. They are clannish and exclusive and marriage with other races is rare. Consequently the spread of American customs among them is very slow and their amalgamation and assimilation does not progress rapidly (1914:36).

Hispanic Churches and Missions

Whereas the majority of Mexicans in the city of Los Angeles in 1914 were classified as nominal Catholics, very few of them "were vitally interested in their religion", according to McEuen. Organized Protestant efforts among the Spanish-speaking people in Los Angeles were just beginning. McEuen located six Mexican churches and five missions sponsored by various denominational groups: Adventists (1), Baptist (4), Congregational (1), Methodist Episcopal (1), Methodist Episcopal, South (1), Nazarene (1), and Presbyterian (2). In addition, there were three missions that were either independent of denominational support or were operated as interdenominational ministries: the Spanish Apostolic Faith Mission, the Sonora Union Gospel Mission, and the Star of Bethlehem Mission. The size of the Protestant community among the Spanish-speaking population was estimated by McEuen to be (1914:38a,94-95):

	No. of Members	No. of Adherents	No. of churches or missions
Adventist	--	--	1
Baptist (Northern)	80	550	4
Congregational	30	50	1
Methodist Episcopal	70	90	1
Methodist Episc.(South)	--	--	1
Nazarene	60	150	1
Presbyterian	200	500	2
Others	--	--	3
Totals:	440	1,340	14

However, since none of the statistics on membership and adherents are given for the Methodist Episcopal Church (South), Pentecostal (Spanish Apostolic Faith Mission), Seventh-Day Adventist, or independent ministries (Sonora Union Gospel Mission and Star of Bethlehem Mission), it seems likely that the total Hispanic Protestant communicant membership could be as high as 550, with about 1,650 adherents. According to McEuen's estimate, the ratio of communicants to adherents (community) is about 1:3 (440 x 3 = 1,320), which is the ratio used here to make the larger projection (550 x 3 = 1,650). Using the median population estimate given by McEuen (30,000), the Hispanic Protestant community was about 5.5 percent of the total Hispanic population.

Comity Council

The superintendents of the Baptist, Congregational, Methodist Episcopal and Presbyterian denominations, who were in charge of ministry to Spanish-speaking people, had by 1914 established a "comity policy" whereby they agreed not to enter neighborhoods occupied by another denomination. Each denomination, therefore, was responsible for a specific area of the city where the Mexican people were concentrated. This comity agreement was an attempt to develop a more efficient ministry by eliminating competition and duplication of efforts. Evidently a fairly harmonious relationship existed between the various Protestant churches involved in ministry to Spanish-speaking people (McEuen 1914:95).

Industrial Schools and Social Work

In addition to the regular church and evangelistic work conducted by Protestant denominations, three industrial schools for Mexican children and young people were also established. The Presbyterians founded the Forsythe School for Mexican girls in 1884. The Methodist Episcopal Church established the Francis DePauw School in 1900, also for Mexican girls, which was under the supervision of the Women's Home Mission Society. A few years later, the Methodists established the Spanish-American Industrial School for Boys (1913) in the city of Gardena. In addition to these three institutions, the Northern Baptists maintained a kindergarten in the Mexican settlement on Fickett Street and also conducted sewing classes for girls at both the Fickett Street colony and the East First Street colony (1914:95-98).

Other organizations that had work among the Mexican population were: the Christian Mission and Industrial Association, the Volunteers of America, the Salvation Army, St. Vincent de Paul Society, the Associated Charities and County Charities, the Fellowship Church and the Spanish American Aid Association. These organizations were engaged in relief and charitable work among the Mexican population (1914:98-99).

Protestant Publications

McEuen reported that the Protestant churches distributed large quantities of Gospel tracts and other evangelical literature among the Spanish-speaking population. The Methodists published a small bi-monthly magazine known as *El Mexicano*, which was devoted to the work of the Methodist Church among the Mexican population. The Presbyterians occasionally published a similar paper, but it had been discontinued by 1914 (1914:93-94).

HISPANIC ADVANCE IN LOS ANGELES AND THE SOUTHWEST: 1921-1925

Writing in the *Annals of the American Academy of Political and Social Science*, the Reverend G. Bromiley Oxnam, pastor of the Church of All Nations (Methodist Episcopal) in Los Angeles, gives the results of his study of Mexicans in Los Angeles in 1921 which was sponsored by the Interchurch World Movement. Oxnam estimated the size of the Mexican population in the city at 30,000 (1921:130) and the size of the Hispanic Protestant community at between 10,000 to 15,000, or consisting of about 3,000 Mexican families (1921:132).

However, Oxnam's population estimate is obviously incorrect for the same reasons mentioned previously in the critique of census figures in McEuen's study. Although the number of "Foreign-born White Mexicans" in Los Angeles County in 1920 was reported as 33,644 (Young 1930:46), it seems reasonable to assume that the total "Mexican" population (both native Americans of Mexican descent and Mexican immigrants) was about 70,000. Thus, the Spanish-speaking population within the city of Los Angeles was probably between 45,000-50,000 in 1920 (*The Latin American* 1918:4).

It is highly unlikely that the Hispanic Protestant community exceeded five percent of the total "Mexican" population, either in the city of Los Angeles or in the county area in 1920. Oxnam's estimate of thirty to fifty percent is obviously absurd. No doubt the proportionate size of the Protestant community declined between 1920 and 1930 due to the rapid increase in the Mexican population which resulted from heavy immigration.

There was, nevertheless, a determined Protestant effort in Los Angeles directed toward the Mexican population. According to Oxnam, Protestant denominations invested more than $350,000 in property, buildings, and assorted equipment to carry on both a religious and social ministry. An additional $260,000 had been raised by the Protestant churches and was designated for the construction of new buildings for ministry to Mexican people. Protestant forces employed sixty-three social workers and directed the activities of several hundred additional volunteer workers (1921:132).

Oxnam refers to the comity council in Los Angeles, mentioned earlier by McEuen, which was established to eliminate the duplication of ministries among the Spanish-speaking people. The mainline denominations were building and directing thoroughly equipped community centers, or settlement houses, in addition to the construction of churches for Spanish-speaking people. The challenge before the organized religious forces working among the Mexican population of Los Angeles was outlined by Oxnam:

> The Churches are organizing to remove the intolerable housing conditions, the menace of adult illiteracy, the inroads of disease and the abnormal poverty situation. Recognizing the close relation of wage scales to these conditions, the churches are likewise concerning themselves with this factor. They frankly face the fact that 80% of the Mexicans have virtually refused to become American citizens and have come to the conclusion that the anti-social conditions prevailing are a major cause of this refusal (1921:132).

Oxnam proposed that the churches accept this challenge and establish a long-range program that would seek to remove the causes of "anti-social forces" and to create social forces that would lead to a higher standard of living for the Mexicans.

The extent of Protestant work among the Spanish-speaking population of the Southwest, according to Rodney W. Roundy, writing in the *Missionary Review of the World* in May 1921, was estimated to include at least 300 Mexican churches, with a communicant membership of approximately 12,000 and an even larger Sunday school membership. The number of those engaged in ministry to Spanish-speaking people in the Southwest totaled over 250 ministers and Christian workers. There were 157 mission school teachers who served as an extension of the ministry of Protestant Mexican churches (1921:366).

According to Roundy, the "Christianization of the Mexican" requires interdenominational cooperation and planning. He encouraged support of "the Permanent Interdenominational Council for Work among Spanish-speaking People in the Southwest," which illustrated the type of cooperation among denominations that he felt ministry to Spanish-speaking people required. Apparently a number of interdenominational projects were underway in May 1921:

> An interdenominational training school for ministers and social workers, an interdenominational paper in the Spanish language, an increasing amount of interdenominational oversight and strategy, working rules of comity covering the whole field and enlisting the allegiance of all concerned are either actively projected or already realized (Roundy 1921:367).

This type of Christian cooperation also appeared in other areas of service to Spanish-speaking people in Puerto Rico, Cuba, the West Indies, Mexico, and Central and South America.

Evidently the extent of Protestant ministry to Spanish-speaking people in the Southwest was subject to wide regional variation. For example, the development of missions among Spanish-speaking people in Texas apparently developed at a much slower rate than did the work in Southern California in the early 1920s. J. M. Carroll, in *History of Texas Baptists*, makes the following comment:

> The work of evangelizing foreigners in Texas has always been a difficult problem.... A very few [workers] have learned to speak Spanish but so far as we know it was not learned with a definite purpose of preaching to Texas Mexicans. *Not one Texas preacher of our denomination has ever gone to any school in order to learn any*

> *foreign language for the purpose of preaching in that language here in Texas.* All the preaching we have ever had among the Texas foreigners who preach to them in their own language have been some of their own people or an occasional return foreign missionary. This significant fact probably accounts in a great measure for our limited success in the work among foreign speaking people in our state (Carroll 1923:586-587; italics mine).

Vernon McCombs, superintendent of the Latin American Mission of the Methodist Episcopal Church for the Southern California-Arizona Conference, in *From Over the Border* (1925), distinguished five religious classes among the Mexican population: The Roman Catholics, the Positivsts or Free Thinkers, the Evangelicals or Protestants, the Modern Fanatics and the Atheistic *Socialistas*. The distinctions between these five classes varied according to locality, the length of residence in the United States, and the socioeconomic status of the immigrant (1925:128).

Roman Catholics composed approximately sixty percent of the Mexican population "made up for the most part of the women, the aged, the ignorant peons, and the old patrician families who have thought they had much to gain in business and social standing by at least nominal adherence to the old established church" (1925:128). Evidently, a large number of Roman Catholics were only nominal adherents to the Church and attendance at Mass was very infrequent, especially by men (1925:128).

The Positivists or Free Thinkers made up about ten percent of the Spanish-speaking population, especially among the middle and upper class immigrants who were well educated. During their course of study in Mexico, many of the better educated Mexicans had been influenced by modern French philosophy (1925:129).

The Evangelicals or Protestants constituted approximately ten percent of the Mexican population, with many from the middle class and quite a number were young people. [This estimate is obviously high; cf. Chapter 2, pp. 34-35.] A considerable number of Evangelicals in the Los Angeles area in 1925 received the Gospel in Mexico. A growing number of young leaders in Evangelical churches were products of Protestant missions and mission schools (1925:129).

Approximately ten percent of the Mexican population was classified as "various fanatical and devisive sects". This classification included Pentecostal groups, New Thought followers, Mormons, Spiritualists, Russelites, Christian Scientists, "Holy Rollers", various members of "Faith Missions", *Independientes*, and other extremists groups. McCombs accuses these groups of being "unscrupulous" and causing the disintegration of some evangelical groups, at least temporarily; they were strongly proselytic also. Evidently McCombs classified Seventh-Day Adventists with the "evangelical churches" since he stated: "At times the Seventh Day Adventists and some of the *other* evangelical groups yield to the temptation to assume this divisive proselyting role" (1925:130; italics mine).

Another ten percent were classified as socialists, atheists, and anarchists. These groups were composed almost exclusively of adult men from the middle and lower classes who reacted strongly to the abuses of the Catholic Church in Mexico, were neglected by Evangelical churches, and were victims of the present industrial system in the United States. They responded to these influences by becoming active and enthusiastic agents of socialism and anarchy, according to McCombs (1925:130).

OVERVIEW OF HISPANIC PROTESTANTISM: 1930-1932

There are two sources of information for this period that make possible a comparative analysis of the data on Spanish-speaking churches within the city of Los Angeles. Robert McLean included as an appendix to *The Northern Mexican* a "Directory of Spanish-Speaking Work in the United States" (1930:27-43). This directory was compiled by the Interdenominational Council on Spanish-Speaking Work, mentioned earlier in Roundy's article (1921:367). McLean gives the names and addresses of fifty-six Spanish-speaking churches and missions in Los Angeles County, including fifteen in the city of Los Angeles for the year 1930. On the other hand, Ortegon's study, "The Religious Status of the Mexican Population in Los Angeles" (1932), lists twenty-eight Hispanic churches in Los Angeles, including fourteen not given by McLean; but McLean's list also has one church not given by Ortegon. This comparison reveals the incompleteness of McLean's directory which only gives churches belonging to the major Protestant denominations (affiliated with the Home Missions Council) while failing to list Pentecostal, Seventh-Day Adventist, or independent churches and missions (Figure 23). However, while acknowledging this limitation, McLean does record at least 367 Spanish-speaking churches in the United States in 1930 which had a total communicant membership of 26,600 (1930:43). The majority of the churches, of course, were in the Southwest: Arizona (33), California (159), Colorado (37), New Mexico (58), and Texas (94) (1930:36-42).

The three largest concentrations of Mexicans in the Southwest in 1930 were located in the cities of Los Angeles, San Antonio, and El Paso, with Los Angeles having the largest Mexican population of any city in the United States. Some observers in this period called Los Angeles "the second capital of Mexico". The number of Mexicans in the city of Los Angeles, according to census figures, increased during the decade of the 1920s by at least 75,500 people, which boosted the Mexican population from 21,600 in 1920 to 97,120 in 1930 (Ortegon 1932:14). However, approximately 30,900 Mexicans were repatriated by the welfare authorities of Los Angeles County during a twelve month period in 1931-1932, which decreased the total Mexican population in Los Angeles to about 66,200 according to Ortegon (1932:65).

The continuing problem of the unreliability of the official census data surfaces again in the estimates given by Ortegon. The 1930 Census did include for the first time, however, "Americans of Mexican descent". The new category defined "Mexican" as: "all persons born in Mexico or having parents born in Mexico who are not definitely white, Negro, Indian, or Japanese." Both McWilliams and Sanchez have argued that this new definition was an attempt to make "Mexicans" a separate race and, therefore, was "obviously misleading and inexact" and under-enumerated the Hispanic population of Mexican birth and descent in the Southwest. McWilliams gave his own estimate of the Mexican population in Los Angeles County for 1930: 385,000 (1968:54-57). However, Governor Young's Mexican Fact Finding Committee gave a lower estimate of 250,000 for the county's Spanish-speaking constituency in 1928. Within the city of Los Angeles, this Committee reported that the Mexican population totaled about ten percent of the city's 1,343,000 inhabitants, or approximately 140,000 (1930:175-176).

Within and adjacent to the city of Los Angeles were five communities where the Mexican population was heavily concentrated. These communities were Belvedere Park, Marvilla Park, Boyle Heights, Palo Verde, Lincoln Park, the Central District, and Rose Hill (cf. Figure 13). Ortegon gives several reasons for the concentration of Mexican immigrants in these five areas:

> The Mexican likes to be with those of his own race. This tendency of the Mexican immigrant is not an accident but the result of certain factors. The most obvious reason, especially at first, is that of language. Naturally they like to live among those who can understand them, *but the strongest permanent cause of living in "colonies" is the attitude of many Americans who think that it is a disgrace to have Mexicans in their neighborhood.* Chiefly for these reasons then the Mexicans of Los Angeles have segregated themselves [or have been forced by strong Anglo pressure] into "little Mexicos" (1932:14, italics mine).

Roman Catholics

The Mexicans in Los Angeles are classified by Ortegon into four religious groups: the Catholics, the Evangelicals, the speculative cult-worshippers, and the Free-Thinkers. Protestant observers (evidently McCombs) estimated that approximately sixty percent of the Mexican population were identified as Catholics, which is a total of 58,270 people by Ortegon's figures; forty percent (38,850) were classified as *faithful adherents*, and twenty percent (19,425) as *nominal adherents* (Figure 24). Catholic spokesmen in Los Angeles listed twenty-six official Mexican Roman Catholic churches; however, this does not include other Anglo Catholic churches where some Mexicans attended. Father LeRoy Callahan estimated that nine-tenths of all Mexicans in the city of Los Angeles were Catholics, but he also divided the Mexican Catholics into two groups: *regular* Catholics and *irregular* Catholics. "Irregular Catholics are those who early in life have been baptized into the church but do not attend the church regularly, some perhaps never attend at all. Then there are the regular Catholics, those who keep up their church duties" (1932:61). According to Father Callahan, about half of nine-tenths of the Mexican population which he lists as Catholics are "regular Catholics", or about 43,700. This figure is close to the estimate of 38,850 given by Ortegon based upon the opinions of several of the Evangelical leaders working among the Mexican population (1932:21,61,67).

Catholic lay participation within the Archdiocese of Los Angeles mainly took place through the Confraternity of Christian Doctrine. This organization of lay volunteers, both men and women, assisted the Sisters in providing classes of religious instruction for children attending the Los Angeles public schools; or where no Sisters were available, they conducted these classes themselves. The Confraternity sponsored mother's clubs and clubs for older boys and girls, which included both religious instruction and recreational activities (1932:61,62).

The Catholic Church in Los Angeles sponsored four community centers: the Brownson House, Santa Rita, Santa Maria, and El Santo Niño Community Centers. In 1932 these four community centers had a combined registration of 2,325 persons who actively participated in their programs and a recorded annual attendance of 167,483 people (1932:63,64). Quoting a Catholic spokesman, Ortegon wrote:

> The primary purpose of these centers is to channel the energies and to develop the character and talents of the individual, and to go far toward setting the spiritual, moral, mental, and physical tone of the neighborhood. With supervised recreation such as dancing,

> dramatics and music, and with organization of social, debating, and religious clubs the Catholic Community Centers aimed to give the youth sane, healthful outlets and to keep them away from public dance halls and pool rooms. The majority of these centers devote a large part of their program to religious training which is mainly of the catechetical type. This work is done by the Sisters of the Holy Family and by the Confraternity of Christian Doctrine, a body of volunteer men and women (1932:63).

Protestant Community

Ortegon estimated that the Protestant Community in Los Angeles was about ten percent of the Mexican population. Twenty-eight Spanish-speaking Protestant churches are listed with a total membership of between 3,200-3,400 (Figures 23 and 24). The size of the Protestant Community, therefore, using the formula "communicant membership x 3 = community", totals between 9,600 and 10,200, or about eight to ten percent of the Mexican population depending on which population estimate is used (97,000 or 140,000) Figure 23 identifies the Hispanic churches in Los Angeles in 1932 based on the studies by Ortegon and McLean.

Religious Cults

The "speculative cults" were composed of the Spiritualists, Theosophists, Russelites (Jehovah's Witnesses) or International Bible Students, and New-Thought systems. Ortegon seems to be unsure of where to classify the "Holy Rollers" (Pentecostals), the Adventists, and the Mormons since he classifies them with the "speculative cults" in one place (1932:22), and then discusses these same groups under the classification of "Evangelical Churches" in a later section of his thesis (1932:53-57). After lumping all the "cults" together, Ortegon estimates that they compose about twenty percent of the total Mexican population, or roughly 19,400 (1932:22). However, since all of these groups combined, except for the New-Thought systems, total only 1,115 according to Ortegon (1932:66), it seems very unlikely that the New-Thought systems make up the remaining 18,300 for Ortegon's twenty percent estimate to be accurate. Nevertheless, in 1932, the city of Los Angeles had one Mormon church (90 members), three Spiritualist churches (109 members), one Theosophist group (10 members), and one International Bible Student (Jehovah's Witnesses) group (15 members) which were composed of Spanish-speaking people (1932:57-60; Figure 24).

Figure 23

HISPANIC PROTESTANT CHURCHES
IN THE CITY OF LOS ANGELES: 1932

Denomination and Church		Membership
Methodist Episcopal Church		
La Plaza		365
Methodist Episcopal Church, South		
La Trinidad		101
Violeta		65
*Misión San Juan		76
Free Methodist Church		
North Main Street Church		77
*Marvilla Park Church		29
Palo Verde Church		34
Independent Churches		
*(four churches are mentioned but the name of only one is given; it is listed with Presbyterians)		100**
Mexican Baptist Churches		
*Iglesia Primera Bautista Mexicana		150
El Salvador (at Christian Center)		119
*Garnet Street		128
Bauchet Street		60
Bethel	(church attendance)	73
Rose Hills	(S.S. attendance)	44
Marvilla Park		71
Belvedere Gardens	(S.S. attendance)	170
Presbyterian Churches		
El Divino Salvador		520
El Siloe		30
*Bethesda Spanish Department		213
*Iglesia Evangélica Memorial, Independent		50
Pentecostal Churches		
*Misión Mexicana, McPherson Church of the Foursquare Gospel		500
*Iglesia Betel, Pentecostal	(S.S. attendance)	200
*(two other churches are mentioned but not named)		50**
Seventh-Day Adventist Churches		
*Boyle Heights Church		101
*Belvedere Mission		40
[McLean adds one "Mexican Nazarene Church"]		50**
Total:		3,416

*Churches not listed by McLean
**Author's estimate

Sources: Ortegon 1932:28-57; McLean 1930:37-39

Communists and Atheists

The Free-Thinkers, or *libre-pensadores*, are distinguished by Ortegon as having a detrimental effect upon society. Free-Thinkers are divided into two groups, the Communists and the Atheists. According to Ortegon, "both the Communists and the Atheists may be seen every Sunday afternoon in the plaza making many fiery and sometimes vile accusations against religion and capitalists. This group is made up exclusively of older men of the middle and lower class" (1932:22,23). Although it is not specifically stated, evidently Ortegon believed that these two groups composed the remaining ten percent of the Mexican population.

SURVEY OF HISPANIC CHURCHES IN LOS ANGELES COUNTY: 1969-1972

No known surveys were made of the total Hispanic Protestant Church situation in the greater Los Angeles area between 1932 and 1969. Several brief studies were done among a few denominations for their own internal use, but no attempts were made to evaluate the growth history of the entire Hispanic Church movement or to discuss its general problems in significant detail. In view of the lack of information in existence on the number, size, distribution, growth characteristics, etc. of Spanish-speaking Protestant churches in Los Angeles County, the author began to accumulate this information in preparation for the present written study.

Directory of Hispanic Protestant Churches

One of my objectives was to compile a directory of Spanish-speaking churches for both Los Angeles and Orange Counties as a preliminary step to an analysis of their growth histories and present problems. Information was needed on the name and location of each church and its denominational affiliation, if any. This directory was difficult to compile and many sources and methods were used: existing directories of denominational and interdenominational organizations, area telephone directories, interviews with pastors and denominational officials, and many hours spent driving through the *barrios* of the two-county area in search of unlisted churches. The first draft of the directory was completed in July 1970 with 211 churches listed. By January 1972, 227 Hispanic congregations were verified to exist in Los Angeles and Orange Counties. The distribution of these churches by cities is given in Figure 25 , with the names and address of each one listed in Appendix III.

The breakdown by denominations for Los Angeles County reveals that the so-called "traditional" Protestant groups accounted for 129 of the total number of churches and about 9,920 communicant members (Figure 26). The average church size for purposes of statistical comparison was 76.3 members, while the Pentecostal group averaged only 62.6 members and accounted for eighty churches and 5,000 communicant members.

The traditional denominations (non-Pentecostal) with the largest number of churches were the following: American Baptist (28), Southern Baptist (24), United Methodist (14), the Seventh-Day Adventists (11), and United Presbyterian (10). The Adventists, of course, are not normally considered to be one of the "traditional Protestant" denominations, but for purposes of this study they were classified as such in order to distinguish between Pentecostal and non-Pentecostal denominations. The largest

Figure 25

NUMBER OF HISPANIC PROTESTANT CHURCHES BY CITY
(January 1972)

<u>LOS ANGELES COUNTY</u>

2	Alhambra
3	Azusa
4	Baldwin Park
1	Bell
1	Burbank
2	Canoga Park
3	Carson
1	Commerce
4	Compton
1	Culver City
1	Downey
5	El Monte
2	Glendale
1	Harbor City
1	Hawthorne
3	Huntington Park
2	Irwindale
5	La Puente
1	La Verne
3	Long Beach
103	Los Angeles (By P.O. Zip areas)
13	Boyle Heights Sta.
12	Central L.A.-Downtown
17	East L.A. Branch
3	El Sereno Sta.
3	Florence Sta.
19	Hazard Branch
3	Highland Park Dist.
2	Hollywood Sta.
9	Lincoln Heights Sta.
9	Lugo Sta.
5	South Central L.A.
5	West Central L.A.
3	West L.A.-Mar Vista
1	Lynwood
1	Maywood
4	Montebello
3	Norwalk
4	Pacoima
3	Pasadena
3	Pomona
8	Pico Rivera
1	Rosemead
4	San Fernando
5	San Gabriel
2	Santa Monica
4	San Pedro
1	Sepulveda
2	South Gate
1	Sun Valley
1	Sylmar
1	Torrance
1	Van Nuys
1	Walnut
1	Whittier
7	Wilmington
209	<u>Total L.A. County</u>

<u>ORANGE COUNTY</u>

3	Anaheim
2	Fullerton
1	La Habra
1	Orange
1	Placentia
8	Santa Ana
1	Stanton
1	Westminster
18	<u>Total Orange County</u>
227	Grand Total

Source: Appendix III, Directory of Spanish Language Protestant Churches in Los Angeles and Orange Counties, California

Figure 26

PROTESTANT-SPANISH LANGUAGE CHURCHES
IN LOS ANGELES COUNTY, 1972

PROTESTANT DENOMINATIONS (NON-PENTECOSTAL)	NUMBER CHURCHES	NUMBER MEMBERS*	AVERAGE CHURCH SIZE*
American Baptist Convention	28	2,390	85.3
Baptist Bible Fellowship	1	75	75.0
Baptist, independent	3	150	50.0
Conservative Baptist Association	3	230	78.0
Church of Christ	4	240	60.0
Christian Church, Disciples of Christ	1	75	75.0
Congregational Church, independent	1	75	75.0
Episcopal Church (non-Protestant)	3	400	133.3
Evangelical Covenant	1	80	80.0
Free Methodist	3	172	57.3
California Yearly Meeting of Friends	1	70	70.0
General Association of Regular Baptists	1	80	80.0
Independent Protestant, interdenominational, or unaffiliated	8	525	65.6
Lutheran Church, Missouri Synod	1	90	90.0
Nazarene, independent	1	65	65.0
Presbyterian, independent	1	60	60.0
Salvation Army	1	90	90.0
Seventh-Day Adventist	11	880	80.0
Southern Baptist Convention	24	1,600	66.7
The Church of the Nazarene	7	350	50.0
United Church of Christ, Congregational	1	70	70.0
United Methodist (Latin American Meth.)	14	1,540	110.0
United Presbyterian Church in the USA	10	615	61.5
Subtotals	129	9,922	76.3
PENTECOSTAL DENOMINATIONS			
Apostolic Assembly of Faith in Christ Jesus	12	1,000	84.0
Assemblies of Christian Churches of N.Y.	1	40	40.0
Assemblies of God (Latin American District Council)	18	1,080	60.0
Assembly of God in Christ, Inc.	1	40	40.0
Church of God (Cleveland, Tenn.)	4	225	56.0
Church of God of Prophecy	2	100	50.0
Latin American Council of Christian Ch.	15	900	60.0
Independent Pentecostal, unaffiliated, or unknown	17	1,020	60.0
Internat. Church of the Foursquare Gospel	10	600	60.0
Subtotals	80	5,005	62.6
GRAND TOTALS	209	14,930	71.4

*Membership data and average church size for 1972 are, in some cases, projections based on earlier statistics from the 1960s.

Pentecostal groups in Los Angeles County were: Assemblies of God (18), Latin American Council of Christian Churches (15), Apostolic Assembly of Faith in Christ Jesus (12), and International Church of the Foursquare Gospel (10). In addition, there were seventeen independent or unaffiliated Pentecostal churches in the county area, or at least there was no known denominational affiliation.

In adjacent Orange County, which is actually part of the Los Angeles metropolitan area, eighteen Spanish-speaking churches were in existence. The Assemblies of God accounted for five of these churches, the American Baptists and Apostolic Assembly both had three, the United Methodists and Free Methodists each had two, and the following denominations each had one: Conservative Baptist, Seventh-Day Adventist, and Southern Baptist. These eighteen churches accounted for approximately 1,285 communicant members. The distribution of Orange County churches by city is given in Figure 25 and names and addresses are listed in Appendix III.

Although the psuedo-Christian sects were not thoroughly investigated as a part of the present study, the following number of Spanish-speaking churches were verified to be in existence in Los Angeles County: Christian Science (1), Church of Jesus Christ of Latter-Day Saints (8), and Jehovah's Witnesses (3). The estimated membership of these churches is about 850.

Geographical Distribution of Hispanic Churches

The Spanish-speaking Protestant churches were plotted on a 72" x 72" wall map of the Los Angeles metropolitan area, with each church represented with a small, red dot. The resulting visual aid showed the geographical distribution of Spanish-speaking churches in both counties, and provided a basis of comparison with the distribution and density of the Spanish-surname population. When the first draft of the "Directory of Spanish Language Protestant Churches in Los Angeles and Orange Counties" was compiled in the summer of 1970, the latest data available on the distribution and density of the Spanish-surname population was from the 1960 census. Since the results of the 1970 census would not be available for several more years, the previous census data served as the basis of analysis for the SSN population.

Three important sources of information provided the needed data on the distribution and density of the SSN population. First, the Western Economic Research Company had compiled a map of Los Angeles County which showed the density of the SSN population by census tracts as a percentage of the total population in 1960. Although it was recognized that changes had occured in many census tracts between 1960 and 1970, it was assumed that the major areas of SSN concentration had changed the least within the county area. Therefore, this map of SSN population density was used to evaluate the distribution of Spanish-speaking Protestant churches in terms of the census tracts having the highest concentrations of SSN people, as well as in census tracts into which Spanish-speaking people were known to be moving (cf. Figure 16; and Appendix I, Figures B,C,D).

The second source of information on the distribution of the SSN population was the Economic and Youth Opportunities Agency of Greater Los Angeles. This government agency had conducted a study of the ethnic composition of the population of Los Angeles County in April 1970. Included in this study were SSN population estimates for 1970, not only for the county as a whole, but also for each Community Action Agency and EYOA Poverty Planning Area (cf. Figure 15). These area divisions and population estimates were used in the present study to evaluate the regional distribution of Hispanic Protestant churches (Figures 27,28).

An important study by Grebler, *et al.*, *The Mexican American People*, provided a convenient classification system for the distribution of the SSN population in Los Angeles County:

> In Los Angeles, our sample households were divided into three equal groups. Replicating the census distributions, one-third of the sample households lived in census tracts with less than 15 percent Mexican Americans. These will be called "Frontier" areas. Another third (Colonies) lived in tracts with more than 43.8 percent Mexican Americans; the remaining third resided in what will be called "Intermediate" areas (1970:305).

This classification system was adopted for use in our study, but the percentage divisions were slightly modified according to the Western Economic Research Company's breakdown: "colony", 45% SSN population or greater; "intermediate" area, 15-44% SSN; and "frontier" area, less than 15% SSN (cf. Figure 15).

When the data from these three sources was integrated with the geographical distribution of Spanish-speaking churches in Los Angeles County, the three-map series, Figures 15, 16, and 27 was the result. When Figures 16 and 27 were compared, the result, as expected, showed that a majority of the Spanish-speaking churches were located in *colony areas* and that the majority of Spanish-speaking departments in Anglo churches were located in *frontier areas*. Both types of churches were found in the *intermediate areas*, with thirteen Spanish departments in intermediate areas and twenty-five in frontier areas (Figures 16, 27 and 28). The breakdown of Spanish departments by denominations was as follows (up-dated to January 1972):

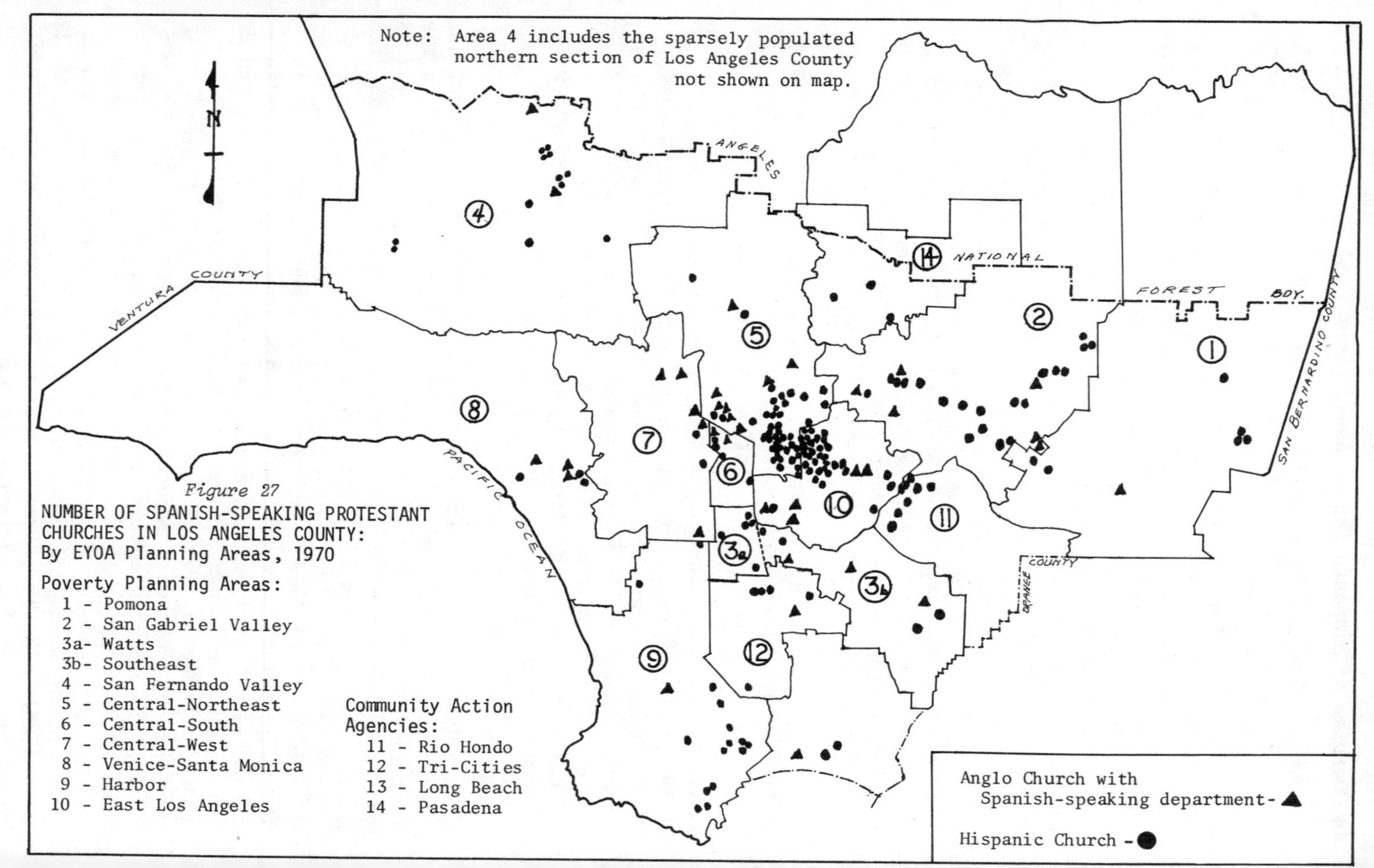

Figure 27

NUMBER OF SPANISH-SPEAKING PROTESTANT CHURCHES IN LOS ANGELES COUNTY: By EYOA Planning Areas, 1970

ANGLO CHURCHES WITH SPANISH DEPT.	NUMBER
American Baptist	12
Church of Christ	2
Disciples of Christ	1
Foursquare Church	2
Independent Pentecostal	1
Independent Protestant	1
Southern Baptist	14
United Methodist	3
United Presbyterian in U.S.A.	2
Total:	38

This important information on the geographical distribution of the SSN population and the distribution of Spanish-speaking Protestant churches in Los Angeles County will be referred to in Chapters Eleven and Twelve as we consider the development of a strategy for Hispanic church growth in the coming decade.

Questionnaire and Interviews

After completing the directory of Hispanic churches and conducting preliminary interviews with denominational officials, it was then possible to develop a two-page printed questionnaire to be used for a mail survey of Spanish-speaking and English-Spanish Protestant churches in Los Angeles County. These forms were sent out in July 1970 with an enclosed, self-addressed envelope, and were personally addressed to the pastor of each church if his name was known.

The purpose of this questionnaire was to obtain statistics of church membership and average attendance so that the size of the total Protestant Community (adherents) and the size of the active church membership could be closely estimated. Information was requested about the history and functioning of each church: when established, language used for services, year when Spanish services were started, seating capacity, age of church buildings, when occupied by present congregation, present membership (Anglo and Hispanic), membership gains and losses during the past year, average weekly attendance at major services, etc. The questionnaire also requested information on the place of birth (country) of church members; where converted to Protestant Christianity (in U.S. or foreign country); the pastor's ministerial service and training; and the church's leadership training program, Sunday school organization and church extension program (see Appendix II for a sample Questionnaire).

Addresses for 185 churches were available when the questionnaires were sent out in July and only thirty-three were returned by October 1970, which amounts to a 16 percent sample of the total number of Spanish-speaking Protestant churches and missions in Los Angeles County. As a check on the accuracy of the information received on the questionnaires, over one-hundred churches were visited and interviews were conducted with denominational officials, pastors, laymen, and community leaders. Also, a pictorial color directory of over seventy churches was compiled based on a cross-section of each denomination.

The data from the sample proved to be a fairly accurate indication (within 6.2%) of the average church membership of Hispanic churches in the county area (cf. Figure 26). According to the sample, the average church size was 77.6 members, with 28.7 family units per church and 2.7 church members per family unit. For churches with less than 100 members, the average attendance at Sunday morning worship services ran 23.5 percent over the communicant membership. Churches with more than 100 members tended to have less attendance than communicant members, with this gap increasing as the size of the membership increased.

Using the previously acquired data on (1) the distribution of the SSN population (Figure 15) and (2) the distribution of Spanish-speaking churches in Los Angeles County (Figure 27), the size of the Hispanic Protestant "communicant membership" and the "Protestant community" were projected for each of the fourteen EYOA Planning Areas in the county (Figure 28). The "index of relative size" of the Protestant community to the total SSN population varies from 192 (1.92%) in the Central-West area of the county to 793 (7.93%) in the Central-South area. According to this estimate, the Protestant Community constitutes about 4.9 percent of the total SSN population in Los Angeles County.

These projections were based on the following formulas: "communicant membership" = the number of Spanish-speaking Protestant churches X 77.6 (average church membership from 1970 survey); and "Protestant community" = communicant membership X 3. "Protestant community" is composed of the following groups: (1) communicant members, (2) non-communicant children of members, (3) unbaptized or other non-member participants, and (4) those who claim to be Protestants based on self-identification (Read, *et al* 1969:48-49; Grebler 1970:487).

Many months later, after denominational histories were compiled and accurate membership statistics were available, the average church size was determined to be about 71.4 members, rather than the 77.6 average of the earlier estimate. The traditional Protestant denominations had a somewhat higher (76.3) average church membership size than did the Pentecostal denominations (62.6) based on a study of twenty-six denominational bodies (Figure 26). The size of the Hispanic Protestant community

Figure 28

ESTIMATED HISPANIC PROTESTANTS IN LOS ANGELES COUNTY: 1970

COMMUNITY ACTION AGENCIES AND EYOA POVERTY PLANNING AREAS[1]	ESTIMATED SSN POPULATION 1970[2]	NUMBER PROTESTANT SPANISH-SPEAKING CHURCHES	(Sp.Dept.)	INDEX OF RELATIVE SIZE[3] (PROTESTANT COMMUNITY)	ESTIMATED PROTESTANT COMMUNICANT MEMBERSHIP[4]
Central-South (6)	19,000	6	(2)	793	2.64%
East Los Angeles (10)	153,000	41	(5)	624	2.08
San Gabriel Valley (2)	101,000	26	(6)	590	1.97
Pasadena (14)	13,000	3	-	537	1.79
Central-Northeast (5)	226,000	52	(8)	536	1.78
Harbor (9)	71,000	16	(1)	525	1.75
Rio Hondo (11)	37,000	8	-	503	1.68
San Fernando Valley (4)	77,000	14	(2)	454	1.51
Tri-Cities (12)	31,000	6	(1)	451	1.50
Southeast (3b)	33,000	7	(3)	442	1.47
Pomona (1)	42,000	7	(1)	388	1.29
Long Beach (13)	22,000	3	(1)	317	1.05
Venice-Santa Monica (8)	48,000	6	(3)	291	0.97
Watts (3a)	42,000	5	-	277	0.92
Central-West (7)	85,000	7	(5)	192	0.64
TOTALS	1,000,000	211	(38)	491 (4.9%)	1.64%

[1] Area numbers are correlated with Figures 16 and 27

[2] Source: Economic and Youth Opportunities Agency 1970:5,7

[3] Index of 100 equals 1.00% of area SSN population

[4] Number of Spanish-speaking churches X 77.6 = estimated communicant membership

("community" = communicant membership X 3) is somewhat less than 4.9 percent estimate of Figure 28. The Protestant community by the new formula totals only 44,770 which is 3.73 percent of the total SSN population of 1.2 million for Los Angeles County in 1970 (cf. Figure 12). The communicant membership is about 1.24 percent or 14,930 compared to the earlier estimate of 1.64 percent in Figure 28.

SSN Religious Affiliation in Los Angeles County

So much for calculations based on logic and hard work. Grebler had a much easier method, perhaps, of determining the size of the Protestant community in Los Angeles County. He simply had his research assistants interview 852 SSN residents of the county and ask them their religious affiliation or preference (1970:472). The result was as follows: "Our Los Angeles...survey data show that only 5 percent of those professing a religion are Protestant" (1970:487). Thus, the test of "self-identification" for determining the size of the Protestant community is proposed.

However, an important question is raised that we must seek to answer if we are to accept the criteria of "self-identification". Can the ratio of communicant church members to the size of the Protestant community be as high as 4:1? This is the ratio that we must accept if we also accept the 5 percent figure, because 5 percent of the 1.2 million SSN population equals 61,500 which is 4:1 X 14,930 (the total communicant membership from Figure 26) Therefore, how can the 4:1 ratio be accounted for?

There are several possible answers, the first of which is that there are many more SSN people who attend Anglo English-speaking churches than are accounted for in the 3:1 ratio. Therefore, we should add another point to the explanation of "Protestant community", which is, "SSN people who are members of or who attend Anglo Protestant churches", or "who identify themselves with these churches even though they may not be active members". The second possibility is that perhaps those who identify themselves as Protestants, but do not actively attend either English or Spanish Protestant church services, are the second or third generation descendents of those early Mexican immigrants who became Protestants in the 1920s or 1930s, but due to the highly migratory character of their lives in that period, they lost contact with the church where they were converted and never renewed strong ties to any other Protestant church. But their children, and perhaps even their grandchildren, have been raised as Protestants rather than Catholics, and for this reason continue to identify themselves as "Protestant". Considering the large number of people in this category, based on personal interviews with SSN people in the community, the 4:1 ratio of communicants to total Protestant community can be assumed to be generally valid.

Assuming the reliability of Grebler's survey of the Spanish-surname population of Los Angeles County in 1965-1966, and projecting his results to include the 1970 SSN population, the following categorization of the total Hispanic population is proposed in Figure 29. The criteria for the classifications of the Catholic population in Figure 29 are as follows: (1) "Practicing Catholics" are those who attend Mass "once a week or more," (2) "Irregular Catholics" are those who attend Mass "one to three times a month," and (3) "Non-Practicing Catholics" are those who attend Mass "a few times a year or less" (Grebler 1970:472,476). The category "Religiously Indifferent or Other Religions" are those members of the SSN or "Hispanic Heritage" population who, regardless of whether or not they were baptized as Catholics in infancy, are now either indifferent to religion in general, are anti-religious, or are members of religions other than Catholic, for example: Protestants, Mormons or other Christian sects, etc.

Concerning the frequency of Mass attendance among Mexican Americans in Los Angeles County, Grebler has written the following important description:

> Large numbers of Catholics in this population do not conform to the norms of the Church.... Mexican Americans in [Los Angeles] fall substantially below the national average in weekly Mass attendance. According to a recent national survey, even respondants with no Catholic schooling attend Mass more regularly than Mexican Americans (for whom Catholic schooling is not reported). Mexican American women attend Mass more frequently than do men, but both range well below Catholics in other surveys (Table 19-2). Similar differences appear when age is controlled, with Mexican-American attendance in Los Angeles markedly low in the 20-29 year age groups (Table 19-3).... Los Angeles Mexican Americans living in more segregated neighborhoods appear to practice somewhat more regularly than those is mixed areas....(1970: 473-474).
>
> The relatively low levels of religious practice and of adherence to some fundamental teachings of the Church [Catholic marriages and birth control, for example] are at least partially related to the Mexican American's low degree of Catholic socialization. This is most evident in their attendance of parochial schools and their participation in religious instruction at public schools. According to estimates for 1966-1967, only 15 percent of the Spanish-surname population in grades 1 to 6 were enrolled in the parochial schools of high-density Mexican-American areas of Los Angeles; and only 57 percent

Figure 29

RELIGIOUS AFFILIATION OF PERSONS OF HISPANIC HERITAGE (SSN) IN LOS ANGELES COUNTY[1] 1970

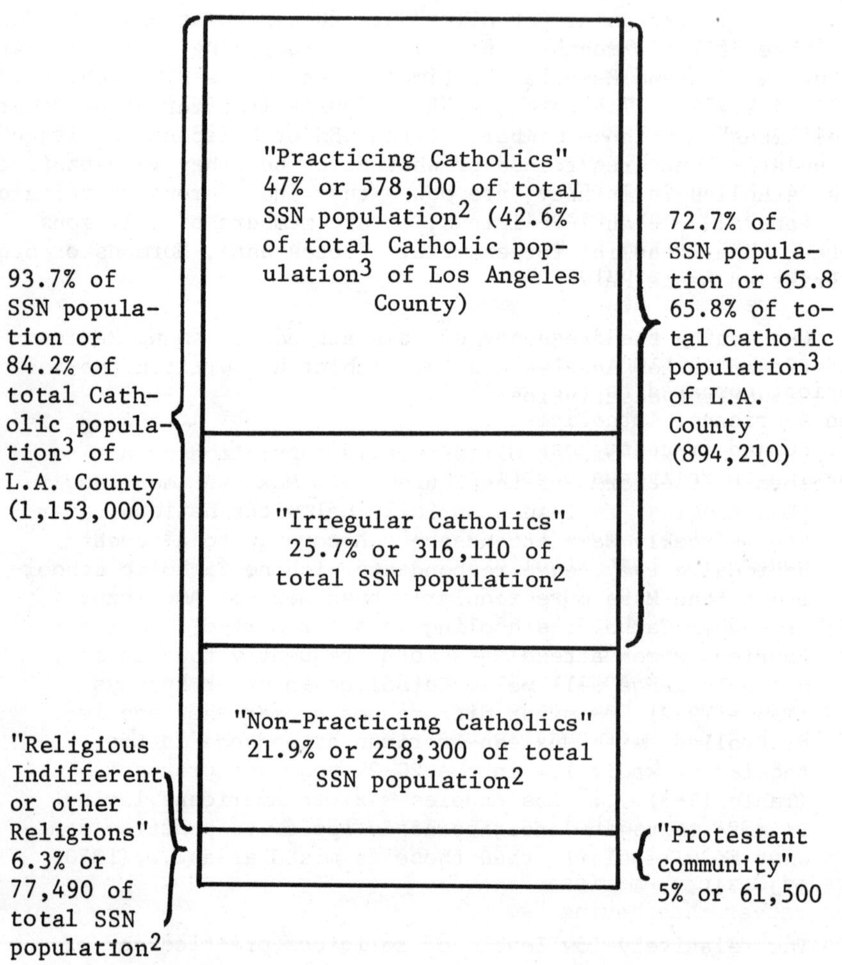

[1]Grebler 1970:472,476,487

[2]Total SSN population of L.A. County in 1970= 1,230,000 (Hebert 1972:1)

[3]Total Catholic population of Los Angeles County= 1,358,000 (The Tidings 1970:1)

received either parochial schooling or so-called CCD instruction (named after the Confraternity of Christian Doctrine). For grades 7 to 12, the corresponding figures were 23 percent and 32 percent. At the junior high and high school level, the Mexican-American participation in CCD classes alone was far below the level for all Catholic students in the same grades (1970:475).

These factors seem to indicate that the religious life of Catholic Mexican Americans follows the general pattern of religious expression in Mexico, and for most of Latin America for that matter. For example, a study made in Mexico in 1958, cited by Labelle and Estrada, indicated that the percentage of weekly Mass attendance for rural and urban populations was 20 percent and 17-18 percent respectively (1964:80). Thus, out of a population that claims to be 94.5 percent Catholic, only about 20 percent of the population attend Mass once each week. Therefore, Grebler's study showing that 47 percent of the Mexican Americans in Los Angeles attended Mass at least once a week is a very high estimate of religious practices among the SSN population, compared to the general trend in Mexico. For most Mexican Americans, Catholicism is a cultural way of life that does not demand frequent Mass attendance; however, many do not feel lacking in religious devotion.

Unfortunately, some Protestants have been overly enthusiastic in downgrading the Catholicism of Mexican Americans because of their low record of Mass attendance. Haselden, for example, only allows the Roman Catholic Church about fifteen percent of the Spanish-speaking population and claims that about eighty percent have "no active church affiliation" (1964:103-104). However, Grebler has shown that at least seventy-three percent of the Mexican Americans in Los Angeles are "active" Catholics (Figure 29).

For American Catholics, the frequency of Mass attendance has been the major test of Catholic devotion, and they too have downgraded Mexican American Catholics as "nominal" church members. But rather than having "weak ties" to the Catholic Church, Hispanic Americans demonstrate ties of a different kind:

> Most Latins have a deeply ingrained faith in God. They see and feel Him in the midst of their poverty, and in their pressing needs they turn to Him with a fervor and humility seldom equalled by many who attend Mass every Sunday. Theirs is a living religion...(Wagner 1966:34).

Nevertheless, Wagner believes that a serious crises exists in American Catholicism in respect to the Spanish-speaking population. Not only does the American Catholic Church have difficulty in identifying with most poverty-level Mexican Americans, but Spanish-speaking Catholics often feel like second-class citizens within the American Catholic Church. According to Wagner:

> There is something very basic lacking in the American Catholic Church, which makes it possible for thousands of Spanish-speaking to leave the Church each year to embrace an alien form of worship. Every indication points to the fact that many more Spanish-speaking leave the Church each year than the Church gains in converts. Large numbers of Spanish-speaking Catholics are looking to other religions for something they cannot find in the Catholic religion. Perhaps the American Catholic Church has become so solidified that it will accept membership only on its own basis and only as long as the individual conforms to its proper development. Basically, this would mean that to be regarded as a good Catholic in the American Church one would have to be in the middle income economically, be able to send his children to the Catholic school, be able to support the structure which is called the parish. Since the Spanish-speaking are not in this position, they have one of two choices: either to forsake all of their background and become as legalistic as the Catholic Anglo or find their expression somewhere else (1966:35).

Many Spanish-speaking Catholics have turned to Protestant churches in an attempt to find a more satisfying religious experience, not only in the earlier period of mass immigration (Gamio 1930:116-118), but also in the last two decades. For example, Crosthwait found that out of 500 Spanish-speaking adults that he surveyed in Galveston, Texas in 1960, 12.3 percent indicated that they were Protestants. But of these, only 1.2 percent had been born into Protestant families, while 85 percent had been converted to Protestantism in the previous twelve years (Wagner 1966:35).

The fact of this exodus from the Catholic Church has important implications for both Catholic and Protestant church leaders who are concerned about the spiritual condition of the Hispanic population. No doubt the number of "non-practicing" Catholics will increase, but whether or not those who turn to Protestantism will find a "satisfying religious experience" is another question. The challenge before the Christian Church, whether Catholic or Protestant, is to make itself relevant to the growing Hispanic population so that the Spanish-speaking masses are able to discover a supernatural Christ who wants to be both Savior and Lord in their daily lives.

Overview of Denominational Histories

The preceeding overview of Hispanic Church development at specific points in time between 1850 and 1972 has set the stage for a more detailed evaluation of the growth histories of all Hispanic Protestant denominations in a vertical or diachronic analysis, which is contained in Chapters 6 through 10.

The objective of the following study is to examine the growth characteristics of the Spanish-speaking churches in the milieu of Southern California and Los Angeles County. Reasons for growth and nongrowth were evaluated from both an internal and external viewpoint: the organizational structure of the church, type of leadership, forms of worship and service, composition of the membership, doctrinal position, self-image, attitude toward the community and the world, relationships with Anglo churches and denominational structures, as well as the external influences such as the location of the church in the community, problems within the community, the attitudes of the community toward the church, etc. It is only when accurate church growth factors are identified and honestly evaluated that realistic solutions to complex socioeconomic and ecclesiastical problems can be proposed.

6.

The Presbyterian Church, U.S.A.

The Presbyterians of America entered the nineteenth century as a united force within the new Republic except for a small group that had formed the Scottish Secession Church. However, disunity was not long in emerging. The Cumberland Presbyterian Church came into existence in 1813 because of policy conflicts with the Synod of Kentucky, which had censured the Cumberland Presbytery (located in eastern Kentucky and Tennessee) in 1802 and then "dissolved" it in 1806. It was not until 1906 that the majority of Cumberland Presbyterian churches reunited with the Presbyterian Church, U.S.A. (Gaustad 1962:87-88).

The Old School and New School Presbyterians separated and formed their own General Assemblies in 1837. This schism resulted from doctrinal differences and the interdenominational Plan of Union (with the Congregationalists) which divided the Presbyterian Church into conservative and liberal wings. The majority of the southern Presbyteries formed the Old School Presbyterians and the New School wing drew its strength primarily from the northern states. However, the causes for division between the Old School and New School Presbyterians were no longer seriously contested by 1869 and the two bodies were reunited in that year (Sweet 1950:261-262,339).

During the early decades of Protestant history in California, the three main branches of Presbyterianism established numerous churches throughout the state, beginning in San Jose and San Francisco in 1849. The Synod of the Pacific (Old School Presbyterian), representing all of the states west of the Continental Divide, was organized in 1851; but only a hand-full of churches existed in California at that time. Early Presbyterian ministry in the northern counties progressed more rapidly than in the south. By 1870, at least forty Presbyterian churches had been established in the north, while no permanent congregation existed in Southern California until 1869 (Drury 1967:94-96). However, an earlier attempt had been made in Los Angeles by James Wood:

> Through the 1850s and early sixties one Protestant minister after another vainly tried to establish a church in the city of the angels. In 1854 the Rev. James Wood arrived to conduct Presbyterian services, but out of the city's entire Protestant population he could muster no more than sixteen worshipers. Shocked at the carnival of drinking and fighting with which the Angelenos observed the Sabbath, he compared Los Angeles in his sermons with the wicked biblical cities of Sodom and Gomorrah. Within a year he threw up his hands and left Los Angeles to its fate. Rather than a city of angels, he said, it was "a city of demons" (Nadeau 1960:43-44).

THE LOS ANGELES PRESBYTERY

The Presbytery of Los Angeles came into existence in 1872 composed of the Southern California counties and the Territory of Arizona. This new Presbytery, which had a total of six churches and five ministers, was part of the new Synod of the Pacific that was organized in 1870 when the Synod of Alta California (New School Presbyterian) and the older Synod of the Pacific were united (Wicher 1927:157).

In 1873, after one year of existence, the Los Angeles Presbytery reported 175 members in six churches and a total of nine ministers. The General Assembly of the Synod of the Pacific, in 1880, transfered the territory of Arizona to the Presbytery of Santa Fe, New Mexico which left the Los Angeles Presbytery with Los Angeles, Riverside and Santa Barbara counties (1927:157).

The growth of the Presbyterian Church in the Los Angeles area followed the general growth of the population which had increased from 11,000 in 1880 to 50,395 in 1890 within the city boundaries (1927:204). The number of churches grew rapidly in Los Angeles and in the surrounding new settlements, where thousands of new Anglo arrivals bought parcels of land and began to build new homes. Most of the new pioneers were mid-westerners who came to California for agricultural purposes and brought with them their previous church commitments. As the population grew, so also did the number of Presbyterians who joined existing Presbyterian churches or formed new ones.

EARLY HISPANIC MINISTRY: 1850-1888

The Presbyterians are the first recorded denomination to initiate ministry to Spanish-speaking people in California. The earliest Presbyterian Sunday school work in California was established about 1850 by Dr. Willey in the Presidio of Monterey, mainly for the benefit of Mexican children. Whereas American Presbyterian ministers were "never indifferent" to the needs of the Mexican population in California, the early ministers "had but little time or opportunity to pay attention to the Spanish population" because they were busy caring for the spiritual needs of the Anglo American settlers who poured into California following the Gold Rush (Wicher 1927:305).

Most of the early Presbyterian ministers were neither interested nor able to adequately minister to Spanish-speaking people in California because of the language barrier. One notable exception, however, was William C. Mosher who served the Pasadena Presbyterian Church in 1875 and 1876, the first two years of its existence, but left this pastorate to become a colpourter among the Spanish-speaking population. Mosher travelled to practically every town and village in Southern California where he distributed thousands of Christian books, gospel tracts, Sunday School papers and constantly preached the message of the gospel to the Mexicans he encountered (1927:305).

The early Presbyterian attempts at ministry to Spanish-speaking people through local Anglo churches were seriously hindered because of the scarcity of capable Anglo leaders who could speak Spanish. However, a Spanish-language ministry was begun by the Presbyterians in the decade of the 1880s. The first Mexican Presbyterian church in Southern California was organized at Anaheim in September 1882 with a total of ten members; but this church lasted only until 1887 when its membership was added to the First Presbyterian Church of Anaheim. The Presbytery of San Francisco, on September 12, 1883, formed a committee to initiate a Spanish-speaking ministry in the Bay area. According to the minutes of April 22, 1884, a Mexican church had been recently organized but nothing further is recorded about this church (1927: 306).

The development of Spanish-speaking work by Presbyterians in Southern California began with the arrival of Carlos Bransby, who came to California after serving with the Presbyterian foreign mission board in Bogota, Colombia. Between 1884 and 1888, Bransby ministered to the Spanish-speaking population in the Los Angeles area and was often assisted by Antonio Diaz, an elderly gentleman who was ordained by the Presbytery of Los Angeles in 1884 (1927: 306). It seems likely that Diaz was the same man that served as pastor of the Fort Street Methodist Episcopal Mexican mission between 1879 and 1882, and later became a Presbyterian (Jervey: 1960:91). Besides regular preaching at the Forsythe School for Mexican Girls operated by Miss Ida Boone on Second Street in Los Angeles, Bransby visited Mexican settlements around Los Angeles and established a mission at Los Olivas (Wicher 1927: 306).

ORGANIZATION OF HISPANIC MINISTRY: 1888-1912

With the arrival in 1888 of A. Moss Merwin, a veteran missionary who served in Chile under the Presbyterian Board, a more organized ministry among Spanish-speaking people was begun in Los Angeles. Merwin became the first Superintendent of the Mexican work in Southern California for the Presbytery and devoted twenty years of his life to an evangelistic ministry among the Mexican population (1927:307,308).

The first Presbyterian Mexican mission in Los Angeles was organized under the leadership of Merwin on September 9, 1888 with only five members. Initially, Spanish-speaking services were conducted in a schoolhouse on Second Street and, for the next ten years, in any available room that could be obtained. About 1898 a lot and building were purchased on Avila Street, but this property was later sold and the church moved to Daly Street (1927:308). Apparently this church became independent of the Presbytery of Los Angeles prior to 1932, since Ortegon records that *La Iglesia Evangelica Memorial* on Daley Street was an independent Presbyterian church (Ortegon 1932:53).

Merwin and his assistants conducted regular services among the Spanish-speaking population in many of the towns surrounding Los Angeles. After the organization of the Mexican Church in Los Angeles in 1888, Merwin established missions at Los Nietos, San Gabriel, Irwindale and San Bernardino, as well as including many other points on his preaching itinerary. Although some of the early missions died out, such as the one at Los Nietos, three of the missions developed into strong churches: Azusa Spanish was organized in 1889 (the name was changed to "Irwindale Spanish" in 1909, and to *"El Divino Salvador"* in 1941); San Gabriel First Mexican was organized in 1891; and *El Buen Pastor* in San Bernardino was established in 1903 (Wicher 1927:308). Alden Case estimated that the communicant membership of the three existing Presbyterian churches in 1897 (Los Angeles, San Gabriel, and Azusa) numbered about 200 people (Case 1897:10). The last church organized under Merwin's leadership was the First Mexican Church of San Diego in 1904.

La Iglesia del Divino Salvador in Irwindale is apparently the oldest Spanish-speaking Protestant church in continuous existence in Southern California. Weekly services are conducted at this church, which is still at the same location and in the original building.

Mary Merwin became the new Superintendent of the Mexican work for the Presbytery of Los Angeles in 1905 following the death of her father, A. Moss Merwin. Before she resigned in 1912, Mexican missions were organized in the growing citrus areas of Redlands and Riverside, which are located about sixty-five miles east of Los Angeles (Wicher 1927:309). *La Iglesia Presbiteriana Casa Blanca* in Riverside was established in October 1910 as "Riverside Mexican", but its name was changed to *Casa Blanca* in 1922. At Redlands, the Mexican mission was organized as *La Iglesia del Divino Salvador* in March 1913. Originally this church was listed as "Redlands Mexican" but became *El Divino Salvador* in 1948. *El Buen Pastor* in Azusa was organized in May 1912, originally as "Azusa Mexican", but was renamed "Good Shepherd" in 1941 (Drury 1967:101).

HISPANIC CHURCH GROWTH: 1913-1930

After 1910, a new era began in the history of Mexican churches and missions in Southern California in response to thousands of Mexican immigrants who poured across the border and settled in colonies and labor camps throughout Southern California. The Presbyterian Spanish-speaking work, which had previously been directed by the various Synods and Presbyteries throughout the Southwest, was coordinated by the Board of National Missions in a unified plan in 1913 under the superintendancy of Robert McLean who had served both in Chile and Puerto Rico prior to his new assignment (Wicher 1927:309). McLean was director of the Mexican work from 1913 to 1918 and "organized churches at strategic centers along the border, and inland, which would get in touch with the Mexican immigrant immediately upon his entrance into the United States" (1927:310). Two of these churches were in Los Angeles: *El Divino Salvador* in Boyle Heights and *Misión La Trinidad*; both were organized in 1914 (Drury 1967:101).

Robert N. McLean, Jr.

Following the resignation of Dr. McLean in 1918, his son, Robert N. McLean, was appointed superintendent of the Spanish language ministry in the Southwest. The younger McLean established new churches at Monrovia (*El Mesias*, 1920), LaVerne (*Emmanuel*, 1921) and Belvedere Park (*El Siloe*, 1922) in Los Angeles County; at Upland (ca. 1922) in San Bernardino County; at Otay and Brawley (ca. 1923) in the Imperial Valley; and in Northern California, at San Jose (ca. 1925) and San Francisco (1926), and a mission in Visalia. By 1927, Presbyterian ministry to Spanish-speaking people in Southern California had grown to include seventeen Spanish churches and seven missions with 1,277 communicant members and about 1660 Sunday school pupils (Wicher 1927:310).

The extent of the national Spanish-speaking ministry of the Presbyterian Church, U.S.A. in 1929 totaled fifty-seven churches, eighteen missions, and one Spanish department, most of which were in the Southwest. Sixty-nine Mexican churches and missions reported 4,765 communicant members (average of sixty-nine members per church) for an increase of 843 members for the year; the estimated total communicant membership was 5,240 (*Annual Report of the General Synod* 1929:44). The Annual Report for 1926 lists seventeen churches in California, five in Arizona, eleven in Colorado, twenty in New Mexico and two in Texas, for a total of fifty-five Presbyterian (U.S.A.) churches in the Southwest; however, no missions were listed in this report.

During 1928 and 1929 McLean conducted a study of the growing Mexican population in the northern states. This study was sponsored by "the Committee on Survey and Research of the Interdenominational Council on Spanish-speaking Work", which is affiliated with the Home Missions Council. The results of McLean's study were published in 1930 entitled *The Northern Mexican*. As an appendix to this report, a "Directory of Spanish-speaking Work in the United States", compiled by the Interdenominational Council, was included. The directory is a valuable source of information for evaluating the extent of Spanish-speaking ministry among the denominations affiliated with the Home Missions Council.

In terms of Presbyterian ministry, McLean reported sixty Spanish-speaking churches and 4,185 communicant members in the Presbyterian Church, U.S.A. and forty-one churches with 2,134 members in the Presbyterian Church, U.S. The distribution of Presbyterian, U.S.A. churches in the Southwest was about the same as given in the 1926 *Annual Report*, whereas Presbyterian, U.S. churches were predominantly located in Texas (McLean 1930:43).

Overview of Growth

The growth of communicant membership in Presbyterian (U.S.A.) churches in California for the period 1905 to 1970 is given in Figure 30, which compares the growth of membership for the entire state of California with that of Los Angeles County. Between 1910 and 1926, the total membership in California increased from about 225 to 1270 communicants, or about 11.2 percent per year. Outside of the county of Los Angeles, membership increased from 75 to 454, while membership in the county grew from 150 to 816. During McLean's superintendency, the number of Mexican churches and missions in California increased from nine to thirty-two for

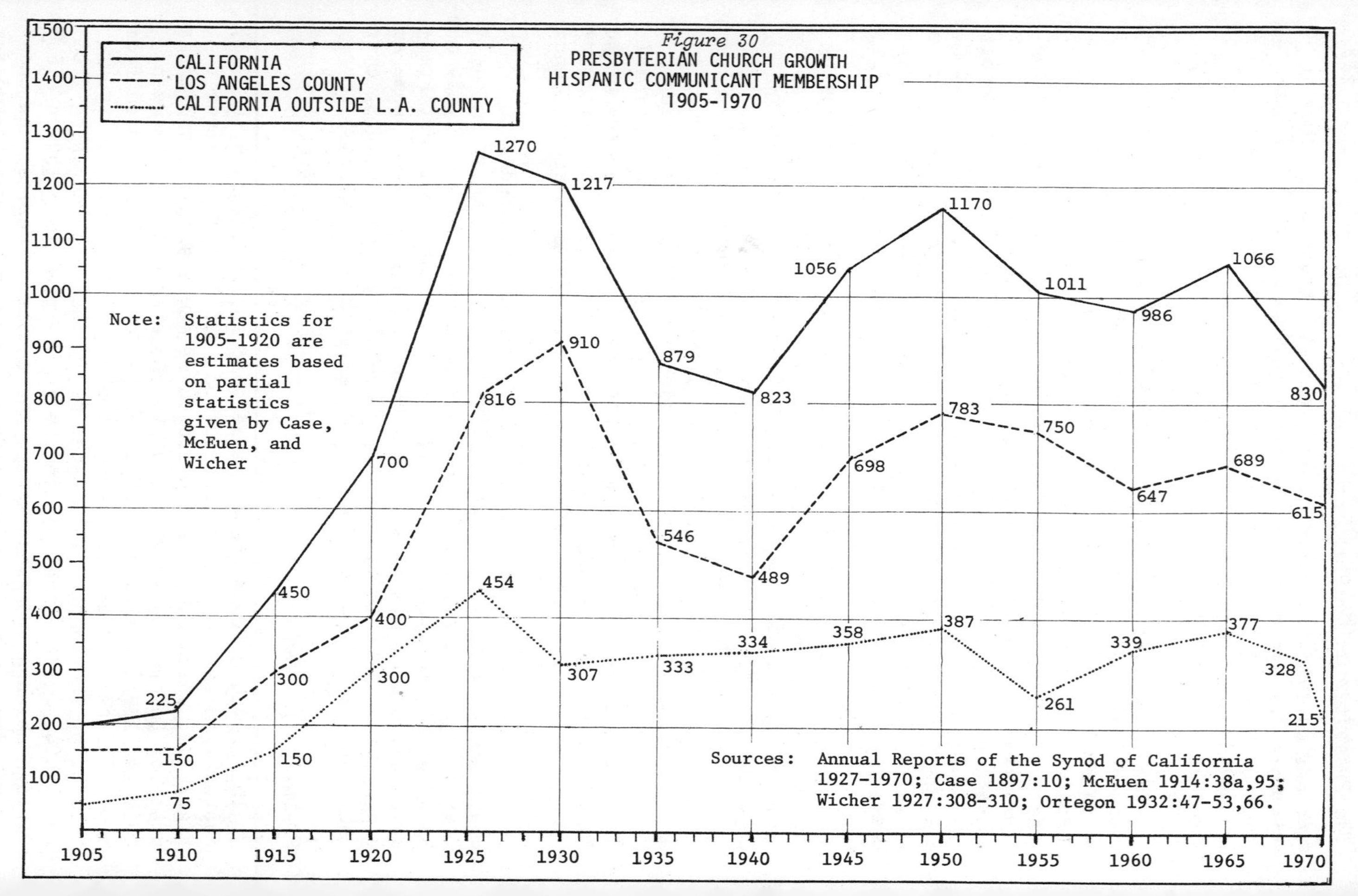

Figure 30
PRESBYTERIAN CHURCH GROWTH
HISPANIC COMMUNICANT MEMBERSHIP
1905-1970

the period 1915 to 1930. Figure 31 shows the distribution of Hispanic Presbyterian churches and missions in the state at the time of McLean's study. Los Angeles County had twelve congregations and about 910 communicant members, with an estimated Presbyterian "community" (adherents) of 2,730.

The rapid increase in Spanish-speaking communicant membership between 1910 and 1930 is obviously related to the rapid immigration of Mexicans to California following the Mexican Revolution. However, Presbyterian growth was not automatic simply because there were more Mexicans in California. Due to the flood of immigrants, however, the Presbyterians reorganized their Spanish language work in 1913 to meet the greater demands for spiritual and social ministry among the rapidly growing Mexican population in the state. Spanish-speaking churches and missions were organized along the border and throughout California for a strategy of continuing ministry among the large Mexican population, which was extremely migratory until the 1940s. Church membership declined in California after 1930 due to the out-migration of Mexicans, including the repatriation of thousands back to Mexico, which resulted from the economic and social hardships of the Depression.

FORSYTHE SCHOOL

The Forsythe School for Mexican Girls opened in Los Angeles about 1884 under the leadership of Miss Ida Boone. Evidently this school was also used for preaching services since Wicher records that both Bransby and Merwin preached there (Wicher 1927: 306-307), and from this congregation the first Mexican church was probably formed in 1888 (Ortegon 1932:53). In 1914, according to McEuen, twenty-two girls boarded at the school but many more were waiting to enter upon the completion of a new building then under construction that would double the capacity of the school. Forsythe School was operated by the Women's Board of Home Missions on a budget of about $2,000 a year (McEuen 1914:96).

By 1932 the school was renamed "Forsythe Memorial School" and was located at the Divine Savior Church in Boyle Heights. Forsythe School offered education beginning with the first grade and continuing through senior high school, with the curriculum paralleling the public school system up through the ninth grade. The senior high curriculum specialized in Home Economics and Religious Education. According to Ortegon:

> The first aim in the school was to train Mexican girls as homemakers with a vision of the people about them and with the technical equipment to meet "that need as lay-workers and members of a Christian community."

Figure 31

HISPANIC PRESBYTERIAN CHURCHES, MISSIONS, AND COMMUNITY CENTERS IN CALIFORNIA: 1930

Church	Pastor
*Alhambra	Heliodoro Pure
Ashland	(unknown)
*Azusa	T. H. Candor
Brawley	S. S. Van Wagner
Corcoran	E. C. Welliver
Elmhurst	H. J. McCall
*El Monte	Victoriano Banuelos
Gilroy	J. B. Guerrero
Hanford	E. C. Welliver
*Hicks Camp	Victoriano Banuelos
*Irwindale	T. H. Candor
La Jolla	Jose C. Rodriguez
*La Verne	Amadeo Maes
*Los Angeles *Divino Salvador*, Boyle Heights Bethesda Church (Spanish Dept.) *El Siloe*, J. M. Ibane Forsythe Memorial School for Girls, Evergreen Street (*Iglesia Evangelical Memorial* Independent Presbyterian, Daley Street)	
*Monrovia	Roman Pasos
National City	Jose C. Rodriguez
*Pasadena	T. H. Candor
Redlands	E. D. Jaramillo
Riverside	James Hayter
Salinas	J. B. Guerrero
San Bernardino	Peter Samana
San Diego	Jose C. Rodriguez
*San Dimas	Amadeo Maes
San Francisco	A. V. Lucero
*San Gabriel	Heliodoro Pure
San Jose	J. B. Guerrero
San Quentin Prison	A. V. Lucero
Solano Beach	Jose C. Rodriguez
Tulare	E. C. Welliver
Upland	Amadeo Maes
Visalia	E. C. Welliver
Woodlake	E. C. Welliver

Presbyterian Community Centers

*El Monte	Home of Neighborly Service, 508 Mt. View
*Los Angeles	Neighborhood House Community Center, Belvedere
*Monrovia	Home of Neighborly Service, 522 E. Duarte
Redlands	Home of Neighborly Service
San Bernardino	Home of Neighborly Service
San Diego	Friendship House
San Francisco	Trinity Center

*Los Angeles County

Sources: McLean 1930:33-39; Ortegon 1932:47-53

> The second aim is to prepare girls for definite Christian training as pastor's assistants or as special teachers of domestic science, and recreation in community centers (1932:48).

The girls lived at the school and helped in various Presbyterian Sunday schools throughout the city. Between 1914 and 1927, the enrollment grew from twenty-two girls to seventy-five, but dropped to forty-six in 1932 (McEuen 1914:96, Wicher 1927:311; Ortegon 1932:48,49).

It is not known when the school ceased to function nor have any studies been made to evaluate its role and contribution within the framework of Presbyterian Hispanic church growth. However, Forsythe School did serve as an acculturation agent between 1884 and late 1930s.

BETHESDA CHURCH

Although several of the early Spanish missions were established as an outreach by interested Anglo churches, Mexican missions usually developed apart from Anglo churches under the supervision of the superintendent of the Presbyterian Spanish work. However, the Bethesda Presbyterian Church in Los Angeles, about 1926, organized a Spanish department on its own initiative. The English and Spanish services were held in the same auditorium at different hours with both groups functioning separately, each with its own pastor, and with both groups having a common church membership (Ortegon 1932:52). In 1927, according to Wicher, the Mexicans and Anglos each had one elder for every twenty-five church members; five elders were Americans (125 members) and four were Mexicans (100 members). The Anglos used the auditorium in the morning and the Mexicans at night. Since the Spanish department at Bethesda had one-hundred members in 1927, it was obviously organized prior to 1927; but that is the year Ortegon gives for its beginning (Ortegon 1932:52; Wicher 1927:310-311).

From a membership of one-hundred in 1927, Bethesda Spanish Department increased to 213 members by 1932 (Ortegon 1932:52). In 1937 "Bethesda Mexican" was organized as a separate church, and the Anglo congregation merged with Mount Washington Presbyterian Church in December 1938 (Drury 1967:101,103). The membership of Bethesda dropped to about one-hundred in 1939, grew to maximum size in the early 1950s with 280, but by 1971 had decreased to 170 members.

IGLESIA DIVINO SALVADOR

Because of the great number of Mexican immigrants that came to Los Angeles between 1910-1913, especially to the eastern sections of the city, McLean organized the *La Iglesia del Divino Salvador* in Boyle Heights in March 1914. By 1927 the membership of this church had increased to 325 communicant members with over 400 in Sunday school (Wicher 1927:310).

Ortegon described the ministry of this church in 1932:

> *El Divino Salvador* enjoyed the privilege of having one of the best equipped churches of the Mexicans of the city. The building is a three story brick structure. The church auditorium seats 227, and 100 more in overflow rooms. The education unit had twenty-two separate classrooms, including two assembly rooms which together seat 200 people (1932:47).

The church also had a print shop for producing Christian literature and the Forsythe School for Mexican Girls was located there in 1932. Two notable Presbyterian leaders served this church, José Falcon and his son, Hubert Falcon. According to Ortegon, the membership of *El Divino Salvador* was 520 communicants with a Sunday school enrollment of 650 pupils; sixty-one young people were enrolled in Christian Endeavor. The value of the church building and land was estimated at $66,379 (1932:47).

However, significant changes have occured in *El Divino Salvador* since its height of ministry during the early 1930s. The Depression had a drastic effect on the ministry of the church, which witnessed the out-migration of whole neighborhoods in the eastern section of Los Angeles. Membership declined from the 1930 high of 403 (this contradicts Ortegon's figure of 520 in 1932) to 116 communicants in 1939. The economic growth of the war years, however, stimulated the migration of Mexican immigrants and their American-born children back to East Los Angeles and other areas of the city and to jobs in manufacturing, construction, and other nonagricultural occupations. Consequently, *El Divino Salvador* recovered somewhat from its period of decline and increased to 162 members by 1950.

But new problems continued to change the character of the church's immediate neighborhood: industrial expansion, freeway construction, and the changing ethnic composition of the area. Many church members were either forced to relocate in other housing areas to the east, or chose to move to better neighborhoods after improving their economic condition. Rather than traveling long distances to their old church in Boyle Heights, many members joined churches in their new neighborhoods (Rodriguez 1969). By

1970, the total communicant membership numbered only seventy-four; but the church continued to meet in the same three-story brick building that had witnessed great success during the early 1930's.

IGLESIA EL SILOE

Organized in the Belvedere section of Los Angeles in 1922, *El Siloe* had a communicant membership of thirty with over a hundred in the Sunday school by 1932. However, there was plenty of room for growth at this church since the auditorium had a seating capacity of 150. In conjunction with *El Siloe* was the Belvedere Neighborhood House under the supervision of the Presbyterian Board of National Missions. This center was a typical neighborhood settlement house characteristic of the 1920s and 1930s. Ortegon recorded the following aims of this center (1932:51):

> To develop and encourage Christian leadership.
> To help our foreign friends to help themselves.
> To discover those aspects of creative ability which are to be found in normal children.
> To provide leisure time activities which will lead to intelligent citizenship.
> To bring all participants to a personal knowledge of Christ.
> To stand as mediator between old and new world customs and habits.

The activities of the Neighborhood House were divided into departments for children, youth, adults, and general activities. In addition to religious instruction, the children's department also sponsored a kindergarten and clubs for boys and girls. The youth department directed club work for young people and Christian Endeavor provided religious instruction. The Neighborhood House also conducted a number of classes for women and a recreational program for men (1932:50-52).

El Siloe failed to develop a large membership for the first forty years of its existence and has only increased to more than one-hundred members in the past decade. By 1960 the membership reached 119 communicants, grew to 195 in 1965, and declined to 144 by 1970. Neighborhood changes also affected *El Siloe* during the 1960s when large sections of the local area were destroyed to make room for freeway construction. The church and Neighborhood House were narrowly missed by one freeway section.

OVERVIEW OF GROWTH: 1930-1972

Presbyterian ministry among Spanish-speaking people in Los Angeles County showed significant development and rapid growth prior to 1926. However, the growth pattern reveals a sharp decline during the years 1930 to 1940 resulting from the economic slump of the Depression years and the decrease in Mexican population (Figure 30). Between 1940 and 1950, the communicant membership increased by 300 members which parallels the economic prosperity of the war years and the increase in Mexican immigration during that same period. Since 1950, however, Presbyterian growth has showed gradual decline, with only a slight increase between 1960 and 1965, while losing over 200 members between 1965 and 1970.

The pattern of Presbyterian church growth among the Hispanic population in Los Angeles County dominated the growth picture of state as a whole (Figure 30), whereas the rest of the state outside of Los Angeles County remained relatively constant for about forty years (1930-1969). Only in the period 1915-1926 did the non-Los Angeles County churches experience significant membership increase (from 150 to 454), which parallels the rapid rate of growth in Los Angeles County during that same period. Looking at the total picture, the rate of Presbyterian church growth and decline closely parallels the pattern of Mexican immigration and the periods of economic prosperity and decline in Southern California. However, the growth rate since 1940 is far below what the potential for growth has been during the past thirty years (compare American Baptist church growth for this same period).

In 1971, only twelve Spanish-speaking Presbyterian congregations remained in California and all but two were in Los Angeles County: *El Buen Pastor* in San Francisco and *El Buen Pastor* in San Bernardino with a total of 215 members. *El Divino Salvador* in Redlands was dissolved in December 1969 and *Casa Blanca* in Riverside was discontinued in May 1970. On the other hand, two new Spanish departments have been started in Anglo churches in Los Angeles County in the past few years (late 1960s): Bethany Presbyterian of Los Angeles and Highland Park Presbyterian. The estimated membership of Hispanic Presbyterian congregations in the county in 1971 was about 615 communicants.

Reasons for a declining pattern of growth among Hispanic Presbyterian churches in California are closely tied to the denomination's policy or strategy of ministry since 1950. Presbyterian strategy has been based upon the idea that Spanish-speaking churches are only a temporary need until acculturation makes a separate language ministry unnecessary. Thus, the Hispanic churches have encountered a multitude of problems due to the denomination's integration policy. This policy demands conformity to Anglo norms and anticipates the disappearance of Hispanic cultural expressions in the life-style of the Church. There are many similarities between the Presbyterians and the United Methodists in this regard, and for this reason the problem will be discussed in greater detail in Chapter Seven. However, there are signs of creative change in the United Presbyterian strategy of Hispanic ministry. [Note: In 1958 the Presbyterian Church, U.S.A. and the United Presbyterian Church of North America merged to form the United Presbyterian Church in the U.S.A.].

NEW GUIDELINES FOR HISPANIC MINISTRY

Alfonso Rodriguez, associate director of the Division of Church Strategy and Development for the Board of National Missions, has written an important report in which he calls for a new sense of mission to the Spanish American population. He also criticizes (what we have called) the "Anglo-conformity" model of assimilation and argues for a bilingual-bicultural approach to Hispanic ministry. Rather than the previous policy of considering Spanish Americans "objects of mission", Rodriguez urges Presbyterians to "look up to these people as responsible agents of mission...as partners in obedience to Jesus Christ and partakers of God's creative activity in today's world." This requires the Church to "discover new structures and new programs of action" (1965: "Planning", 3-4; "Program", 1-3,6).

After briefly describing the extent and diversity of the nation's Spanish American population, Rodriguez calls Presbyterians to a "sense of urgency" concerning their mission to Spanish Americans:

> *Undoubtedly, the Spanish Americans make up the largest single field in the U.S.A. for Protestant witness and service*...[therefore,] it is a categorical imperative that the Spanish Americans be considered, essentially and also for all practical purposes, as an integral part of the mission of the Presbyterian Church in the U.S.A. today (1965: "Background", 3; author's italics).

Rodriguez urges both the Anglo American and Hispanic churches to assume "evangelistic responsibility" for Spanish Americans and to develop a "team relationship" within a common geographical area. There must be a "generous investment of resources" by the whole Church in the recruitment and training of bilingual leadership among both Anglos and Hispanic Americans; the establishment of both indigeneous Spanish-speaking churches and outreach ministries by English-speaking Anglo churches in their local neighborhoods; and the production and distribution of Spanish-speaking literature for evangelism, Christian education, worship, stewardship, and leadership education. For Anglo churches, this means the appointment of a Spanish-speaking associate pastor who is capable of providing the leadership required to lead the church into an "all-inclusive" ministry to their total community (1965: "Background", 3-4).

This ministry requires Presbyterians to confront "the socio-economic dimension of the Gospel" as they seek to relate themselves to the local Hispanic population, according to Rodriguez. Interdenominational cooperation, both on the local and national levels, is also required to demonstrate the unity of the Gospel and the Church's common mission in the world (1965: "Background", 4-5).

To aid the United Presbyterian Church in developing creative ministry to Spanish Americans, Rodriguez urged support of the Hispanic-American Institute at Austin, Texas, and the Hispanic American studies program being developed by Austin Presbyterian Seminary, the Episcopal Seminary of the Southwest and the State University of Texas (1965: "Program", 3-5).

Although only a proposed institution in 1965, the Hispanic-American Institute was established in May 1966 with Jorge Lara-Braud as its director. This interdenominational Institute is supported by various Presbyterian, Methodist, Lutheran, Episcopal, and Christian Church bodies in the Southwest as well as by the National Council of Churches. The purpose of the Institute is to provide

> an ongoing program of ecumenical advocacy for the advancement of Mexican-Americans, and for the promotion among supporting denominations of more relevant bilingual and bicultural ministries (Lara-Braud 1971a:1).

From June 1970 to April 1971, the Institute staff (four Mexican Americans) provided consultative services on mission strategy to many denominations; developed and disseminated research materials dealing with major socioeconomic issues relative to the well-being of Mexican Americans; held special seminars for theological students and professors on Hispanic ministry in the Southwest; conducted fact-finding investigations on social problems; provided legal assistance to individuals and groups who claimed their civil rights were violated; granted scholarship aid to various individuals engaged in undergraduate, graduate, or post-seminary level programs; and provided other forms of technical, research, or special assistance to both individuals and organizations (1971: 1-3).

Although it is not known to what extent Presbyterian policy has been revised according to the strategy urged by Rodriguez, or the degree of "success" of the Hispanic-American Institute, nevertheless these guidelines for Hispanic Presbyterian ministry reveal the direction of change within the denomination. These guidelines reflect the Hispanic American's desire for self-determination in religious as well as secular matters within American society.

7.

Methodism in Southern California

When the Methodist Episcopal Church entered the present state of California, great internal tensions had eroded the unity of Methodism. The division of the Church into northern and southern branches over the slavery issue occurred at the General Conference of 1844 in New York, when a Plan of Separation was proposed. The formal separation took place at the Louisville Convention in May, 1845, when representatives of the southern annual conferences met and voted overwhelmingly to form a new denomination, the Methodist Episcopal Church, South. From 1848 to the start of the Civil War, the two major branches of American Methodism experienced a tense period of growing bitterness towards each other. It is in this context that Methodism arrived in California during the Gold Rush period and began to take root.

METHODIST EPISCOPAL CHURCH, SOUTH: 1852-1939

The Pacific Annual Conference of the Methodist Episcopal Church, South was formed in San Francisco in April, 1852. The southern Church began its ministry in Southern California in 1854, when the Los Nietos Methodist Church was organized under the leadership of a layman, Alexander Groves. The first Methodist ministers arrived in the Southland in 1855: J. T. Cox went to El Monte and E. B. Lockley to Los Angeles. By 1858 the southern Church had established the Los Angeles District, but it only lasted one year. Thus, both the northern and the southern Methodists had meager beginnings in Southern California during the early pioneer period (Jervey 1960:25,26).

Civil War Problems

Southern Methodism progressed slowly in the southern counties during the Civil War years, but occasional services were conducted in various places. J. C. Stewart arrived in Southern California in 1862 and established societies in Carpenteria and San Bernardino. The Conference report for 1864 shows only fifty-six members and thirty-nine probationers in the Los Angeles District. The Civil War and the slavery issue generated considerable hostility and bitterness against southern Methodist ministers and laymen. While visiting California in 1864, Bishop H. H. Kavanaugh was arrested for a brief time and accused of being a spy for the Confederacy. By 1867, J. E. Miller was the only southern Methodist minister that remained in Southern California (Jervey 1960:26,27).

Los Angeles District

The Pacific Annual Conference created the Los Angeles Mission District in 1868 which consisted of the Los Angeles station, the Los Angeles circuit, the San Bernardino mission, the Santa Barbara circuit and San Simeon. In September 1868, the first Quarterly Conference was held in Los Angeles by the southern Methodists. Six new appointments were added to the Los Angeles District in 1869: Los Nietos circuit, El Monte, San Buena Ventura circuit, San Luis Obispo circuit, San Diego and San Luis Rey circuit (1960:27,28).

Los Angeles Conference

Between 1852 and 1870, the Pacific Annual Conference encompassed the entire state of California. However, in October 1870, the Los Angeles Conference was organized with only ten ministers in an area that included all of Southern California and Arizona. It was not until 1922 that Arizona became a separate conference (1960:28).

Notable progress occurred in Southern California in the years following the formation of the Los Angeles Conference due to the rapid population growth of the area. In 1870 the first annual conference reported only two church buildings and a total membership of 475 people. By 1900, thirty churches reported more than 2,000 members, with five of these churches in Arizona; by 1922 the Los Angeles Conference had grown to sixteen churches with 4,512 members. When the Los Angeles District along with the entire Methodist Episcopal Church, South united with the northern Methodists to form "the Methodist Church" in 1939, the district reported twenty-two churches with 8,509 members (1960:31-35).

Spanish-Speaking Ministry

The Los Angeles Conference initiated a ministry among the Spanish-speaking population in 1895, but this work was discontinued after only one year. However, in 1908 James R. Toberman, a former mayor of Los Angeles, established a deaconess home in Los Angeles as a tribute to his son. The Homer Toberman Deaconess Home, which opened in 1904 under the supervision of the Women's Home Missionary Society, served as a base for city mission work. This home was used as a temporary residence for young Mexican working girls and offered day classes in sewing. In addition, night classes were offered for Chinese who desired to learn English (Jervey 1960:42-43).

In 1913 the Deaconess Home was relocated in East Los Angeles, where it served as both a mission and a clinic for the growing concentration of Mexicans in that area who were in desperate need of health and welfare services. In addition to the clinic, clubs for boys and girls were organized, along with classes in sewing and cooking for older young people and adults, also a night school (1960:43).

By 1937, Homer Toberman Settlement House had outlived its usefulness in an area that was now heavily industrialized and had lost most of its former residents who had moved to better housing areas. Basically for financial reasons, the Settlement House combined its efforts with the Community Chest and was re-established on North Grand Avenue in San Pedro. The Settlement House and Clinic continued to provide needed community services for many years in the harbor area (1960:43-44).

The scope of the ministry to Spanish-speaking people in the Los Angeles area was never very extensive by the Methodist Episcopal Church, South. In addition to the work at Homer Toberman Settlement House and Clinic, only a few Mexican churches came into existence in Southern California. The mission at Homer Toberman on Violet Street in East Los Angeles was developed in conjunction with *La Trinidad* Methodist Church which began about 1913 (McEuen 1914:95). Ortegon reported that in 1932 there were three southern Methodist churches in Los Angeles: *La Trinidad* with 101 members, *Iglesia Violeta* with sixty-five members, and *Misión San Juan* with seventy-six members (1932:35-36). Evidently, *Iglesia Violeta* was an outgrowth of the mission at Homer Toberman Settlement House since both are listed at the same address by Robert McLean in his "Directory of Spanish-speaking Work in the United States" (1930:37). At unification in 1939, eleven southern Methodist Spanish-speaking charges with 936 members from the Los Angeles and Arizona Conferences became part of the united Conference (*Journal* 1939 and 1940).

METHODIST EPISCOPAL CHURCH BEGINNINGS: 1851-1876

During the early years of California statehood, the majority of the population was concentrated in the north, especially in the area around San Francisco. It was in the "Bay City" that the California Conference of the Methodist Episcopal Church was organized in August 1851, which was four years after the first Methodist church was established in California at San Francisco. Methodism developed more rapidly in the northern part of the state than in the southern "Cow Counties" (Jervey 1960:16).

Beginnings in Los Angeles

According to Methodist historian Edward Jervey, the first Protestant minister to visit Los Angeles was Henry Kroh, a missionary of the German Reformed Church, who arrived in November 1849. The first known Protestant sermon preached in Los Angeles was given by John R. Brier in June 1850. Brier was a Methodist probationer from the Iowa Conference of the Methodist Episcopal Church (1960:16).

The first Conference appointment to Southern California was Adam Bland, who came as a missionary to Los Angeles in February 1853. When Bland arrived in Los Angeles, not only were there few Methodists in the city, but there were also only a few Anglo American residents. Shortly after his arrival, Bland rented the El Dorado Saloon located on Main Street near the Mexican Plaza, and this became the first Methodist chapel. Bland's wife opened a school for girls at this same location soon thereafter. The Los Angeles circuit took Bland as far north as Ventura and Santa Barbara where he established new preaching points in his attempts "to find and make more Methodists." After a year of pioneer effort in the Southland, Bland returned to Northern California but left the Los Angeles District with five stations: Los Angeles, Santa Barbara, San Diego, El Monte and Tulare. However, only two of these stations had pastors. Evidently, the Los Angeles District was discontinued in 1855 (1960:16-19).

The California Conference withdrew all the Methodist ministers from Southern California in 1858 because of the opposition they encountered due to their attitudes on the slavery question. There was "growing sectional conflict in the ranks of these Methodist preachers" as the Civil War approached. After the end of the Civil War, Bland returned to Los Angeles and reopened the work that was abandoned in 1858. The Methodist Episcopal Church has been in continuous existence in Southern California since 1867 when a Quarterly Conference and "love feast" was conducted in Los Angeles with thirty people in attendance (1960:19).

Methodism progressed slowly in Southern California until the land boom of the late 1860s. Real estate speculation in Los Angeles and San Diego and the potential for agricultural development in the surrounding areas stimulated rapid growth in these two cities. The land boom of the late 1860s and early 1870s brought many people to Southern California who had previously been Methodists or who were receptive to Methodism upon their arrival. Methodist growth in the Southland increased to the point that the California Annual Conference re-established the Los Angeles District in 1870. In spite of the collapse of the land boom in 1875, due to over-speculation, many new settlements were established in the Los Angeles basin that grew into permanent towns (Jervey 1960:19-20).

Southern California Conference

When the California Annual Conference met in 1875, it was reorganized in two sections: the Southern California Conference and the Northern California Conference. Rapid growth among both the churches and the general population in Los Angeles County was responsible for the creation of the Southern California Conference: between 1850 and 1875, the population of the city of Los Angeles increased from 1,610 to 8,453 and the population of the county increased from 3,530 to 24,344. The new conference was formally organized in September 1876 under Bishop William L. Harris. When organized, the Southern California Conference consisted of "13 church buildings, 9 parsonages, 1257 members, 24 ministers in full relation and 3 men on trial" (1960:20).

THE METHODIST EPISCOPAL CHURCH: 1876-1939

Although the Southern California Conference was organized in 1876, it was not until after 1886 that the Methodist Episcopal Church experienced rapid growth. When the Santa Fe Railroad was completed to Los Angeles in that year, a period of intensive growth was experienced by the Conference, especially between 1886 and 1889 before the collapse of the land boom which attracted thousands of people from the Midwest and East to Southern California. During the year 1887 alone, the Southern Pacific brought over 120,000 people to Los Angeles and the Santa Fe averaged three daily passenger trains from the East (McWilliams 1946:118). Methodist membership increased from 3,909 to 5,175 in one year, 1886-1887. Between 1886 and 1889, the number of preaching appointments increased from eighty to 130. Los Angeles really came of age during the land boom of the 1880s, which resulted in permanent growth for the city and the rest of Southern California (Jervey 1960:52).

While the rapid population growth of Los Angeles and its surrounding towns presented unusual opportunities for rapid church growth, Methodism in Los Angeles suffered both from a lack of funds and from uncoordinated efforts, according to Jervey. However, some progress was made in inter-church cooperation. The *City Evangelization Union* was organized in Los Angeles in 1895 "for the purpose of establishing mission services and Sunday Schools in needy sections of the city, planting new churches in unoccupied territory, in helping churches struggling with burdens of debt" (Jervey 1960:53). However, this organization was forced to disband after only one year, although a committee of concerned laymen and ministers continued to meet together and worked out an aggressive plan of evangelism for a seven-year period.

In 1904, the *Los Angeles City Missionary Society* was organized by the Methodist Church to strengthen weak churches and to organize new Sunday schools and churches in the rapidly growing sections of the city. In 1914 this organization was renamed the *Los Angeles Missionary and Church Extension Society* with responsibility for church development in the entire Los Angeles District, which included the city of Los Angeles. In 1920, Methodist churches from all over the district cooperated to pledge over $100,000 toward the building fund for the proposed Plaza Community Center and the Church of All Nations, which ministered to the city's ethnic minority groups (1960:53-54).

When the third great period of economic prosperity exploded upon Southern California in the early 1920s as the result of oil production, the motion picture industry, the tourist trade and extensive land promotion schemes, this created a migration into Southern California that McWilliams characterized "as the largest internal migration in the history of the American people" (1946: 135). However, Jervey reported that over fifty percent of Methodists migrating to Southern California were being lost to Methodism for several reasons: "(1) the lack of suitable buildings, (2) the tremendous heterogeneousness of people who came from all parts of the country, and (3) the 'countless bootleg religions' which drew many earnest but undiscriminating Methodists". Whereas the total population of the area increased by seventy percent during a five-year period in the 1920s, the Southern California Conference increased by only eighteen percent (Jervey 1960:55-56).

Jervey makes the following summary statement concerning Anglo Methodist church growth in the period 1876 to 1939:

> The Southern California Conference as a whole showed a continual growth since the organization in 1876. Starting with a little more than 1,200 members, by 1939 she could count more than 90,000. Only during the five

> years of the Depression, 1930-1935, did a decrease take place. Throughout the history of the Conference many churches were started in communities but later had to be discontinued because of financial reasons or the simple factor of community stagnation. Others which were started have continued to grow and today are strong ones in the United Conference (1960:59).

MINISTRY TO MINORITY GROUPS

The California Conference of the Methodist Episcopal Church began to minister early in its history to many of the racial and ethnic minorities that made up the state's heterogeneous population, although "tremendous racial prejudice prevented any significant advance for some years" (1960:85).

The first Chinese Methodist church was organized at San Francisco in 1870, but Los Angeles did not have a Chinese mission until 1887. Ministry to the Japanese population was organized by the California Conference in 1886 and the Japanese Mission Conference was created in 1900 (1960:85-86). Work among Koreans was initiated in 1909 in Los Angeles and among Filipinos at Pasadena in 1916 (1960:86-87).

Ministry among negroes in Los Angeles was initiated by the Conference in 1888 with the organization of Wesley Chapel. At unification in 1939, there were only five Negro Methodist churches in Southern California (1960:90). Although Methodist missionary activity among Indians in the Conference territory began in 1877, Jervey states that "the bitterness of years of frontier warfare was not conducive to much Christianization." The Yuma, Arizona Methodist Indian Mission was started in 1903 and was the extent of Methodist Indian ministry (1960:90).

Ministry to the Portuguese and Italian immigrants in California was the responsibility of the Latin American Mission which came into existence in 1920, mainly to minister to the growing numbers of Spanish-speaking people in the state. The Portuguese work was completely confined to northern California, while the Italian activity, which began in 1919, was centered in Los Angeles (1960:87).

HISPANIC CHURCH BEGINNINGS: 1880-1910

The Methodist Episcopal Church began its ministry among Mexicans in Los Angeles in 1879 when the Fort Street Methodist Church established a Spanish-speaking mission under the leadership of Antonio Dias, who was an ordained minister. The Southern California Annual Conference of 1880 reported that eighty people had become church members through the Fort Street Mexican Mission (Jervey 1960:91). This mission was apparently discontinued in 1882 (1960:93). Dias later became a Presbyterian minister about 1884, and assisted Carlos Bransby in establishing several Presbyterian missions in the Los Angeles area (Wicher 1927:306-307).

Greater progress was made in the Methodist ministry to the scattered Mexican colonies along the Southern California coast during the decade of the 1880s, beginning with a mission near Santa Barbara about 1881. The growing response to Methodist activity among the Mexicans was often "bitterly assailed" by Roman Catholic priests, but this only intensified the evangelistic fervor of the Mexican Methodist pastors. By 1900 Mexican missions were established in all three districts of the Southern California Conference, from San Diego to Santa Barbara and eastward as far as Riverside and Redlands; but this early missionary activity "was sporadic and lacked cohesion and dynamic leadership" (Jervey 1960:91).

About 1898 the Grace Methodist Church in Los Angeles sponsored a Mexican mission under the leadership of J. H. Limbs, a local preacher of Mexican ancestry, and Mrs. A. M. Whitson, who had been a teacher in South America. By 1900 this mission was organized as "the Mexican Methodist Church of Los Angeles" with seventeen members and a Sunday school enrollment of fifty-seven (Davila 1957:1). From the beginning of this project, classes and clubs were organized for Mexican girls and women. With assistance from the Women's Home Missionary Society, the Women's work was expanded in 1899 to include a sewing school in a rented house.

In 1900, Mrs. Francis DePauw donated a large house on Hewitt Street to the Women's Society for the purpose of establishing a home and school for Mexican girls. The new institution had a successful beginning and it was soon necessary to expand the facilities to add more classrooms and living accomodations. The *Francis DePauw Home* was relocated on Sunset Boulevard in Hollywood in 1902 where there was more room for expansion; this became its permanent location until the 1960s (Jervey 1960:93).

SPANISH AND PORTUGUESE DISTRICT: 1911-1920

Ministry to Spanish-speaking people in Southern California by the Methodist Episcopal Church was disorganized and sporadic prior to the arrival of Vernon M. McCombs in 1910. McCombs served as superintendent of the North Andes Mission in Peru from 1906 to 1910, but was forced to return home because of ill health. After regaining his strength, McCombs accepted the invitation of Dr. F. M. Larkin, superintendent of the Los Angeles District, to become the new director of Spanish work for the Conference in May 1911 (McCombs, Mrs. Vernon 1959:1). Jervey states that "Vernon McCombs came to this new responsibility not only with extensive experience but also with an understanding of the people and many of their problems" (1960:91). Until his retirement in 1946, McCombs provided capable and inspiring leadership and personally recruited many of the workers who came to assist in the expansion of Methodist ministry among Spanish-speaking people for thirty-five years (McCombs, Mrs. Vernon 1959:1-3).

The Spanish and Portuguese District of the Southern California Conference was organized in October 1912 under McCombs' leadership. The Spanish-speaking ministry was centered in Southern California, along with the later Italian work, while ministry to the Portuguese was primarily in the northern part of the state, mainly in East Oakland and Hanford. The progress of this work was reported in the eleven consecutive volumes of *El Mexicano* (originally, *El Mejicano*) from April 1913 to January 1923, published by the Spanish-American Mission Association as the official organ of the District. For many years, this journal was printed by the Spanish American Institute Press in Gardena. The editor of *El Mexicano* and chairman of the Methodist Historical Society, F. Ray Risdon, wrote in 1924:

> If one were to undertake to write a history of the Latin American work of the Methodist Episcopal Church in the Pacific Southwest, one would not need to refer to other sources of information than the twelve Annual reports rendered by Dr. Vernon M. McCombs since 1912. In fact, these dozen classics, taken together, constitute a full, accurate and authentic record of the achievements, growth and progress of this work under his continuous superintendency during the past thirteen years (1924:1).

First District Report

At the end of the first year of the Spanish and Portuguese District (October 1913), McCombs reported that evangelistic services were held at several points, with permanent work started at San Pedro, Compton, Watts, Long Beach, Whittier and in various sections of Los Angeles. Five regular circuits were maintained within the District, which included seven charges and six outstations. Gains for the year were: probationers increased from 23 to 101; total membership more than doubled from 113 to 220; three Sunday schools with 123 enrolled increased to eight Sunday schools with 259 enrolled; adherents increased from 300 to 1200; and the number of charges increased from three to seven (*El Mexicano*, Vol. 1, No. 6:3). Concerning this growth, McCombs stated: "About one-half of our Mexican churches are made up of people who have come to California [from Mexico] within recent months" (Vol. 1, No. 6:6).

The five circuits of the District came into existence between 1911 and 1913 through the efforts of McCombs and several Mexican pastors and laymen, along with valuable assistance from a growing number of Anglo American women missionaries and volunteer helpers. Financial backing for the Spanish language ministry came from the annual budgets of the Southern California Conference of the Methodist Episcopal Church, the Women's Home Missionary Society, numerous Epworth League chapters, and the contributions of Methodist men and women in the growing number of Anglo American churches throughout Southern California.

The first two women missionaries in the Spanish and Portuguese District, in addition to Mrs. McCombs, were Esther Turner and Elizabeth Vincent. Miss Turner, who served in Mexico prior to coming to Los Angeles about 1910, was supported by the Women's Home Mission Society. Esther was often quoted as saying: "Whenever you pray, do not say 'Amen' until you have said, 'Bless the Mexicans'" (*Methodist Archives* 1952:1). Mrs. Vincent, a returned missionary from Chile, came to assist in the work in 1911; she was supported by the "J.O.C. Class" of the First Methodist Church of Los Angeles (McCombs, Mrs. Vernon 1959:1 and *El Mexicano*, Vol. 1, No. 1:5).

In addition to one Anglo American pastor, Royal Weaver at Pasadena, there were five Mexican pastors serving Spanish-speaking congregations and outstations in the District by 1913: Enrique Narro at Los Angeles, Ambrosio C. Gonzalez at Santa Ana, Antonio Jiminez at Downey and Lankershim, Francisco Olazabal at Compton, and Samuel Goitia at Anaheim. The two lady missionaries, Esther Turner and Elizabeth Vincent, were mainly involved in house-to-house visitation in several areas of the District. Although all of these efforts were primarily evangelistic, early attempts were made to care for the sick and diseased at a little clinic on Bloom Street in connection with the First Mexican Methodist Church of Los Angeles. In October 1913, Narro reported that over fifty patients were being treated every week at the free clinic. Concern for the social needs of the growing Mexican population soon led to the development of additional welfare and health services within the District (Vol. 1, No. 1:5 and No. 6:7).

Among the estimated 200,000 Spanish and Portuguese-speaking population of California in 1913, McCombs and his co-workers began to make known the Gospel of God's love and to care for the spiritual and temporal needs of thousands of new arrivals, as well as for the continuing needs of the older residents. After two years of ministry, McCombs wrote:

> Gospel lights glow heavenly welcome in Los Angeles, Pasadena, Santa Ana, Anaheim, Fullerton, Lankershim, Compton, Downey and Rivera. Scores of copies of the Scriptures have been sold and distributed. Many thousands of good tracts have been carefully sown.... The American churches in Santa Ana and Pasadena have done heroically in aid. These brethren are responding nobly at all new points. Their fruits will soon appear (*El Mexicano*, Vol. 1, No. 1:2).

The next two sections illustrate how the Spanish-speaking ministry in the District progressed under McCombs' leadership and the type of cooperation that was necessary from Anglo American Methodist churches for the successful expansion and development of this ministry. When McCombs accepted the superintendency in 1911, only two small Mexican missions were in existence in Southern California, one in Los Angeles and the other in Pasadena.

Pasadena

The Pasadena Mexican Mission began in 1907 under the leadership of Oliver C. Laizure, who was at that time District Superintendent. Speaking at the dedication of the new institutional Mexican church building at Pasadena in September 1915, "Laizure told of the organization of the church after an outdoor meeting of seventeen persons, and the growth of the membership until twenty-four persons were meeting in a room twelve feet square" (*El Mexicano*, Vol. 4, No. 3:2).

Royal A. Weaver served as pastor from 1908 to 1914 when meetings were held in this same windowless little chapel that was constructed for $200. In 1913, McCombs stated that "brother and sister Weaver have toiled faithfully for over three years under handicaps that no American pastor can appreciate" (Vol. 1, No. 6:4). Weaver organized a number of "cottage prayer meetings" that met on Friday evenings in various Mexican homes throughout Pasadena, which had a significant influence on the progress of the work among the Spanish-speaking population. These small group meetings were held

> ...preferably in the homes of those who, because of prejudice or some other cause, such as sickness in the family, do not get out to the services at the Mission. These meetings are presided over by different members of the church, who take turns in leading. We have already seen good results from these gatherings, for the people where the meetings are held thus hear the gospel, lose some of their prejudice and eventually become interested to the

> extent that they attend the regular means of grace (Vol. 1, No. 2:3).

After aiding several ministerial candidates with their conference studies, Weaver requested a transfer to another charge so that a Mexican pastor could be appointed to expand the work on the Pasadena circuit (Vol. 1, No. 6:4).

Francisco Olazabal was appointed to the Pasadena circuit for the year 1914 after serving there for part of the previous year, while also conducting house-to-house visitation in Compton with assistance from his mother (Vol. 1, No. 2:2,7; No. 7:6). Evidently, Olazabal was ordained as a deacon in Mexico prior to his arrival in Southern California, because at Pasadena he entered third-year studies in preparation for ordination as an elder. In October 1913, Enrique Narro and Antonio Jimenez became the first two Mexican pastors to be ordained as deacons in the Southern California Conference (Vol. 2, No. 4:11). Olazabal, along with Narro and Jimenez, were the first to be ordained as elders in the Spanish District, which took place in 1917 (Vol. 5, No. 3:3), the year Olazabal was transfered to the San Francisco-Sacramento circuit (Vol. 6, No. 1:9) and Ambrosio C. Gonzales was appointed to Pasadena (Vol. 9, No. 1:3).

The Anglo Methodist churches of Pasadena had an early and continuing interest in work among the Spanish-speaking population. Under the leadership of Matt Hughes, the First Methodist Church gave strong financial backing to the development of a new building for the Mexican church which was constructed and dedicated in 1915 at a cost of $6,000. An additional $3,700 was given to the Spanish American Institute in Gardena (Vol. 2, No. 4:6). Cooperative effort among the four Anglo Methodist churches in Pasadena through a Latin American Committee resulted in: (1) adequate financial support for the Mexican pastor; (2) choosing a good location and lot for the new Mexican church; (3) workers assigned for music, the sick, and the poor; (4) a city-wide fund drive to eliminate indebtedness and provide an adequate institutional plant for Spanish work; (5) a Mexican night school for the community with a faculty of eight; (6) distribution of food, clothing, and other items to needy families through the "Muchacho School" located near the church; and (7) organization of the "Bonita Cooperative Laundry", which employed many of the Mexican women of the church (Vol. 4, No. 2:6).

By 1920 the Latin American Committee helped establish a "Mexican Hotel" for young working men which was located a few blocks from the Mexican Methodist Church; this hotel was managed by Aaron Gonzales, brother of the pastor. In August 1920, McCombs wrote: "This Pasadena [Mexican] church has been honored of God in raising up half of the students in the Bible Training Department of the Spanish American Institute. Three of them were recruited by the Mexican Hotel..." (*Journal*, 1920:15-16).

The Pasadena circuit by 1920 regularly served East Pasadena-Lamanda Park, the Lincoln district, and Glendale under the pastoral leadership of Ambrosio Gonzalez. Teodoro Mata, who was a "local preacher," conducted Sunday afternoon services at Lamanda Park. Social functions on the circuit centered around the mother church in Pasadena (1920:15).

Los Angeles

The second Mexican mission in existence when McCombs began his ministry in Southern California was the Bloom Street Mission in Los Angeles. Evidently, McCombs began to preach in Spanish at the Bloom Street Mission soon after his arrival in Los Angeles, prior even to his appointment as Superintendent of the Spanish Work:

> Vernon was attending Spanish classes at the University of Southern California, also doing some teaching there, when U.S.C. students asked him to go down to the little Sunday School at Bloom Street. One of these students and Sunday School Superintendent then (no pastor) was Mrs. Ruth Iliff Nordahl...(McCombs, Mrs. Vernon 1959:1).

Beginning in the early Spring of 1911, probably in April, Vernon assisted at Bloom Street where the mission met in a rented store-front building. Although no specific date is given for the start of this mission, it apparently began during the winter of 1910-1911. Vernon's diary records: "at Mexican church Los Angeles, Bloom Street, good order, good number, and the Spirit's power," dated May 23, 1911 (1959:1). Concerning the Conference year 1911-1912, McCombs wrote: "Last year under American workers it [Bloom Street] was merely an irregular mission with very few adult Mexicans, and its gifts came largely from the workers" (*El Mexicano*, Vol. 2, No. 4:5-7).

By October 1913, the Bloom Street Mission was a fully organized church with a full-time pastor (Enrique Narro), Sunday school, Epworth League, Junior League, prayer meeting, mother's classes, English classes and the regular preaching services. Also, a free medical clinic, staffed by volunteer physicians, and a parsonage were added to the church during 1913 (Vol. 1, No. 6:

From this humble beginning, the Plaza Methodist Episcopal Church emerged a few years later and became one of the strongest Hispanic churches in Southern California for over fifty years. The inspiration for the development of this church came from

Enrique Narro who, in 1913, said: "I have a vision of a large and respectable church up near the Plaza, a church great in numbers and in holiness" (Vol. 1, No. 3:6).

Eucario M. Sein was appointed pastor of the Bloom Street Mission in December 1913 for the conference year that began in October (McCombs, Mrs. Vernon 1959:1). Sein had previously served in Mexico as general secretary of the International Sunday School Association from 1905 to 1913, but conditions in Mexico worsened and caused the resettlement of the Sein family in Laredo, Texas (Vol. 2, No. 2:2 and No. 4:6). Sein came to Southern California in October 1913 to attend the annual conference and to give an address about conditions in Mexico. McCombs was very impressed with Sein's experience and ability and invited him to return from Texas with his family: "We expect his return within a few weeks to aid in the work in Los Angeles and environs. We admire his ability and good nature, and covet him in evangelistic and institutional work" (Vol. 1, No. 6:7).

Evidently, McCombs had caught Narro's vision for a large Plaza church that would more adequately minister to the growing Mexican population around the old Los Angeles Plaza, where hundreds continuously gathered for lengthy conversations and discussions about the turmoil in Mexico and their travels from remote ancestoral villages. The little chapel on Bloom Street was obviously inadequate, even unattractive to many Mexicans and at a poor location; it was over a mile from the Plaza in a neighborhood largely Italian (*El Mexicano*, Vol. 2, No. 4:6). Therefore, McCombs' vision increased for a large, centrally located and attractive Mexican church near the Plaza:

> We do not feel it wise to make extensive improvements on our present little church, because it is not centrally located among the Mexicans. When we can receive some aid we shall proceed to provide the Mexicans with a suitable and central institutional church--for all classes of Mexicans in Los Angeles and the hundreds who circulate through the city. If we may have such a man as Eucario M. Sein during the coming year, it will help solve this problem (Vol. 1, No. 6:4).

Sein brought his family to Los Angeles in February 1914 and began his important ministry at the Bloom Street Mission, which was renamed "the First Mexican Methodist Episcopal Church of Los Angeles." After struggling along in the Bloom Street chapel for six months, a hall was secured for $40 per month at 110 Commercial Street, which faced the Post Office and was near the Plaza. Evangelistic meetings were started on Tuesday evenings at the Plaza, sponsored by the Mexican Epworth League, with large crowds in attendance. This important beginning caused McCombs to exclaim:

> Here, where revolutions are fathered and financed; here, where Spain most deeply intrenched her life in our soil; here, where social sores will increasingly fester with the coming of diverse multitudes and great wealth and industries calling for unskilled labor such as Mexicans; and here, in the heart of this city, Los Angeles, we have this year gotten a secure foothold... But the folly of our long continuing to pay $500 a year in rent for a single room, two blocks from the Plaza, is apparent to all. Will you pray and earnestly aid in securing a lot for a Plaza church?... When we have a lot we can then begin to do a really constructive work for the Mexicans who throng that Plaza and who scatter out from there (Vol. 2, No. 4:6-7).

Pastor Sein's salary and rents were provided for largely through the First Methodist Church of Los Angeles, with assistance from South Pasadena, Vermont Square and Boyle Heights Methodist churches, who considered him their "Mexican assistant pastor." Since Sein's family consisted of seven boys and one girl, the job of providing for their financial needs presented quite a challenge (Vol. 2, No. 4:7).

Beginning of Plaza Church and Community Center

When the First Mexican Methodist Church relocated on Commercial Street, the Bloom Street building was developed as a free clinic and welfare center. However, "with the myriads of Mexican people in Los Angeles and vicinity, and continuing to come, and practically no welfare work being done among them, Dr. McCombs felt the great need of Methodists launching out in it" (*Methodist Archives* 1956:2). On the recommendation of a teacher in South Pasadena, McCombs contacted Katherine Higgins in Pennsylvania and invited her to come to Los Angeles and serve as a social worker and to head the welfare department. Miss Higgins arrived in May 1915 after leaving a good position and coming at a considerable financial sacrifice, since no funds were then available to develop the welfare department (McCombs, Mrs. Vernon 1959:2).

Katherine's first project was to survey the social conditions and needs of the Mexicans in Los Angeles, and to submit her findings to the Board of Home Missions. While awaiting funds to begin the welfare work, Miss Higgins assisted McCombs in fund raising activities for church development and for the Spanish American Institute. With no funds forthcoming to establish the welfare department, Katherine took positive action:

> Realizing a remedial and educational health program was badly needed, and there being no funds to launch such a

> work, 150 second-hand coffee sacks, marked "Opportunity Bags", were placed in the homes of Epworthians for their cast-off clothing. When filled they were brought to the Bloom Street Mission, the contents sold and with the money Clinical equipment and medical supplies were purchased. And in the Fall of 1915 a Medical Clinic was opened, admission being 5 cents. The clinic was opened every morning with a religious service which was appreciated by the patients. Then sewing and other classes for mothers, clubs and classes for children and youth, English classes for all, welfare work, and a Mission Sunday School were started (1956:3).

Miss Higgins and her mother made the first "Opportunity Bags" and this successful venture resulted in the later development of the Goodwill Industries in Southern California (McCombs, Mrs. Vernon 1959:2).

The vision and promotion of Vernon McCombs for the establishment of a "Plaza Institutional Church" that would minister to the growing religious, moral, and social needs of the Mexicans in Los Angeles resulted in the organization of a Board of Trustees "to care for the property interests and to have authority to receive annuities and bequests" to make McCombs' vision a reality. This board was incorporated in July 1916 as "the Methodist Board of Latin American Missions" with Robert J. Taylor, pastor of the Vermont Square Methodist Church, as president (*El Mexicano*, Vol. 5, No. 1:5; No. 2:6). The Board decided to purchase a $25,000 lot on the northeast corner of the Plaza, on Marchessault Street (now Sunset Boulevard), from the Huntington Land Company (McCombs, Mrs. Vernon 1959:2). This lot was acquired in January 1917 and the expansion of the ministry soon followed:

> On this lot stood an old adobe building, a landmark, the former headquarters of General Fremont, but later one of the worst vice dens in the City. This old building was cleaned and some of the work moved into it from Bloom Street, but for health reasons and the frequent callers of the former occupants, it was advisable to wreck it. There were no funds to buy another building but Mr. and Mrs. J. C. Lennox gave two lots, which were sold and the funds used to erect two portable buildings. One housed the Plaza Mexican Methodist Church, the other, the Clinic, Employment, Educational, Day Nursery, Kindergarten, Welfare Work and the Plaza Goodwill Industries Store. Another landmark on Olvera Street was used for the Work Shop, or Industrial Work (*Methodist Archives* 1956:3).

By April 1918 the Methodist Board of Latin American Missions had changed its name to "Plaza Community Center" and had occupied the temporary buildings on the Plaza lot (*El Mexicano* Vol. 6, No. 4:4). The motto of the Center was "Helping folks to help themselves." The two portable structures at the Plaza were dedicated in December 1917 but were already too small by September 1918 to meet the growing needs of the Plaza Church and Community Center (Vol. 7, No. 1:3).

Between 1919 and 1921, the Plaza Community Center continued to develop a full program that offered help to every member of the family, where problems were met "by faith, prayer and practical work of the people at the Mission" (Schermerhorn 1953:2). Hatherine Higgins wrote:

> Already many people have learned of this [that the Plaza Community Center was always ready to be a friend to all] and are coming to us with confidence that we will "help them to help themselves," in giving them advice and help along some of the following lines: Employment, labor troubles, education, matrimony; all kinds of domestic troubles; placing of orphan children, juvenile court wards, inmates of county and city jails; justice in court cases, legal matters; health.
>
> "The duty of the church is not only to call men to God, but to put God into the life of the community. *Its fundamental task is to change the relationships that underlie wrong conditions.*"
>
> We are here for the purpose of helping to change the unchristian conditions of this community, and thus make better our city, state, and nation (*El Mexicano*, Vol. 6, No. 4:4; italics mine).

The work begun by Miss Higgins with "Opportunity Bags" in 191[illegible] at the old Bloom Street Mission developed into a profitable and useful ministry by providing employment for needy Mexicans in collecting, repairing and utilizing the clothing and other donated items. The Plaza Goodwill Store opened for business in one of the temporary buildings on the new Plaza lot in March 1918.

The Board of Home Missions, at McCombs' recommendation, broug[illegible] Frederic H. Blair from Boston to become the social and religious director of the Plaza Goodwill Department of the Community Cente[illegible] Blair is credited with much of the expansion of Goodwill Industries in Southern California, serving with this organization fro[illegible] 1919 to 1950 and advancing to become the Regional Director of th[illegible] West Coast Goodwill Industries (Jervey 1960:104-105). At its be[illegible]ginning in 1919, the industrial department of Plaza Community

Center was loosely affiliated with the National Bureau of Goodwill Industries of the Methodist Church, but in 1921 the department was incorporated under its own board of directors: "all equipment, merchandise, 25,000 bags out in homes and the Woman's Auxiliary were transferred to the new organization" (*Methodist Archives* 1956:4). Goodwill Industries original purpose of aiding and employing needy Mexicans and other nationalities changed during the Second World War to providing employment for the handicapped and disabled veterans (Jervey 1960:105).

Spanish American Institute

The success of the Francis DePauw Home and School for girls in Hollywood prompted the Southern California Conference to establish a similar institution for Mexican boys. The "Spanish American Industrial Training School for Boys" was incorporated in 1909 for the purpose of ministering to boys in the same way that the Francis DePauw Home aided Mexican girls:

> The need for a school where Spanish-speaking boys might receive an industrial education had been recognized for many years. It was a group of concerned Christians from the First Methodist Church of Pasadena which put that need in material shape by launching the project of such an institution under the auspices of the Southern California Conference of "The Methodist Episcopal Church" (*Spanish American Institute* 1971:1).

Nothing much was accomplished towards the actual establishment of the school until McCombs arrived to take charge of the Spanish language ministry for the Conference in 1911. McCombs called together an interested group of Christian laymen and began to make concrete plans for the development of this institution as authorized by the Conference. "A Board of Directors was formed and, after several years of work, enough funds were raised to justify the purchase of land and equipment for a building. Several sites were considered before the Gardena 'ranchito' was selected" (1971:1).

The Spanish American Institute (its official name since 1914) opened in Gardena, midway between Los Angeles and the San Pedro harbor, in September 1913 with John Howe the first superintendent. Support for the establishment of the school in Gardena came from Charles Lewis, pastor of the Gardena Methodist Church, who was an enthusiastic friend and fund-raiser of the school for many years. The Gardena Church and a committee of business men in the community raised $1,200 in cash and pledges toward the purchase of property (*El Mexicano*, Vol. 1, No. 1:4). "Established on a ten acre campus, it provided agricultural training, instruction in a multitude of crafts from iron work to commercial arts, and a standard secondary education" (Jervey 1960:94). Eventually the school was enlarged to thirty acres and several new buildings were added through contributions from many churches in the Conference (*Spanish American Institute* 1971:5).

The purpose and goals of the Spanish American Institute were clearly defined by Richard H. Silverthorn, the seventh superintendent of the school:

> First and foremost, the Christian group of men who founded the school had in mind that it would be a Christian character building institution where Mexican boys would be given an opportunity; second, to develop and train boys along vocational lines so that they are able to take their place in the world prepared to accomplish a first-class job; third, to produce leaders who will be a credit to their own race and become outstanding citizens (1971:3).

Although the Institute offered the equivalent of public school education from elementary grades through high school during the early years of its existence, after 1928 the boys attended local public schools and supplemented their program with vocational and religious instruction at the Institute (1971:5). Jervey makes the following comment concerning the quality of the educational program of the school:

> Many of the boys have made excellent records in the public schools. Greater still, the overwhelming majority have gone out to take up their places as Christian citizens in the world, fully equipped with an education and a skill. Some have become fine ministers. The germ of this achievement lies in the Bible Training Class begun at the institution after its opening (1960:95).

One of the most significant developments in the history of the Spanish American Institute was the establishment of the *Bible Training Department* in January 1920, under J. D. Gilliland, for the preparation of young Mexican men for the Christian ministry. Six men were enrolled in ministerial preparation the first year: "These young men are in the school five days in the week and then go out to regular appointments for pastoral work every Saturday and Sunday. They have done a very excellent work, both in school and in their charges" (*El Mexicano*, Vol. IX, No. 1:12). Because a considerable number of Mexican Methodist charges were close to the Institute, several student appointments were made from the most promising young men (Vol. IX, No. 1:5). Four of the most successful young pastors in the District were graduates of the first class: Benito Garcia, Cristobal Valencia, Emilio Hernandez and Francisco Quintanilla (*Journal* 1922:19).

An excellent example of the value of the Bible Training Department is found in the training and ministry of Francisco Quintanilla, who was converted at the Mexican Methodist Church in Pasadena after fleeing from the ranks of the revolutionary army in Mexico. Because of his gifts and potential, Francisco was invited by McCombs to attend the Bible Training Department, one of three young men recruited by the Pasadena Mexican Church (Smith 1933:68-72). After entering the Institute in January 1920, Francisco was sent by McCombs to the Mexican community at Watts, only a few miles north of Gardena, to have services in the homes of interested people. Quintanilla was quoted as saying:

> After a few months, I was able to organize a Sunday School with six persons. This was in the spring of 1920. Our organization was effected in the American Methodist Episcopal Church in Watts and for two years we held our services in that church.... In 1920 we began without any members and now we have 250 members in full communion. In 1920 we began our Sunday School with six persons and now we have an enrollment of more than 400 (1933:73).

In September 1920, McCombs wrote:

> This year Francisco Quintanilla took the field as a student pastor from the Spanish American Institute. If anybody doubts the statement of Francisco's friends that he has served for months under "Pancho" Villa as officer in the revolutionary armies of Mexico, such doubts are allayed on beholding his whirlwind efforts and success every time he turns around, whether it be on his charge or in public address at Arbamar and in the churches. He is very modest and has won, not only the hearts of the Mexicans and the Americans on his circuit, but also of the faculty and students at the Institute. He holds regular services with a growing attendance, having now some thirty Mexicans attending, at each point [Compton and Watts]. His earnest prayer is for a church building at Watts (*El Mexicano*, Vol. IX, No. 1:6-7).

The Watts Mexican Methodist Church, under the leadership of Quintanilla, grew to become one of the largest and most influential Mexican churches in the Southern California Conference for over forty years, until it disbanded in 1964 after the heavy out-migration of Mexicans from that area.

Another important feature of the Spanish American Institute was the social function it served in training Christian young men who were potential husbands for the young Mexican ladies being trained at the Francis DePauw School in Hollywood or at the National Training School for deaconesses in San Francisco. According to McCombs, "It is particularly true in this work that the wives of our pastors are as important as the pastors themselves" (*Journal* 1920:18). The record shows that many Institute students did marry girls from the Francis DePauw School and, hopefully, "lived happily ever after" (*Spanish American Institute* 1971:12).

Epworth Leagues

The Southern California Conference concentrated its early youth ministry in the Sunday school programs of the local churches. However, in order to develop a more extensive youth program, the Epworth League of the Methodist Episcopal Church was organized in 1899. Epworth League chapters multiplied rapidly among the Conference churches, and district conventions and summer institutes were held to train and challenge young people in Christian discipleship. Chapters were organized in many of the growing Spanish-speaking churches throughout Southern California, which served the valuable function of training youth leadership in the churches and encouraging young men for the ministry (Jervey 1960:61-62).

The first Epworth League chapters to be organized in the Spanish and Portuguese District were at Bloom Street Mission (sometimes referred to as "Los Angeles Spanish") and at Santa Ana Mexican Methodist Church during the 1912-1913 Conference year (*El Mexicano*, Vol. 1, No. 6:3,5). The Mexican Epworth League District was organized in December 1915 at Santa Ana where the first conference of Mexican Epworth Leagues was held with 140 representatives attending from all over the Conference (Vol. 4, No. 3:3).

Several Epworth League "Gospel teams" were organized to participate in inspirational and evangelistic meetings within the District. As early as October 1914, the Plaza Epworth League chapter sponsored open-air services on Tuesday evenings at the Plaza under the supervision of Eucario Sein, pastor of the First Mexican Methodist Church of Los Angeles (Vol. 2, No. 4:6). By September 1918, Sein was preaching to large crowds at the Plaza every Sunday afternoon in an "open-air forum" under the continued sponsorship of the Epworth League (*The Latin American* 1918:11). Other Gospel teams conducted services in Mexican and Anglo American churches and missions throughout the Conference, as well as street meetings at many Mexican colonies in Southern California (Stowell 1924:124). McCombs mentions that two youth groups were especially significant and inspiring, the Plaza Gospel Team and the Santa Ana Choral Club: "These fascinating Gospel groups of well-organized and irresistible Mexican youth, numbering eight each, are constantly moving among the Mexican and leading American churches with great effect" (*Journal* 1922:20).

Ministerial Qualifications

The Southern California Conference established high standards of education for new ministers as early as 1881. The General Conference of the Methodist Church in 1896 prescribed specific books or courses for ministerial preparation which the Southern California Conference readily adopted. A candidate was required to score at least sixty-five percent on each level of training before advancing to the next step and full ordination. In 1910 the Conference adopted the requirement that a candidate for the ministry have at least a high school education. The Conference adopted a resolution in 1918 requiring candidates to have a bachelor's degree from an accredited college or university in addition to being a graduate of a theological seminary (Jervey 1960:75-76).

In the Spanish-speaking churches and missions in the Southern California Conference, the above educational qualifications for the ministry were modified to allow for the socioeconomic hardships that existed among the thousands of Mexican immigrants. However, specific courses of instruction for ministerial candidates in the Hispanic churches were established and higher levels of education were often sought by candidates whenever possible. Ministerial training began with the District granting a license to preach to a promising layman, which carried the distinction "lay or local preacher." After completing the prescribed course of study, the candidate would be ordained a "deacon" by an ordination council representing the District. The next level of ministerial attainment was ordination as an "elder". This is the process of training given in the autobiography of Ambrosio C. Gonzales in *El Mexicano* in June 1917 (Vol. 5, No. 4:4,5).

Formal preparation for the pastoral ministry in the Spanish and Portuguese District, and later in the Latin American Mission, was developed through the Bible Training Department of the Spanish American Institute in Gardena, beginning in early 1920. Many of these students served weekend pastorates on nearby circuits. For older men, or those unable to attend the Institute, instruction was given by Eucario Sein at the Plaza Bible Training School which began in October 1920; all of these men had pastoral assignments (McCombs, Mrs. Vernon 1959:3 and *Journal* 1922:19). It is not known when these programs were terminated.

District Progress to 1920

The Mexican population of California, especially in Southern California and Los Angeles, increased significantly between 1910 and 1920 mainly as the result of the revolutionary conditions in Mexico which sent hundreds of thousands of refugees fleeing northward. The number of Mexicans in Los Angeles increased from an estimated 20,000-30,000 in 1913 (*El Mexicano*, Vol. 1, No. 7:4) to over 50,000 by 1918 (*The Latin American* 1918:4). In 1920 Los Angeles was reported to be the fourth largest "Mexican city" in the world (*Journal* 1920:26).

The extent of ministry in the Spanish and Portuguese District increased to thirty-three preaching places in California, with thirteen organized circuits and 644 total members (both active and inactive) by September 1919. However, only one Mexican Methodist church existed within the city of Los Angeles and its membership totaled only 147 with 200 adherents. The majority of the circuits were located in Southern California and only three were outside of Los Angeles and Orange counties; Hanford (Portuguese), Santa Paula and Calexico (*El Mexicano*, Vol. 8, No. 1:3-9).

The scope of Methodist church growth between 1912 and 1920 is *not* adequately reflected in the statistics of communicant church membership as recorded in the annual reports of the District. A more accurate indication of growth is seen in the occasional mention of the number of adherents or converts in *El Mexicano*. For example, although the total communicant membership is given as 644, the annual report for 1919 states: "The adherents include about 2,000 of those who are finding increasing hunger to worship at our temples and to know our fellowship" (Vol. 8, No. 1:8). By 1920, the total number of conversions recorded in the history of the District was given by McCombs as over 1,500 with 266 recorded conversions during the conference year 1918-1919 and 452 for 1919-1920 (*Journal* 1920:26 and McCombs 1930:6).

Because of the marked difference between the number of recorded conversions and adherents and the number of communicant members added during the decade, it is necessary to look for valid reasons for this difference. The most obvious reason, when one examines the history of the period, is that a great number of Mexicans, who were recent arrivals in Southern California from the chaos in Mexico, formed a large floating population that migrated to and from the city of Los Angeles for many years (McEuen 1913:4). Another reason for the lag in membership was the policy among Methodists to require a longer probationary period for new Mexican converts than for Anglo Americans prior to becoming full members (*El Mexicano*, Vol. 2, No. 4:7). Added to these problems was the growing number of inactive or non-resident members among the Mexican churches and missions. After relocating in a new area, Spanish-speaking Methodists were not always able to find and worship in a Methodist congregation. Therefore, some Methodist members became active members of other denominational or independent churches throughout the Southwest, while migrating members of other religious groups would sometimes be attracted to a local Methodist church for this same reason (Vol. 8, No. 1:7).

By September 1919 the thirteen circuits of the District were being served by about thirty-five ministerial and lay workers, both Mexicans and Anglo Americans, who were receiving some salary allotment from the Conference. These workers sold and gave away over 2,400 Bibles and held or assisted in over 4,650 worship and evangelistic services during the 1918-1919 conference year (Vol. 8, No. 1:9). McCombs added:

> The most notable gain of the year is the growing company of fine young Christian workers, who, like eager steeds, are awaiting the opportunity to run the race of the ministry and of other Christian work. For four Quarterly Conferences, we issued ten licenses to preach. Superintendent A. Ray Moore will soon have his hands full of this brand-new crop he is getting ready for at the Spanish American Institute, namely: Mexican young men as divinity students (Vol. 8, No. 1:9).

An example of the type of dedication of the Methodist workers during this pioneer period of Mexican missions is seen in the following comment by McCombs concerning pastor Tirre, who served the Huntington Beach-Westminster circuit in 1919:

> Luis P. Tirre came to us during the year to supply this Beet Empire circuit from Huntington Beach.... Folks throughout the circuit regard him as a wonder in pastoral work and success. He has English classes scattered from Huntington Beach to Artesia, 21 miles away, where thirty Mexicans have united in night school and health center and mothers' meetings. This means a ride of 42 miles for Brother Tirre, on his bicycle, once or twice a week.... He also serves Wintersburg, Balboa, Talbert, and Los Alamitos, and supervises our local preacher, Celso Esparza, at Westminster and Stanton.... It is hoped to inaugurate a bilingual American pastor at some of the points on this circuit, and to provide an auto, partly with Centenary funds (Vol. 8, No. 1:7-8).

Based upon information concerning Spanish-speaking churches and missions of the District as reported in *El Mexicano* for the period prior to the founding of the Latin American Mission in 1920, the chronological record of the expansion and development of the various charges is given in Figure 32.

Figure 32

THE METHODIST EPISCOPAL CHURCH
SPANISH AND PORTUGUESE DISTRICT 1911-1920

Year Established	Name of Church or Mission[1]	Founders or Early Leaders
1911-1912	*Missions at Los Angeles and Pasadena were strengthened	Weaver, McCombs
	Anaheim circuit: Anaheim, Fullerton and Placentia	Samuel Goitia
	Santa Ana circuit (first organized institutional church)	A. C. Gonzalez
1912	Organization of the Spanish and Portuguese District of the California Conference in October	McCombs, Supt.
1912-1913	*Downey circuit: Lankershim, Rivera, Montebello and other preaching points	Antonio Jimenez
	*Evangelistic services at San Pedro, Compton, Long Beach, Watts and in various sections of Los Angeles	McCombs, Narro, Olazabal, Turner and Vincent
1913	*Los Angeles Spanish Church organized (was Bloom Street Mission, 1910)	Enrique Narro
1913-1914	Santa Paula circuit	Enrique Narro
	Santa Ana circuit: Delhi Sugar Factory and El Modeno	A. C. Gonzalez
	*Long Beach circuit: Watts and Santa Monica	Elias Montoya
1914	*Los Angeles Spanish renamed, "First Mexican Methodist Episcopal Church" and relocated on Commercial Street	Eucario Sein
1914-1915	Santa Ana circuit: Artesia	A. C. Gonzalez
	*Rivera-Olinda circuit: Richfield, Yorba Linda and La Habra	Emilio Hernandez
1915-1916	El Modeno Mexican Chapel	A. C. Gonzalez
	*San Fernando circuit	Leonardo Flores, A. C. Gonzalez
	Westminster-Huntington Beach circuit: Los Alamitos	Tranquilino Gomez
	Fillmore, Ventura and Moorpark circuit: Piru	Vicente Mendoza
	Santa Paula circuit: Limoneira and Sespe	Antonio Jimenez

Year Established	Name of Church or Mission[1]	Founders or Early Leaders
1916	Anaheim Mexican Church (mission 1912)	Enrique Narro
	*Los Angeles and Watts circuit	Sein & Higgins
	San Francisco-Sacramento circuit	Francisco Olazabal
1916-1917	*Long Beach circuit: Zaferia	Alfonso Sanchez
	*Watts mission	Emilo Hernandez
	*Pasadena circuit: Lamanda Park	A. C. Gonzalez
	*Puente circuit: El Monte	Miguel Narro
	Santa Ana circuit: Westminster and Garden Grove	Vicente Mendoza
	Santa Paula circuit: Fillmore, Ventura, Moorpark, Piru and Nordoff	Antonio Jimenez
	Calexico circuit	Ore, lay preacher
1917	*Los Angeles: First Mexican Methodist Church relocated in temporary buildings on Plaza lot	Eucario Sein
1918-1919	*Compton-Watts circuit	Emilio Hernandez
	*Long Beach circuit: Perris Road	Alfonso Sanchez
	*Santa Monica circuit: Ocean Park, Sawtelle, The Palms and Venice	Herbert Sein & Benito Garcia
	Santa Paula circuit: Simi	Antonio Jimenez
	*Pasadena circuit: Lincoln District, Glendale and Tropico; and the Mexican hotel	A. C. Gonzalez
	Santa Ana circuit: Orange	J. C. Nava
	Westminster-Huntington Beach circuit: Wintersburg, Balboa, Talbert and Artesia	Luis P. Tirre, Celso Esparza
	Calexico circuit: new church to be built two blocks from the border	Manuel Madrigal
1919-1920	*Watts Mexican Church (meets in Anglo church building); Compton	Francisco Quinilla
	*Santa Monica Mission	Gavino Garcia
	*Glendora Mission	Benito Garcia
	*San Fernando circuit: Lankershim, Van Nuys and Owensmouth	L. C. Flores
	Bakersfield Mission (Puente Mission was exchanged for Bakersfield Congregational)	Emilo Hernandez, Ezequias Durán
	Selma circuit	Stephen Dominguez
	San Francisco Mission	Herbert Sein

After the first mention of a circuit, only additions are given

Los Angeles County

Source: *El Mexicano* 1913-1920

THE LATIN AMERICAN MISSION: 1920-1941

Due to the rapid growth and the potential for continued development among the Spanish and Portuguese-speaking Methodist churches and missions, which stretched from the Mexican border to San Francisco, the Spanish and Portuguese District was reorganized as the "Latin American Mission" in August 1920, under the continuing superintendency of Vernon McCombs. Bishop Adna Wright Leonard of San Francisco formally organized the Mission to expand the area of ministry begun by McCombs and his co-workers in Southern California to include all of California and Nevada, western Arizona and Lower California in Mexico (*El Mexicano*, Vol. IX, No. 1:13).

Decade of Progress: 1920-1930

Whereas the period 1910 to 1920 represents a pioneer decade in the establishment of Spanish-speaking churches and missions, the next decade is the history of the growth and expansion within the circuits previously established, the training of leadership for the churches, and the physical development of church buildings and parsonages. Figure 33 shows the overall growth trends of this period.

In analyzing the decade of the 1920s, McCombs gave the following summary and explanation concerning the data given in Figure 33:

> During the decade the number of workers has been reduced from 62 to 41. We have necessarily lost fields such as Tia Juana, carried on now by the W.H.M.S.; Van Nuys and Monterey, surrendered to another denomination; the Goodwill Industries work has been separated from the Plaza Community Center, and the Filipino work given over to the supervision of the Superintendent of the Chinese Work. Notwithstanding these losses, the church membership more than doubled. Several have joined American churches, not counting also over 100 students at the Spanish American Institute and Frances DePauw who are members of other churches. The Sunday School membership nearly trebled. The total giving has been multiplied by four, and pastoral self-support increased nearly nine times, and total self-support more than five times (1930:7).

The significance of the increase of property values lies in the fact that many of the churches and missions in existence in 1920 were meeting in temporary facilities or in buildings that were rapidly outgrown; but by 1929 most of the churches were located in their own buildings, with greatly improved facilities for

Figure 33

LATIN AMERICAN MISSION
GROWTH TRENDS DURING THE 1920s

	1920	1929
Number of circuits	21	29
Mexican	18	23
Portuguese	2	2
Italian	1	2
Other Spanish	0	2
Number of workers	62	41
Local preachers	14	17
Ordained pastors	8	17
Women workers	18	0
Other workers	22	7
Church membership (total)	1,131	2,895
Full members	686	1,586
Inactive/nonresident	131	705
Probationary	314	604
Number of Sunday schools	28	44
Total Sunday school enrollment	1,386	3,355
Adults baptized	36	95
Total converts to date	1,510	7,976
Church buildings	10	33
Parsonages	3	21
Total giving	$ 3,123	$ 12,952
Total property value	$60,700*	$460,200*

*Note: The 1920 and 1929 figures of "Total property value" do not include the Spanish American Institute or the Munger Building; however, the 1929 figure does include $291,000 listed for the Plaza Community Church and Plaza Community Center.

Sources: McCombs 1930:6; McCombs, Mrs. Vernon 1959:3; *Journal* 1920 and 1929, Statistician's Report

worship and service and a far greater stability of the work. In 1920 there were only ten church buildings in the twenty-one circuits of the Latin American Mission, whereas in 1929, with twenty-nine circuits, thirty-three church buildings were in existence. Equally significant for the decade is the fact that, although the total membership only doubled, the total giving quadrupled, which indicates the improved socioeconomic status of the Mexican Methodist constituency. However, the majority of the funding necessary for the construction of new churches and parsonages during the decade came not from the Spanish-speaking churches themselves, but from the Anglo American churches of the Conference and from Methodist Home Missions allocations.

McCombs described the early 1920s as a period of "moral and spiritual community revival," where "the beautiful feet of the evangels of the gospel of peace are, for the first time, bringing the open Bible, with its moral ideals, its practical, democratic, inter-racial fraternity, and all its wealth of character and faith efficiency" (*Journal* 1922:18). Although not strongly reflected in the statistics of full membership for the first part of the decade, McCombs stated that:

> There seems to be an unusual earnestness and enthusiasm for soul-winning and new membership in the congregations, so scattered and handicapped as to equipment and helpers.... Even in the present time of unemployment, the dear members have followed their heroic pastors in efforts to secure tithers, as at Bakersfield, Long Beach, Rivera and Santa Paula; self-support, as at Santa Ana and Rivera; better equipment, as at San Fernando, Santa Monica and Bakersfield; putting the Bible in every home, as in Rivera and Selma; and pushing on of a larger social and cultural program in nearly all the charges (1922:19-20).

McCombs goes on to describe the sources of this revival energy:

> There have been many contributing factors: a larger volume of prayer in these days of distress and difficulty; there has been more emphasis upon music and the learning of new hymns; the pastors and programming their work and moving toward definite objectives, with a dawning consciousness among our people of the great objectives of the present Methodist movement (which largely began or took form with the Centenary), including conversions, church membership, daily intercessors, and the family altar, tithers and life-service Christian workers (1922:20).

These efforts--among the largely displaced Mexican population that was searching for a new sense of identity, security, and greater social mobility--resulted in 6,466 recorded conversions during the decade, the number of "full active members" more than doubling, growth in the number of Sunday schools from twenty-eight to forty-four, and the Sunday school enrollment increasing by 250 percent (Figure 33).

Although some writers, in discussing the history of Mexican Methodist work in the 1920s, stress Methodist commitment to the "social gospel" during this period, it is obvious after a study of the readily available historical data that McCombs did not compartmentalize "sin" as being either distinctively "institutionally transmitted", or "as a failing of the individual". But rather, he represents "an interesting transitional blend of missionary evangelism and social gospel ideology" (Grebler 1970: 491). Whereas the "social gospel ideology", as a form of theological liberalism, did not stress personal evangelism or individual conversions but rather the social reformation of American society or "institutional salvation", the record shows that McCombs believed that transformed communities and "social uplift" was the result of the conversion of individuals within the community who would then have the spiritual and moral resources to effect permanent changes of "institutional evils" within their communities (*Journal* 1922:17-21).

However, the "institutional church" has been notoriously slow in recognizing the true nature of "social evil" and in taking significant corrective action against major social problems. Here we must make a distinction between "surface problems" and "root problems". Much of the Social Gospel activity expresses a "band-aid mentality" that was directed against surface problems, rather than being a commitment to serious social surgery. The position that the Gospel of Christ demands radical changes of social structures, as well as of individuals, has been argued by the more recent advocates of a "Theology of Liberation" (Gish 1970:113-142).

The charge that

> early missionaries of the Southwest, when campaigning for funds to support their missionary activities, did not explore with the churches the need of reaching these people with a Christian message, but the fact that conversion made "worthy citizens" out of typical Mexicans (Galvan 1969:96-97)

cannot accurately be made against Vernon McCombs. The record in *El Mexicano* reveals McCombs genuine attitude and motivation concerning Methodist ministry among the Spanish-speaking population:

> [The Mexicans] are coming to us in the United States "like doves to their windows," thinking that Mexicans will have in this land what everybody seems to have in abundance. But the fact is that they are worse off here than there, as many of them tell us. For we have not yet provided for these "strangers within our gates" ...Mexicans are a noble people who should be "given a chance," which is precisely what they have never had. The masses reflect this neglect in well-known conditions.
>
> Generous friends all over California stand ready to do all these needy multitudes require to help them "to learn to walk alone," as one Mexican pastor put it. But all such aids of food, clothing, supplies for home and work, medical service, classes, employment, recreation, lodging, training in trades, personal work, Gospel appeal and "brotherly life" generally must be organized and systematized or they may become destructive charity rather than the desired constructive work of giving capacity. "There is no help like the help which helps folks to help themselves."
>
> To neglect this call to us amid our Gospel and temporal plenty will deaden our sympathies and store up vials of social and civic evil for our children, if not for ourselves...
>
> I believe that the Los Angeles Plaza Institutional church will [soon] be brought to pass. It will be a miracle of achievement, for *prejudice and inertia have worn ruts so deep that they have become graves for the souls and bodies of the Mexicans these decades past.*
>
> Just seventy years ago the United States had taken over more than half of Mexico; *what have we done for the people we then took under our care?* (Vol. 5, No. 1:2-3).

Concerning evangelism, McCombs wrote in 1930:

> The Methodist Episcopal Church with its serious and inviting spiritual, winsome, influential leadership and program of evangelism is equaled by no other [denominational effort] particularly in this region [Southern California] (1930:18).

The objectives of the Latin American Mission, according to McCombs, were: "saving souls" and evangelism, social uplift of racial communities, trained leadership, providing material equipment, self-support and self-direction, co-ordinating cognate grou

organization for the permanence of the work, enlisting entire communities in "Evangelical Christianity", enriching cultural programs, larger strategy and values "in our great task", team work with the general Methodist program of Centenary quotas (cf. Sweet 1950:404), assisting World Service Cultivation, co-operating with the Interdenominational Comity Council, and enlisting support and workers for missions (McCombs 1930:3). McCombs' strategy was more than the traditional evangelistic thrust of the "Fundamentalists", and it represents a significant attempt toward ministry to the "whole man" based on the example of the teaching, preaching, and healing ministry of Jesus (cf. Matthew 4:23-24).

However, McCombs believed that "destructive forces" were at work against the task of bringing Mexican people to a definite commitment to Evangelical Christianity and to active membership in Methodist churches:

> Great subtle movements are here competing in the plastic humanity represented by 500 thousand people for whom the Latin American Mission is responsible. They include godless, irreligious, subtly-tempting settlement houses, fiestas and clubs who are vying with enriched programs often supported by the Community Chest for the time and talents of our hundreds of thousands of young people. Among other subtle movements disorganizing the work are the Pentecostal movement, the Roman Catholic Church especially strong and active among the Latins and, in this part of the country, the Communists who are anti-church, and other independent movements. Vice, bootleggers, youthful criminals, are exceedingly active and in contact with our Latin peoples. Gradually the race prejudices and antipathies are being broken down by work such as we carry forward (McCombs 1930:18).

Opposition to Methodist ministry in Southern California occured in an earlier period, as well:

> [At Long Beach] Socialists and members of the Independent Mexican church have stirred up trouble concerning pastors being given salaries. Nevertheless, the people from the Pacific Electric section and others round about are coming out now, and that means an interest in the Gospel (*El Mexicano*, Vol. 2, No. 4:5).

The Latin American Mission continued to grow and develop under McCombs leadership, however, in spite of competition from other religious and social organizations or from disruptive influences within some of the churches, namely the growing Pentecostal* influence. The chronological history of Mexican Methodist growth during the 1920s is given in Figure 34. Jay Stowell, in *Methodism's New Frontier*, attributes this growth to a combination of factors:

> The large new influx of Mexicans; new leadership; a Centenary program which gave new courage and provided enlarged resources for the work; and, in some cases, loyal community cooperation on the part of Americans in the communities touched, particularly involving help in the erection of new buildings and the maintenance of a general attitude of good will toward the work (1924:126).

In 1930, McLean reported that twenty-two Methodist Episcopal Mexican churches and missions were in existence in Los Angeles County (1930:37-39). However, many of these were only temporary missions that later ceased to exist. Only nine churches or missions listed by McLean were still in existence by 1940 and only six remained beyond 1960.

Development of Plaza Mexican Church and Community Center

When W. T. Gilliland was appointed Superintendent of Plaza Community Center in 1921, he began a serious campaign to erect the proposed Plaza Church and Community Center, along with the full cooperation of McCombs and pastor Sein, and with the support and encouragement of the Board of Trustees. The construction of the new Plaza Church was given first priority and the Community Center building was to follow as a second stage of development. By December 1922, the temporary buildings that had stood on the Plaza lot since 1917 were moved to the corner of Sunset Blvd. and New High Street in anticipation of beginning the construction of Plaza Church. However, due to a lack of funds, the actual construction was delayed until 1925 and the church was not ready for occupancy until April 1926. The Plaza Community Center building, which was planned to be four stories and a basement, remained uncompleted until further fund raising by Gilliland in 1927 brought in another $25,000. By December 1927 the basement and first two floors were occupied (*Methodist Archives* 1952:2; and Gilliland 1925:1,2).

The many departments of Plaza Community Center, some of which had struggled along in small temporary quarters for over ten years, now occupied the newly completed building next to Plaza

---

*Note: This paragraph should not be construed to imply that the Pentecostal Movement is not commited to Evangelical Christianity, but rather that Pentecostalism was a disruptive force within Methodism during the 1920s.

Figure 34

THE METHODIST EPISCOPAL CHURCH
LATIN AMERICAN MISSION: 1920-1930

Year Established	Name of Church or Mission	Early Leaders
1920	Organization of Latin American Mission (Aug.): California, Nevada, Western Arizona and Lower California (Mexico) with twenty-one circuits and 817 full-members (includes inactive).	Vernon McCombs
1920-1921	Fillmore circuit (was with Santa Paula)	J. R. Wood
	Sacramento circuit	Ralph Rader
1921-1922	*West Long Beach Mission	Alfonso Sanchez
	*Downey Sunday school organized on Rivera circuit	Benito Garcia, Mrs. Widaman
1922-1923	*Pasadena: Lamanda Park Mexican	Carlos Andueza
	Mountain View Latin American	Bonifacio Durán
	Orange-El Modeno circuit	Ricardo Schade
	*Owensmouth-Van Nuys circuit	Ezequias Durán
1923-1924	Artesia-Stanton circuit	Tranquilino Gomez
	Fullerton Mexican	Leandro Lopez
	Mesa, Arizona Mexican	Alma Blew
	Stockton Latin American	Cristobal Valencia
	San Francisco Filipino	
	San Francisco Italian	Lucius Martucci
1924-1925	Moorpark circuit	Feliciano Chavez
	Tia Juana-San Ysidro circuit	
1926	*Dedication of the new Plaza Mexican Church (April)	Eucario Sein
1927	*Dedication of Plaza Community Center building (December)	W. T. Gilliland
1927-1928	Monterey Latin American	
1928-1929	Pittsburg Mexican	Alfonso Lara
1929-1930	Selma circuit (was with Bakersfield)	

*Los Angeles County

Source: *LAM Journal* 1920-1930

Church, which stood facing the birthplace of the city of Los Angeles. The Center offices were located on the second floor, with the first floor entirely devoted to the clinic which consisted of several departments staffed by volunteer doctors and specialists: dental; eye, ear, nose and throat; and general medical departments. The remainder of the building was occupied by the welfare, recreational, educational, legal and employment departments, in addition to the Christian Training School (*Methodist Archives* 1952:2).

Organized in October 1920, the Plaza Christian Training School offered "instruction in Christian doctrines and in practical methods of church work," with classes meeting four afternoons each week and all instruction in Spanish. (Stowell 1924:124) When the school began, pastor Sein of Plaza Church was the only instructor, but by 1924 the faculty had increased to six members. At that time Stowell wrote: "The school is particularly for the Mexican and other Spanish-speaking young people, who have been converted and called to special Christian service, without having earlier opportunities for adequate training (1924:124) Training was offered to men already serving circuits in the district. In addition, new workers who were unable to devote full-time to theological study in the Bible Training Department of the Spanish American Institute in Gardena were trained in the part-time program at the Plaza school and served student pastorates on the week-ends. The first class to receive instruction in this new program under pastor Sein included twelve students, five of whom were: Benito Garcia, Cristobal Valencia, Benjamin Cortez, Leonardo Flores and Ezequias Durán (*Journal* 1922:19). It is not known how long this school was in existence, but Christian workers continued to receive instruction through 1928 (Gilliland 1928:2).

In 1923 the Plaza Children's Home was established in a rented house in Los Angeles because of an urgent need for a home to care for many young children who were left without parents during the influenza epidemic of that year. This was the only Protestant orphanage for Hispanic Americans in Southern California. Property was later purchased in Sierra Madre and the Children's Home was moved to permanent facilities where it remained until the Home was closed in 1954 (*Methodist Archives* 1952:2; 1956:4).

During the difficult years of the Depression, the staff of Plaza Community Center struggled under serious financial strain and amidst the growing needs of hundreds of Mexicans and Anglos who came to their doors for assistance. Somehow the payments were made on the new building, but no funds were available to finish the remaining two floors. Moreover, the work load of the clinic was seriously curtailed in 1935 when the second floor was remodeled to house the Methodist Headquarters of the Southern

California Conference, which had been forced to move from its previous location. Up to that time, the Center had continuously sought to expand its services to the Spanish-speaking community, but this discouraging situation resulted in a drastic reduction of its services. Schermerhorn reports that, at this time, "Dr. Gilliland, after fifteen years of strenuous service, gave up his work as superintendent" (1953:2).

About 1939, when the Bishop of the Southern California-Arizona Conference moved his office from San Francisco to Los Angeles, the third floor of the Community Center was completed to meet the expanding needs of the Methodist Headquarters. It was not until 1949, however, that the final phase of construction was begun on the fourth floor of the building. The top floor was completed at a cost of $57,000 and occupied in April 1950 by the various departments of the Methodist Headquarters staff (*Methodist Archives* 1952:3).

District Gains and Losses: 1920-1940

During the late 1930s definite changes were taking place in the community surrounding Plaza Mexican Methodist Church and Community Center, which had long been located in a predominantly Mexican neighborhood. According to Schermerhorn: "In the period 1937-1940 great changes were made in the areas adjacent to the Plaza, with the building of the new Union Station, the enlargement of the Civic Center, and the moving in of industry" (1953:3). Not only were large numbers of Mexicans displaced by civic and industrial expansion, but thousands more were "repatriated" by Los Angeles County civil authorities in order to ease the pressure of unemployment and the over-loaded welfare rolls. Grebler states that "between 1931 and 1934 the Los Angeles Department of Charities launched 15 special trainloads averaging 1,000 Mexicans each," which sent relief recipients back to Mexico with the assistance of the Mexican government (Grebler 1970:524). However, most of those shipped back "home" to Mexico did not go voluntarily, but were forced to leave houses and belongings, families and friends, regardless of their citizenship status. Others returned entirely of their own volition to rural villages or to the growing cities and towns of Mexico where they hoped to survive the ravages of the Depression.

Membership statistics for the Methodist Episcopal Church reflect the outmigration of Mexicans from Los Angeles County and the Southwest during the early 1930s, especially in the growing numbers of nonresident members: "There is a dubious gain in nonresident and inactive members of 238, the number now being 1,299. Many of these members have gone back to Mexico and with whom letters, in very many cases, are being exchanged" (*Journal* 1935: 21). Plaza Mexican Church, for example, decreased in communicant membership from 265 in 1930 to 212 in 1935, but by 1940 membership had grown to 316. The overall statistics for Los Angeles County reveal that communicant membership within the Latin American Mission declined between 1930-1935, from 832 members to 816 (Figure 35).

The financial hardships of the Depression years along with the declining Mexican population are reflected in the slow down in the number of new churches or missions begun during the 1930s. Only four new charges are recorded for the period 1930-1934--Simi, Ventura, Burbank and Costa Mesa--and none are reported between 1935-1941.

The Latin American Mission District was enlarged during the years 1932 through 1936 to include all of Arizona, New Mexico, Texas, Colorado and Kansas. In 1932 this district had forty-six circuits, fifty-four churches, sixty-five Sunday schools, 2,321 full-members (includes inactive), and a Sunday school enrollment of 4,740 (*Journal* 1932). However, in 1937 the district resumed its previous geographical dimensions, which included the entire state of California, western Arizona, and the adjacent border region in northern Mexico.

The unification of the two major branches of Methodism, which had separated in 1845 over the slavery question, took place in 1939 when the Methodist Episcopal Church and the Methodist Episcopal Church, South (along with the smaller Methodist Protestant Church which had separated in 1830) merged to form "the Methodist Church". Before unification, McCombs reported thirty-seven Spanish-speaking churches with 2,940 full-members (includes inactive) in the Latin American Mission of the Methodist Episcopal Church (*Journal* 1939). At unification, the Methodist Episcopal Church, South added eleven Spanish-speaking churches with 936 full-members (includes inactive): (1) California added *La Trinidad*, Los Angeles; *El Mesias*, Inglewood; and Dinuba. (2) Arizona added Tucson, Phoenix, Prescott, Nogales, Miami-Claypool and Sonora-Hayden circuits (*Journal* 1940). When these two Latin American Conferences were united, Vernon McCombs was appointed Superintendent and Dr. Lawrence Reynolds, who was director of the southern Church's Spanish-speaking ministry, resigned and went into retirement (*Methodist Archives* 1956:7).

THE LATIN AMERICAN PROVISIONAL CONFERENCE: 1941-1956

In July 1941 the Latin American Mission was reorganized as the Latin American Provisional Conference within the geographical boundaries of the Southern California-Arizona and the (Northern) California-Nevada Annual Conferences. Between 1941 and 1956, five major geographical district reorganizations took place

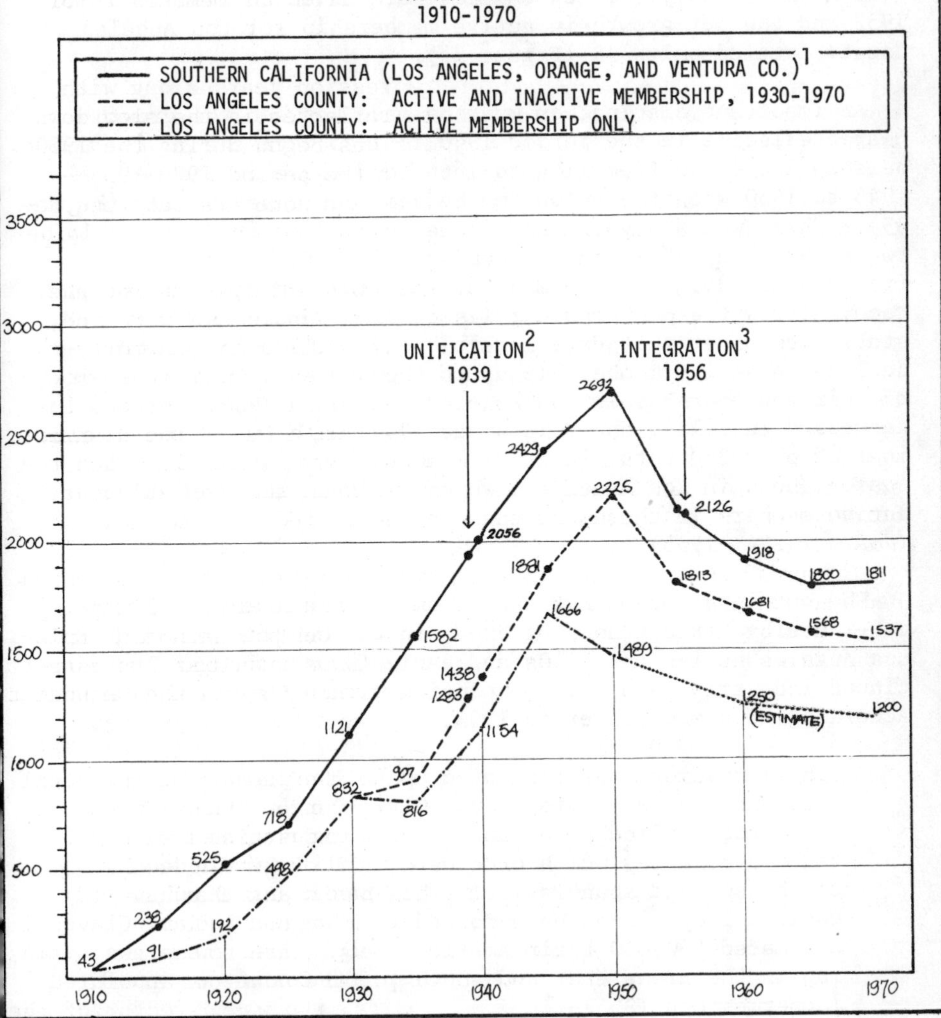

Notes:

[1]Statistics for Southern California include full members/active, 1910-1934 and 1955-1970; Full members/active and inactive, 1935-1954.

[2]Unification of Methodist Episcopal Church and M.E., South in 1939; M.E., South added two churches and 190 communicant members (included in 1940 statistics).

[3]Integration of Latin American Provisional Conference with Southern California-Arizona Annual Conference of the Methodist Church

Sources: *El Mexicano* 1913-1920; *Latin American Journal* 1920-1940; *Journal of the Latin American Provisional Conference* 1941-1953; *Journal of the So. California-Arizona Conference of the Methodist Church* 1954-1970.

within the Latin American Provisional Conference, with churches being shifted from one district to another with great frequency. These changes, however, were not necessitated due to rapid growth, since only two new charges were added between 1940 and 1953 and the net growth in active membership for Los Angeles County totaled only 335 (Figure 35).

An important distinction must be made between the growth characteristics in the period 1940 to 1945 when the *active* membership increased from 1154 to 1666, and those in the period 1945 to 1950 when the *active* membership decreased by 177 (Figure 35). There was a significant increase in *inactive* membership between 1945 and 1950 when the number of inactive members rose from 289 to 736. By 1955 many of the inactive members had been removed from the membership rolls of the churches so that the statistics after that date more closely reflect the continuing decline in active membership up to the present. Out of a total of thirteen churches in Los Angeles County in 1955, eight had decreased in full-membership since 1950, with two churches eliminating over 350 total inactive members (*La Plaza* and *El Buen Pastor*, both in Los Angeles), which reflects the decline in active members in these churches in the period 1945 to 1950 (*Journal* 1941-1955).

The outmigration of Mexicans from the Plaza area and from other nearby Mexican housing areas in the Central District of Los Angeles during the 1940s and early 1950s resulted from continued industrial and civic expansion within those neighborhoods. According to one observer in 1953,

> [This] movement has continued up to the present time, until now freeways, railways, Civic Center, Union Station, Post Office Annex and certain industries have taken over areas which once were full of little Mexican houses and shanties.... This has meant that the Mexican people have been forced to move and today an estimated 250,000 Latin American people are now living in the areas east and south [of the Downtown area] (Schermerhorn 1953:3).

For this reason it was necessary to relocate the Plaza Community Center from its Plaza lot to East Los Angeles in 1954. From this new beginning, in an area with a greater concentration of Mexican American and other Latin peoples, the community center and clinic was able to fulfill its charter obligation of ministering to the Spanish-speaking population, first in a rented building and then in new facilities which were dedicated in January 1960 (Jervey 1960:96). Thus, McCombs' vision and concern for ministering to the "whole man" has been continued in the new heart of the Mexican population.

Changes were also taking place administratively and structurally within the Latin American Provisional Conference. Vernon McCombs retired from the superintendency in June 1946 and was succeeded by H. M. Hilliard, and later by L. P. Tirre and Doroteo Venegas (*Methodist Archives* 1956:7). In 1948 the General Conference of the Methodist Church took initial action regarding the integration of the various Provisional Conferences (which represented racial and ethnic minorities) into the Annual Conferences within which they were located geographically.

Bishop James Baker appointed a Committee on Integration in 1949 composed of representatives from the Provisional Conferences, the Southern California-Arizona Annual Conference, and the (Northern) California-Nevada Annual Conference. In 1953 when a special committee representing the Latin American Provisional Conference and the two Annual Conferences met, a vote was taken indicating that the overwhelming majority of both laymen and ministers favored integration. It was further decided that final integration would be completed by June 1956, which was presumed to be sufficient time to affect salary increases for Spanish-speaking ministers to bring them up to the standards of the Annual Conferences, and to prepare the Spanish-speaking churches for merger with the Anglo Conferences (Jervey 1960:180-181).

At integration in 1956, twenty-seven ministers and 2,375 members from the Metropolitan and Arizona districts of the Latin American Provisional Conference were transferred into the Southern California-Arizona Annual Conference, while the North District was incorporated into the (Northern) California-Nevada Annual Conference; the Metropolitan District included Los Angeles and Orange counties (*Journal* 1956:64). The statistical report for 1955 reported that Los Angeles County's twelve Spanish-speaking Methodist churches had a communicant membership (both active and inactive) of 1813, and Orange County's five churches totaled 340 communicant members (1955:335).

RECENT DEVELOPMENTS IN HISPANIC METHODISM: 1956-1971

The record of Hispanic Methodist church growth for the decade of the 1950s is one of gradual decline in Los Angeles County and Southern California, and this pattern has continued to the present (Figure 35). It is important to analyze the possible reasons for this decline, as well as to consider the proposed solutions of Methodist churchmen.

A Critique of Integration

Whereas one might be easily tempted to attribute Hispanic Methodist decline since 1950 to external factors, such as the outmigration of the Spanish-speaking population from neighborhoods where several large Hispanic churches were located for many years (*La Plaza* in Los Angeles and *El Buen Pastor* in Watts), it is clear from a comparison of Methodist growth patterns with those of other denominations and from the writings of Hispanic Methodist churchmen that the major reasons for this decline are internal factors.

If a comparison is made between the growth patterns of the Hispanic churches among the United Presbyterians, the American Baptists, the Southern Baptists, and the United Methodists, it is easy to see major differences in rates of growth. The American Baptist communicant membership almost doubled between 1950 and 1970 along with a net increase of fifteen churches (Figure 43). Hispanic Southern Baptist membership grew 375 percent between 1960 and 1970 in Los Angeles County (Figure 51) with twenty-four new churches and missions coming into existence since 1950. By contrast, the Presbyterians and the Methodists both have a similar history of declining numbers of Hispanic churches and membership, and it is these two groups that have "forced" a policy of integration on their respective Spanish-speaking churches and ministers. Thus, it appears that the attitudes and tensions involved in the process of Hispanic integration within the dominant Anglo denominational structure has strongly contributed to the decline of the Hispanic Methodist Church in Southern California.

Eliaz Galvan contends that the movement toward integration was the result of indirect pressure from the Civil Rights Movement and direct pressure from "liberal" church leaders who were opposed to the continued existence of segregated ethnic bodies within the denominations affiliated with the National Council of Churches. Therefore, the steps taken by the Methodists to integrate the Provisional Annual Conferences, especially in the case of the Latin American Conference, was a move to eliminate a strong source of embarrassment to Methodist leadership in ecumenical circles. And furthermore, according to Galvan, the Anglo leadership saw integration as an "opportunity to ameliorate the financial burden which the small Spanish-speaking churches were causing" to the Board of Missions. Galvan argues that Anglo denominational leaders originally conceived of the ethnic church "only as a step in the acculturation process of the individual, thus, having a temporary function...", but they later viewed "the ethnic church as an obstacle to assimilation; thus, integration of segrated bodies was seen as the solution to many problems" (1969:102-103).

The results of integration for the Hispanic Methodist churches in Southern California, according to Galvan, were the following:

> Among denominational officials there is a general dismay that "integration" has not worked. The second, or third generation of Mexican-Americans are not transferring in mass to the Anglo churches. On the other side, the Spanish-speaking ministers fell into a demoralizing state when they lost control over their work and saw the closing of many of their churches. *More than ten years have passed after integration and the Latin churches have experienced a decrease in their membership without a substantial increase of Spanish-surnamed persons in the Anglo churches, and a critical shortage of leaders.*
>
> What went wrong? Many Latin ministers claim that integration was unfair to them. They were not given equal status when received into the larger conference. Others affirm that their increase in salary was about the only good thing that came from integration. Still others would say that they were not ready for integration, that the haste with which the Anglo conferences and the Board of Missions preceeded have damaged the work among the Spanish-speaking population (Galvan 1969:103-104, italics mine).

Integration was seen as a "cure-all" for the complex problems of inter-relationships between the Anglo-dominated conferences and the ethnic churches. However, there is a long history of "discriminatory attitudes and practices among the Anglo membership"; reluctance to invest the necessary funds for church development within the sphere of "Home Missions" while huge sums were invested in "Foreign Missions"; strong paternalism among Anglo churchmen who retained the reigns of leadership in the denominational structure and in the institutions that served the Spanish-speaking population; and failure to update the theological education of Hispanic ministers and to recruit new leadership, especially in Southern California (1969:104-106).

Therefore, integration was indeed unfair to a large number of Spanish-speaking pastors who had long lived under the double standard imposed on them by the Anglo-controlled hierarchy that refused to take the Hispanic Church seriously, to prepare the Spanish-speaking congregations for full participation within American Methodism, or to respect their cultural differences and allow them the freedom of self-determination.

The New Face of Hispanic Methodism

Several recent articles in Methodist publications, together with policy statements from Hispanic church leaders, point to creative and constructive change within the United Methodist Church. The most important changes are in respect to the self-determination of Hispanic congregations and their revitalization as viable instruments for mission among the growing Hispanic population of the United States.

The Congregation in Mission. There is a growing conviction among younger Hispanic church leaders, according to Joel Martinez in *Response* (1970:25), that "there is unparalleled opportunity for the Hispanic United Methodist congregation to be in mission to the people whose mother tongue is Spanish." Whether or not the Hispanic Church responds to this opportunity will largely depend upon its ability to leave behind its "mentality of survival" and to develop the resources with which to successfully "engage in mission" to the total Hispanic community. The survival mentality of Spanish-speaking congregations was a reaction to many years of hostility that they faced in the *barrios* of the Southwest because of their Protestant convictions and their "rejection" of the historic folk-Catholic heritage of the majority of the residents of the *barrios*. But the Hispanic Church also reacted "to the subtle indifference of the general church and its agencies...and this hampered its engagement in mission more than any other factors" (1970:25).

Self-determination and Shared Resources. The future strength of the Hispanic Methodist Church and the development of her resources as a mature and responsible component of American Methodism will no doubt depend upon the response that the United Methodist Church gives to its Hispanic constituency by way of both "allowing" and encouraging self-determination, and by sharing her resources with the struggling Spanish-speaking congregations. "Especially significant," according to Martinez, "is the new attitude of the Board of Missions with regard to self-determination in the area of program development and the administration of funds" (1970:25). In the light of the Hispanic American cultural renaissance in the Southwest, it is imperative that Methodism be truly united in its efforts to provide creative and well-trained leadership "that will bring direction to the total Hispanic community as it discovers anew its history, its culture and its capabilities" (1970:25). Martinez argues his point well:

> Now, in the time of the rebirth of hope, the Hispanic-American masses will move ahead with new confidence and dignity. Their role in the Southwest will be decisive. They will be shaping the institutions, the systems, the

> policies of the area in the days to come. It will be the church that lives among the people--that is, in the barrio--that will make its influence felt.
>
> The congregation that speaks the language, appreciates the culture, and pitches its resources and leadership into the service of the people will be the congregation which will get a hearing. None else need apply.... *Only as the congregation in its life and the general church in its attitude and support appreciate this potential for mission will the opportunity in all its fullness be seized* (1970:26, italics mine).

Development of Hispanic Caucauses. The movement toward self-determination and shared resources as a policy of the Methodist Board of Missions toward the Hispanic Church and other ethnic churches has not come about without internal stress. For example, in October 1970, an appeal for more attention to be paid to Hispanic American problems was made by Dr. Ignacio Castuera, who represented the Latin American Methodist Action Group of the Southern California-Arizona Conference before a meeting of the Board of Missions. His recommendations were:

> A $1 million nationwide scholarship fund for Hispanic-Americans, the establishment of an Hispanic-American center for theological and socioeconomic studies and the hiring of at least 50 more Hispanic community organizers for work in "barrios" (Dart 1970c).

Because integration is viewed by many Hispanic leaders as "robbing" the Hispanic Methodist Church of whatever voice it had in denominational affairs, these churchmen have joined forces with their fellow-pastors, both in local Methodist conferences and nationwide, to form Hispanic "caucuses". These action groups seek to present their case before their respective Conferences and national Methodist bodies: "Some conferences have formally recognized these groups and have delegated to them certain authority and funds," according to James Davis (1970:5). Davis believes that the crucial question faced by the United Methodists is

> how to harmonize [racial and ethnic] differences into a working unity without destroying creative differences... [since] minority groups within geographic conferences are searching for ways to preserve their own unique identity, to control their own destiny, and to strengthen the ministry to their people (1970:6,49).

Theological Education for the Hispanic Church. One of the most hopeful new thrusts within the Hispanic Methodist Church, in cooperation with the United Methodist Conference, is in the area of leadership education for creative ministry among the Hispanic population of the Southwest. Whereas the majority of the older Hispanic Methodist pastors were trained on a Bible Institute level at either the Lydia Patterson Institute in El Paso, Texas or at the Spanish American Institute in Gardena, California, the majority of the younger pastors and church leaders have received a graduate-level training at Perkins Theological Seminary in Texas or at the School of Theology at Claremont, California. Unfortunately, neither Perkins nor Claremont seminaries has offered a bilingual program geared to the continuing needs of the Hispanic Methodist Church, either for the recruitment and training of new ministers, or for the in-service training of present ministers.

However, the Spanish American Institute (S.A.I.) in Gardena took definite action during 1970 "to shift the emphasis of S.A.I. more directly into ministerial education and enablement for Spanish-speaking churches" by establishing a Center of Latin American Churchmanship. The director of S.A.I., Richard Acosta, has outlined the rationale and the priorities for this new Center (Acosta 1971:1-2; n.d.:1-3):

> Since Metropolitan Los Angeles is probably the major Spanish-speaking center in the Southwest, the churches are faced with extraordinary challenges in church development and strategy, ethnic selfconsciousness, and radical politics. To meet the needs of a rapidly changing society, the Institute could be re-directed to serve more individuals by helping develop Latin church leadership. This revision in policy, in cooperation with the School of Theology at Claremont, could be a significant step in responsibly fulfilling the traditions of Spanish American Institute in the future. This will include:
>
> a) Recruitment of ministerial students
> b) Establishment of tuition and financial aid funds for these students
> c) Conducting of weekend institutes for Latin laymen interested in full-time service as lay-ministers
> d) Conducting of retreats and institutes to train laymen in Churchmanship relevant for today
> e) Working through LAMAG [Latin American Methodist Action Group], MARCHA [Methodists Associated Representing the Cause of Hispanic Americans] and COHAM [Council on Hispanic American Ministeries] to train ministers and laymen for community action

f) Providing a center for re-training of missionaries to Spanish-speaking countries
g) Sponsoring a program of Spanish language instruction [to train bilingual ministers and leaders for community action]
h) Inviting churchmen and theologians from Spanish-speaking countries for study and lecturing
i) Sponsoring cultural activities [in Hispanic churches and in the community to increase the pride of the Latin people in their cultural heritage]
j) Creating of a Spanish library and archives
k) Possible sponsorship of a Chair of Spanish American Studies at the School of Theology

The changing character of the Spanish American Institute reflects the up-to-date needs of the Spanish-speaking Methodist churches in a rapidly changing urban society. For almost sixty years, the Institute served the Hispanic community by providing education and job skills for Mexican boys "who were normally excluded from such advantages because of ethnic prejudice and vocational exclusiveness." However, due to the high cost of maintaining such an institution, the curtailment of denominational and private funding, the increasing problems of meeting state licensing requirements, and "the changing character of institutional responsibilities of the Church", the Board of Directors have redefined the Institute's role to one of ministerial education and church revitalization (*Spanish American Institute* 1969:1; Acosta 1971:1).

These proposed changes in the function of the Institute do not mean, however, that it will be absorbed into another organization, but that it will continue "its role of mediating the two cultures by shifting its emphasis" and still maintain its autonomy (*Spanish American Institute Subcommittee* 1970:1). The Institute, according to this proposal, would

> ...relocate to the campus of the School of Theology at Claremont in a relationship that would be similar to that enjoyed by the Disciples Seminary Foundation. The Institute would retain its corporate charter and structure, its board, and its relation to the United Methodist Church. But it would integrate its program into the School of Theology and the academic and research facilities of the School would be available to the Institute (*Spanish American Institute* 1969:1).

Community Development. Along with the renewed emphasis on ministerial education, both the training of new ministers and in-service training for present pastors, the Hispanic Methodist Church is exploring the creative possibilities of providing community leadership through "community action organizers." The Hispanic cultural renaissance in the Southwest forecasts a long-term commitment to Spanish language ministry by Methodist congregations, not for mere survival but for constructive engagement with the problems and needs of the Hispanic population. It is in the local community that a local church must provide creative leadership if it is to be a "congregation-in-mission". "Our main task", said Richard Acosta, "shall be a new thrust into the development of leadership for decisive community guidance and action.... Constructive Christian social concern shall be furthered through the training of ministers and laymen for *community action*" (n.d.:2).

Martinez mentions a new United Methodist program called "Indigenous Community Developers" that is being sponsored by the National Division of the Board of Missions (1970:25-27). This program "provides financial assistance to local congregations for the hiring of a person to work on the staff of the church in the area of community development." The local congregation seeks to relate itself to the *barrio* in a significant way by creating a local policy committee for community development composed of representatives from both the church and the community. The goals of one such church, Emmanuel United Methodist in El Paso, Texas, were the following:

> The recruitment and mobilization of lay and clergy leadership in community service programs and movements for social change; developing new forms of service and ministry; relating to existing community service programs sponsored by other denominations relating to community-wide organizations and agencies in order to strengthen the ties between the leadership of the church and the community (Martinez 1970:27).

This kind of involvement, stimulated by the concern of a local church to be a servant to its community in behalf of Christ, will no doubt have significant and permanent implications within the Hispanic community as it strives for equal opportunity, greater mobility, and creative self-expression within American society. This is the new face of Hispanic Methodism.

OVERVIEW OF GROWTH IN HISPANIC METHODISM: 1910-1971

The patterns of Methodist growth fall into three main periods. From *the beginning* of organized Spanish-speaking ministry in 1911 and continuing until 1930, the Spanish and Portuguese District, reorganized as the Latin American Mission in 1920, experienced its greatest proportionate growth in relationship to total church membership. For example, Figure 36 shows that the number

Figure 36

HISPANIC METHODIST BAPTISMS
(Number Baptisms per 100 Church Members per Year)
1914-1931

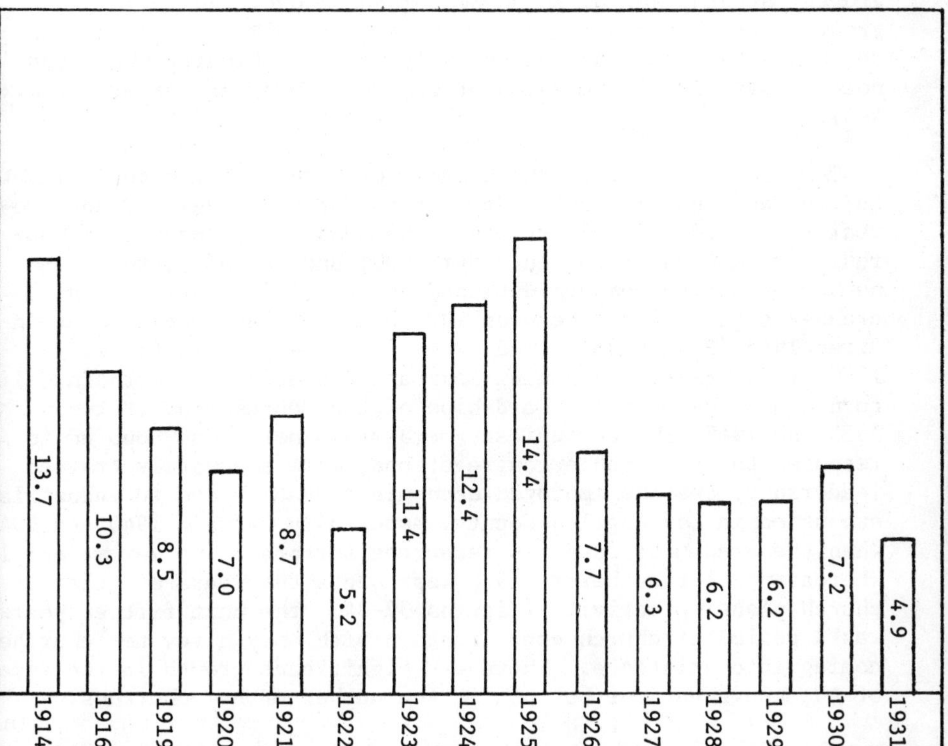

:es: *El Mexicano* 1914-1920;
Latin American Journal 1920-1932

of baptisms per one-hundred church members per year between 1914 and 1926, although 1920 and 1922 were low years, was much higher than in the period 1926 to 1931. If records were available, no doubt the period 1910 to 1914 would also show a similar high proportionate growth based on the number of baptisms. This agrees with the data available on the number of recorded conversions between the years 1913 to 1931, which shows that 1915 and 1916 had the highest number of conversions per one-hundred church members per year: 68.4 for 1915 and 47.2 for 1916. The next highest year was 1924 with 46.7 conversions per one-hundred church members. Some churchmen might expect this to be a normal growth pattern, but as Ralph Winter has shown, the period of greatest proportionate growth can occur at any time in the history of a movement, not necessarily in the beginning years and not necessarily in the years of greatest numerical growth (n.d.: 4-5).

The second period in the history of Methodist growth begins in 1930 and ends in 1945. Statistics for Los Angeles County reveal the following: First, that the number of inactive or nonresident members increased after 1930; and secondly, that the number of active members declined between 1930 and 1935, increased significantly between 1935 and 1945, and declined again after 1945 (Figure 35). The slump in membership in the early 1930s reflects the declining Mexican population in Southern California and the economic hardships of the Depression. Between 1935 and 1945, the communicant membership more than doubled in response to more stable congregations, more adequately trained leadership, and the improved economic situation due to industrial expansion in Los Angeles County, especially between 1940 and 1945 when the area mobilized its resources for producing war materials. Whereas the period before 1930 represents the years of greatest church planting activity (Figures 32-34), the next fifteen years was a period of church consolidation with only a few new churches coming into existence. There was significant growth in the size of the congregations but not in the number of new churches.

The final period in the history of Hispanic Methodism, 1945 to 1971, is characterized by a continuing decline in active communicant membership. Although the statistics on full-membership (both active and inactive members) point to 1950 as the peak year of Methodist growth, the record of active membership in Los Angeles County shows that the causes for the later decline had their origin in the mid-forties (Figure 35). Two basic reasons have been given for this decline: the outmigration of the Mexican population from some of the older *barrios* because of urban renewal, industrial expansion, and freeway construction; and the internal changes in the Latin American Provisional Conference, both preceding and following the integration of the Spanish-speaking churches into the Anglo, English-speaking Southern California-Arizona Annual Conference. Integration resulted in the closing of some of the struggling Hispanic churches and, in some cases, the consolidation of several neighboring congregations to form one stronger church.

Although the reasons for the decline of Hispanic Methodism in Los Angeles County are complex and generalizations overlook contributing factors, it seems evident that the greatest cause of demoralization and decline among the Hispanic churches has its origin in the attitude and policy of Anglo churchmen who held to the Anglo-conformity model of assimilation. Since the Spanish-speaking congregation was believed to be only a temporary expedient until integration and assimilation occured, no long-range planning was given to Hispanic Church development, especially in terms of ministerial recruitment and education or to leadership education within the local congregations. This is the principal reason for the continued existence of struggling Hispanic churches who have had to make the rapid transition from a paternalistic mission-oriented relationship with the Anglo-dominated Conference to one of "equal partnership", although the inequities of the past still produce frustration and contribute to the present decline in the strength of Hispanic Methodism.

Both the problems and the potential of Spanish language ministry present a continuing challenge to the United Methodist Church in Southern California, a challenge that can only be met by a commitment to Hispanic self-determination and shared resources. Hopefully, the recent change in policy by the Methodist Board of National Missions will stimulate Hispanic Church development and will aid in the establishment of the Center of Latin American Churchmanship as proposed by Acosta of the Spanish American Institute. The new program of Indigenous Community Developers also has great potential for stimulating the Hispanic congregation in mission to its immediate neighborhood, both evangelistically and in constructive social action.

Although the years 1945 to 1971 present a general picture of stagnation, demoralization and decline, the decade of the 1960s does reveal a growing number of Spanish-speaking departments in Anglo churches and the establishment of several new Hispanic churches in Los Angeles County. At least seven Spanish departments have been established since 1958 and two new autonomous churches have come into existence. Communicant membership in the Spanish departments totals about 250 people. Estimates by Hispanic church leaders indicate a very low ratio of Hispanic communicants in Anglo churches which do not have a Spanish-speaking department. But, hopefully, the new trend of Hispanic church development will continue and increase throughout this decade and will establish a new pattern for later years.

8.

The Northern (American) Baptist Convention

Since the American Baptist Hispanic churches and missions comprise the largest number of congregations in Los Angeles County, and due to the wealth of available data, a thorough narrative of their history is required. To provide the setting in which the Spanish-speaking ministry has developed in Southern California, a brief summary of the origin and development of the Southern California Baptist Convention will be given, along with an analysis of growth patterns in the English and Spanish language churches.

SOUTHERN CALIFORNIA BAPTIST CONVENTION

The first association of Baptists in Southern California was organized in 1869 in El Monte with five churches and 118 members; this was the origin of the Los Angeles Baptist Association (Hine 1966:31). The association was only nominally affiliated with the California Baptist State Convention, since the strength of the State Convention was in Northern California. In 1892 the Los Angeles Association was reorganized to form four associations--Santa Barbara, Santa Ana Valley, San Diego and Los Angeles-which constituted the new Southern California Baptist Convention (SCBC), a sister organization to the Northern California Baptist Convention. At the national level, the SCBC officially recognized the Northern Baptist Convention in 1908, the year after its formation, and became affiliated with the new denomination in January 1912 (1966:91-93,107).

Anglo Baptist churches in the Southland multiplied rapidly along with the exploding population of the area, so that by 1920 there were ninety-nine churches with 22,975 members. By 1965, the number of churches had grown to 285 and the number of church members to 114,600. The growth by decades was (Hine 1966:93):

1920-1929	Net growth of sixty-five churches
1930-1939	Thirty-two churches established, but a net gain of twenty-six
1940-1949	Seventy-one new churches; a net gain of forty-five
1950-1959	New churches totaled seventy-three with a net gain of forty-five

The uneven growth among Anglo Baptists in Southern California between 1920 and 1970 reflects the changing economic and religious conditions, fluctuations in population growth, and the changing urban situation. Especially significant was the out-migration of Anglos from urban neighborhoods to the suburbs in an attempt to escape from the problems of minority group influx during the 1930s and 1950s. The decade of the 1930s witnessed the beginning of heavy losses among Baptists in Southern California due to the economic decline of the Depression years, and in part to theological differences. The Fundamentalist-Modernist controversy dominated the religious life of the 1930s (1966:164-165).

The founding of Baptist churches during the period 1940 to 1960 strongly reflects the tremendous population growth of the war and post-war eras in Southern California, whereas the high mortality rate among the churches is evidence of Baptist failure to adjust to the problems of changing urban conditions. For example, between 1940 and 1950, seventy-one new churches were formed but twenty-six went out of existence; and between 1950 and 1960, while seventy-three churches were organized, twenty-eight ceased to exist.

The growth pattern of individual churches, especially in the metropolitan areas of Los Angeles County and particularly within the city of Los Angeles, as in other major American cities, reflects the pressures of interaction between the older Anglo church constituency and the growing minority population. Many churches in Los Angeles were "forced" either to disband, to merge with other churches, or to relocate in other areas of the city or in the suburbs as minority groups rapidly moved into their inner-city neighborhoods. The Anglo church members fled to the safety of the suburbs of Los Angeles, or to the security of conservative Orange County which is part of the Los Angeles metropolitan area (1966:164-165).

In the decade of the 1950s, the Southern California Baptist Convention also experienced competition from other Baptist groups who were entering the Southland in large numbers, most notably the Southern Baptist Convention; although some churches were lost to the newly formed Conservative Baptist Association that came into existence because of theological dissension within the Northern Baptist Convention between 1943 and 1947 (Hine 1966:164 and Torbet 1963:436). In 1950, the Northern Baptists changed their name to "the American Baptist Convention".

Concerning the growth of the Southern California Convention during the past decade, Hine states:

> While many churches have continued to grow and new churches have been founded since 1960, American Baptists in Southern California, as in many other places, have been decreasing somewhat in number. The high point was 1960 when the Convention reported 117,075 members. In 1964, the number had dropped to 114,603. Baptisms per year also dropped from 5,778 to 4,406. Actually, the decrease as measured in relation to the population of Southern California began a decade earlier.... The reasons for and the meanings of this are not clear. Most of the decrease has taken place in Los Angeles, where the *failure to discover ways to minister to changing neighborhoods* is as evident as in other large cities. Since life in most of the churches seems to be growing in health, the decrease probably reflects general conditions and some still lingering ambiguities concerning the proper nature of the American Baptist witness (1966:166, italics mine).

EARLY HISPANIC CHURCHES AND MISSIONS: 1900-1910

Prior to 1910, the Southern California Baptist Convention had made few attempts to minister to the Spanish-speaking Mexicans who were scattered throughout the Southland. The First Baptist Church of Santa Barbara has the distinction of being the first church in the Convention to initiate evangelistic work among the Mexicans in Southern California. Established in March 1901, the Mexican mission in Santa Barbara was pastored by C. T. Valdivia who also ministered in many of the surrounding towns and successfully established a mission in Oxnard in 1903. However, these two missions had disbanded by 1910 (Ellis 1938:90).

Ministry to Mexicans in Los Angeles was initiated by Miss Nina Morford in 1902, who also conducted a "Chinese Baptist Night School" (Ellis 1938:146). Between 1905 and 1907, the First Baptist Church of Los Angeles established a Mexican mission on Rio Street, but this mission went through several years of strife before it became part of the Anderson Street Mission under the leadership of the Troyers, and eventually was developed into *La Iglesia Bautista El Salvador* in 1915 (Troyer 1934:49; Ellis 1938:130-132). The Calvary Baptist Church sponsored a Mexican Mission in 1910 which became the First Mexican Baptist Church in 1912 (1938:128).

DR. AND MRS. L. E. TROYER: 1911-1917

The development of Baptist ministry to Spanish-speaking people in Southern California followed the appointment of the Reverend and Mrs. L. E. Troyer as general missionaries for Spanish work under the Southern California Baptist Convention in 1911. After serving as Baptist missionaries in Puerto Rico, and later in Pueblo, Mexico, the Troyers returned to Los Angeles in 1910 due to the ill health of L. E. Troyer, and were asked to be Superintendents of the Mexican ministry early the next year (Troyer 1934:146-147).

First Mexican Baptist Church

Beginning with the two missions in Los Angeles, the Troyers were instrumental in establishing the First Mexican Church in its own building. Since no funds were available from the Convention for development of the Spanish-speaking missions, the Troyers faithfully trusted that God would provide supporters for the expansion of the ministry: one gift of $2,500 was received for the construction of the church building, and members of the Southern California Baptist Convention Board of Directors contributed $600 for the purchase of the lot (1934:23-26).

Rio Street Mission

When the Troyers arrived in Los Angeles in the winter of 1910-1911, contact was made with a Mexican mission on Rio Street that had once been under the care of the First Baptist Church. Concerning the origin of this mission, Quiñones wrote:

> the First Baptist Church of Los Angeles sponsored a Spanish Baptist Mission under lay leadership.... At the beginning, they met in the homes of the people and by 1906 they had congregational meetings under a tent where they were known as the Baptist Mission of the New Testament.... (1966:16).

However, a group of dissenting members from the First Baptist Church, who had organized themselves as "Grace Church", were supervising the work of the mission since the only Spanish-speaking member at First Baptist was one of the "departing brethren" (Troyer 1934:49). The Rio Street Mission was not affiliated with the Southern California Baptist Convention for most of 1910 through 1912 (Ellis 1938:131).

Iglesia Bautista El Salvador

In 1913 the Grace Baptist Church allowed the Rio Street Mission to come under the supervision of the Troyers, after much prayer and diplomacy by the Troyers. For a brief time, the mission continued to meet in a rented building on Rio Street; but when a lot on North Anderson Street was given to the Troyers, a chapel was constructed for the Mexican mission and the Rio Street buildings was used to open a Russian-speaking ministry (Troyer 1934:49-51). When the Anderson Street Mission was opened in 1914, Mateo Carceller was called as pastor. Under his leadership, with assistance from the Troyers, this mission was organized as *La Iglesia Bautista El Salvador* in 1915 (Ellis 1938:130-132); however, the annual reports of the Southern California Baptist Convention listed this church for several years as "North Anderson Street Mexican".

Santa Barbara and Oxnard

During their first year in Southern California, the Troyers re-established the Mexican mission in Santa Barbara which had been discontinued some years previously for lack of Spanish-speaking workers. The Troyers rented a building for the new mission and enlisted Antonio Jimenez to develop the work among a large colony of Mexicans. The First Baptist Church of Santa Barbara provided the salary for the new pastor and his wife (Troyer 1934:28-32). A few miles down the coast at Oxnard was the mission established by Valdivia, but it had also disbanded prior to the Troyers' arrival; a new work was begun that eventually developed into an organized church, *El Buen Pastor*, in 1928 (1934:33,34).

When the Troyers concluded their second year of ministry in January 1913, additional missions had been developed in nearby Long Beach and Bandini, and in distant Bakersfield, Corona, and San Diego; two stations were added in Los Angeles, as well (*SCBC Annual Report* 1913:36).

Bandini Mission

During the course of the Troyers early missionary labors in Los Angeles and in the surrounding towns where new Mexican colonies were rapidly growing due to heavy immigration, the Troyers came upon a labor camp located near the Los Angeles River and the eastern city limits of Los Angeles, called Bandini. Most of the people in this settlement in 1912 were employed at the Simons

Brick Yard located nearby, and the land upon which they built their shacks and houses was owned by the Simons Company (cf. Grebler 1970:311). The Troyers bravely went to the president of the company in Los Angeles and persuaded him to allow a Mexican mission to be opened at Bandini using company buildings (Troyer 1934:38-42).

Garnet Street Church

In 1913 another mission began in an unused building at the Simons City Brick Yard, on the edge of the Boyle Heights section of Los Angeles. Because there was such a transformation in the lives of his workers, Walter Simons offered the Troyers a lot on Garnet Street on which to build a more permanent mission. Work on the new building began on Thanksgiving Day, 1913, at Garnet and Seventh Streets. Within a few weeks, the newly established Garnet Street Mission was growing rapidly (1934:43-48). After the City Mission Society took over supervision of the Garnet Street field in 1919, the mission was organized as Garnet Street Baptist Church and a new building was constructed in 1922 (*SCBC Annual Report* 1922:104). The Lorena Heights Mission was developed as a branch of the Garnet Street Church around 1923, after Villanueva and the "auto chapel" spent several months in the area (*SCBC Annual Report* 1923:99).

Overview of Growth: 1911-1917

The accomplishments of the first seven years of organized Northern Baptist work among the growing Mexican population in the Southland were significant. Many Anglo churches were enlisted to help expand the Spanish language ministry. Their help included giving financial aid, providing places of worship, and appointing new workers to assist the Troyers in missions already opened and in developing new missions in responsive areas. By 1918, when Dr. J. F. Watson's term (1912-1918) as Executive Secretary of the Southern California Baptist Convention came to an end, at least thirteen missions and two Mexican churches had been established through the labors of the Troyers and their co-workers. The total number of Mexican churches and missions established by Baptists in Southern California between 1911 and 1917 is shown in Figure 37.

The valuable leadership and inspiration of the Troyers, beginning in 1911 and continuing to the death of Mr. Troyer in 1917, laid a valuable foundation for the expansion of Spanish-speaking ministry throughout Southern California. Following the death of her husband, Mrs. Troyer continued to serve as a missionary for many years and wrote two valuable books describing the opening of Baptist missions in the Southwest: *The Sovereignty of the Holy Spirit (Revealed in the Opening of our Mexican Missions of the South-West)* and *Protestant Missions to Catholic Immigrants;* both published in 1934.

Figure 37

NORTHERN BAPTIST MEXICAN CHURCHES
AND MISSIONS: 1911-1917

Year Established	Name of Church or Mission	Founders or Early Leaders
1911-1912	*First Mexican Church, Los Angeles (mission 1910)	Lucas Ruiz
	Santa Barbara Mission (re-established)	Antonio Jimenez
	Oxnard Mission (re-established)	Antonio Jimenez
	*Bandini Mission	Janie Duggan
	*Long Beach Mission (temporary)	
	Bakersfield Mission	C. T. Valdivia
	Corona Mission	Hattie Greenlaw
	San Diego Mission	Janie Duggan
1913	*Garnet Street Mission	Hallie Embre
	*Lorena Street Mission	Swedish Baptist
	*Rio Street Mission (established 1905; Independent 1910-12)	Troyers
1914	*No. Anderson Street Mission (was Rio St.)	Troyers
	Garden Grove Mission	Marcos Castillo
	*Monrovia Mission (temporary)	
1915	*San Pedro Mission	R. Q. Martinez
	*El Salvador Baptist Church (was No. Anderson Street Mission)	Mateo Carceller
	San Diego, second mission	Lucas Ruiz
1916-1917	Several outstations/preaching places	

*Los Angeles County

Sources: Quiñones 1966:17-18; Ellis 1938:128-132; and *SCBC Annual Reports* 1913:36; 1914:16; 1916:47 .

EXPANSION OF HISPANIC MINISTRY: 1918-1939

The superintendency of the Spanish work, left vacant by the death of Mr. Troyer in 1917, was filled the following year by the appointment of Edwin R. Brown who had recently arrived from Pueblo, Mexico. Brown became the Field Executive for the Mexican ministry under the American Baptist Home Mission Society, which made him responsible for an extensive area that now stretched from Michigan to California. The Spanish language ministry in Southern California was co-sponsored by the Southern California Baptist Convention under the leadership of Dr. W. F. Harper, the Executive Secretary from 1918 to 1929. Responsibility for Mexican missions within the city of Los Angeles was shared with J. B. Fox, Secretary of the Los Angeles Baptist City Mission Society (Ellis 1938:148).

Cooperating Agencies

Two additional mission agencies participated in opening and developing churches and missions among the Spanish-speaking population in the Southland. The *Women's Home Mission Society* provided many needed workers who were especially important to the ministry of the Baptist Christian Center in Los Angeles. Of the ten women missionaries involved in the Spanish-speaking ministry in the United States in 1930, three were serving in Southern California (McLean 1930:28). *The American Baptist Publication Society* played a central role in the development of new Mexican missions by providing colporteurs, also known as *"Chapel Car Missionaries"*, who spent several months in new mission areas distributing Christian literature, organizing Sunday schools and preaching services, and laying the foundations for the establishment of a permanent mission (Hine 1966:104-106). In 1930, Southern California had two chapel car missionaries devoting full-time to Spanish-speaking extension work: P. J. Villanueva and M. P. Enriquez (McLean 1930:27).

Organization of Mexican Baptist Work

In 1923 the Spanish-speaking churches and missions in the Southern California Baptist Convention were organized into the Mexican Baptist Convention which operates as a separate language department within the State Convention. However, the Superintendent of the Mexican Work, Edwin R. Brown, continued to provide needed leadership for the Spanish churches and supervised the establishment of new churches and missions until his resignation in 1938 when he became a full-time professor at the Spanish American Baptist Seminary. Separate women's and young people's organizations came into being for Spanish-speaking people (Ellis 1938:148).

By 1954 three regional conventions of Spanish-speaking Baptists had been organized within the American Baptist Convention: the Northern California Mexican Baptist Convention, the Southern California Mexican Baptist Convention, and the Spanish American Baptist Convention composed of churches in the Midwest. The Spanish-speaking Baptists in the Midwest belong to one of three associations within the Spanish American Convention: the Michigan Spanish American Baptist Association, the Great Lakes Spanish American Baptist Association, and the Central Spanish American Association (Leavenworth and Froyd 1954:15).

Chronological History of Mexican Churches and Missions

Although it is difficult to document the exact date when some of the Mexican missions were established in Southern California, the period 1910 to 1935 is obviously when the greatest number of missions were started, especially during the years 1925-1929 (Figure 38). Ellis traced the origin and development of Baptist churches in Southern California prior to 1938 and contributed valuable information on the development of Mexican missions in this period of rapid growth. Ellis' data closely agrees with the chronological record of Hispanic growth given in Figure .

During the administration of W. F. Harper (1918-1929), according to Ellis, fifteen Mexican missions were established in the area supervised by the Southern California Baptist Convention *outside* of the city of Los Angeles: five missions were organized into churches by 1938, five were abandoned or relocated and renamed because of the resettlement of members of these congregations in other areas, and five were still operated as missions (Ellis 1938:148). Based on the historical data for the entire Southern California area, eleven Mexican Baptist churches and twenty-four missions were established between 1918 and 1929; thirteen missions and six churches were in Los Angeles County.

Under the leadership of Otto S. Russell, who was Executive Secretary of the SCBC from 1930 to 1939, at least eight Mexican missions were established in Los Angeles County. Evidently, seven Spanish-speaking missions were also developed under the supervision of J. B. Fox of the City Mission Society between 1919 and 1938. Of these, five were organized churches in 1938 and two were still classified as missions (1938:148). The chronological history of the establishment of Mexican churches and missions during the 1930s is given in Figure 39.

Figure 38

MEXICAN BAPTIST GROWTH: 1918-1929

Year Established	Name of Church or Mission	Founders or Early Leaders
1918	*Watts mission, L.A.	
	*Boston Heights mission, L.A.	
	*Mexican mission (North Broadway field)	Mrs. A. M. Petty
	*Bauchet International Mission, Mexican Dept.	Pablo Ayon
1919	Corona Latin American Baptist Church (mission in 1901; re-established in 1912)	
	Colton mission (later First Mexican ca. 1921)	Alberto Cordova
1920	*Christian Center, L.A. (Settlement House, El Salvador Baptist Church)	
1921	*Spanish-American Baptist Seminary at Christian Center	Dr. Detweiler
1922	*San Pedro Mexican Baptist Church (mission 1915)	R. Q. Martinez
	*Marvilla Park Mexican mission	Hallie Embre
ca. 1922	*Wilmington mission (temporary)	
1923	*Garnet Street Mexican Baptist Church (mission 1913)	
	*Hollenbeck Avenue mission (became Bethel Mexican Baptist ca. 1931)	Hallie Embre, Alberto Morales
	Meadowbrook mission, San Bernardino	First Baptist
ca. 1923	Banning mission (church 1925)	
1924	San Diego First Mexican Church (mission 1918)	
	El Cajon mission, San Diego	
	Beaumont mission	
	*Pacoima mission (church 1928)	Lankersheim Baptist, San Fernando Baptist
	*Marvilla Park Mexican Baptist Church (mission 1922; became Bethania 1945-1946)	
	*Rose Hill Mexican Mission (church 1927)	
1925	Banning Mexican Baptist Church (mission ca. 1923)	Beulah Simpson
	Lemon Grove Mission, San Diego	
	Calvary Mission, San Diego	
	TiaJuana Mission (church 1931)	
	*Belvedere Park Mexican Mission (church 1927)	Samuel Ortegon

Year Established	Name of Church or Mission	Founders or Early Leaders
1926	*Venice mission (church 1938)	San Pedro Mexican
	*West Pico Street Mission	
	*Harbor City Mexican Mission (church 1950)	
1927	*Rose Hill Mexican Baptist Church (mission 1924)	
	*Belvedere Park Mexican Baptist Church (mission 1925; became Park Vista 1963)	Samuel Ortegon
	Anaheim-Fullerton mission (Anaheim, church 1934)	Anaheim & Fullerton Baptist churches
1928	Oxnard, Good Shepherd Mexican Church (mission 1903; re-established 1912)	
	*Pacoima, Good Shepherd Mexican Church (mission 1924)	Prendez
1929	Placentia mission (sponsored by Fullerton Baptist Church)	Villanueva, Janeway
	Independencia mission	Anaheim Mexican
	La Habra mission (church 1933)	Villanueva
	La Jolla mission	
	Manzanilla mission	Garden Grove Mexican, Antonio Jiminez

*Los Angeles County

Sources: Ortegon 1932; Troyer 1934; Ellis 1938; Quiñones 1966; and *SCBC Annual Reports*

Growth Factors

At least five major factors influenced the growth rate of Hispanic churches and missions during this period of rapid development: the migratory character of the Mexican population, strategic concentrations of Mexicans, trained leadership, improved church facilities, and the evangelistic concern of Hispanic Baptists.

The migratory character of the Mexican Population. Many Mexican missions were only temporary congregations that never develope into permanent churches because of the high migration rate of the Spanish-speaking population in California prior to World War II. For this reason, wrote Ellis, "the growth in membership of Mexicar Baptist churches and missions before 1920, had been very slow, anc quite in proportion to the age of the work in each place" (1938: 149). During the 1930s, not only was the traditional dependence upon seasonal agricultural employment in various sections of

Figure 39

MEXICAN BAPTIST GROWTH
1930-1939

Year Established	Name of Church or Mission	Founders or Early Leaders
1930	Brawley Mexican mission	O'Compo, Beulah Simpson
	Tijuana Primera Bautists (mission 1925)	
	*Bethel Mexican Baptist Church (was Hollenbeck Avenue Mission, 1923	Armando Alvarado
ca. 1930	*South Park Street Baptist Church, Mexican Mission or Department	Langford
1931	Shafter Mission (church 1932)	Prendez, Shafter Baptist Church
1932	Shafter First Mexican (mission 1931)	
	Carpenteria mission	Villanueva, Santa Barbara Mexican
1933	Camarillo mission	Villanueva, Escalera
ca. 1933	Sawtelle mission	Venice Mexican, Argueta
	*Wilmington mission (temporary)	
1933	La Habra First Mexican Church (mission 1929)	
1934	Anaheim First Mexican Church (mission 1928)	
1935	Colonia Juarez, Wintersburg Rd., Huntington Beach	Antonio Jiminez
1936	Lompoc mission	Santa Barbara Mexican
1938	*Venice First Mexican Church (mission 1926)	
	Riverside Mexican mission (church 1942)	
	Blythe mission	

*Los Angeles County

Sources: Ortegon 1932; Troyer 1934; Ellis 1938; Quiñones 1966; and *SCBC Annual Reports*

California a continuing factor in the migratory character of Mexican immigrants and their American-born families, but also the socioeconomic difficulties of the Depression years caused the population to be "extremely migratory and fluctuating," according to Ellis (1938:149).

This factor helps to explain the apparent contradiction between the recorded active church membership and the number of conversions and baptisms per year in Mexican Baptist churches and missions. For example, of the four organized Mexican churches in 1920, the newly organized church at Santa Barbara was the largest in membership (eighty), *El Salvador* and First Mexican in Los Angeles each had fifty members, and Corona had about forty-five members. The membership of these churches fluctuated significantly from year to year, although the number of baptisms was often between fifty and seventy per year during the 1930s. This means, of course, that the Hispanic membership was also extremely migratory in most of the churches and missions, which caused difficult problems in building up strong self-supporting churches composed of mature Christians. Even though the strategy of the City Mission Society was to develop missions in strategic areas where strong Hispanic churches could grow, the main problem was one of trying to determine how long an area would be "strategic" when the Mexican population was so highly migratory.

Strategic Concentrations of Mexicans. There were sections of Los Angeles and adjacent county areas, especially the area east of the city limits that is now generally known as "East Los Angeles", where large colonies of Mexicans settled, more or less permanently, and where several permanent churches were established. Hallie Embre organized a mission in Marvilla Park in 1922 when several members of the Garnet Street Mexican Church moved into this new housing area. Growth was so rapid that a church was organized and buildings were erected by 1924 (Troyer 1934:75).

Belvedere Park was developed in typical Southern California real estate boom fashion, with small lots offered in a hilly area that had been bypassed by other land promotion schemes. The area was mostly settled by Mexican immigrants who bought small plots of land and built small houses, which can still be seen today in this section of Los Angeles County that is still "just beyond" the city limits. Mrs. Troyer observed the development of Belvedere Park and recorded:

> This great new section of Belvedere was being opened up for the Mexican people, a district lying about midway between the Marvilla Park Church and our First Mexican Church. We were called out one day and stood in amazement at the countless little houses that were going up on every hand. We were amazed at the development, for

> we had passed through this territory three months before and there was not, at that time, a single house standing. We visited the nearest real estate office and found there was only one lot that could be bought (1934:75-76).

Mrs. Troyer bought the available lot and it was taken over and developed by the Southern California Baptist Convention. The "auto chapel" was loaned for six months to initiate the work on that field, which resulted in the conversion of "a large and earnest group of people" who were organized to form the Belvedere Park Mexican Baptist Church in 1927, only two years after the mission had been established (Troyer 1934:76; Ellis 1938:150).

Trained Leadership. A principal factor in the growth of Mexican Baptist churches in Southern California since 1921 was the location of the Spanish American Baptist Seminary in Los Angeles which provided trained leadership for the churches and missions (Ellis 1938:148). This seminary has trained a majority of the Mexican Baptist (Northern Baptist Convention) pastors for the United States, and even some for Mexico and Central America. Many of the students in the seminary served as pastors in local churches during their course work in Los Angeles, which gave the Mexican churches and missions a definite leadership advantage over many other Spanish-speaking congregations in other parts of California and the Southwest until the early 1960s (1938:194).

Prior to the establishment of this seminary, the tendency among Mexican Baptist churches in California was to ordain and call to the ministry any promising young man who had the ability to speak well in public, regardless of his educational background. According to Ortegon, the only qualifications for the ministry were that a man have a conversion experience and demonstrate good speaking ability. The new minister's education was then advanced "though a Minister's Conference in an American Association or Convention, or through the teaching of an American pastor who spent special time teaching the new convert preacher." These young men were usually encouraged to complete their high school education, if possible (1950:214-215).

The quality of Mexican pastoral leadership in the early years of Baptist development showed continued improvement. By 1938 there were several pastors with both college and seminary degrees, another with a university degree, and fourteen were graduates of theological seminaries out of a total of fifty-three Mexican Baptist pastors within the Northern Baptist Convention. The two pastors with both college and seminary degrees were Samuel M. Ortegon and John R. Janeway, who were both serving churches in the Los Angeles area (Ellis 1938:151).

Improved Church Facilities. The Los Angeles Baptist City Mission Society served a most important function during this period of rapid Baptist church growth by making funds available for the construction of new church buildings for Spanish-speaking missions. The new buildings that were provided for the First Mexican Baptist Church in Los Angeles in 1936, which had begun as a mission in 1910 and was an organized church by 1912, no doubt were one of the principal reasons for the church's continued increase in membership during the late 1930s and into the 1950s. The peak membership of First Mexican occured in 1950 when 421 members were recorded.

Adequate church facilities do not in themselves insure continued growth in membership. But if a church is experiencing rapid growth because the spiritual and social needs of its members are being met by the quality of their congregational life, then new buildings, or expanded or remodeled facilities, can help to stimulate continued growth. However, when a church obtains new buildings, the members often expect the new facilities to do all the work for them--that is, they expect that the new buildings will "in themselves" draw people to the worship services. Consequently, the acquiring of new facilities has sometimes been a contributing factor in the *decline* of some churches because of changes of attitude by members of the congregation once they were comfortable in their new surroundings. Some congregations have stopped "caring" for people in the community, have become preoccupied with their own "family life", and have degenerated to a "professional" level of ministry: "we pay the pastor to teach, preach, evangelize, and care for the sick and elderly." A warning was given by Ellis that is still true today: "As better churches are built and better equipment is provided, there seems to be a tendency to relax individual efforts, and to expect the church building to draw the people" (1938:152).

Evangelistic Concern. In evaluating growth factors among the Mexican Baptist churches in Southern California one of the most outstanding characteristics of Mexican Christians was *their evangelistic zeal*, especially among the most recent converts. According to Ortegon:

> It was not difficult to enlist evangelists for the conversion of the Mexican immigrant since almost every converted Mexican Baptist became in turn a zealous and active evangelist, whole families were won through the zeal and devotion of converted fathers, mothers, brothers, sisters, and uncles. The most influential Mexican Baptist churches were born during this period [1910-1923] in this manner (1950:114).

Ellis tabulated the number of baptisms recorded by several of the largest churches and found that the First Mexican Baptist Church baptized 371 new converts in the eighteen year period 1920 to 1938, whereas *El Salvador* recorded only 267 baptisms and Santa Barbara 216. According to Ellis, "Few churches in Southern California can boast as good a record in this respect, and most observers agree that this has been the chief element in the progress and success of the Mexican Baptist Churches." The average number of baptisms for these three churches computed on a yearly and monthly basis, however, was small:

Church	No. Bapt. per year	No. Bapt. per mo.
First Mexican Baptist	20.6	1.7
El Salvador Baptist	14.8	1.2
Santa Barbara Mexican Baptist	12.0	1.0

By examining the period 1921 to 1930 in terms of the number of baptisms per year in proportion to the total number of communicant church members in Mexican Baptist churches and missions, a more specific growth picture emerges. Figure 40 indicates that the

Figure 40

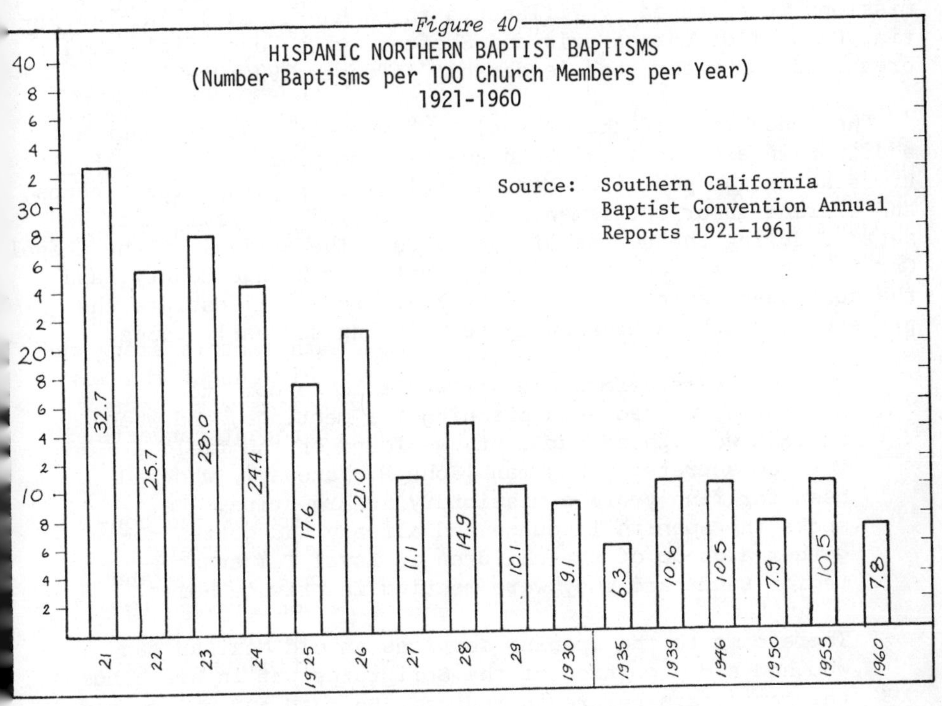

highest percentage of the growth in church membership took place between 1921 and 1926, based on the data available. No doubt the period before 1921, if statistics were available, would show an equally high percentage of growth in relation to the number of church members. In comparison to the record of Methodist baptisms for the same period (Figure 36), the number of Baptist baptisms per hundred members per year was more than double that of the Methodists. However, the growth of both the Baptists and Methodists was severely curtailed during the Depression years (cf. Figures 35 and 43).

Chapel Car Ministry

The development of new Mexican missions in Southern California was the result of many contributing growth factors. For example, in 1923, an Anglo widow in Santa Ana gave $20,000--part of the fortune left by her late husband--to the work of Mexican missions. This large gift was used to provide an automobile, living quarters, and a tent for Gospel services that were used by P. J. Villaneuva, a gifted evangelist and colporteur who served with the American Baptist Publication Society. For over eight years, Villaneuva planted churches and missions in Southern California, occasionally assisted by Mrs. Troyer. Between 1924 and 1933, new missions were opened by Villaneuva in La Habra, La Jolla, Placentia, Camarillo, Carpenteria and Shafter, with "each field well organized and under good leadership" (Troyer 1934:94-95).

The innovation of the "Chapel Car" ministry was an important addition in expanding the Spanish-speaking ministry of the Baptists among the scattered Mexican colonies, railroad labor camps, and migrant labor settlements where thousands of immigrants had settled during the decade of the 1920s. The arrival of the Chapel Car in the citrus community of Placentia in Orange County, and the subsequent events narrated by Mrs. Troyer, illustrate the procedure used by a missionary team during the early 1930s:

> For two years before the car was able to come to Placentia, we had been planning for meetings, and when at last we pithced our tent, we found on the field a very consecrated young man [John R. Janeway], who had been for five years a missionary in Argentina. He spoke the Spanish language and already had gotten together a group of the children in Loyal Temperance Legion Band, and they were meeting in private homes.
>
> There came to the opening services an old Mexican man who had had a portion of the Scriptures put in his hands thirteen years before in Mexico. He read and understood [but] he brought upon himself a great amount of dissension; in fact, the neighborhood made it so uncomfortable for

> him that he came to the United States, where he was told there was religious freedom. He came at great sacrifice....
>
> There were no funds available [for a chapel], so we continued the services and had a vacation school for another month...[then] the Holy Spirit laid it upon the heart of a dear old Mexican man to give us a piece of property on which there was a little house, where we might hold our services while the needed chapel was being built.
>
> Arrangements were made by our Convention Board to take over the property, and they offered a contribution of $1000, to be matched by a like amount from the field. Mr. Bassitt, the active chairman of the missionary committee of the Fullerton [Baptist] Church, proceeded to raise a like amount, and under his direction, and with the cooperation of other members of the Fullerton Church, the building was erected, and today we have a beautiful chapel, adequate to our needs in that field (1934:96-99).

Janeway became the pastor of the mission at Placentia, supported by the Fullerton Baptist Church and helped by a legacy left by the Anglo widow for the development of Spanish missions. When a Mexican chapel was built at Anaheim a few years later, the Fullerton Church helped in a similar manner as it had at Placentia, in cooperation with the First Baptist Church of Anaheim who largely supported the pastor of the new mission (1934:99-100).

Anglo-American Attitudes

Mrs. Troyer expressed a deep concern about the attitude of many Christians in Anglo churches who seemed to be "greatly interested" in foreign missions in distant lands, but showed no interest in Mexican missions in their own local area (1934:101). Reflecting on the involvement of the Fullerton Baptist Church, Mrs. Troyer wrote:

> Just consider for a moment how our mission work would be advanced on our whole field if our American churches actually felt a like obligation in the task which the Lord has laid upon them in the bringing of these multitudes to our very doors (1934:100).

"Mother" Troyer was very unhappy with many Anglo churches that reflected an inadequate concept of the nature of the Christian mission, especially in terms of the mission of each local congregation

This unfortunate attitude seemed to characterize many of the churches in Los Angeles at the time Mrs. Troyer wrote in 1934. Many older Anglo churches, when the composition of the local neighborhood changed because of the influx of large numbers of foreign-speaking nationalities, sold their property in the old neighborhood and moved to a new area where many of their former white Anglo neighbors had migrated. An exception to this pattern, however, was the South Park Baptist Church in Los Angeles where the minister attempted to meet the needs of his changing community by providing worship services in English, French, Italian and Spanish (1934:107).

On the positive side, the origin and development of some Mexican churches and missions in Southern California was due to the initiative of individual Anglos or Anglo churches who became concerned about the spiritual and social welfare of the rapidly growing Mexican population in their local areas, and attempted to do something to meet their needs. According to Quiñones:

> Mexican Baptist growth during the first quarter century period from 1910-1935 was a period characterized by the building of foundations and extensive growth. The growth was [mainly] due to the deep zeal and devotion of the missionaries whose concern and dedication made possible the ministry to Spanish-speaking people in California (1966:17).

There are scores of examples of Anglo churches who began missions or departments for Spanish-speaking people, as has been previously shown. But in proportion to the number and resources of Anglo churches and the needs among the Mexican immigrant population that numbered about 250,000 to 300,000 in Los Angeles County in 1930, the Anglo Protestant response was very weak and inadequate.

Los Angeles Baptist City Mission Society

The Los Angeles Baptist City Mission Society (LABCMS) was established in 1906 to aid in establishing and developing Baptist churches within the city of Los Angeles. In 1913 a committee was organized to initiate work among the rapidly growing foreign language population in the city, which included Italians, Russians, Syrians, Japanese and Chinese, in addition to the large concentration of Mexicans (Hine 1966:112,132).

James B. Fox was the first executive officer of the Society. When Fox was appointed "city missionary" in 1911, he was responsible for achieving greater progress in the development of city mission churches among many nationalities, in enlisting the cooperation and support of a larger number of established Baptist churches for the Society, and in raising larger sums of money to finance the Society's overall ministry. The jurisdiction of the City Mission Society extended to one mile beyond the city limits, although the authority of the Society within the city was only vaguely defined (Hine 1966:113).

Comity Council. One of the important developments in Los Angeles by 1914 was the organization of a Comity Council composed of the Superintendents of the Northern Baptist, Congregational, Methodist Episcopal and Presbyterian Spanish language ministries (McEuen 1914:95). As early as 1910, the Southern California Baptist Convention had discussed the possibilities of interdenominational cooperation and a comity agreement, but it was probably not until 1913 that a satisfactory agreement was worked out. In that year, the board of directors of the City Mission Society appointed a committee "to invite representatives of other denominations to a conference on the work among the foreign-speaking people of the City of Los Angeles." It was in this conference, or one like it, that a comity agreement was adopted by the cooperating denominations (Hine 1960:132).

The Comity Council was organized under the leadership of James Fox of the LABCMS. The purpose of the council was to eliminate overlapping and competition among the various denominations working in the city of Los Angeles. Each denomination was given responsibility for specific sections of the city, and the other groups agreed not to establish new missions in those areas (Ellis 1938:144,145).

Funds for Expansion. Prior to 1919 the City Mission Society was somewhat dependent upon the Baptist State Convention for both its funding and its program, but in that year the Northern Baptist Convention recognized the LABCMS as a "Class A Standard City Mission Society," which greatly increased its status and funding. In 1920 the Society experienced the greatest advance in its history when over $50,000 was provided for the construction of new buildings and the development of new missions (1938: 134-135).

Several changes took place in 1919 regarding the relationship between the LABCMS and the Spanish language ministry in the city. Mrs. Troyer states that the Society "at that time...took over the supervision of the Mexican churches in the city that up to this time had been provided for by the State Convention." Secondly, the Society started sharing "with the Convention and the Home Mission Society in the payments of the salaries of the pastors on these fields" (Troyer 1934:143).

During the decade of the 1920s, increased funding through several private donors and the State Convention made extensive growth possible, so that by 1931 the Society was supervising fifty-six mission churches, many of which were among minority groups (Hine 1966:146). In the period 1919 to 1928, the City Mission Society established thirty-two churches in Los Angeles, including several Mexican missions (Ellis 1938:100). Between 1928-1938, thirteen churches were established and eleven missions organized: one Anglo American, eight Mexican, two Japanese (1938: 102). The City Mission Society has continued to provide salary supplement to pastors within the city and to assist in the development of Hispanic churches and Spanish-speaking departments in Anglo churches. As late as 1970, nine Spanish-speaking pastors received partial support from the Society (*SCBC Annual Report* 1970:88).

Strategy of Ministry. In 1938 Ellis interviewed the executive secretary of the LABCMS, J. B. Fox, and gave this summary of the society's strategy of ministry:

> In what seemed to be stabilized fields *permanent missions or churches* were established. If necessary, the first building might be erected by the Society without help from the community, church, or mission. If growth made a second, or an enlarged, building necessary, the church was asked to appoint a building committee to cooperate with the Society, and to assume at least one-half of the cost of building. When a third unit was necessary, the church was expected to assume the entire cost, but the Society would assist with a loan from the revolving fund set aside for that purpose. However, there were some fields where there was little, if any prospect of developing a permanent church organization. It was the policy in such cases, where there was a sizeable community or national group, to meet temporary needs by establishing *temporary missions* (1938:133-134; italics mine).

The overall strategy of the society was to provide places of worship in *strategic communities*, "believing this to be the best means of evangelizing the people and advancing the Kingdom of God" (1938:142). The goal of the City Mission Society was stated by Fox in 1934:

> We believe that the Baptists can make their best contribution...by following the Christ of the New Testament and by being true to his gospel through well-planned organization of denominational churches and missions where we can *preach and teach the gospel with enthusiasm and in the power of the Holy Spirit,* and *persuade the people to accept Christ* and *assume the responsibility of Christian living and service*. Our churches must

> more and more stand for the Christian life. Our weakness has been fear to stand for real Christian living (Hine 1966:146, italics mine).

In addition to developing missions in strategic locations, Dr. Ralph Mayberry, who was the executive secretary of the Society from 1937 to 1956, believed that *capable and experienced leadership* was also required for healthy growth to take place in mission churches, as well as developing an *adequate basis of support* from the Anglo American Baptist constituency (1966:147).

Baptist Christian Centers

When the Los Angeles Baptist City Mission Society was upgraded to the status of a "Standard City Mission Society" and assumed responsibility for the Mexican missions within the city, additional funds became available from the Convention for the construction of new buildings. Apparently, some of these funds were used to build the Baptist Christian Center at North Anderson and First Streets in Boyle Heights, along with assistance from the Northern Baptist Home Mission Society and the Women's Home Mission Society (Troyer 1934:50,144).

The first unit of the Christian Center or Community House, completed in 1920, provided a chapel for *Iglesia Bautista El Salvador* and classrooms for a "Training School for Ministers and Workers for Spanish-speaking People" (*SCBC Annual Report* 1921: 93-94). The second unit was completed in 1921 and housed a clinic, kindergarten, day nursery, home economics department, and living quarters for several women missionaries. By 1923, the Christian Center functioned as an international settlement house with varied activities for many nationalities, which included: *Iglesia Bautista El Salvador*, the Mexican Department of the International Baptist Seminary, a Japanese Mission, a Hungarian mission, the Boy's Club Department and additional services already mentioned (*SCBC Annual Report* 1923:99-101). By 1932, the Industrial and Relief Department was added under the supervision of the Women's Auxiliary of LABCMS (Ortegon 1932:41).

The Northern Baptists established many "Christian Centers" in the Southwest, the Midwest, and some northern states, mainly for the benefit of the Spanish-speaking population. For example, McLean reported that eight "community centers" were sponsored by the Northern Baptists in at least six states: Los Angeles and Fresno, California, and in Arizona, Colorado, Missouri, Indiana, and Wisconsin (1930:27-28,36-43).

The role of Baptist settlement houses was discussed by Ortegon: "The primary purpose was to win the Mexican to the knowledge of

Christ and to help him adjust himself to the social and economic environment in which he found himself so bewildered" (1950:119). Strong emphasis was given to helping people learn English, but courses were also offered in arts and crafts, home economics, and clerical skills. Clinical and medical services were provided at nominal cost.

Social workers at these centers were "particularly interested in helping second generation young sons of immigrants in selecting trades and clerical positions" (1950:120). With assistance from the Christian Centers, high school and college graduates were placed in "gainful occupations". Help with job placement was a necessary function of Baptist centers, according to Ortegon because

> Generally speaking, the people of the United States regarded second and third generation Mexican [Americans] like the rank and file of Mexican immigrants. Even when the second generation Mexican [American] finished high school, he found great difficulty finding appropriate employment...[however,] as a consequence of the work of these centers, American-born Mexicans obtained an all around advantage over the Mexican immigrants; they had steady jobs, somewhat higher wages and more skilled occupations (1950:120).

Racial prejudice, occupational and other forms of social discrimination were very real problems for the Spanish-speaking population in Southern California, both for Mexican immigrants and their American-born children. Concerning this situation in the late 1940s, Ortegon wrote:

> The environment in which the Mexican lives has a great deal to do with his educational condition. Employment, prejudices, and vocational restrictions prevent him from attaining his highest ambitions and capabilities, and from utilizing fully what he has learned in the American society. Because he is faithful, dependable and anxious to please, American employers find it easy to exploit him. The sharp discrimination by our American society against his full use of our schools, parks, theatres, restaurants, and other social organizations prevents him from learning in a normal manner American ways of speech, conduct, and ideology. Undue American publicity given him when he commits a crime, gives him a bad reputation in the community (1950:207).

HISPANIC ADVANCE: 1940-1960

While the initial growth of Hispanic Baptist churches and missions between 1910 and 1940 was the result of consecrated efforts by both Anglo missionaries and early Hispanic Baptist leaders, the progress and growth of the churches during and after the Second World War came about mainly through the efforts of Spanish-speaking pastors who with great dedication built up their congregations and ministered to the needs of their people. This period is characterized by continued growth in membership, increased giving and progress in self-support, but with little growth in the number of new churches and missions. However, there was considerable progress in improving the quality of church facilities (Quiñones 1966:21-22).

Record of Growth

The membership of the Hispanic churches and missions in the Mexican Baptist Convention in Southern California totaled 1,850 in 1939, and by 1946 had grown to 2,158. In 1960, Hispanic membership reached the 2,500 mark (Figure 43). Of the thirty-three Spanish-speaking churches and missions in Southern California in 1960, fifteen were located in Los Angeles County and four in Orange County. Hispanic Baptist membership in Los Angeles County increased from 1,016 in 1939 to 1,565 in 1960. Although thirteen new churches came into existence between 1940 and 1959, there was a net gain of only three congregations in Southern California. Five missions were also established by the Convention across the Mexican border in Baja California and they are still in existence (Figure 41).

Self-Support

The economic prosperity of the 1940s in Southern California brought advances in the area of self-support to the Hispanic Baptist churches. Commenting on this important advance, Quiñones stated:

> By the early forties, because of opportunities opened to them, the Spanish-Americans in the churches were able to face up to the challenge and responsibilities of church support. The churches in California led the way in assuming self-support and also in purchasing the properties and buildings wherein they worshipped. What began in the early forties took gigantic strides in the period 1950-1960. Many churches not only bought the properties from the State Convention, but assumed the responsibility of pastor's salaries (1966:24).

Figure 41

HISPANIC BAPTIST CHURCHES
AND MISSIONS: 1940-1959

Year Established	Name of Church or Mission
1940	Ensenada mission (became Primera del Sauzal)
ca. 1940	*Resurrection Baptist
1942	Riverside First Mexican (mission 1939)
1945	Ensenada mission (later, Primera Bautista) *Torrance Mexican mission (dissolved 1959)
1946	*Bethania Baptist (was Marvilla Park) *West Los Angeles Mexican mission (was Venice?), (name changed to Barrington Ave. in 1957)
1948	*Unida Bautista, formed when Resurrection was dissolved Santa Maria First Mexican Church Mexicali mission (became Primera Bautista)
1950	Bakersfield First Mexican Church (mission 1913) *Harbor City Mexican church (mission 1926) *Los Angeles, Santa Barbara Street Mission
1953	*Rose Hill became Emmanuel Baptist (new building, new location)
ca. 1955	Ontario mission
1957	*Hispana Bautista, Los Angeles *West L.A. Mission became Barrington Ave. (established 1946)
1958	*Del Valle Baptist Church, Pacoima Tijuana mission (became El Calvario) Tecate mission (later, Tecate Bautista) *Lorena Baptist, Spanish Department

*Los Angeles County

Source: *SCBC Annual Reports* 1940-1960

In 1947, only twelve Spanish-speaking churches were self-supporting out of 218 Hispanic Baptist churches in the United States (Northern and Southern Baptist Conventions). Ortegon reported that eighty churches provided fifty percent of their pastor's salary, seventy-five churches provided thirty-three percent, thirty-eight provided twenty percent, and ten churches contributed only twelve percent. Of the twelve self-supporting congregations, seven were in Southern California and six were in Los Angeles County (1950:127,239-240).

Thus, the situation had changed considerably since 1938, when Ellis reported:

> Because of the poverty of the members and the economic uncertainty which goes with common labor, the pastors themselves are afraid to try self-support or to urge self-support on their churches, and there is not a single self-supporting Mexican Baptist Church up to this time.... The 3,616 members in the Mexican Baptist Churches and Missions of the Northern Baptist Convention gave last year [1937-1938] a total of $24,000 [less than $8 per capita], of which $3,200 was for missionary purposes (1938:152).

By 1955, twelve Spanish-speaking churches within the Mexican Baptist Convention in Southern California were self-supporting, in terms of pastoral support. Nine churches were in the process of buying or had bought their properties from the State Convention. The remaining churches were encouraged by the Convention to draw up definite plans and to move toward self-support "as soon as practical and possible" (*SCBC Annual Report* 1955:97).

A special committee appointed by the Southern California Baptist Convention in 1954 "to review the cooperative work of the Convention and the Mexican Baptist Convention in Spanish-speaking work" adopted the following resolution in their report to the 1955 Convention:

> That the pastors and leaders of the Spanish-speaking work throughout Southern California area are to be commended for their continuous, courageous and untiring efforts in the cause of Christ in face of great difficulties, misunderstandings and unsettled economic conditions of many of the Spanish-speaking peoples... it is recognized that the average salary of the missionary pastor is inadequate and that good leadership in the ministry is lost because men cannot support a family on such salaries; therefore, it is recommended that efforts shall be made by both Conventions to assist the churches in areas where it is deemed wise,

in a satisfactory salary plan, which would be agreeable and workable (*SCBC Annual Report* 1955:97-98).

The matter of self-support was, and continues to be, a formidable obstacle to the Hispanic churches throughout Southern California, and especially in the greater Los Angeles area where a majority of the churches are concentrated. The policy of the American Baptist Convention, according to Quiñones, defines "self-support" in terms of a local church no longer receiving financial aid of any kind from the Convention (1966:24).

This policy created severe hardships for most Spanish-speaking churches in the period 1940-1960 because the majority of their constituents were in the lower income bracket. These churches lacked the resources to adequately support a full-time pastor and to keep up with operating expenses and the repair and maintenance of the church properties. Sometimes self-support has been forced upon a church by the Convention through a gradual withdrawal of funds, while other churches have themselves decided to try self-support because of "personal pride". This often leaves the Spanish-speaking pastor with less than a subsistance salary and greatly limits the resources available for the development of the church's overall ministry within the local community (1966: 24-25).

However, the prosperity of the post-war era in Southern California affected the socioeconomic level of a large portion of the Spanish-speaking population by giving them greater financial stability. Some of the churches, therefore, acquired the resources to relocate in more adequate structures or to build new facilities utilizing the manpower of their congregations. As late as the 1950s, older Anglo church buildings were available in urban neighborhoods due to the out-migration of Anglos who had achieved middle class mobility and resettled in the mushrooming suburbs throughout Los Angeles and Orange counties. In this period, Hispanic churches, with some financial assistance from the Convention, could buy land and build new structures, although the rising cost of land in the Los Angeles basin soon made this prohibitive.

Distribution and Size of Congregations

Leavenworth and Froyd conducted a survey of Hispanic Baptist churches within the American Baptist Convention in 1954 and reported ninety-four churches distributed in the following states: California (48), New York (11), Michigan (7), Illinois (6), Arizona (6), Kansas (6), Missouri (Kansas City, 2), Minnesota (2), and one each in Indiana, Iowa, Nebraska, Ohio, Pennsylvania, and Wisconsin (1954:11). The largest group of existing churches were established prior to 1920 (at least 30), followed by the five-yea periods 1925-1929 (18), 1945-1949 (13), 1940-1944 (12), and 1935-1939 (12). The majority of Spanish-speaking churches in California, Kansas, and Illinois were organized prior to 1929, whereas the majority of churches in the other states were founded after 1929 (1954:43, Table VII).

The size of Hispanic congregations showed strong regional variation with California and New York having the only churches with more than 200 members: California (4) and New York (2). Of the total ninety-four Hispanic churches, sixty-one percent had fewer than fifty members and less than two percent had over one-hundred members. Leavenworth and Froyd reported that, "in contrast to the situation found generally among [Anglo] American Baptist churches, the [Hispanic] Sunday schools tend to be larger than the churches" (1954:12). Approximately thirty-six percent of the Sunday schools had less than one-hundred members, whereas about seventeen percent had greater than one-hundred members. Of California's forty-eight churches, only nine (19%) had more than one-hundred members and six of these were in Los Angeles County where the median church size was 118.2 members. About fifty-four percent of the Hispanic churches in California had fewer than fifty members, and the median church size was only 79.3 members. Therefore, it is understandable that all but ten Hispanic pastors in California required a subsidy to maintain an average salary of $2,400 annually (1954:12, Tables VIII and IX).

Cultural Integration

A strong movement toward cultural integration spearheaded by the public school system, Anglo public opinion, and government agencies became a dominant influence in the decade of the 1950s. Its goal was the total assimilation of minority groups into the dominant Anglo American cultural "melting pot". Leavenworth and Froyd wrote that "the virtually complete cultural isolation of the Spanish-speaking population of a generation ago is slowly breaking down." However, "Pastors generally, backed up by the substantial core of their laity, were found to be resisting this trend" (1954:17). The General Convention report for 1955 noted "that a beginning has been made in teaching the Sunday School classes in English, as well as all youth and young peoples work" (1954:97). In response to Anglo American pressure which demanded conformity to their cultural ideal, cultural isolation was breaking down somewhat among Hispanic Baptist churches in Southern California. However, total assimilation is an unreal and unnecessary goal and it has had a crippling effect upon the self-image of thousands of Spanish-speaking school children. The shift toward bilingualism among the Hispanic churches in Southern California had its beginnings in the 1950s, however.

SPANISH AMERICAN BAPTIST SEMINARY

Founded in 1921 by the Home Mission Society, the Spanish American Baptist Seminary was originally affiliated with the International Baptist Seminary of East Orange, New Jersey, and for nine years was located at the Christian Center. Although sponsored by the Home Mission Society, the seminary was evidently a joint venture with the Southern California Baptist Convention and the City Mission Society. The board of directors of the institution included representatives from the State Conventions of Northern and Southern California, Arizona and Colorado, and from the American Baptist Home Mission Society (Leavenworth and Froyd 1954:6).

When the seminary was incorporated in May 1927, funds were requested from the Northern Baptist Convention for the erection of separate seminary buildings, rather than continuing to use the facilities of the Christian Center (Ellis 1938:194). Many individuals contributed to the building fund for the seminary an over $60,000 was received. Walter Simons of Simons Brick Co. pro vided all of the brick and tile needed for the buildings as a mem orial to his father (Troyer 1934:194). Located in East Los Angeles, the Spanish American Baptist Seminary was built at a cost of $75,000 and was dedicated in October 1930 (Ellis 1938:19 Ortegon gives us a picture of the seminary's facilities in 1932:

> The new building is a two story brick structure of Spanish colonial architecture. There are rooms for thirty-eight single students and apartments for five married students. There are also seven class rooms with modern equipment, two offices, a moderately well supplied library and a very beautiful chapel with a Spanish mission atmosphere (1932:39).

In addition to Dean Detweiler, the seminary faculty included A. B. Howell, Mrs. Carlotta Medina, Mrs. Luisa Cordova, and Miss Menita Huse who taught during the early years of its existence (Troyer 1934:145-147). Detweiler served as president from 1921 to 1943 and was succeeded by Samuel F. Nelson who held this position until 1954 when he resigned to work with the American Bible Society in Mexico. After serving for two years as "acting president", Benjamin Morales became president of the seminary and continued until 1963. Dr. José Arreguin was appointed interim president in that year and served until the seminary was closed in 1964 (Quiñones 1966:19-20).

Rationale for Establishing the Seminary

The seminary was founded to provide spiritual leadership for the growing number of Mexican immigrants who surged across the border between 1910 and 1921, and who were heavily concentrated in the Southwest. The Spanish language ministry of the Northern Baptist Convention was centered in Colorado, Arizona, and California. According to Leavenworth and Froyd,

> Ministers were needed and they were needed in great haste--ministers of Mexican origin who understood the culture of their people and were at home in their native tongue. *The urgency of this situation determined the early character of the school.* Spanish became the language of the classroom. Provision for preparatory work was made available to those who had only meager schooling or no formal schooling at all. Short term courses were available to those who were too old to take the regular course, which in the beginning was only three years. In the early curriculum, subjects frequently appeared which were usually found on the elementary and the high school level. The main job of the seminary was *to take prospective ministers where they found them,* give them as much training as they could in the time available, and then send them out to provide leadership to the rapidly growing number of churches and missions. Immediacy and urgency became strong governing factors in the determination of curricular offerings (1954:6-7, italics mine).

Ortegon stated that the Seminary had a three-fold task in 1932:

> *First,* to prepare men and women to be pastors and missionaries for the Mexicans of the United States. *Second,* to educate leaders of the United States and elsewhere to a larger knowledge of the Bible and better methods of Christian work through its correspondence department. There were enrolled last year more than forty in this department from the United States and six from Latin-American countries. In the *third* place, the Seminary prepares the local Mexican Bible School workers for better service by holding night classes and institutes (1932:39, italics mine).

However, out of 252 students who entered the seminary between 1921 and 1952, only 107 graduated from one of the four programs of the seminary, and only sixty-six graduates entered the pastorate (Leavenworth and Froyd 1954:8; Table V). The mortality rate at the Spanish American Baptist Seminary was considerably higher than the drop-out rate at other theological schools in the United States. Of the seventy-seven pastors of Spanish-speaking churches in 1952, fifty-seven percent (forty-four pastors) received their training at S.A.B.S., twenty-three percent (eighteen pastors) were trained at other seminaries (mainly in Puerto Rico and

Mexico), fourteen percent (eleven pastors) were products of Bible institutes, and six percent received miscellaneous training (1954:13, Table IXX). As early as 1938, the Seminary had made a significant contribution in leadership training for Northern Baptist Spanish-speaking churches:

> Under the leadership of President Detweiler, the school has continued to train most of the Mexican Baptist ministers for this country and some for Mexico and Central America. Their students have done a great work in the Mexican Baptist Churches and Missions of Southern California (Ellis 1938:149).

Rationale for Closing the Seminary

After forty-three years of operation, the Spanish American Baptist Seminary concluded its classroom instruction in 1964 and turned over its assets to a Scholarship Fund for Spanish-speaking young people desiring to enter the field of Christian service. The rationale for closing the seminary revolved around four dominant factors: *First,* the majority of the incoming students in the early 1960s were from Latin America rather than from the United States; the foreign students required instruction in Spanish and few of them returned to serve in their native countries, while the American students had a limited knowledge of Spanish and required instruction primarily in English. *Secondly*, limited financial resources created budgetary problems at a time when additional funds were needed to broaden the curriculum and increase the size of the faculty; also, this came at a time when the seminary had been recently transferred from the jurisdiction of the Home Mission Society to the Board of Education and Publication of the American Baptist Convention. In the *third* place, because the seminary was not an accredited institution, its graduates did not meet the ordination requirements of the Anglo Convention which greatly hindered their mobility within the denomination where the emphasis was upon the development of a more highly educated ministry. *Fourthly,* the decision to discontinue the seminary came from the Department of Theological Education rather than from the Home Missions Society which had a greater understanding of the problems and needs of the Hispanic ministry Hence, with its limited experience with the Spanish American Seminary, the Department of Theological Education did not see the necessity of continuing the institution, especially with all of the problems that faced its continuation (Madsen 1971:1-2).

Apparently, the rationale that led to the closing of the seminary was based on the assumption that Spanish-speaking people in the United States, and in particular the constituency of the Hispanic Baptist churches and missions, would in the near future become *assimilated* into the dominant Anglo-American socie with a corresponding loss of Hispanic cultural identity. There was a strong trend among American Baptists at this time toward the integration of Spanish-speaking Baptists into Anglo churches and the elimination of a need for Spanish services and churches. Therefore, the closing of the seminary was based on false presuppositions for two good reasons: (1) The rapidly growing Spanish-speaking population in Southern California refuses to be "melted down" or assimilated; and (2) the continuing demands for pastoral leadership education among Hispanic churches has recently led to the establishment of the Hispanic Urban Center in Los Angeles.

THE DECADE OF THE 1960s

Vahac Mardirosian, who grew up in Tijuana, Mexico and comes from an Armenian family, became the Director of Spanish Work for the Southern California Baptist Convention in 1959 and has provided inspiring leadership in several key areas. Under Mardirosian's leadership, a Commission on Spanish Work was organized in 1962 that "effectively represents" Mexican Baptist churches in Southern California in relationship to the State Convention. The Commission is composed of representatives of the Southern California Baptist Convention, the Mexican Baptist Convention and area representatives. According to Hine, "Since 1959 Mr. Mardirosian has led the Spanish work to significant gains in pastors' salaries and education, evangelistic outreach, tithing enlistment, and missionary outreach" (1966:174).

While serving as chairman of the Education Issues Committee, Mardirosian backed Mexican American student demands before the Board of Education of Los Angeles City Schools during the 1968 student boycott. He also headed the strategy committee of the Council on Spanish American Work, an interdenominational agency that has coordinated Spanish language ministry in the Southwest since about 1912 (Dart 1968:1,6).

Mardirosian resigned as Director of Spanish Work for the state convention in November 1970 after being appointed Director of the new Hispanic Urban Center by the National Hispanic Caucus. At the annual meetings held at San Diego in 1970, the Southern California Baptist Convention was renamed the "American Baptist Churches of the Pacific Southwest." In September 1971, David Luna became the new Director of Spanish Work for the Pacific Southwest.

Growth Trends

The high cost of land in the 1960s along with the rising cost of building materials and labor has seriously hindered the construction of new church buildings, whether Anglo or Hispanic. Thus, it has been impossible for a Spanish-speaking church, with or without aid, to relocate and build a new plant. Occasionally, a Hispanic congregation has been able to relocate by selling their old property in a run-down neighborhood and buying new church facilities vacated by Anglos in neighborhoods rapidly becoming Spanish-speaking.

The out-migration of Spanish-speaking people from East Los Angeles to other communities within the city of Los Angeles and in the suburbs has stimulated many Anglo churches to organize Spanish departments. Since 1958 at least twelve Spanish-speaking departments have been established in communities with a growing Hispanic population. Figure 42 shows the growth picture from 1960 to 1971 among Hispanic Baptist churches and Spanish departments in Anglo churches.

The communicant membership of Spanish-speaking churches and departments in the Southern California Baptist Convention showed a definite increase in the rate of numerical church growth for the period 1960 to 1970 (Figure 43). From a total membership of 2,500 in 1960, Hispanic Baptists in Southern California increased to 3,130 members in 1970, while Los Angeles County grew from 1,565 members to 2,390 by 1970. Although this is a very slow rate of growth compared to Protestant and Pentecostal church growth in Latin America where the average annual growth rate of Evangelicals is ten percent (Read 1969:49), Hispanic Baptist church growth in Southern California exceeds that of all other large Protestant denominations, except Southern Baptists. Hispanic Baptist church growth averaged 2.3 percent per year for the decade of the 1960s.

In terms of the number of churches and departments established, Hine reported that between January 1945 and January 1966 ten Spanish-speaking churches were planted in Southern California and seven missions in Baja California; this includes eight Spanish departments (1966:155). In the decade of the 1960s, seven Hispanic churches were organized along with one mission and thirteen Spanish departments. The growth of Spanish-speaking departments in Anglo churches is a recent development, mainly since 1965 when twelve departments came into existence (Figure 44).

THE HISPANIC URBAN CENTER

The Hispanic Urban Center was established in Los Angeles in 1971. The concept of an "Urban Center" was first proposed in July 1970 by a committee representing the Hispanic American Caucus of the American Baptist Convention. The Hispanic Urban Center came into existence at a meeting of the National Hispanic Caucus in Green Lake, Wisconsin in September 1970, when the original proposal was accepted with slight modification. The Caucus

Figure 42

HISPANIC BAPTIST CHURCHES
AND MISSIONS: 1960-1971

Year Established	Name of Church or Department
1960	*Latin American Mission, Monterey Park (moved to East Los Angeles in 1963)
1961	*Feliz de Lincoln Heights, Los Angeles
1962	*Florence Avenue Baptist, Los Angeles (was Anglo)
1963	*Park Vista Baptist Church, Los Angeles (was Belvedere Park Mexican--new location and building; also gained members from Bethania when it dissolved) *First Baptist Church of Los Angeles, Spanish Dept.
ca. 1963	Santa Ana, Primera Bautista (was Garden Grove Mexican, Orange County)
1964	[Tijuana mission; became Puerta Abierta] Spanish American Baptist Seminary dissolved
1965	*First Baptist of Long Beach, Spanish Dept. *Nueva Vida Bautista, West Los Angeles-Culver City *Norwalk Temple Baptist, Spanish Dept. *Alhambra First Baptist, Spanish Dept. Thermal, Spanish Dept.
1966	*Huntington Park First Baptist, Spanish Dept.
1967	*La Resurección, Los Angeles *Sun Valley, Hispana Bautista *Santa Monica First Baptist, Spanish Dept. *Sylmar First Baptist, Spanish Dept.
1968	*Maywood First Baptist, Spanish Dept. *Torrance First Baptist, Spanish Dept.
1969	*Los Angeles Temple Baptist, Spanish Dept.
1970	*Hollywood First Baptist, Spanish Dept.
1971	*Ebenezer Baptist, Huntington Park (was Florence Avenue Baptist, 1962)
Unknown	Bakersfield First Baptist, Spanish Dept. (Kern County)

*Los Angeles County

Source: *SCBC Annual Reports* 1960-1971

Figure 43

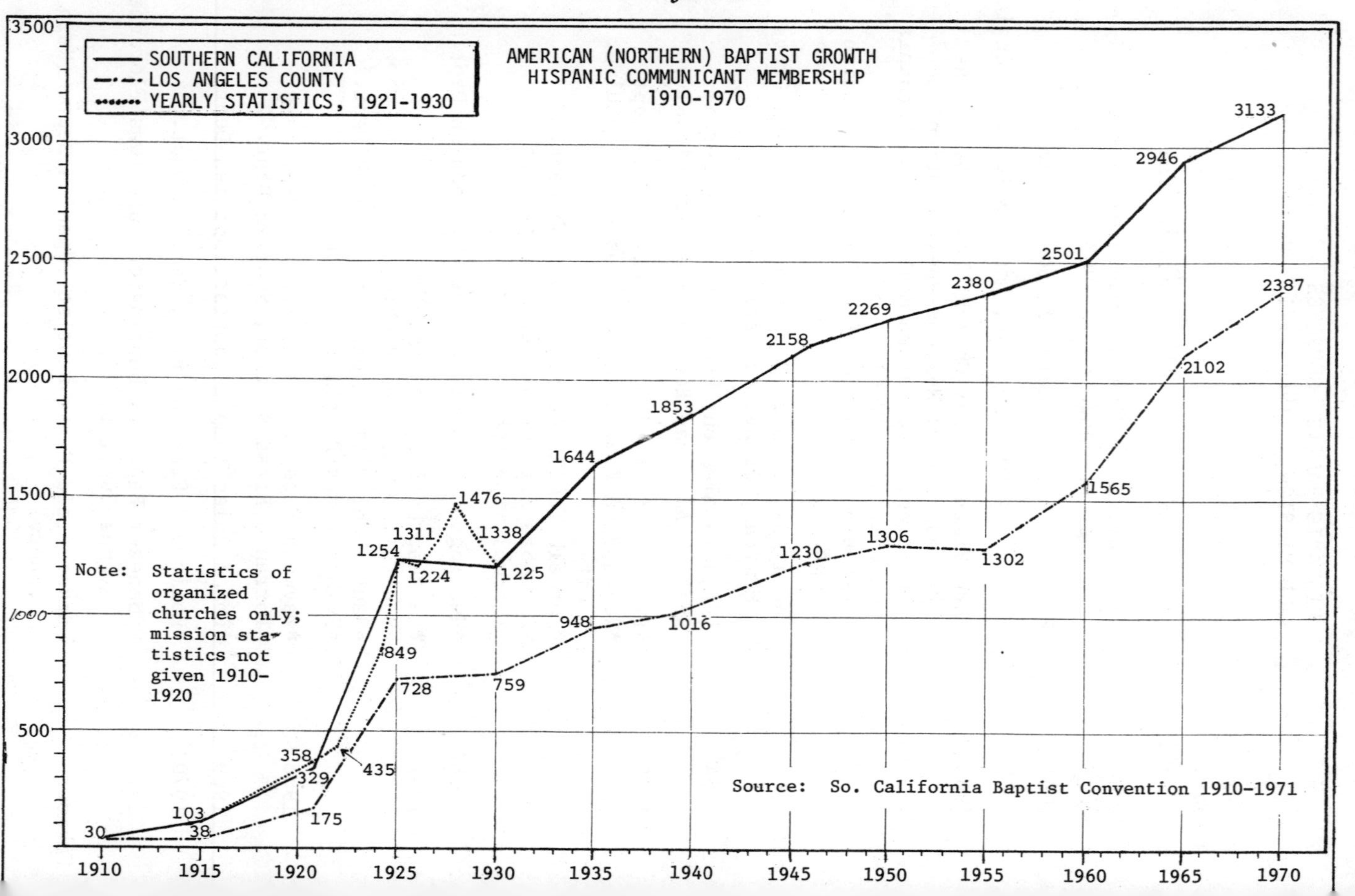

AMERICAN (NORTHERN) BAPTIST GROWTH
HISPANIC COMMUNICANT MEMBERSHIP
1910-1970
SOUTHERN CALIFORNIA
LOS ANGELES COUNTY
YEARLY STATISTICS, 1921-1930
Note: Statistics of organized churches only; mission statistics not given 1910-1920
Source: So. California Baptist Convention 1910-1971
3500
3000
2500
2000
1500
1000
500
1910
1915
1920
1925
1930
1935
1940
1945
1950
1955
1960
1965
1970
30
103
38
358
329
175
435
849
1254
1224
1311
1476
1338
1225
728
759
1644
948
1853
1016
2158
1230
2269
1306
2380
1302
2501
1565
2946
2102
3133
2387

appointed Vahac Mardirosian as director and Luis Fidel Mercado as academic dean and charged them with the responsibility of implementing the establishment of the Urban Center.

Prior to January 1971, the Center existed only on paper, but at that time it was incorporated and a board of directors appointed. After securing a $50,000 loan from the American Baptist Extension Corporation, the Hispanic Urban Center was established at 1201 East First Street in the Boyle Heights District of Los Angeles, in the same buildings that at one time housed the Baptist Christian Center and El Salvador Baptist Church beginning in 1921. These were the same facilities used by the Spanish American Baptist Seminary during the first nine years of its existence (Mercado 1971:1,4).

The establishment of the Hispanic Urban Center represents a new thrust in Hispanic leadership development because the American Baptist Home Mission Society has now gone on record in support of Hispanic American *self-determination*, and with this a commitment to *cultural pluralism* (American Baptist Home Mission Society 1971:1-2). This represents a definite shift in strategy since the closing of the Spanish American Baptist Seminary in 1964 when the rationale was "toward a more integrated approach to theological training for the Spanish language minister" based on the "Anglo conformity" model of assimilation (Shinto 1970:4). The rationale for the new Hispanic Urban Center was given by Shinto:

> In 1970...the Hispanic American Caucus believes that the new situation with the rising cultural awareness and new life in the congregations merits a new thrust in leadership development. Therefore, the Caucus proposed that the American Baptist Convention and its related agencies develop a Spanish Urban Center which will create a bilingual, bi-cultural theological, educational and history program...(1970:4).

The Hispanic Urban Center is a multi-purpose institution designed to serve various specific needs within the Hispanic American communities. The primary goal of the Center is to become an accredited higher education institution under the sponsorship and direction of an accredited college in the greater Los Angeles area. This is necessary to develop a college level supplementary program that includes accredited courses in Hispanic American culture, history and language, as well as biblical and religious studies. In respect to ministerial training

> The candidates for the ministry were expected to pursue a course of studies leading to the B.A. degree in the sponsoring institution or any other accredited college

> or seminary of college level, and to take the supplementary program of the Center. Courses taken at the Center would count for the B.A. It was the expectation that the person receiving this type of education would be able to step into a pastorate in one of the Hispanic churches of the American Baptist Convention. The proposal as a whole puts a heavy emphasis on the need for qualified leadership to assume pastoral responsibilities in the Hispanic community (Mercado 1971:1-2).

Related to this is a proposed program of in-service education for pastors currently serving in local Hispanic churches. Courses will also be designed for Spanish-speaking pastors who have recently arrived from Latin America to acquain them with Mexican American culture and patterns of ministry.

Another stated objective is for the Center to be a catalytic agent in the East Los Angeles *barrio* "for the development of social services and community groups which would spin off into independent agencies" (1971:2). Because of this concern, the Center became involved in a community action program to orient Anglo Americans to the problems of Mexican American youth in the public schools. Consequently, a program of in-service training for elementary public school teachers who work with Spanish-speaking children in the Los Angeles Unified School District was launched in the Fall of 1971. This program is accredited by Occidental College and was developed under contractural arrangements with the Los Angeles Unified School District.

Although the initial development of the Center has been at the under-graduate level in providing in-service training for public school teachers, the Center planned to develop graduate level programs as soon as the details could be worked out with an accredited theological seminary and graduate school. In preparation for this important step, Dr. Luis Fidel Mercado was assigned the responsibility of preparing a proposal on theological education that would be relevant to the needs of the Hispanic community. The Board of Directors of the Center also appointed an Ad Hoc Committee on Theological Education to advise and work with Mercado (1971:2,5).

The Hispanic Urban Center is committed to "flexibility in style service with a minimum of capital investment, and the growth of the church through trained leadership" (Shinto 1970:7). Needless to say, this Center represents an important and creative new expression of the growing maturity and resourcefulness within the Hispanic Church in the vital area of leadership education and development.

OVERVIEW OF HISPANIC GROWTH: 1910-1970

The quantitative dimension of Hispanic church growth among American Baptist churches in Southern California between 1910 and 1970 is represented in Figure 43. The majority of church planting took place between 1910 and 1935 when seventeen churches and forty-six missions were established, or an average of two or three churches or missions per year. However, out of a total number of sixty-seven churches and missions established by 1935, only twenty-eight were still in existence, which is mainly attributed to the migratory character of the Spanish-speaking population at that time. By contrast, in the period 1935 to 1970, most of the Hispanic congregations established became permanent churches and reflected a more stable socioeconomic condition among the large Mexican American population.

Figure 44

HISPANIC CHURCHES, MISSIONS AND DEPARTMENTS
ESTABLISHED IN SOUTHERN CALIFORNIA
1910-1970

Year Reported	Number Existing Churches/Missions	Period Reported	No. Churches Established	No. Missions Established	No. Spanish Depts. in Anglo Ch. Est.	Total No. Established	Accumulative Total
1910	2	1900-1909	0	4	-	4	4
1915	10	1910-1914	1	13	-	14	18
1920	11	1915-1919	3	7	-	10	28
1925	22	1920-1924	4	9	-	13	41
1930	27	1925-1929	5	11	-	16	57
1935	28	1930-1934	4	6	-	10	67
1939	30	1935-1939	1	3	-	4	71
1946	29	1940-1946	1	0	-	1	72
1950	30	1947-1949	2	2	-	4	76
1955	31	1950-1954	3	1	-	4	80
1960	33	1955-1959	1	2	1	4	84
1965	37	1960-1964	4	1	1	6	90
1970	45	1965-1969	3	-	12	15	105

Source: *SCBC Annual Reports*, and Figures 37-39, 41-42.

American Baptist historian Leland Hine summarized the Spanish-speaking ministry in Southern California in this way:

> By far the most extensive foreign language work done by Baptists in Southern California has been among the Spanish-speaking Mexicans. As would be expected, this work has experienced all of the problems to which work with minorities is heir. Help from the majority group has often been insufficient. As usual, the tendency to give occasional gifts without relating to these folk as brethren in Christ has appeared. The Mexicans, in turn, have sometimes received help without accepting responsibility. Within the group all the problems of acculturation have been magnified by the easy possibility of returning home [to Mexico] (1966:173-174).

Although this is a generally accurate statement, Hine has obviously "overlooked" the fact that by 1965 eighty percent of California's Spanish surname population were native-born Americans, and that "home" for over half the state's Mexican American population was the greater Los Angeles area.

9.
The Holiness and Pentecostal Bodies

American church history has many examples of new religious groups being formed outside of the older denominational structures when renewal from within was considered improbable or impossible by members of a revitalization movement. There are many similarities in the historical origins of the Adventists in the period 1830-1840, the Holiness bodies of the late 1800s, and the Pentecostal groups at the beginning of the twentieth century. These three movements have been regarded as "disruptive elements" by the mainline denominations and have sometimes been denounced as departures from orthodox Christianity or as excessively emotional and anti-intellectual. Nevertheless, each movement has provided important corrective influences to "cold orthodoxy" and has helped to strengthen Christian convictions in American society, especially among the lower socioeconomic classes. [The Adventists will be considered in a later section.]

THE HOLINESS MOVEMENT

At the close of the Civil War, the Holiness movement came into being in various parts of the country as a reaction against the moral laxity and irreligion of the postwar era. Initially, this movement took the form of Methodist camp meetings where the doctrine of entire sanctification "as a work of grace distinct from and subsequent to justification" became its distinctive feature (Clark 1937:72-73). According to Williard Sperry, Wesley's doctrine of "entire sanctification" or perfection has continuously stimulated reform movements within Methodism that have sought to recover this emphasis which Methodism originally stressed (1946: 98).

William Warren Sweet identifies the Holiness movement as a reaction against formalized religion within the larger denominations and a return to "heart religion":

> As the great denominations came more and more to be controlled by business methods and dominated by men of wealth, as the services tended to become more formal, and as ministers and choirs donned their robes, and cushions were placed in the pews, people of limited means came to feel more and more out of place (1950: 352).

The desire for "holiness" or "perfectionism" is seen by Sweet as a protest movement by the common man who finds in the doctrine of the "second blessing" a spiritual recompense for his lack of the material blessing; thus, he feels estranged from the churches composed of the growing middle class who dominate the leadership of the institutionalized church. The result of this cleavage was the withdrawal from the older denominations of many who identified with the Holiness movement and the formation of independent religious bodies (1950:352-353).

The presence of certain doctrinal differences within the Holiness movement in terms of the manifestation of "sanctification" in the life of the Christian resulted in later divisions within Holiness groups, as well as a major distinction between Holiness and Pentecostal bodies. Timothy Smith has distinguished between "the Oberlin and Wesleyan types of perfectionism": the Oberlin type views perfection as attainable through a process of growing in grace, whereas the Wesleyan teaching of sanctification sees it as an instantaneous gift of grace by the Holy Spirit, a "second blessing" (Gaustad 1962:121). According to Gaustad,

> As the movement attracted other groups, it became necessary to draw a further distinction between those for whom the Spirit's gift of "entire sanctification" was (as it was for Wesley) marked by a life of disciplined devotion to God; and those for whom this gift had its immediate manifestation in the form of ecstatic trances, glossolalia and extreme emotionalism. Sometimes the word "holiness" is reserved for the former, the term "pentecostal" for the latter (1962:122).

More than twenty-five Holiness and Pentecostal bodies came int existence between 1880 and 1926 (Sweet 1950:353), and the rate of growth of these groups, compared to the older "Colonial families" (Anglican, Baptist, Congregational, Lutheran, and Presbyterian) has been phenominal. The greatest contrast in rates of church growth occured between 1910 and 1930, when the "Holiness familie grew 240-300 percent compared to the slight growth of the older denominations (Gaustad 1962:121, Figure 101). While the newer Holiness and Pentecostal denominations, "filled with youthful vigor and holy vitality, [have] in the present century spurted ahead, burying last year's statistics under a mass of new adherents, new churches, and new territories," it is obvious that their rates of growth have declined considerably since 1930, although still much higher than the mainline denominations (1962: 121-122).

Free Methodist Church

One of the earliest schisms within Methodism due primarily to "agitation on the subject of perfectionism and the practices common thereto" resulted in the formation of the Free Methodist Church in 1860. This movement, led by B. T. Roberts and Joseph McCreary, protested against

> worldly practices, decline of sanctification, membership in secret societies, admission of unconverted persons, departure from primitive simplicity, renting of pews, indulging in questionable amusements, choir singing, building of costly churches and similar practices (Clark 1937:63).

From its organization in Pekin, New York, the denomination grew to 1,200 churches with about 50,000 members by 1926 (1937:64).

The Pacific Coast Latin American Conference was organized in 1930 under the General Missionary Board of the Free Methodist Church of North America. In that year, McLean reported ten churches in existence with 300 members, eleven pastors (both lay and ordained), and four teachers at two schools (1930:43). Both the "Mexican Young Men's Training Home" and the "Mexican Young Ladies' Training Home" were operated in connection with The Los Angeles Pacific College (now known as Azusa Pacific College). Nine Spanish-speaking churches were located in California and one in Arizona: Los Angeles (two churches), Wilmington, Santa Ana, Chino, Atwood, Merced, and Modesto in California; and Chandler, Arizona (1930:29,36-39).

Ortegon gives a brief description of the three Free Methodist Hispanic congregations that were located in Los Angeles in 1932. The North Main Street Church (now First Free Methodist) had a membership of seventy-seven and a Sunday school enrollment of 120. The headquarters of the Conference were also located at this church, which also had a small medical clinic that ministered daily to the Mexican residents of the area. The other two churches were housed in "very old and inadequate" buildings: Palo Verde Church with thirty-four members and seventy enrolled in Sunday school; and Maravilla Park Church with twenty-nine members and a Sunday school enrollment of sixty (1932:35-36,66). Concerning the pastoral leadership, Ortegon wrote:

> Of the three Mexican ministers of this denomination only the pastor has had what we may call a formal education, and his training ceased in his sophomore year in college. One pastor has a very limited formal education, although he has had three years of Bible training. The third pastor has not even an eighth-grade education. He is at present taking a Bible course (1932:36).

The twenty-third Annual Session of the Latin American Conference in 1963 reported eight Spanish-speaking churches in the Los Angeles District with 342 total members (includes Junior, Adult Preparatory, and Adult members), or an average of 42.7 members per church. Churches were located in Atwood, Chino, Los Angeles, Montebello, Moorpark, Placentia, Santa Ana and Wilmington. Only three of these (Los Angeles, Montebello and Wilmington) were located in Los Angeles County, but they accounted for half (172 members) of the total membership of the district. The San Diego District had nine churches and 324 members, but only two of these were in California (San Diego and National City) and the others in Baja California, Mexico. The church in San Diego was the largest Free Methodist Hispanic congregation in California (111 members), followed by First Church in Los Angeles with eighty-eight total members (*Yearbook* 1963:444-445).

The record of growth among Free Methodist Spanish-speaking congregations between 1930 and 1972 shows a net increase of one church in California, while the total membership increased from 300 in 1930 to approximately 485 in 1972. The average church size remains small: 48.5 members per church in California in 1963 and 57.3 average for Los Angeles County's three churches. The picture is one of a few small churches barely holding their own through biological church growth--it is a picture of stagnation. There is, however, a Christian school, the Light and Life Day School, located in Los Angeles that operates in English but is predominantly for Mexican American students. This school has been financed by the Home Missions Board of the Free Methodist Church, but plans are now underway to transfer it to local contro

The Church of the Nazarene

The Holiness movement had achieved considerable influence in Southern California by 1884. This "disruptive" influence led the Southern California Conference of the Methodist Episcopal Church to warn Methodists against certain "Union Holiness Bands", although the doctrine of perfection was reaffirmed by the conference. The leaders of the Holiness sects were characterized as "irresponsible, insubordinate, erratic and fanatical, who reject the advice and control of pastors and official boards and set themselves forth as the special exponents and exemplars of holiness" (*Methodist Annual Minutes* 1884:14-15). The Holiness movement caused considerable schism and dissension within Methodist circles in the late 1880s (Jervey 1960:111).

Phineas F. Breese, who by 1892 had held leading Methodist pastorates in the Southern California Conference and served as Presiding Elder of the Los Angeles District, was strongly influenced by the Holiness movement in the early 1890s. Consequently, Breese left the Methodist Church and organized "the Church of the Nazarene" in October 1895. Breese had fallen into disfavor with the local Methodist leadership because of two factors: first, his strong support for the Holiness movement; and secondly, his participation in a three-month evangelistic campaign with some of the leading preachers of the National Holiness Association (Jervey 1960:112).

Growth Through Mergers. The initial aim of Breese and his followers was to advance "perfectionism" and to organize a church composed of common people who were often neglected by the larger denominations. The Church of the Nazarene joined forces with similar evangelical Holiness groups in Los Angeles to form a stronger association. In 1907 the Los Angeles Association merged with the Association of Pentecostal Churches of America which had been organized in 1895 in Brooklyn, New York; the new organization was called the "Pentecostal Church of the Nazarene". The Holiness Church of Christ, organized in Texas in 1904 through the merger of the Holiness Church and the Independent Church of Christ, united with the Church of the Nazarene in 1908 at Pilot Point, Texas. In 1919, in order to disassociate themselves from the growing Pentecostal movement that emphasized "speaking in tongues" as the evidence of sanctification, the Nazarenes dropped the word "Pentecostal" from their official title and has since been known as "the Church of the Nazarene" (Jervey 1960:111-113; Clark 1937:74). According to Clark, this organization

> ...is to all intents and purposes a Methodist sect. Its ministers and members originally were nearly all drawn from the Methodist fold. Five of the first seven general superintendents had formally been Methodist preachers, and the other two had been closely identified with Methodism and had obtained their holiness views from that church. The Nazarene polity is Methodistic, its *Manual* being little more than a modified Methodist *Discipline*. The sect makes no attempt to conceal its borrowings from Methodism; on the contrary it claims the heritage and avows that it is a reversion to original Wesleyism (1937:74-75).

Statistics of Anglo Membership. The Church of the Nazarene, with headquarters in Kansas City, Kansas, has a growing reputation as one of the nation's "givingest churches". With more than 100,000 members in the United States, the Nazarenes have an annual contribution per church member that is double the amount of most Protestant denominations (*Los Angeles Times* 1971a).

There are two districts of the Church of the Nazarene in Southern California. In May 1971, the Los Angeles District, with headquarters in Pasadena, listed seventy-nine congregations with 10,598 communicant members. The District's Sunday school enrollment had increased by 1,290 for a total of 21,252. The per capita giving averaged $259 for the year ending May 1971. The Southern California District (Orange County) lists eighty-eight congregations and a total membership of 13,983. The Sunday school enrollment increased to 28,874 and the per capita giving rose to $251 (*Los Angeles Times* 1971a).

Hispanic Ministry. The ministry of the Church of the Nazarene to Spanish-speaking people in the Southwest was organized in 1930 as *Distrito Suroeste* (now *Distrito Occidental Latino-Americano*). The District is now organized into seven zones: Los Angeles, Fronteria (West Coast of Baja California), Del Valle (apparently, San Bernardino, Riverside and San Diego counties), Del Norte (Northern California), Del Sol (Arizona), Del Este (Chihuaua, Mexico), and Rio Colorado (Mexicali and Colorado River Valley, Mexico).

In 1969 the Latin American District had twenty-seven churches and missions in the Southwest and thirty-four in Mexico, for a total of sixty-one. The geographical distribution of Spanish-speaking Nazarene Churches in the Southwest in 1969 was: California 16 (Northern California 3, Southern California 13), Arizona 6, New Mexico 2, and Texas 3 for a total of twenty-seven churches in the Southwest. Figure 45 shows the changes between 1930 and 1969 in the Latin American District, an increase of nine Spanish-speaking churches in the United States compared to twenty-three new churches in Mexico.

Although the Spanish-speaking district was organized in 1930, annual statistical reports could only be obtained for the period 1946-1969. However, McLean's report shows that the Church of the Nazarene had eleven churches with 415 members in the Southwest in 1930: four in California, three in New Mexico, and one in Texas. There were eight pastors serving the eleven churches under the supervision of a Superintendent of Mexican Work, E. Y. Davis, of Pasadena, California. The churches in California were located at Los Angeles, Pasadena, San Diego, and Ontario (McLean 1930:33,43).

Figure 45

HISPANIC NAZARENE CHURCHES
DISTRITO OCCIDENTAL LATINOAMERICANO
1930-1969
75
70
65
60
55
50
45
40
35
30
25
20
15
10
5
MEX. UNKNOWN
U.S. 11
(27)
MEX. 9
U.S. 18
(27)
MEX. 10
U.S. 17
(42)
MEX. 21
U.S. 21
(50)
MEX. 22
U.S. 28
(57)
MEX. 28
U.S. 29
(61)
MEX. 34
U.S. 27
1930
1946
1950
1955
1960
1965
1969

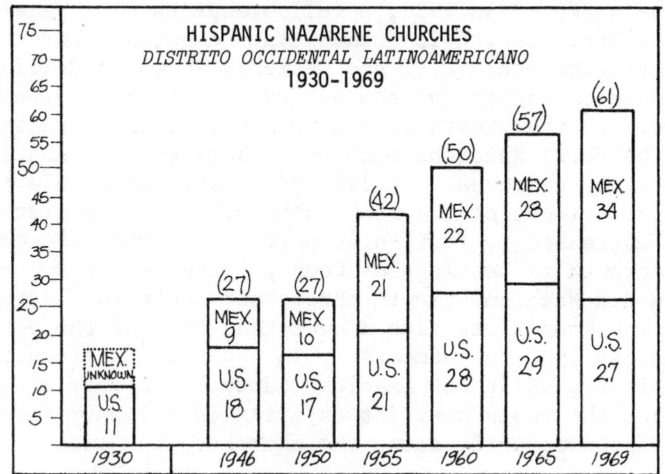

Sources: McLean 1930:33,43; Church of the Nazarene, General Assembly Proceedings 1946-1970

Figure 46

HISPANIC NAZARENE CHURCH GROWTH
(COMMUNICANT MEMBERSHIP)
1930-1969

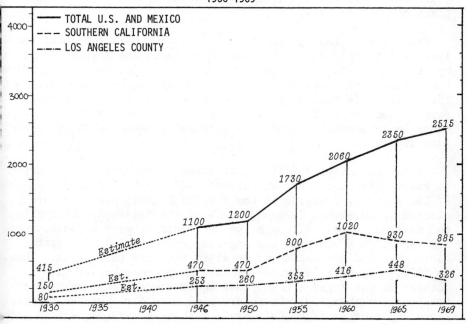

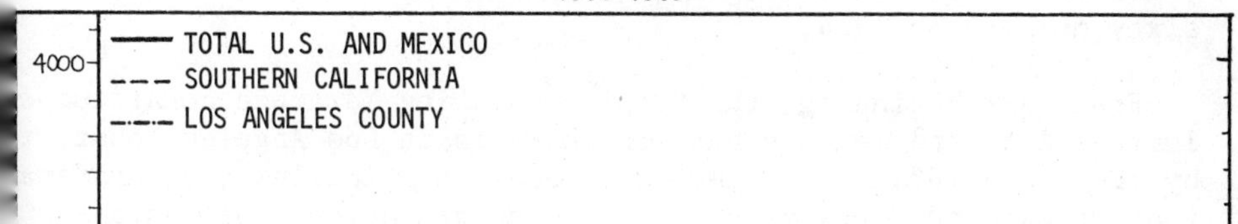

TOTAL U.S. AND MEXICO
SOUTHERN CALIFORNIA
LOS ANGELES COUNTY
4000
3000
2000
1000
Estimate
Est.
Est.
415
150
80
1100
470
253
1200
470
260
1730
800
353
2060
1020
416
2350
930
448
2515
885
326
1930
1935
1940
1946
1950
1955
1960
1965
1969

Based on the statistics of the annual report for 1946-1969 and McLean's report in 1930, a reliable picture of Nazarene growth emerges. Growth in communicant membership for the total district (Southwestern U.S. and Mexico), Southern California, and Los Angeles County for the period 1930-1969 is given in Figure 46. Church growth in Southern California more than doubled the total Nazarene membership between 1950 and 1960 and added four new churches. In 1950, Southern California composed thirty-nine percent of the membership of the whole district, but this increased to forty-nine percent by 1960. By comparison, Hispanic growth in Los Angeles County increased at a much lower rate than did Nazarene growth throughout Southern California; the county's growth was also slower than that of the total district. After 1960 the membership in Southern California decreased slowly, while Los Angeles County had a very slight increase; but the whole district experienced a twenty-five percent increase, predominantly among the churches in Mexico.

The first Spanish-speaking Nazarene church in Los Angeles, *La Primera Iglesia del Nazareno*, was located on North Broadway in the Bunker Hill section of the city. In 1914, according to McEuen, this church had a membership of sixty and actively ministered to about 150 people (1914:38a,95). Thus, Nazarene ministry to the Mexican population of Los Angeles began only a few years after the founding of the denomination in 1895, since several years were required to organize a Spanish-speaking church with sixty members by 1914.

From this beginning, the Spanish-speaking Nazarene constituenc increased to 253 members and six churches in Los Angeles County by 1946. In addition to the churches in Los Angeles and Pasadena that were founded prior to 1930, new congregations were established in Santa Monica, San Fernando, Pomona, and in the Boyle Heights section of Los Angeles. Other churches came into existence in Cucamonga, Upland, San Bernardino, and San Diego by the late 1940s.

In the decade of the 1950s, missions or churches were started at Puente, El Monte, Azusa, Pacoima, and in the Belvedere section of Los Angeles. Outside of Los Angeles County, churches were planted in Cucamonga (Second Church of the Nazarene), Escondido, and National City. Although two new churches were added between 1960 and 1970 (*Cuatro* in Los Angeles, and Ontario), at least seven churches had ceased to exist in Southern California. Thus, in 1970, only seven Spanish-speaking Nazarene churches were located in Los Angeles County and their communicant membership totaled less than 330. There are nine Hispanic churches in existence in other parts of California with about 900 Members (Figure 46).

According to the present District Superintendent, Juan Madrid, most of the Spanish-speaking Nazarene pastors have received their training at the Spanish American Nazarene Seminary in San Antonio, Texas. Madrid also confirmed the fact that Nazarene churches in Mexico were growing much faster than the churches in the Southwest (Madrid 1969).

Nazarene churches in Los Angeles County appear to be static and introverted and in need of greater vitality, both in the quality of their congregational life and in ministry to their local communities. According to a recent report, however, the Nazarenes have committed themselves to an "Evangelism-In-Depth" strategy during 1972 (*Latin America Evangelist* 1972:4). It will be interesting to see how this effects both Anglo and Hispanic Nazarene churches in the Southwest during the next few years.

THE PENTECOSTAL MOVEMENT

The modern Pentecostal movement had its popular beginning in 1906 at the famous Azusa Street Mission in Los Angeles. From an unlikely beginning in an old frame building that once housed a Methodist congregation, located in a heavily industrialized section to the east of the Downtown area, led by a one-eyed Negro pastor, Charles J. Seymour, the Pentecostal revival drew seekers from afar and spread the movement around the world. The news of supernatural signs and wonders, a second Pentecost, was broadcast from the "Apostolic Faith Gospel Mission" and had a special appeal to members of the Holiness movement who were seeking an instantaneous "second blessing" (Nichol 1966:32-37). Although there were antecedent occurances of the "baptism of the Holy Spirit" with accompanying glossolalia prior to 1906--for example, the Camp Creek (North Carolina) revival in 1892 and the Topeka, Kansas outpouring (Charles F. Parham) in 1901--it was the Azusa Street revival that caused the movement to be identified as the "outpouring of the Latter Rain" (Clark 1959:100-101).

Theological Distinctives

Doctrinally, Pentecostal churches are placed in the radical or left wing of the Protestant Reformation (Nichol 1966:3) and in the left-wing of the Holiness movement (Clark 1959:85,100). Nichol argues that Pentecostals, in general, are basically Fundamentalists and their doctrinal position is almost identical to the National Association of Evangelicals (NAE), founded in 1942. In fact, many Pentecostal groups originally joined that organization, but fifteen of the major Pentecostal denominations later formed their own interdenominational organization, in 1948, known as the Pentecostal Fellowship of North America (Nichol 1966:2-5). The doctrinal statement of this new organization was identical to that of the NAE except for Article Five, which states:

> We believe that the full gospel includes holiness of heart and life, healing for the body and the baptism of the Holy Spirit with the initial evidence of speaking in other tongues as the Spirit gives utterance (1966:4).

It is this emphasis on the "full gospel" which separates the Pentecostal churches from most of the traditional Protestant bodies, although the growth of the charismatic movement since the late 1960s has created a new openness to an "experiential encounter with the Holy Spirit" within the mainline Protestant denominations. This, along with the revolutionary Catholic Pentecostal movement and charismatic manifestations among the Jesus People have prompted many observers to speak of "Neo-Pentecostalism" as a new, dynamic force within the Christian Church (Hills 1973:23-25,33).

Causes of Initial Growth

In the early decades of this century, Pentecostalism grew rapidly among thousands of Christians who had been conditioned to expect supernatural occurrences through exposure to the "divine healing" campaigns of John A. Dowie and A. B. Simpson. In addition, many early Pentecostal leaders had been nurtured in the Holiness movement, and they considered this new outpouring of the Spirit as the consummation of their search for sanctification and vitality of religious experience (Nichol 1966: 54-55).

Rather than a new emphasis on doctrine or church government, as had occurred in some of the previous revitalization movements within American Christianity, it was the early Pentecostals' emphasis on "esthetic experience" that drove people of all ages to the altar to seek the baptism of the Spirit with its resultant charismatic gifts.

As was true of the Holiness movement which preceeded it, Pentecostalism was mainly a revitalization movement among the lower socioeconomic classes who were reacting against the "spiritual lethargy" of middle class religion which emphasized "form" rather than "spirit"--orthodoxy of belief rather than of practice. According to Nichol,

> ...the early Pentecostals did not consider themselves to be a separate entity. They thought of themselves as a movement within the Christian church, used of God to revitalize it.... The thrust of the Pentecostal message during the early years was directed at the nominal Christian, the lethargic believer, rather than to the unconverted. The view was that the Holy Spirit baptism was

considered to be an enduement of power for more effective Christian service by those who were already followers of Jesus Christ (1966:55-56).

Causes of Early Opposition

Few main-line church leaders were sympathetic to the Pentecostal movement which, by 1915, had begun to cause serious dissension and strife within thousands of denominational churches. Ministers and missionaries who supported, or even some who were only sympathetic to, the new emphasis on the baptism of the Holy Spirit were forced to resign from their positions within the older denominations (1966:70-72). The anti-Pentecostal sentiment soon caused thousands of church members to leave their denominational churches and to form congregations composed only of Pentecostal believers. These new groups worshiped in private homes or in rented store-front buildings until they grew strong enough to purchase or build regular church buildings (1966:56).

Initial opposition to Pentecostalism was based on a wide range of criticism by Protestant church leaders and by a majority of their communicant members. The basic issue was, and continues to be, doctrinal. Most Protestants have long taught that a major distinction should be made between being "baptized with the Spirit" and being "filled with the Spirit". Traditionally stated, this distinction is seen in the often repeated formula: "There is one baptism with the Spirit (at conversion) but many fillings of the Spirit". The scripture passages usually cited for this distinction are: I Cor. 12:13 and Eph. 5:18-20 (cf. Stott 1964, *The Baptism and Fullness of the Holy Spirit*). Therefore, the Pentecostal emphasis on the "baptism in the Spirit", and speaking in tongues as a sign of this baptism, has usually been considered doctrinal heresy by main-line Protestants.

Anti-Pentecostal sentiment increased by 1920 and led to official church censure of many who claimed to have received the Pentecostal experience. In addition to the dissension and confusion caused by Pentecostalism within denominational churches over the doctrinal issue, church leaders opposed the movement for a growing number of reasons: (1) the abuse of tongue-speaking, prophecy, and "faith healing"; (2) the attitude of spiritual pride that was often manifested by those who had received the baptism; (3) the emotionalism displayed by both those who were seeking and those who had received the baptism; (4) the psychological manipulation and coersion used by some Pentecostals to "bring" this experience to others; (5) the anti-intellectualism of many early Pentecostals; (6) the strong ascetic and "other worldly" emphasis of the movement in general; (7) some occassional instances of immoral behavior; and (8) the strongly proselytic tactics of Pentecostals who claimed they were the "true church" (Nichol 1966:74-80).

Reasons for Continued Growth

Nevertheless, the Pentecostal movement continued to grow and to satisfy the felt needs of many Americans, especially among the lower classes, who had not found a meaningful religious experience within the older denominational structures. The mass evangelistic and healing campaigns of Pentecostal preachers--who often felt the call to "evangelize" but *not* to pastor churches--had a great appeal to the common man who believed in and desired to have a supernatural encounter with God by means of His Holy Spirit.

Pentecostal meetings allowed for spontaneous audience participation--singing, praying, hand-clapping, use of musical instruments, tongue-speaking and use of other spiritual gifts, public testimony of the grace and power of God, etc. Thus, Pentecostalism provided an emotional release for many who were frustrated and suffering due to the numerous sorrows and injustices that they encountered in their troubled world. According to Nichol,

> Thus it might be said of Pentecostals that they did not seek to save the world, but rather to save individuals out of a world which they felt was getting progressively worse, and that this approach gained them many adherents in the hard, lean years just prior to and following World War I (1966:66).

Pentecostalism has been described by Swiss sociologist Christian LaLive d'Epinay (1969) as "the haven of the masses" on the basis of his study of Pentecostalism in Chile, which underlines the point made above by Nichol. The element of "hope" among the oppressed classes "for heavenly deliverance from earthly woes" has been a strong contributing factor to the growth of Pentecostalism during the early years of the century in the United States (Sweet 1950:422), as well as during the past half-century in Latin America where Pentecostals outnumber all other evangelicals by a ratio of greater than two to one (Read, *et al.*, 1969:58)

Other significant growth factors have been: (1) the "thus said the Lord" attitude of Pentecostals who are convinced that God is an all-powerful, supernatural being, who manifests Himself by means of His Holy Spirit to transform and heal sinful men, and to endow them with the gifts of His Spirit in order to accomplish His redemptive purpose in the world; (2) the example of sacrifice and devotion with which many Pentecostal preachers and evangelists have served the Lord, usually among the disposessed peoples of the world; (3) the pattern of leadership training characteristic of Pentecostals, especially their emphasis on and recognition of the role of the laity in their churches, and their failure to make a strong distinction between the clergy and the laity;

(4) the principle of establishing "indigeneous churches", that is, churches that are "self-governing, self-supporting, and self-propagating" (Hodges 1970:24); (5) the unstructuredness of congregational worship, service, and institutional life that allows for spontenaity, self-expression, and exercise of the gifts of the Spirit; (6) an equalitarian expression of congregational life in which mutual esteem, brotherly love, and community-relatedness (among members of the local "family" of believers) provide meaningful interpersonal relationships and group solidarity for new converts and for the continuing needs of older believers; and (7) an enthusiastic dedication to all types and and methods of evangelism by the rank-and-file membership, which is geared to disciple men to Jesus Christ and incorporate them into a local congregation of believers where they are cared for as part of the family and taught the Word of God and the elements of personal discipleship (cf. Gonzalez 1969:119-120; Nichol 1966: 54-69; Read, *et al.*, 1969:313-325).

Internal Dissension

While external opposition was growing against the new movement from denominational sources, Pentecostalism was also experiencing internal dissension centered principally around "leadership and authority" on the one hand, and "acceptable principles of organization and practice" on the other hand (Nichol 1966:81).

During the early years of Pentecostalism, the movement was led by outstanding charismatic leaders who had introduced people to the experience of Holy Spirit baptism. In the rural areas of Tennessee, North Carolina, and Georgia, A. J. Tomlinson organized the "Church of God" in 1907, which traced its origin to the Christian Union established in 1886.

In Kansas and Texas, Charles F. Parham was the recognized leader of the early Pentecostals. Parham published the first Pentecostal periodical known as *The Apostolic Faith*, organized the first interstate conferences of Pentecostal believers, and issued the first ministerial licenses to a growing number of followers.

Los Angeles area Pentecostals looked to William J. Seymour and those in the Portland, Oregon-Seattle, Washington area recognized Florence Crawford as their leader. Pentecostals in the Midwest and East recognized the forceful leadership of William H. Durham, editor of the *Pentecostal Testimony* (1966:81-82).

However, Nichol states that "not a single one of the early Pentecostal leaders could speak for the entire movement.... The inevitable result was an invidious partisanship" (1966:82-83).

But rather than looking to human leaders and their authority, many early Pentecostals relied on "the leading of the Holy Spirit" for guidance and discernment regarding matters of organization and practice in the daily life of the church.

The previous denominational orientation and training of early Pentecostal leaders no doubt was a strong factor influencing the development of church polity, ordinances, and modes of worship, and which brought these leaders into conflict with one another. Pentecostals quarreled over the principles of organization vs. independency, the doctrine of sanctification, the question of utilizing glossolalia or prophecy as a basis of church administration and guidance, the question of whether or not tongue-speaking *always* accompanies the baptism in the Holy Spirit, and the "Jesus only"-trinitarian controversy. Other lesser issues--for some Pentecostals they were major issues--concerned "dress, entertainment, eating habits, physicians, divorce, and so forth" (1966:85-93).

At present there are at least eight major Pentecostal denominations, as well as over twenty smaller groups, within the United States (1966:99-157). Added to these are thousands of independent Pentecostal churches that are spread across the country. It is interesting to note that only about half a dozen Pentecostal groups have a significant ministry to Spanish-speaking people, according to studies made in New York City (Wicher 1960:35-40) and Los Angeles (Holland 1970).

THE HISPANIC PENTECOSTAL CHURCHES

The following sections provide a brief analysis of Pentecostal groups who are involved in Hispanic ministry in the greater Los Angeles area, as well as comparative glimpses of other areas.

Church of God (Cleveland, Tennessee)

Founded in Union Grove, Tennessee in 1907 by A. J. Tomlinson, the Church of God traces its origin to the Christian Union, founded in 1886 in Monroe County. This earlier group was led by an ex-Baptist preacher, R. G. Spurling, who, due to opposition from his fellow Baptists, organized an independent body "as a reformation movement to restore primitive Christianity and bring about the union of all denominations" (Clark 1959:100). Later, under the leadership of William F. Bryant, the movement adopted the name "The Holiness Church" (1902).

It was under Bryant's ministry in Cherokee County, Tennessee, about 1896, that a large group of adherents received the baptism of the Holy Spirit, accompanied by the gift of tongues. This event was known as the Camp Creek revival and is regarded by Church of God historian Charles W. Conn as the true beginning of the modern Pentecostal movement (Nichol 1966:18; Clark 1959: 100-101).

When Tomlinson organized the Church of God in 1907, only five churches and 150 members, in North Carolina, Georgia, and Tennessee, were founding members. By 1936, over 1,000 churches were affiliated with the Church of God. According to Gaustad, "in 1950 there were 3,368 churches and approximately 175,000 members, with the group's strongest representation in the following states: Georgia, Florida, Alabama, North Carolina, and Tennessee" (1962: 125). Nichol reports that by 1966 the denomination was composed of 3,411 ordained ministers, 3,575 churches, and an inclusive membership of 205,465 (1966:102).

In terms of Hispanic ministry, the 1964 *Yearbook* of the Church of God listed three Spanish-speaking congregations in Los Angeles County, with a combined communicant membership of about 170. The largest was the First Spanish Church of God in the Belvedere District with eighty members; the smallest was City View Church of God in Boyle Heights, with only seventeen members. The Montebello Spanish Church of God was reported to have seventy-five communicants. All three of these churches had Spanish-surname pastors in 1964. Another *Iglesia de Dios* was located in Pacoima in 1970, but the relationship between this church and the Cleveland, Tennessee group is unknown.

By contrast, the Church of God, Spanish District Council for the East, had ten affiliated churches in New York City with an estimated membership of 750 in 1960. The Spanish District was organized in 1950 and includes churches in Chicago, Illinois; Lansing, Michigan; and Toledo, Ohio in addition to those in New York City. The total communicant membership for the District was estimated at about 1,000 in 1960. Although affiliated with the Church of God (Cleveland, Tennessee), the Spanish District is functionally autonomous, with local church contributions channelled to the Overseer of the Spanish District and none going to the Cleveland headquarters (Whitam 1960:38).

The Church of God of Prophecy

A. J. Tomlinson served the Church of God from 1909 to 1919 as an able administrator and with distinction, although he was "somewhat egotistical and autocratic". However, after 1920, there was growing dissatisfaction with Tomlinson's administration of denominational funds, which led to his impeachment in 1923 (Nichol 1966:137-138).

Tomlinson and his loyal followers insisted that they were the original Church of God. However, the group from which Tomlinson was expelled brought court action against him which demanded that his followers "desist and refrain from claiming or representing themselves to be connected in any way with the Church of God" (1966:138). Therefore, the expelled group organized "The Tomlinson Church of God" which continued under Bishop Tomlinson's leadership until his death in 1943. His son, Milton, succeeded him as General Overseer, and the name of the denomination was changed to "The Church of God of Prophecy" in 1953. Doctrinally, this group is fairly representative of the Holiness wing of the Pentecostal movement. But in church practices, the Church of God of Prophecy maintains a rigid position against women taking part in church business meetings, immoderate dress, worldly amusements, and mixed bathing (1966:140).

As of 1963, the denomination reported 1,383 churches, with 39,195 members and 3,813 bishops, deacons, and evangelists. In addition, the missionary activity of the Church of God of Prophecy includes 810 "native ministers and missionaries" in fifty countries (1966:139).

Two Spanish-speaking churches are known to be affiliated with the Church of God of Prophecy: one is in El Monte and the other in the Boyle Heights section of Los Angeles. The total communicant membership of these congregations is estimated to be about 100.

The Assemblies of God

The largest Pentecostal denomination in America, The Assemblies of God, came into existence at Hot Springs, Arkansas in 1914. Eudorus N. Bell, editor of the Pentecostal organ *Word and Witness*, had called upon fellow Pentecostals to meet at Hot Springs for a "general council" of likeminded church leaders. Bell gave five basic reasons for having such a conference (Nichol 1966:110):

(1) to achieve better understanding and unity of doctrine,
(2) to know how to conserve God's work at home and abroad,
(3) to consult on protection of funds for missionary endeavors,
(4) to explore the possibilities of charting churches under a legal name, and
(5) to consider the establishment of a Bible training school with a literary division.

More than 300 delegates arrived for the April conference and took up "the urgent question of unifying the diverse, scattered, oftimes competing efforts of a multitude of Pentecostal groups that had come into existence during the previous two decades" (Gaustad 1960:122). The first General Council of the Assemblies of God succeeded in uniting more than 500 ministers in an acceptable system of national organization, without violating the sovereignty of the local affiliated churches.

It was not until 1916 that a "Statement of Fundamental Truths" was adopted by the Assemblies of God, which was a matter that the first conference failed to resolve. The Assemblies' doctrinal position is basically Trinitarian and Arminian; it recognizes the ordinances of water baptism by immersion and the Lord's Supper; it ascribes to a progressive view of sanctification (which represents the convictions of the Baptist rather than the Holiness wing of Pentecostalism); and it is strongly premillennial (Nichol 1966:112).

General Growth. In 1918 the Assemblies of God established their headquarters in Springfield, Missouri. At that time, the communicant membership of their 200 churches totaled approximately 10,000 members, and it included more than 500 ministers and 90 missionaries (Gaustad 1960:123, Nichol 1966:112). By 1966, this denomination reported 8,452 churches, 8,159 ordained ministers, and a total membership of about 556,000 in the United States (1966:114). Latourette records that between 1919 and 1955 the Assemblies of God experienced a membership increase of 436 percent (1969:19).

The distribution of churches in 1950 was largely in the states of Texas (930), California (721), Oklahoma (479), and Arkansas (455) (Gaustad 1960:123). The Assemblies of God have carried forth an extensive home and foreign mission program, with hundreds of foreign language churches in the United States and approximately 12,500 foreign churches with a membership of over 985,000 (Nichol 1966:113).

Hispanic Districts. The most extensive foreign-language ministry of the Assemblies of God within the United States has been among the Spanish-speaking people. There are two major districts serving the Hispanic population: the Spanish Eastern District which covers most of the United States east of the Mississippi River, and also Puerto Rico; and the Latin American District which includes the area west of the Mississippi, as well as Illinois, Indiana, Michigan, and Wisconsin. In 1966 the Spanish Eastern District reported 158 Spanish-speaking congregations, with the majority in New York State (67) and Puerto Rico (45); the Latin American District listed 337 congregations, with the heaviest concentrations in Texas (121) and California (97) (General Council of the Assemblies of God 1966:312-333).

By contrast, Mexico, in the same year, reported 364 assemblies, 587 ministers, and 25,000 church members (*La Luz Apostolica* 1966:6), compared to 450 Spanish-speaking assemblies in the United States with about 21,500 communicant members.

The annual report of the Latin American District for 1970 records 13,500 communicant members and 402 churches, with the Pacific Conference (Arizona, California, Hawaii, Idaho, Oregon, and Washington) contributing 5,450 members and about 140 churches. This means that the average church size in the Pacific Conference is about 40 members, whereas the Latin American District, in general, averaged only 33.6 members per church. The district had an increase of thirteen churches during 1969 and 1,328 reported conversions (only 3.3 conversions per church per year). And although the western district reported sixty-two new churches for the period 1965-1969 compared to the eastern district's gain of fifty-two, the net gain in churches, at least for the Latin American District, was only eleven (from 391 in 1965 to 402 in 1969--includes missions and preaching points). The net gain in communicant membership for this same period in the western district was only thirty members--from 13,469 in 1965 to 13,499 in 1969 (Latin American District Council, 1966:28; 1970:24).

Los Angeles. In terms of Los Angeles County, the Spanish-speaking congregations of the Assemblies of God numbered eighteen in 1971 and had an approximate membership of 1,080. At this time, the City of Los Angeles contained seven congregations and the following cities had one: Compton, El Monte, Huntington Park, La Puente, Lynwood, Norwalk, Pico Rivera, Pomona, San Fernando, San Pedro, and Torrance. Five Assembly of God churches with about 300 members were located in Orange County. Santa Ana had three congregations and Fullerton and Stanton each had one. The average church size for assemblies in Los Angeles and Orange Counties in 1971 was sixty members. Of the ninety-seven Spanish-speaking assemblies in California, fifty-two were in Southern California and forty-five were in the northern part of the state.

Figure 47 indicates when each of the churches in Los Angeles and Orange Counties became affiliated with the Latin American District Council, but these dates do not necessarily reveal the year when each church was founded. For example, *El Aposento Alto* was founded by Alice Luce in 1918, but it is not officially listed by the Latin American District Council until 1938. According to Natividad Nevarez, *La Sendera de la Cruz* was founded as a mission in 1923 (Nevarez 1970). Other assemblies no doubt were founded as missions prior to the dates given in Figure 47.

The growth of Assembly of God congregations in the two-county area, by decades, reveals the following:

1930-1939	3	congregations	established
1940-1949	3	"	"
1950-1959	3	"	"
1960-1969	14	"	"

Figure 47

GROWTH OF ASSEMBLIES OF GOD: 1934-1970
LOS ANGELES AND ORANGE COUNTIES

Date affiliated with LADC	Location and/or Name
1934	Los Angeles, *La Puerta Abierta*
1938	Los Angeles, *El Aposento Alto*
1938	Los Angeles, *El Sendero de la Cruz*
1940	Stanton
1948	Compton
1948	San Fernando
1958	Santa Ana, *El Sinai*
1958	Santa Ana, *El Calvario*
1959	Los Angeles, *La Luz*
1960	Pomona
1961	El Monte
1961	San Pedro
1961	Torrance
1961	Pico Rivera
1961	Fullerton
1961	Los Angeles, *La Nueva Jerusalén*
1962	Los Angeles, *La Antioquia*
1962	Los Angeles, *El Calvario*
1963	Santa Ana, *El Gethsemani*
1963	Norwalk
1967	La Puente
1967	Lynwood
1969	Huntington Park

Source: Vigil 1970

This record is actually one of net growth since there were some churches or missions that did not last for more than a few years after they were founded, while others were disbanded due to the heavy outmigration of Spanish-speaking people from neighborhoods where a church had ministered for many years.

However, in terms of permanent growth of congregations, the decade of the 1960s accounted for the largest number of new churches (14) and eleven of these were added between 1960 and 1965. This indicates that church planting has been an important part of the strategy of the Assemblies of God in the Los Angeles area during the past decade. Their success in planting new churches during this period also indicates that *the Spanish-speaking population has not been unresponsive to evangelism and church planting efforts*, at least in the neighborhoods where the Assemblies have concentrated their energies.

A Brief History of Hispanic Development. Permanent Spanish-speaking ministry by the Assemblies of God in the United States began in Ricardo, Texas in 1915 when young Henry C. Ball, then only nineteen, baptized thirteen new converts on July 4, nine of whom received the baptism in the Spirit that same afternoon (Ball 1970:2). Recalling this experience, Ball recently wrote:

> This started a movement that has continued to this day [1970]. People came from as far away as 15 miles to hear and see what the Lord was doing. Soon our people were scattered all over South Texas to pick cotton. Wherever they went they held services at night. Soon I was receiving letters to go and meet the new believers in several South Texas places. These believers from different towns requested me to supply them a pastor. Since we had no men to act as such, we simply appointed the best qualified men to lead the small congregations (1970:2-3).

There were three reported cases of Pentecostal ministry among Spanish-speaking people prior to the outpouring in Ricardo, Texas, according to Ball (1966a:2):

> Before 1915 brother George Montgomery of Oakland, California had initiated work among the inhabitants of Nacozari, Sonora, Mexico where there was a mine. But this little work was not formed into an assembly.
>
> Antonio Rios Morin began a little work in Uvalde, Texas before this outpouring but it did not last although there are believers still as a result of his work.

In Pasadena, Texas some Latins attended the English-speaking Assemblies of God church. They were saved, and although they worshipped sometimes apart in their own language, they did not form their own established assembly until much later.

The first "Mexican Convention" of the Assemblies of God was held in January 1918 at Kingsville, Texas, located six miles north of Ricardo. There were seven workers present under the leadership of Ball, who was appointed shortly thereafter as the first superintendent of Mexican work in the United States, a position which he held until 1939. It was at Kingsville that the first Assemblies of God chapel was constructed and the small congregation was served by Ball and José Garza. Ball had moved his small group from Ricardo to Kingsville after a hurricane destroyed their canvas chapel in August 1916 (Ball 1966a:2).

In May 1918, Ball accepted a new pastorate in San Antonio, Texas where the small congregation was meeting in a rented hall. The following month, Ball married Sunshine Louise Marshall, a former missionary in Mexico. The second Latin convention was held in San Antonio in November with ten preachers present. One of those in attendance was Francisco Olazábal, who became a great evangelist and later founded the Latin American Council of Christian Churches (1966b:2).

Ball and his new bride left San Antonio in November 1918 to visit several new congregations in California. Alice E. Luce, who had been an Anglican missionary in India prior to being baptized in the Spirit and who had worked with Mrs. Ball in Mexico until forced to leave by the Revolution, had arrived in Los Angeles early in 1918 and, by the time of the Balls' arrival, had established a growing congregation in a rented room near the Mexican Plaza. This mission was called *El Aposento Alto* and, together with a small congregation in San Jose, constituted the extent of the Assemblies of God ministry in California. Although, by 1918, several hundred Latins were affiliated with the Assemblies of God in congregations in Texas, Arizona, California, and Colorado, most of these groups were meeting in private homes or in rented rooms, with Kingsville, Texas having the only church building. The second church, *Templo Cristiano*, was constructed in San Antonio, Texas in October 1919 after the Ball's return (1966b:2; 1970:3).

By the time of the fourth annual Mexican convention, which met in Houston in December 1920, the state of Texas had over 500 communicant members who were scattered among dozens of cities and towns. New missions were reported throughout Northern Mexico, and in Arizona and New Mexico as well (1966b:2; 1966c:6).

Attending the convention in Houston were Fred and Flora Steele and Francisco and Natividad Nevarez from Los Angeles, California. These workers evidently took over the mission started by Miss Luce when she returned to Texas to initiate a series of Bible conferences for the training of believers, since there were no Bible institutes or seminaries in existence at that time. It was under the leadership of C. Fred Steele, in 1923, that the first temple was constructed in Los Angeles, *El Aposento Alto* (Ball 1966c:3).

In an interview with Natividad Nevarez in July 1970, she reported that her husband had served as pastor of *El Aposento Alto* after Steele and that the Azusa Street revival had had a tremendous influence on the early growth of Pentecostalism in the Los Angeles area. Many people were healed and baptized in the Holy Spirit, which drew many interested people to the nightly services. There were few ordained Pentecostal ministers in those days, but many lay-workers conducted vacation Bible schools, led services in house churches, and "evangelized" their neighbors. Between 1916 and 1930, the Spanish-speaking people were reported to have been very open to the evangelistic efforts of enthusiastic Pentecostal converts, which resulted in many conversions and the establishment of several new missions. But after about 1930 the Spanish-speaking Catholic community began to oppose "proselytic" activity and signs appeared in the windows of a multitude of houses, which stated: "We are a Catholic family"--Protestants stay away! (Navarez 1970).

For many years the Spanish-speaking work of the Assemblies of God was organized under the "Mexican Convention". This included all of the Latin work in the United States (including at one time a Portuguese ministry), Mexico, El Salvador, and Guatemala, and for some time Cuba also. Later, the name was changed to "the Latin American Convention". However, in 1929, the Hispanic ministry was reorganized as the Latin American District Council of the Assemblies of God in the U.S.A., and separate districts were formed for Mexico, Central America, and for the eastern United States (includes Puerto Rico). It was not until 1939, however, that the "Latin American District Council of the Assemblies of God" was incorporated under the Laws of Texas (Ball 1966c:11; 1966e:4).

During the 1920s, assemblies were established in California at San Francisco, San Jose (both Spanish and Portuguese groups), Santa Paula, San Diego, and several missions in Los Angeles, including *El Sendero de la Cruz* in 1923 (1966e:4). Beginning in 1924 and continuing into the 1930s, an "evangelistic truck", equipped with beds and other useful items, traveled throughout Texas "sowing the Word of God everywhere". Victoriano Boviero was the first evangelist who used the truck and he was followed in later years by Felix and Blasa Flores, and in the 1930s, by Kenzy Savage (1966c:11; 1966e:11). The 1930s also witnessed the rapid expansion of assemblies in Colorado: Pueblo, Grand Junction, and Denver (1966e:4).

During the early years of Hispanic ministry, there were scores of Anglo American missionaries, pastors, and lay-workers who participated in planting new congregations and instructing new believers in the faith. Many of the early Spanish-speaking congregations began their services in Anglo Assembly of God churches, until they could afford to rent a room or construct a small chapel of their own. There was a definite attempt by many Anglo workers to learn to understand and preach in Spanish in order to communicate the Gospel to large numbers of Mexicans in the Southwest.

Beginning in September 1916, Ball began to publish a magazine in Spanish, entitled *La Luz Apostolica*, for his growing and scattered flock. This monthly periodical soon became the official district council magazine and has been published continuously since that time. Also in 1916, Ball and his helpers began to print tracts and other Christian literature in Spanish on a small hand press. As the need for literature grew, Ball published tracts, pamphlets, hymnbooks, teaching materials, etc. through local print shops. By 1925, Ball had set up his own print shop with a Linotype press in San Antonio (1966c:11). The Spanish literature department continued to grow until the need for more and better publications, in 1947, led to the establishment of *Editorial Vida*, which became the Spanish Literature Division of the Gospel Publishing House of the Assemblies of God in Springfield, Missouri. According to Spence, "30 Latin American countries and 63 denominations use the Spanish literature offered by *Editorial Vida*" (n.d.:11). Ball was director of *Editorial Vida* from 1946 to 1961, when he "retired" to San Antonio and promptly established a new assembly (n.d.:7-11,15).

In 1965, Ball summarized the growth of the Hispanic ministry of the Assemblies of God in the Western United States as follows:

> In the first convention held in Kingsville, Texas in January 1918, we were seven workers, and I believe only two had been ordained. By the second meeting of the Latin American District Council held in San Jose, California on November 16-20, 1930...we had 38 ministers who were ordained and 79 licensed men. And in 1935 when we held the Council in Dallas, Texas there were 41 ordained ministers, 96 licensed men, and 37 exhorters. Thirty years later in 1965, we have 190 ordained ministers, 314 licensed men, 199 exhorters.

> Today, the meetings of the four conferences...count more ministers than we had in the Convention for many years of our history. These meetings are held in enormous auditoriums, and the North Central Conference, which is the smallest of our four conferences, holds its meetings in enormous church buildings which are very beautiful. To God be the glory! (1966f:4).

The Latin American Bible Institutes. During the early 1920s, Alice Luce and Henry and Sunshine Ball conducted a series of Bible conferences throughout Texas for the strengthening of Spanish-speaking believers (1966c:3). According to Ball, these conferences

> awoke a deep hunger for a knowledge of the Word of God, and our pastors felt a need to better prepare themselves for the ministry. Many of these pastors, before entering the ministry, had been humble workers. And so, like the apostles, it was their dedication to the Lord and the fullness of the Holy Spirit on their lives that made them powerful champions of the Truth (1966d:3).

By 1920, several denominational ministers, who had been trained in theological seminaries (for example, Alice Luce and Francisco Olazábal), were baptized in the Holy Spirit and joined the Assemblies of God. When the more poorly trained pastors saw how useful was the preparation of the denominational ministers, they began to aspire for additional training.

The result was that, in 1926, two Bible institutes were founded for the training of pastors and lay workers, one in San Antonio, Texas and the other in San Diego, California. Both institutes were opened in October and both were named "the Latin American Bible Institute". However, the school in San Diego was known for many years as "the Berean Institute" (1966d:3).

These training schools have continued to serve the Latin American District Council of the Assemblies of God until the present time. Many of the denominations' Spanish-speaking leaders, both in the United States and in Mexico, were trained at these institutions, especially at the one in Texas. Concerning the early curriculum Ball wrote:

> We lacked text books that were adequate for these institutes, and Sister Luce, having the best preparation of anyone, began the arduous task of preparing the lessons. These lessons were printed in the publishing house in San Antonio, and many times we were in a hurry to keep ourselves ahead of the classes.... The lessons of sister Luce were bound in two volumes and served well in the institute for years (1966d:3).

The Latin American Bible Institute in San Antonio was established in the annex of *Templo Cristiano*, with nine students, on October 4, 1926. Two members of this first class became well-known leaders in Mexico: Juan C. Orozco, who became superintendent of the Convention; and Ruben Arevalo, who also served as superintendent in Mexico and pastored a large congregation in Mexico City, where he founded the Elim Bible Institute. Other members of the first class have become church leaders in the United States: Josue Cruz and Horacio Menchaca (Ball 1966d:3).

Many of the early teachers of the Texas institute were returned missionaries from Latin America or eventually became missionaries: Fannie Van Dyke (Venezuela), H. May Kelty (Argentina and Cuba), Alta Wetmore (Mexico), Laura Kritz (with later service in Costa Rica and Mexico), and Henry and Sunshine Ball (who served two years in Chile, 1941 to 1943) (1966d:3).

Ball was the first director of the Texas Bible school, where he served from 1926 to 1940 in addition to being the superintendent of Latin work in the U.S. from 1917 to 1939 (Spence n.d.: 7-8). The Latin American Bible Institute was originally located in San Antonio, but in 1935 it was relocated to a ranch near the small town of Sespamco, Texas. From there it was moved to Ysleta (now part of El Paso) in 1945 (1966d:3).

The Berean Institute in San Diego, California began offering instruction on October 1, 1926 and graduated its first class of three in 1928. Initially, both institutes offered a two-year program but this was later expanded to three years. Alice Luce was the founder and first director of the Berean Institute and was affiliated with the school for many years. In 1935, the California Bible institute was moved to La Mesa, and then to Los Angeles in 1941. Since 1950, it has been located on a four acre plot in La Puente, to the east of Los Angeles (1966d:3; 1966f:4; Latin American Bible Institute, 1970:3,9).

In 1969, an important study was made of the Latin American Bible Institute in California by Jesse Miranda, in which he evaluated the stated objectives of the institute and its role within the Spanish-speaking churches of the Assemblies of God. Bible schools play an important role within the strategy of this denomination as seen by the fact that many of their graduates become pastors and lay leaders in local churches. The declared purpose of the La Puente Bible institute, according to Miranda, is to prepare young men and women for Christian service in a "missionary and evangelistic" context (1969:26-27).

Between 1926 and 1935, twenty-five young people were graduated from the institute (Latin American Bible Institute 1970:9); between 1953 and 1968, 155 completed the three-year program

(Miranda 1969:21). Of this latter group, forty-seven graduates were surveyed and the results showed that the majority (36) were then serving as pastors or other church workers, with only eight indicating their present ministry was "missionary" and none listed "evangelist" (1969:29-30). In addition, Miranda surveyed thirteen seniors and forty-seven graduates of the institute, together with ninety-one Assembly of God ministers. The results of this survey are shown in Figure 48.

Figure 48

RANKING OF CHURCH WORK IN RELATION TO TIME CONSUMPTION

Category	13 Seniors	47 Graduates	91 Ministers
Preaching	63	166	337
Teaching	60	157	330
Administration	41	118	297
Visitation	40	115	278
Personal Evangelism	32	99	168
Counseling	28	82	125

Source: Miranda 1969:35

Miranda argues that the Latin American Bible Institute at La Puente has an over-emphasis on the preparation of "missionaries" and "evangelists" while neglecting the "settled needs for educational ministry of the local church" (1969:36). There is a definite lack of correlation between the declared objectives of the institute, the performance of the students after graduation, and the continuing needs of local churches, according to Miranda who was professor of Bible and Religious Education at the La Puente institute.

Evidently, Miranda's study has influenced the curriculum of the institute by the addition of more courses on Christian education, as reflected in the 1970-1971 catalog. And, although the section on "Aims and Ideals" still states that "the whole outlook of this school is missionary and evangelistic", there seems to be a broader emphasis now on the preparation of Spanish-speaking young people for Christian service by not only continuing the strong emphasis on learning the Word of God, but also giving them practical training in Christian education for all ages, in addition to training in various methods of evangelism (Latin American Bible Institute 1970:4-10).

During the 1969-1971 school terms, about fifty single students were living at the dormitories of the Bible institute, while another thirty day school students drove to classes.

Since there were no living accomdations at the school for married students, no doubt some of the commuting students were married, or were young people from the local area who were permitted to live off-campus. In addition to regular day school classes, the La Puente institute also offered evening classes in Spanish for the training of older laymen from local churches, as well as offering basic ministerial training (Melendres 1970).

Summary of Hispanic Ministry. The Spanish-speaking Assemblies of God came into existence because there were few churches, especially in the early years of the Pentecostal movement, that accepted the outpouring of the Holy Spirit with the initial sign of speaking in tongues as evidence of having received the fullness. Ball states that "the goal was not to separate ourselves from another church, nor to give them competition, nor to look for proselytes among them, but to be a blessing" (1966b:2). But in the early days when members of denominational churches were receiving the baptism of the Holy Spirit, "many times they were despised by their pastors and by other members, so we had to provide them with a congregation of believers of the same testimony in order to strengthen them in the faith" (1966b:12). Ball claims that he and the early members of Assembly of God congregations "never taught or believed, that we were 'the exclusive people of God', for we know that the church does not save, but only the Lord" (1966b:12).

Concerning the method of pastoral support, Ball commented:

> Many people prophesied in the first days of our movement that it would soon pass away like the wind, that we did not have a salaried ministry paid by a mission board, and that we would fail because our ministers would look for salaries in other churches. Very few of our men have done this. We believe that a minister is worthy of a salary; we don't have any scruples against giving a salary to our ministers, but we do believe that the local assembly ought to pay the salary of their own pastor. You can tell by a man's attitude if he is only working for a salary or if he is divinely called by God to feed the congregation and to win souls for our Savior (1966f:4).

This section of the Assemblies of God now closes with Ball's thoughts concerning the present state of relationships between his denomination and the main-line Protestant groups:

> Little by little the denominations are recognizing us, not as "stealers of sheep", but as brothers in Christ with an important message for the world, that of the fullness of the power of the Holy Spirit. Many

> denominational churches have received the fullness of the Spirit without the necessity of uniting themselves with the Pentecostal movement. Thanks be to God for their favorable attitude in spite of the fact that there are still some ministers against it [the baptism of the Holy Spirit]; and others, it is a shame to say, who are not born again because they deny the virgin birth of Christ and other fundamental doctrines of the Word of God (1966f:10).

The Apostolic Assembly of the Faith in Christ Jesus

Among the many people who attended the famous Azusa Street Apostolic Faith Mission in Los Angeles were several Mexicans. Luiz López was baptized there in 1909 and before long the mission had produced its first Mexican preacher, Juan Navarro. Evidently, both López and Navarro were Protestants prior to their arrival in Los Angeles; but upon hearing the Pentecostal message, they were convinced of its truth and received the baptism in the Holy Spirit (Cantú 1966:6).

The Apostolic Doctrine. López and Navarro also received another baptism which had great significance for the movement among Spanish-speaking people that soon followed. These Mexican believers accepted the doctrine that they should be rebaptized *only* in the name of Jesus Christ and that this is *"el verdadero bautismo que salva"* (the true baptism that saves). According to the official history of the Apostolic Assembly, this baptismal practice dates from about 1909, which is several years prior to the controversy which erupted over the "Jesus Only" vs. Trinitarian baptismal formula that sharply divided the early Pentecostals (1966:6).

The First Leaders. In 1912, Navarro baptized twenty-two year-old Francisco F. Llorente in San Diego, soon after Llorente had arrived from his home in Acapulco, Mexico. This young man had received the message of salvation in San Diego from a group of Anglos who were followers of "the Apostolic Faith" (the name used by "Jesus Only" Pentecostals). Early in 1913, Llorente, who felt called to preach the Gospel and had been ordained as an evangelist by the San Diego Apostolics, himself baptized his first two converts, María and Rita Serna (1966:6,62).

Llorente traveled to Colton, California in 1914 where he met Marcial De La Cruz, who was converted and baptized by Llorente. After receiving the baptism of the Holy Spirit, De La Cruz joined Llorente and Navarro and together they traveled throughout Southern California during 1914-1915, establishing groups of Spanish-speaking believers in Colton, San Bernardino, Riverside, Los Angeles, and Watts (1966:6,62). In 1914, McEuen listed a

"Spanish Apostolic Faith Mission" on North Hill Street in Los Angeles (1914:38a). According to Gaxiola, "all these churches met in private homes; there were no ministerial requirements and anyone who felt called could start a church, either in his own home or in the home of another family" (1970:157).

These early Mexican believers adopted practices quite different from those of Anglo or Negro Pentecostals, in that Llorente and his fellow evangelists taught that their churches should not have women preachers, that women should have their heads covered during public worship services, and that water baptism should be administered only in the name of Jesus, citing passages such as Acts 2:38 and I. Tim. 2:12 (1970:157).

The "Jesus Only" Controversy. The dispute among Pentecostals over the so-called "Jesus Only" heresy grew to serious proportions following the 1913 Worldwide Pentecostal Camp Meeting held at Arroyo Seco, California. Since most Pentecostals, when praying for physical healing, "preface their rebuke of the illness with the phrase, 'In the name of Jesus...,'" it was natural that many would be inspired by the power of the "wonderful name of Jesus" to see a contradiction between texts like Acts 2:38/John 3:5 and the traditional Trinitarian baptismal formula of the older Protestant Churches. It was at the Arroyo Seco camp meeting that John G. Scheppe and others asserted that "*true* baptism *must* be only 'in the name of Jesus' rather than 'in the name of the Father, and of the Son, and of the Holy Ghost'" (Nichol 1966: 89-90).

The result was that, in 1915, many influencial Pentecostal leaders, such as Bell, Goss, Opperman, and Rodgers of the newly formed Assemblies of God (1914), accepted the new teaching and were rebaptized "in Jesus' name". When the General Council of the Assemblies of God committed themselves to a Trinitarian position in the "Statement of Fundamental Truths", which appeared in 1916, over 150 ministers withdrew from the Assemblies of God and formed a new Pentecostal body, the Pentecostal Assemblies of the World. According to Nichol, "the proponents of the [Jesus Only doctrine] denied that there are three Persons in the Godhead, asserting instead that there are three manifestations of one Person, namely, Jesus" (1966:117).

Eventually, several "unitarian" Pentecostal denominations came into existence. Although the Pentecostal Assemblies of the World was originally formed as an interracial body, its "white constituents" withdrew in 1924 and organized the Pentecostal Church, Inc. which mainly represented the states in the Mississippi River Valley. In 1931, the Pentecostal Assemblies of Jesus Christ was formed from churches in the North Central, Middle Atlantic, and South Atlantic States, which had not united with the former group. However, these two groups merged in 1945 to form the United Pentecostal Church, which is now the largest "unitarian" Pentecostal denomination in the United States, with 1,800 churches and 200,000 members in 1965 (1966:118-119).

The Mexican Pentecostal ministers in California who adhered to the "Jesus Only" doctrine soon became affiliated with the Pentecostal Assemblies of the World. In 1916, according to Gaxiola,

> Navarro, Llorente, and De La Cruz, together with others, had credentials [from the Pentecostal Assemblies of the World] and to Llorente was given the vague title of "Mexican Representative" before that body.... This was one of the few organizations of the name of Jesus Christ which had the recognition of the government at that time and many ministers were affiliated with it, although in reality it was a system in which each minister was at liberty to go and preach in whatever place he wished and to organize his church in accordance with the method which seemed to him the most proper (1970:161).

Antonio C. Nava. In 1916, Marcial De La Cruz was preaching among the migrant labor camps in the Imperial Valley when he encountered Antonio Nava from Nazas, Durango, Mexico. Nava listened to the Apostolic message but remained unconvinced. However, he accompanied De La Cruz for a period of six months until they arrived in Los Angeles where Nava was dramatically converted and baptized in the Holy Spirit. Nava remained in Los Angeles for several months where he met Llorente, who was then (1917) pastoring a small Apostolic church at Angeles and Aliso Streets near the Downtown area. Later, Nava accompanied De La Cruz to Riverside where the former saw a vision and felt called to the ministry. Using the small church in Riverside as their base of operation, De La Cruz and Nava conducted evangelistic meetings throughout Southern California during 1918-1919. In September 1919, following his ordination, Nava went to Yuma, Arizona where he formed a congregation of thirty people, most of whom had been members of local Methodist and Baptist Spanish-speaking churches (Cantú 1966:7,65-66).

After several months Nava journeyed to Calexico, located on the California side of the border across from Mexicali, Mexico. There, in the house of Luiz and María Herrera, Nava established the first Apostolic mission in Imperial Valley. During the rest of 1920 and the following year, Nava preached the Apostolic message along the border and was successful in organizing churches in Mexicali and Colonia Zaragoza. Nava, who continued as pastor of the church in Calexico until 1928, became the second

"Presiding Bishop" of the Apostolic Assembly following the death of Llorente in September of that year (1966:66).

The Apostolic Faith in Mexico. Although the churches founded by Nava in Baja California were not the first Apostolic congregations in Mexico, they did provide a bridge between the two Apostolic organizations that emerged on both sides of the border. The birth of the Apostolic message in Mexico has been traced by Gaxiola to a family named Valenzuela, who immigrated to Los Angeles from Villa Aldama, Chihuahua in early 1914 to escape the dangers and turmoil of the Revolution. In Los Angeles, Romana Valenzuela and her husband were converted to the Apostolic faith, although both had been devoted Catholics in Mexico. Concern for their families in Chihuahua finally forced them to return to Villa Aldama where they excitedly shared the Apostolic message. Twelve members of Romana's family were baptized in the Holy Spirit and spoke in tongues in November 1914. According to Gaxiola, this is the first known case of the Pentecostal experience in Mexico (1970:4-5). From this beginning, the Apostolic faith spread to Chihuahua, Durango, Coahuila, and to other states in Mexico, so that by 1932 twenty-six congregations were established with about 800 members (1970:81,140-141).

Apostolic Growth in California. Meanwhile, Llorente and De La Cruz continued to organize small congregations of believers in California and to seek out new leadership for the Apostolic movement. Between 1916 and 1919, at least a dozen pastors were ordained and given responsibilities for new congregations stretching from San Francisco to the Mexican border. While spending part of their time in secular work and as much time as possible in evangelism, Llorente carried the Apostolic message north from Los Angeles and De La Cruz and Nava carried it south from San Bernardino and Riverside (Cantú 1966:7-8).

During these early years of Apostolic ministry, the young church leaders "had to depend on their own initiative and resources and to a great degree this was a blessing because they had to begin from the bottom without outside help" (Gaxiola 1970: 162). Although many of the first Mexican pastors and evangelists had credentials from the Pentecostal Assemblies of the World, that organization exercised no control or supervision of the growing Spanish-speaking work. There was only a loose organizational thread between the Hispanic Apostolic leadership and the Indianapolis, Indiana headquarters of the licensing agency.

By 1925, there were at least twenty-three struggling churches and twenty-five pastors scattered throughout California, Arizona, New Mexico, and Baja California who composed the Spanish-speaking Apostolic Faith movement (Figure 49). Gaxiola has given a very descriptive insight into the difficulties of church planting and

Figure 49

CONGREGATIONS OF THE APOSTOLIC ASSEMBLY
1925

Location	Pastor
National City, Ca.	Francisco F. Llorente *(Pastor General)*
*Calexico, Ca.	Antonio L. Nava *(Anciano Ejecutivo)*
*San Bernardino, Ca.	José L. Martínez *(Secretario General)*
Santa Paula, Ca.	Bernardo Hernández *(Asistente Secretario)*
Redlands, Ca.	Pedro Zavala
*Otay, Ca.	Isaías G. Ceceña
Watsonville, Ca.	Valentin García
*Bakersfield, Ca.	Juan R. Ridríguez
Chino, Ca.	Margarito G. Vargas
Watts, Ca.	Arturo Hermosillo
*Brawley, Ca.	Agustín Cerros
El Rio, Ca.	Jesús Torres
*Indio, Ca.	Ramón Ocampo
Westmoreland, Ca.	Miguel C. García
San Francisco, Ca.	Antonio Arias
Thermal, Ca.	Sotero Carranza
Madera, Ca.	Manuel E. Soto
Jimtown, Ca.	Bernardo Hernández (1922)
Cucamonga, Ca.	Filomeno Carranza (1922)
Yuma, Arizona	Filomeno Carranza
Lordsville, New Mexico	Tomás Martinez
Mexicali, Mexico	Antonio Nava and Ramón D. Ocampo (1919-1921)
Colonia Zaragoza, Mexico	Antonio Nava and Ramón D. Ocampo (1919-1921)

*Only church buildings in existence

Source: Cantú 1966:10d,17-18,20d,80,98

of building stable congregations among the migrant Mexican population in California in the 1920s:

> The task was not easy and the progress was slow and painful. In the beginning the majority of the converts were workers in the fields, entire families of migrants who followed the harvests in California. They worked all day in the fields and at night they had a worship service that lasted four or five hours. They sang and preached with all the fervor and enthusiasm which only recently converted men can have. They composed their own hymns and sang them accompanied by the guitar and they spoke in tongues and prayed with all the strength of their lungs. The non-convert who lived in the same camp either joined them or left. The summer was a "time of mites" in more than one sense. The whole family got into an old dilapidated Ford and went to harvest fruit, vegetables and souls. The inconveniences didn't bother the children; they learned to love the church and they grew up in the middle of a family which found in the new religion all that they needed, spoiled and cared for by all the members of the church who were now a new family (1970:163).

In this pioneer period of church development, a new Apostolic Faith congregation in one place might only last until the harvest was completed. But gradually the migrant workers began to put their roots down in various places where they could find stable employment and buy a small lot. According to Gaxiola,

> some went to California for the summer and returned to their homes in Texas for the winter; but by 1928 many believers had permanent homes in Brawley, El Centro, Indio, Riverside, [Los Angeles], Bakersfield, Delano, Fresno, Salinas, San Jose, Modesto and other places (1970:163).

Without having the "advantage" of bank loans and savings accounts, the humble Pentecostal believers managed to build simple churches. The land was donated by some members of the congregation, others contributed small sums of money and manual labor, with the end result that when the new temple was dedicated, it was free of debt and built with the love and devotion of a strong "family" of believers.

Organization of Apostolic Movement. In December 1925, the leaders of the growing movement met together in San Bernardino for their first general convention. The twenty-seven pastors who were present recognized the necessity of establishing uniform ministerial qualifications, of deciding various doctrinal matters, and of effecting a better organizational structure.

In addition to these matters, the convention decided that their movement should have the official name "The Church of the Apostolic Pentecostal Faith" (Cantú 1966:9-17).

Evidently, out of about twenty Apostolic congregations represented in the movement, only seven were meeting in regular church buildings, with the rest holding services in private homes. The seven temples were located in Calexico, Brawley, Otay, Indio, San Bernardino, Bakersfield, and Tulare (1966:17-18). The estimated communicant membership of the Spanish-speaking Apostolics in 1925 was about 700.

Dissension and Schism. The following year, a small group of ministers, led by José L. Martínez of San Bernardino, led a revolt against the majority leadership of Francisco Llorente by demanding "a doctrinal purification, the purging of the ministry, and a new name for the movement" (Gaxiola 1970:164). However, according to Lorenzo Salazar, president of the Apostolic Assembly in 1970, the major issue was that of the financial structure of the movement, specifically the requirement concerning tithing.

The unfortunate result of this conflict was that Martínez, who was elected Secretary General at the first convention in 1925, withdrew from the Apostolic Assembly along with at least six other ministers and formed their own movement in 1927. This group of churches organized themselves as "The Apostolic *Christian* Assembly of the Name of Jesus Christ", some of which are still in existence (one such church was located in Irwindale--Los Angeles County--in 1971 and had a membership of fifty) (Cantú 1966:19).

Period of Turmoil. This schism did not have a serious effect upon the Apostolic Assembly due to its continued growth by the addition of churches in Arizona, New Mexico, Texas, and Baja California. In addition, most of the ministerial body was united behind their young movement, although there was a time of discouragement and dissatisfaction in the movement during the period 1928-1929.

First, Llorente lost his wife, Josefina, in 1928 and his own health began to decline. And according to Gaxiola, "Nava, who was one of the principal pillars of the organization, had returned to Mexico with the intention of remaining" (1970:164). While Nava was away in Mexico, Llorente died of a heart attack in September of 1928, which left the Apostolic Assembly "practically leaderless".

However, the Secretary General, Bernardo Hernández, assumed command and called for a ministerial convention in Indio at the end of the yar. There it was decided by the majority of ministers to wait for Nava's return from Mexico, while De La Cruz,

Torres, and Hernández looked after the most urgent matters. Nava came back to California in March 1929 and was elected President of the Apostolic Assembly at the fifth general convention at Indio (Gaxiola 1970:164).

Incorporation of Movement. Nava proposed a major change in the movement by recommending that the Apostolic Assembly become incorporated under the laws of California and sever their relationship with the Pentecostal Assemblies of the World. Nava's proposal was enthusiastically accepted by the ministerial body and they were inspired by the new direction the movement was taking. The sixth general convention met at San Bernardino in March 1930, where the incorporation plan was ratified by the assembly. The new name of the organization became "The Apostolic Assembly of the Faith in Christ Jesus" (Cantú 1966:26).

The 1930s. Due to the economic hardships of the early 1930s, accompanied by the large-scale movement of migrant farm workers back to Mexico, the Apostolic Assembly did not experience much growth. No annual conventions were held during 1931 and 1932. However, between 1925 and 1935, the following churches were apparently standing firm: San Francisco, El Rio, Bakersfield, Watts, Jimtown, San Bernardino, Chino, Redlands, Westmoreland, Indio, Otay, Tulare, Brawley, and Calexico in California; Yuma, Arizona; El Paso, Texas; and Mexicali and Colonia Zaragoza in Baja California. Apostolic evangelists were also active in this period and held campaigns in many new towns: Saticoy, Oxnard, Santa Paula, North Hollywood, Pacoima, Van Nuys, Santa Ana, Corona, Chino, Fowler, Caruthers, Wasco, San Jose, and Fresno (1966:73). De La Cruz and Tereso Gamba pioneered in Arizona and New Mexico (1966:76).

The 1930s were also a period of both schism and internal organization. A small group of churches in New Mexico, led by Pedro Banderas, left the denomination over the continuing problem of tithing--which the Apostolic Church requires of every member (Cantú 1956:29-32)--and these churches joined the United Pentecostal Church (Cantú 1966:31,35). However, on the positive side, the first annual Apostolic youth convention was held in Otay in 1934. In addition to the young people's work, organizations for men and women also were developed (1966:30).

The 1940s. The first issue to face the Apostolic Assembly in this decade was *the relationship between the Church in the United States and the brethren in Mexico.* Not only were there legal matters to resolve, but also various doctrinal and practical differences had arisen between the two groups. In 1940-1941, a committee was appointed to study these problems and to make recommendations to the general convention. Meeting in Otay in 1944, representatives from the Apostolic Assembly of Faith in

Christ Jesus on both sides of the border agreed on a "Treaty of Unification", which resolved most of the problems and bound the two organizations in Christian brotherhood (1966:32-33).

Between 1942 and 1945, many young men from Hispanic Apostolic churches were drafted into the armed services during World War II, which raised *the issue of "war and peace"* among church leaders. The Apostolic Assembly decided that, while they were obligated by the scriptures to "obey human ordinances" and to support their government in time of war, nevertheless, they insisted that their young men only serve in a non-combatant role (Cantú 1956: 55-56). While many men served in the Army Medical Corp. and in other support capacities, other young men entered approved courses of study in Bible institutes, colleges and seminaries in preparation for the ministry, which also made them exempt from military service (Cantú 1966:34-35).

In terms of *the ongoing work and expansion* of the Apostolic Assembly, the mobilization of the nation for defense and the rationing of consummer products and building materials severely restricted the construction of new churches and parsonages. In addition, travel was hindered by the shortage of automobile parts, gasoline, and oil (1966:35).

Beginning in 1946, the Apostolic Assembly and the United Pentecostal Church began to discuss the possibilities of greater spiritual unity, fellowship, and cooperation, especially in terms of the planting of churches in new areas. The result of these discussions was *the establishment of a "Fraternal Alliance" between the United Pentecostal Church and the Apostolic Assembly of the United States and Mexico,* which took place in Dallas, Texas in 1947. The most significant outcome of this pact was the mobilization of the combined forces of these organizations in joint missionary work in Central America, initially in Guatemala, Nicaragua, and El Salvador (1966:36-37).

In 1949, the Apostolic Assembly gave serious consideration to its *program of Christian Education*, which resulted in many improvements for all age groups within the local churches. Sunday schools and vacation Bible schools had been organized since the early days of the movement, but often the quality of instruction was not the best. Desiring to improve their teacher training program and to up-grade the methods of instruction, the Apostolic Assembly commissioned Daniel Morales and Elizar Rodríguez, students at the Apostolic Bible College in Tulsa, Oklahoma, to prepare guidelines for the organization of better Sunday schools, not only for the instruction of children, but also for youth and adults.

The Department of Christian Education, in cooperation with the youth federation, "Mensajeros de Paz", organized the Apostolic Bible Training School in Hayward, California in 1949. The Secretary of Christian Education, Ernesto Cantú, developed a correspondence course in systematic Bible study for pastors and lay workers, in addition to the day school program of the new training school (1966:38,46).

1950-1971. Post-war economic growth in Southern California and the increasing immigration of Mexicans, both legal and illegal, greatly effected *the growth and expansion of Spanish-speaking Apostolic congregations.* Between 1950 and 1962, forty-two new temples were dedicated: California (20), Arizona (6), Texas (7), New Mexico (3), Colorado (3), and Illinois (3). Work in the Midwest was begun in 1952 in Chicago and other areas where large numbers of Spanish-speaking people had migrated. Much of the Hispanic Apostolic growth in this period was due to special campaigns of "faith healing" conducted by evangelists and pastors, mainly in the Southwest (1966:40-42,47-48).

Between 1958-1960, *two problems challenged the internal life of the Apostolic Assembly*, one was apparently resolved while the other continues to cause concern and demands openness and wisdom by church leaders. Problems again arose concerning the relationship between the Church in Mexico and the United States. Meeting in San Diego, representatives of both groups resolved that each national movement should have the freedom of internal organization and development in a manner most conducive to its own growth and progress, and that the continuing causes of irritation and conflict between the two groups should be patiently dealt with in a spirit of brotherhood and cooperation.

The second major problem that arose in this period was a cultural clash between the older Mexican immigrants and their native-born children and grandchildren, who were rapidly becoming acculturated to the Anglo American value system and life styles. The older generation was resisting the changes of dress, attitudes, and behavior that they witnessed in their young people. Many older church leaders felt uncomfortable outside the familiar circle of friends and acquaintenances who had also immigrated from Spanish-speaking countries (Gaxiola 1970:165-166).

These leaders reacted to the problems of acculturation among their young people by treating it as a "spiritual problem", as rebellion against parental authority and the authority of the church. There were concerted efforts in the early 1960s to resolve the problem by prayer and exhortation, calling on the young people to return to "the paths of holiness and purity". The conflict between generations continues to trouble the church and family life of the Apostolic Assembly, just as it does among many other Spanish-speaking denominations as they struggle with the problems of acculturation (Cantú 1966:45-46).

Nevertheless, *the Apostolic Assembly continued to multiply congregations and to benefit from the rising socioeconomic level of its members during the post-war era.* Evangelists and missionaries were sent out from the established churches to open new areas in Washington and Oregon, Pennsylvania and Florida in the mid-1960s. Missionaries were also sent to Costa Rica and Italy in 1964, and to Honduras in 1965 (1966:49).

The older districts of the Hispanic Apostolic movement continued to build new temples and expand their limited facilities as they grew in numbers and prosperity. The newer districts slowly added new congregations as enthusiastic evangelists and new converts spread the Apostolic message to new towns and communities. Between 1962 and 1966, twenty-three new temples were dedicated: California (16), Texas (4), and New Mexico, Iowa, and Pennsylvania (one each) (1966:49).

The latest statistics available on the Apostolic Assembly reveal that, in 1968, the total communicant membership in the United States was about 8,000 with 152 churches located in the following states: Arizona (9), California (88)--southern counties (37) and northern counties (51)--Colorado (6), Illinois (3), Iowa (1), Michigan (4), New Mexico (10), Pennsylvania (1), Texas (26), Utah (1), Washington (2), and Wisconsin (1). In addition, there were 349 ordained or licensed ministers serving the Spanish-speaking churches, missions, and preaching places. The national average church size was 53 members (Gaxiola 1970: 165; Apostolic Assembly 1967). By comparison, the Apostolic Assembly in Mexico reported 435 churches and 14,670 communicant members in 1968, with an average church size of only 34 members (Gaxiola 1970:76,81,140-141).

Los Angeles County. Of the estimated forty Spanish-speaking Apostolic churches in Southern California in 1971, twelve were located in Los Angeles County: Bell Gardens, Burbank, Canoga Park, Compton, Culver City, El Monte, Long Beach, East Los Angeles, San Pedro, Torrance, West Whittier, and Wilmington. Adjacent Orange County had three congregations: Anaheim, Orange, and Santa Ana. The total communicant membership of the Apostolic assemblies in Los Angeles County was estimated to be 1,000. Orange County contributed another 250 members.

General Evaluation. The strength of the Apostolic Assembly has been its strong leadership and discipline, and its ability to form a strong "family unit" of believers in each congregation and between congregations (cf. Gaxiola 1970:163). Nida made the following observation about the Apostolic Assembly in Mexico which is equally true about the Church in the United States:

> [*La Iglesia Apostólica de la Fe en Cristo Jesús*] is an indigenous church which has relatively strong leaders who represent a close psychological approximation to the old *patrón* system, but are for the most part amazingly close to their people (1965:106).

Thus, the cultural orientation of rural Mexico, with its "small community" attitudes and social structures (Redfield 1967:4) which characterized most Mexicans in the period of mass immigration (1910-1930), expressed itself in the socio-religious structure of the Apostolic Assembly that came into existence during this same period.

At the time of the first general convention in 1925, the Apostolic Assembly adopted *an organizational structure similar to Methodism*. The body of ministers organized a *Mesa Directiva* (Executive Board) with the following officers: *Pastor General, Anciano Ejecutivo, Secretario General,* and *Asistente Secretario* (Cantú 1966:17). The term of office for these officials varied at different times in the history of the movement, but the office of President or Presiding Bishop was held by Francisco Llorente from 1925-1928, Antonio Nava 1929-1950, Benjamín Cantú 1950-1963, Antonio Nava 1963-1966, Efraín G. Valverde 1966-1970, and Lorenzo Salazar 1970-. In later years the following officers were added to the Board of Directors: Treasurer and Assistant Treasurer, Secretaries of Missions and Christian Education, and Superintendents of Men's, Ladies', and Young Peoples' Societies. These officials are now elected to a four-year term of office and may be reelected only once to the same office (Cantú 1956:2).

The Apostolic Assembly is divided into various districts (thirteen in 1970), each of which is under the supervision of a Bishop who is elected to office by a majority of the ministers of his district, subject to the approval of the "Qualifying Commission" (three members of the Board of Directors) (1956:22-23). The ministers of the local congregations are appointed and subject to removal by the District Bishop; the local church is consulted but the final decision is made by the Bishop. Sometimes the Supervising Bishop allows the local church to call their own pastor. Pastoral changes are normally made at district conventions or regional pastors meetings (Salazar 1970).

All *church buildings and properties* are held in the name of The Apostolic Assembly of Faith in Christ Jesus, a California corporation. The local minister is held responsible for these church properties and the Board of Directors of the Assembly "may not dispose of these without previous consent of the pastor and the majority of the members of the congregation" (Cantú 1956:21,43).

The principle of self-support is strongly adhered to in the Apostolic Assembly and tithing is considered the duty and obligation of *every* member. In addition, "no local church shall be exempt of its obligation of remitting a tenth of its tithes and offerings to the General Treasury of the Assembly"...(Cantú 1956:32). The tithes of the pastors and elders of each district are remitted monthly to the District Treasurer for the support of the Bishop and the administration of the district (1956:29).

Although the local church is responsible for supporting its pastor, many pastors are working either part-time or full-time in secular work, thus reducing the financial load of many, small struggling congregations. Local funds are used for the maintenance and administration of the local church as well as for "a plan of assistance for widows, orphans, the sick, and others in need" (1956:31-32).

The Apostolic Assembly has maintained a consistent *policy of lay and ministerial training* which has contributed to its stability and growth. The local congregation is organized under the leadership of its pastor who is aided by "an assistant pastor, one or more Evangelists, Ordained Deacons and Would-Be-Deacons [Probationary Deacons], a Secretary and Treasurer" (1956:46). The leadership training program begins with the pastor who seeks out spiritually gifted and qualified men to assist in the ministry of the local church. The following minimum requirements must be met by those aspiring to the rank of *Ordained Deacon:*

1. A person must believe and practice the doctrine of our Lord Jesus Christ.
2. He must be baptized by immersion in the name of Jesus Christ.
3. He must have been endowed with the Gift of the Holy Spirit with the evidence of speaking in other tongues.
4. He must have a good testimony in his church.
5. He must know how to read and write.
6. He must pay his tithes regularly.
7. He must be a faithful member of a local church for a minimum period of one year.
8. He must be in accord with the doctrinal, economic, and organizational system of the Assembly.
9. He must be willing to study the courses necessary for his ordination.
10. He must be approved, upon termination of his trial period, by a Qualifying Commission (1956:35).

Candidates for the office of Ordained Deacon are interviewed by the local pastor who must secure the approval of the Supervising Bishop before the candidate is accepted as a *Deacon on Probation* or *Would-Be-Deacon*. There is a minimum probationary period of one year which begins with a service of consecration at a regional ministers conference:

> The objective of this trial period is to determine whether the candidate is vocationally suited for the ministry and to permit him to acquire the necessary experience in the work to which he will be assigned by his pastor, and to also acquire the cultural and biblical knowledge necessary to be a good Minister of the Lord (1956:36).

During this probationary period laymen are given responsibility for conducting mid-week services of worship and evangelism, usually meeting in private homes. They are expected to make converts from the world and to teach them how to walk with the Lord. According to Salazar, this method of home services led by deacons has been a major growth factor among Apostolic churches. During 1969-1970, for example, the congregation in Compton baptized over 100 new converts through their house-church ministry (Salazar 1970).

In addition to receiving this type of practical training, probationary deacons are required to complete a special course of ministerial studies (probably by correspondence from the Apostolic Bible College in Hayward, California). If he satisfactorily completes this probation period, and is approved by an Examining Commission (composed of at least three pastors), then he can be ordained at the next district convention or regional ministers meeting (Cantú 1956:35-37,46).

Ordained deacons assist the local pastor in church administration and other pastoral responsibilities, including the visitation of church members and ministering to their needs. In the larger churches, one of the ordained deacons who fulfills all the requirements for the pastorate may be chosen as *Assistant Pastor*. Through this new area of responsibility, capable men receive the added experience and qualifications for advancement to full pastoral positions (1956:44-45).

Evangelists are also appointed from among the ordained deacons if they demonstrate the special gift of preaching the Gospel and of winning people to the Lord. An evangelist may pioneer in a new area or he may work under the pastor of a local church. Some churches may have several evangelists helping in their local ministry. The ordained deacons and evangelists are all "laymen" in the normal sense that the traditional denominations use this term, that is, they work in secular employment and hold services and do pastoral visitation or evangelism in the evenings and on weekends, rather than spending their full time in church work (1956:44-45).

The next rank of leadership above that of the local pastor is the position of *Assistant Elder*. Certain pastors, who through their experience and ability demonstrate superior leadership qualities, may be chosen by the district bishop to supervise other congregations in addition to their own. These men aid the bishop by checking on the progress and evaluating the problems and needs of congregations in the district. When church disciplinary action is needed, an assistant elder is present to aid the local pastor in his obligation. District bishops are usually nominated from among the acting assistant elders of each district (1956:22-29).

Thus, a strong pattern of leadership emerges from this evaluation of the Apostolic Assembly which is based upon the personalities and spiritual gifts of individual leaders. The charisma of these men, whether they be local pastors or bishops, has provided a functional substitute for the *patrón* of the old feudal system of rural Mexico, which still appears to be a strong cultural force within the lives of rural-oriented immigrants. Leadership within Apostolic churches is based on spiritual qualifications rather than on education, on the power of the Holy Spirit rather than on theological degrees:

> If a person [can] lead a church to grow in grace and manifest a divine compassion to reconcile men to God in Christ, Pentecostals judge that man a pastor, appointed not by men but by God. Men are eager to know if there is a power which can save them from their sins, cleanse them, hold them from falling back into sin, and help them to know and find God. Men will listen to this kind of Gospel. The Pentecostal pastors can preach this Gospel effectively because they are just like other men.... [They] are not separated from them by clericalism (McGavran 1963:119).

By all indications, the strength of the Apostolic movement among the Spanish-speaking population has *not* been in the larger cities of the Southwest, but rather in the small towns and migrant labor camps. For example, in Southern California most of the congregations are located in the agricultural districts rather than in the larger urban areas where the Spanish-speaking population is heavily concentrated. This situation is even more pronounced in Northern California, where only one out of fifty Apostolic churches is located in a large urban center. Thus, there is a strong possibility that the majority of the Apostolic churches are ministering to agriculturally-oriented people who compose the lower socioeconomic class of the Hispanic community, many of whom are Mexican immigrants. It is to this segment of the population that the Apostolic pattern of leadership, worship, and family-relatedness will continue to have great appeal.

There is a growing problem of introversion, however, among some churches as the older immigrants and their native-born children achieve greater upward social mobility. Enough acculturation has taken place among some congregations to cause a social barrier to exist between them and the more recent arrivals, who are still at the bottom of the social ladder in terms of income, acculturation, and English-language ability. Apostolic church leaders are no doubt aware of this problem, but it will be their ability to respond creatively in building a strategy of ministry that takes into consideration the needs of recent immigrants, as well as the continuing needs of the more acculturated church members, that will determine the character of their future growth.

The Latin American Council of Christian Churches

One of the least known Hispanic Pentecostal denominations is the *Concilio Latino-Americano de Iglesias Cristianas*, founded by Francisco Olazâbal in 1923. However, Olazâbal himself was well known among several Spanish-speaking denominations during the early years of the Pentecostal movement, as well as among the Latin American Mission of the Methodist Episcopal Church.

Francisco Olazâbal. During the years 1913 to 1917, Olazâbal was a Methodist minister in California, where he served on several circuits in both the southern and northern counties. After his arrival in Southern California from Culiacân, Sinaloa, Mexico in early 1913, Olazâbal was appointed to the Compton area as an evangelist. Already an ordained deacon at the time of his arrival, young Olazâbal was aided by his mother in house-to-house visitation among the railroad and farm labor camps of Compton and Watts (*El Mexicano*, Vol. 1, No. 2:2; No. 7:6).

Olazâbal was an excellent preacher and evangelist according to *El Mexicano*, the organ of the Latin American Mission, which often mentioned his addresses before both Anglo and Hispanic gatherings (Vol. 1, No. 2:5,7; No. 4:7; No. 7:6). From October 1913 to October 1916, Olazâbal served the Pasadena mission, one of the two Spanish-speaking Methodist missions that had been established by 1913; the other one was the Bloom Street Mission in Los Angeles. Olazâbal spearheaded a fund drive among Anglo Methodist churches to raise money for the Pasadena Mexican Church, which was constructed in 1915 for $6,000. In addition to his pastoral responsibilities, Olazâbal taught at a night school for

Spanish-speaking people, helped establish a cooperative laundry for Mexican women, and conducted evangelistic campaigns in other circuits (Vol. 2, No. 4:6; Vol. 4, No. 1:11; No. 2:6).

At the annual Methodist conference in October 1916, Olazâbal was appointed to the San Francisco-Sacramento circuit. There he aided two Mexican missions established by Anglo churches: Grace Methodist of San Francisco and the First Methodist Church of Sacramento (Vol. 5, No. 3:5-6). In early 1917, Olazâbal was ordained as an elder and continued his ministry on the San Francisco-Sacramento circuit through September 1917 (Vol. 5, No. 3:3; Vol. 6, No. 1:9). However, while in San Francisco, Olazâbal was strongly influenced by the Pentecostal movement and left the Methodist Church in the Fall of 1917 to become a Pentecostal evangelist (Vol. 6, No. 1:9 [No further mention is made of Olazâbal in *El Mexicano* after this issue]; *Journal of the Latin American Mission* 1920:26).

Olazâbal attended the second convention of the Assemblies of God which met in San Antonio, Texas in November 1918. By this time he apparently had already been ordained as a minister with the Assemblies. Although Ball gives the date of Olazâbal's ordination as September 24, 1916, the correct date must have been either 1917 or 1918, since Olazâbal was still serving at the Pasadena Methodist Mission in September 1916 (Ball 1966b:2; *El Mexicano* Vol. 5, No. 1:12; Vol. 6, No. 1:9).

From November 1918 to at least the Fall of 1920 Olazâbal pastored an Assemblies of God mission, *Buenas Nuevas*, in El Paso, Texas. However, he withdrew from the Assemblies of God in January 1923, apparently as a result of a disagreement with Ball and other Assembly leaders, and organized his own group of churches with a large number of followers. Nevertheless, Ball paid him the following high tribute:

> [Brother Francisco Olazâbal] was a great evangelist and his withdrawal from our movement caused great disturbances of a serious nature. Undoubtedly, we would be more advanced than we are today if he had stayed with us in the evangelization instead of founding his own new movement. However, many new souls have found the Lord in his movement and we give thanks to the Lord for having had him with us and for the success that he has found apart from us (Ball 1966c:3).

The Latin American Council of Christian Churches was founded by Olazâbal in March 1923, shortly after leaving the Assemblies of God (*Concilio Latino-Americano de Iglesias Cristianas* 1962:23). Not much is recorded about this famous evangelist after 1923, except for the following quotation from Clark:

> The growth of [the Pentecostal movement] among the Spanish-speaking people [of New York City] is largely due to the evangelistic work of the Rev. Francisco Olazabal, who was a Methodist preacher of some prominance in Mexico and California before he entered the [Pentecostal movement] (1959:105).

Many Spanish-speaking churches in the New York area came into existence through the evangelistic efforts of Olazábal and Abram Rodríguez about 1936. These churches were predominantly composed of Puerto Ricans and, evidently, were loosely related to the Latin American Council. However, there was a split in this growing movement following Olazábal's death in the late 1930s, with the churches in the New York area establishing their own organization, *The Assembly of Christian Churches* (Rodríguez 1970). In 1960 this organization had sixty-four churches in the New York metropolitan area and about 4,000 baptized members (Whitam 1960: 38-39).

Miguel Guillén. After Olazábal died, the leadership and expansion of the Latin American Council of Christian Churches became the task of Miguel Guillén, who continued as president until his death in July 1971 (*El Mensajero Cristiano* 1971:1). According to a brief history included in the catalog of the Cladic Seminary in Los Angeles:

> Under the brilliant leadership of Dr. Guillén, the organization [the Latin American Council of Christian Churches] has expanded greatly. It is now considered to be one of the largest Latin American religious organizations in America. The growth of this religious corporation has been without the backing of a great denomination or long-established institution (Cladic Seminary 1958).

According to Arturo R. Muñiz, who is now president of this organization, Guillén wrote a history of the movement which will soon be published by the Latin American Council (Muñiz 1971).

Size and Distribution. While it is true that this organization has developed without the support of an Anglo denomination, its claim to be "one of the largest" Spanish-speaking denominations means that it ranks third behind the Latin American District Council of the Assemblies of God (an organization independent of, but affiliated with, the General Council of the Assemblies of God) and the Apostolic Assembly of Faith in Christ Jesus. In terms of size, the Latin American Council of Christian Churches had 105 affiliated churches in the United States in 1971, with an approximate membership of 4,200. The breakdown by states was the following: Arizona (2), California (27), Colorado (7), Illinois (3), Indiana (4), Michigan (5), New

Mexico (2), Ohio (2), and Texas (53). In addition, there are fifty-five churches in Mexico with about 2,200 baptized members (*El Mensajero Cristiano* 1971:15).

The distribution of churches in California reveals that twelve congregations were located in Northern California, while Southern California had fifteen, all of which were in Los Angeles County. In 1971, the county area had Latin American Council churches in the following cities: Azusa, Baldwin Park, El Monte, La Puente, Los Angeles (Boyle Heights-2, Belvedere, Vernon, and Watts), Pico Rivera (2), San Gabriel, San Pedro, and Wilmington. The communicant membership of these churches totaled about 900. Compared to Latin American Council churches in other large U.S. cities, Los Angeles and San Antonio both had five congregations, while Houston, Texas, had eight (1971:15).

The Cladic Seminary. The official training institution for pastors and other Christian workers is the Cladic Seminary, located on Whittier Boulevard in the Boyle Heights section of Los Angeles. This school is housed in an old movie theater where the congregation of *El Refugio* meets for its services. This Bible institute was founded in September 1954 and has a Three-Year Ministerial Course, a Two-Year Missionary Course, and a special one-year course for older ministers. Only the regular Ministers Course has a minimum educational requirement, a High School Diploma. All instruction is given in Spanish and at least five courses are offered in Spanish grammar and composition (Cladic Seminary 1958). About twenty-five students were enrolled in 1971 and the majority were young people.

Doctrine and Organization. The Latin American Council is Trinitarian and does not seem to have any doctrinal deviations from other "orthodox" Pentecostal denominations. However, the organizational structure is very authoritarian. Only the president of the denomination is elected by a general convention, which meets every two years, and he appoints six *Síndicos* (Trustees) which include the following officers: General Superintendent, Secretary, and Treasurer. These trustees (seven including the President) compose the *Comité Ejecutivo* which administers five departments: *Hacienda* (Finance), *Propiedades* (Property), *Asuntos Ministeriales* (ministerial Business), *Literatura*, and *Misiones* (*Concilio Latino-Americano de Iglesias Cristianas* 1962:2-10).

The Latin American Council is divided into *thirteen districts* (eight in the United States and five in Mexico), each of which is administered by a District Committee appointed by the President and composed of a president, secretary, treasurer, and a field supervisor.

In each *local church*, the pastor, who is appointed by the *Comité Ejecutivo*, nominates two candidates for each position on *"La Junta Official"* which must have at least three members but not more than eleven. The pastor serves as president of this church council and appoints a secretary and treasurer. Although this structure gives the pastor strong powers in the administration of the local church, he must receive a vote of confidence from a majority of the congregation "every six months." If the pastor loses the confidence of his church, then the Executive Committee must investigate the situation through its district representatives and find a workable solution to the problem, which may mean the replacement of the pastor (1962:10-11,15-16, 26).

The *categories of church workers* include exhorters, licensed preachers, and ministers. The *exhorters* receive a credential which allows them to assist the pastor in the ministry of the local church, including the direction of a mission; but they are not authorized to officiate at any of the church ordinances (communion, baptism, or marriage ceremonies). After serving a year trial period, exhorters may request to be licensed by the Council. The *licensed preachers* are authorized to serve as pastors, assistant pastors, and evangelists, as well as officiating at all church ceremonies except for marriages. Licensed preachers must serve a four-year probationary period before becoming eligible for full-ordination to the ministry. Women may hold the positions of exhorters, licensed preachers, and evangelists, but they may not officiate at the church ordinances (1962:18-21).

All local *church property* is held in the name of the Latin American Council of Christian Churches as are all building funds and church checking or savings accounts, which are administered by the District Treasurer. Only the pastor's monthly salary and a "petty cash" fund of $50 can be withheld by the local church. In addition, *every church and worker must send his monthly tithe to the Treasurer of the Executive Council* (1962:11-12,22,24).

This evaluation reveals the strongly authoritarian structure of the Latin American Council of Christian Churches. Many of the conclusions reached concerning the Apostolic Assembly could be applied to the Latin American Council as well. The *patrón* pattern is very much in evidence. There has been even less change in the highest administrative offices of this denomination (only two presidents between 1923 and 1971) than in the Apostolic Assembly. The Latin American Council has had very little interaction with other Pentecostals and can be classified as among the most conservative and introverted of the Pentecostal denominations.

The International Church of the Foursquare Gospel

Founded by Aimee Semple McPherson in 1921, the Foursquare Gospel Church was composed of people who were attracted by her particular brand of Pentecostal fervor. Early in 1921, while conducting an evangelistic campaign in Oakland, California, "Sister Aimee"

> became fascinated by the prophetic vision of four faces (those of a lion, man, ox, and eagle) recounted in Ezekiel 1:4-10, and she immediately associated them with the four points which she incessantly emphasized in her gospel preaching: Salvation, Holy Spirit baptism, healing, and the second coming of Christ (Nichol 1966:120).

Thus was born her new emphasis on "the Foursquare Gospel". After calling a ministerial conference a few days later, over 1,000 followers signed a doctrinal statement in support of Mrs. McPherson's views, and out of this conference came The Foursquare Gospel Association (1966:120-121).

Growth 1923-1966. Although not incorporated until 1927, the International Church of the Foursquare Gospel established its "mother church", Angeles Temple, at the north end of Echo Park in Los Angeles in 1923. This impressive church had a seating capacity of 5,300 and was constructed at a cost of about 1.5 million dollars. By 1925, there were at least thirty-two affiliated churches in Southern California, and by 1966, the number of churches had grown to 741 nationwide, with a communicant membership of about 89,200 (Clark 1959:115; Nichol 1966:121-122).

Angeles Temple Bible School. Many of these churches were founded by students who graduated from the "Evangelistic and Missionary Training Institute", now called LIFE Bible College, which was started at Angeles Temple in 1923. Over 100 missionaries are now serving in twenty-six countries and many of them received their training at this institute (1966:122).

Hispanic Ministry. At least twenty-one of the Foursquare Gospel churches in the United States were Spanish-speaking congregations in 1971. These churches were located in only three states: California (11), Arizona (1), and Colorado (9). All of the Spanish-speaking congregations in California were in the southern half of the state, with all but one (El Cajõn) located in Los Angeles County. The following cities had Hispanic Foursquare Gospel churches: Baldwin Park, Canoga Park, Compton-Willowbrook, La Puente (Spanish Department), and San Gabriel. Each of these Los Angeles suburbs had but one Spanish-speaking congregation, while the City of Los Angeles itself had five: Angeles Temple Spanish Department; Boyle Heights Pan-American;

El Sereno Foursquare; *El Gethsemani* (south-central district); and Belvedere Pan-American. The total communicant membership for Los Angeles County was about 600 and the national Hispanic membership totaled approximately 1,050.

El Buen Pastor. Interestingly enough, the first Spanish-speaking church affiliated with the Foursquare Gospel Movement, *Misión Mexicana McPherson*, established in 1929 in Boyle Heights, is still in existence but does not presently belong to the Foursquare Church. Mrs. McPherson took a special interest in the establishment of this mission and contributed $12,000 (in 1930!) to build an impressive California mission stucco-type structure, with an auditorium that seated 500 people (Ortegon 1932:53).

The first pastor of the McPherson Mexican Mission was Antonio Gamboa, who is still its pastor, although the name of the church has been changed to *El Buen Pastor*. Gamboa completed six years at the Lydia Paterson Institute in El Paso, Texas prior to coming to California about 1927. After his arrival in Los Angeles, he enrolled in the Plaza Training School for Methodist pastors and became a licensed preacher. However, he left the Methodist Church and joined the Pentecostal movement about 1928, where he eventually became involved with The Foursquare Gospel Church. In 1929, Gamboa established the denomination's first Spanish-speaking mission, which had an amazingly rapid growth to about 500 members by 1932. While pastoring this mission during its first year, Gamboa attended and graduated from the "Angeles Temple Bible School" (1932:53-54).

Although not particularly sympathetic to the Pentecostal movement, Ortegon gives us an interesting insight into the ministry of this church in the early 1930s:

> The work of [*Misión Mexicana McPherson*] is essentially evangelistic. It is given impetus by the healing services which appeal strongly to the Mexican mind. Services are held every night at 7:30 p.m. and extend sometimes to 11:30 p.m. There are no clubs, no industrial centers. The main feature is the evangelistic service. There is, however, in this church a woman's [sic] society which has once a week a sale of old clothing for the needy. It also gives away bread and groceries. The pastor states that during the present economic crises the church feeds 400 every week (1932:54).

Gamboa has been the pastor of *El Buen Pastor* for over forty years, where he has witnessed many ethnic population changes in the Boyle Heights area. However, his church, now independent and interdenominational, continues to maintain a membership of about 400 communicant members, although the average Sunday morning attendance is only about 200.

General Evaluation. Most of the Spanish-speaking Foursquare Gospel churches were established after the mid-1940s and many of them are pastored by graduates of either LIFE Bible College in Los Angeles or the Foursquare Spanish Bible School in Denver, Colorado. Most of the Spanish-speaking churches in Los Angeles County are operated as autonomous Hispanic congregations, but there are two churches that function as a Spanish department of an Anglo church: La Puente and Angeles Temple. Although the Hispanic ministry of the Foursquare Gospel Church is not very large, most of the ministers evidently are graduates of Bible institutes and many of them are under forty years of age.

Independent Pentecostal Churches

In terms of the number of independent Pentecostal churches in Los Angeles County, the pattern there is distinctly different from that in New York City where at least 117 churches were listed as "other, independent, unknown" but definitely Pentecostal, according to Whitam (1960:50). By comparison, Los Angeles County only had seventeen "independent Pentecostal churches," some of which may have inter-church affiliations although they do not belong to any of the larger Pentecostal denominations. The location of churches of this type in Los Angeles County was as follows: Baldwin Park (1), Los Angeles (13), Sepulveda (1), and Wilmington (2). The estimated communicant membership of these seventeen churches was about 1,020. In addition, one church in Huntington Park is listed as "Assembly of God in Christ, Inc.", while in Wilmington, the Assembly of Christian Churches of New York has one congregation of forty members. [See Appendix III for the names and addresses of these churches.]

10.

Other Protestant Groups/Christian Sects

The importance of a balanced perspective in the historical analysis of Hispanic Protestantism in Los Angeles County now leads us to a brief consideration of a number of other denominational bodies. Some of the following groups only have a few Spanish-speaking churches in the county area, others have had a much shorter record of ministry among the Hispanic population than denominations previously considered, and still others have received only a brief analysis due to the limited data available from which to trace their growth histories. Finally, a brief report is given concerning two non-Protestant "Christian" sects to further balance the total picture of Hispanic non-Catholic religious life in Los Angeles.

THE CONGREGATIONAL CHURCH (UNITED CHURCH OF CHRIST)

The growth of Congregational churches in America prior to 1800 was closely tied to the history of New England where, in 1620, the first "Congregational" church was founded at Plymouth, Massachusetts. This distinguishing name pointed, of course, to a "congregational" form of church government in contrast to that of the Church of England and its episcopal polity. Although Congregational influence and strength was spurred on by the Great Awakening in the mid-1700s, Congregational churches did not expand rapidly on the western frontier. "As late as 1830," according to Gaustad, "nine-tenths of the Congregational churches were still in New England. There simply were no Congregationalists of the Middle and Southern Colonies to move into newly opened territories" (1962:59). When Congregationalism did expand, it followed the trail of migration from the New England states to New York, Ohio,

Illinois, Michigan, Wisconsin, and Iowa. By 1906, one-third of all Congregational churches were still in New England, another third were in the five midwestern states just mentioned, and the remaining one-third were distributed throughout the remaining states (1962:13-16,59-60).

Cooperation and Merger

Congregational expansion from the New England States has mainly been the result of cooperation and merger with other denominations. Concerning the early cooperation with the Presbyterians, Gaustad has written:

> Through the cooperative effort of the Plan of Union (1801) and the American Board of Home Missions, which was organized in 1826 to execute this Plan, Congregationalists worked with Presbyterians in planting churches in the West, in forwarding mission efforts among the Indians, and in establishing centers of higher learning (1962:62).

When the Plan of Union was rejected by the Congregationalists in 1852, the Presbyterians had already absorbed a large proportion of migrating New Englanders to the detriment of the Congregationa[l] Church (Sweet 1950:221,339). However, by 1849, Congregational ministers had founded the first of many Congregational churches in California; by 1950 this was the only state west of the Missis sippi River with more than 200 Congregational churches (Gaustad 1962:61, Figure 51).

The pattern of interdenominational cooperation by the Congregationalists, which began with the Plan of Union, continued through the American Board of Commissioners for Foreign Missions (1801) and the American Board of Home Missions. Later, a new social awareness following the Civil War resulted in Congregational leadership in the "social gospel" and in early ecumenicity Two Church mergers in recent years increased the united membership to an all-time high of about 2,250,000 nationally by 1960. In 1931, the Congregational Church merged with the General Convention of the Christian Church to form the Congregational Christian Churches. And in 1957, merger of this body with the Evangelical and Reformed Church created the United Church of Christ (Gaustad 1962:62-63).

Spanish-speaking Ministry

The earliest record of Congregational activity among the Spanish-speaking population of California comes by way of Alden Case's tract promoting the California Spanish Missionary Society. This interdenominational society, as we have seen, was establishe in 1897 by Case and his supporters who sought to develop Mexican churches and missions in the southern part of the state. Case was a Congregational missionary in Mexico with the American Board of Commissioners for Foreign Missions prior to his coming to Pomona, California and initiating Spanish-speaking ministry in that area. Many of the early Mexican missions--at Redlands, Chino, Santa Ana, San Bernardino and Piru--were aided by local Congregational churches, although Methodists and Friends also contributed valuably to Case's ministry (Case 1897).

By 1930 the Congregational Home Mission Society was responsible for five Spanish-speaking churches in the Southern California Congregational Conference. It is assumed that these churches came into existence mainly due to the labors of Case and his fellow workers. McLean reported Congregational churches or missions in Pomona, Chino, Puente, Ontario and East Highland, although in his statistical summary only two organized churches are listed with 125 members. In addition, five community centers ministered to the broad social needs of the Mexican population (McLean 1930:28,37-38,43).

However, by 1969, the *Yearbook of the United Church of Christ* reported only three Hispanic churches in Southern California and a total membership of only 169. The Barstow Mexican Congregational Church, which was formally organized in 1932, had forty members and seventy-four enrolled in Sunday School in 1969. The missions in Chino and Pomona were both listed as "churches" in 1920. Chino had fifty-eight members and seventy-five Sunday School scholars in 1969. *El Buen Pastor* in Pomona, the only Congregational Church (U.C.C.) that was still in existence in Los Angeles County in 1969, had a Sunday School enrollment of eighty-five and seventy-one church members. There is, however, another Congregational church in the county, Bethany Congregational on Ditman Avenue in Los Angeles, but it is independent of the United Church of Christ and its origin and development are unknown.

THE CALIFORNIA YEARLY MEETING OF FRIENDS

The Quakers sponsored evangelistic work among the Mexican population in Whittier in the 1890s, which later resulted in a mission sponsored by the First Friends Church. According to David LeShana in *Quakers in California*, the Whittier Friends took an active part in the ministry of Alden Case, a Congregational missionary from Pomona, beginning in March 1898, when they united their efforts with the "International Spanish Society" (officially known as the California Spanish Missionary Society). Several Quakers served on the board of directors of this society, "thus giving it needed support and direction" (1969:131).

However, the Spanish-speaking ministry did not have a permanent basis until the Reverend and Mrs. Ervin G. Taber arrived in Whittier in 1902. The Tabers, who had been missionaries with the Friends in Mexico, were called by the Women's Missionary Board of California Friends to work among the Mexican population in Southern California. A home and school for Mexican girls was opened in 1909 in the home of Philena B. Hadley, but this ministry was apparently of short duration. Sometime later, another home for girls was established and continued for a number of years, along with a Spanish-speaking Sunday School (Arnold and Clark 1933:278).

The development of these early efforts into a permanent Mexican church awaited the arrival of Enrique Cobos in 1915. This Mexican evangelist held services in several locations in and around Whittier before a new church and parsonage were finally erected in April 1922. A Mexican chapel had been previously established (November 1915) in the section of East Whittier known as "Jimtown", which was near the old Pico Mansion where the first governor of California had lived. Apparently these were the only Friends-sponsored Mexican missions and churches in California up to the present (1933:279; LeShana 1969:131).

The Spanish-speaking church established by Cobos was still in existence in 1972, but it is now located in Pico Rivera and English is used for worship and instruction. The Pico Rivera Friends Church is one of the few Hispanic churches in Southern California that has switched to an all-English format, although the majority of churches now use English in their Sunday school programs. This congregation has used English since 1958 when the church moved into its new building in a predominantly Mexican housing area. This sixty-nine member congregation is served by an Anglo pastor and has been self-supporting since 1963. Plans were being made to establish a bilingual church in Montebello during 1972, according to the pastor.

DISCIPLES OF CHRIST/CHURCHES OF CHRIST

The "antimission movement" in the early 1800s (see Clark 1937:200) caused serious dissension within Baptist circles and was one of the major reasons for the withdrawal of thousands of Baptists to form Disciples of Christ congregations in the late 1820s (Sweet 1950:273). However, one of the principal advocates of antimission views, Alexander Campbell, who with his followers were nominally Baptist from 1813 to 1830, after separating from the Baptists and organizing the Disciples, changed his mind in 1844 and adopted the opposite position. This led to a reactionary party within the Disciples led by those who had strong antimission convictions and, together with the anti-organ advocates, eventual polarized the membership into "progressives" (Disciples) and "conservatives" (Churches of Christ). By 1906, this schism was recognized by a religious census taken by the federal government, although the official division into two separate bodies was not completed until 1926 (Clark 1937:212-217; Gaustad 1962:64-65).

The Churches of Christ, according to statistics for 1936, reported 3,800 churches and over 300,000 members. Most of these congregations were in the Southern states and were about eighty-five percent rural. Operating on the principle that they "speak where the Scriptures speak and are silent where the Scriptures are silent," the Churches of Christ oppose the use of all musical instruments, church societies and organizations of all kinds. Their ministers are unordained and are chosen by the local groups; they have no conferences, presbyteries, synods, assemblies, or other ministerial or ecclesiastical bodies; and they do not affiliate with any interdenominational agencies. According to Clark, "There is nothing distinctive about them save their 'anti' attitude in the matter of organs and missionary societies... *They carry on no organized home mission, social service, or other benevolent activity,* though they are intensely evangelistic... and are not opposed to foreign missions" (1937:214-215).

Nevertheless, by 1972, the Churches of Christ had initiated "home missions" among the Spanish-speaking population in Southern California. Four Spanish-speaking churches or missions within Anglo churches were reported in Los Angeles County. Three of these congregations were in the City of Los Angeles and the other one was located in the neighboring city of Montebello. It is estimated that the combined membership of these Spanish-speaking congregations is 200-250. Although the dates of origin are not known, apparently all four were established fairly recently (since 1960). Three of the churches are pastored by Anglos, with the fourth church having a Spanish-surnamed pastor.

By contrast, the Christian Church, Disciples of Christ have only one Spanish-speaking church in Los Angeles County, located in the Cyprus Park district of Los Angeles. In addition, there are at least three other congregations that have the "Christian Church" label but are independent of the Disciples. One of these churches, *La Iglesia Fundamental Cristiana "La Trinidad"* (110 members), originated as a breakaway movement from *La Trinidad* United Methodist Church in 1963; and it is now meeting in the buildings that once housed the Spanish American Baptist Seminary on Indiana Street.

THE SOUTHERN BAPTIST CONVENTION

The first Anglo Southern Baptist church in Los Angeles County was organized on November 14, 1937, and in 1943 five churches met to organize the Los Angeles Southern Baptist Association. These five Anglo churches had a combined membership of 408 in 1943. By 1969, four Southern Baptist Associations had been formed in Los Angeles County composed of 143 churches and a combined membership of 50,956 (Los Angeles Southern Baptist Association Brochure, 1969).

Overview of Hispanic Growth

The ministry of the Southern Baptist General Convention to Spanish-speaking people in California began in 1949 when Jesús Rio arrived in Los Angeles from San Antonio, Texas. Rio organized the first Spanish-speaking Southern Baptist church in the state, now known as *Primera Iglesia Bautista*. Later, in 1950, Rio organized the *Primera Iglesia Bautista* in San Jose, California. From this small beginning in 1949, the Spanish language ministry increased to sixty-one churches and missions by April 1969: twenty-seven were in Northern California and thirty-four in Southern California (Southern Baptist General Convention of California, *Language Missions Directory*, 1969).

The Southern Baptist Convention began its ministry to Spanish-speaking people in the Los Angeles area within a dozen years after the establishment of the first Anglo Southern Baptist church. Since 1950, when the first Spanish language church was organized, Southern Baptists have planted eleven Hispanic churches and thirteen Spanish departments in Anglo churches within Los Angeles County. Three or four additional Spanish churches or departments were organized during this period, but these were either discontinued or merged with other existing churches. Figure 50 shows the location of Southern Baptist Spanish-speaking churches and departments in Los Angeles and Orange Counties. Although only two Hispanic churches were established by 1955, five new churches came into existence by 1960, and seven more were added by 1965. Beginning in 1968, many Spanish-speaking departments were established in Anglo churches in an attempt to integrate Mexicans, Cubans, Puerto Ricans, and other Latins into Anglo American churches. By 1971 thirteen Spanish departments were in existence, which is more than the total number of separate Spanish language churches.

The rate of increase in Spanish language membership in Southern Baptist churches in Los Angeles County is shown in Figure 51. From the bridgehead in 1949, the communicant membership has grown to 1,394 with an increase between 1955 and 1965 of 280 percent, a between 1965 and 1969, an increase of 204 percent. It is estimat

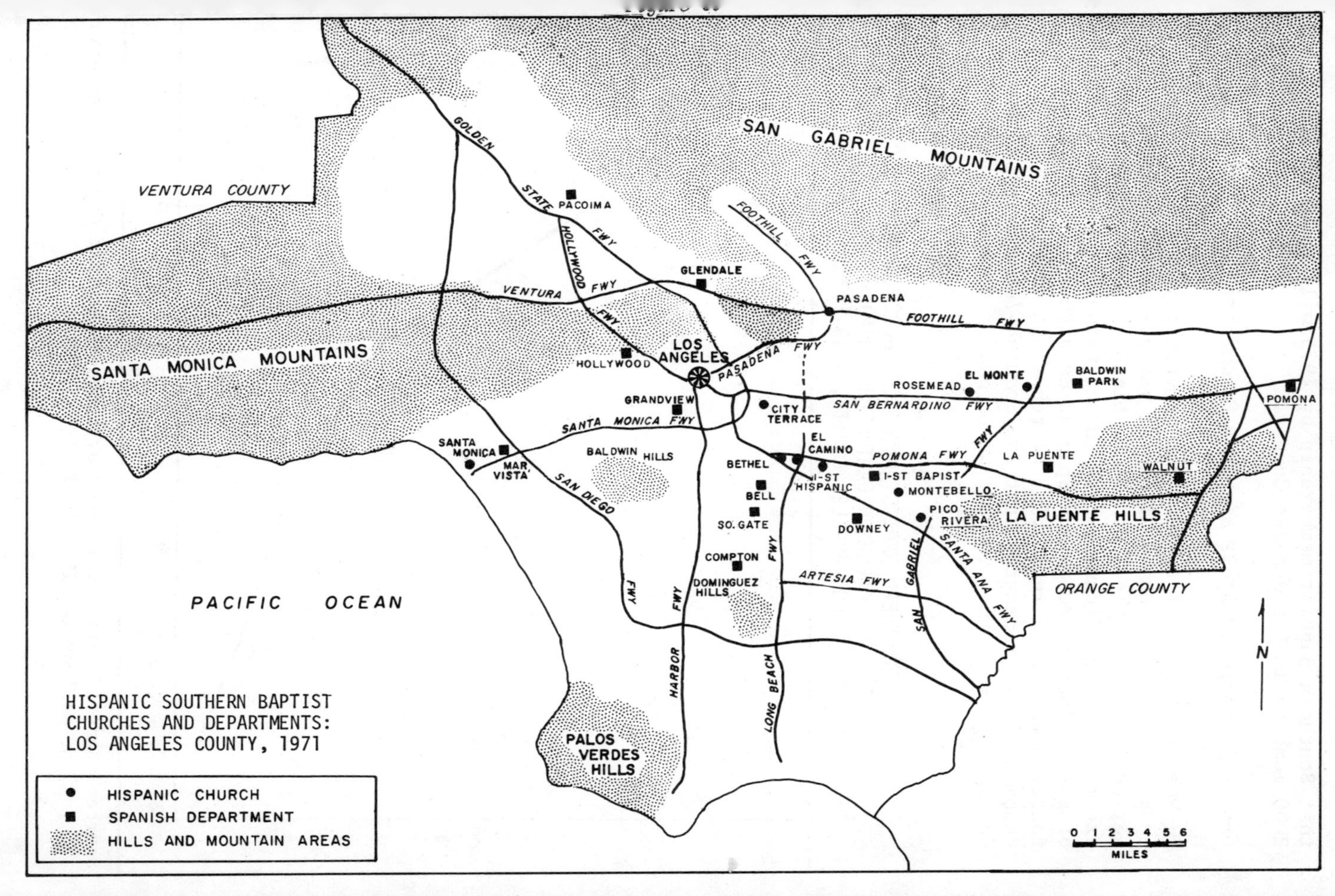

HISPANIC SOUTHERN BAPTIST
CHURCHES AND DEPARTMENTS:
LOS ANGELES COUNTY, 1971

that Southern Baptist membership by 1975 will be about 1800 to 2000 members in Los Angeles County.

Growth Compared to Other Hispanic Denominations

Whereas the total communicant membership in other Spanish language denominations declined at various rates during the period 1950-1971, the Southern Baptist churches and missions experienced significant growth in and through the organization of twenty-four churches and Spanish departments. This growth factor among Southern Baptist churches, in contrast to other denominations, indicates that *the Spanish language population in Los Angeles County was not unresponsive to evangelistic*

Figure 51

SOUTHERN BAPTIST HISPANIC CHURCH GROWTH
(COMMUNICANT MEMBERSHIP)
LOS ANGELES COUNTY, 1949-1975

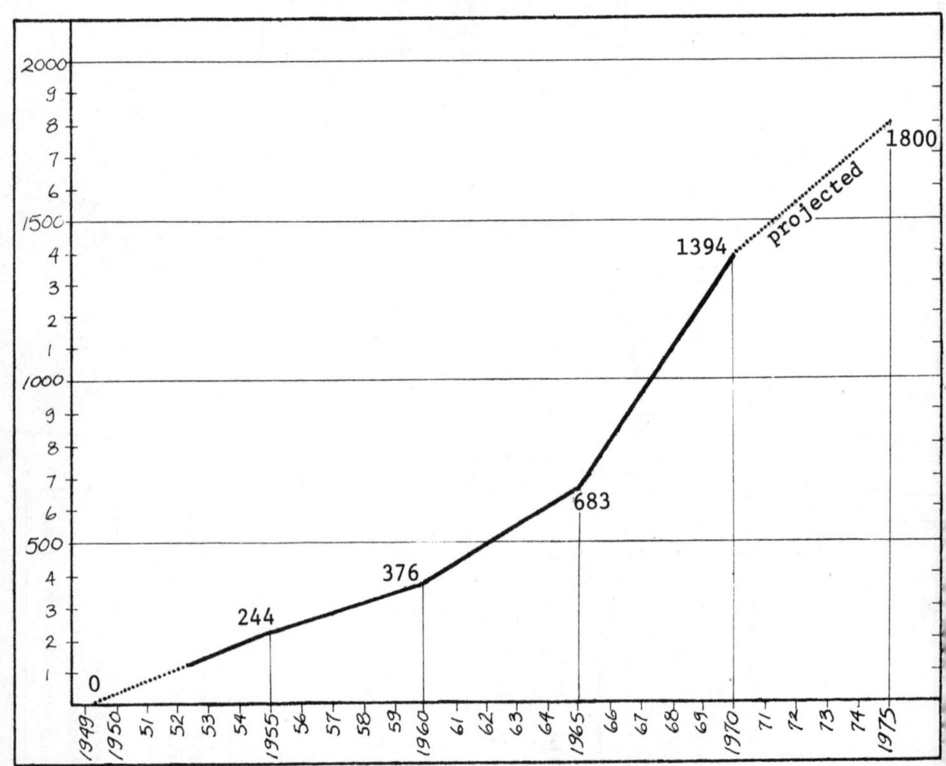

Source: Annual Statistical Reports, Southern Baptist General Convention of California, 1950-1970

efforts among them between 1950 and 1970. In fact, it shows that if other denominational groups had been organizing and developing their own ministry among Spanish-speaking people in the area with the same enthusiasm as the Southern Baptists, then their own growth would have shown significant membership increase as well.

Reasons for High Growth Rate

Since the rate of immigration from Mexico and the migration of Spanish-speaking people from other areas of the Southwest to California increased significantly between 1950 and 1970, it is quite possible that many Spanish-speaking Southern Baptists from Texas migrated to Southern California and provided the nucleus for the Spanish churches and departments that were established in Los Angeles County and Southern California in this period.

However, the increase in membership in Southern Baptist churches because of "conversion growth" seems to be a significant factor in the history of Southern Baptist Spanish-speaking ministry in Southern California. It is estimated that the communicant membership of Hispanic Southern Baptists in California was about 3,650 members in 1970.

Evaluation of Present Ministry

Eugene Wolf, Southern Baptist missionary to Spanish-speaking people in Los Angeles County, contributed the following information concerning Southern Baptist churches and missions in the area. Although some of the older churches have now reached a plateau in their rate of growth, most of the churches are continuing to experience increases in membership. Several of the churches are composed primarily of Cubans, such as the churches at Bell, Santa Monica and Glendale. Also, Los Angeles Bethel Baptist and Grandview Baptist Spanish Department have a growing number of Cubans, Puerto Ricans and other Latin Americans. Other churches, like the First Baptist Church of Baldwin Park Spanish Department, have a large number of illegal Mexican aliens who are either members or who attend the worship services; this means that the congregation is highly mobile with many returning to Mexico from time to time (Wolf 1970).

Leadership Training

The pastoral leadership of the Southern Baptist Spanish language churches in Los Angeles County includes many who are serving part-time while working in secular employment and others who are lay-pastors. To meet the need for continuing education for pastoral and lay leadership in the churches, leadership training classes were organized by the Southern Baptists and were held on

Monday nights during 1969 and 1970 at El Camino Baptist Church in Los Angeles. Wolf and several Hispanic pastors taught classes on personal evangelism, Sunday school administration, and Bible doctrine; about twenty laymen attended. The Southern Baptist Spanish-speaking pastors have a monthly Saturday morning breakfast meeting at a local restaurant, where area business is conducted in addition to a time of inspiration. The only known Spanish language leadership training institution for Southern Baptists is located in San Antonio, Texas, where many of their pastors and lay workers are trained; this is the Mexican Baptist Bible Institute which was established in 1926. However, a growing number of workers receive college and seminary training in the English-speaking institutions of Texas.

Growth Compared to Texas and U.S. Totals

Southern Baptist Mexican churches and missions in Texas for the year 1967-1968 totaled 368 with a communicant membership of about 34,250. Sixty-five Mexican churches had an estimated membership of 9,850 and 303 Mexican missions had a membership of 24,390. The estimated average "church" membership of Mexican Baptist churches in Texas, based upon a sample of twenty-one congregations, was 151.6 members. The "mission" average was 80.5 based upon a sample of forty-five missions. The Associations in Texas with the largest number of Mexican churches and missions were: Magic Valley, Lower Rio Grande, Blanco, San Antonio, El Paso, Frio River, Union, Staked Plains, Corpus Christi and Dallas (Baptist General Convention of Texas 1968).

The total scope of Southern Baptist ministry among Spanish-speaking people in the United States is indicated by the fact that, in 1964, there were 510 Spanish language congregations and 580 missionaries (both husbands and wives) in the Convention (Haseldon 1964:105). By 1970 this ministry had increased to at least 540 Spanish churches and missions, with about 44,200 communicant members.

THE CONSERVATIVE BAPTIST CHURCH/OTHER BAPTISTS

The Northern Baptist Convention, like the Disciples and other groups, has had its share of dissention and schism. Polarization between "modernists" and "fundamentalists" within the Convention resulted in several withdrawal movements, beginning in the 1920s and continuing into the 1940s. Some of the most important points of disagreement were open communion, alien immersion, comity agreements, and the "inclusive policy" of the Foreign Mission Society (Sweet 1950:407-408; Torbett 1963:433-434).

In 1933 dissatisfaction with theological liberalism within the Northern Baptist Convention, together with the denomination's cooperation with the Interchurch World Movement and the Federal Council of Churches of Christ in America, resulted in the withdrawal of about fifty churches and the organization of the *General Association of Regular Baptist Churches (GARB)*. By 1946 the GARB constituency had grown to over four hundred churches in twenty-six states, with California being one of its strongest supporters (Torbet 1963:433-435). At present, only one Hispanic congregation in Los Angeles County is affiliated with this denomination; it is the Calvary Baptist Church in Boyle Heights.

The Fundamentalist reaction within the Northern Baptist Convention continued during the decade of the 1940s. A major issue among conservatives was the alleged "inclusive policy" of the Foreign Board which, according to its critics, allowed the appointment of missionaries who denied the virgin birth of Christ (Torbet 1963:399-401). Consequently, the Conservative Baptist Foreign Mission Society was organized in 1943 as an alternative society within the Northern Baptist Convention. Its purpose was to appoint only those who annually signed a doctrinal statement which guaranteed their allegiance to the "Fundamentals of the Faith". The failure of the Convention to recognize and support the new Foreign Society eventually led to the organization, in 1947, of *The Conservative Baptist Association of America (CBA)*; the next year, the new Association launched a Home Missions Society. By 1962, membership had grown to over 300,000 in 1,350 churches nationwide (1963:435-436,477,512).

Hispanic ministry among Conservative Baptists in Southern California has been sponsored by the Home Missions Society, which supports several Anglo missionaries in the Los Angeles area. Beginning in the mid-1950s, Spanish-speaking churches and missions were organized in several southland counties, so that by 1972 seven Hispanic congregations were in existence. Los Angeles County has three churches: East Los Angeles, Commerce, and Norwalk. Two smaller congregations are located in Orange County at Fullerton and Santa Ana. Other churches or missions are located in Ontario (San Bernardino County) and Riverside (Riverside County); and two missions have been established in Tijuana (Baja California, Mexico). These congregations have formed *La Asociación de Iglesias Bautistas Conservadoras* and have cooperated in several leadership training conferences in the past few years. The combined membership of the Hispanic churches and missions in California is estimated to be between 400-450.

Other *independent* Hispanic Baptist churches are located in Los Angeles County, from La Puente, to Los Angeles, and south to Wilmington; but their combined membership totals only about

150 people. In addition, the *Baptist Bible Fellowship* has an affiliated Spanish-speaking church in South Gate. It is reported that this is the only Hispanic congregation of that denomination.

THE SEVENTH-DAY ADVENTIST CHURCH

The Adventist message originated with William Miller, a Baptist preacher from upstate New York, who, in 1831, began to lecture on his theories concerning the return of Christ and the approaching end of the world. Based on a premillenial interpretation to the Scriptures, Miller calculated that Christ would return to "cleanse the sanctuary", that is, to purge the world of sin and rebellion, between March 1843 and March 1844. After Miller gathered a following of about 50,000 people from various denominations by 1844, the predicted time of Christ's return passed and Miller's followers were greatly disappointed. "Some returned to their denominational affiliation; some forsook Christianity and its apparently misleading book; some continued to look for Christ's imminent return," according to Gaustad (1962:113-114).

Birth of Adventist Bodies

Since many were convinced that the chronological calculations of Miller and another Adventist, John Couch, were correct, the "cleansing of the sanctuary" was reinterpreted to be a "heavenly sanctuary" rather than one on earth. Thus, Miller and the Adventist message were vindicated and the movement continued to grow. According to Clark, "Miller's doctrine was at first received with complacency by ministers and laymen of the denominations and his followers did not sever their ecclesiastical connections" (1937:38). However, the Adventist movement was soon denounced by denominational leaders, whereupon separate congregations of Adventists were formed in various locations (1937:34-39).

The Seventh Day Adventist Church is the largest group in existence that traces its origins to Miller's prophecy. The first church was apparently organized in 1844 in Washington, New Hampshire when a previous Adventist group, having been influenced by Seventh Day Baptists, accepted Saturday as the Christian Sabbath. Adventists were inspired by the prophecies of Mrs. Ellen White, who encouraged others by her dreams and visions which began in 1842. She became an outstanding Adventist leader and "contributed to the movement a mass of instruction which the faithful received as next to the Bible in spiritual authority" (1937:39). Clark characterized Seventh-Day Adventists as evangelical and orthodox because they accept the major principles of Protestant theology, whereas their distinctive doctrines are: the unique interpretation of the second advent, the observation of Saturday as the scriptural Sabbath, and in acknowledging the inspiration of Mrs. White (1937:41). It was in Battle Creek, Michigan that the name "Seventh-Day Adventist" was officially adopted by a large Adventist group in 1860 and where the General Conference was organized in 1863 with 125 churches and 3,500 members (Gaustad 1962:115).

Although the original Adventists urged the selling of all their property and the discontinuance of manual labor in preparation for the imminent return of Christ, the Seventh-Day Adventists have built a virtual kingdom here on earth (Clark 1937:36, 40). Battle Creek became the Adventist-inspired capital of health and cereal foods which were developed to supplement and enrich the diet of most Adventists who are vegetarians. The use of alcohol, tea, coffee, and tobacco were condemned and, although meat was not forbidden, Adventists were urged to eat only "natural foods". This emphasis on physical health also led to the development of medical and educational institutions in America and in many foreign countries (Gaustad 1962:115).

In 1960 there were over 3,000 Seventh-Day Adventist churches in the United States with a combined membership of approximately 310,000 (1962:115). The largest number of Adventists were reported in California, where the Southern California Conference had ninety churches and twenty-five church schools and academies in 1971. Adventist churches have been organized among many ethnic groups in the three counties of the Conference (Los Angeles, Ventura and Santa Barbara). Spanish-speaking congregations constituted the largest group.

Hispanic Adventist Churches

Ortegon reported that in 1932 only two "Seventh-Day Adventist Mexican Churches" were organized in Los Angeles. Actually, only one was an officially recognized church, the Boyle Heights Mexican Church, but a mission had been organized in Belvedere that later achieved church status. The combined membership of these two congregations totaled 141, together with an average attendance in Sabbath school of one-hundred students. Although no community centers were sponsored by the Adventists, the White Memorial Hospital (also known as the College of Medical Evangelists) served a large Mexican constituency in the Boyle Heights area (1932:55-56).

From this beginning in the late 1920s, Spanish-speaking Seventh-Day Adventist churches grew to ten congregations in Los Angeles County by 1971. The newest Spanish language congregation to be organized is in Glendale with a membership of eighty. Within the city of Los Angeles, churches are found in Boyle Heights,

Lincoln Heights, Belvedere, and the Central District. Other churches in the county are located in Carson (was Wilmington Spanish), Pico Rivera, San Fernando, San Gabriel (Temple City Spanish), and Van Nuys. The estimated total communicant membership of Hispanic Adventist churches in Los Angeles County is about 800-900. Several other Hispanic congregations were reported in Oxnard, Santa Paula, and Santa Ana.

National statistics for 1960 reveal that sixty-eight Spanish-speaking Adventist churches were in existence with a reported membership of approximately 5,000. In addition, eight institutions (hospitals, schools or community centers) that ministered to the Hispanic population were sponsored by the denomination. Sixty-five percent of the Hispanic Adventist constituency was located in the West and the Southwest; one-fifth of all Spanish-speaking Adventist churches were located in Southern California (Grebler 1970:488). Compared to the denomination as a whole, Hispanic Adventists accounted for 1.7 percent of the total communicant membership and 2.3 percent of the total number of churches.

OTHER DENOMINATIONAL/INTERDENOMINATIONAL GROUPS

The First Covenant Church of Los Angeles has a Spanish-speaking congregation meeting in its facilities on Francisco Street in the Central District. *Iglesia Cristiana Evangelica* has a membership of about eighty persons and is served by an Anglo pastor who is a returned missionary from Latin America. This group has attempted to establish rapport with the heterogeneous Hispanic peoples in the Downtown area by sending teams of church members door-to-door and handing out booklets which explain city and county services that are available to them, such as health, education, and welfare. Recreational activities are also available to young people in the church's gymnasium, which has been a valuable outlet for residents in this transient neighborhood.

The Parish of East Los Angeles of the *Episcopal Church* has conducted Spanish-speaking services since the mid-1950s. The three congregations that compose the parish had a combined membership of 397 Hispanic Americans in 1970 out of a total parish membership of 422. Father John B. Luce and his two assistant ministers served the Church of the Epiphany in Lincoln Heights, Saint Bartholomews in El Sereno, and the Church of the Resurrection in East Los Angeles. Father Luce has been active in the *Chicano* civil rights movement and the Parish of East Los Angeles has a definite "activist" stance. Although the Episcopal Church does not consider itself a "Protestant" denomination, it has been included in this study.

The small number of Spanish-speaking *Lutheran churches* in Southern California does not require a separate evaluation of the Anglo denominational structure, nor of the various histories of each synod. There were no Lutheran-sponsored Hispanic congregations in California in 1930, according to McLean's study. However, the Joint Synod of Ohio and Other States reported three congregations and 266 members, apparently all in Texas. These Hispanic churches were supervised by the Board on Mexican Missions of the Evangelical Lutheran Church with headquarters in Victoria, Texas (McLean 1930:30,43).

By 1965 the Lutheran Church-Missouri Synod had ten organized Spanish-speaking congregations in the United States. Texas had five Hispanic churches and the following states had one congregation each: New York, New Jersey, Florida, Illinois and California. *La Santa Cruz* Lutheran Church was organized in the Boyle Heights section of Los Angeles in 1957. According to the statistical report for 1965, this church had ninety communicant members and fifty-six Sunday school pupils and was served by an Anglo pastor (*Statistical Yearbook* 1965:19). Apparently, Angelica Lutheran Church initiated a Spanish-speaking ministry in 1971 in response to the in-migration of Hispanic Americans in its local community, located near McArthur Park in Los Angeles.

The City Terrace Mennonite Brethren Church, although not technically a "Spanish-speaking church", has a strong Hispanic constituency with many bilingual members. There are sixty-five Hispanic Americans in the church's ninety-member congregation. Spanish is used by some of the church's "witnessing teams" that have conducted a door-to-door canvass in local neighborhoods. A Spanish-speaking adult Sunday school class has been organized for those who have started attending the church as a result of the neighborhood canvass.

The Belvedere Gardens Corps of the *Salvation Army* has had an Hispanic constituency and Spanish language ministry since 1933. This congregation now has eighty-one communicant members and moved into a new building in 1966.

The *Asociación de Iglesias Evangelicas del Sur de California* dates its origin to 1908 when Domingo A. Mata, a Presbyterian pastor from Los Angeles, was elected president of this interdenominational organization. Although it is now known whether the present participating denominations and churches were active in this organization from its beginning, it is assumed that most of them were charter members in 1908. The membership of the Association in May 1951 included the following groups: The Friends, American Baptists, Congregational, Salvation Army, Church of God, Methodists, Free Methodists, Church of the Nazarene, Presbyterians in U.S.A., as well as several independent churches. An annual convention is held for the member churches, mainly for inspirational purposes (1969:18, and Chronological Table on inside back cover).

NON-PROTESTANT CHRISTIAN SECTS

Only two groups will be discussed in this section, the Jehovah's Witnesses and the Church of Jesus Christ of Latter Day Saints, although a third group is also in existence. The latter is the Church of Christian Science, which only had one church where Spanish language services were conducted in 1970, the Eleventh Church of Christian Science on Guirado Street in Los Angeles.

Jehovah's Witnesses

Jehovah's Witnesses, originally known as "The Zion's Watch Tower Tract Society" and for many years referred to as the International Bible Students' Association, was classified as "the most vigorous propagandists of all the Adventists" by Clark, although not technically listed as an Adventist body (1937:45).

Origin and Doctrine. Founded in 1872 by Charles Taze Russell in Pennsylvania, Witnesses teach that Christ returned to the "upper air" in 1874 to initiate His "second coming" in progressive stages. Since 1914 Christ has ruled in His heavenly, millennial Kingdom having brought to an end the "times of the Gentiles". Christ's spiritual return in 1914 marked the "beginning of the end times" when He began to call out 144,000 "witnesses" and is sending them forth "to bear testimony to the name of Jehovah and to His Theocratic Government" (Van Baalen 1960:290, 294-297). These witnesses will proclaim the Kingdom message until Christ's final return to earth to confront Satan's forces in the great Battle of Armageddon, which will be followed by the judgment of the nations and the beginning of the eternal kingdom. In addition to the 144,000 witnesses, there shall be "other sheep" that shall also enter the eternal age (1960:298-299).

Opposition and Growth. Claiming not to be a denomination and opposing all Protestants and Catholics alike, Jehovah's Witnesses have thrived on persecution and have received their share of it. Opposition has mostly come from the Witnesses' "denial of practically every major doctrine of the Christian faith, from the Trinity and the deity of Christ to the bodily resurrection from the grave and the visible second advent of our Lord" (Martin 1957:11). Other sources of difficulty have been the refusal of members of this society to serve in the armed forces, to salute the flag, and to receive blood transfusions. Nevertheless, there were over 4,000 congregations of Jehovah's Witnesses in 1960 with a constituency of more than 250,000 in the United States (Gaustad 1962:117-118). Most of this growth has resulted from a vigorous campaign of door-to-door literature distribution and "evangelism" by zealous witnesses, and from lectures conducted in local meeting places for those who have been influenced by their literature.

Hispanic Ministry. Not much is known about the influence of Jehovah's Witnesses among minority groups in Southern California. Only one small Spanish-speaking congregation of "Russelites" was reported in Los Angeles by Ortegon in 1932, numbering about fifteen persons. There were possibly other Spanish language groups unknown to Ortegon that were located in Los Angeles County. However, it was reported that "the work has been going on for a period of eight years without conspicious success." Ortegon further comments:

> Their work is carried on from house to house by the zealous members. Each member is given a set of books, translations of Judge Rutherford's books, whom they consider a great prophet of God, and they go from house to house either selling the books or giving away magazines in which the doctrines of the Russelites are explained.... Their services resemble more a class lecture than a worship service (1932:59-60).

The success of this organization among Spanish-speaking people in Los Angeles County in 1972 does not appear to be very good. Only three congregations are to be found in predominantly Spanish-speaking neighborhoods throughout the county area: one each in East Los Angeles, Cyprus Park and El Sereno.

Latter Day Saints

The Church of Jesus Christ of Latter-Day Saints (Mormons) was organized by Joseph Smith in 1830, after receiving (so he claimed) a series of revelations from the angel Moroni which resulted in Smith's writing of the *Book of Mormon.* This book is purported to be the history of the Nephites and the Lamanites, both descendents of the lost tribes of Israel, who migrated to the American continent hundreds of years prior to the European colonization.

Migration to Utah. After gaining a following in New York, Smith led his faithful disciples to Ohio, Missouri, and then to Illinois, where by 1844 the Mormon community numbered from 8,000 to 15,000. However, the colony at Nauvoo experienced much persecution, especially due to the community's finances, the doctrine of the Mormon Church, and integrity of Smith. After the slaying of Smith in 1844, several groups of Mormons left Illinois for other locations, but it was the group led by Brigham Young that created a Mormon "Zion" on the western frontier. Young's pioneer group left Illinois in 1846 and traveled west to the present state of Nebraska and on to Utah in 1847 where a colony was established in the Salt Lake Valley. By 1870 the population of Utah had grown to 86,000 and about ninety-five percent were reported to be Mormons. Another colony was established at San Bernardino, California in 1851 but most of these settlers returned to Salt Lake City during the Civil War (Gaustad 1962: 82-87).

Mormon Growth. The growth of Mormonism from sixteen churches in 1850 to nearly 1.5 million members in 1960 is a remarkable record considering the opposition they have received for many years of their history. Opposition has come both from Protestants who object to Mormon theology, and from government sources who sought to eliminate the practice of polygamy. The strength of the Utah-based Church of Jesus Christ of Latter-Day Saints continues to be in the western states, primarily in Utah, California and Idaho. The other branch of Mormonism, *the Reorganized Church of Jesus Christ of Latter-Day Saints* with headquarters in Missouri, has had a much slower growth pattern: from 18,000 members in 1884 to about 150,000 in 1960 (1962:86).

Gaustad mentions one factor that has greatly aided the world-wide expansion of the Utah branch of Mormonism:

> [One principal growth factor] is the practice of sending a great number of young men on a mission, foreign or domestic, on behalf of the Church. In pairs, the young men take the world as their parish--teaching, preaching, sowing the seed which (often in the form of the *Book of Mormon*) is left behind to germinate. Priding itself on its nonclerical, nonprofessional ministries, the Utah Church takes with great seriousness the priesthood of every believer. And even should the young evangelist in his two- or three-year missionary endeavor fail to win a single convert, he himself returns to his daily work a confirmed, convinced, earnest disciple of the Palmyra prophet (1962:86).

Hispanic Mormonism. Early contact between the Mormons and the Mexicans in the Southwest inspired missionary activity among them, beginning in the 1870s. Since Mexicans were classified by the Mormons as basically of American-Indian stock, the Mormons felt a special obligation to convert them "to the true faith". However, according to Grebler, there was discrimination against the Mexicans: "Despite the special place in Mormon theology for Mexicans, the Mormons developed what one author has called a 'pioneer attitude', in which the 'subordinate peoples' continue to occupy a subordinate position" (1970:506).

Nevertheless, the growth of Hispanic Mormon congregations has been quite outstanding if Grebler's information is correct: "Some 15,000 members are claimed [in the United States] which would make the Mormons one of the largest denominations among Mexican Americans" (1970:506). Concerning Mormon organization and growth, Grebler comments:

> At the present time there are two branches of the "Spanish American Mission"--one in San Antonio and one in East Los Angeles. A few of the missionaries are Mexican Americans (the number varies from year to year). More are Anglos (often descendants of the Mexican colonists) who have a special knowledge of Mexicans. If they cannot support themselves, they are assisted by their local stakes. To fill missionary vocations, young men are apparently sent with equal ease to canvass fields in Mexico or the United States. Within the United States they have been sent freely to both urban and rural areas. They are frequent visitors to migrant camps, for example. In recent years, however, work has concentrated on the urban mission. In any case, most of the work has been conducted among the poorer Mexican Americans (1970:506).

Los Angeles County. Not much is known about the specific growth of Hispanic Mormon congregations in Los Angeles County. Ortegon lists only one "Mexican Mormon Church" in Los Angeles in 1932 and it had a membership of ninety persons. "There is no pastor," wrote Ortegon, "but the church is under the charge of a president who does not get any salary and does his work free of charge" (1932:57). This congregation did not have its own building but met in a rented hall. Evidently, the Hispanic ministry was partially supported by the "American Board" of Home Missions.

In 1971, the Church of Jesus Christ of Latter-Day Saints had eight Spanish-speaking congregations in Los Angeles County and one in Orange County at Garden Grove. Five Hispanic churches were located in Los Angeles: two in East Los Angeles, two in Belvedere, and one in the West Central District. Other churches were situated in Glendale, Baldwin Park, and Compton. The total communicant membership may be as high as 500-600 for Los Angeles County.

* * * * *

In retrospect, we have analyzed, in Part I, the process of Mexican immigration, and of Mexican American urbanization and assimilation. We have considered the socio-cultural mosaic of urban Los Angeles County, the more rural setting of the

Southwest in general, and the complexity of Hispanic American socioeconomic and political problems in historical perspective. Then, in Part II, we traced the history of Hispanic Protestant Church development in Southern California, with special reference to Los Angeles County.

The dynamics within the numerous Hispanic denominations and congregations, and their relationships to Anglo-dominated ecclesiastical structures, reflect the tensions and ambiguities of Anglo/minority group relations in general. Protestant denominations, in addition to being religious organizations, are social institutions that reflect the beliefs, attitudes, and behavior of the dominant society, with all of its conflicts and incongruities. Therefore, in Part III, our analysis of the religious dimension in Hispanic Los Angeles will have a dual focus: first, on Anglo Protestant attitudes, policies, motives, and goals in relationship to Hispanic ministry; and secondly, on the internal and external dynamics of Hispanic church growth itself.

PART III

An Analysis of the Religious Dimension in Hispanic Los Angeles

Introduction

In Part II (Chapters 5-10) we traced the origin and development of Hispanic Protestant churches and denominations in Southern California. This analysis dealt mainly with three major groupings of Hispanic churches: the older Protestant groups (Congregationals, Baptists, Methodists, and Presbyterians), the Holiness churches (Free Methodist and Nazarene), and the Pentecostal groups (Apostolic Assembly, Assemblies of God, Church of God, Foursquare, and the Latin American Council of Christian Churches). As an introduction to Part III, a brief historical overview of Hispanic Church development will be given based on the three categories of church bodies.

HISTORICAL DEVELOPMENT OF TRADITIONAL PROTESTANT GROUPS

In regard to the older Protestant denominations, the history of their Hispanic ministry in Southern California can be divided into four distinct stages of development. The first stage, termed the pioneer period or missionary phase, began in the Los Angeles area during the mid-1870s and continued until about 1910. During this period, Anglo missionaries--many of whom had prior experience in Latin America--began evangelistic ministries among the Spanish-speaking population and established the first "Mexican missions" in Southern California. For the Presbyterians, Mosher (late 1870s), Bransby (1884-1888), and the Merwins (1888-1912), and for the Congregationalists, Alden Case (1896-1917), were the first such Mexican mission specialists to attempt organized efforts for their respective denominations. In addition, in 1897, Case established the interdenominational "California

Spanish Missionary Society", which was supported mainly by the Methodists, Congregationalists, and Quakers.

The second period of development, which began about 1910 and lasted until the mid-1930s, was characterized by extensive church planting and the organization of segregated Mexican conferences. Although the Los Angeles Presbytery appointed a "Superintendent of Mexican Work" in 1888 (A. Moss Merwin), it was not until 1913 that the Presbyterian Board of National Missions organized a unified plan of Hispanic ministry for Southern California and Arizona. The Methodist Episcopal Church organized its Hispanic ministry in 1911 with the appointment of Vernon McCombs as Superintendent of the Spanish and Portuguese District in Southern California. Also in 1911, the Southern California Baptist Convention (Northern Baptist) appointed its first general missionaries (Mr. and Mrs. L. E. Troyer) for Mexican ministry. However, it was not until 1923 that a separate Mexican Baptist Convention was formally organized within the State Convention.

The third period, from the mid-1930s to the mid-1950s, was characterized by the continued development of established Hispanic churches, especially in the area of self-support. Although few new churches or missions were established during this period, there was generally substantial growth in the size of congregations and in the development of church facilities. Comparing the growth of the seven largest Hispanic churches in Los Angeles County between 1915 and 1970 reveals that four of the seven reached their maximum size between 1950 and 1955, one reached its peak about 1930, and the remaining two churches achieved their maximum growth between 1960-1965 (Figure 52).

The final stage, which began in the mid-1950s, was a period of integration in Southern California. Whereas the American Baptist integration movement took the form of establishing Spanish-speaking departments in Anglo churches (fourteen departments were established between 1955 and 1970), the Methodists and Presbyterians eliminated their respective segregated conferences and the Hispanic pastors and churches merged with the parent bodies. The American Baptists, along with the newly organized Southern Baptist Hispanic ministry that began in 1949 were the only two traditional Protestant bodies that continued to emphasize the planting of new churches and the expansion of their Hispanic ministries during the 1950s and 1960s. By contrast, the Methodists and Presbyterians have continuously declined numerically since 1950, both in terms of churches and membership, although several new Spanish-speaking departments were added in Anglo churches. We have previously considered various reasons for this decline (cf. Chapters Six and Seven).

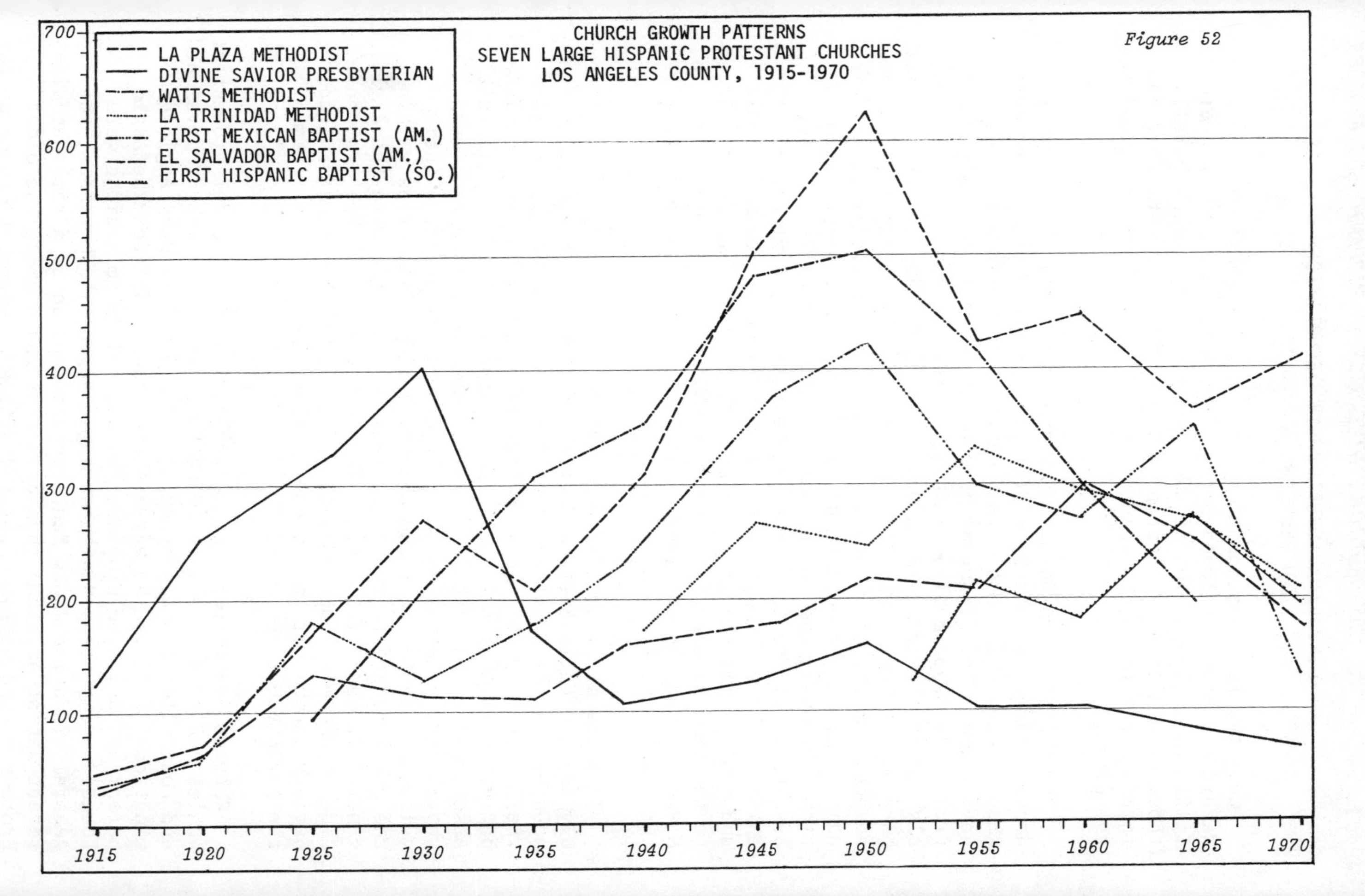
Figure 52
CHURCH GROWTH PATTERNS
SEVEN LARGE HISPANIC PROTESTANT CHURCHES
LOS ANGELES COUNTY, 1915-1970
LA PLAZA METHODIST
DIVINE SAVIOR PRESBYTERIAN
WATTS METHODIST
LA TRINIDAD METHODIST
FIRST MEXICAN BAPTIST (AM.)
EL SALVADOR BAPTIST (AM.)
FIRST HISPANIC BAPTIST (SO.)
700
600
500
400
300
200
100
1915
1920
1925
1930
1935
1940
1945
1950
1955
1960
1965
1970

HISTORICAL DEVELOPMENT OF HOLINESS AND PENTECOSTAL GROUPS

Only two Holiness denominations, the Free-Methodists and the Nazarenes, have developed Spanish-speaking churches in Southern California. The stages of their development closely parallel those of the older Protestant groups, with both denominations forming segregated conferences in 1930 which have continued to the present.

The history of several of the major Hispanic Pentecostal denominations is notably different from the Hispanic Protestant groups previously considered. Two major Pentecostal bodies have received no financial help or other forms of assistance from Anglo denominations. In fact, neither the Apostolic Assembly nor the Latin American Council of Christian Churches (LACCC) have parent Anglo organizations from which support could be received. On the other hand, the Foursquare Gospel churches are administered as a department within the Anglo parent denomination. However, the Latin American District Council of the Assemblies of God functions between these two extremes: it exists as an autonomous body (incorporated in Texas in 1939) and most of its churches are self-supporting; but it is related to the General Council of the Assemblies of God in Springfield, Missouri, and has received various types of assistance from the parent body.

In terms of paternalism and indigeneity, the Apostolic Assembly and the Latin American Council (LACCC) are the most indigenous of all the Hispanic Protestant denominations, being virtually free from all Anglo paternalism because of their unique pattern of Hispanic leadership and development. The Hispanic Assemblies of God should be rated next in this regard, even though some paternalism no doubt has been present in their development due to the leadership of Anglo missionaries within the movement and to the functional relationship with the Anglo-controlled General Council. The Foursquare churches are considered the most paternalistic of the major Pentecostal denominations because of the strong control exercised over them by the Anglo power structure.

Whereas Spanish-speaking churches related to older Protestant bodies and to Holiness denominations were established, developed, and controlled largely by Anglo missionaries and by Anglo denominational leaders who administered the funds from the Anglo parent bodies, some Hispanic Pentecostal denominations were founded and developed without Anglo support. Therefore, the general situation among Pentecostals represents a somewhat different set of problems than does that found among the older Protestant and Holiness-related Hispanic congregations of Southern California. This fact should be kept in mind as we discuss Hispanic church problems in Chapters Eleven and Twelve.

11.

The Anglo Dimension in Hispanic Church Development

There is a serious need for Anglo churchmen to thoroughly evaluate the history of their relationships with Hispanic Protestant churches, to honestly recognize their numerous shortcomings, and to seek the revitalization of attitudes, strategies, and programs that will stimulate creative ministries and lead to mutually beneficial relationships between Anglos and Hispanic Americans and their respective churches. In this regard, the principles of "integration" and "inclusive membership" need to be reexamined, redefined, and incorporated into the life-styles of Anglo churches, with due consideration given to the Hispanic cultural renaissance taking place in the Southwest, their renewed desire for bilingual and bicultural identity and acceptance, and the growing movement toward Hispanic self-determination within the heterogeneous socio-cultural reality of American society in the decade of the 1970s and beyond. Rather than accepting stereotypes and generalizations about Hispanic Americans, concerned Anglos must be ready to listen, to observe, and to learn from their Hispanic neighbors.

OVERVIEW OF ANGLO-HISPANIC RELATIONSHIPS

Although many Spanish-speaking churches were established in Southern California between 1870 and 1930, with the initiative for church planting coming from Anglo missionaries who had returned to the United States after serving in Latin America, the development of most Spanish-speaking congregations was independent of large-scale Anglo Protestant interest or involvement (cf. Galvan 1969:95-97). Nor have many Anglos or their churches been involved in Hispanic ministry in Southern California between 1930 and the present.

There were mixed motives among Anglos for launching "Mexican work" in the Southwest. Some Anglos had a genuine compassionate concern for the plight of poverty-stricken Mexicans (e.g. Alden Case). Other Anglos were mainly concerned with "saving souls" (Troyer 1934), or with improving the morals of an "ignorant and immoral people" (McEuen 1913:Vol. 2, No. 1:5). Some "noble" Anglo Protestants provided money to build small wooden halls for Mexican worshippers because "some of the American Protestant churches resented the appearance of a Mexican in their congregations" (Ortegon 1932:12). One of the principle arguments used to secure Anglo support for Mexican missions was that converting Mexicans to Protestantism would protect the socioeconomic *status quo* in the Southwest (Anglos exploiting "cheap" Mexican labor), and would preserve Anglo American cultural institutions--the principle of "Americanization through evangelization" (cf. *El Mexicano*, Vol. 1, No. 7:5 [November-December 1913]; Vol. 6, No. 4:2-3 [April-June 1918]; and Grebler 1970:490-493).

The use of Mexican mission "specialists" and the development of segregated Mexican church associations allowed Anglo Protestants to fulfill the Church's evangelistic mandate, as well as to "make worthy American citizens out of 'typical' Mexicans" by converting them to Protestantism, without bringing Mexicans into direct contact with middle-class Anglos or their churches (cf. Grebler 1970:490-491). Thus, in the missionary and segregated conference stages of Hispanic church development,

> A handful of Spanish-language churches ministered almost exclusively to new immigrants, using predominantly Mexican-born and Mexican-trained ministers under the direction of Anglo evangelists. Like most missions, the Mexican Presbyterian mission practiced segregation from the outset--at first because of Anglo hostility to Mexicans, and later because it was considered the easiest way of accomplishing the mission (1970:490).

The general Anglo-Protestant estrangement from Hispanic Americans in Southern California is clearly seen in the citrus-belt communities described by McWilliams (1946:219; 1948:217-221) and by Griffith (1948:190-193). From the early 1900s, the bulk of the Anglo Protestant middle and upper classes in the citrus-belt communities were supported either directly or indirectly by the agribusiness. Anglo Protestant citrus growers, their churches, and their communities maintained an effective "isolation-insulation" system to separate themselves from the lower-class work force. Mexican nationals and their native-born children have been the major source of "cheap labor" for California agribusiness from World War I to the present.

The discriminatory attitudes and policies of older citrus-belt churches were often carried over into the new suburban churches that emerged after World War II in the growing new housing areas of Southern California. These new communities, built upon land where citrus groves and vegetable farms once stood, were created in response to over six million new residents, both from the majority society and from various ethnic and racial groups, who have migrated to the Southland from other parts of the U.S. since the mid-1940s.

Not only have suburban Anglo churches in Los Angeles County--both older and newer congregations--failed to minister to a growing minority population in their changing communities, but a majority of Anglos in urban churches have been guilty of even greater failure in this regard: first, because low-income Mexicans and Negroes have migrated heavily into deteriorating urban neighborhoods where they have been deliberately shunned or otherwise ignored by most Anglo churches; and secondly, because Anglo Protestants have fled in mass from urban to suburban neighborhoods, or from one urban neighborhood to another, to escape from the pressure of minority group influx in their quest for "safe" neighborhoods--insulated, homogeneous, and middle-class (cf. Winter 1962:15-66).

Urban renewal projects and freeway construction have eliminated many sections of older ethnic neighborhoods in Los Angeles, which has forced thousands of blacks and Latins to relocate in other low-income areas of the city and suburbs. A small portion of the minority population has been absorbed into urban and suburban middle-class neighborhoods in Southern California, but these are the lighter-skinned ethnics that have successfully acculturated to middle-class Anglo society. Most blacks and darker-skinned Latins have not been allowed to integrate, but rather have been continually frustrated by imposed restrictions as to where they could live, work, and worship (cf. Chapter 4).

It is both ironic and tragic that while many Anglo Protestants have given various degrees of support to foreign and home mission programs through denominational and/or interdenominational organizations, these same Anglos and their churches have often been indifferent to the plight of disadvantaged minorities, while failing to have fellowship with brown or black worshippers or to accept responsibility for ministry among the rapidly growing minority population in their local communities.

These failures of Anglo Protestant concern and involvement with Spanish-speaking people have been equally true in respect to other minority groups (e.g. American Indians and Asians) in Southern California for over one-hundred years (cf. Wollenberg 1970; Heizer and Almquist 1971). This kind of Christian "double-mindedness", while usually covert in recent years, has had visible manifestations in the form of discriminatory policies in housing, education, employment, church attendance and membership, and many other policies and practices supported either directly or indirectly by individual Christians, local churches, and denominational bodies. Only within the past ten or fifteen years has the social conscience of *some* Anglo Evangelicals (cf. Wirt 1968, *The Social Conscience of the Evangelical*) been sufficiently aroused--or perhaps it would be better to say "disturbed" --by the Negro civil rights movement, or by the movement to organize migrant farm workers as symbolized by the nationwide "Grape Boycott" led by Cesar Chavez--to the point of reevaluating their "social ethics" and developing a more just and "Christian" attitude toward the problems of racial and ethnic minorities within American society.

ANALYSIS OF ANGLO PROTESTANT ATTITUDES AND POLICIES

The perspective that many Anglos have toward minority groups in American society has often been strongly biased and distorted. Prejudice and discrimination continue to be serious problems that hinder the relationships of Anglos with their Spanish-speaking neighbors. The attitudes that many Anglo Protestants have toward minority groups in general may also distort their perspective of the problems and opportunities of Spanish-speaking Protestant churches and of ministry among the Hispanic population.

Anglo Middle-Class Distortion

Many Anglos have been victims of a middle-class subculture ("ethclass") bias that has distorted their perspective of minority group problems (Gordon 1964:47-54). Most Anglos "bought" the idealized concept of America taught in the public schools that visualized American society as "the land of opportunity" wherein existed "liberty and justice for all". In reality, however, equal opportunity and justice for "all" meant for *all Anglos*, or at least for *most* middle-class Anglos. But "all" has never included either American citizens or alien residents who were unable to conform to "WASP" standards or who resisted acculturation. On the one hand, Anglos have insisted on "behavioral assimilation" (acculturation) while refusing to allow "structural assimilation" (cf. Figure 17); and on the other hand, many Spanish-speaking Americans have resisted the "Americanization" or "Angloization" process, choosing rather to retain their cherished cultural heritage.

The distorted "ethclass" perspective of middle-class Anglos is clearly seen in their attitudes about poverty and those living in the poverty cycle. Most financially secure Anglos (as well as some middle-class blacks and Hispanic Americans) believe that the poor are themselves to blame for their own poverty. Rather than considering that the economic problems of the lower classes are mainly the result of limited educational and employment opportunities, low wages, seasonal periods of unemployment, poor health, and similar problems, the majority of middle-class Anglos believe that poverty is the result of laziness, unwise spending habits, immorality, drunkenness, and other character defects among those living in poverty (cf. pp. 56-57). In other words, most Anglos view the problems of the lower classes as being "behavioral" rather than "structural" in nature. However, a realistic appraisal of the nature and causes of poverty reveals that the problem has *both* behavioral and structural dimensions, and that something like a "subculture of poverty" does in fact exist (cf. pp. 56-65, "The Subculture of Poverty").

Protestant "Ethclass" Distortion

The new American middle-class has a distorted view of itself and of American society in general, which is also reflected in Anglo Protestant church life. Anglos in a large metropolitan area, like Los Angeles, "associate with one another on the basis of similar occupations, prestige, income, residence, and style of life" (Winter 1962:71). The pressure of conformity--to relieve status anxiety--"means that families associate with other families whose residence, income, and style of life reflect a comparable position on the economic ladder" (1962:71).

This fact is no where more evident than in Anglo Protestant churches in urban areas, where the typical congregation is an extremely homogeneous social and economic group--a highly exclusive "fellowship". The Anglo middle-class congregation is first and foremost "an economic peer group" and secondarily "a believing and worshipping fellowship"; its survival depends on its ability to recruit new members from among social and economic peers. The middle-class congregation, then, becomes a vehicle of Anglo Protestant social and economic group identity (1962: 70-82). Commenting on this tendency, Kyle Haseldon wrote:

> ...[Anglo] Protestant churches in the United States occupy and serve the middle strata of American society.

> They are socially as well as racially homogeneous. Such churches become ingrown and soon confuse the people's economic, social, and political interest with the gospel. They tend to acquire the coloration and some of the same customs of a social club and to lose their distinctiveness from the secular world. In such a setting the Jesus Christ who is Lord of all life is tamed and made the defender of the status quo (1964:161).

The distorted perspective of Anglo middle-class Protestants shows itself in their relations with ethnic and racial minorities. It is tragic that many Anglo Protestant churches insist that Hispanic Americans become "Anglicized" in order to become "good" Christians (1964:73). There is obviously great confusion over what constitutes "supercultural" Christianity (Kraft 1971), since many Protestant groups seem to identify Puritan morality, the Protestant Ethic, an unquestioning "Patriotism", and Americanization with biblical faith and orthodoxy.

In terms of Protestant ministry among the Spanish-speaking, many Anglos assume that through evangelism and/or social service Hispanic Americans will somehow become more acceptable to the larger society; that is, they will become acculturated to Anglo middle-class culture. However, Christian ministry is not something that is done to make others more acceptable to a dominant group, rather it is a service of love that has as its object the well-being (spiritually, as well as physically, socially, and psychologically) of a specific person or group. The warning of Clyde Kluckholn in *Mirror for Man* is still needed (1949:269):

> Americans have generally accepted diversity as a condition, but only some Americans have embraced it as a value. The dominant note has been that of pride in destroying diversity through assimilation.... Order is bought too dearly if it is bought at the price of the tyranny of any single set of inflexible principles, however noble these may appear to be from the perspective of any single culture [or subculture].

Anglo Americans have consistently failed to respect the dignity of the individual, treating Hispanic Americans and other minorities as objects to be manipulated by the dominant society for their selfish interests. While many Anglo Protestants voice their concern for man "as a living Soul", thus directing their efforts at "saving souls", they consistently deny Hispanic Americans of human dignity by perpetuating dehumanizing and oppressive socioeconomic conditions under which many Spanish-speaking Americans are forced to live.

Whereas Anglos, in general, tend to have a distorted perspective of Hispanic Americans and their socioeconomic problems, Anglo Protestants have an equally distorted view of Hispanic Protestant churches, their origin and development, and their contemporary problems.

For example, the problems of self-support among Hispanic churches related to the mainline denominations are viewed by many Anglo church leaders to be the result of poor stewardship among Hispanic church members, their "inherent laziness", or weak Hispanic leadership. But Mexican Americans generally have less education, have been restricted to low-paying "blue-collar" jobs, and consequently have considerably less earning power than do most middle-class Anglo churches. Moreover, the operating expenses and pastors' salaries, both of Anglo and Hispanic churches, require a certain basic minimum due to the high cost of living in urban and suburban areas within Los Angeles County. Hispanic congregations are considerably smaller and have less income than Anglo churches, but they have many of the same expenses. Consequently, Hispanic congregations are forced to pay their pastors lower salaries and have less capital available for the maintenance and repair of church buildings, or for the purchase of new property and the construction of more adequate church facilities.

The perspective of many Anglo Protestants is further distorted by a comparison of their own church with known Hispanic churches in terms of the attractiveness of the buildings, the "quality" of the neighborhood, the growth of the membership, and the professional quality of the pastors. By way of illustration, whereas Anglo churches in Los Angeles County tend to grow or decline in response to members who "transfer-in" or "transfer-out", Hispanic Protestant churches have historically grown through "conversion growth"; that is, by recruiting new church members from among their nominal Catholic relatives, friends, and neighbors. This major difference in the type of membership growth gives the casual Anglo observer a distorted picture of both his own church and Hispanic churches. If Anglo churches in Southern California only grew through conversion growth--the conversion of Anglos from our materialistic, Protestant-oriented but non-Christian society--then their rate of numerical increase would be drastically reduced. Although few Anglo churches are growing through significant conversion-growth, many large, conservative Anglo churches are experiencing continued membership gains by attracting disenchanted church members from other Protestant denominations (cf. Kelley 1972; Towns 1973:12-19).

The majority of Anglo Protestants in Los Angeles County lack an awareness of the existing needs, problems, and opportunities for ministry among Spanish-speaking Protestant churches in their local communities. This lack of knowledge and exposure is due to the continuing "isolation-insulation" system maintained by Anglos toward Mexican Americans. Some Anglos no doubt rationalize their noninvolvement with the Hispanic minority by assuring themselves that *all* Latins are "fervent" Catholics, that Protestantism and Latin culture are incompatible, etc. (cf. Haseldon 1964:89-101). In this context, Spanish-speaking departments in Anglo churches can become a bridge to personal and group awareness among Anglos by helping them to gain a sympathetic understanding of Hispanic Americans, an appreciation of Hispanic culture and language, a concern for Hispanic problems and frustrations, and a realization that many Latin Americans are highly responsive to Evangelical Christianity.

Continuing Anglo-Hispanic Tensions

Although there are unlimited opportunities for Anglos in Los Angeles County to interact with Hispanic Americans and to build bridges of mutual understanding, respect, and acceptance within a pluralistic society, nevertheless, continuing tension exists in Anglo and Hispanic Protestant relationships. Grebler made the following analysis of the dynamics of change within Protestantism, in respect to the interaction of Church and society and the effect this has on Anglo and Hispanic Protestant relationships:

> ...churches have...acted as acculturative agencies for Mexican Americans. They were concerned with this group before some of the other institutions of society, including the schools, began to be involved. Americanization has played an important role in the activities and goals of both the Catholic Church and various Protestant denominations. Shifts from segregation to integration and from paternalism to greater self-determination, the development of institutional structures and church specialists for coping with the group's needs, the growing emphasis on social action--these trends mirror significant changes in the larger society. In fact, one can read the history of the churches' role among the Mexican American people as an illustration of social change in this country. It spotlights the slowness and difficulty of institutional adaption. Change in basic institutional *assumptions* (for example, questioning of established values, addition of new values) has been under way for close to three generations, with only recent signs of change in institutional *functioning* (Grebler 1970:588).

Many Protestant churches, reflecting the ambiguities and contradictions of American society in general, have failed to participate in or to encourage evangelical outreach to Hispanic Americans, nor have they encouraged or supported the growth of segregated Hispanic churches and conferences. A great many Anglo Protestants have been reluctant in allowing Hispanic Americans to attend their worship services and Sunday schools, even refusing church membership to Hispanic Americans when their local communities have a rapidly growing SSN population. Although a small percentage of Anglo churches allow the more acculturated Latins--those who have only a slight accent or none at all--to attend or to become members of their churches, many Protestant churches make little pretense about not having an "inclusive" membership; they make it perfectly clear to the occasional black or brown visitor that their church is an "exclusive" club for Anglos.

Where Protestant churches have assisted "autonomous" Hispanic congregations or sponsored Spanish-speaking missions or departments in their own churches, Anglos tend to treat Latins as "second-class citizens" and relegate them to a subordinate and inferior position in their personal contacts with them. The attitude of Anglo "superiority" has intensified intra-ethnic tensions within numerous Spanish-speaking departments in Anglo churches, as well as in segregated Hispanic congregations receiving Anglo "help". This attitude of superiority has hindered creative interaction between Anglos and Latins; it no doubt has had a detrimental affect on Hispanic departments and churches, in terms of internal body-life and their outreach in their local communities. Although in the 1960s and continuing to the present many Spanish-speaking departments have been established in Anglo churches--mainly in Baptist churches, but including departments in Foursquare, United Methodist, and United Presbyterian churches--the attitudes of Anglos and their relationships with Latins have been varied and contradictory.

Ideally, the integration movement among Protestant congregations should represent a desire for "inclusive" ministry within the local community--a conscious attempt to establish "a representative congregation" (Winter 1962:147-151) composed of all classes, races, and ethnics in the church's neighborhood, perhaps inspired by Jesus' prayer in John 17 or by other scriptural passages dealing with the composition of the Christian Church, the Body of Christ (cf. Acts 11:1-18, Ephesians 2:14-21, James 2:1-8, and Revelation 7:9-17). In reality, however, many Protestant churches are divided by class, culture, and race, in addition to a myriad of other issues and problems. Too often, a local congregation is composed of numerous power groups and "cliques", each one preoccupied with their own special interests to the detriment of the edification and unity of the congregation and its ministry within the community.

Because of continuing Anglo ethnocentricity and the dominance of the Anglo-conformity model of assimilation, the majority of Anglo church members "naturally" assume that establishing a Spanish-speaking department will aid the acculturation of Latins to the values and behavior of Anglo middle-class society. Acculturation is viewed only as a one-way process--to make the language and behavior of Latins acceptable (or at least tolerable) to the dominant society. The attitude of Anglo cultural superiority, perhaps mixed with lingering racial prejudice and "subconscious" discriminatory practices, continues to frustrate Hispanic Americans who attend and seek to participate in a local "fellowship of believers". Spanish-speaking departments, therefore, may have their greatest "success" among Latins who have already committed themselves to acculturation--to gaining Anglo acceptance by leaving their Mexican, Puerto Rican, or Cuban cultural "baggage" behind in their quest to become "first-class" citizens.

MOTIVES AND GOALS FOR HISPANIC MINISTRY

The majority of Anglo Protestant churches in Los Angeles County, throughout the history of the Hispanic American Church, have failed to develop a creative strategy of dynamic interaction with Spanish-speaking churches of their respective denominations in carrying out the Church's evangelistic mandate within Hispanic communities in Southern California. Most Anglo churches have also failed to become active agents of social justice, either by combating continuing prejudice and discrimination among Anglos, or by initiating corrective social action to eliminate both the causes and effects of social injustice among the Hispanic population.

It is true that some churches are more aware of these problems than others, and some have actively participated in various denominational programs of evangelism or social action among Latins. On the one hand, conservative Protestant churches are more disposed to participation in evangelistic outreach among various minority groups but have usually avoided, or have refused to participate in, social welfare or social action type programs. There is a great reluctance among conservative Anglo middle-class churches to even *consider* the possibility of participating in social action geared to changing unjust socioeconomic structures for the benefit of low-income minority groups. The Anglo middle-class forms a large part of the "Establishment" and they are, therefore, staunch defenders of the *status quo*. On the other hand, most liberal churches have actively participated in "Social Gospel" activities, while usually neglecting traditional types of evangelistic outreach within their local communities.

Many liberal churches, however, have been guilty of token participation in social welfare programs, while refusing to become involved in corrective social action to change unjust social structures. For example, the settlement house and community center types of programs, especially during the 1920s and 1930s, were welfare activities that acted as a "conscience palliative" to liberal Anglo Protestants, while allowing the average Anglo parishioner to maintain his social distance from racial and ethnic minorities (cf. Grebler 1970:504).

By the mid-1960s, Presbyterian and Methodist community centers, while continuing their traditional function as referral agencies for minorities in the inner-city, had become active in community-organizing efforts aimed at achieving greater socio-economic and political power for poverty-level minorities. "Increasingly", according to Grebler, "urban Mexican Americans came to be treated not just as a particular people but as victims of society's collective failures" (1970:498). Another expression of social involvement to achieve desired structural changes in American society is the work of the Migrant Ministry, sponsored by the National Council of Churches of Christ in the U.S.A., which has supported Chavez' union organizational efforts among Mexican American farm workers (1970:500-502). The rationale for this type of ministry is not the traditional needs of organized religion but the need for social justice, which is a legitimate Christian concern.

Although today the same polarity exists between conservatives and liberals on the issue of evangelism *or* social action as it did when the Social Gospel controversy raged during the early 1900s, the situation now is far more complex than in the earlier era. Mexican Americans in the post-World War II period have developed a strong minority group consciousness, with greater political awareness and participation being the correlary of increasing social mobility, which has made them restless for beneficial structural changes in the socio-economic-political *status quo* that is controlled by the institutions of the dominant society.

Many Mexican Americans seriously question the relevance of religious institutions--Catholic and Protestant--which refuse to stand with suppressed minorities in their struggles for social justice within American society. Have institutional churches, whether the Catholic Church or the various Protestant denominations, forfeited their right to be heard because of lack of involvement in improving socioeconomic conditions among Mexican Americans and in bringing social justice to the *barrios* of Southern California? Social *service* is not enough, social *action* is required--that is, *changing* unjust social structures that have created and that maintain injustice for the nation's minorities, especially blacks, Indians, and Hispanic Americans. This type of corrective action is a biblical and moral imperative.

To raise the issue of evangelism *or* social action is to ask the wrong question. Not only are *both* evangelism and social action needed, but we need to critically reevaluate what *authentic* evangelism and social action really are, both from a biblical perspective and in the light of the concrete historical situation which faces the Church today. That is what the late Kenneth Strachan did in *The Inescapable Calling*, when he discussed the importance of "disinterested" service (not influenced by regard to personal advantage) as an authentic expression of true Christian discipleship (1968:73-74):

> At the heart of the gospel preached and demonstrated by Jesus Christ were concern and compassion for man in every aspect of his life.... He demanded of his disciples deeds of mercy apart from any ulterior or selfish motives.... These [deeds] were not for purposes of propaganda; they represented instead a genuine expression of concern for others.
>
> The implications of this for Christian witness today are perfectly clear. Only a genuine disinterested service to others outside the family, a service which looks to no recompense, which is not a concealed means to an end (e.g. the acquisition of more church members), can properly reveal the love of God and the gospel of free grace. Only such service can deliver the Christian and the Christian Church from the self-interest and self-centeredness that are at the root of the pharisaism condemned by Christ.
>
> In the complexity of modern society, it follows then that social concern and action will form an essential part of the Christian witness. The church cannot remain indifferent to the pressing problems that confront men today. In the faithful discharge of his witness, some expression of concern, some social action must find a place. In faithfulness to the biblical injunction, and without being diverted from the church's mission to proclaim the gospel, that concern must be expressed. The important thing is that this imperative be recognized, and that the door be opened for Christian hearts to find the means of that outreach in individual, informal, and collective service to society. This is the badge of true Christianity.

TOWARD A STRATEGY OF MINISTRY AMONG HISPANIC AMERICANS

If concerned Anglo churchmen and their parishioners are to engage in "disinterested" service among the rapidly growing Hispanic population in Los Angeles County, then they must become aware of both the diversity of change taking place among Hispanic Americans and the reasons for this social unrest. Changes are occuring because Americans of Hispanic heritage have rejected Anglo dictated models of assimilation and are demanding equal rights and opportunities as guaranteed to them by the U.S. Constitution--the right to "life, liberty, and the pursuit of happiness." Recent new voices and movements of change--the Hispanic cultural renaissance in the Southwest, farm labor unionization and boycotts, militant *Chicano* power protests, and the organization of Mexican American community action groups and political parties--reveal to wide-eyed Anglos that even greater changes lie ahead for Hispanic Americans.

It is within this context that a strategy of ministry among Hispanic Americans must be developed that reflects biblical priorities and that is relevant to the felt-needs of the Hispanic community. Anglo church leaders and their congregations should explore the possibilities for creative ministry among Spanish-speaking people in their local neighborhoods, rather than ignoring their presence or fleeing to other areas in search of "safe" communities. The relevance of the "Good News" concerning Jesus Christ must be effectively communicated across cultural barriers by Anglos who have gained a sympathetic understanding of the various felt-needs and aspirations of their Hispanic American neighbors.

Evaluating the Problem: The Church in a Changing Community

Within the older residential areas of Los Angeles County, numerous Anglo churches have witnessed significant changes in the composition of their local neighborhoods. For some churches the transition has been slow but gradual, while for others the change has occurred with overnight swiftness. Some Anglo middle-class churches, realizing their deteriorating neighborhoods are attracting more and more low-income Negroes or Mexican Americans, find themselves in a dilemma.

Acknowledging that a church which ignores community changes cannot survive in the long run, and witnessing the increasing flight of Anglos from the local neighborhood and from its own membership, a local congregation needs to consider available options. Some of the church's members, perhaps a majority, may want to sell the church properties and relocate in some other part of the city or in an adjoining community. The congregation that relocates elsewhere has, by moving, written off the old neighborhood and communicated its symbolic exclusion to the in-migrating minority population.

The church that stays in a changing neighborhood, but attempts to remain an Anglo island in a predominantly Negro or Spanish-speaking area, becomes even a more forceful example of Anglo middle-class exclusiveness and intolerance. When less and less of its Anglo members are willing to commute back to the church for Sunday and weekday activities, a church may be forced either to sell its facilities or to reestablish contact with its local community. However, those who have been excluded from an Anglo inclave for several years are not likely to attend such a church when its doors are finally opened to them, since an almost unbridgeable gap has been created between the Anglo congregation and the new residents of the community (cf. Wilson and Davis 1966:82).

On the other hand, an Anglo congregation that, from the very beginning, decides to remain where it is and to minister to whoever moves into the community may really discover what the incarnation of Christ was all about. Such a congregation may experience a new kind of dying, one that springs forth to new life, vitality and relevance. However, the road to "inclusive" ministry involves a definite risk (1966:127):

> ...the loss of the old and familiar for the new and unknown. Success is not assured, but this should not discourage any Christian group from making the effort. Churches which have ministered to all people have found it to be one of their most significant experiences.

Two major factors to be considered before a congregation decides its future course are: (1) the need for a continuing Christian witness in the local community and (2) the possible consequences of the church's decision, either to stay or to leave. A church facing this situation should ask itself the following question: "What is our responsibility to the people who will be living in the community in the years ahead"? (1966: 61). The church that decides to stay and *serve* its changing community, by proclaiming the "good news" of the Kingdom of God and by making visible in a particular spot in the world what "citizens of the Kingdom" ought to be like, will be following in the footsteps of the Son of Man.

As the vision of opportunity for creative ministry in one's local community becomes clear, it will be necessary for church leaders--both the pastoral staff and lay leaders--to think in terms of defining ultimate objectives, establishing long-range and short-range goals, and mobilizing itself for action. Strachan expressed it this way:

> ...in the definition of goals and the formation of plans it is necessary to keep in mind that the objectives are not to launch artificial, temporary efforts of evangelism, but rather to develop a pattern of church worship, life, fellowship, and service that will be a communal witness in itself and at the same time will provide for and foster the individual witness of its members in the concrete situations of civic life.
>
> To that end it is helpful to remember that the local congregation exists for three purposes: (1) to nourish and support the spontaneous witness of its members who are scattered strategically throughout the community; (2) to furnish that additional and authoritative declaration of the gospel and its implications for all of life which is not possible to the individual members; and (3) to make visible through its communal life, fellowship, and service a foreseeing of the kingdom of God, thus supporting the message preached. The goal of every preparatory effort therefore should be to impart to the entire congregation a vision of the church's responsibility, or its potential ministry in the community, and of the part each member may play in its fulfillment (1968:87-88).

Gaining a Sympathetic Understanding of Hispanic Americans

Concerned Anglos must gain an understanding of how acculturation affects the thinking and behavior of Hispanic Americans and of the stresses and tensions involved in the acculturation process. Individual and group need-levels of Hispanic Americans, in relation to multi-cultural, urban, and poverty-level experiences, need to be closely examined.

For the Latin immigrant or the Hispanic American "in-migrant" from rural areas of the U.S. who has recently arrived in metropolitan Los Angeles, the trauma of relocating one's family in a new country or urban area, the experience of cultural isolation and often of rejection while attempting to acquire a new cultural orientation, the effort to learn a new and difficult language while living in a segregated neighborhood, the struggle of making new friends, of trying to provide for one's family needs on an inadequate income, and of countless other adjustments is an extremely difficult and "shocking" experience for most new urban dwellers.

On the other hand, not all Hispanic Americans in growing Spanish-speaking housing areas in Los Angeles County are recent arrivals from rural areas or from across the southern border. Many new Hispanic residents in changing neighborhoods are displaced persons--displaced by unemployment, urban renewal, or freeway construction--from other parts of the county or from other cities in the Southwest. Any specific *barrio* contains Hispanic Americans in various stages of the acculturation process, with different levels of English-language proficiency, and with a wide range of attitudes, problems, and aspirations for themselves and their families. Colony, Intermediate, and Frontier Areas throughout Los Angeles County (cf. Figure 16) represent a variety of unique situations, with many similarities and yet with startling contrasts between areas, each of which requires continuous, first-hand exposure in order to understand the dynamics of change (or lack of it) and the felt-needs of its Hispanic residents (cf. pp. 87-105).

The disorientation that comes with cross-cultural experiences, with urbanization, and with poverty-level frustrations is not easily understood by Anglos who have not experienced "culture shock", rural-to-urban migration, or poverty. But it is these stresses that should become a major concern of Anglo churchmen and their congregations as they seek to minister in Christ's behalf to their Spanish-speaking neighbors--to minister to the "whole man" with compassionate, "disinterested" service. Churches should reach out to disoriented people in their local communities--those disoriented culturally, socio-economically, and spiritually--letting them know that they are respected, accepted, and cared for by the visible Body of Christ, thereby helping them to know and experience the reality of Jesus Christ in their daily lives. The local church is responsible for ministering in Christ's behalf to the various racial and ethnic groups within its immediate neighborhood and within the larger community. Regardless of linguistical, cultural, or socio-economic barriers, the "people of God" must reach out to others where they are, in whatever circumstances, in a relevant and concrete manner. Failure to develop an "inclusive" fellowship that reflects the composition of the local community is to betray the Liberating Christ who came to set all men free from self-centeredness, pride and bigotry (cf. James 2:1-26).

Anglo Protestants should be leaders in breaking down barriers of prejudice and discrimination against Hispanic Americans and other minorities in order to demonstrate the liberating power of the Gospel of Christ. Forgiven and liberated men have a joyful obligation to love and accept *all* men without prejudice or discrimination, thereby, bearing witness to the Lordship of Christ. The Christian is obligated by the radical demands of the Gospel to demonstrate a new social ethnic which, in the context of contemporary American society, should lead him to individually and collectively protest against social injustice and to stand with oppressed minorities in their struggles for structural integration and equal opportunity. Anglo Christians must also balance their social concern with evangelistic action: both vertical and horizontal reconciliation are demanded by the Gospel (cf. Luke 4:14-21; 10:25-37).

Developing a Strategy of Ministry

Two basic approaches to implementing Hispanic ministry will be considered in this section. The first is a *simplistic approach* that has often characterized many Anglo churches in their attempts to "minister" to Spanish-speaking people. This approach is not recommended, however.

1. Secure an ordained Spanish-speaking pastor or lay-minister, pay him a few dollars per week, and turn him loose to conduct services in Spanish in the church basement or in a nearby mission annex. (Characteristic Anglo Attitude: "We'll pay him to minister to people we don't want to have anything to do with, but our theology demands that we do something.")

2. Expect that eventually the Spanish-speaking worshippers will learn to speak English, will learn good citizenship, will accept the Anglo "Establishment", will not get involved in community social issues, will become highly acculturated ("Americanized or gringoized"), and will eventually achieve middle-class respectability. (Characteristic Anglo Attitude: "Given enough encouragement, the 'inferior Mexican' will become a respectable citizen and will learn to be thrifty, honest, dependable, and moral by accepting the attitudes and values of the dominant society--the Protestant Ethic--and by leaving behind his Mexican, Cuban, or other Latin cultural baggage.")

3. Then, and only then, will "we" (Anglo-Protestants) let "them" (various and assorted Latins) become members of our congregation. (Characteristic Anglo Attitude: "You must become a 'good' Anglo Protestant in order to be a 'good' Christian.")

A more creative approach to Hispanic ministry is obviously needed. The *problem-solving* model of ministry, which represents the opposite end of the spectrum from the "simplistic approach", will now be presented in outline form. There are, of course, many degrees of variation between these two approaches to Hispanic ministry which have characterized scores of Anglo churches, especially during the decade of the 1960s and into the 1970s:

1. Share your interest and concern for Hispanic ministry with others, discuss the issues with them, and stimulate their interest and concern.

2. Form an action group with some structural relationship to a decision-making body (i.e., the Board of Deacons, or Board of Elders, etc.) composed of interested laymen in your local church (a member of the pastoral staff should be an ex-officio member).

3. Read and discuss the available literature on Hispanic Americans, especially the literature dealing with Mexican Americans in the Southwest and with specific local problems (cf. Bibliography).

4. Investigate the actual situation in your community in respect to the Hispanic population and their socio-economic and political problems:

    4.1 Where are Spanish-speaking housing areas located? Which are Colony, Intermediate, and Frontier Areas? Which are older *barrios* and which are changing neighborhoods? What is the rate of SSN population increase or decline in each area?

    4.2 How many SSN pupils attend local public and private schools? What is the number and percentage of enrollment in each school, in each school district? What special educational problems exist? What is the drop-out rate of SSN pupils in each school? What are the reasons for this? Are there bilingual-bicultural programs, "English as a Second Language" (ESL) programs, etc.?

    4.3 What employment opportunities are there for Hispanic Americans of various skill levels and occupations in your local community? What percentage of SSN workers are employed in the major industries in your area? Are there "equal employment opportunities" for Latins in each major industry? Is there evidence of discrimination in employment?

4.4 What is the breakdown and distribution of various SSN nationalities in your community? How many Mexican Americans, Cubans, Puerto Ricans, Central and South Americans, etc.? What is the percentage of native-born, mixed parentage, and foreign-born of each national group?

4.5 What is the rate of acculturation among the SSN population, as generally indicated by the language spoken in the home--Spanish, bilingual, or English? (cf. pp. 121-123).

4.6 Is there evidence that the SSN population is achieving upward social mobility in your local area, with accompanying degrees of structural, marital, identificational, attitude receptional, behavior receptional, and civic assimilation? (cf. Figure 17).

5. Conduct an openminded investigation of the problems of Anglo prejudice and discrimination against Hispanic Americans: the problems of unequal opportunities in education, employment, housing, and recreation; and the denial of civil rights because of gerrymandering, voting restrictions, "police brutality", and other grievances articulated by *Chicano* groups. Interview Mexican American community leaders, "brown power" spokesmen, and other social activists to be exposed to their points of view. Discuss these issues with them.

6. Investigate the religious dimension among SSN people in your community:

6.1 Determine the number and distribution of autonomous Spanish-speaking Protestant churches. Discuss with their pastors and laymen the needs, problems, and opportunities of Hispanic ministry.

6.2 Determine the number and distribution of Spanish-speaking departments in Anglo churches or missions sponsored by Anglo churches. Interview pastors and laymen both from Anglo and Hispanic congregations and discuss opportunities, problems, and strategies of ministry.

6.3 Determine the size of the Hispanic Protestant communicant membership in your community, including past and present growth patterns. What are the reasons for growth and nongrowth among various churches and denominations?

6.4 Determine the percentage of SSN Catholic population in your local area, the number and distribution of Catholic churches with Spanish masses, SSN priests, and Anglo churches where Latins attend, etc. Evaluate the type and percentage of Hispanic Catholic membership--active, nominal, and inactive. Investigate the type of involvement of the Catholic Church in community-organizing efforts and other forms of social action.

7. Evaluate the role and function of the local congregation in the missionary plan of God. Questions such as the following should be studied and discussed: What is the Church of Christ and why is it in the world? What is the mission of the Church? Why does the local church exist and what are its functions? What is the role of the pastor, of the laity, etc.?

8. Study and discuss the three general types of ministries that characterize Anglo Protestant churches:

8.1 Vertical reconciliation: Our only concern should be evangelism or preaching the Gospel--the mission of the Church is to make disciples or to win converts

8.2 Horizontal reconciliation: How can we say that we love God if we don't love our neighbor and become involved with him in his socioeconomic and political struggles? Jesus came to proclaim "good news" to the poor and to liberate the oppressed people of the world. Therefore, social action against all forms of injustice must be a primary concern of the church.

8.3 Balanced vertical and horizontal reconciliation: The ministry of Jesus was three-fold--proclaiming good news of the Kingdom of God, teaching responsible discipleship, and healing those who were oppressed. His life-style was a prophetic witness to the truth He proclaimed. Therefore, each local congregation of Jesus' disciples today must go and do likewise, which means *both* authentic evangelism and social action.

9. Evaluate the history of Protestant Anglo-Hispanic relationships: Anglo-conformity vs. cultural pluralism, paternalism vs. self-determination, "exclusive" vs. "inclusive" ministry, etc.

10. Determine the most effective type of ministry to those outside your local congregation (the church's external ministry):

10.1 "Come-structure"--minister only to people who attend your worship services and church school; wait for the people to come to you.

10.2 "Go-structure"--strategic penetration by members of your congregation into individual homes and into the community as agents of reconciliation (both vertical and horizontal); go where the people are and minister to them in Christ's behalf.

11. Discuss priorities of ministry to various age groups: adults, youth, and children. Determine the most effective means of ministering to each age group according to their felt-needs.

12. Evaluate specific objectives of ministry to Hispanic Americans:

 12.1 Meaningful worship experiences

 12.2 Building a "healing fellowship"--emphasis on body-life

 12.3 Relevant Christian education for various age groups

 12.4 Home cell groups: evangelistic Bible studies, growth groups for new Christians, reflection groups for mature disciples, etc.

 12.5 Leadership education for developing teachers, counsellors, lay-pastors, youth leaders, recreation directors, cell group leaders, specialists in outreach to people with special needs, community organizers, action group leaders, etc.

 12.6 Youth center for multi-ministry: recreation, counselling, building friendships, development of spiritual life, community awareness, meaningful community involvement, etc.

 12.7 Community-related involvement: developing greater awareness of community social problems; organizing action groups to improve the "equal opportunities" for all members of the community, to protest against social injustice in concrete situations, and to produce corrective social action against the structures of injustice; organizing ESL classes for all age groups and supplementary education programs for school drop-outs; organizing a food-cooperative for low-income families, etc.

13. Make definite plans for action and carry them out: establish both short-range and long-range goals; evaluate possible obstacles to achieving these goals and how you plan to accomplish them; determine resources needed (personnel, materials, equipment, facilities, finances); adopt a budget; draw up a calendar of activities; assign and train personnel; provide for needed material resources; and implement your goal-oriented strategy. Goals should be *obtainable* and *measurable* (work through the decision-making body related to your action group).

14. At periodic intervals (3 months, 6 months, or 12 months), conduct thorough evaluation sessions to determine the strengths and weaknesses of your strategy; to redefine your priorities, goals, and programming; and to implement an improved strategy that will accomplish your objectives within a specific time period.

By way of summary, the steps in the problem-solving model are as follows (this model was adapted from an unpublished paper prepared by the Office of Worldwide Evangelism-in-Depth and presented at the "Alajuela Consultation on Evangelism-in-Depth" in Alajuela, Costa Rica, in August 1971):

1. Research: discover the facts and define the problems
2. Analysis of problems, obstacles, trends, opportunities
3. Goal setting:

   3.1 OBJECTIVES: establish specific priorities and objectives for church renewal, meaningful social action, and evangelistic penetration in the local community in terms of desired conditions or activities. Priorities should be determined based on the strengths and weaknesses of the local church, the congregation's expressed desire for renewal, the situation in the community, and the missionary nature and calling of the Church of Jesus Christ.
   3.2 Set GOALS which are *short-range* (with specific dates); *attainable* (within the realm of practical possibility); *measurable* (level of achievement can be measured at any stage of development); and which *activate* the chosen methodology.

4. Program selection and implementation

   4.1 Consider several general methods, plans, and approaches for resolving problems and for achieving objectives.
   4.2 Determine resources needed (personnel, materials, equipment, facilities and finances); allot budget; draw up a calendar of activities; assign and train personnel.

4.3 Implement strategy.

5. EVALUATION: periodically measure progress and revise goals accordingly (distinguish between long-range *objectives* and short-range *goals*).

Of course, this suggested "problem-solving" model is not exhaustive of the possibilities for creative ministry by Anglos among Hispanic Americans, but rather it is representative of the type of strategy that some Anglo churches are attempting to implement within their local communities. The desired objective, however, is that local Anglo congregations or groups of churches will begin to study and reflect on the nature of Christian mission; will discover the missionary character of the Church as the Servant of Christ, including the responsibility of each local congregation of Jesus' disciples to really be the "people of God" within their local communities for the glory of God; and will become active agents of God's reconciliation (both vertical and horizontal) in the world, while demonstrating a prophetic witness to the Lordship of Christ and to His coming Kingdom.

Two Adaptations of the Problem-Solving Model

Religious revitalization does not often come about when a church or group of churches adopts a "packaged" program of evangelism, renewal, or social action. It is my conviction that the problem-solving model offers the best approach to church revitalization when built into the life-style of a local congregation; it is equally relevant as a denominational renewal strategy.

Two organizations that offer assistance to churches interested in developing a problem-solving strategy are: Indepth Evangelism Associates (IDEA), 10871 Caribbean Blvd., Miami, Florida 33157; and The Center for Parish Development, 329 East School Street, Naperville, Illinois 60540.

IDEA provides consultive services to a local congregation (or a denomination) to guide it through the various stages of the problem-solving methodology, specifically to aid in the development of an "in-depth" evangelistic strategy. This process helps a church to define biblical goals and priorities; to evaluate its past and present growth and ministry; and to mobilize its total resources for effective witness and service in the light of the needs and opportunities for ministry in its local community. Several denominations and dozens of local congregations are experimenting with this evangelism-renewal strategy, which will no doubt receive widespread interest during "Key '73". An introductory booklet, entitled "Goal-Oriented Evangelism-in-Depth", is available from IDEA on request.

The Center for Parish Development is a mission agency of the United Methodist Church and is located at Evangelical Theological Seminary in Naperville, Illinois. The Center was "established on the conviction that the worshipping congregation is a valid and enduring expression of the universal church, that it has legitimacy and meaning in society today, and will continue to be significant tomorrow" (The Center for Parish Development, "Report to Supporting Churches", 1972:1).

As a mission agency, the Center "helps people in the local church, and those agencies concerned with the life and ministry of the parish, more effectively to discover and fulfill their mission as disciples of Jesus Christ in this time of rapid social change" (1972:1). As a model-building agency, the Center coordinates "a planned process of experimentation, testing, and evaluation in carefully selected settings...in which new models for the missional congregation and new alternative designs for church life are created" (1972:1).

Eight long-range model-building experiments were in process during 1972, or were planned for 1972-1973, under the Center's sponsorship. "Each experiment is being developed in such a way that it can be shared with and adapted to other communities and congregations" (1972:1). The following model-building experiments were planned for a duration of one to four years (1972:1-2) urban strategies (18 congregations in Flint, Michigan); congregational renewal (one church in Baraboo, Wisconsin); small-urban clusters (five congregations in Beloit and seven congregations in Racine, Wisconsin); district renewal strategy (the Waterloo District, Iowa); small rural congregational renewal (planned); rural cluster (planned); inner-city congregation (Gary, Indiana); and multiple-staff ministries (planned).

As a service agency, the Center helps local congregations discover creative ways to participate in mission by offering the following services: consultation, training, evaluation research, think-tank conferences, and resource development. In addition, the Center publishes reports on its model-building experiments (see Dietterich and Weis, 1973) and sends out a monthly bulletin called "The Center Letter".

12.

The Hispanic Dimension in Protestant Church Development

A series of important questions remain for our consideration as we approach the end of our study on the religious dimension in Hispanic Los Angeles, even if only partial answers can be found for some of them. What does the overall picture of one-hundred years of Hispanic church growth look like? What is the state of the Hispanic Church today? What does all that has been said up to this point mean in terms of understanding the growth patterns of the various Hispanic denominations in Los Angeles County, the socio-religious process of "church growth" itself, the patterns of Hispanic leadership development, and the role of leadership in movements of directed change? What of the Hispanic Church tomorrow? What *forms* will the Hispanic Church take? Can a balanced strategy of evangelism and social action be developed over the wide spectrum of Hispanic Protestant denominations in urban Los Angeles? How can Anglo and Hispanic church leaders, together with their respective congregations and denominational structures, interact with one another in creative tension to produce a healthy partnership that has as its goal the revitalization of the Church of Jesus Christ, as manifested in the attitudes, beliefs, and behavior of local congregations of believers, so that the Church will demonstrate a credible witness to the Lordship of Christ as His servant of reconciliation and liberation in the world?

ONE-HUNDRED YEARS OF HISPANIC CHURCH GROWTH

The development of Spanish-speaking Protestant churches in Southern California should be viewed from several perspectives:

from the perspective of Anglos and of Hispanic Americans, and from the perspective of the traditional Protestant denominations and of the Pentecostal churches. Each perspective will be different and each will provide corrective balance to the total picture. On the one hand, Hispanic churchmen of the traditional denominations acknowledge the role that Anglos have had in the planting of many Spanish-speaking congregations in Southern California; but on the other hand, Hispanic church leaders and laymen have often had a more decisive role in the origin and development of Hispanic Protestant churches. This is especially true among the Pentecostal denominations which have had little Anglo participation in the development of their congregations. Therefore, in this section, we will mainly evaluate the history of Hispanic church planting from the Hispanic American perspective and analyze the general growth patterns of each major Hispanic denomination.

The Mainline Protestant Denominations

The "simplistic approach" to initiating Spanish-speaking ministry, considered earlier, was in wide usage prior to 1930, as well as in the "integrated" church era that began in the late 1950s. Often a gifted "native" Spanish-speaking evangelist (someone with a gift of oratory but not necessarily with secular or theological education) was retained by an Anglo congregation which had some special interest or concern for the growing Hispanic population in their local area. Spanish-speaking services were conducted in the Anglo church on Sunday afternoons and at special times during the week, or in a separate "Mexican chapel" on more or less the same time schedule as the Anglo "mother" church. The main emphasis was on evangelism, although some social welfare efforts were also sponsored by local Anglo churches. After initial Anglo sponsorship, with Anglos providing the original chapel and paying the pastor's salary, many Spanish-speaking congregations became independent of Anglo sponsorship and control and were maintained as segregated Hispanic congregations. On the other hand, numerous Mexican chapels ceased to exist for lack of indigeneous leadership or because the Hispanic population was highly migratory, being mainly dependent on seasonal agricultural employment.

Another approach was for Anglo denominational bodies to appoint "Mexican mission specialists" (usually returned Anglo missionaries from Latin America), who were given responsibility for supervising the denomination's existing Mexican mission program and for establishing a segregated Hispanic church conference. Included in this responsibility was the recruitment and training of indigeneous pastors and lay workers, both for the existing missions and for establishing new congregations in growing Hispanic population centers. Usually these centers were located in agricultural areas, but there were also several large neighborhoods in Los Angeles where Mexican immigrants settled, mainly in the central district and in eastern sections of the city and the adjoining county area, as well as in small "pocket" settlements throughout the city (cf. Chapter 3).

Following the appointment of Mexican mission specialists (ca. 1900-1915), there seem to have been fewer cases of Anglo church sponsorship and a growing dependence on the "specialists" to minister to the Hispanic population on behalf of the Anglo parent denomination, which sponsored the "Mexican work" through the annual denominational budget. From about 1900 to 1930, numerous institutions also were established by the larger Anglo denominations to minister to the growing Mexican population--Bible institutes and seminaries, community centers, clinics, welfare agencies, schools, orphanages, child-care centers, and various types of cooperatives. With few exceptions, however, these institutions were established, supported, and controlled by Anglos who were motivated by "Americanization" goals and who saw evangelism and social service as a means of achieving the acculturation of Mexicans to the norms of the dominant society. Few Mexican Americans were given positions of leadership and decision-making responsibilities within these Anglo-dominated institutions.

During the 1920s, the Presbyterians, Methodists, and Northern Baptists established heavily-subsidized "institutional" churches among the Mexicans in Los Angeles. Large congregations were developed in modern facilities that offered a wide variety of ministries to the "whole man"--*El Divino Salvador* Presbyterian Church and *El Salvador* Baptist Church and Community Center in the Boyle Heights area, and *La Plaza* Methodist Church and Community Center in the Downtown area are the best examples of this multi-dimensional ministry. Except for the United Methodists, most of these institutional-type ministries have ceased to exist, a factor mainly attributed to denominational cutbacks during the Depression and to integration policies since the Depression.

Nevertheless, scores of autonomous Spanish-speaking churches were planted in Southern California, both by Anglo missionaries and by Mexican-born evangelists and lay workers, prior to 1930. Many of the first Hispanic congregations became "mother" churches as smaller "daughter" missions came into existence through the evangelistic efforts of their lay members, sometimes with special assistance from Mexican evangelists or from Anglo church workers. Early Hispanic church growth was mainly due to the zealous evangelism of new converts and their lay pastors (Ortegon 1932:26), who enthusiastically shared their new faith in Christ with their relatives, friends, and neighbors in the growing Mexican housing areas in Los Angeles County and throughout Southern California.

According to Quiñones, "While the initial work was started by Anglo missionaries, the progress and phenomenal growth has been due to the Spanish-speaking pastors who have given of their lives to the building of churches and ministering to the people" (1966:21-22).

New Spanish-speaking congregations were organized following successful house-to-house visitation efforts, literature distribution, child evangelism classes, special evangelistic services, and home Bible study groups. Often the newly-converted would initially meet for worship, study, and fellowship in private homes or in the shade of a nearby grove of trees, later constructing a small chapel on donated land with volunteer labor, and eventually accumulating the resources to build a larger church building, often with several Sunday school rooms and sometimes with a social hall or parsonage.

Where Anglo sponsorship was involved, meetings were often begun in a Gospel tent, in a rented hall, or in a nearby Anglo church building. There are numerous cases where Anglo Protestants assisted a new Hispanic congregation of their denomination either by donating plots of land or building materials, offering volunteer labor, providing furnishings for the church and parsonage, or some combination of these factors. Large sums of money were also given by some benevolent Anglos to aid in the development of Mexican missions, usually at the intercession of Anglo missionaries (cf. Troyer 1934).

The most consistent type of Anglo assistance, however, was apparently in the form of denominationally-dispensed salary supplements, which enabled Hispanic pastors to provide for themselves and their families while ministering to their poverty-stricken congregations. Other pastors either struggled along on their small church incomes, or worked part-time in secular employment when they could find work.

During the early 1930s, many Spanish-speaking congregations were dissolved when the majority of their members returned to Mexico--either voluntarily or by forced repatriation sponsored by Los Angeles County welfare authorities. Although all denominational efforts among the Hispanic population in the Los Angeles area were severely influenced by the Depression, the Hispanic Presbyterian ministry was the most seriously affected; their 1940 communicant membership dropped to about half of what it was in 1930 (Figure 53). Few new congregations were established during the 1930s, since the energies of most Hispanic churches were used to maintain their survival in the midst of severe unemployment, food shortages, and the declining Mexican population (cf. Figure 2).

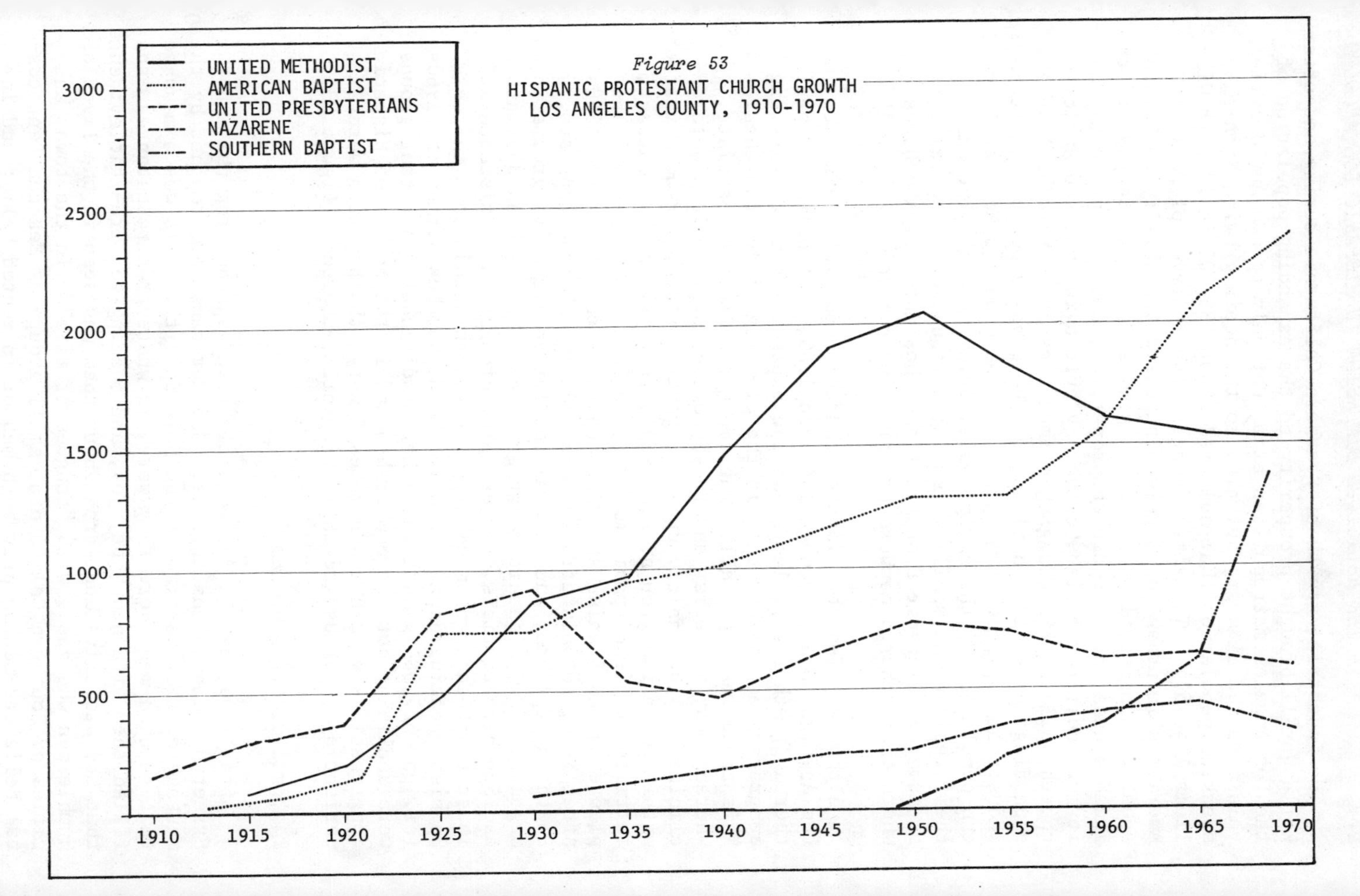

Figure 53

HISPANIC PROTESTANT CHURCH GROWTH
LOS ANGELES COUNTY, 1910-1970

The industrial growth of Southern California during and after World War II brought prosperity to the expanding population of the Los Angeles metropolitan area, not only to new Anglo arrivals from the midwest, but also to the again growing Spanish-speaking population that numbered about 385,000 in 1948 (McWilliams 1948:57). The rising general income level of Mexican Americans in urban Los Angeles increased the ability of Spanish-speaking congregations to become self-supporting, to pay off the indebtedness on their church properties, and to improve the quality of their facilities, either by purchasing vacated Anglo church buildings in changing communities or by refurbishing and expanding their older buildings. There was a notable shift to industrial employment among Los Angeles County's Mexican American population by the early 1950s, which not only increased their residential mobility, but also resulted in the relocation of numerous Hispanic Protestant churches into neighborhoods where their church members had previously moved.

Although a few new Hispanic churches came into existence in Los Angeles County between 1940 and 1960, most of the Hispanic church growth was reflected in the expanding size of existing congregations, rather than in the planting of new churches. This trend was especially true among the American Baptists, whereas many Methodist and Presbyterian congregations were declining by 1960, mainly due to a general state of demoralization within these two groups. The Southern Baptists, by contrast, initiated their Hispanic ministry in Los Angeles in 1949 and planted seven Spanish-speaking congregations during the 1950s. After 1960, notable efforts were made by American Baptists, Southern Baptists, and several smaller conservative groups in organizing new Hispanic congregations. The American Baptists and Southern Baptists, for example, brought into existence at least fourteen autonomous Hispanic churches and about thirty Spanish-speaking departments in Anglo churches during the 1960s (cf. pp. 327,384). Whereas other traditional Protestant groups were declining both in membership and in the number of Hispanic congregations within Los Angeles County, the Baptists were experiencing vigorous growth in Hispanic membership (Figure 53).

The Pentecostal Denominations

After 1906, as the Pentecostal "fire" spread from the Azusa Street Mission in Los Angeles, many Mexicans were touched by the message of the "baptism in the Holy Spirit". This was a message that reached men where they were, in whatever circumstances, and filled them with new hope, joy, and meaning to life--the evidence that God was alive and cared about them was seen in the lives of humble men who spoke with "tongues of fire". In the towns and cities of Southern California, small groups of Mexican Pentecostal believers met in private homes or in rented halls; and in the countryside while following the crops, they met around the campfires and on the river banks near where their small shacks stood. There were few church buildings in those early years because the destitute Mexican immigrants were highly migratory, moving from place to place with the cycle of planting, cultivating, and harvesting of the crops of California's multimillion dollar "agribusiness".

Enthusiastic Pentecostal believers were forced out of churches of the traditional denominations because the Pentecostal doctrine was considered heretical by the mainline groups. Nevertheless, *few* organized groups of Spanish-speaking Pentecostals were in evidence in Los Angeles by 1915 (cf. McEuen 1914:38a). The situation changed during the 1920s, however, when at least ten permanent congregations with a total of about 1,000 members came into existence in the Los Angeles area. Although most of these churches were small, at least one congregation numbered close to 500 members, while another Pentecostal church had over 200 in Sunday school (Ortegon 1932:53-54).

The growth picture of Hispanic Pentecostal churches is sketchy at best, but there is evidence that by 1940 fifteen or so congregations were functioning in Los Angeles County. By 1950, about twenty-five churches had been established in the county with a total membership of about 1,450. A clearer record of growth emerges during the 1950s and 1960s, however.

The Assemblies of God, for example, organized at least fourteen new Hispanic congregations in Los Angeles and Orange Counties during the 1960s, with the membership of these churches totaling about 840 in 1971. By comparison, only eight permanent congregations were established prior to 1960, and these eight churches accounted for about 500 members in 1971 (cf. pp. 346-348).

The Apostolic Assembly of the Faith in Christ Jesus has a growth history in the Los Angeles metropolitan area similar to the Assemblies of God. By 1950, although approximately thirty-five Apostolic assemblies were in existence throughout the state, only four permanent congregations had been organized in Los Angeles and Orange Counties. During the 1950s, three new congregations were organized within the two-county area, which brought the total number of churches to seven. Between 1960 and 1971, however, eight new congregations were established which more than doubled the number of Apostolic assemblies in the Los Angeles basin.

Unfortunately, neither the record of growth of the Latin American Council of Christian Churches (fifteen congregations), nor of the Church of the Foursquare Gospel (ten Hispanic congregations), was available for comparison within Los Angeles County. However, the history of Hispanic church development among the Assemblies of God and the Apostolic Assembly shows a trend similar to the recent expansion in the number of Baptist congregations in the area. Approximately seventy-five percent of the total number of congregations established within Los Angeles and Orange Counties by the Assemblies of God and the Apostolic Assembly were planted since 1950. The Assemblies of God planted sixty-one percent of their present churches between 1960 and 1971, whereas 53.5 percent of the Apostolic assemblies were established during that same period.

Pentecostal growth during the 1960s resulted from strong evangelistic outreach, not only on the part of ordained ministers, but also through the efforts of committed laymen. Most Pentecostal groups often have extended evangelistic and healing campaigns in their local churches, where lay members are expected to bring their relatives, friends and neighbors and to encourage them to trust God for physical healing and deliverance for the soul. Those who make decisions for Christ are usually baptized and added to existing local churches.

However, another pattern also exists that has resulted in significant growth among some Pentecostal groups. The Apostolic Assembly, for example, has a definite strategy of evangelistic outreach by which key laymen conduct services in their own homes or in the homes of interested friends or neighbors. This "house-church" approach is not new, of course, but it is having significant results in the urban context of Los Angeles County. New converts from "house-churches" are baptized in the local Apostolic assembly and are incorporated into the larger fellowship of believers. The Compton assembly is reported to have added over one-hundred new members in one year (1969-1970) through evangelistic outreach in home meetings (Salazar, Lorenzo 1970).

Summary of Hispanic Growth Patterns

The patterns of growth among the various Hispanic denominations in Los Angeles County present a complicated picture of growth, stagnation, and decline, especially from the 1950s through the early 1970s. Whereas some older Protestant groups were experiencing declining membership (United Presbyterians and United Methodists), and others were merely maintaining a mediocre level of membership (Nazarene, Free Methodist, Congregational, and Friends) still others were experiencing rapid growth both in membership and in the number of new congregations (American Baptist, Southern Baptist, Seventh-Day Adventist, and nearly all of the Pentecostal groups).

Although there are many neighborhood and community growth variables within Los Angeles County, the general situation is one of rapid growth among the Hispanic American population in many areas of the county--from 9.6 percent of the total population of Los Angeles County in 1960 to 17.5 percent in 1970 (Figure 54). In terms of numerical increase, the Hispanic population more than doubled in ten years (refer to Figures 15 and 16 and Appendix I for the distribution and growth of the Hispanic population in Los Angeles County between 1960 and 1970). Figure 54 also compares the estimated growth pattern of the total Hispanic Protestant communicant membership in Los Angeles County with the general growth of the Hispanic American population between 1900 and 1970.

In response to the growing opportunities for ministry among the Spanish-speaking people in Los Angeles County, approximately ninety-five new Spanish-speaking congregations were organized by the various Protestant denominations during the decade of the 1960s. At least thirty-five Spanish-speaking departments were established in Anglo churches, in addition to about sixty autonomous Hispanic congregations. The total membership increase for the decade was approximately 6,500 communicants, with more than fifty percent of the total Pentecostal membership being added during the 1960s compared to about thirty-seven percent of non-Pentecostal membership. Figure 55 gives the estimated growth in communicant membership for all Hispanic Protestant churches from 1900 to 1970, with a comparison of estimated growth patterns for the Pentecostal and non-Pentecostal groups. The distribution of Hispanic membership and churches among the various denominations in Los Angeles County in 1970 is shown in Figure 56. Refer also to Figures 25-29 for a complete breakdown of Hispanic churches by denomination and for their geographical distribution within Los Angeles County.

Some obvious questions need to be asked by every Hispanic church and denomination: How does our growth compare with the tremendous opportunities for ministry that are ours in growing Hispanic neighborhoods throughout Los Angeles County? What are we doing to develop a relevant strategy of ministry within these growing neighborhoods? What types of ministry should we develop that will meet the multitude of felt-needs among our Hispanic neighbors? How can we minister to the "whole man" in Christ's behalf?

ANALYSIS OF GROWTH AND OBSTRUCTION

Within each association of Hispanic churches can be found congregations that are in various stages of growth or decline. Churches that are basically "extroverted" (humanitarian and liberal), as well as those that are fundamentally "introverted" (pietistic

Figure 54

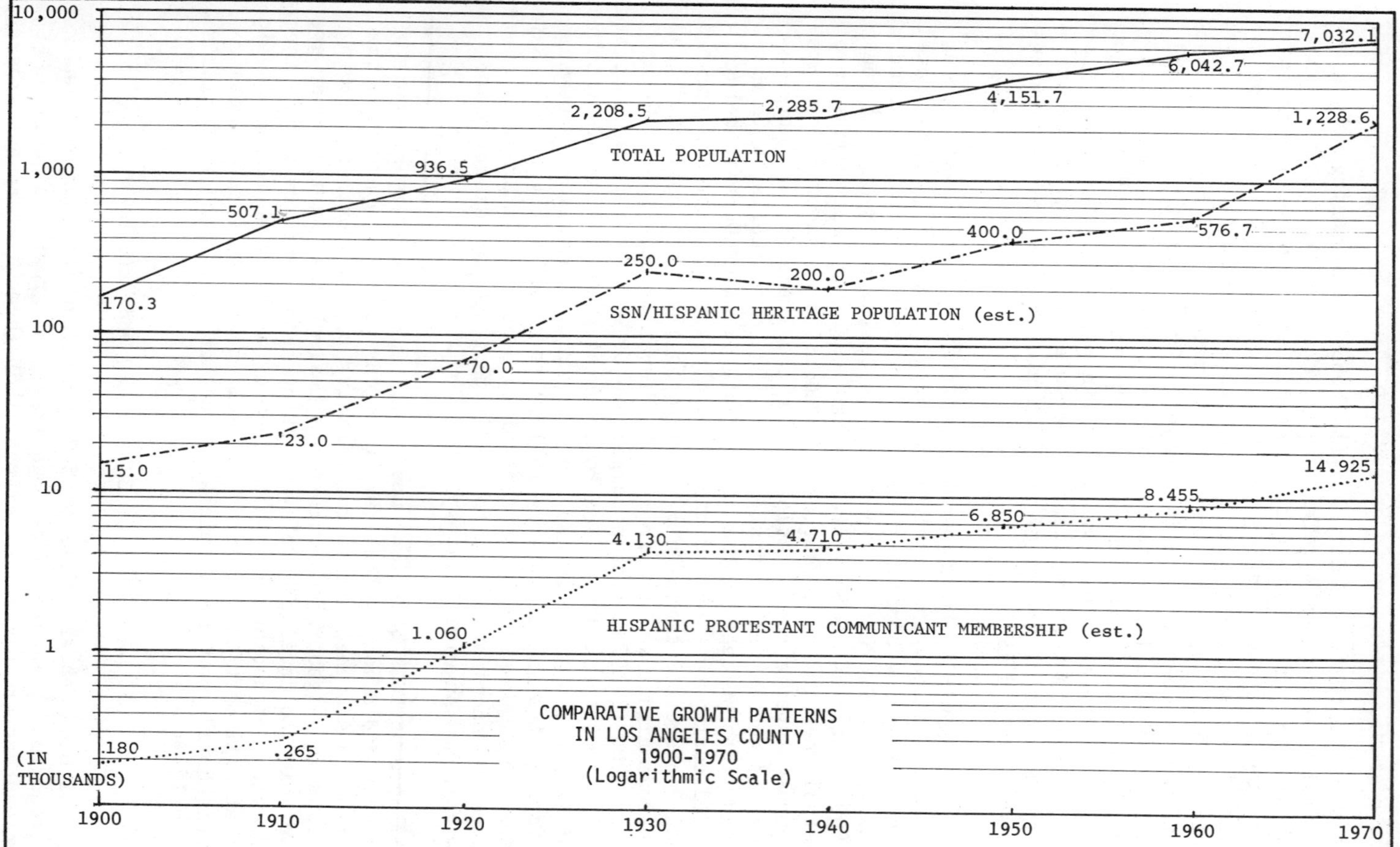

COMPARATIVE GROWTH PATTERNS
IN LOS ANGELES COUNTY
1900-1970
(Logarithmic Scale)

10,000
1,000
100
10
1
(IN THOUSANDS)

TOTAL POPULATION
170.3
507.1
936.5
2,208.5
2,285.7
4,151.7
6,042.7
7,032.1

SSN/HISPANIC HERITAGE POPULATION (est.)
15.0
23.0
70.0
250.0
200.0
400.0
576.7
1,228.6

HISPANIC PROTESTANT COMMUNICANT MEMBERSHIP (est.)
.180
.265
1.060
4.130
4.710
6.850
8.455
14.925

1900
1910
1920
1930
1940
1950
1960
1970

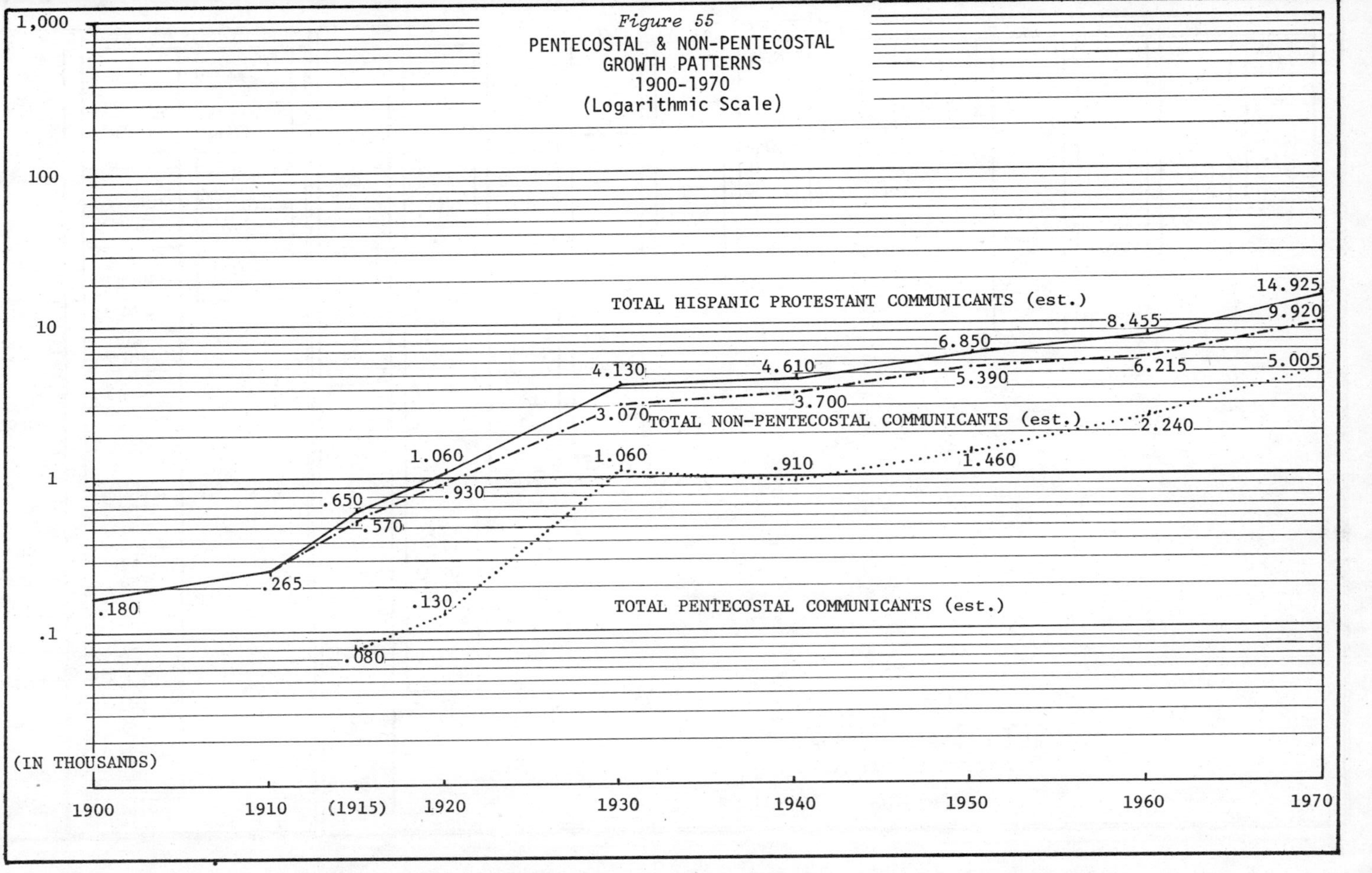
Figure 55
PENTECOSTAL & NON-PENTECOSTAL
GROWTH PATTERNS
1900-1970
(Logarithmic Scale)
1,000
100
10
1
.1
(IN THOUSANDS)
1900
1910
(1915)
1920
1930
1940
1950
1960
1970
TOTAL HISPANIC PROTESTANT COMMUNICANTS (est.)
TOTAL NON-PENTECOSTAL COMMUNICANTS (est.)
TOTAL PENTECOSTAL COMMUNICANTS (est.)
.180
.265
.650
.570
1.060
.930
.080
.130
4.130
3.070
1.060
4.610
3.700
.910
6.850
5.390
1.460
8.455
6.215
2.240
14.925
9.920
5.005

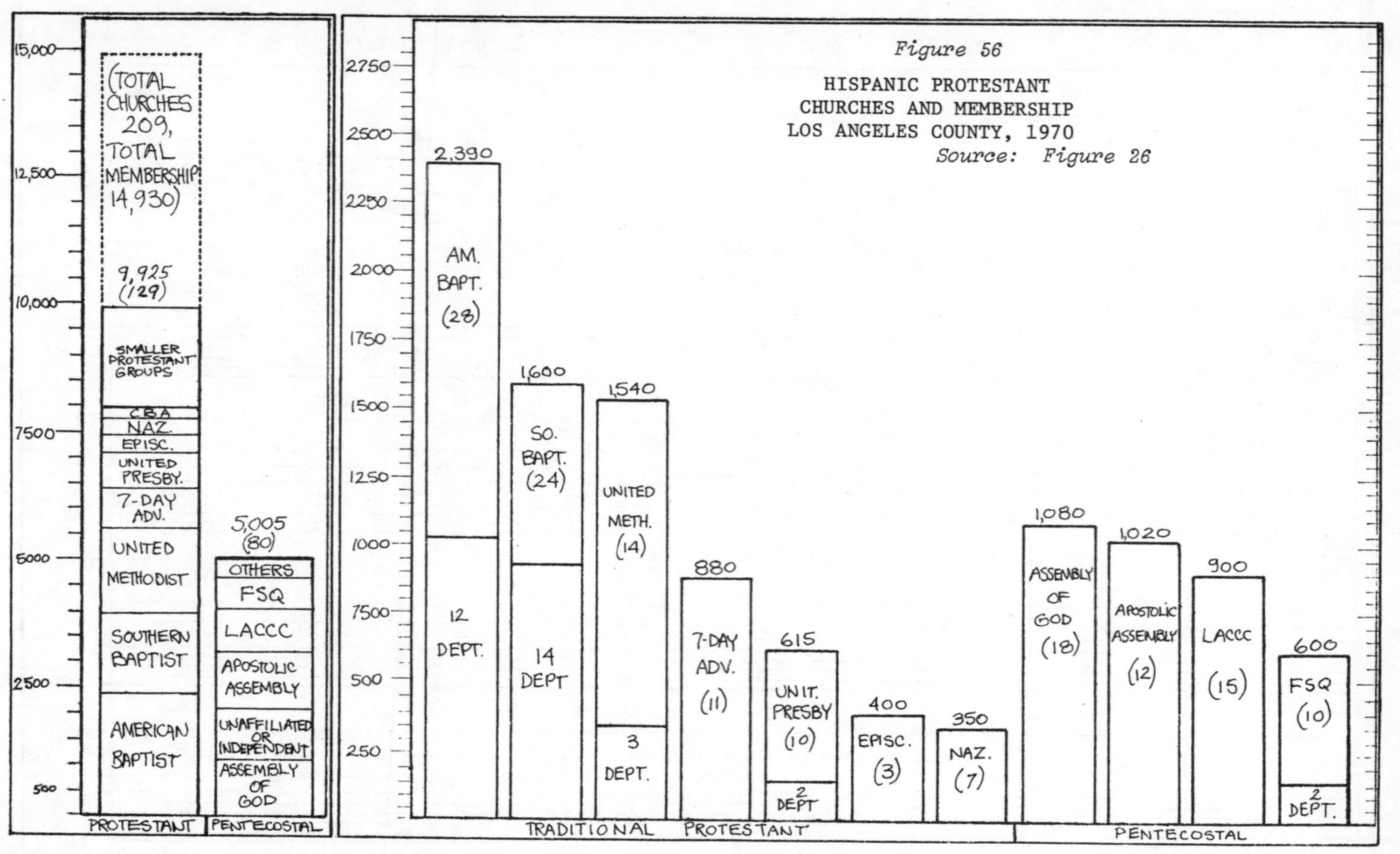
Figure 56
HISPANIC PROTESTANT
CHURCHES AND MEMBERSHIP
LOS ANGELES COUNTY, 1970
Source: Figure 26
15,000
12,500
10,000
7500
5000
2500
500
(TOTAL CHURCHES 209, TOTAL MEMBERSHIP 14,930)
9,925 (129)
SMALLER PROTESTANT GROUPS
CBA
NAZ.
EPISC.
UNITED PRESBY.
7-DAY ADV.
UNITED METHODIST
SOUTHERN BAPTIST
AMERICAN BAPTIST
5,005 (80)
OTHERS
FSQ
LACCC
APOSTOLIC ASSEMBLY
UNAFFILIATED OR INDEPENDENT
ASSEMBLY OF GOD
PROTESTANT
PENTECOSTAL
2750
2500
2250
2000
1750
1500
1250
1000
7500
500
250
2,390
AM. BAPT. (28)
12 DEPT.
1,600
SO. BAPT. (24)
14 DEPT
1,540
UNITED METH. (14)
3 DEPT.
880
7-DAY ADV. (11)
615
UNIT. PRESBY (10)
2 DEPT
400
EPISC. (3)
350
NAZ. (7)
1,080
ASSEMBLY OF GOD (18)
1,020
APOSTOLIC ASSEMBLY (12)
900
LACCC (15)
600
FSQ (10)
2 DEPT.
TRADITIONAL PROTESTANT
PENTECOSTAL

and conservative), may be experiencing either growth, stagnation, or disintegration based on a series of internal and external growth variables.

The Dilemma of the Introverted Hispanic Church

Radically introverted Hispanic congregations are the result of a survival mentality, a legacy of the past, that has created an inhibited life-style among a majority of their church members which often hinders them from engaging in creative ministry, either among themselves or within their local communities (cf. Martinez 1970:25-26).

Most Hispanic congregations in Southern California have long existed in the midst of nominally-Catholic Mexican American *barrios* which have been generally hostile to Protestants. Hispanic Protestants often feel cut off from their Catholic neighbors; family relationships are sometimes strained because of Catholic-Protestant tensions; and, many times, it is the Protestant convert who willfully cuts off close contact with his Catholic relatives and friends to avoid mutual hostilities, uneasiness, and perhaps embarrassment (cf. Sumner 1963:117-119; Clark 1959:22-23,98-99).

Contributing to the climate of hostility has been the strongly individualistic conversion pattern of a majority of Hispanic Protestant churches. New converts within most conservative churches are expected to leave family and friends behind in order to follow Christ, identifying themselves instead with their new "brothers and sisters in Christ". On the other hand, Protestant converts have often encountered hostility, deep resentment, and sometimes ostracism from their Catholic families and friends. When new converts are rebaptized and join a Protestant church, these acts are often considered as a betrayal of their Catholic family, their Hispanic folk-Catholic heritage, and "la raza" (cf. Sumner 1963:116,118).

The obvious response to this climate of hostility by many Hispanic Protestant churches has been the adoption of "a mentality of survival", a persecuted-minority complex, characterized by a passive acceptance of the problems of this "present evil world" and a retreat into the "fellowship of believers". This tendency was further strengthened by the vigorous anti-Catholic stance and the "Fundamentalist" ideology of many of the early Anglo missionaries who supported a dualistic separation between the sacred and the secular, between the Church and the world, between evangelism and social action (Grebler 1970:494-495; also see Miguez-Bonino 1967:191-197).

Not only has there been considerable hostility between Catholics and Protestants in the *barrios* of the Southwest, but sectarian exclusiveness and competition have also existed between various Protestant groups. Whereas members of the older Protestant denominations have openly interacted with one another across denominational lines, Pentecostal groups have usually maintained a rigid social separation from non-Pentecostals. This semi-isolation has resulted both from the traditional hostility toward Pentecostal churches exhibited by mainline denominations as well as from Pentecostal exclusiveness. The same tension has existed between the Seventh-Day Adventists and other Protestant groups for these same reasons (cf. Clark 1959:22-23,96-99,111-117; Sumner 1963:118-121; Grebler 1970:504-505).

The introversion of many Hispanic Protestant churches has been further intensified by consistent Anglo rejection and discrimination in general, and specifically by Anglo Protestant exclusion and neglect (Grebler 1970:496). Spanish-speaking Protestants have often felt estranged from their Anglo Protestant denominational brethren because of several related factors: (1) the low tolerance level of Anglos in respect to cultural and class diversity; (2) the paternalism that characterizes Anglo Protestant relationships with Hispanic churches; and (3) the general indifference of middle-class Anglo churches in respect to the problems of the Hispanic minority.

In respect to paternalism, the tendency to introversion has no doubt been strengthened among the traditional Protestant denominations by the long history of Hispanic church dependence upon Anglo subsidies, which were obviously necessary due to the "benumbing poverty" of the Mexican American minority especially in the pre-World War II era (Ellis 1938:152). Stewardship education and self-support were slow in coming to many Spanish-speaking congregations. Financial dependence, either in the form of salary supplements or denominational ownership of the church buildings, has often bred a psychological dependence that has had a crippling effect on Hispanic church leadership. The traditional exclusion of Hispanic church leaders from participation in the decision-making process at the denominational level, in respect to institutional goals and functions, leadership training, program development, and the administration of funds for Hispanic ministry, is a continuing sign of Anglo paternalism and the lack of Hispanic self-determination.

In summary, a series of related factors in the origin and development of the Hispanic Protestant Church has contributed to the creation of a multiplicity of introverted congregations: (1) the general hostility against Protestants in Mexican American *barrios*, especially the hostility of Catholic relatives and neighbors; (2) the Fundamentalist ideology--with its accompanying ascetism, hyper-individualism and anti-Catholicism--which characterized most Anglo Mexican mission "specialists" and which was generally adopted by Hispanic Protestants; (3) the exclusiveness and competition between various Protestant groups, especially between Pentecostals and non-Pentecostals and between the Seventh-Day Adventists and all other Protestant groups; (4) the cultural imperialism, prejudice, and discrimination of the dominant Anglo society toward Hispanic Americans; and (5) the exclusion, indifference, and paternalism demonstrated toward the Hispanic Church both by Anglo middle-class churches and by the Anglo denominational Establishment.

Not every Hispanic denomination or congregation was influenced by these factors to the same degree, nor did each one respond to these and other conditioning factors in the same way. Therefore, a variety of introverted religious subsocieties have come into existence, each with an identifiable "subculture"--its own characteristic life-style (Gordon 1964:38-40,47-49). There are, of course, many common characteristics between many of these subsocieties.

Although the introverted church, in general, conceives of its mission as "saving people from the world," many congregations are frustrated in fulfilling their mission because of the "sealed-off" character of their church-community relationships (cf. Clark 1959:117). Church members tend to be completely involved in the program of their local congregations, so that little time or opportunity is available for developing meaningful relationships across denominational lines or with their non-Protestant neighbors, or for significant community involvement. Their "church-life" constitutes the whole sphere of existence for many faithful Hispanic church members, as Grebler illustrates from an interview with a Baptist spokesman:

> The Spanish people are trained to serve *their church*, not the Kingdom of God. We find faithful people who come to church three days a week. They serve the church; they come and clean it; they bring flowers to the church; they cook for the church; they do everything for the church--the local congregation. But they never serve in the community (1970:495).

The introverted Hispanic church has an intensely traditional orientation, a strong desire to preserve the meaningful symbols of the past and a tendency to be rigidly conservative about the present and the future. In the midst of increasing disorientation and change, this basic conservatism is an attempt to preserve the cohesiveness and solidarity of the communal group, because the ethnic church has become the basis of Hispanic Protestant social identity (cf. Winter 1962:110-11; Burma 1970:443).

What Makes Churches Grow?

One would expect that the most radically introverted Hispanic congregations would be the most isolated from their local communities and, therefore, either static or declining in membership. On the other hand, one might also expect that the least introverted Hispanic churches--those that might be called "extroverted" (the least pietistic and the most oriented to social action)--would have the highest potential for growth, since they have the greatest interaction with their local communities. However, this is not necessarily the case.

Much of recent Hispanic church growth in Los Angeles County (cf. Figures 53 and 55) has taken place among conservative Hispanic churches which represent various degrees of introversion, rather than among the so-called "liberal" Hispanic churches related to the mainline Protestant denominations which are more community-oriented (Grebler 1970:498-499). Although United Methodist and United Presbyterian Hispanic congregations are generally declining in membership, not so with American Baptist Hispanic congregations. Even though the American Baptist Convention is generally considered a "liberal" body (cf. Kelley 1972: 88-99), their Spanish-speaking counterparts are far more conservative and generally fall into the "introverted" category, which may be true of some of the Methodist and Presbyterian Hispanic congregations as well (Grebler 1970:494-504). Grebler observes that most Hispanic Protestant churches "are conservative theologically and socially, irrespective of denominational affiliation" (1970:494). The present study is a confirmation of that fact. The conclusion, therefore, is not simply to say that conservative Hispanic churches are growing and liberal churches are declining. The dynamics of church growth are far more complex than that.

The Complexity of Church Growth. "The growth of a specific church," according to David O. Moberg in *The Church as a Social Institution*, "depends upon *a complex set of interacting factors* which make some grow rapidly while others barely hold their own, decline in size, or even die" (1962:212; italics mine). The problem, of course, is how to unravel this "complex set of interacting factors" which causes varying rates of church growth among denominational bodies, and even among individual local churches within each denominational family.

The simplist approach to isolating and evaluating growth factors is to divide the problem into internal factors and external factors. What are the *internal factors* that cause some churches to have high growth potential, while others demonstrate low potential for growth? On the other hand, what are the *external factors* that influence a religious subsociety's growth--the environmental factors over which a local church or group of churches have little or no control?

There are many ways to classify the internal growth factors in the life of a religious subsociety. Anthropologist Alan R. Tippett, of the Institute of Church Growth in Pasadena, California, divides "church growth" into three related factors:

> ...in my own research I have been rather impressed by the disclosure that, time after time, quantitative, qualitative, and organic growth go together. They are often different manifestations of the same latent life and power (1970:61).

Tippett then goes on to explain the use of these three terms:

> Discipling and perfecting...are different but related kinds of growth--one the quantitative intake due to evangelistic outreach, the other the qualitative development to maturity within the congregation. Without the former the congregation would die. Without the latter it would produce neither leaders nor mature members. Without maturity and leadership there would be no organic growth of "the Body" (1970:63).

Of the three dimensions of growth defined by Tippett, the qualitative dimension is the most difficult to analyze, because "quality" has a wide range of subjective meanings to different people and it is the most difficult to measure. On the other hand, the quantitative dimension (membership growth) is fairly easy to analyze and measure. The organic dimension, while more difficult to measure than the quantitative dimension, is becoming more accesible to analysis because of the growing amount of verifiable data on group dynamics and organizational functioning.

Dissatisfaction with the term "qualitative" has led some concerned observers of the Church Growth movement (i.e., of Dr. Donald McGavran and the Institute of Church Growth; cf. Tippett 1973) to seek for more descriptive terms that are more easily subject to measurement. One such observer, Orlando Costas, who jointly serves with the Latin American Biblical Seminary and the Institute of In-Depth Evangelism in San José, Costa Rica, evaluates "church growth" from the theoretical perspective of what the Church of Christ ought to be ideally and discusses four dimensions of growth: numerical, organic, conceptual, and incarnational (1973a:1-2).

> By *numerical* expansion is understood the recruitment of persons for the Kingdom of God by calling them to repentance and faith in Jesus Christ as Lord and Savior of

their lives, and their incorporation into a local community of persons which, having made a similar decision, worship, obey and give witness, collective and personally, to the world of God's redemptive action in Jesus Christ and His liberating power.

By *organic* expansion is meant the internal development of a local community of faith; i.e., the system of relationships which is built among its members--its form of government, financial structure, leadership, types of activities in which its time and resources are invested, etc.

By *conceptual* expansion is meant the degree of consciousness that a community of faith has with regards to its nature and mission to the world; i.e., the image that the community has formed of herself, the depth of her reflection on the meaning of her faith in Christ (knowledge of Scripture, etc.) and her image of the world.

By *incarnational* growth is meant the degree of involvement of a community of faith in the life and problems of her social environment; i.e., her participation in the afflictions of her world; her prophetic, intercessory and liberating action in behalf of the weak and destitute, the intensity of her ministry to the poor, the brokenhearted, the captives, the blind and the oppressed (Lk. 4:18-21).

Costas further describes these four interacting dimensions of church growth as follows:

Each of these areas deals with a number of variables that involve a holistic missionary interaction with the world. The *numerical* deals with the personal life and struggles of the people of the world; their coming into repentance and faith in Christ and their incorporation into the community of faith. The *organic* deals with indigeneity and culture; i.e., God's mission manifesting itself at the level of community life in terms of a cultural and structural development. In other words, the community of faith as taking form in culturally relevant terms, not as a foreign entity, but as an indigenous organism. The *conceptual* penetrates both the psychological as well as the logical spheres of the life of the church in the light of her own identity, her image and understanding of her faith and of the world. The *incarnational* affects the church sociologically, for it deals with her involvement in

> the collective and structural problems and struggles of society (1973a:2).

For Costas, this is the only type of "church growth" that can be said to legitimately reflect God's missionary action in the world:

> Such growth is a missionary imperative. It is the type of growth that God wants and that the world needs. For it makes the church what it should be--the community for others--and the gospel what it was meant to be --the joyous glad tidings of a new order of life. Such a church is a servant of the world for God's sake. Her growth is, therefore, neither imperialistic nor alienating, for it is an expansion in service, in liberating action, *which generates hope and announces the advent of the* [*Kingdom of God*] (1973a:2).

For the Church of Christ to fulfill this missionary purpose, the four interrelated dimensions of growth outlined by Costas must function in creative balance and produce a community of believers whose ideology (the conceptual dimension), life-style (the incarnational dimension), organizational structures and functions (the organic dimension), and reproduction (the quantitative dimension) bear prophetic witness to the fact that Christ is indeed the only Savior and Lord of mankind and that the Kingdom of God is foreseen in the communal life of the "people of God" in the historical present.

In reality, however, the local church is often a faint shadow of what the Church of Christ ought to be; its ideology is often warped and distorted by race, culture, and class; its life-style often betrays the radical demands of the Gospel of Christ; its organizational structures, forms, and traditions often obstruct healthy "body life"; and its reproductive energies are often dissipated in selfish activities which fail to disciple men to Jesus Christ. How can the local church become a valid expression of the true Church of Jesus Christ? It must be revitalized by bringing the four dimensions of growth back to a balanced state of equilibrium. In order to help the local church and its denominational family achieve revitalization, we need to understand the general process by which religious subsocieties are revitalized.

The Process of Revitalization. Religious subsocieties, as well as all social organisms, exist in the tension between stability and change, organization and disorganization, revitalization and disintegration or entropy (loss of energy). "Like all energy systems," observes Kelley, "social organizations are entropic--they gradually run down--they are subsiding toward a state of rest" (1972:96). Even the strongest religious subsocieties, given enough time, run into periods of increasing stress, distortion, and decline; there is a need for revitalization to alleviate the effects of organizational decay or dysfunctionalism.

Borrowing Anthony Wallace's model, the process of religious revitalization may be diagrammed as follows (1956:264-281):

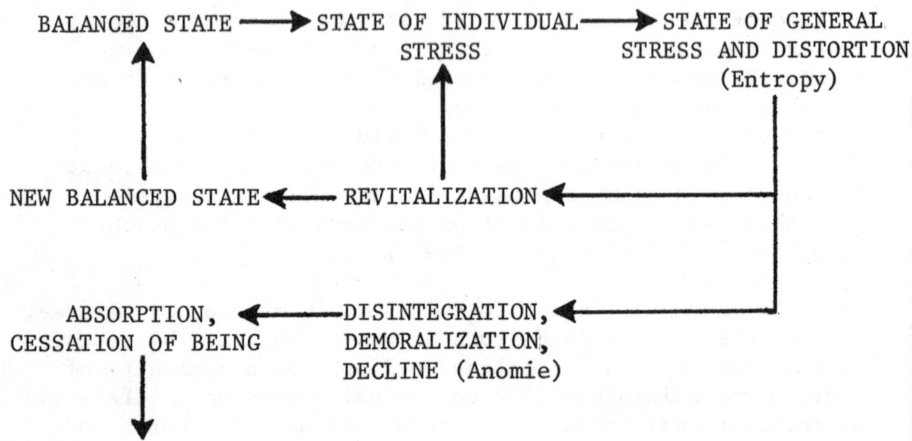

Briefly described, the revitalization process functions in the following manner:

1. *Balanced State*. When a society maintains approved techniques for satisfying "felt-needs" among its members so that the society, as an organism, is able to operate with efficiency while maintaining "chronic stress" within tolerable limits, that society is experiencing a steady state of moving equilibrium.

> Gradual modification or even rapid substitution of techniques for satisfying some needs may occur without disturbing the steady state, as long as (1) the techniques for satisfying other needs are not seriously interfered with and (2) abandonment of a given technique for reducing one need in favor of a more efficient technique does not leave other needs, which the first technique was also instrumental in satisfying, without any prospect of satisfaction (Wallace 1956:268-269).

In other words, a balanced state of equilibrium is achieved in a religious subsociety by minimizing stress, distortion, and disintegration and by maintaining maximum satisfaction of the group's felt-needs, while constantly adapting to resistance and change.

2. *Individual Stress*. Every member of a given society maintains "a mental image of his society and its culture, as well as of his own body and its behavioral regularities, in order to act in ways which reduce stress at all levels of the system" (1956: 266). This mental image Wallace calls "the mazeway", which is a construct of "the cell-body-personality-nature-culture-society" system or field, as organized by the individual's own experience, that includes perceptions of both

> ...the maze of physical objects of the environment (internal and external, human and nonhuman) and also of the ways in which this maze can be manipulated by the self and others in order to minimize stress. The mazeway is nature, society, culture, personality, and body image, as seen by one person (1956:266).

The state of increasing individual stress occurs when, with the passage of time, individual members of a society "experience increasingly severe stress as a result of the decreasing efficiency of certain stress-reducing techniques" (1956:269). Various types and degrees of change may take place within the religious subsociety, but "there is a continuous diminution in its efficiency in satisfying needs" (1956:269).

> While the individual can tolerate a moderate degree of increased stress and still maintain a habitual way of behavior, *a point is reached at which some alternative way must be considered*. Initial consideration of a substitute way is likely, however, to increase stress because it arouses anxiety over the possibility that the substitute will be *less effective* than the original, and that it may actively interfere with the execution of other ways. In other words, *it poses the threat of mazeway disintegration* (1956:269; italics mine).

3. *General Stress*. According to Wallace:

> The prolonged experience of stress, produced by failure of need satisfying techniques and by anxiety over the prospect of changing behavior patterns, is responded to differently by different people. Rigid persons apparently prefer to tolerate high levels of chronic stress rather than to make systematic adaptive changes in the mazeway. More flexible persons try to reduce stress by addition or substitution of mazeway elements with more or less concern for the *Gestalt* [patterns and organization] of the system (1956:269).

In this state, the society undergoes internal distortion, and loss of energy (entropy), resulting in a lack of harmony and mazeway disintegration:

> ...as the inadequacy of existing ways of acting to reduce stress becomes more and more evident, and as the *internal incongruities* of the mazeway are perceived, symptoms of anxiety over the *loss of meaningful life* are also becoming evident: *disillusionment* with the mazeway, and *apathy* toward problems of adaptation, set in (1956:270; italics mine).

4. *Period of Revitalization.* "A revitalization movement is defined as a deliberate, organized, conscious effort by members of a society to construct a more satisfying culture," or a more satisfying socio-religious system (1956:265). Revitalization is a special kind of change phenomena: the persons involved in the process of revitalization must perceive that their system is unsatisfactory, and they must innovate to establish a new system that will satisfy their felt-needs.

Wallace states that religious revitalization movements may undergo at least six major steps: (1) mazeway reformulation, (2) communication, (3) organization, (4) adaptation, (5) cultural and behavior transformation, and (6) routinization (1956:270-275). To be completely successful, a revitalization movement must pass through *all* of these stages. However, many movements are abortive, with their progress arrested at some intermediate point in the revitalization process. Success or failure in determining the fate of any given movement will depend on two major variables: the relative "realism" of the new doctrine or conceptual framework, and the amount of force exerted against the new movement by its opponents (1956:278).

5. *New Steady State.* Once a new mazeway has been created and the new system has proved itself viable, and once the new movement has solved its problems with routinization, a new steady state may be said to exist. The character of this state will be different in pattern, organization, and traits from the earlier steady state, and it will also be significantly different from that of the period of general stress and distortion (1956:275).

The choices available to a society in the process of revitalizing itself and achieving a new balanced state of equilibrium are threefold, according to Wallace: (1) *to revive* a traditional system that passed out of existence for a variety of reasons (often if this choice is made, it denotes "a myth of the golden past"); (2) *to import* a foreign system that holds high promise of meeting the society's felt needs and achieving a new balanced state; and (3) *to create* a new system, that is neither a revival of the past or an importation of a foreign system, but a new option that conceives of a desired "endstate", a future *Utopia*, as the ideal system (1956:275).

However, a fourth option is also available, although it could be considered part of Wallace's third choice. This option includes: (1) a rejection of values, symbols, and practices from the old system that are incompatible with the new reality, and which themselves are part of the problem of anxiety and stress within the society; and (2) the incorporation of those values, symbols, and practices of the past which are meaningful and which enrich the society's life-style, together with the integration and adaptation of new values, symbols and practices which will make the religious subsociety more meaningful, relevant, and satisfying (cf. Costas 1973b:8).

In summary, revitalization is necessary among churches composed of second, third, and subsequent generations of Christians because churches run into periods of decline, variously known as fatigue, entropy (loss of energy), or anomie (normlessness). In the state of general stress, the four dimensions of growth become seriously out of balance; they demand critical self-evaluation by the subsociety and revitalization to bring the organism to a new state of moving equilibrium. Continuous revitalization is also possible if, in the period of increasing individual stress, the church is open to change and continuously practices critical self-evaluation, taking the necessary corrective action to alleviate stress by meeting the general felt-needs of a majority of her members.

This revitalization process, of course, does *not* exclude the ministry of the Holy Spirit, but represents a continuous openness to the work of the Spirit and a healthy response to His illuminating, guiding, and healing ministry within the life of the Church and of her individual members. Balanced four-dimensional church growth, in my opinion, is a biblical imperative and represents an openness and responsiveness to the revitalizing work of the Spirit within the Body of Christ, and within each local fellowship of believers (cf. Rev. 1-3, Christ's message to the seven churches).

The Quantitative Measurement of Social Strength. While recognizing that the four dimensions of church growth are interrelated factors that must be kept in balance, membership statistics (the quantitative dimension) can be used as an indication of the "social strength" of a religious subsociety--its vitality as a social organism. Dean Kelley, in his recent study of American Protestant Church life entitled *Why Conservative Churches are Growing*, stresses this important point (1972:16):

> Though membership statistics are not the only index of social strength, yet they do point to a certain inescapable, irreducible, quantifiable "thereness" in an organization, which has some direct and discernible relation to its existence and success. That is, organizations are made up of members. Whatever its optimum size, an organization that is losing this essential substance is in a distinctly different state from one that is gaining it. If a man is progressively losing weight, he and his family and friends begin to worry about his health. There may be many reasons for the loss--and it may indeed be a healthy one--but his physician will want to be quite sure he knows what is going on and that he has the process under control, since diminution can proceed only so far. Beyond that there is no patient left. The physician can usually determine by secondary symptoms whether the loss is healthy or not.
>
> Likewise with organizations: consistent loss of substance is an important change which may have various explanations, but its causes need urgently to be known, lest it prove fatal.

Religious subsocieties are in a constant process of change, although the rate and degree of change may vary widely--from a steady state to a condition of increasing individual stress, to general stress and distortion, and to either revitalization and a new steady state or to disintegration and cessation of being. Membership gain or loss is an important part of understanding this process of change and can be used as a measurement of an organization's vitality or social strength, especially in a comparative study of the membership statistics of several religious subsocieties, which draw their membership from the same ethnic minority population within the same geographical area. This, of course, is what we have done in terms of Hispanic Protestant churches within Los Angeles County. We have noted that the social strength of some Hispanic denominations is declining, while at the same time the social strength of other groups is increasing.

Although we have evaluated the process of religious revitalization in general, we need to get a better understanding of what constitutes "a balanced state of equilibrium." Differentiation must be made at this point between the idealized concept of balanced four-dimensional church growth postulated earlier and the sociological reality that a "distorted" view of the Gospel of Christ, as in Mormonism for example, may produce a religious ideology with its corresponding life-style, organizational functioning, and disciple-making activity which creates a religious subsociety, in spite of widespread opposition and even persecution, that has amazing vitality and is growing in social strength (cf. Kelley 1972:56-77). What are the factors, then, that tend to create a "strong" religious subsociety, regardless of ideological orthodoxy to the Gospel of Christ, which will help us to understand the internal growth dynamics of Hispanic Protestant churches in Los Angeles County?

Internal Growth Factors of "Strong" Religious Groups. Kelley maintains that (1) the strength and vitality of religious organizations depends on the nature of the *demands* they make upon their adherents, and (2) the degree to which those demands are met by *commitment* (1972:47-55; Kelley's full argument is developed in pp. 36-96 of his study). This hypothesis is highly relevant for our present study, since this is the same conclusion that I have reached through the process of being a participant observer in numerous religious subsocieties, and as a result of studying the conclusions of Anthony Wallace (1956:264-281), Max Weber (1963:46-79), David Moberg (1962:73-99,212-220), and other sources.

The dominant internal growth characteristics of a "strong" religious subsociety, in my opinion, are the following:

1. The inspirational or charismatic quality of its leaders; the relative "realism" of their doctrine or message as a "meaning-orientation" system ("mazeway" reorientation); and their ability to recruit disciples and followers (communication) and to establish a permanent, supportive religious community (organization and routinization of the movement).

2. The commitment of its members to its "ideology" (a system of values, beliefs, and goals with prescribed attitudes and behavior); the identification of their ideology with "ultimate Truth" or authority (absolutism); the acceptance of a closed system of meaning and value.

3. The degree of identification of each member with the group (positive group identity); their participation in the life-style of the group (cultural and behavioral transformation); their loyalty to the group; and their willingness to obey its sanctions and discipline (group conformity and separation).

4. The missionary zeal and proselytic effectiveness of the group: the participation, eagerness, and dedication of each member in communicating the ideology of the group (degree of mobilization), regardless of opposition

(degree of fanaticism); their ability to communicate the "message" without distortion; and their ability to persuade outsiders of the "truth" of the message--to disciple others to their ideology and life-style.

5. The ability to maintain organizational strength, vitality, and relevance: the functional effectiveness of the group in defining and maintaining status and role models; satisfying the "felt-needs" of the majority of its members; maintaining the commitment, loyalty, and discipline of its membership (internal cohesion and solidarity); providing adequate financial support; recruiting, training, and developing new leadership; mobilizing its members in the constant propagation of its ideology; recruiting and indoctrinating new disciples; and expanding the organization into new geographical areas by organizing new cell groups of disciples among responsive segments of the population.

6. The group's ability to maintain maximum cohesion, vitality and functional effectiveness while keeping stress, anxiety and disintegration to a minimum; this includes adaptation to resistance and change through a process of continuous revitalization, thus maintaining a balanced state of equilibrium.

The significance of these internal growth factors to an understanding of Hispanic church growth in Los Angeles County should be obvious. While it is true that some Hispanic churches are growing and others are declining because of differences in the internal "strength" of each subsociety, growth and decline should be viewed in relationship to the process of revitalization and to "the biblical ideal" of balanced four-dimensional church growth.

This approach may lead us to raise questions about biblical interpretation and authority, supracultural norms for the church, and the problem of subcultural distortion in understanding the teaching of scripture. However, if the Old and New Testaments are regarded as "the only rule of faith and practice", then a religious subsociety has a standard by which to evaluate itself as an organism, as an historical expression of the Body of Christ.

We have suggested four dimensions of church growth that can be measured and compared with biblical norms, and we have discussed the process of revitalization in terms of how a religious subsociety can bring the four dimensions of growth back into a balanced state of equilibrium. On the other hand, our analysis of the growth dynamics of religious subsocieties leads us to conclude that a certain combination of internal growth factors, coupled with favorable external factors, will produce a "strong" religious subsociety that experiences significant growth, regardless of the subsociety's "orthodoxy" in terms of biblical norms. The subsociety may be in a balanced state *sociologically*, but the religious group may be a poor reflection or even a distortion of the biblical norms as represented in our idealized model of "balanced four-dimensional church growth". Since churches grow because of a combination of favorable internal and external factors, at this point we need to consider the external growth factors that have influenced Hispanic church growth in the Los Angeles metropolitan area.

External Growth Factors Within Los Angeles County. It appears that many introverted Hispanic churches are providing members of the Hispanic community with a new "meaning-orientation" system (cf. Kelley 1972:36-55) which meets their particular felt-needs (for a discussion of "felt-needs", see Aronoff 1967:1-17 and Nida 1954:261-262). The heterogeneity of the Hispanic population in Los Angeles County means, however, that a wide range of felt-needs are in evidence--from those of the least acculturated members of the lower classes to those of the highly acculturated members of the upper classes. The following question, therefore, needs to be asked: Within this range of variables, *which* felt-needs are being met, by *which* religious groups, among *which* segments of the Hispanic population?

Some highly introverted Hispanic congregations, mainly Pentecostals, preach an exclusivistic message, place rigid demands on their members, and receive a high level of commitment in return, which has produced a cohesive religious subsociety that appeals to certain types of people within the local community (cf. Willems 1967:122-153). Many Spanish-speaking residents of urban Los Angeles County are extremely disoriented personally and socially due to the loss of traditional social structures, the impersonalization of the urban milieu, and the demoralization of poverty. They are "uprooted" people who are searching for something to make life meaningful, for a sense of "belonging" (cf. Poblete and O'Dea 1962:195-199).

The SSN population of Los Angeles County more than doubled between 1960 and 1970 (cf. Figure 54), which means that hundreds of thousands of Spanish-speaking people have migrated to Los Angeles from other areas of the Southwest, or from Mexico or other Latin countries. These "in-migrants" often experience several years of extreme disorientation in the transition from a rural to urban environment, from agricultural to industrial employment, from loss of family and friendship ties to establishing new primary group relationships, from traditional social structures to acculturation into a new social matrix. For some migrants the transition is only from rural to urban poverty, but for others it involves a shift from socioeconomic *immobility* to achieving some measure of upward socioeconomic progress (cf. Chapters 1-4).

The uprooted suffer from strong feelings of anxiety, guilt, alienation, isolation, loneliness, and loss of meaning in life, which leads them in a quest for "community" (i.e., group acceptance, identification, and solidarity). Personal and social disorientation leads men to seek for integration, status, and membership in a new personal community (i.e., the restructuring of primary group relations and reorientation to meaningful life). A state of "anomie" (disorder, normlessness) may temporarily exist among the uprooted regardless of socioeconomic class; but for the impoverished lower classes who are caught in the poverty cycle (cf. Figure 9), disorientation and demoralization may become a permanent mode of existence by developing into a subculture of poverty (cf. Poblete and O'Dea 1962:195-199; Willems 1967:83-86,122-126; Ireland 1968:1-12; and Moynihan 1968:187-200)

However, other Hispanic Americans have been able to improve their socioeconomic level due to a variety of upward mobility factors, which we have previously considered in Chapter 2. For example, the native-born Mexican American who is a second generation urbanite, has acquired a high school or college education, is a highly-skilled craftsman or "white collar" worker, and is thoroughly acculturated to Anglo middle-class society, has developed or is in the process of developing a "meaning-orientation" system quite different from that of a poverty-stricken Mexican migrant worker who has just arrived in East Los Angeles, let's say, from rural Mexico via the harvest cycle in Brownsville, Texas; Tucson, Arizona; and Brawley, California.

Although there is no "specific" documentary evidence to suppor the following hypothesis, two general explanations are proposed t account for recent Hispanic church growth in Los Angeles County. First, the growth of Hispanic Pentecostal churches since 1960 is the result of their special appeal to the uprooted lower classes among the Hispanic population, who find in the introverted Pentecostal subsocieties a new sense of "community" (cf. Poblete and O'Dea 1962:199-206; Winter 1962:139-147). Secondly, the growth of non-Pentecostal churches (mainly American Baptist and Southern Baptist) is the result of their special appeal to socially mobile Mexican Americans, who find in Spanish-speaking departments in Anglo churches: (1) greater opportunities for acculturation for themselves and for their children; (2) reduced status anxiety by increased identification with Anglo Protestants (the prestige group) without forsaking the Hispanic congregation, which continues to be the main focus of social identity for many Hispanic Protestants; and (3) a new sense of "community" within the context of an "organization church" (most Anglo churches sponsoring

Spanish-speaking departments are large, successful, multi-staffed churches with diversified ministries), which appeals to the higher acculturation level expectations of socially mobile Hispanic Americans (cf. Sumner 1963:115-121; Winter 1962:93-96, 124-132).

Thus, highly introverted Hispanic congregations have a greater appeal to the lower-class "uprooted" elements within the Hispanic population, whereas Spanish-speaking departments in Anglo churches have a stronger appeal to emerging middle-class Mexican Americans, who are consciously seeking greater acculturation and participation within the framework of Anglo society. Spanish-speaking departments also draw other upwardly mobile Latins (large numbers of Cubans, Puerto Ricans, and Central Americans), who are recent arrivals in urban Los Angeles and are also suffering from being uprooted.

On the other hand, highly acculturated middle-class Hispanic Americans, who are comfortably bilingual or fluent only in English, tend to associate only with Anglo churches, while having little to do with ministry among the Spanish-speaking population. It appears that there are a growing number of "Hispanic" Americans in this category. For example, in 1964, the Director of Spanish Work for the American Baptists reported: "Even now we have more Spanish American people in the memberships of Anglo churches than in our forty Spanish-speaking churches [in Southern California]" (The Southern California Baptist Convention 1964). Obviously, the acculturation level of Hispanic Americans has a decisive role in determining the type of church where they attend and become members.

Other external church growth factors include the general predisposition of Hispanic Americans toward the particular message and life-style communicated by a given Hispanic Protestant church, or in some cases by an Anglo Protestant church. The predisposition of each individual will be influenced by a series of personal variables: his religious background (indifferent, nominal, or active Catholic/Protestant/other); his felt-need for a more personal religious experience (often subconscious); and his interest level in Protestant-oriented religious life based on a general exposure to Protestants, his friendship contacts with them in his local neighborhood or in a work situation, and the possible influence of Protestant relatives. An individual may attend and later join a particular Protestant church because friends or relatives have invited him, previous contacts with church members have stimulated an interest in deepening his personal religious commitment, and he needs the fellowship and acceptance of a new personal community--because the "message" (ideology) and life-style of the group meet his particular need for a new meaning-orientation system ("mazeway" reorientation).

This, of course, is the primary function of "religion"--to provide individuals with a meaningful and satisfying personal and group experience in relationship to God and their neighbors (see Figure 8 for other variables that may influence the "receptivity-resistance" axis; cf. McGavran 1970:216-232).

An Evaluation of the Small Congregation. One of the chief characteristics of Hispanic congregations in Los Angeles County is their small relative size (Figure 57) compared to Anglo congregations. The small congregation, whether Anglo or Hispanic, represents many problems for the mainline denominations because such churches are rarely self-supporting, nor do they have the resources to provide for adequate facilities for worship and Christian education, unless of course the small membership also has a high average income and is able to provide for itself financially. Few, if any, Hispanic congregations are that well off financially.

The majority of Hispanic congregations in the Los Angeles metropolitan area are small and mainly composed of lower-income Mexican Americans, although a growing number of lower-middle class churches have emerged since the late 1950s. An illustration of the low income status of Hispanic churches in the mid-1950s is seen in the following statistics on the American Baptists: out of ninety-four Spanish-speaking churches affiliated with the American Baptist Convention throughout the United States, sixty-one percent had fewer than fifty members. In California, only nine Hispanic churches (19.6%) out of forty-six had more than 100 members, four (9%) had between 100-150 members, one (2%) had 150-200 members, three (6.5%) had between 200-250 members, and one (2%) had 350-400 members. Of those that had less than 100 members (37 churches or 80.4%), twelve churches (26%) had 50-100 members, fifteen churches (33%) had 26-50 members, and ten churches (22%) had less than twenty-five members. Consequently, in California and Arizona, seventy-eight percent of the Hispanic pastors in the American Baptist Convention, in 1954, were dependent upon salary subsidies from the denomination so that they could continue to serve their small churches (Leavenworth and Froyd 1954:11-15; Tables VIII and XIV).

Nor was the general situation much improved by 1970, when the author determined that the average congregational size among Pentecostal denominations in Los Angeles County was 62.6 members per church, compared to 76.3 members per church among the non-Pentecostal denominations (Figure 57). The average congregational size for the total number of Spanish-speaking Protestant churches was 71.4 members per church (cf. Figure 26). Thirty-eight percent of the pastors served on a part-time basis, while working part-time or full-time in secular employment, and forty-one percent of the pastors received part (or in some cases, all)

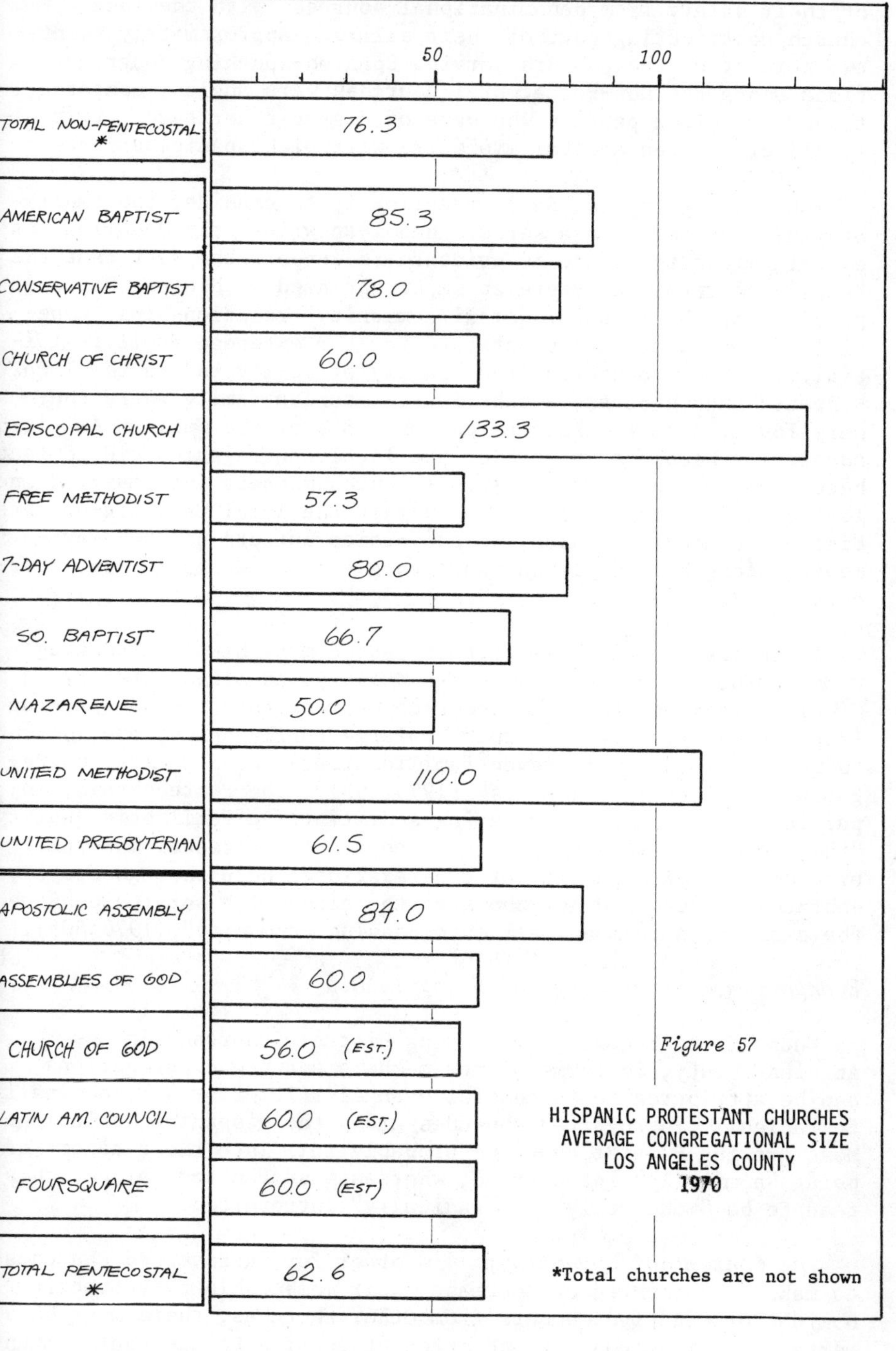

Figure 57

HISPANIC PROTESTANT CHURCHES
AVERAGE CONGREGATIONAL SIZE
LOS ANGELES COUNTY
1970

*Total churches are not shown

of their salary from denominational sources, with the local church contributing part of their salary. Approximately twenty-two percent of the pastors serving Spanish-speaking congregations among the non-Pentecostal churches were Anglos, compared to seventy-eight percent who were of Hispanic heritage. Virtually all of the Pentecostal ministers were of Hispanic heritage.

Whereas the typical Anglo reaction is to consider the small Hispanic congregation a serious handicap within the denomination's overall ministry, there is evidence to support the fact that the "small congregation" meets an important need within the Hispanic population--the need for "small community" relationships, especially as a functional substitute for the extended family. Initially, for new converts, the "family of believers" in the local Hispanic church became a substitute extended family where they were loved, accepted, and cared for. But as the Mexican American population became more stable, the local congregation did in fact become a real extended family, as church members intermarried and formed an isolated social group within the local Catholic-oriented Hispanic community. Also the conversion pattern of "web movements" along kinship lines was strongly in evidence in some churches and denominations.

A combination of these factors caused many Hispanic congregations to have a strong familistic quality, as illustrated by Grebler's comment that "at one time most of the Spanish-speaking [Baptist] churches were formed by large family units; one church in California had only seven families represented in its congregation of ninety-two members" (1970:495). The Pentecostals, in particular, are noted for having a distinctive familistic quality: "the atmosphere is one of total acceptance: personal and family problems are made public for congregational help through prayer; embraces between pew neighbors at the close of a service enhance the sense of a warm and all-encompassing community" (1970:505).

Evangelism, Conversion, and Discipleship

Much of the recent growth among Hispanic churches in Los Angeles County, in terms of new members and new congregations, can be attributed to successful evangelistic efforts by nominally to radically introverted churches among the Hispanic population. Most growing Baptist churches probably fall into the category of being "nominally" introverted, whereas most Pentecostal churches tend to be "moderately" or "radically" introverted.

The Context of Evangelism. In order for introverted churches to make new converts or increase their membership by attracting nominal or inactive members from other churches, there must be a certain level of contact and interaction with the general community outside of their particular religious subsociety. However, for many introverted churches, this increased contact with "the world" is only a temporary expedient for the sake of accomplishing their mission of "winning souls" *from* the world. Contact with the unconverted community is only *tolerable* for members of introverted religious subsocieties to permit them to earn a living, to shop, to attend school, to participate in certain restricted recreational activities, and to evangelize "the lost".

Many introverted Hispanic churches, while consciously avoiding all activities that could be labeled as "social gospel", seek to develop an effective evangelistic outreach within their local communities. "Soul-winning" activities may include house-church ministries, sending teams of laymen door-to-door to witness for Christ and to distribute religious literature, or sponsoring evangelistic rallies in the local church, in a public meeting place, or sometimes in a large tent erected in a vacant lot. Some conservative churches, mainly Pentecostals, maintain a continuous evangelistic format, with services almost every night of the week geared to "winning the lost". For special "revivals" or evangelistic crusades, an evangelist is usually brought in from outside the local area. These efforts are geared to lead the unconverted out of "the world" to God, which is often subconsciously interpreted to mean leading them out of "sinful vices and pleasures" into a building-centered church program--into fellowship and identification with their particular religious subsociety.

The internal dynamics of "strong" religious subsocieties mean that their members are highly motivated to communicate their special "message", which may be a unique interpretation of the Second Coming of Christ (Jehovah's Witnesses), a belief in a special extra-biblical revelation (Mormonism), or a particular doctrine or experience such as the "baptism of the Holy Spirit" (Pentecostalism). Most non-Pentecostal Protestant groups differ from one another in their definitions of "orthodoxy", their forms of baptism, their organizational structures, and their concepts of Christian ethics and behavior. Pentecostal groups are also divided on these issues, but their main differences are related to the gifts and ministry of the Holy Spirit--how these gifts are manifested, how they are to be used, etc.--particularly concerning the gifts of "speaking in tongues" and divine healing. While the majority of these groups claim to preach "the Gospel of Christ", their interpretation of what constitutes "the Gospel", how people are converted, and how new converts should live as disciples of Christ is closely tied to their unique ideology and life-style--to their particular religious subsociety.

Understanding Biblical Conversion. Since the process of "conversion" and the expected results of conversion are socially as well as theologically defined by a religious subsociety (cf.

Moberg 1962:421 ff.), we need to ask the question, what is "biblical conversion" and how does it take place? *Theologically*, biblical conversion is a turning to God in repentence and faith in response to the illuminating and convicting power of the Holy Spirit as one encounters the risen Christ through the presence, witness, and service of His Body in the world, the Church of Jesus Christ. *Psychologically*, biblical conversion is a reorientation of the human personality around the person of God. Where man once lived out his life in open rebellion against God and in a state of alienation against his neighbors, he now responds to the love and mercy of God in creaturely obedience. He begins to learn what it means to love God with his whole heart, mind, soul, and strength and to love his neighbor as himself (cf. World Council of Churches 1968:36-37; Moberg 1962:421-440).

The new Christian, therefore, begins to creatively explore a whole new series of relationships with God, with the community of believers, with his family and friends, and with those co-members of his society in general that are outside of Christ. Because each man is a "man-in-society", his new relationships are both shaped and distorted by his cultural milieu and his socio-economic status (his "ethclass"). Therefore, he must continuously be open and responsive to the Holy Spirit's guidance and illumination in working out what he conceives to be "the will of God". The new Christian, with constant reference to the revelation of God in the scriptures and God's saving acts in history, must develop a culturally relevant Christian ethic as a critique upon his relationships with his family, his neighbors and friends, and with the structures of society in which he finds himself enmeshed.

The community of believers, in each culture and subculture, must determine for themselves what is the will of God in their unique situation, but they must also see themselves in historical perspective--in the perspective of the scriptures and of church history--and learn from the mistakes of the past. Jesus never intended for His Church to merely be an introverted religious subsociety, but rather it was meant to be "a community for others" sent into the world as He was to reconcile men to God and to each other (cf. John 17).

The role of the Advocate. Since the process of proclaiming and authenticating the Gospel of Christ is intended to lead the receptors of the message to a crisis encounter with Jesus Christ, it is important to examine the role of the advocate in the decision-making process. What problems are involved in being an advocate of the Gospel--as an Anglo American seeking to persuade Latins to become responsible disciples of Jesus Christ, as a Latin seeking to win other Latins? To what are the receptors of the message of Christ converted? Are they converted to the religious "ideology" of the advocate who has shared his faith, to the message and life-style of a particular local church or denomination? Are they converted to a distorted understanding of the Gospel?

As much as we would like to believe that new "disciples" are only converted to Jesus Christ, it is obvious that many people have been converted, often unconsciously, to a distorted religious ideology, to a narrow denominational perspective and tradition, to a particular form of church government, or to a charismatic religious leader other than Jesus Christ. Often a Christian's loyalty and commitment is to a religious subsociety, and to its ideology and subculture, rather than to Jesus Christ and the Universal Body of Christ (cf. World Council of Churches 1968:44-47).

The role of the advocate can be misdirected by personal and subcultural bias, doctrinal distortion, biblical ignorance or misguided zeal, as well as by dishonesty, greed, pride, or immorality, in specific cases. Consequently, some of the charges of "proselytism", directed against specific individuals or groups for using unethical means of persuasion, are valid criticisms. The charge of proselytism has often been made against *any* evangelistic attempt to persuade members of a non-Christian religion to become a Christian, or by some Christian denominations as a charge against other denominations or local churches who attempt to "steal their sheep". The term "proselytism", as usually defined, means: "the making of a convert, especially to some religious sect, or to some opinion, system, or party" (Lindsell 1966:225). However, the term, in its broader usage, has a positive connotation also.

Throughout the New Testament, Jesus' disciples proclaimed the "good news" about Him and persuaded men to commit themselves to Him as their Lord and Savior, while also becoming part of a local community of believers who were seeking to know and do the will of God. *The necessity of a decision* concerning Jesus Christ as one hears the message of reconciliation is obligatory by the inherent nature of the Spirit-directed message ("He will convict the world of sin, of righteousness, and of judgment," John 16:8-11). The use of unbiblical and unethical methods of persuading people to change their religious convictions by psychological manipulation or by physical, material, or social coercion is condemned, however. Because the resurrection of Jesus Christ from the dead validates His claim to be the *only* Lord and Savior of mankind, *the Christian Church must seek to persuade all men, by every legitimate method, to personally encounter Christ by faith.*

The practice of proselytism, when defined as "denominational aggrandizement", must be rejected by all branches of the

Christian Church. But the message of God's reconciliation in Christ must be communicated to *all* men, so that *all* may have the option of encountering Christ in the historical present.

Genuine Discipleship and Authentic Evangelism. Converted men must commit their lives to Jesus Christ, never to a church or denomination which proclaims an exclusivistic religious ideology. To be a genuine "Christian" is to be a disciple of Jesus Christ and uniquely related to the universal Body of Christ; to be a disciple of Christ is to demonstrate to one's local community that Jesus is "alive and well", and that allegiance to Him makes an emphatic difference in the quality of one's life for the common good of all men, especially in terms of increased moral righteousness and social justice (cf. Lindsell 1966:111-122).

Commitment to Jesus Christ requires a revolutionary quality of life. The nature of the obedience that Jesus requires of His followers is a call to "radical discipleship". The Christian is called to be an "eternal revolutionary", who shares the message of a living Christ with those around him in the hope and expectancy that they too will be *reconciled* to God and to their neighbors, will commit their lives to Him alone, will faithfully do all that He commanded, and thus become responsible members of His Body, the Church Universal (cf. Gish 1970:79-142).

"Authentic" evangelism, then, is the "reconciled community" bearing witness by word and deed, through the power of the Holy Spirit, that Jesus Christ is the only Lord and Savior of mankind; it is the "people of God" communicating by a *credible* witness as "salt" and "light" in the world that God has manifested His love for all men in Jesus Christ, who sacrificially reconciled men to God and to their neighbors through His death and resurrection, and that He calls all men to be His faithful disciples and responsible members of His Church.

It is the *credibility* of the Church's witness to Jesus Christ in this present alienated world that is on trial. While the quality of the Church's life-style in the world often strongly negates its message, alienated men are still seeking to establish the credibility of Jesus and demand of His followers: "Show me that you are redeemed and then I will believe in your Redeemer!" (quoted in Voelkel 1971:140).

It is encouraging that a growing number of "nominally" introverted Hispanic congregations are becoming notably less "sealed-off" from their communities as they attempt to follow the example of Jesus and give themselves in loving service to their neighbors in "authentic" evangelism and social action, rather than expending their creative energies exclusively in "soul winning" activities. A growing number of Hispanic pastors and laymen are beginning to seriously ask themselves important questions about their church's ministry: How can we *genuinely* demonstrate to our community the truth of the Christian message that we proclaim? How can we give *credible* testimony today to the life and ministry of Jesus--who *proclaimed* the "good news" of the Kingdom of God, *taught* the ethics and behavior required of those entering the Kingdom, and *healed* those who were "oppressed" as evidence of His sovereign authority and His loving compassion? What kind of life-style does our church need today in order to *demonstrate* to our community that Jesus is indeed the Lord and Savior of the world?

The openness to ask these kinds of questions usually results from an increasing awareness that getting a person to make "a decision for Christ" is *not the end but the beginning* of the process of discipleship (cf. Coleman 1963, *The Master Plan of Evangelism*). No doubt a troubled pastor's growing concern for the *kind* of disciples (cf. Kelley 1972:104) that he is making has led him to ask serious questions about his overall ministry, especially when the majority of his time is spent "oiling" the organizational machinery in his local church or trying to keep all the church leaders on speaking terms with one another, rather than in discipling men to Christ and in ministering to those with serious problems.

Through the process of serious biblical and sociological study and reflection, a concerned pastor can gain greater insight into the problems of "the introverted church" and can then confront one of the central problems of Christian ministry: how to disciple men to Jesus Christ rather than to a distorted religious subculture. This process of study and reflection will hopefully lead an increasing number of concerned pastors to weep with compassion over the needs of their "Jerusalem" as did Jesus, while at the same time seeking to develop a balanced strategy of "authentic" evangelism (discipling men to Jesus Christ) and liberating social action (changing unjust social structures as well as ministering to those suffering the effects of social injustice). This dual-strategy is a legitimate response to Jesus' command, not only to "love God" wholeheartedly and to seek to bring others to know and love Him, but also to "love your neighbor as yourself" by caring for our neighbor as a "whole" person--physically, psychologically, and socially as well as "spiritually" (cf. Luke 10: 25-37, NEB).

Evangelism and Church Growth. Returning to the sociological dimension, evangelistic activity, an indication of the commitment, discipline, and missionary zeal of members of a particular religious subsociety, usually results in the conversion of outsiders and the successful incorporation of some of the new converts into the "fellowship of believers", thus increasing the "social strength of that subsociety. Evangelism, however, as traditionally understood (i.e., proclaiming the Gospel of Christ for the purpose of making "disciples"), *may have a variety of results* depending on the advocate's concept of the Gospel, his ability to communicate the "message" (verbally and non-verbally--not only by "words" but also by actions and life-style), the predisposition of his hearers towards the message "received" (the meaning of the message as interpreted by the receptors), and the historical "moment" (the context) in which the communicative event takes place (cf. Tippett 1967:3-8).

The appeal of a specific "message" as understood by a specific individual in a specific historical context is conditioned by numerous factors, as we have already seen. However, if a local congregation or association of churches are experiencing significant membership growth, it means that some important aspects of their message and life-style are relevant for those who are being attracted to their particular religious subsociety (González 1969: 115-124). According to Justo González, in *The Development of Christianity in the Latin Caribbean*,

> ...relevance without growth is nonsense, both practically and theologically. Theologically, because the New Testament clearly shows that God's plans include the formation of a body of believers who give witness to him, but who also gather together to "break the bread," and to whom God adds "those who are to be saved." Any interpretation of the mission of the Church that has no room for this aspect of it implies a twisted understanding of the gospel itself. Practically, the claim to relevance without growth is nonsense because it is difficult to see how a body can be relevant to its situation and still not attract others who wish to join it, or at least hear its message (1969:116).

On the other hand, many nongrowing Hispanic churches are in a state of demoralization, of general stress and distortion, as they wrestle with problems concerning the credibility and relevance of their religious organizations. For some, the present struggles will lead to revitalization and renewal ("mazeway" reorientation), to increasing relevance and a meeting of felt-needs, while for others, the present demoralization is but a prelude to increasing disintegration, decline, and eventual death. González' observation concerning the problem of relevance among mainline ("historical") Protestant churches in the Caribbean area is equally true of the situation among some of the Protestant churches in the Los Angeles area:

> It is difficult to see how organizations so involved in institutional matters can be very relevant in a world that is so rapidly changing. Indeed, a large number of young people, driven to despair by their churches' irrelevance, have left them, often to join political parties of the radical left or simply to pursue their lives in a manner they take to be more relevant to the real problems of their people. Others are working within the Church seeking to lead it to take action on the crucial issues of our times. These, however, have often been led to bitter struggles with other church leaders, and the result has been an atmosphere of misunderstanding and mistrust that prevents the Church from growing, being relevant, or showing the nature of reconciliation. This divisive spirit has been heightened by the false alternative between church growth and relevance, so that in many instances whole churches are being polarized between groups that argue for one or the other. The tragedy of this situation is even greater if one takes into consideration that, once again, it turns the attention of the Church inwards, so that the question of growth and relevance often becomes a matter to be solved by inner ecclesiastical politics, and those who are concerned for church growth as well as those who are concerned for relevance find very little time or energy to devote to one or the other (Gonzalez 1969:122).

ANALYSIS OF HISPANIC PROTESTANT LEADERSHIP

The key to the future relevance of the Hispanic Protestant Church in metropolitan Los Angeles is the quality of her leaders and their commitment--both pastors and laymen, and through them the rank-and-file membership of each local church, in Spanish-speaking, bilingual, and English-speaking congregations--to "authentic" evangelism and liberating social action among the growing Hispanic American population. Introverted churches and ill-prepared leadership will continue to hinder the Hispanic Church from being a relevant voice and prophetic witness to the Lordship of Jesus Christ in the rapidly changing *barrios* of Los Angeles County, where the Hispanic minority is awakening from its oppressed condition and achieving greater participation and mobility within the "fragmented metropolis" that is America's third largest city. The role of Hispanic Protestant leaders as agents of directed change, within their religious subsocieties and within their local communities, must be seen in the context of the historical patterns of Hispanic leadership training, the crisis in Hispanic leadership that emerged in the 1950s and that continues to the present, the status of Hispanic leadership in Los Angeles County today, and emerging new forms of Hispanic leadership training.

Patterns of Hispanic Leadership Training

The first Hispanic pastors and evangelists in Southern California often were men with a high level of natural ability. They were chosen as leaders because of their gifts for ministry, and they were generally well-liked and respected by their congregations. Many had little formal education, but their gifts and devotion to "the work of the ministry" resulted in permanent accomplishments in terms of changed lives, organized congregations of believers, and the general progress of Hispanic ministry within their respective denominations.

The patterns of leadership training among the various Hispanic denominations have varied widely, but the major difference between groups has been the strong emphasis among mainline denominations for formal ministerial training, as opposed to the informal or "on-the-job" training that has characterized Pentecostal denominations and some of the smaller non-Pentecostal groups. This difference in emphasis was less true during the early stages of Hispanic church development, however.

Prior to 1920, the leadership pattern among the Northern Baptists was for new Spanish-speaking pastors to be trained by observing and duplicating the forms of worship, church administration, and pastoral ministry that they found in Anglo churches. This pattern of informal training is explained by Quinoñes:

> In the early days much of the [pastoral] training came through personal study and that which they could receive through the services in the Anglo church. The mission services were held on Sunday afternoon in Spanish. In the morning the Spanish-speaking pastor would attend the English-speaking church and from the English-speaking pastor he would receive the lesson for the Sunday School and would then stay for the worship service to listen to the sermon. The Sunday School gave him his teaching preparation and the sermon his theology. On Wednesday, he would attend Prayer Service in the English-speaking church and on Thursday he would assume the responsibility in his own church. This gave him training in administration and showed him the way to lead services (1966:22-23).

Evidently, the Methodists had a similar practical training program for Hispanic ministers, but with stronger tutelage by Anglo pastors and specific courses of instruction for each level of ministry. Under the supervision of an Anglo pastor, Methodist Spanish-speaking pastoral candidates progressed from being a licensed "local preacher", to ordination as a "deacon", and eventually to full pastoral ordination as an "elder" (*El Mexicano*

1917, Vol. 5, No. 4:4-5). The Presbyterians had a similar program of leadership training during this early period of Hispanic church development.

The flood of Mexican immigrants that poured into Southern California between 1910 and 1920 also produced a rapid increase in the membership of existing Spanish-speaking Protestant churches and missions, and led to the planting of many new congregations among the growing Mexican population. Concern for the pastoral needs of these growing churches led to the establishment of formal programs of leadership training by the Methodist Episcopal Church and the Northern Baptists during the early 1920s.

Two pastoral training programs were launched by the Methodists in Los Angeles County during 1920. The first one was the Bible Training Department at the Spanish American Institute in Gardena, initiated in January, and the other one was the Plaza Christian Training School at the Plaza Mexican Methodist Church in Los Angeles, which began in October. The training at Gardena was a residence program for the formal education of ministerial candidates who also served student pastorates on the weekends, whereas the Plaza Christian Training School was a part-time program of in-service training for pastors who were already serving on local circuits (*El Mexicano* Vol. IX, No. 1:5,12; *Journal of the Latin American Mission* 1922:19).

The Northern Baptists established the Spanish American Baptist Seminary in 1921, originally at El Salvador Baptist Church and Christian Center in Boyle Heights; and later, in 1930, it was housed in its own buildings farther east, on Indiana Avenue, in the Belvedere-Marvilla Park area. This seminary, as well as the Methodist training programs, accepted ministerial candidates with little or no formal education, gave them preparatory work, and assisted them through two to five years of formal ministerial training in theology, Christian education, and pastoral studies. These programs were geared to give prospective ministers, or those already serving in pastoral appointments, as much training as possible in the time available, and to send them forth to meet the leadership needs of rapidly growing numbers of Spanish-speaking churches and missions (cf. Leavenworth and Froyd 1954:5-9).

Despite these efforts to provide trained leadership for Spanish-speaking churches among the mainline denominations, the educational level of Hispanic pastors in the 1940s was still quite low. Grebler reports that a survey of 300 Baptist ministers in the Southwest during the late 1940s showed only twenty-five percent "who had received high school, college, or seminary training," while thirty percent "had received no education at all" (1970:495).

Leavenworth and Froyd's survey of the educational background of students entering the Spanish American Seminary between 1921 and 1952 revealed the following: thirty-three percent had elementary schooling but did not finish, another twenty-four percent were high school graduates, seven percent were graduates of Bible schools, and twelve percent had some college training (1954:8 and Table IV). Thus, at least fifty-seven percent of all entering students had less than a high school education.

Of 252 students admitted to the seminary between 1921 and 1952, fifty-eight percent (146) withdrew or were dropped, while the majority of those who stayed (67 students out of 106) went on to complete the four-year diploma program. However, out of the original 252 students, only twenty-six percent (66) entered the pastorate, while another ten percent (26) entered other kinds or religious work; forty-four percent (110) were employed in secular occupations (1954:8).

Looking at the other side of the picture, Leavenworth and Froyd reported that, out of seventy-seven Hispanic American Baptist pastors surveyed in the U.S., eleven (14%) only had Bible institute training, eighteen (23.4%) had received their training in seminaries other than the Spanish American Baptist Seminary, and forty-four (57%) were trained at the Los Angeles seminary. Evidently, about five percent of the pastors had received no formal ministerial training (1954:Table XII).

In respect to other denominations prior to the 1960s, the majority of Hispanic ministers of the Methodist Church were trained at the Bible institute level, either at the Spanish American Institute in Gardena, California or at the Lydia Patterson Institute in El Paso, Texas. Among the Pentecostals, the Assemblies of God established two Latin American Bible Institutes during 1926, one in San Antonio, Texas and the other in San Diego, California. The latter institute was later moved to La Mesa (1935), then to Los Angeles (1941), and finally to La Puente (1950), in eastern Los Angeles County.

Between 1926 and 1968, 180 students were graduated from the Latin American Bible Institute, with the majority of the graduates serving as pastors or other church workers--church officials, Sunday school teachers or department heads, Bible school workers, etc. Miranda conducted a survey of forty-seven graduates of the institute and found that fifteen (32%) were presently serving as pastors, three (6.4%) were assistant pastors, two (4.3%) were wives of pastors, and eight (17%) were "missionaries"; the other nineteen (40.4%) were lay workers in the churches (1969:21,29; Latin American Bible Institute 1970:9).

Prior to 1970, the only other training institutions in California for the preparation of Spanish-speaking ministers and Christian workers were: (1) the Apostolic Bible Training School of the Apostolic Assembly, established in 1949 at Hayward; (2) the Cladic Seminary of the Latin American Council of Christian Churches, founded in 1954 and located on Whittier Blvd. in East Los Angeles; and (3) the Evangelical Bible Institute in La Puente, established about 1960. The latter institute is an independent and interdenominational school affiliated with the Independent Fundamental Churches of America; it provides training for young people primarily from Mexico for evangelistic ministry in Mexico, with few workers being trained for Christian ministry in local Spanish-speaking churches, either as laymen or as pastors. Each institution requires a high school diploma for admission and offers a three-year ministerial course, as well as shorter courses for lay workers.

Since the Apostolic Bible Training School and the Cladic Seminary were the only pastoral training institutions of their respective denominations, it probably means that only a few of their ministers even have a Bible institute level education. However, the majority of laymen in Spanish-speaking churches probably have not finished high school, although a small number of lay leaders have completed special one or two-year courses in their respective Bible institutes.

The Pentecostal pattern of leadership recruitment and training appears to have some practical advantages over that of the mainline denominations which stress higher education for Hispanic ministers, although the requirements for ordination and service in most non-Pentecostal churches have been lower, until more recent times, for Hispanic pastors than for Anglos. For one thing, most of the Pentecostal congregations are composed of lower-class Mexican Americans who have little education, low paying jobs, and a slow rate of upward social mobility and acculturation. Candidates for the Pentecostal ministry are usually chosen because of their proven abilities and spiritual gifts, and not on the basis of completing a prescribed course of ministerial education that includes college and seminary. Many young pastoral candidates never complete their "formal" training in one of the Pentecostal Bible institutes or Bible colleges because they are called to pastor a church or to start a new mission during their course of study, and "serving the Lord" takes priority over formal preparation.

The strong familistic quality of Pentecostal congregations and the high level of commitment of church members, coupled with a heavy emphasis on tithing, means that the Pentecostal pastor is the spiritual leader of a church "family" that gives sacrificially to meet the financial needs of their pastor, the local church, and the evangelization of their neighbors. However, about fifty percent of the Pentecostal ministers supplement their church salaries by working in secular employment on a part-time or full-time basis, depending on what their family needs are. While this limits their time for pastoral ministry, it also brings them closer to the laymen of their congregations because they share common work situations and common experiences of sharing their faith in the laymen's world. This keeps many Pentecostal pastors from becoming a special ministerial "class" that is cut off from the common problems of their lay members, while they still receive the special "status" of being "a chosen servant of the Lord."

For most Pentecostal churches, there have been no Anglo church bodies from which to obtain salary supplements or loans for church development, although many Pentecostal groups are obviously growing in membership and new churches without outside funds. The mother-daughter relationship between older congregations and younger churches and missions means that resources of personnel, funds, and materials are shared to stimulate the growth and development of newer congregations. The rising income level of some Pentecostal churches has also helped to stimulate growth by making more resources available for church development, including many new church buildings.

This, of course, is not to suggest that one pattern of leadership training is "better" than another, but rather to point out that the leadership patterns of various Hispanic churches are "different" based on socioeconomic and acculturation variables, and on the status and role models of different denominations. It should be noted that significant differences also exist between Pentecostal groups in terms of the educational level of their ministers, with the Assemblies of God and Foursquare ministers showing a higher level of academic training. These two groups are among the few Hispanic Pentecostal denominations that have formal ties to Anglo denominational structures, and no doubt that Anglo influence has raised the academic aspirations of their Spanish-speaking pastors.

The Crisis in Hispanic Leadership

Beginning in the 1950s and continuing to the present, a serious crisis has existed in Hispanic church leadership, which has revealed itself in two important dimensions: first, many Hispanic pastors are poorly trained academically; and secondly, many Hispanic churches are not recruiting and training enough new pastors for their existing churches. For example, among the American Baptists in the mid-1950s, many pastors were discouraged by their poor church salaries, the necessity of having to work part-time or full-time in secular employment to provide for their families, and the unlikely prospect of being called to pastor one of the larger, more "rewarding" (financially, as well as spiritually and socially) congregations of their denomination.

In response to the question, "Why are the Spanish-speaking churches in this country failing to produce for the ministry?" Leavenworth and Froyd found that, among American Baptists,

> ...the most frequently mentioned deterrents to the ministry were the bleak salary prospects and the attitudes of the present ministry. As to prospects for improvement of the salary situation, the ministers feel trapped. Where their relations to the denomination do not prevent it, the almost universal practice is to get jobs on the side. The "best" churches are held by men who are "hanging on" to them. This situation is common conversation among adults and can't be prevented from filtering down to young people. Observing how ministers and their families had to live, young people repeatedly said they wanted none of it.
>
> Perhaps even more serious than the economic deterrent is the negative attitude of the ministers themselves. A ceiling seems to have settled over the outlook of many. They have lost heart about reproducing their kind. Many actually seek to dampen the appearance of any enthusiasm about the ministry.... This problem of morale among ministers about their work was found to be acute and widespread (1954:27-28).

This general state of demoralization, not only among American Baptist Hispanic pastors but also among most mainline Protestant denominations, has been due to: (1) the isolation of their small, struggling congregations from Anglo American society in general, and specifically from the Anglo Protestant churches of their respective denominations; and (2) the leadership drain that has continued to rob Spanish-speaking churches of members who are achieving more education and acculturation, improving their economic status, moving into better houses and neighborhoods, and joining Anglo churches. The increasing acculturation differences between Spanish-speaking parents and their English-speaking children create severe intergenerational conflicts and often lead to an exodus of the more acculturated members from the Spanish-speaking churches. Grebler quotes a Baptist spokesman as saying:

> Transfer from a Spanish-speaking congregation to an English-speaking congregation means they are lost in a sense to our Spanish ministry and church. And these are the people we need because they are the leadership

> material.... One of our main problems is the recruitment and training of able personnel for our pastorate.... Most of them are born in Mexico or another country in Latin America. Very few native-born Americans have become ministers in our Spanish-speaking churches (1970:497).

The continuing problem of pastoral recruitment is verified by the author's survey of thirty Hispanic American Baptist pastors in Los Angeles County in 1971, which showed the following differences in nationality: Argentina, 2 (6.7%); Costa Rica, 1 (3.3%); Cuba, 9 (30%); Guatemala, 1 (3.3%); Mexico, 12 (40%); Mexican-American, 4 (13.3%); and Puerto Rico, 1 (3.3%). Obviously, the recruitment and training of Mexican American ministers for predominantly Mexican American, Spanish-speaking congregations in the Los Angeles area has been a serious problem, at least for the American Baptists, and no doubt for other groups as well.

The Status of Hispanic Leadership in 1970

A broader picture of the status of Hispanic American leadership, based on responses to questionnaires sent by the author, in July 1970, to 188 Spanish-speaking churches in Los Angeles County, reveals the following information on the age, nationality, education, and pastoral training and experience of twenty-seven Hispanic American pastors who were distributed among seventeen denominations (the size of the sample was 14.4%): the average age of the pastors was 42.6 years (median age was 44.5 years); their place of birth was the United States (44%), Mexico (26%), and other Latin American countries (33%); the level of education showed that twenty-two percent had not completed high school (or *secundaria* in Latin America), while seventy-four percent were high school graduates; thirty-three percent of the pastors were graduated from both a college and Bible institute (11%), or a college and seminary (22%); the number of Bible institute graduates was thirty percent, college graduates fifty-six percent, and seminary graduates thirty-seven percent (possibility of multiple answers); the location of training received above the high school level was Los Angeles and vicinity (33.3%), California--including Los Angeles and vicinity (40%), Texas (8%), other states (24%), Cuba and Argentina (8% each), and Mexico, Puerto Rico, and Brazil each with four percent; the average number of years in the pastorate was 15.7 years, the average number of years as pastor of their present church was seven years, and the number of pastors who had been in the same church for their entire pastoral experience was thirty-three percent.

In terms of ministerial employment and salary sources, the following data was obtained from the 1970 survey: sixty-two percent were full-time pastors, twenty-two percent were part-time pastors who also worked part-time in secular employment, four percent were employed full-time in secular work and served as part-time pastors, and eight percent were retired or otherwise self-supporting and pastored their church on a part-time basis without salary; fifty-nine percent of the pastors received no salary subsidies of any kind, while forty-one percent received part or all of their salary from denominational sources.

The author's 1970 survey also revealed the following specific information concerning Pentecostal ministers (size of sample was 15%): the average age was forty-seven years (median age was 45.5 years); the nativity status was the United States (58.3%), Mexico (25%), and Puerto Rico (16.6%), with no Cuban or other Latin American origin emerging in the sample; 33.3 percent had not completed their high school education, whereas 66.6 percent were high school graduates; 8.3 percent had no formal training for the ministry and another 8.3 percent had some Bible institute training, although they had not graduated; half of the pastors were graduates of Bible institutes, with 16.7 percent having been graduated from both a Bible institute and a Bible college, while another 33.3 percent were *only* Bible college graduates; fifty percent of the pastors were employed full-time by their churches and received 100 percent of their salary from the local church; twenty-five percent of the pastors worked part-time in secular employment while also receiving a small salary from the local church, whereas 8.3 percent had part-time jobs in addition to their pastoral responsibilities and received salary subsidies from their denominations; and, in conclusion, 16.6 percent of the pastors were self-supporting, usually retired men who were living on Social Security, and donated part of their time to pastoral work without receiving a formal salary from the local church.

Figure 58 compares Pentecostal ministerial data with that of all Hispanic pastors in the 1970 sample, in terms of age, nativity, education, type of employment and salary source. Whereas seventy percent of all Hispanic pastors were between the ages of 30-49, only 57.4 percent of the Pentecostals were found in this age group; the number of pastors under forty years of age was twenty-five percent of the Pentecostals, compared to thirty-three percent of all ministers. The Pentecostals had a higher percentage of Mexican American pastors than did non-Pentecostal groups, about the same percentage of Mexican-born pastors, and far fewer ministers from other Latin American countries.

In respect to educational attainment and salary sources, fewer of the Pentecostal ministers were high school graduates, and none of the Pentecostals in the sample had received the "standard" seven years of preparation that many mainline Protestant denominations require. On the other hand, many Anglo pastors in English-

Figure 58

HISPANIC MINISTERIAL SURVEY
LOS ANGELES COUNTY
1970

Age of Ministers:

Age	% Pent.	% All	Compared to % Am. Bapt. Pastors in 1954*
20-29	8.3	4	16.2
30-39	16.7	29	5.4
40-49	41.7	41	46.0
50-59	8.3	11	24.3
60+	25.0	15	8.1
Median age:	45.5	44.5	46.0
Average age:	47.0	42.6	-

Nativity of Ministers:

	Pent.	Al
% U.S.	58.3	41.
% Mexican	25.0	26.
% Other	16.6	33.

Ministerial Training:

Pentecostal	All	
33.3%	26.0%	Less than High School
66.7	74.0	Completed High School
50.0	29.6	Bible Institute graduate
50.0	55.6	College graduate
16.7	11.1	Bible Institute and College
-	37.0	Seminary graduate
-	22.2	College and Seminary
16.7	11.1	No formal ministerial training

Type Employment and Salary Source:

Pentecostal	All	
50.0%	38.0%	Part-time church
50.0	62.0	Full-time church
8.3	41.0	Received denominational subsidy
91.7	59.0	No denominational subsidy

Source: Responses from 27 Hispanic pastors in Los Angeles County, July-October 1970; 17 denominations represented (sample size was 14.4% based on 188 questionnaires sent out).

*Leavenworth and Froyd 1954:Table XI.

speaking Pentecostal denominations, or in many of the smaller non-Pentecostal groups, only have a Bible institute or Bible college-level education. Denominational salary subsidies were almost nonexistent among Hispanic Pentecostal ministers, but a higher percentage of the Pentecostals served their churches on a part-time basis and worked either part-time or full-time in secular employment.

In terms of lay leadership training, the 1970 survey revealed that about fifty-five percent of the Hispanic churches either had leadership training courses in their local churches or participated in denominational or interdenominational leadership institutes, such as those that have been sponsored by the Greater Los Angeles Sunday School Association. Of the eighteen Spanish-speaking churches that reported lay leadership training during the period July 1969 to July 1970, an average of 8.3 persons per church received this training, or a total of 150 people. However, it was not known whether the language of instruction was Spanish or English, nor the quality of the instruction received.

New Forms of Leadership Training

Whether the Hispanic Church continues to maintain a "mentality of survival", or whether she confronts the problems of the *barrios* and becomes a prophetic witness to the Lordship of Christ, will largely be determined by the awareness, attitudes, and commitment of her leaders. The type of training that church leaders receive today and in the near future is of crucial importance in producing a new state of awareness, new attitudes, and new commitment to biblical priorities and to meeting the multitude of felt-needs among the Hispanic American population. The challenge for the Hispanic Church is to engage herself in "authentic" mission and service among those whose mother tongue is Spanish.

Recent Trends and Problems in Ministerial Training. From the late 1950s to the early 1970s, a younger generation of Hispanic ministers within mainline denominations, often aided by scholarship funds, have usually been trained in a similar manner as have Anglo ministers; that is, they have completed four or more years of college or university training and three to five years of graduate-level studies in theological seminaries. The majority of their classroom instruction was given by Anglo professors and was often geared to the middle-class Anglo student. However, since the late 1960s, some of the younger ministers have taken courses in the growing number of Mexican American studies centers in Southern California.

The younger Hispanic ministers have usually received their seminary training at one or more of the following institutions: Methodist pastors have normally attended either Perkins

Theological Seminary at Southern Methodist University in Texas, or the School of Theology at Claremont, California (this school was formerly located at the University of Southern California and is now jointly operated with the Disciples Seminary Foundation). American Baptist students usually have attended California Baptist Seminary (now, the American Baptist Seminary of the West) at Covina, or, until 1964 when the school was closed, some students were trained at the Spanish American Baptist Seminary in East Los Angeles. There are no other denominational seminaries in the Los Angeles area, although two interdenominational institutions are in existence which have no doubt trained a few Hispanic American ministers: Fuller Theological Seminary in Pasadena and Talbot Theological Seminary in La Mirada.

Somewhere in the course of their college or university training, some of the Hispanic American students decided to enter the Christian ministry and followed through with this decision by attending and graduating from a theological seminary, in addition to completing other denominational requirements for ordination. After being ordained to the ministry, they were called or assigned to a local congregation, usually as pastor of an autonomous Hispanic congregation or as an assistant pastor in charge of a Spanish-speaking department in an Anglo church; only a few Hispanic pastors have been called to serve as senior pastors of Anglo churches, although some are serving in multi-racial and multi-ethnic churches, usually in the inner-city.

The present crisis in Hispanic leadership training is that no accredited seminary program exists in the Los Angeles area (as of October 1973) that is geared to the specific needs of Spanish-speaking or bilingual ministry. Consequently, many of the younger Hispanic American pastors feel that much of their course work was largely irrelevant to their present ministry, as do the few black pastors who have been trained in these same programs. Not only that, but many of the younger Anglo pastors also feel that their seminary courses were not geared for relevant and practical ministry, in terms of the problems they are now facing in their churches and communities.

Many young Hispanic ministers have an awakened social conscience and are impatient for meaningful change, whereas most of the older ministers have learned to live with the Anglo Establishment and generally support the *status quo*. Some Hispanic ministers, often younger men and usually from the mainline denominations, have become discouraged with the slowness of change from within their churches, and have committed themselves and their talents to the *Chicano* civil rights movement. By contrast, Reies Tijerina, one of the well-known radical leaders in the *Chicano* movement is a former Pentecostal minister who left his church after falling into disfavor with his denominational brethren

(Galvan 1969:117). On the other hand, a number of Hispanic ministers from mainline denominations are active both as church and community leaders; this dual activity is notably less true of ministers in the smaller non-Pentecostal denominations or of Pentecostal pastors (1969:118-120).

New Proposals and Prospects for Ministerial Education. Beginning in 1969 and continuing to the present, several new programs of Hispanic leadership training have been proposed, but none has yet been implemented at the graduate seminary level. As early as November 1969, J. Richard Acosta, director of the Spanish-American Institute (United Methodist) in Gardena, proposed a new future for the Institute, a center of Latin American Churchmanship, which would concern itself with the recruitment and training of Hispanic pastors for United Methodist congregations, the retraining of newly arrived Latin American pastors who need orientation to the local situation, and training institutes and conferences for Hispanic laymen (Acosta 1969:1-4).

The Hispanic Urban Center in Los Angeles, proposed in 1970 and established in 1971, is sponsored by the American Baptist Convention and is under the directorship of the Rev. Vahac Mardirosian. The Center was to develop an accredited college-level supplementary program for public school teachers, as well as a program of biblical and religious studies, leading to a B.A. degree in the sponsoring institution, probably Occidental College. Candidates for the ministry were expected to take their major course work at the sponsoring college or university, while also taking the supplementary program at the Hispanic Urban Center. "It was the expectation that the person receiving this type of education would be able to step into a pastorate in one of the Hispanic churches of the American Baptist Convention" (Mercado 1971:2). In addition, the Center was to develop a program of in-service training for pastors already serving in Hispanic churches.

The long-range plan was to eventually offer courses on both the under-graduate level and the graduate level in cooperation with accredited graduate schools and seminaries. Unfortunately, the proposed biblical and religious studies program has not yet been developed, although the supplementary program for public school teachers was initiated during the school year 1971-1972.

Several events that occured during 1972 and 1973 are encouraging signs that an accredited program of Hispanic theological education may soon become a reality in the Los Angeles area. In the first place, early in 1972, the Spanish Evangelical Theological Society of the U.S.A. (*Sociedad Teológica Evangélica Hispana*) was established with Ismael E. Amaya as president, H. O. Espinoza as secretary, and C. Peter Wagner as advisor, all of whom are residents of Southern California. This organization is affiliated with *La Fraternidad Teológica Latinoamericana*, and its purpose is to stimulate theological studies and interaction among Hispanic Americans (Espinoza 1972).

Secondly, in July 1972, the Latin American Biblical Seminary of San José, Costa Rica, following up on the success of its regional center and extension seminary program in New York City (January-March 1972), sent Dr. George Gay to the Los Angeles area to explore the possibilities of establishing a similar regional center and extension program. Initial reports from Dr. Gay indicated that there was wide-spread interest among Hispanic pastors for a program of interdenominational theological studies, and that the pastors were favorable to the idea because of the Latin American Biblical Seminary's "strongly evangelical" reputation and because of the seminary's past and present role in training pastors from all over Latin America (Gay 1973a:1-5).

Thirdly, in October 1973, an "*ad hoc* committee on theological education" for Hispanic Americans, under the chairmanship of H. O. Espinoza, was formed in Los Angeles following the visit of the Rev. Cecilio Arrastía of New York City, who has been commissioned by the American Association of Theological Schools (AATS) to study the need for Hispanic theological education throughout the United States. This study has not yet been completed, but the *ad hoc* committee planned to have "a formal and serious consultation" on theological education for Hispanic pastors and laymen of the greater Los Angeles area during February 1974 (Gay 1973c:1).

Finally, the possibility exists that Fuller Theological Seminary in Pasadena may establish a program for Hispanic pastors, "within the next few years," similar to their present program for black pastors. The present program includes a year of pre-theological orientation in black studies before students begin the regular theological program, which leads to the M.A. degree (Gay 1973b:1).

Hopefully, some combination of the aforementioned programs for the recruitment and training of new Hispanic pastors, for the re-orientation of Latin American ministers who have relocated in Southern California, and for the in-service training of local Hispanic pastors will soon be a reality. Denominational as well as interdenominational programs are necessary if the leadership needs of the Hispanic Church are to be met, and if new Hispanic congregations are to be established in the Los Angeles area in proportion to the rapidly growing Hispanic population that numbered 1.2 million in 1970.

Guidelines for Future Leadership Training Programs. Future programs of Hispanic leadership training must take into consideration the diverse needs of the heterogeneous Hispanic American population in Los Angeles County, the need for various levels and types of leadership education, the diversity that exists among the various Hispanic Protestant congregations and their denominational families, and the changing religious environment in the *barrios* of Los Angeles because of the renewal taking place within the Roman Catholic Church since the Second Vatican Council, including the growing Catholic Charismatic Movement (cf. Ranaghan 1969, *Catholic Charismatics*).

In terms of the levels and types of Hispanic leadership training, future programs should: (1) make provision for training *both* pastors and laymen at various educational levels--high school, Bible institute, junior college, college or university, and post-graduate; (2) train Christian leaders for bilingual and bicultural ministries--*fluency* must be developed in *both* Spanish and English; (3) train Christian workers *both* for church-directed and community-directed ministries, including community organization and development; and (4) train Christian workers for church-related ministries, denominational and interdenominational, and for para-ecclesiastical and non-denominational ministries (e.g. student ministries, such as Young Life, Campus Life, Inter-Varsity Christian Fellowship, Campus Crusade for Christ, etc.).

The training of Christian workers for church-directed ministries should receive top priority in future program development because the revitalization and renewal of local congregations hangs in the balance.* Included in this category of leadership training are many vital areas: (1) leaders for "small groups" within the local church (cf. Reid 1969, *Groups Alive--Church Alive*), including discipleship groups (cf. Trueblood 1961, *The Company of the Committed*; Coleman 1963, *The Master Plan of Evangelism*) and "body life" ministries (cf. Stedman 1972, *Body Life*); (2) teachers, helpers, and advisors for the church's Christian education program--children, youth, and adults; and (3) advisors, teachers, and group leaders for a creative program of lay ministries through the local church, which should include evangelism, church planting, and action groups for social involvement (cf. Hodges 1973; Gerber 1973; McGavran and Win 1973; and Sexton 1965).

Past leadership training institutes and conferences for Hispanic pastors and laymen have only touched the surface of the

---

*Community-directed ministries must not be neglected; but at the same time, a proper base must be built for social action ministries as part of the revitalization process, especially in terms of "mazeway" reorientation and the incarnational dimension of church growth.

existing needs or of the possibilities for creative leadership development. In May 1969, a Spanish Church Growth Seminar was held at Fuller Theological Seminary in Pasadena, sponsored by the Institute of Church Growth at the Seminary, and with church leaders from many Spanish-speaking groups participating. The following problems in Hispanic church life were discussed: the church location, multiple nationalities, language differences, the generation gap, leadership development, theological education, the spirit of rebellion in our time, the social dimension, and the bicultural church, in addition to the principles and dynamics of church growth itself.

During a series of four Tuesday evenings between February 23, and March 16, 1971, an "Academia de Capacitación Teológica", sponsored by the Congress on Hispanic American Ministries (COHAM) of the National Council of Churches, was held at *Iglesia Bautista Park Vista* in East Los Angeles. The program included a general conference session each evening and a series of five elective classes taught by church leaders from mainline denominations on the following themes: "The Theology of Hope", "Christian Education for Today", "Urban Ministries", "Youth and the New Spirituality", "the Church and Social Problems", and "The Layman and His Church".

Beginning in 1971, Campus Crusade for Christ International, with headquarters in San Bernardino, California, began to develop a "Minorities Lay Ministry" program to train black and brown church leaders in the following areas: (1) how to live an abundant Christian life; (2) how to effectively share Jesus Christ with members of your family, friends and neighbors; (3) how to train other laymen in your church; and (4) how to evangelize each neighborhood in each community through the members of the local churches after they are trained. Lay Institutes for Evangelism have been held at Arrowhead Springs and in local Hispanic churches, both in English and in Spanish, to mobilize Hispanic pastors and laymen in spontaneous and planned evangelism within their churches and neighborhoods.

In November 1970, the Greater Los Angeles Sunday School Association (GLASS) included Spanish-speaking general conferences and workshops in its convention program, which was held at the First Baptist Church of Van Nuys. A small turn-out was reported at these special Spanish-speaking training sessions, although other Hispanic church leaders and teachers attended the regular English-speaking meetings. Since the majority of the Sunday school classes for children and youth within the Hispanic churches of Los Angeles County are in English, with only the adult classes using Spanish, the problem of low attendance in the Spanish-speaking workshops is understandable. On the other hand, many Hispanic churches have a hard time finding enough qualified bilingual or English-speaking teachers and counsellors for children's and youth ministries.

Obviously, more pre-study, discussion, planning, and promotion are required if future Christian education workshops are to speak to the educational and leadership needs of Hispanic churches: (1) a thorough study is needed of Christian education problems among the churches of Los Angeles County, especially in terms of language and acculturation levels among the churches (see Gaxiola's discussion of language and acculturation problems within the Apostolic Assembly, 1970:165-170); (2) the future large-scale training of Hispanic leadership will probably be more effective on a regional institute basis, where training sessions are held one night each week for four to six weeks, rather than at the three-day annual GLASS convention because of transportation, cost, and time problems; (3) to really do the job, a bilingual team of educational consultants and workshop leaders should be formed on an interdenominational basis to hold city-wide institutes for ten to twelve neighboring churches, either for a week-long series of evening sessions or for four or five consecutive Monday or Tuesday evenings, for example; and (4) the regional or area institutes will be much easier to promote, should result in a higher percentage of participation from local churches, and ought to produce a significant change in the quality, enthusiasm, and effectiveness of Christian education programs in local Hispanic churches.

THE HISPANIC CHURCH TOMORROW

Since each Hispanic congregation and their respective denominations or subsocieties exist in the tension between stability and change, disintegration and revitalization, the future relevance and growth of these churches will depend upon the ability of church leaders--both pastors and laymen--to make adaptive changes within their religious subsocieties to meet the changing felt-needs of their members, while keeping stress and distortion to a minimum. Church leaders in subsocieties that are currently experiencing general stress and distortion must gain a greater understanding of the various "techniques"* for reducing stress

*Because there are a great many "stress producing" situations among Hispanic churches, only a few examples will be given here to illustrate "stress reducing" techniques: study and reflection groups to aid "mazeway" reorientation, open discussion sessions to "clear the air", organic restructuring to permit greater flexibility and creative development of leadership models and roles, action groups working out problem-solving strategies for greater community involvement, etc.

and meeting felt-needs; they must aid the process of "mazeway" reformulation so that church members come to a new understanding of the priorities of scripture--the Lordship and Saviorhood of Jesus Christ; the nature and mission of the Church; the ministry and gifts of the Holy Spirit; the role of pastoral leadership, of the laity, and of the local "fellowship of believers" in the missionary plan of God--and to a new commitment to Jesus Christ, to fellow members of the Body of Christ, and to their local communities as agents of reconciliation and liberation.

The turning point in the lives of many discouraged church leaders has often come with the awakening realization that the church is not an end in itself, that the church does not exist for itself, but that *"the church exists for the world"* (Come 1964:19). Justo González expressed it this way:

> The object of Christian proclamation is not to pull people out of the society in which they have been placed by God, but rather to reconcile them with God and their neighbors so that the will of God may be done in that society (1969:115-116).

The Church of Christ, by her very nature as the *community of the reconciled*, has been sent into the world by Christ as a *reconciling community* to "declare the wonderful deeds of Him who called [us] out of darkness into His marvellous light" (I Peter 2:9), out of alienation into true fellowship with God and man, and to call men out of that same darkness and alienation into fellowship with God and with their neighbors (cf. Blauw 1962:126-136). The congregation-in-mission is a body of Jesus' disciples who accept their commission as "agents of reconciliation" and who go forth to risk their lives, as did Jesus, in ministry to the world, so that men may *know* and *do* the will of God.

The Hispanic congregation, in particular, must be a congregation-in-mission within the *barrios* of Los Angeles County and the Southwest. Rather than continuing as a backward-looking, introverted organism with a "mentality of survival" and committed to cultural and religious conservatism (to the socio-religious *statu quo*), the Hispanic congregation must develop a new self-image as a "reconciling community" and commit herself to "authentic" evangelism and liberating social action. She must not remain isolate from and indifferent to the problems and frustrations of the *barrios*, but rather she must risk her very life to demonstrate the reality of the message she proclaims: "Jesus Christ is Lord". The Hispanic Church must become a culturally relevant vehicle for carrying the freedom and power of the Lordship of Christ to the heterogeneous Hispanic population of the Southwest, that is now slowly emerging from a state of socioeconomic and political oppression in search of equal opportunity and self-determination.

Appendix I.

Hispanic Population Changes in Los Angeles County: 1960-1970

Figure A

SSN POPULATION
LOS ANGELES COUNTY, 1960

District and City*	% SSN	Number SSN
Central Los Angeles District	24.9	201,340
Boyle Heights	66.8	50,140
Downtown	14.9	3,870
East Los Angeles	67.1	70,765
El Sereno	37.4	11,025
Elysian Park	32.5	7,950
Highland Park	7.7	2,595
Hollywood	5.1	4,275
Lincoln Heights	56.9	17,865
Mt. Washington	34.5	5,225
Silver Lake	7.3	1,800
Westlake	14.9	10,340
Wholesale	37.4	5,990
Wilshire	5.4	3,595
South-Central District	9.6	79,010
Bell, Bell Gardens	7.8	5,205
Central	17.0	3,610
Compton, Willowbrook	10.7	6,620
East Compton	9.7	5,365
East Inglewood	6.7	2,980
Exposition Park	8.5	4,890
Florence, Graham	17.8	12,200
Huntington Park, Maywood	5.2	2,830
Santa Barbara	10.0	5,905
So. Vermont, Greenmeadows	12.8	11,150
University	27.7	5,755
Watts	8.8	6,355
Harbor District	9.5	35,005
Dominguez	11.2	6,630
East Torrance	7.7	3,700
San Pedro	9.6	3,290
Wilmington	29.3	16,790
Long Beach District	3.7	18,960
Artesia, Dairy Valley	17.7	2,390
Hawaiian Gardens	13.1	2,075
Paramount	9.1	2,480
Terminal Island	14.5	260
West Long Beach	6.1	1,840
Southwest District	3.7	18,670
Lawndale	9.0	2,000
Leimert	5.6	2,425
Redondo Beach	5.8	2,825

*Partial listing based on communities with greater than 5.0% SSN population

District and City	% SSN	Number SSN
West District	5.1	23,260
South Santa Monica	9.2	4,410
Venice, Del Rey	12.0	7,505
West Los Angeles	8.2	3,430
San Fernando Valley District	6.1	46,390
Canoga Park	5.8	3,260
Mission Hills	8.9	2,840
Pacoima	25.9	10,235
Panorama City	5.2	2,400
San Fernando	31.5	5,070
Sunland	5.2	1,530
Sun Valley	7.2	2,460
Sylmar	8.6	2,725
Verdugo Hills District	4.2	11,905
Atwater, Glassel	13.3	4,795
Foothill District	2.9	9,410
Central Pasadena	8.3	2,600
Monrovia	5.1	2,440
San Gabriel Valley District	10.1	27,310
Alhambra	5.8	3,180
El Monte	14.7	9,870
Monterey Park	13.1	4,695
Rosemead	7.6	1,200
San Gabriel	15.5	3,490
So. San Gabriel	15.0	3,930
East San Gabriel Valley District	9.6	28,930
Azusa	17.8	6,040
Baldwin Park	12.4	4,560
Covina Highlands	5.1	1,480
Industry	12.7	3,400
La Puente	23.5	9,270
Rio Hondo District	12.6	55,225
La Mirada-Santa Fe Springs	12.9	12,200
Montebello	22.6	7,255
Norwalk	14.9	13,250
Pico Rivera	29.7	14,600
Pomona District	9.2	9,630
Claremont, La Verne	9.7	2,700
Pomona	9.0	6,915
Los Angeles County total	9.6	576,700

Sources: Welfare Planning Council 1965; U.S. Census of Population (1960), Final Report PC (2)-1B, 1963

Figure B

SPANISH SURNAME PUPIL ENROLLMENT
LOS ANGELES COUNTY SCHOOL DISTRICTS[a]
1970

	District	No. SSN enrollment 1970	Percent SSN enrollment 1970	Increase in no. SSN enrollment 1966-1970
2	Alhambra City Elementary	4,522[b]	25.5[b]	257[c]
17	East Whittier City Elem.	1,325	12.6	287
18	El Monte Elementary	3,463	34.5	1,155
21	Garvey Elementary	3,590	53.4	987
35	Lawndale Elementary	1,228	19.5	528
36	Lennox Elementary	720	24.2	102[d]
37	Little Lake City Elem.	1,812	28.1	160
39	Los Nietos Elementary	1,884	69.6	-183
43	Mountain View Elementary	3,114	50.8	752
54	Rosemead Elementary	648	24.0	183
	Rowland Elementary	3,097[b]	23.2[b]	977[c]
57	San Gabriel Elementary	938	23.2	279
61	So. Whittier Elementary	1,305	29.6	422
64	Valle Lindo Elementary	717	57.8	174
68	Whittier City Elementary	2,356	37.9	759
101	Alhambra H.S. District	2,730	28.9	*e*
109	El Monte Union H.S.	2,464	34.1	244[d]
	La Puente High School	2,813[b]	23.0[b]	*e*
117	Whittier Union H.S.	3,172	21.9	99[d]
U- 3	Burbank Unified	1,512	10.0	341
U- 7	Glendale Unified	2,209	8.8	952
U- 8	Long Beach Unified	4,243	6.1	910
U- 9	Lynwood Unified	1,737	20.1	933
U-10	Montebello Unified	13,600	52.4	1,694
U-15	Bonita Unified	1,125	14.8	290
U-17	Paramount Unified	1,946	19.2	775
U-18	Pomona Unified	3,925	17.2	599
U-19	Santa Monica Unified	1,750	12.3	544
U-21	Baldwin Park Unified	4,494	34.8	955
U-24	West Covina Unified	1,214	9.0	302
U-25	Azusa Unified	3,381	26.4	237
U-27	Duarte Unified	869	16.8	362
U-29	Los Angeles Unified	141,450	22.0	3,240
U-32	Pasadena Unified	2,666	9.2	618
U-34	El Rancho Unified	9,602	66.8	116[d]
U-35	Bassett Unified	3,749	43.2	496
U-37	Norwalk-La Mirada Unified	7,183	22.8	533[d]
U-38	ABC Unified	3,934	21.4	659
U-39	Compton Unified	4,462[e]	11.4	518[c]
U-41	Rowland Unified	3,851	26.0	*e*
U-42	Hacienda-La Puente Unified	8,579	28.4	*e*
	Hudson Unified	5,747[b]	28.4[b]	860[c]
	TOTAL: Los Angeles County	279,521	19.1	60,638

Notes: [a]Selected districts based on percent of SSN enrollment or numerical increase in SSN enrollment 1966-1970

[b]1969
[c]1966-1969
[d]1969-1970
[e]District Change

Source: Los Angeles County Board of Education 1966-1971

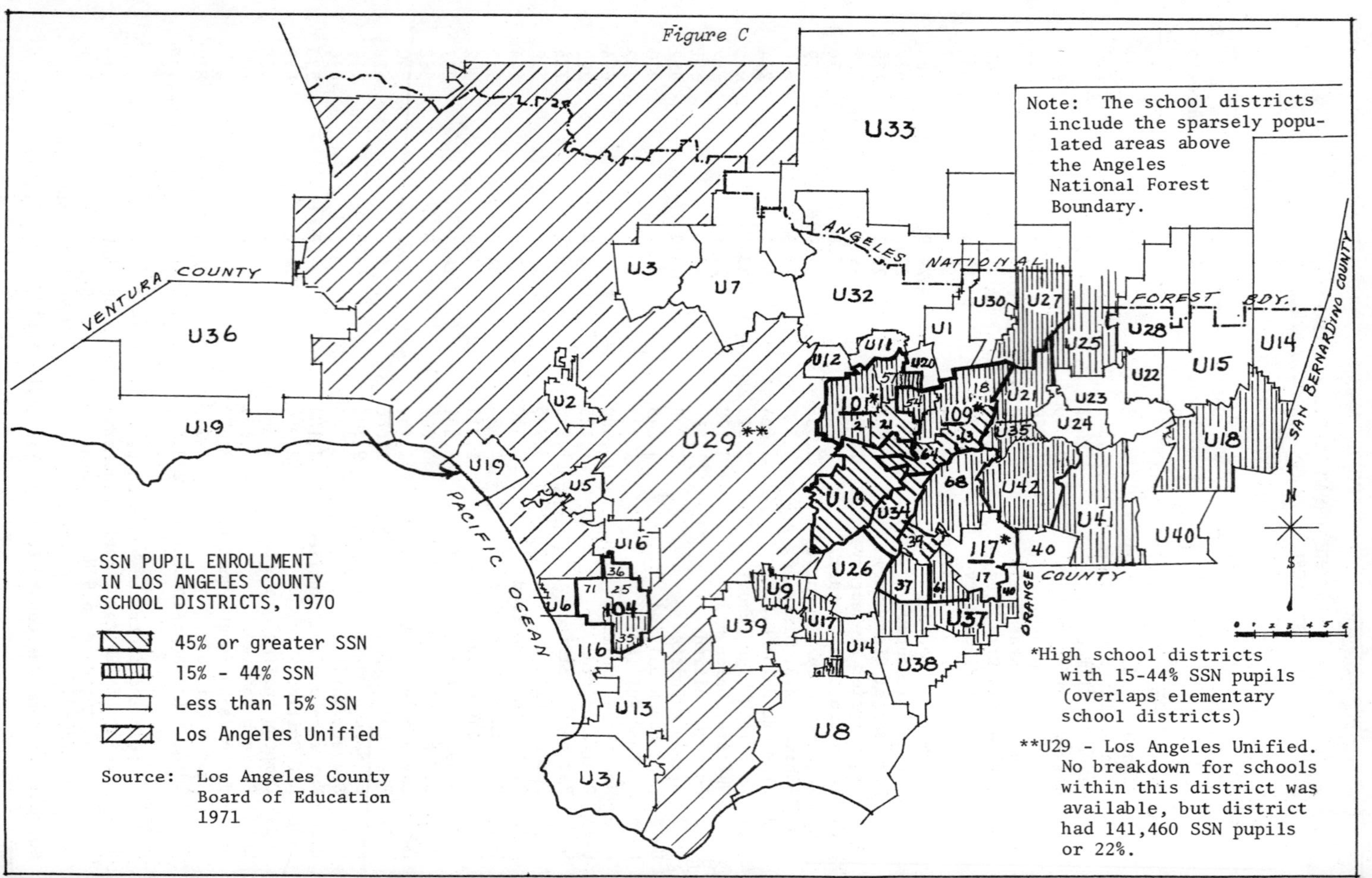
Figure C
Note: The school districts include the sparsely populated areas above the Angeles National Forest Boundary.
VENTURA COUNTY
SAN BERNARDINO COUNTY
ORANGE COUNTY
ANGELES NATIONAL FOREST BDY.
PACIFIC OCEAN
U36
U19
U33
U3
U7
U32
U2
U5
U29**
U16
U6
116
U13
U31
U12
U11
U20
U1
U30
U27
U25
U28
U22
U15
U14
U18
U21
U23
U24
U35
101*
109*
117*
U10
U34
68
U42
U41
U40
40
U26
U9
U17
U14
U39
U38
U37
U8
104
SSN PUPIL ENROLLMENT IN LOS ANGELES COUNTY SCHOOL DISTRICTS, 1970
45% or greater SSN
15% - 44% SSN
Less than 15% SSN
Los Angeles Unified
Source: Los Angeles County Board of Education 1971
*High school districts with 15-44% SSN pupils (overlaps elementary school districts)
**U29 - Los Angeles Unified. No breakdown for schools within this district was available, but district had 141,460 SSN pupils or 22%.

Figure D

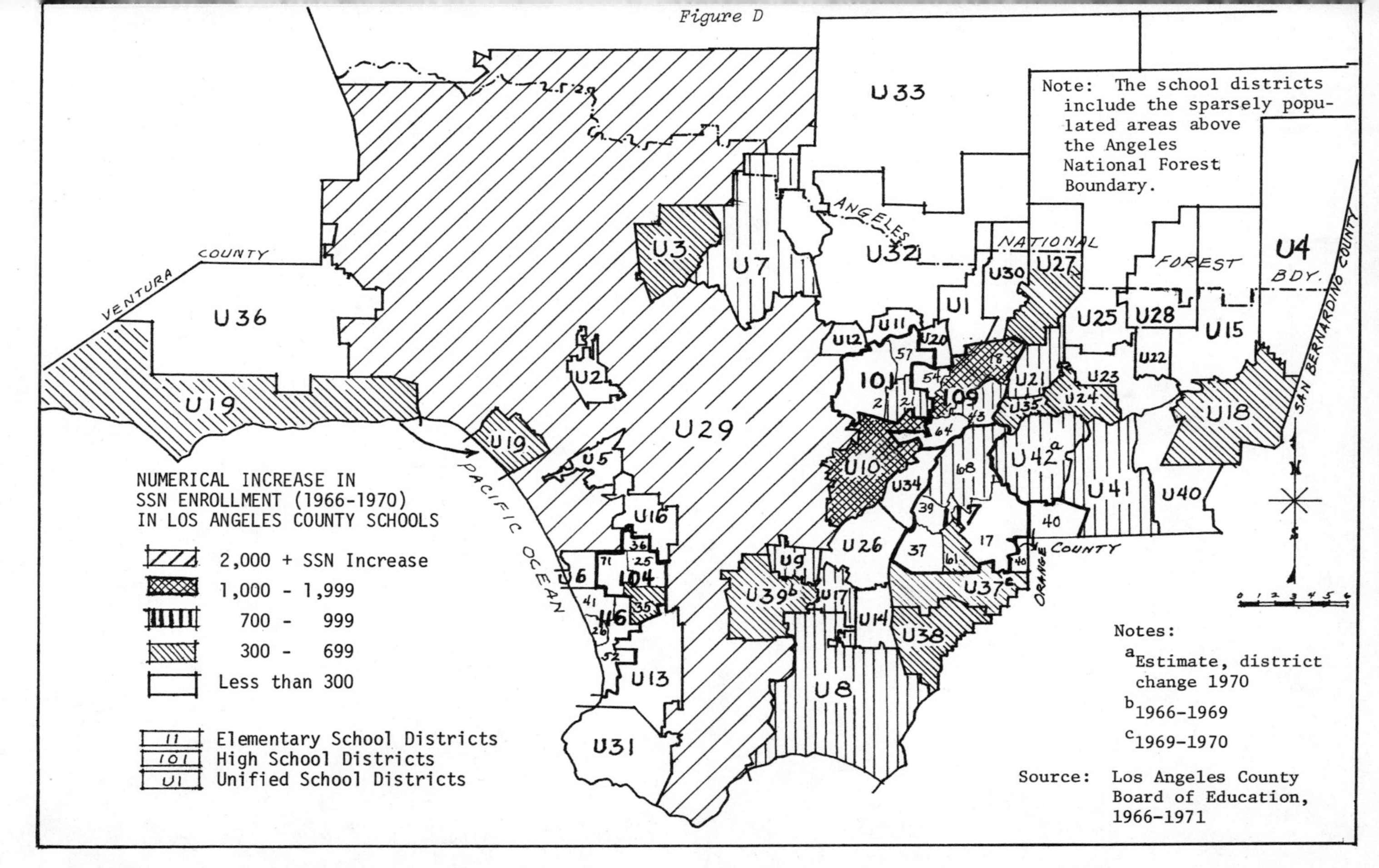

Note: The school districts include the sparsely populated areas above the Angeles National Forest Boundary.
ANGELES NATIONAL FOREST BDY.
VENTURA COUNTY
SAN BERNARDINO COUNTY
ORANGE COUNTY
PACIFIC OCEAN
U33
U32
U36
U19
U3
U7
U2
U29
U5
U16
U6
U13
U31
U4
U15
U28
U25
U22
U23
U24
U18
U27
U30
U1
U11
U12
U20
U21
U35
U42^a
U41
U40
U10
U34
U26
U9
U39^b
U17
U14
U38
U37^c
U8
101
109
104
116
117
NUMERICAL INCREASE IN
SSN ENROLLMENT (1966-1970)
IN LOS ANGELES COUNTY SCHOOLS
2,000 + SSN Increase
1,000 - 1,999
700 - 999
300 - 699
Less than 300
Elementary School Districts
High School Districts
Unified School Districts
Notes:
^a Estimate, district change 1970
^b 1966-1969
^c 1969-1970
Source: Los Angeles County Board of Education, 1966-1971

Appendix II.

Hispanic Church Survey Questionnaire, 1970

SURVEY OF SPANISH-SPEAKING OR BILINGUAL CHURCHES, MISSIONS, AND DEPARTMENTS

Name of church ______________________________

Address ______________________________
(street) (city) (zip)

Church phone ______________ Denomination ______________

Pastor's name ______________________________

Address ______________________________
(street) (city) (zip)

HISTORY & ATTENDANCE

1. What year was your church established? ____________.

2. What year were Spanish services started? __________ English services? __________; Bilingual services? __________.

3. How many people can your building seat for a worship service (maximum number)? __________.

4. What year was your present building constructed? __________; OR, when did your church move to the present building? __________.

5. What was your average weekly attendance for the past year (July 1, 1969 through June 30, 1970)?

SUNDAY SCHOOL		MORNING WORSHIP		EVENING WORSHIP	
Spanish		Spanish		Spanish	
English		English		English	
Bilingual		Bilingual		Bilingual	

SPANISH-SPEAKING MEMBERSHIP (except**)

1. What was your total membership as of July 1, 1970?

**Total members		Total members gained '69-'70	
**Total Anglos		By baptism	
Total Spanish		By transfer	
Total dropped '69-'70		By profession of Faith	

2. Total number of family units (households) in your church? __________

3. What are your qualifications for church membership? __________
____
______________________________ (minimum age __________)

NATIVITY OF SPANISH-SPEAKING MEMBERS

1. How many of your members were born in the United States? In Latin American countries? (please estimate)

2. How many of your members were converted to Protestant Christianity while in the United States? [ ]
In Latin countries? [ ]

(country)	(number)
U.S.A.	
Mexico	

Page 2 - SURVEY OF SPANISH-SPEAKING OR BILINGUAL CHURCHES, MISSIONS, AND DEPARTMENTS

THE PASTOR: SPANISH CHURCH, MISSION OR DEPARTMENT

1. What is your age?__________ 2. Where were you born?__________________

3. How many years have you served as a pastor?__________________

4. What year did you become the pastor of this church?__________________

5. What pastoral training have you received? (name and place of schools attended and degrees received)__________________

____

____

6. What is the highest public school grade completed?__________________

7. Is your church income your main means of support?__________________

8. Do you work part-time in secular work?__________________

9. Do you receive part of your salary from your denomination or home missions department?__________________

SPANISH LEADERSHIP TRAINING & CHURCH EXTENSION

1. Did your church have a teacher or leadership training course during 1969-1970?* What kind and how long?__________________

____

2. Do you plan to have such training during 1970-1971?*__________________

3. How many people completed this training during '69-'70?__________________

4. How many people attended other leadership training courses in 1969-1970?

__________ Where?__________________

5. How many Sunday school teachers does your church now have?

TOTAL TEACHERS:

Kindergarten thru grade 6	☐	Grades 10, 11, 12	☐
Grades 7, 8, 9	☐	College age (18-21)	☐
		Adult (over 21 yrs)	☐

6. Has your church established any branch churches, Sunday schools, or home Bible study groups? When, what type, and how many?

____

____

7. Do you plan to establish one of these ministries during '70-'71? What kind, when, and where?__________________

____

*NOTE: 1969-1970 or 1970-1971 refers to the period July 1-June 30

ARE YOU INTERESTED IN KNOWING THE RESULTS OF THIS SURVEY?__________________

PLEASE COMPLETE the questionnaire within 10 days and return it in the envelope provided. Thank you.

Appendix III.

Directory of Hispanic Churches in Los Angeles and Orange Counties, 1972

DIRECTORY OF SPANISH LANGUAGE
PROTESTANT CHURCHES IN LOS ANGELES COUNTY
CALIFORNIA

ALHAMBRA 91802*

Iglesia Bautista El Salvador (AB)
919 S. Garfield Ave.
576-0377

First Baptist Church (AB)
Spanish Dept.
101 S. Atlantic Blvd.
284-3207

AZUSA 91702

El Buen Pastor (Pres)
611 N. Alameda Ave.

Ebenezer Assembly of God
540 Azusa Ave.

Iglesia Belem (LACCC)
244 S. Soldano Ave.

BALDWIN PARK 91706

First Baptist Church (SB)
Spanish Dept.
4620 N. Main Ave.
337-4722

Iglesia Del Redentor (IP)
3739 N. Monterey Ave.
962-4226

El Buen Pastor (LACCC)
5108 N. Elton Ave.

*Zip code area numbers

BALDWIN PARK (Cont.)

Iglesia Foursquare
13749 E. Monterey St.

BELL 95340

First Baptist Church (SB)
Spanish Dept.
4009 E. Gage St.
582-5356

BURBANK 91501

Asamblea Apostolica
553 E. Santa Anita Ave.

CANOGA PARK 91303

Asamblea Apostolica
6914 Eton Ave.

Pan-American Foursquare
7056 Millwood Ave.

CARSON 90502

Asamblea Apostolica
1708 E. Carson St.

Carson Spanish S.D.A.
21828 S. Dolores Ave.

Ebenezer (AG)
226 E. Dominguez St.

COMMERCE 90022

First Baptist Church (CBA)
5102 E. Kinsie St.
Los Angeles
268-9623

COMPTON

First Baptist Church (SB)
Spanish Dept.
1019 N. Harris Ave. 90220

Iglesia Betania (AG)
1942 E. El Segundo Blvd.
90222

Asamblea Apostolica
2343 E. El Segundo Blvd.
90222

Primera Iglesia Cuadrangular de Willowbrook (FSQ)
12726 S. Mona Blvd. 90222

CULVER CITY 90230

Asamblea Apostolica
11724 W. Culver Blvd.

DOWNEY 90241

Rio Hondo Baptist Church (SB)
Spanish Dept.
11543 S. Paramount Blvd.
869-3213

EL MONTE

Primera Iglesia Bautista del Sur (SB)
3712 N. Cypress Ave., 91731
443-5755

Templo Bethel (LACCC)
3949 N. De Garmo Ave., 91731

Iglesia de Dios de la Profecia
12348 Denholm Dr., 91731

Asamblea Apostolica
3924 Cobswell Rd., 91732

El Tabernaculo de Fe (AG)
2324 N. Durfee Ave., 91732
332-2938

GLENDALE

First Southern Baptist Ch.
Spanish Dept.
725 N. Central, 91203

Glendale Spanish S.D.A. Ch.
c/o Broadway United Methodist
901 E. Broadway, 91209

HARBOR CITY 90710

First Mexican Baptist (AB)
1201 W. 255 St.

HAWTHORNE 90250

Bethesda Presbyterian Ch.
(Calvary Chapel-temp. location)
12515 S. Acacia Ave.

HUNTINGTON PARK 90255

First Baptist Church
Spanish Dept. (AB)
2662 E. Clarendon St.
587-2265

Templo Bethesda (AG in Christ, Inc.)
7921 S. Pacific Blvd.

Iglesia del Señor (AG)
c/o Huntington Park S.D.A. Ch.
6300 Stafford St.

IRWINDALE 91706

Asamblea Apostolica Cristiana, Ir
5135 N. Irwindale Ave.

El Divino Salvador (Pres)
5120 N. Irwindale Ave.

LA PUENTE

Iglesia Evangelica (Ind Bapt)
14864 E. Valley Blvd., 91747
336-9022

Misión Cristiana (LACCC)
13852 E. Valley Blvd., 91746

LA PUENTE (Cont.)

El Buen Samaritano (AG)
330 Santa Mariana St., 91746
330-7931

La Puente Foursquare Church
Spanish Dept.
15017 E. Fairgrove, 91744

First Southern Baptist
Spanish Dept.
California & Fairgrove
P. O. Box 326, 91745
330-4084

LA VERNE 91750

Immanuel Presbyterian Church
Ave. A & Second St.

LONG BEACH

Asamblea Apostolica
726 Dawson Ave., 90813

First Baptist Church
Spanish Dept. (AB)
1000 N. Pine Ave., 90813
432-8447

Latin American Methodist
1350 N. Redondo Ave., 90804

LOS ANGELES

Boyle Heights 90033

Unida Bautista (AB)
132 N. Chicago St.
269-5755

Calvary Baptist Ch. (GARB)
206 S. St. Louis St.
262-4631

El Buen Pastor (IP)
1524 E. Pleasant Ave., 90033
AN 3-0680

The Church of God of
Prophecy (P)
2446 E. Houston Ave.
265-3558

(Store Front Church-IP)
1525 E. Brooklyn

LOS ANGELES

Boyle Heights (Cont.)

Boyle Heights Latin American
Nazarene
213 S. Breed
262-0134

Bethsaida Tabernaculo (IP)
1925 E. 1st St.
269-6221

Community House of God (IP)
2302 E. 2nd St.
AN 3-1163

Mission Sinai (LACCC)
2003 E. Brooklyn Ave.
261-9284

El Divino Salvador (Pres)
515 N. Echandia St.

Spanish-American S.D.A.
1825 E. Michigan Ave.

La Nueva Jerusalén (AG)
601 N. Echandia St.

City View Church of God
2308 City View Ave.

Central L.A. - Downtown

Angeles Temple (FSQ)
Spanish Dept.
1100 N. Glendale Blvd., 90026
484-1100

Temple Baptist Church (AB)
Spanish Dept.
427 W. 5th St., 90013

Bethany Presbyterian Church
Spanish Dept.
1629 Griffith Park Blvd. 90026
664-2176

Echo Park Methodist Church
Spanish Dept.
1226 N. Alvarado, 90026

Iglesia Pentecostal (IP)
200 N. Mountain View, 90026
629-2947

LOS ANGELES

Central L.A. (Cont.)

Fourth Church of the Nazarene
1602 W. Temple St., 90026

Bethel Temple (IP)
Spanish Dept.
1250 Bellevue, 90026

Hispana Bautista (AB)
1700 S. Toberman St., 90015
749-4976

Temple Methodist (LAM)
1575 W. 14th St., 90015
385-3361

Misión Antioquia (AG)
1200 S. Kenmore, 90015

Iglesia Cristiana Evangelica (Evangelical Covenant)
Spanish Dept.
8515 S. Francisco St., 90017

La Plaza Mexican Methodist (LAM)
115 E. Sunset, 90012
628-5773

East Los Angeles 90022

First Baptist of East L.A. (AB)
1120 S. McDonnell St.
262-2302

El Camino Baptist Ch. (SB)
537 S. Sydney Dr.

First So. Baptist Ch.
Spanish Dept.
715 S. Bradley
728-4812

First Spanish Baptist Ch. (SB)
601 S. Ferris
263-6666

Iglesia Bautista Fundamental (CBA)
942 S. Ford Blvd.
268-8152

LOS ANGELES

East Los Angeles (Cont.)

United Methodist Church of East L.A.
700 S. Gerhart
721-8023

El Mesias (LAM)
4526 E. Brooklyn Ave.
268-6003

Iglesia Cristiana (Ind)
543 S. Fetterly St.
263-0505

Evangelical Mexican Memorial Church (Ind)
215 S. Fetterly St.

Roca de La Eternidad Pentecostes
4329 E. Floral Dr.

Templo El Eden (P)
1400 S. Eastern Ave.
262-2811

Belvedere Church of God
200 N. Humphreys

La Puerta Abierta (AG)
5017 E. Olympic Blvd.
261-8397

Misión La Luz (AG)
739 S. Belden Ave.

"El Siloe" Asamblea Apostolica
701 S. Ferris

Fundamental Bible Church (Ind)
700 S. Hoefner St.

"El Siloe" Presbiteriana
4408 E. Dozier St.

El Sereno 90032

Immanuel Baptist (AB)
4540 Huntington Dr. South
221-0021

El Sereno Foursquare Church
5007 E. Navarro

LOS ANGELES

El Sereno (Cont.)

El Sereno Church of Nazarene (Ind)
5333 E. Alhambra Ave.
221-8412

Florence 90001

Florence Baptist (AB)
7311 S. Miramonte Blvd.
588-0240

Florence Ave. Methodist (LAM)
1951 E. Florence Ave.

El Sendero de La Cruz (AG)
6508 S. Holmes
582-1750

Hazard-Belvedere 90063

First Mexican Baptist (AB)
101 S. Gage Ave.
264-1928

Eastminster Community Presbyterian
3729 E. Brooklyn Ave.

Templo de Bethel (IP)
510 N. Marianna St.
269-7995

Iglesia Bautista "La Resurección (AB)
4006 E. Ramboz Dr.
261-4445

Park Vista Baptist (AB)
4200 E. Michigan Ave.
268-4604

City Terrace Mission (SB)
3364 E. City Terrace Dr.
265-4947

La Trinidad First Methodist (LAM)
3565 E. 1st St.
261-2337

Latin American Free Methodist
213 S. Dacotah St.
264-0396

LOS ANGELES

Hazard-Belvedere (Cont.)

Ejercito de Salvación
140 N. Eastman Ave.
P. O. Box 63196
263-7577

"La Trinidad" Iglesia Fundamental Cristiana (Ind)
481 S. Indiana
269-2788

City Terrace Methodist (LAM)
4018 City Terrace Dr.
264-0468

Pan-American Foursquare
420 N. Rowan Ave.

Primera Iglesia Cristiana de City Terrace, Inc. (Ind)
3246 E. City Terrace Dr.
264-0476

Mission Israel Pentecostes (IP) (was, 3425 E. Brooklyn, present address unknown)

El Aposento Alto (AG)
3505 E. Michigan
268-4586

Iglesia Evangelica Pentecostal (LACCC)
3501 E. Gleason St.
263-6644

Templo de Bethel (LACCC)
4205 E. Hammel
269-7995

Ditman Spanish S.D.A. Church
203 S. Ditman Ave.

City Terrace Mennonite Brethren (English service)
1441 N. Herbert
262-7804

Highland Park

Highland Park Presbyterian Spanish Dept.
115 N. Ave. 53, 90042
256-4171

LOS ANGELES

Highland Park (Cont.)

Cypress Park Christian Church (Disciples of Christ)
Spanish Dept.
1145 N. Cypress Ave., 90065

El Principe de Paz (IP)
719 N. Cypress Ave., 90065
CA 1-3755

Hollywood 90028

First Baptist Church (AB)
Spanish Dept.
6682 W. Selma Ave.

First So. Baptist Church (SB)
Spanish Dept.
1528 N. Wilton Place
466-9631

Lincoln Heights 90031

Feliz de Lincoln Heights (AB)
2012 E. Mozart St.
225-6702

Church of the Epiphany (Episcopal)
2808 Altura
222-1322

First Mexican Nazarene Church
124 S. Ave. 22
225-8877

El Calvario (AG)
1943 N. Workman St.

Templo El Gethsemani (FSQ)
308 Ave. 17
222-0089

Iglesia de Cristo
2500 N. Sichel St.
221-9260

Lincoln Heights Church of Christ
2451 N. Workman St.
245-0862

Lincoln Heights Spanish (S.D.A.)
2422 E. Manitou Ave.

LOS ANGELES

Lincoln Heights (Cont.)

Church in the Valley (Ind)
3709 Rolle St.
245-3361

Lugo 90023

Lorena Baptist (AB)
1100 S. Lorena St.

Bethel So. Baptist (SB)
709 S. Spence
268-6611

Boyle Heights Foursquare
1025 S. Indiana St.

Primera Iglesia Bautista Fundamental Mexicana (Ind Bapt)
1245 S. Indiana
264-2548

Bethany Congregational (Ind)
800 S. Ditman
261-6463

La Santa Cruz Lutheran (Missouri Synod)
2747 E. Whittier Blvd.
269-7989

Belvedere Nazarene Church
1153 S. Gage St.
263-8278

(Store Front Church-P)
2733 E. Whittier Blvd.

Templo de Refugio (LACCC)
2804 E. Whittier Blvd.
269-6171

South Central L.A.

Church of Christ
7911 S. Vermont, 90044
752-8787

Iglesia Juan 3:16 (IP)
9616 S. Vermont, 90044

LOS ANGELES

South Central L.A. (Cont.)

Iglesia Rosa de Saron (IP)
8229 S. San Pedro, 90044
778-2760

Templo Bethel de Watts (LACCC)
10512 S. Wilmington, 90002
566-4495

Iglesia El Salvador (LACCC)
1811 E. 41st St.
90058

West Central L.A.

Bethesda Presbyterian
1075 W. 35th St., 90007

Central Seventh-Day Adv.
Spanish Dept.
650 W. 21st St., 90007

Grandview So. Baptist (SB)
Spanish Dept.
925 S. Grandview, 90006

Rosewood Ave. Methodist
Spanish Dept. (LAM)
591 N. New Hampshire Ave.
662-1194 90004

First Baptist Church (AB)
Spanish Dept.
760 S. Westmoreland Ave.
384-2151 90005

West Los Angeles-Mar Vista

Barrington Ave. Baptist
Spanish Dept. (AB)
1903 S. Barrington Ave., 90025

Nueva Vida Bautista (AB)
11312 W. Washington Blvd. 90066

Mar Vista So. Baptist
Spanish Dept. (SB)
11811 Venice Blvd., 90066

LYNWOOD

Capilla "Sinai" (AG)
11820 S. Wright Rd., 90262

MAYWOOD

First Baptist Church (AB)
Spanish Dept.
3759 E. 57th St., 90270
585-1428

MONTEBELLO

First Spanish Baptist Church (SB
904 W. Oakwood, 90640
728-2025

Montebello Free Methodist
207 N. Montebello Blvd., 90640

Montebello Spanish Ch. of God
145 S. 4th St.

Montebello Church of Christ
2445 W. Via Acosta St., 90640
721-0031

NORWALK

Iglesia "Buenas Nuevas" (AG)
11910 E. Alondra Blvd., 90650
697-8280

Carmenita Baptist Church (CBA)
P. O. Box 628, 90650
Claressa St. & Vieudelou Ave.

PACOIMA

"El Valle" Baptist Church (AB)
10705 Telfair St., 91331
899-8268

First Spanish Baptist (AB)
13131 S. Mercer St., 91331
833-2457

First Southern Baptist
Spanish Mission (SB)
14055 S. Van Nuys Blvd., 91331
889-1800

Iglesia de Dios (P)
13443 S. Van Nuys Blvd., 91331

PASADENA

Latin American Methodist
c/o Hartzell Methodist
2428 E. Colorado Blvd., 91109
793-3959

PASADENA (Cont.)

Mexican Church of the Nazarene
1141 N. Lincoln Ave.,
794-9268

Templo Bautista "Sinai" (SB)
1740 N. Sierra Bonita Ave.
796-8934

POMONA

Iglesia Congregacional Mexicana (UCC)
819 S. White Ave., 91766
(714) 622-5378

Templo de La Fe (AG)
583 W. 10th St., 91766

White Ave. So. Baptist
Spanish Dept.
675 S. White Ave., 91766

PICO RIVERA

Pico Rivera Friends Church
4550 S. Lexington Rd., 90660
699-6707
(English Service)

Lirio de los Valles (AG)
8247 Whittier Blvd., 90661

First Spanish Baptist Ch. (SB)
9133 Mines Ave., 90660
692-4863

Pico Rivera S.D.A. Spanish
5058 S. Cord Ave., 90660

Iglesia Bethsaida (LACCC)
9147 E. Perkins Ave., 90660

El Buen Samaritano (LACCC)
4127 S. Zola St., 90660

Pico Park Methodist Ch. (LAM)
P. O. Box 508, 90660
692-9055

Pico Rivera Methodist Ch. (LAM)
7267 S. Serapis Ave., 90660
695-4415

ROSEMEAD 91770

First So. Baptist Church
Spanish Dept.
7878 E. Hellman Ave.
573-5644

SAN FERNANDO 91340

El Mesias United Methodist Church (LAM)
467 S. Kalisher St.

San Fernando Nazarene
1002 Mott Ave.
365-1813

La Trinidad (AG)
1150 O'Melveny

San Fernando Spanish S.D.A.
508 S. Maclay St.

SAN GABRIEL 91771

San Gabriel Union Church (Ind)
Spanish Dept.
Las Tunas & Pine Ave.
287-0434

Iglesia Four Square
113 E. Mission Dr.
728-4580

First Presbyterian Church
219 E. Mission Dr.

Iglesia "Bethel" (LACCC)
708 E. Sunset

Temple City Spanish S.D.A.
5116 N. Rosemead Blvd.

SANTA MONICA 90405

First Baptist Church (AB)
Spanish Dept.
2601 Pico Blvd.

Santa Monica Spanish Mission (SB)
1520 Pearl St.
396-7617

SAN PEDRO

First Mexican Baptist (AB)
305 N. Centre St., 90731
Mail: P.O. Box 1168, 90733
833-2457

Iglesia "Sion" (AG)
555 W. 12th St., 90731

Asamblea Apostolica
1009 S. Centre, 90731

Central Tabernaculo (LACCC)
236 N. Mesa St., 90731

SEPULVEDA 91343

Pentecostal Christian Assembly of Van Nuys, Inc. (IP)
9145 Burnet Ave.

SOUTH GATE

Immanuel Baptist Church (SB)
Spanish Chapel
10263 S. San Carlos, 90282
567-2937

Iglesia Bautista Hispana (BBF)
3420 E. Ardmore, 90280
567-0281

SUN VALLEY 91352

Spanish Baptist Church (AB)
11140 W. Saticoy St.
765-0705

SYLMAR 91345

First Baptist Church (AB)
Spanish Dept.
13361 W. Glenoaks Blvd.
367-7040

TORRANCE 90502

First Baptist Church (AB)
Spanish Dept.
2118 W. Carson St.

VAN NUYS 91408

Van Nuys Spanish S.D.A.
15059 Saticoy Ave.

WALNUT 91789

First So. Baptist Church
Spanish Chapel
19648 Camino De Rosa
595-3110

WHITTIER 90606

Asamblea Apostolica
5724 S. Esperanza Ave.

WILMINGTON 90744

Wilmington Free Methodist
1021 N. Fries Ave.

Asamblea Apostolica
1508 E. Robidoux

Iglesia Galilea Pentecostal (LACCC)
1303 E. Mauretania

Iglesia Cristiana Puerta del Cielo (P)
(Assemblies of Christ Ch. of New York)
1330 E. Mauretania

Primera Iglesia Bautista (Ind)
1241 Watson

Iglesia Cristiana "Roca de Salvación" (IP)
1244 N. Avalon Blvd.

Misión Iglesia Cristiana (IP)
2440 N. Avalon Blvd.

DIRECTORY OF SPANISH LANGUAGE PROTESTANT CHURCHES IN ORANGE COUNTY CALIFORNIA

ANAHEIM

First Mexican Baptist Ch. (AB)
1015 N. Patt St., 92801

Asamblea Apostolica
1106 N. Homer St., 92801

El Sinai (LAM)
2885 W. Ball Rd., 92804
(714) 827-7910

FULLERTON

El Buen Pastor (AG)
336 E. Truslow Ave., 92631
(714) 635-5069

Immanuel Baptist Church (CBA)
c/o Rev. George Boman
6336 S. Citrus Ave.
Whittier, 90601
(Meets at VFW Hall
1201 W. Commonwealth St.)

LA HABRA 90631

First Mexican Baptist Ch. (AB)
612 W. Fourth St.

ORANGE 92666

Asamblea Apostolica
537 Palm St.

PLACENTIA 92670

Placentia Free Methodist
925 S. Melrose Ave.

SANTA ANA

First Mexican Baptist (AB)
5022 W. Hazard Ave.
Santa Ana, 92703
(714) 839-0044

SANTA ANA (Cont.)

El Gethsemani (AG)
3818 W. 5th St., 92703
(714) 531-7798

Asamblea Apostolica
223 N. Harper St., 92703

El Gethsemani (LAM)
709 W. 6th St., 92702

Spanish-American S.D.A.
117 W. McFaddon St., 92702
(714) 543-6220

Templo Calvario (AG)
1808 W. 8th St., 92702
(714) 776-8004

El Templo Sinai (AG)
307 E. McFaddon St., 92702

Santa Ana Free Methodist
1600 Myrtle St., 92703

STANTON 90680

La Hermosa (AG)
10901 S. Beach Blvd.
(714) 527-1065

WESTMINSTER 92683

First So. Baptist Church
Spanish Dept.
7001 Main St.

Bibliography

AARONS, Leroy F.
1972 "Lettuce Boycott: Is it Just a 'Cesar' Salad?", *The Miami Herald* (August 20), Section H:3.

ABBOTT, Walter M. (ed.)
1966 *The Documents of Vatican II*. New York: Association Press.

Apostolic Assembly of the Faith in Christ Jesus
1967 *Ministerial and Church Directory: 1967-1968*. El Monte, California: Office of the Treasurer, Apostolic Assembly.

ARMSTRONG, John Milton
1949 "A Mexican Community: A Study of the Cultural Determinants of Migration". Unpublished Ph.D. Dissertation, Yale University (m/f used).

ARNOLD, Benjamin F. and CLARK, Artilissa D.
1933 *History of Whittier*. Whittier, California: Western Printing Corporation.

ARONOFF, Joel
1967 *Psychological Needs and Cultural Systems*. Princeton, New Jersey: D. Van Nostrand Company, Inc.

Asociación de Iglesias Evangélicas Del Sur de California
1969 *62 va. Gran Convención* (May 14-18). "Directorio de Iglesias y sus Pastores", pp. 15-17. "Constitución", pp. 18-22. "Tabla Cronológica de los Presidentes de Nuestras Convenciones", p. 25.

AUSTIN, Lee
1970 "Recall Election Viewed as Crucial to Pasadena School Integration", *Los Angeles Times* (October 11), Section L:1,4.

1971(a) "Mexican-Americans Ask Better Schools", *Los Angeles Times* (March 19). [Section and page number unknown.]

1971(b) "Minority Enrollment to Reach 50% in Pasadena", *Los Angeles Times* (March 24), Part II:6.

1971(c) "Schools Face Dilemma of Segregated Classes", *Los Angeles Times* (June 6), Section G:1,3.

BALL, Henry C.

1966 "Historia de los primeros 50 años de las Asambleas de Dios Latinas", *La Luz Apostolica*, Vol. 50, Nos. 7-12; Vol. 51, Nos. 4-6, 10, 12. [Trans. into English by Mary Anne Voelkel, 1971. Typewritten.]

1970 "Short History of the Spanish Assemblies of God". Typewritten. [This brief article was written by Ball in response to the author's personal request and was received in Pasadena on October 10, 1970.]

Baptist General Convention of Texas

1968 *Texas Baptist Annual: Statistical Report*. Fort Worth: Baptist General Convention (Southern Baptist).

BARNETT, H. G.

1953 *Innovation: The Basis of Cultural Change*. New York: McGraw Hill Book Company, Inc.

BAYARSKY, Nancy and Bill

1972 "The Raveled Street of Wear", *Los Angeles Times West Magazine* (February 6) pp. 4,7,10,12.

BEALS, Ralph Leon and HUMPHREY Norman D.

1957 *No Frontier to Learning: The Mexican Student in the United States*. Minneapolis: University of Minnesota Press.

BEAN, Walton

1968 *California: An Interpretive History*. New York: McGraw-Hill Book Co., Inc.

BERKENSHAW, Jack

1969 "Spanish Speaking Face Profusion of Problems", *Los Angeles Times* (July 20), Section G:1,3.

BERNSTEIN, Harry

1972(a) "Many Reportedly Enter 'Job Market' via Crime", *Los Angeles Times* (March 21), Part II:1,12. [Survey of youth workers in East L.A. and Watts conducted by the Manpower Research Center at UCLA, Institute of Industrial Relations.]

1972(b) "Illegal Alien Job Law: Many Turn Selves In", *Los Angeles Times* (March 25), Part II:1,12.

BERNSTEIN, Harry and DEL OLMO, Frank
1971 "Garment Shops: Hiring of Alien Workers Grows", *Los Angeles Times* (September 14), Part I:1,15.

BEVERIDGE, William I.B.
1957 *The Art of Scientific Investigation.* New York: Vintage Books, Random House.

BLAIR, Bertha, LEVELY, Anne, TRIMBLE, Glen
1959 "Spanish-speaking Americans: Summary and Conclusions", adapted from *Spanish-speaking Americans.* New York: Home Missions Research Unit of the Bureau of Research and Survey, Home Missions Division National Council of Churches of Christ in the U.S.A.

BLAUW, Johannes
1962 *The Missionary Nature of the Church.* New York: McGraw-Hill Book Co., Inc.

BRADSHAW, Malcolm R.
1969 *Church Growth Through Evangelism-in-Depth.* South Pasadena, California: William Carey Library.

BROOM, Leonard and SHEVKY, Eshref
1952 "Mexicans in the United States--A Problem of Social Differentiation", *Sociology and Social Research,* 36 (January-February): 150-158. Also in Burma (ed.), *Mexican-Americans in the United States: A Reader,* pp. 427-434. Cambridge: Schenkman Publishing Company, Inc.

BURGER, Henry G.
1969 "'Ethnonics': Converting Spanish Speakers' Ethnography for Directed Change", *Practical Anthropology* (November-December): 241-251.

BURKE, Vincent J.
1972 "1 of 6 Californias of Latin Heritage", *Los Angeles Times* (January 8), Part I:1,29.

BURMA, John H. (ed.)
1970 *Mexican-Americans in the United States: A Reader.* Cambridge: Schenkman Publishing Company, Inc.

BURMA, John H.
1954 *Spanish-Speaking Groups in the United States.* Durham, North Carolina: Duke University Press.

CABRERA, Y. Arturo
1971 *Emerging Faces: The Mexican Americans.* Wm. C. Brown Company Publishers.

California Department of Industrial Relations, Division of Labor Statistics and Research.
1964 *Californians of Spanish Surname.* San Francisco: California Department of Industrial Relations, Division of Fair Employment Practices.

1968 *Negroes and Mexican Americans in South and East Los Angeles; Changes Between 1960 and 1965 in Population, Employment, Income and Family Status.* San Francisco, Fair Employment Practices Committee.

California. San Fernando Valley State College, Northridge, Library.
1968 *Brown Black Bibliography.*

California State Board of Education, Bureau of Intergroup Relations
1967 *Racial and Ethnic Survey of California Public Schools, Part One: Distribution of Pupils, Fall 1966.* Sacramento: California State Department of Education.

1969 *Racial and Ethnic Survey of California Public Schools, Part One: Distribution of Pupils, Fall 1967.* Sacramento: California State Department of Education.

1970 *Distribution of Racial and Ethnic Groups in California Public Schools* (October 1969). Sacramento: Californi State Department of Education.

1971 *Racial and Ethnic Distribution in California Public Schools* (October 1970). Sacramento: California State Department of Education.

California University at Los Angeles. Mexican-American Study Project.
1965-1968 *Advance Reports.* Nos. 1-11.

California University at Los Angeles. Institute of Industrial Relations.
1968 *Directory of Organizations in South and East Los Angeles.* Los Angeles: The Institute of Industrial Relations.

California University at Santa Barbara Library
1969 *Mexican-Americans: A Bibliography.*

CANTU, Ernesto S.
1956 *Constitution or By-Laws of the Apostolic Assembly of the Faith in Christ Jesus in the United States of America.* Los Angeles: Apostolic Assembly.

CANTU, Ernesto S. (ed.)
1966 *Historia de la Asamblea Apostólica de la Fe en Cristo Jesús: 1916-1966.* Mentone, California: Sal's Printing Service.

CARROLL, J. M.
1923 *A History of Texas Baptists.* Dallas: Baptist Standard Publishing Company.

CARTER, Thomas P.
1970 *Mexican Americans in School: A History of Educational Neglect.* New York: College Entrance Examination Board.

CASAVANTES, Edward J.
1969 *A New Look at the Attributes of the Mexican American.* Albuquerque, New Mexico: Southwestern Cooperative Educational Laboratory, Inc.

CASE, Alden
1897 *Foreign Work at Home for our Spanish Neighbor.* California Spanish Mission Society. Pamphlet.

CASTRO, Mike
1971(a) "New Bishop Seeks Change by Working Within the Establishment", *Los Angeles Times* (March 7), Part II:1,3.

1971(b) "Cuban Exiles Squeezed between Two Cultures", *Los Angeles Times* (October 31), Section M:1,4,5.

1972 "$1.9 Million OK'D For Hicks Camp", *Los Angeles Times* (January 7), Part II:7.

Catholic Almanac
1969 "Padres", in "News--October 1969", p. 99.

The Center for Parish Development
1972 "Report to Supporting Conferences". Mimeographed. Naperville, Illinois: The Center for Parish Development (United Methodist Church).

CHAMBERLIN, Ubiana
1970 "Death of the Barrio", *Pasadena Eagle* (March 19). [Section and page number unknown].

Church of the Nazarene. General Assembly Proceedings.
1946-1970 Kansas City, Missouri.

Cladic Seminary
1958 *Catalog: 1958-1959*. Los Angeles: Cladic Seminary, Latin American Council of Christian Churches.

CLARK, Elmer T. (rev. ed.)
1959 *The Small Sects in America*. Nashville: Abingdon-Cokesbury Press (orig. 1937).

CLARK, Margaret
1959 *Health in the Mexican-American Culture*. Berkeley: University of California Press.

COHEN, A. K. and HODGES, H. M., Jr.
1963 "Characteristics of the Lower-Blue-Collar Class", *Social Problems*, 10:303-334.

COLEMAN, Robert E.
1963 *The Master Plan of Evangelism*. Old Tappan, New Jersey: Fleming H. Revell Company.

COLEMAN, William J.
1958 *Latin American Catholicism*. Maryknoll, New York: Maryknoll Publications.

COME, Arnold B.
1964 *Agents of Reconciliation*. Philadelphia: The Westminster Press.

Concilio Latino-Americano de Iglesias Cristianas
1962 *Constitución y Reformas*. Brownsville, Texas: Concilio Latino-Americano de Iglesias Cristianas.

COSTAS, Orlando E.
1973(a) "Church Growth as a Goal of In-Depth Evangelism". Mimeographed. San José, Costa Rica: Institute of In-Depth Evangelism.

1973(b) "La crisis de la iglesia evangélica en América Latina". Mimeographed. San José, Costa Rica: Institute of In-Depth Evangelism.

DART, John
1968 "Protestant Clergy Leads Fight for Mexican-American Goals", *Los Angeles Times* (April 5), Part II:1,6.

1969 "Chicano-Catholic Conflict: A Split over Philosophy", *Los Angeles Times* (December 31), Part I:1,10.

1971(a) "New L.A. Bishop Expects No Problems with Identity", *Los Angeles Times* (February 16), Part II:1,5.

1971(b) "Latin Church Group to Push Drive for Voters", *Los Angeles Times* (February 20), Part I:26.

1971(c) "'Padres' Elect Texas Bishop in Rare Move", *Los Angeles Times* (October 14), Part II:8.

DAVIE, Michael
1972 "California, Here We Come", *The Miami Herald* (August 13), Section CW:1.

DAVILA, N. B.
1957 "Information on: Plaza Community Center". Typewritten. Claremont: Methodist Historical Society Archives, School of Theology at Claremont (United Methodist Church).

DAVIS, James H.
1970 "United Methodists and Minorities", *Response*, Vol. 2, No. 10:5,6,49.

DAVIS, Nolan
1972 "The Archbishop in Motion", *Los Angeles Times West Magazine* (March 12): 7-12.

DIEBOLD, Robert
1970 "Pomona Schools Given Ultimatum by Chicanos", *Los Angeles Times* (April 30):1,3. [Section unknown].

DIETTERICH, Paul M. and WEIS, James C.
1973 "An Experiment in Local Church Renewal: The First United Methodist Church, Barabao, Wisconsin". Mimeographed. Naperville, Illinois: The Center For Parish Development.

DRURY, Clifford M.
ca. 1946 *A Chronology of Protestant Beginnings in California*. San Francisco: The Centennial Committee of the Northern California-Western Nevada Council of Churches.

1967 "Chronological List of Churches", *Minutes of Annual Session*, Appendix C:94-108. United Presbyterian Church in the U.S.A., Synod of California.

DWORKIN, Anthony G.
1970 "Stereotypes and Self-Images Held by Native-born and Foreign-born Mexican Americans", in Burma (ed.) *Mexican Americans in the United States: A Reader*, 397-409. Cambridge: Schenkman Publishing Company.

Economic and Youth Opportunities Agency of Greater Los Angeles, Research and Evaluation Division
1970 "Ethnic Composition of the Population of Los Angeles County, April 1970." EYOA Working Paper No. 2. Los Angeles: EYOA.

El Mensajero Cristiano
1971 "Templo Bethel, Harlington, Texas", Año 46, No. 11:1. "Iglesias y Cambios de Pastores", Año 46, No. 11:15. Brownsville, Texas: Concilio Latino-Americano de Iglesias Cristianas.

El Mexicano. Vol. I-XI (April 1913-June 1923).
1913-1923 Official Publication of the Spanish American Mission Association; later the Latin American Mission of the Methodist Episcopal Church. Gardena, California: Spanish American Institute Press.

ELLIS, Ivan
1938 "Origin and Development of Baptist Churches and Institutions in Southern California." Unpublished M.A. Thesis, University of Southern California.

ESPINOZA, H. O.
1972 Personal correspondence, March 21.

FEAGIN, Joseph R.
1971 "Most Blame Poor for Poverty, Survey Finds", *Los Angeles Times* (June 24). [Section and page unknown].

FOGELSON, Robert M.
1967 *The Fragmented Metropolis: Los Angeles, 1850-1930*. Cambridge, Massachusetts: Harvard University Press.

FOLEY, Thomas J.
1971 "'Brown Power' Parley Opens this Weekend", *Los Angeles Times* (October 22), Part I:18,19.

FORBES, Jack D.
1966 *Mexican-Americans: Handbook for Education*. Berkeley, California: Far West Laboratory for Educational Research and Development.

Free Methodist Church
1963 *Yearbook*. Arizona-Southern California Conference of Free Methodist Church.

FRODSHAM, Stanley H.
1926 *"With Signs Following": The Story of the Latter-Day Pentecostal Revival*. Springfield, Missouri: Gospel Publishing House.

FULLER, Elizabeth
1920 *The Mexican Housing Problem in Los Angeles*. Monograph No. 17. Los Angeles: U.S.C., Southern California Sociological Society.

GALARZA, Ernesto
1964 *Merchants of Labor: The Mexican Bracero Story*. Santa Barbara, California: McNally and Loftin.

GALARZA, Ernesto, GALLEGOS, Herman, and SAMORA, Julian
1969 *Mexican-Americans in the Southwest*. Santa Barbara, California: McNally and Loftin.

GALVAN, Elías Gabriel
1969 "A Study of the Spanish-Speaking Protestant Church and Her Mission to the Mexican-American Minority." Unpublished Rel.D. Dissertation. Claremont, School of Theology.

GAMIO, Manuel
1930 *Mexican Immigration to the United States*. New York: Harper & Row, Publishers.

GAXIOLA, Manuel J.
1970 *La Serpienta y la Paloma*. South Pasadena: William Carey Library. "The Church in the United States", Appendix, pp. 155-171. [Translated to English by Mrs. Edna Sawnor, November 1971. Typewritten.]

GAY, George A.
1973(a) "Informe de Jorge Gay sobre las posibilidades y necesidades de un Centro Regional en Los Angeles." Mimeographed. San José, Costa Rica: Seminario Bíblico Latinoamericano.

1973(b) Personal correspondence, August 15.

1973(c) Personal correspondence, October 3.

General Council of the Assemblies of God.
1966 *Directory: Assemblies of God*. Springfield, Missouri: General Council of Assemblies of God.

GERBER, Vergil
1973 *A Manual for Evangelism/Church Growth*. So. Pasadena, California: William Carey Library.

GILLAM, Jerry
1971 "Democrats Unveil Redistricting Plan", *Los Angeles Times* (October 7), Part I:3,30.

GINSBERG, Mitchell
1972 "Social Worker's Chief Calls Subsidy Welfare", *Los Angeles Times* (February 2), Part I:23.

GISH, Arthur G.
1970 *The New Left and Christian Radicalism.* Grand Rapids: William B. Eerdmans Publishing Company.

GLAZER, Nathan and MOYNIHAN, Daniel P.
1963 *Beyond the Melting Pot.* Cambridge, Massachussets: The M.I.T. Press.

GONZALEZ, Justo L.
1969 *The Development of Christianity in the Latin Caribbean.* Grand Rapids: William B. Eerdmans Publishing Company.

GORDON, Milton M.
1964 *Assimilation in American Life: The Role of Race, Religion and National Origins.* New York: Oxford University Press.

GREBLER, Leo
1966 *Mexican Immigration to the United States.* Mexican American Study Project, Advance Report 2. Los Angeles: Division of Research, Graduate School of Business Administration, University of California at Los Angeles.

GREBLER, Leo, MOORE, Joan, GUZMAN, Ralph C., *et al.*
1970 *The Mexican-American People: The Nation's Second Largest Minority.* New York: The Free Press.

GREENWAY, Roger S.
1973 *An Urban Strategy for Latin America.* Grand Rapids: Baker Book House.

GRIFFITH, Beatrice
1948 *American Me.* Boston: Houghton Mifflin.

GUZMAN, Ralph
1969 "Brown Power: The Gentle Revolutionaries", *Los Angeles Times West Magazine* (January 26). [Page number unknown.]

HALL, Edward T.
1959 *The Silent Language.* Greenwich, Connecticut: Fawcett Publications, Inc.

HARLEY, Ron
1970 "Why They Signed with the Union", *The Farm Quarterly* (September-October). [Reprint copy distribution by UFWOC.]

HARTMIRE, Wayne C.
1969 "The Delano Grape Strike: The Farm Workers' Struggle for Self Determination". Los Angeles: California Migrant Ministry.

HASELDON, Kyle
1964 *Death of a Myth.* New York: Friendship Press.

HEBERT, Ray
1970 "County Planners Tell of Peril in Population Rise", *Los Angeles Times* (April 15), Part II:1,5.

1971 "Study Ranks Blighted Communites of L.A.", *Los Angeles Times* (February 28), Section C:10.

1972 "L.A. County Latin Population Grows 113%: Other Whites Decrease in Last Decade", *Los Angeles Times* (August 18), Part I:1,26.

HEIZER, Robert F. and ALMQUIST, Alan J.
1971 *The Other Californians: Prejudice and Discrimination under Spain, Mexico, and the United States to 1920.* Berkeley: University of California Press.

HELLER, Celia S.
1966 *Mexican-American Youth.* New York: Random House.

HELM, June (ed.)
1968 *Spanish-Speaking People in the United States.* Seattle: University of Washington Press.

HERBERG, Will
1960 *Protestant-Catholic-Jew: An essay in American Religious Sociology.* Garden City, New York: Anchor Books, Doubleday & Company, Inc.

HERNANDEZ, Luis F.
1969 *A Forgotten American: A Resource Unit for Teachers on the Mexican American.* New York: Anti-Defamation League of B'nai B'rith.

HERRING, Hubert
1956 *A History of Latin America.* New York: Alfred A. Knopf.

HILLS, James W. L.
1973 "The New Charismatics 1973", *Eternity*, Vol. 24, No. 3:23-25,33. Philadephia: The Evangelical Foundation, Inc.

HINE, Leland D.
1966 *Baptists in Southern California.* Valley Forge, Pennsylvania: Judson Press.

HODGES, Melvin L.
1970 *Growing Young Churches*. Chicago: Moody Press.

1973 *A Guide to Church Planting*. Chicago: Moody Press.

HOLLAND, Clifton L.
1970 "Directory of Spanish Language Protestant Churches in Los Angeles and Orange Counties in California (July 1, 1970)". Xeroxed.

HOUGH, Joseph C., Jr.
1968 *Black Power and White Protestants*. New York: Oxford University Press.

HOWARD, John R. (ed.)
1970 *Awakening Minorities: American Indian, Mexican American, Puerto Rican*. New Brunswick, New Jersey: Trans-Action Books, Adeline Publishing Company, Rutgers University.

HUEGEL, John
n.d. "A Bridge Into Mexico". Mimeographed. Pasadena: School of World Mission, Fuller Theological Seminary.

IRELAN, Lola M. (ed.)
1967 *Low Income Life Styles*. Washington D.C.: U.S. Department of Health, Education and Welfare, Welfare Ad., Division of Research.

JERVEY, Edward Drewry
1960 *The History of Methodism in Southern California and Arizona*. Historical Society of the Southern California-Arizona Conference. Nashville: Parthenon Press.

JOSEPHY, Robert
1965 *The Great West*. New York: American Heritage Publishing Company.

Journal of the Latin American Mission (Southern California Conference of the Methodist Episcopal Church).
1920-1940 Gardena, California: The Spanish-American Institute Press.

Journal of the Latin American Provisional Annual Conference.
1941-1953 Los Angeles: The Methodist Church.

Journal of the Southern California-Arizona Conference of the United Methodist Church.
1953-1969 Los Angeles: The Methodist Publishing House.

KEESING, Felix M.
1958 *Cultural Anthropology: The Science of Custom.* New York: Holt, Rinehart, and Winston.

KELLEY, Dean M.
1972 *Why Conservative Churches are Growing.* New York: Harper & Row.

KIBBE, Pauline R.
1946 *Latin Americans in Texas.* Albuquerque: The University of New Mexico Press.

KLUCKHOHN, Clyde
1949 *Mirror for Man.* New York: McGraw Hill.

KRAFT, Charles H.
n.d. "Communicating the Supracultural Gospel to Culture-Bound Man." Mimeographed. Pasadena: School of World Mission, Fuller Theological Seminary.

La Luz Apostolica
1966 "R. C. Orozco in Mexico", Vol. 51, No. 4:6. [Organ of the Latin American District Council of the Assemblies of God, Albuquerque, New Mexico.]

LABELLA, Yvan and ESTRADA, Adriana
1964 *Latin America: In Maps, Charts, Tables.* No. 2: "Socio-Religious Data". Mexico D.F.: The Center of Intercultural Formation.

LADD, George Eldon
1964 *Jesus and the Kingdom: The Eschatology of Biblical Realism.* New York: Harper & Row.

LALIVE d'EPINAY, Christian
1968 *El refugio de las masas: estudio sociológico del protestantismo chileno.* Santiago, Chile: Editorial del Pacífico, S.A.

1969 *Haven of the Masses: A Study of the Pentecostal Movement in Chile.* New York: Friendship Press.

LANDES, Ruth
1965 *Latin Americans of the Southwest.* New York: McGraw-Hill.

LARA-BRAUD, Jorge
1971(a) "The Hispanic-American Institute in 1971". Photocopy. Austin, Texas: The Hispanic-American Institute.

1971(b) "Bilingualism for Texas: Education for Fraternity" Austin, Texas: Texas Conference of Churches. [A position paper written for the Texas Conference of Churches.]

Latin America Evangelist
1972 "News", Vol. 52, No. 2:13. Bogota, New Jersey: Latin America Mission.

The Latin American. Pamphlet.
ca. 1918 Los Angeles: The Spanish and Portuguese District of the Southern California Conference, Methodist Episcopal Church.

Latin American Bible Institute of California
1970 *Catalog: 1970-1971.* La Puente: Latin American Bible Institute, Latin American District Council of the Assemblies of God.

Latin American District Council, Assemblies of God
1970 *Informe Bianual.* Albuquerque, New Mexico: Latin American District Council.

LATOURETTE, Kenneth S.
1969 *Christianity in a Revolutionary Age. The 20th Century Outside of Europe*, Volume 5. Grand Rapids: Zondervan Publishing House (orig. 1962).

LAZERWITZ, Bernard
1964 "Religion and Social Structure in the United States," in Louis Schneider (ed.), *Religion, Culture, and Society.* New York: John Wiley and Sons.

LEAVENWORTH, Lynn and FROYD, Milton
1954 "The Spanish American Baptist Seminary and Its Task". Photocopy. Los Angeles: Hispanic Urban Center Library

LEIREN, Hall
1970 "Mexican-American Courses Promised", *Los Angeles Times* (April 12), Section G:4.

LENSKI, Gerhard
1961 *The Religious Factor: A Sociological Study of Religion's Impact on Politics, Economics, and Family Life.* Garden City, New York: Doubleday & Co., Inc.

LEONARD, Olin E. and JOHNSON, Helen W.
1967 *Low Income Families in the Spanish-Surname Population.* Agricultural Economic Report No. 112. Washington D.C. Department of Agriculture, Economic Research Service.

LE SHANA, David C.
1969 *Quakers in California*. Newberg, Oregon: The Barclay Press.

LESLIE, Ruth R.
1923 "The Protestant Movement in Mexico". Unpublished M.A. Thesis, College of Missions.

LEWIS, Oscar
1959 *Five Families: Mexican Case Studies*. New York: Basic Books.

1960 *Tepaztlán: Village in Mexico*. New York: Holt, Rinehart and Winston.

1961 *The Children of Sánchez*. New York: Random House.

1964 *Pedro Martínez*. New York: Vintage Books.

1966 "The Culture of Poverty", *Scientific American*, Vol. 215, No. 4:19-25.

1968 "The Culture of Poverty", in Moynihan (ed.) *On Understanding Poverty*. New York: Basic Books.

LINDSELL, Harold (ed.)
1966 *The Church's Worldwide Mission*. Waco, Texas: Word Books.

LINTON, Ralph
1945 *The Culture Background of Personality*. New York: Appleton-Century-Crofts.

LOFSTEDT, Anne Christine
1922 "A Study of the Mexican Population in Pasadena, California." Unpublished M.A. Thesis, University of Southern California.

LOORY, Stuart H.
1970 "Nixon Welcomes Diaz Ordaz to Coronado with State Dinner", *Los Angeles Times* (September 4), Section B: 1,2.

Los Angeles County Board of Education, Office of Superintendent of Schools.
1966-1971 Unpublished school district reports based on the annual "Racial and Ethnic Survey" of Los Angeles County Schools.

Los Angeles Southern Baptist Association
1969 No Title. Pamphlet describing area ministries and containing a church directory. Los Angeles: Office of Mission Secretary.

Los Angeles Times
1971(a) "Nazarenes Thriving in Membership, Finances" (May 29). [Section and page no. unknown.]

1971(b) "Southland: Latins Hit New Alien Work Law" (November 17), Part I:2.

1971(c) "Most Blame Poor for Poverty, Survey Finds" (June 24). [Section and page no. unknown.]

1971(d) "Young Chicanos Actively Recruit for New Party" (August 30), Part I:3,23.

Lutheran Church-Missouri Synod
1965 *Statistical Yearbook*. St. Louis: Department of Research and Statistics, Missouri Lutheran Synod.

LUZBETAK, Louis J.
1963 *The Church and Cultures, An Applied Anthropology for the Religious Worker*. Techny, Illinois: Divine Word Publications.

1966 "Christopaganism", *Practical Anthropology*, 13:115-121.

MC COMBS, Vernon Monroe
1925 *From Over the Border, a Study of the Mexicans in the United States*. New York: Council of Women for Home Missions and Missionary Education Movement.

1930 "The Latin American Mission". Typewritten. Report from Superintendent of the Latin American Mission, Methodist Episcopal Church.

MC COMBS, Mrs. Vernon M.
1959 Personal correspondence to Dr. Ragsdale, November 12. Claremont, California: Methodist Historical Society Archives, School of Theology at Claremont.

MC EUEN, William W.
1913 "The Mexicans in Los Angeles", *El Mexicano*, Vol. 1, No. 7:4-5 (Chapter 1); Vol. 1, No. 8:4-5 (Chapter 2); Vol. 2, No. 1:4-5 (Chapter 3). Gardena: Spanish American Institute Press.

1914 "A Survey of the Mexicans in Los Angeles". Unpublished M.A. Thesis, University of Southern California.

MC GAVRAN, Donald A.
1965 "Social Justice and Evangelism", *World Vision Magazine* (reprinted article). Monrovia, California: World Vision.

1966 *How Churches Grow*. New York: Friendship Press (original copyright 1959, World Dominion Press).

1970 *Understanding Church Growth*. Grand Rapids: William B. Eerdmans Publishing Company.

MC GAVRAN, Donald A. (ed.)
1965 *Church Growth and Christian Mission*. New York: Harper & Row, Publishers.

MC GAVRAN, Donald A. and ARN, Win
1973 *How to Grow a Church*. Glendale, California: Regal Books Division, Gospel Light Publications.

MC GAVRAN, Donald, HUEGEL, John and TAYLOR, Jack
1963 *Church Growth in Mexico*. Grand Rapids: William B. Eerdmans Publishing Company.

MC LEAN, Robert Norris
1928 *That Mexican! As He Really Is, North and South of the Rio Grande*. New York: Fleming C. Revell Co.

1930 *The Northern Mexican*. New York: Home Missions Council.

MC NAMARA, Patrick H.
1968 "Bishops, Priests, and Prophecy: A Study in the Sociology of Religious Protest." Unpublished Ph.D. Dissertation, University of California at Los Angeles.

MC WILLIAMS, Carey
1946 *Southern California Country*. New York: Duell, Sloan and Pearce.

1968(a) *The Mexicans in America*. New York: Teachers' College Press, Teachers' College, Colombia University.

1968(b) *The Mexicans in America: A Student's Guide to Localized History*. New York: Teachers' College Press.

1968(c) *North From Mexico: The Spanish-Speaking People of the United States*. New York: Greenwood Press (original copyright 1948).

MACKIE, Steven G. (ed.)
1970 *Can Churches be Compared?* Research Pamphlet #17. New York: Friendship Press.

MADGE, John
1965 *The Tools of Social Science.* Garden City, New York: Anchor Books, Doubleday & Co., Inc.

MADSEN, Paul
1971 No Title. Mimeographed. [A report dealing with the closing of the Spanish-American Baptist Seminary in Los Angeles and presented at a meeting of the *Ad Hoc* Committee on Theological Education on October 26. American Baptist Headquarters, Los Angeles.]

MADSEN, William
1964 *Mexican-Americans of South Texas.* New York: Holt, Rhinehart & Winston.

MARTIN, I. G.
1937 *Dr. P. F. Bresee and the Church He Founded.* Kansas City: Nazarene Publishing House.

MARTIN, Walter R.
1957 *Jehovah's Witnesses.* Grand Rapids: Zondervan Publishing House.

MARTINEZ, Joel N.
1970 "Hispanic Congregation: Survival to Engagement", *Response*, Vol. 2, No. 10:25-27. Cincinatti: Joint Committee on Education and Cultivation, Board of Missions of United Methodist Church.

MARTINEZ, John R.
1966 "Leadership and Politics", in Julian Samora (ed.) *La Raza: Forgotten Americans.* Notre Dame: The University of Notre Dame Press.

MATTHIESSEN, Peter
1969 *Sal Si Puedes: Cesar Chavez and the New American Revolution.* New York: Random House.

MELENDREZ, Simón
1970 Personal interview, July 29. [Pastor of "El Aposento Alto" Assembly of God Church in East Los Angeles.]

MERCADO, Luís Fidel
1971 "The Hispanic Urban Center, Los Angeles, California." Typewritten.

Methodist Episcopal Church, Southern California Conference
1884-1918 *Methodist Annual Minutes*

The Methodist Church
1950-1955 *General Minutes of the Annual Conferences of the Methodist Church in the United States, Territories and Cuba.* Chicago: Council on World Service and Finance, Statistical Office of the Methodist Church.

Methodist Historical Society Archives
ca. 1952 "The Plaza Community Center". Author unknown. Typewritten. Claremont, California: School of Theology Library.

ca. 1956 "God Sees the Present and the Future". Author unknown. Typewritten. Claremont, California: School of Theology Library.

Mexican American Population Commission of California
1971 "Mexican American Population in California: October 1970, with Projections to 1980." San Francisco: MAPC of California.

The Miami Herald
1972 "Teamsters, Chavez OK Grape Pact" (September 29), Section MH:2A.

MIGUEZ-BONINO, José
1967 "Main Currents of Protestantism", in Samuel Shapiro (ed.) *Integration of Man and Society in Latin America*, pp. 191-201. Notre Dame: University of Notre Dame Press.

MOBERG, David O.
1962 *The Church as a Social Institution: The Sociology of American Religion.* Englewood Cliffs, New Jersey: Prentice-Hall, Inc.

MOORE, Joan W.
1967 *Mexican-Americans: Problems and Prospects.* Institute for Research on Poverty, University of Wisconsin. Madison: University of Wisconsin Press.

MOORE, Joan W. with CUELLAR, Alfredo
1970 *Mexican Americans.* Englewood Cliffs, New Jersey: Prentice-Hall.

MORIN, Raúl
1966 *Among the Valient: Mexican Americans in World War II and Korea.* Alhambra, California: Borden Publishing Company.

MOYNIHAN, Daniel P. (ed.)
1968 *On Understanding Poverty*. New York: Basic Books, Inc.

MUÑIZ, Arturo R.
1971 Personal Correspondence, December 6. [President of the Latin American Council of Christian Churches.]

NADEAU, Remi
1960 *Los Angeles: From Mission to Modern City*. New York: Longmans, Green, and Co.

1965 *City-Makers: The Story of Southern California's First Boom, 1868-76*. Los Angeles: Trans-Anglo Books.

NAVA, Julian
1969 *Mexican Americans: Past, Present, and Future*. New York: American Book Co.

NELSON, Eugene
1970 "Who Is César Chávez?", in Manuel P. Servín (ed.) *The Mexican Americans: An Awakening Minority*. Beverly Hills: The Glencoe Press.

NEVAREZ, Natividad
1970 Personal interview, July 29. [Wife of Francisco Nevárez, one of the early Assemblies of God pastors in Los Angeles--ca. 1916-1930.]

Newsweek
1971 "A Survey of U.S. Catholics: Has the Church Lost Its Soul?" (October 4):80-89.

NICHOL, John Thomas
1966 *Pentecostalism*. New York: Harper & Row, Publishers.

NIDA, Eugene A.
1954 *Customs and Cultures*. New York: Harper & Brothers.

1960 *Message and Mission: The Communication of the Christian Faith*. New York: Harper & Row, Publishers.

1961 "Christopaganism", *Practical Anthropology* (January-February), 8:1-15.

1965 "Culture and Church Growth" in McGavran (ed.) *Church Growth and Christian Mission*. New York: Harper & Row, Publishers.

NIEBUHR, H. Richard
1956 *Christ and Culture.* New York: Harper Torchbooks, Harper & Row Publishers.

del OLMO, Frank
1971(a) "Latin Leaders Report Few Gains Since Riot", *Los Angeles Times* (August 30), Section 1:3,22

1971(b) "Chicano Party Says it Defeated Alatorre in 48th District", *Los Angeles Times* (November 18), Part I; 3,22.

1971(c) "Raza Unida: Barrio Power?" *Los Angeles Times* (December 13), Part II:1,10.

1972 "Chicanos Divided by Sympathy for Aliens, Fear for Own Jobs", *Los Angeles Times* (March 25), Part II:1,12.

ORTEGON, Samuel M.
1932 "The Religious Status of the Mexican Population of Los Angeles." Unpublished M.A. Thesis, University of Southern California.

1950 "Religious Thought and Practice Among Mexican Baptists of the U.S., 1900-1947," Unpublished Ph.D. Dissertation, University of Southern California.

OXNAM, G. Bromley
1921 "Mexicans in Los Angeles from the Standpoint of the Religious Forces of the City," *Annals of the American Academy of Political and Social Science* (January), 93: 130-133.

PARKER, Richard
1972 "Are You Really Part of the Middle Class?", *Tropic* magazine, *The Miami Herald* (November 26), pp 22,24,26.

PASTIER, John
1971 "It's a Car, It's a Bus, It's a Train--It's a Mess," *Los Angeles Times* (October 21), Part II:7.

PATTISON, E. Mansell
1966 "Closed Mind Syndrome: An Analysis of Current Data," *Christian Medical Society Journal* (Spring):7-11.

PAZ, Octavio
1961 *The Labyrinth of Solitude: Life and Thought in Mexico.* New York: Grove Press.

PEÑALOSA, Fernando
1963 "Class Consciousness and Social Mobility In a Mexican-American Community (Pomona, California)." Unpublished Ph.D. Dissertation, University of Southern California.

1967 "The Changing Mexican American in Southern California", *Sociology and Social Research*, LI, No. 4:405-417.

PITT, Leonard
1966 *The Decline of the Californios: A Social History of Spanish-Speaking California, 1846-1890*. Berkeley: University of California Press.

POBLETE, Renato and O'DEA, Thomas
1962 "Sectarianism as a Response to Anomie", in Robert Lee (ed.) *Cities and Churches*. Philadelphia: The Westminster Press.

POMEROY, Earl
1965 *The Pacific Slope: A History of California, Oregon, Washington, Idaho, Utah, and Nevada*. New York: Alfred A. Knopf.

The Presbyterian Church in the U.S.A.
1926,1929 *Annual Report of the General Synod in the U.S.A.*

1926-1958 *Annual Report of the Synod of California.*

QUIÑONES, Horacio
1966 "A Short History of the Baptist Church Among the Spanish-Speaking People." Mimeographed.

QUIRK, Robert E.
1960 *The Mexican Revolution, 1914-1915: The Convention of Aguascalientes*. New York: W. W. Norton & Co.

RAMOS, Samuel (Trans.)
1962 *Profile of Man and Culture in Mexico*. Austin: University of Texas Press.

RANAGHAN, Kevin and Dorothy
1969 *Catholic Pentecostals*. New York: Paulist Press Deus Books.

READ, William R., MONTERROSO, Victor M., and JOHNSON, Harmon A.
1969 *Latin American Church Growth*. Grand Rapids: William B. Eerdmans Publishing Co.

REDFIELD, Robert
1967 *The Little Community/Peasant Society and Culture*. Chicago: Phoenix Books, University of Chicago Press.

REID, Clyde
1969 *Groups Alive--Church Alive.* New York: Harper & Row Publishers.

RISDON, Ray
1924 "Report of the Historical Society." Typewritten, dated April 9. Claremont, California: Methodist Historical Society Archives, School of Theology at Claremont.

ROBERTS, W. Dayton
1967 *Revolution In Evangelism.* Chicago: Moody Press.

RODRIGUEZ, Abram
1970 Personal interview with Taylor Pendley, January 28. Typewritten. [Rodríguez was one of the founders of the Assemblies of Christian Churches of New York, along with Francisco Olazábal.]

RODRIGUEZ, Juan
1969 Personal interview, November 2. [Pastor of Divine Savior Presbyterian Church in Los Angeles.]

ROUNDY, R. W.
1921 "The Mexican in Our Midst", *Missionary Review of the World* (May):361-366.

ROWITCH, Robert
1971 "Gang Violence: A Grim Reality Evades Solution", *Los Angeles Times* (August 2), Part I:1,20.

RUBEL, Arthur J.
1966 *Across the Tracks: Mexican Americans in a Texas City.* Austin: University of Texas Press.

RYCROFT, W. Stanley and CLEMMER, Myrtle M.
1963 *A Factual Study of Latin America.* New York: COEMAR, United Presbyterian Church in the U.S.A.

SALAZAR, Lorenzo
1970 Personal interview, September 23. [President of the Apostolic Assembly of the Faith in Christ Jesus, Los Angeles, California.]

SALAZAR, Ruben
1963 "Spanish-Speaking Angelenos: A Culture in Search of a Name", *Los Angeles Times* (February 24-March 1). A series of six daily articles. Reprint.

1970 "Mexican Americans Come Out 2nd Best in High School Course", *Los Angeles Times* (May 15, Editorial Page). [A series of articles on Mexican Americans appeared every Friday on the Editorial Page of the *Los Angeles Times*, February 6-August 28.]

SAMORA, Julian
1971 *Los Mojados: The Wetback Story*. Notre Dame: University of Notre Dame Press.

SAMORA, Julian (ed.)
1966 *La Raza: Forgotten Americans*. Notre Dame: University of Notre Dame Press.

SANCHEZ, George
1967 *Forgotten People: A Study of New Mexicans*. Albuquerque: Calvin Horn.

SAUNDERS, Lyle
1960 "'Anglo' and Spanish-Speaking Americans: Contrasts and Similarities", *Practical Anthropology*, VII; No. 5: 193-204.

SCHERMERHORN, Charles M.
1953 "Preliminary Report for the Southern California-Arizona Annual Conference." Dated May 1. Mimeographed

SCHOLES, William E.
1966 "The Migrant Worker" in Samora (ed.) *La Raza: Forgotten Americans*. Notre Dame: The University of Notre Dame Press.

SCOTT, Robin F.
1970 "The Zoot-Suit Riots" (pp. 116-124), "The Sleepy Lagoon Case and the Grand Jury Investigation" (pp. 105-115), in Servín (ed.), *The Mexican Americans: An Awakening Minority*. Beverly Hills: Glencoe Press.

SERVIN, Manual P.
1970 *The Mexican-Americans: An Awakening Minority*. Beverly Hills, California: Glencoe Press.

SEXTON, Patricia Cayo
1965 *Spanish Harlem*. New York: Harper Colophon Books, Harper & Row, Publishers.

SHELDON, Paul M.
1966 "Community Participation and the Emerging Middle Class," in Samora (ed.), *La Raza: Forgotten Americans*. Notre Dame: University of Notre Dame Press.

SHEVKY, Eshref and LEWIN, Molly
1949 *Your Neighborhood: A Social Profile of Los Angeles.* Los Angeles: The Haynes Foundation.

SHEVKY, Eshref and WILLIAMS, Marilyn
1949 *Social Areas of Los Angeles.* Los Angeles: University of California Press.

SHINTO, William
1970 "Proposal: American Baptist Spanish Urban Center." Dated July 4. Photocopy.

SIMMEN, Edward (ed.)
1971 *The Chicano.* New York: New American Library, Times-Mirror Company.

SIMPSON, George E. and YINGER, J. Milton
1965 *Racial and Cultural Minorities.* New York: Harper & Row, Publishers.

SMITH, Clara G.
1933 "The Development of the Mexican People in the Community of Watts, California." Unpublished M.A. Thesis, University of Southern California.

Southern Baptist General Convention of California.
1969 *Language Missions Directory.* Fresno, California: Office of Language Missions.

Southern California Baptist Convention (Northern/American Baptist Association)
1900-1970 *Proceedings of the Southern California Baptist Annual Convention.* Los Angeles: S.C.B.C.

1964 "Spanish Baptist Work in Southern California." Pamphlet. Los Angeles: Director of Spanish Work, S.C.B.C.

Spanish-American Institute
1969 "A Draft of Proposal for the Board of the Spanish-American Institute." Dated November 19. Mimeographed.

1971 *Spanish American Institute: 1913-1971 Service to Boys.* Gardena, California: The Spanish American Institute.

Spanish-American Institute Subcommittee
1970 "Minutes of the Meeting on Purposes." Dated June 25. Mimeographed.

SPENCE, Inez
n.d. *Henry C. Ball: Man of Action.* Heroes of the Conquest Series, Number 13. Springfield, Missouri: Foreign Missions Dept., Assemblies of God.

Stanford University, The Center for Latin American Studies
1969 *The Mexican American: A Selected and Annotated Bibliography.* Stanford: California University Press.

STEDMAN, Ray C.
1972 *Body Life.* Glendale, California: Regal Books Division, Gospel Light Publications.

STEINBECK, John
1973 *The Grapes of Wrath.* Harmondsworth, England: Penguin Books Ltd. [Original copyright 1939.]

STEINER, Stan
1969 *La Raza: The Mexican Americans.* New York: Harper & Row, Publishers.

STINGLEY, Jim
1970 "El Monte, County to Reexamine Hicks Camp Improvement Plan", *Los Angeles Times* (January 1), Part 6:1,2.

STOTT, John R. W.
1964 *The Baptism and Fullness of the Holy Spirit.* Downers Grove, Illinois: Inter-Varsity Press.

STOWE, David M.
1970 *Ecumenicity and Evangelism.* Grand Rapids: Zondervan Publishing Co.

STOWELL, Jay S.
1921 *The Near Side of the Mexican Question.* New York: Geo. Doran Co.

1924 *Methodism's New Frontier.* New York: Methodist Book Concern.

STRACHAN, R. Kenneth
1968 *The Inescapable Calling.* Grand Rapids: William B. Eerdmans Publishing Co.

SWEET, William Warren
1950 *The Story of Religion in America.* New York: Harper & Row, Publishers. [Original copyright 1930.]

SUMNER, Margaret L.
1963 "Mexican American Minority Churches, U.S.A.", *Practical Anthropology*, 10:115-121.

TAYLOR, Ron
1971 "UFWOC--Is it Union or Social Reform", *The Fresno Bee* (August 12). [Reprinted copy distributed by UFWOC.]

THOMPSON, Warren S.
1955 *Growth Changes in California Population*. Los Angeles: The Haynes Foundation.

THOMAS, William L., Jr. (ed.)
1959 "Man, Time, and Space in Southern California", *Annals of the Association of American Geographers*, Vol. 49, Number 2:1-118. Lawrence, Kansas: Allen Press.

THRAPP, Dan L.
1970(a) "McIntyre Retires from Archdiocese", *Los Angeles Times* (January 22), Part I:1,14.

1970(b) "Catholics Organize Diocesan Council to Push Aid for Latins", *Los Angeles Times* (February 14), Part II:1.

1971(a) "Southland Parish", *Los Angeles Times* (May 22). [Section and page unknown.]

1971(b) "Chicanos Issue Call for Own Catholic Church", *Los Angeles Times* (October 16). [Section and page unknown.

The Tidings
1970 *1970 Catholic Directory, Archdiocese of Los Angeles*. Los Angeles. [Official Catholic newspaper of the Archdiocese of Los Angeles.]

TIPPETT, Alan R.
n.d. "Religious, Group Conversion in Non-Western Society." Research-in-Progress Pamphlet Series, Number 11. Pasadena: School of World Mission, Fuller Theological Seminary.

n.d. "Patterns of Religious Change in Communal Society." Mimeographed. Pasadena: School of World Mission, Fuller Theological Seminary.

1969 *Verdict Theology in Missionary Theory*. Lincoln, Illinois: Lincoln Christian College Press.

1970 *Church Growth and the Word of God*. Grand Rapids: William B. Eerdmans Publishing Company.

TIPPETT, Alan R. (ed.)
1973 *God, Man and Church Growth*. Grand Rapids: William B. Eerdmans Publishing Company.

TORBET, Robert G. (Revised)
1963 *A History of the Baptists*. Valley Forge: The Judson Press.

TORGERSON, Dial
1971 "Which Way for Echo Park--Inner City Oasis or Slum?" *Los Angeles Times* (September 19), Section C:1-3.

TOWNS, Elmer L.
1973 "Trends Among Fundamentalists", *Christianity Today* (July 6):12-19.

TROYER, Mrs. L. E.
1934 *The Sovereignty of the Holy Spirit Revealed in the Opening of Our Mexican Missions of the Southwest*. Los Angeles: Student Benefit Publishing Co.

TRUEBLOOD, Elton
1961 *The Company of the Committed*. New York: Harper & Row, Publishers.

TUCK, Ruth D.
1946 *Not With the Fist: Mexican Americans in a Southwest City*. New York: Harcourt, Brace & Co.

TURNER, Craig
1971 "Mexican American Group will Protest School Plan", *Los Angeles Times* (December 13), Part II:6,7.

1972 "Rosemead Faces New Problem of Suburban Poor", *Los Angeles Times* (January 16), Section L:1,5.

The United Presbyterian Church in the U.S.A.
1959-1970 *Minutes of the Annual Session of the Synod of California*

The United Presbyterian Church in the U.S.A., Synod of California
1967 *Minutes of Annual Session*, Appendix C: "Chronological List of Churches" by Clifford M. Drury, pp. 94-108.

United States Bureau of the Census
1963(a) *1960 Census of Population: Persons of Spanish Surname*. Final Report PC (2)-1B. Washington D.C.: U.S. Government Printing Office.

1963(b) *Congressional District Data Book* (88th Congress). Washington D.C.: U.S. Government Printing Office.

1963(c) *U.S. Census of Population 1960*. Vol. I, *Characteristics of the Population*, Part 6, "California". Washington D.C.: U.S. Government Printing Office.

1966(a) *Special Census Survey of South and East Los Angeles Areas: November 1965* (Tech. Series #17). Washington D.C.: U.S. Government Printing Office.

1966(b) *Characteristics of South and East Los Angeles Areas: November 1965* (Tech. Series #18). Washington D.C.: U.S. Government Printing Office.

1967 *County and City Data Book*. Washington D.C.: U.S. Government Printing Office.

U.S. Census of Population and Housing, 1960
1962 *Census Tracts: Los Angeles-Long Beach, California*. Washington D.C.: U.S. Government Printing Office.

U.S. Commission on Civil Rights, California State Advisory Committee
1968 *Education and the Mexican American Community in Los Angeles County*. Washington D.C.: U.S. Government Printing Office.

U.S. Commission on Civil Rights
1968 *The Mexican American*. Washington D.C.: U.S. Government Printing Office.

U.S. Inter-Agency Commission on Mexican American Affairs
1968 *The Mexican American: A New Focus on Opportunity*. Testimony presented at Cabinet Meeting on Mexican American Affairs at El Paso, Texas, October 26-27. Washington D.C.: U.S. Government Printing Office.

VALENTINE, Charles A.
1971 "Deficit, Difference, and Bicultural Models of Afro-American Behavior", *Harvard Educational Review*, Vol. 41, No. 2:137-157.

VALVERDE, Katie (ed.)
1969 *Direcciones de los Supervisores, Pastores, Misioneros, y Evangelistas*. Los Angeles: Asamblea Apostólica de la Fe en Cristo Jesús.

VAN BAALEN, Jan Karel
1960 *The Chaos of the Cults*. Grand Rapids: William B. Eerdmans Publishing Co.

VASQUEZ, Richard
1970 *Chicano*. Garden City, New York: Doubleday & Co., Inc.

VIGIL, A. F.
1970 Official correspondence with the Secretary of the Latin American District Council of the Assemblies of God, Albuquerque, New Mexico. [This letter contains the date when each assembly in Los Angeles and Orange Counties became affiliated with the Latin American Council.]

VILLARREAL, Jose Antonio
1966(a) "Mexican Americans in Upheaval", *Los Angeles Times West Magazine* (September 18): 20-30.

1966(b) "Mexican Americans and the Leadership Crises", *Los Angeles Times West Magazine* (September 25): 44-50.

VOELKEL, Janvier W.
1971 "The Eternal Revolutionary: Evangelical Ministry to the University Student in Latin America." Unpublished M.A. Thesis, School of World Mission, Fuller Theological Seminary.

WAGLEY, Charles and HARRIS, Marvin
1955 "A Typology of Latin American Subcultures", *American Anthropologist*, Vol. 57, No. 3:428-451.

WAGNER, C. Peter
1971 *Frontiers in Mission Strategy*. Chicago: Moody Press.

WAGNER, John A.
1966 "The Role of the Christian Church", in Julian Samora (ed.), *La Raza: Forgotten Americans*. Notre Dame: University of Notre Dame Press.

WALLACE, Anthony F. C.
1956 "Revitalization Movements", *American Anthropologist*, Vol. 58 (April): 264-281.

1961 *Culture and Personality*. New York: Random House Inc.

WEBER, Max (Trans. by Ephraim Fischoff)
1963 *The Sociology of Religion*. Boston: Beacon Press. [Original copyright 1922.]

WEIGERT, Andrew J., D'ANTONIO, William V., and RUBEL, Arthur J.
1971 "Protestantism and Assimilation Among Mexican Americans: An Exploratory Study of Minister's Reports", *Journal for the Scientific Study of Religion*, Vol. 10, No. 3:219-232.

Welfare Planning Council, East Central Area
1968 "Churches: Catholic and Protestant in the East Central Area." Mimeographed. Los Angeles: Welfare Planning Council.

Welfare Planning Council, Los Angeles Region Research Department
1965 *Social Profiles: Los Angeles County*. Los Angeles: Welfare Planning Council.

WEST, Richard
1971 "Reagan Signs State Ban on Hiring Illegal Aliens", *Los Angeles Times* (November 9). [Section and page unknown.]

Western Economic Research Company
1960 "SSN Population by Census Tracts, 1960: Los Angeles County." Map. Reseda, California.

WHITAM, Frederick L.
1960 "A Report on the Protestant Spanish Community in New York City (July 1960)." New York: Department of Church Planning and Research, Protestant Council of the City of New York.

1962 "New York's Spanish Protestants", *Christian Century*, LXXIX (February 7): 162-164.

WHITLEY, Oliver R.
1964 *Religious Behavior: Where Sociology and Behavior Meet*. Englewood Cliffs, New Jersey: Prentice-Hall, Inc.

WICHER, Edward Arthur
1927 *The Presbyterian Church in California: 1849-1927*. New York: Frederick H. Hitchcock (The Grafton Press).

WILLEMS, Emilio
1967 *Followers of the New Faith: Culture Change and the Rise of Protestantism in Brazil and Chile*. Nashville: Baird-Ward Printing Co. (for Vanderbilt University).

WILSON, Robert L. and DAVIS, James H.
1966 *The Church in the Racially Changing Community*. New York: Abingdon Press.

WINTER, Gibson
1962 *The Suburban Captivity of the Churches*. New York: Macmillan Co.

WINTER, J. Alan (ed.)
1971 *The Poor: A Culture of Poverty or a Poverty of Culture*. Grand Rapids, William B. Eerdmans Publishing Company.

WINTER, Ralph D.
1970 *The Twenty-Five Unbelievable Years 1945-1969*. So. Pasadena, California: William Carey Library.

n.d. "Quality or Quantity". Mimeographed. Pasadena, California: School of World Mission, Fuller Theological Seminary.

WIRT, Sherwood Eliot
1968 *The Social Conscience of the Evangelical*. New York: Harper & Row, Publishers.

WIRTH, Louis
1945 "The Problem of Minority Groups", in Ralph Linton (ed.) *The Science of Man in the World Crises*. New York: Columbia University Press.

WOLF, Eric R.
1955 "Types of Latin American Peasantry: A Preliminary Discussion", *American Anthropologist*, 57:452-471.

WOLF, Eugene
1970 Personal interview, March 5. [Wolf is a Southern Baptist Home Missionary working among the Spanish-speaking population of Los Angeles.]

WOLLENBERG, Charles (ed.)
1970 *Ethnic Conflict in California History*. Los Angeles: Tinnon-Brown, Inc.

WOODS, Francis J.
1949 *Mexican Ethnic Leadership in San Antonio, Texas*. Washington, D.C.: The Catholic University of America Press.

World Council of Churches
1968 *Drafts for Sections*. Prepared for the Fourth Assembly of the World Council of Churches, Uppsala, Sweden. Geneva: World Council of Churches.

YINGER, J. Milton
1970 *The Scientific Study of Religion*. New York: The Macmillan Company.

YINGER, J. Milton and SIMPSON, George E.
1956 "The Integration of Americans of Mexican, Puerto Rican, and Oriental Descent", *Annals of the American Academy of Political and Social Science* (March), pp. 124-131.

1957 *Religion, Society and the Individual: An Introduction to the Sociology of Religion.* New York: The Macmillan Company.

YOUNG, Governor C. C. of California, Mexican Fact Finding Committee
1930 *Mexicans in California.* San Francisco: State of California Building.

About the Author

Clifton L. Holland was born in Little Rock, Arkansas on July 9, 1939, but has lived in Southern California the majority of his lifetime. He received all of his primary and secondary education in Los Angeles County, was graduated from the Moody Bible Institute (Diploma, General Bible) in Chicago, BIOLA College (B.A., Bible) in La Mirada, California, and Fuller Theological Seminary, School of World Mission (M.A., Missions) in Pasadena, California. In addition to ten years experience in military and civilian electronics (including four years in the U.S. Air Force), Holland has served on the staff of four churches in Los Angeles and Orange Counties, in the areas of Christian education, youth ministries, and pastoral visitation. Since April 1972, he has been a missionary with the Latin America Mission in San José, Costa Rica, where he is on the staff of the Institute of In-Depth Evangelism. Holland is editor of the bulletin *In-Depth Evangelism Around the World* and co-director of *Indepth Publications*. He is married to Linda Ives and is the father of two children: Richard (12 years) and Suzan (11 years).

The author grew up in a welfare family and lost his father before the age of two. In his teens he became a juvenile dilinquent and dropped out of high school to spend four years in the military. On returning to civilian life, he worked full time to put himself through college and seminary, supporting a family at the same time. His varied experiences in secular and religious employment and cross cross-cultural ministry have given him a unique insight into the religious dimension in Hispanic Los Angeles.